Walking with Śiva
Cognitive Roots of Indian Art, Archaeology and Religion

With Reference to Tala and Dakṣiṇa Kośala

Walking with Śiva

Cognitive Roots of Indian Art, Archaeology and Religion

With Reference to Tala and Dakṣiṇa Kośala

Kalyan Kumar Chakravarty

Vol. I: Text

Aryan Books International
New Delhi

Dedicated to

The Unknown Artists of India

WALKING WITH ŚIVA
Cognitive Roots of Indian Art, Archaeology and Religion

ISBN: 978-81-7305-596-6 (Vol. I)
978-81-7305-598-0 (Set)

Published in **2018** by
Aryan Books International
Pooja Apartments, 4B, Ansari Road, New Delhi-110 002 (India)
Tel.: 23287589, 23255799; Fax: 91-11-23270385
E-mail: aryanbooks@gmail.com
www.aryanbooks.co.in

Designed and Printed in India by
ABI Prints & Publishing Co., New Delhi

Contents

Acknowledgements

The Directorate of Archaeology and Museums, Government of Madhya Pradesh and Chhattisgarh deserve my unreserved appreciation for taking up surveys and excavations under my direction. I could not have completed this work without my colleagues in the Directorate, of whom I can name only a few like G.L. Raikwar and Rahul Kumar Singh in Bilaspur, and V.P. Nagaich, Naresh Pathak and G.K. Chandrol in Raipur and Bastar. Chemists and engineers from Bhopal including V.K. Vajpeyi, Satish Chaturvedi, Shashi Sekhar Singh and A.P. Singh have helped in chemically and structurally conserving and restoring the excavated structures and fragments, making it easier to inspect them. Successive Commissioners at Bilaspur, notably Manoj Kumar, Subhash Majumdar, B.S. Baswan have rendered invaluable infrastructural assistance in the survey of related sites and environmental upgradation of the site of Tala. Dr. Ramlal Kashyap, former Vice-Chancellor, Agricultural University, Bilaspur, rendered yeoman's service in identifying the flora in Tala art. It is impossible to adequately thank the drivers, local guides and enthusiasts, who have taken me to different sites and given me valuable clues. My daughter Sayantani, who was born the year in which my Ph.D. thesis came to fruition in 1991, has kept my zest alive by accompanying me in further expeditions. Gratitude is due to my wife Minati who has accompanied me to remote sites, pointed out and discussed significant features, helped organize my material, patiently allowed me to take long months away from her for research, and constantly egged me on to refine, finish and publish my work, spread through decades. I owe an undying debt to my deceased parents, Nilima and Hiralal Chakravarty, who kept me focused on my research, despite many painful ailments. Mrs. Chandra, Mary Carmen Lynn acted like my elder sister, enveloping me with unobtrusive generosity and hospitality, through my days of research at Harvard.

O.P. Misra, Rajvaidya, M.K. Sasankan, Ravi Goel and P.A. Mohammed, at the Directorate of Archaeology and Museums, Madhya Pradesh, at Bhopal, Jayaprakashan, Manoj Jain, Imtiaz Khan, Rawat at the Indira Gandhi Rashtriya Manav Sangrahalaya, Bhopal, Joy Kuriakose, Prema Nair, at the Indira Gandhi National Centre for Arts (IGNCA), New Delhi, Saini at Raipur, Sushil Gaur, Jaya Kaushal and Sudarshan at the Delhi Institute of Heritage Research and Management, Om Prakash and Pallavi Moitra at Lalit Kala Akademi, helped me trace, collate, classify, process and edit archival material. Thanks are due to Pravin of Cultural Informatics

Lab (CIL) at IGNCA, who systematically digitized, edited and arranged the photographs, to Shri P. Jha, Director, CIL, IGNCA, who supervised the operation, and to Dr. Ajay Kumar Mishra and Dr. Kishor Kumar Tripathy, who checked the text.

No words are adequate for thanking Late Dr. Pramod Chandra, Emeritus Professor of Fine Arts, Harvard University, who suggested the unique and unparalleled quality of the site, guided my explorations, specially in Vidarbha, provided me with photographs, books and references, and, encouraged me to examine my premises with critical and constructive doubt. I must also thank Late Prof. M.A. Dhaky who personally directed the photographic documentation of the site at Tala by the American Institute of Indian Studies. Late Profs. Krishna Deva, N.P. Joshi, K.D. Bajpai visited the site and offered illuminating comments about the iconography. Profs. John Rosenfield, Oleg Grabar, David Mitten and Eduard Sekler at Harvard equipped me with tools to place Indian art and architecture in the backdrop of Asiatic, European, Classical arts and global architectural history. Profs. Oscar Handlin, Harrison White, David Maybury Lewis at Harvard induced in me a deep commitment to the intangible elements of the arts and culture of hinterland communities. Thanks are also due to Mr. Robert Bednarik, Dr. Rekha Morris, Prof. G. C. Tripathi and Prof. K. D. Tripathi for the careful and critical reading of the text. Last but not the least, appreciation is due to Mr. Vikas Arya of Aryan Books International for his personal care in scrutinising the work and flawless publishing of the book.

Finally, I must thank the many known and unknown voices from the past, retrieved from archaeological and literary relics and records, which have helped me repossess the cultural world of Dakṣiṇa Kośala in the fifth and sixth century by recollection and recapitulation.

Photo Credits

The photographs of Tala and Chhattisgarh sites are derived mostly from my field survey. The photographs of some sites like Maheshpur in Chhattishgarh have come out of the survey by the Directorate of Archaeology and Museums, Raipur, specially by its Dy. Director, Mr. G.L. Raikwar. The photographs of Sirpur in Chhattisgarh and Mānsar in Maharashtra have been taken by my colleagues in State Archaeology, Chhattisgarh with the help of Mr. A.K. Sharma, the senior excavator, retired from the A.S.I. and the A.S.I. office, Raipur. Several photographs of Indian sites including Pavnār in Maharashtra are drawn from the personal archive of Dr. Pramod Chandra. Thanks are due to Dr. Priti Trivedi, Head, Department of Ancient Indian History, Culture and Archaeology, R.T.M University, Nagpur for the recent photograph on the back cover of the twelve-headed Mahāsadāśiva image in the University Museum. Read Central Museum in caption of Pl. 47 as University Museum.

I am grateful to Mr. Chedilal, late chief draughtsman, Directorate of Archaeology and Museums, Govt. of Madhya Pradesh for providing plan, elevation, find sites of objects for Tala temples; to K.P. Varma, Directorate of Archaeology, Govt. of Chhattisgarh for supplying plans of Chhattisgarh temples; and, to Chhattisgarh Tourism Board, for some photographs of archaeological sites.

Appreciation and acknowledgement are due to the American Institute of Indian Studies, for photograph nos. 47, 138-39, 154-55, 202-05, 207-08, 276, 278, 288-91, 313, 382-84, 390, 402-03, 407, 439-41, 443-44, 555, 559, 569, 571, 621-26; and, to the Indira Gandhi National Centre for the Arts, Archive, for nos. 4-5, 14-16, 26-30, 104, 126, 145-53, 216-17, 232-35, 341-42, 408, 542, 563-64

Abbreviations

JOURNALS

AA	*Artibus Asiae*
AAS	*Artibus Asiae Supplementum*
AARP	*Art and Archaeology Research Papers*
AB	*Ars Buddhica (Bukhyo Geijutso)*
ABORI	*Annals of the Bhandarkar Oriental Research Institute*
AHRS	*Andhra Historical Research Society*
AIIS	American Institute of Indian Studies
AIND	*Ancient India*
AI	*Art International*
AJP	*American Journal of Philology*
AMG	*Annales de Musée Guimet*
AO	*Acta Orientalia*
AOSP	*American Oriental Society Publication*
ARA	*Artes Asiatiques*
ARO	*Ars Orientalis*
AROR	*Archiv Orientalni*
ARAA	*Archives of Asian Art*
AS	*Asiatische Studien*
ASIAR	*Archaeological Survey of India, Annual Report*
ASIPR	*Archaeological Survey of India Progress Report*
ASIPR WI/EI	*Archaeological Survey of India. Progress Report, Western India/Eastern India*
ASR	*Asiatick Researches*

BDCRI	*Bulletin of the Deccan College Research Institute*
BMAUP	*Bulletin of Museums and Archaeology in Uttar Pradesh*
BMPGB	*Bulletin of Museum and Picture Gallery, Baroda*
BPWM	*Bulletin of the Prince of Wales Museum*
BSOAS	*Bulletin of the School of African and Oriental Studies*
BV	*Bhāratīya Vidyā*
CII	*Corpus Inscriptionum Indicarum*
CR	*The Calcutta Review*
EA	*Etudés Asiatiques*
EAW	*East and West*
EI	*Epigraphia Indica*
GOS	*Gaekwad Oriental Series*
HAS	*Hyderabad Archaeological Series*
HOS	*Harvard Oriental Services.*
HTR	*Harvard Theological Review*
IA	*Indian Antiquary*
IAL	*Indian Arts and Letters*
IAR	*Indian Archaeology – A Review*
IC	*Indian Culture*
IF	*Indian Folklore*
IGNCA	Indira Gandhi National Centre for the Arts
IHQ	*Indian Historical Quarterly*
IIJ	*Indo Iranian Journal*
IIRINS	*Indian Institute of Research in Numismatic Studies*
IMB	*Indian Museum Bulletin*
JAAC	*Journal of Aesthetics and Art Criticism*
JAIH	*Journal of Ancient Indian History*
JAHRS	*Journal of the Andhra Historical Research Society*
JAOS	*Journal of the American Oriental Society*
JBBRAS	*Journal of Bombay Branch of the Royal Asiatic Society*
JESI	*Journal of the Epigraphical Society of India*
JIH	*Journal of Indian History*
JISOA	*Journal of the Indian Society of Oriental Art*
JKHRS	*Journal of Kaliṅga Historical Research Society*
JMPIP	*Journal of M.P Itihās Parishad*
JNSI	*Journal of the Numismatic Society of India*
JOIB	*Journal of the Oriental Institute of Baroda*
JOR	*Journal of Oriental Research*

JRASB	*Journal of the Royal Asiatic Society of Bengal*
JRASGBI	*Journal of the Royal Asiatic Society of Great Britain and Ireland*
JRSEAMC	*Journal of the Royal Society for the Encouragement of Arts, Manufactures and Commerce*
JSAS	*Journal of South Asian Studies*
JUPHS	*Journal of the Uttar Pradesh Historical Society*
KV	*Kala Vaibhav*
LK	*Lalit Kalā*
LP	*Liṅga Purāṇa*
MASI	*Memoirs of the Archaeological Survey of India*
MHSP	*The Mahākośala Historical Society Papers*
MII	*Man in India*
MS	*Monumenta Serica*
ND	*Numismatic Digest*
NIA	*New Indian Antiquary*
NLR	*New Left Review*
NS	*Numismatic Supplement*
NURS	*Nagpur University Research Series*
NUJ	*Nagpur University Journal*
ON	*Orientalia Neerlandica*
OHRJ	*Orissa Historical Research Journal*
PAIOC	*Proceedings of All India Oriental Conference*
PIHC	*Proceedings of the Indian History Congress*
PO	*Poona Orientalist*
PRB	*Prabuddha Bhārata*
PRP	*Prācya Pratibhā*
PU	*Purāṇa*
PUJ	*Poona University Journal*
QJAHRS	*Quarterly Journal of Andhra Historical Research Society*
QJMS	*Quarterly Journal of the Mythic Society*
RAA	*Revue des Artes Asiatiques*
SAA	*South Asian Archaeology*
SAUJ	*Sāgar University Journal*
SUJ	*Sambalpur University Journal*
VBA	*Viśva Bhāratī Annals*
VIJ	*Visveshvarānand Indological Journal*
VSMV	*Vidarbha Saṁśodhana Maṇḍala Vārṣika*
WZKM	*Weiner Zeitschrift für die Kunde des Morgenlandes*

WZKSO	*Weiner Zeitschrift für die Kunde Sūd-und Ostasiens*
ZDMG	*Zeitschrift der Morgenlandische Gipselschaft*

TEXTS

AB	*Aitareya Brāhmaṇa*
AgP	*Agni Purāṇa*
AgS	*Aśvalāyana Gṛhya Sūtra*
ASS	*Āpastambha Śrauta Sūtra*
Asup	*Atharvaśiras Upaniṣad*
Av	*Atharvaveda*
BhaP	*Bhaviṣya Purāṇa*
BhP	*Bhāgavata Purāṇa*
Bhrup	*Bhṛgūpaniṣad*
BrP	*Brahmāṇḍa Purāṇa*
BrS	*Bṛhat Saṁhitā*
Brup	*Bṛhadāraṇyaka Upaniṣad*
BS	*Brahma Sūtra*
BSS	*Baudhāyana Śrauta Sūtra*
BvP	*Brahmavaivarta Purāṇa*
Chup	*Chāndogya Upaniṣad*
GaP	*Garuḍa Purāṇa*
Gup	*Gaṇapati Upaniṣad*
HvP	*Harivaṁśa Purāṇa*
Jup	*Jābālyupaniṣad*
KaP	*Kālikā Purāṇa*
KB	*Kauśitakī Brāhmaṇa*
Kaup	*Kauśitakī Upaniṣad*
KuP	*Kūrma Purāṇa*
LP	*Liṅga Purāṇa*
MatP	*Matsya Purāṇa*
Maiup	*Maitrāyaṇi Upaniṣad*
MarP	*Mārkaṇḍeya Purāṇa*
Mbh	*Mahābhārata*
MS	*Maitrāyaṇi Saṁhitā*
Mup	*Muṇḍaka Upaniṣad*
PP	*Padma Purāṇa*
Prup	*Praśna Upaniṣad*
PS	*Pāśupata Sūtras*

RV	*Ṛgveda*
Samp	*Śāmba Purāṇa*
SB	*Śatapatha Brāhmaṇa*
SiP	*Śiva Purāṇa*
Shp	*Śāradā Purāṇa*
SkP	*Skanda Purāṇa*
SR	*Śatarudrīya*
Sup	*Śvetaśvatara Upaniṣad*
TB	*Taittirīya Brāhmaṇa*
TS	*Taittirīya Saṁhitā*
Tup	*Taittirīya Upaniṣad*
VaP	*Vāmana Purāṇa*
VarP	*Varāha Purāṇa*
VayP	*Vāyu Purāṇa*
VayS	*Vāyavīya Saṁhitā*
VdP	*Visṇudharmottara Purāṇa*
VG	*Vyāsa Gītā*
VP	*Visṇu Purāṇa*
VS	*Vājasaneyī Saṁhitā*
YS	*Yajurveda Saṁhitā*

List of Illustrations
(Vol. II)

FIGURES

Architecture at Tala: Plans

Architecture in Chhattisgarh: Plans

Architecture of Jethani

Architecture of Devarani

94. Devarani, from north, Gaṇeśa shrine embedded in later platform, c. 7th cent. AD.
95. Devarani, from east, candraśālā on later platform, c. 7th cent. AD.
96. Devarani, north, snake catching mouse on vedībandha of later platform, c. 7th cent. AD.
97. Devarani, north, snake chasing mouse. c. 7th cent. AD.
98. Devarani, north, brick āmalakas and slab found on later platform, c. 7th cent. AD.

Architecture in Chhattisgarh and Vidarbha: Temples

99. Garh Dhanaurā, Kānker, Bastar, Chhattisgarh, foundations of Viṣṇu group temple, c. 5th-6th cent. AD.
100. Brick plinth of ruined temple at Garh Dhanaurā, c. 5th-6th cent. AD.
101. Brick mouldings on shrine at Bhoṅgāpāl, Bastar, Chhattisgarh, c. 5th-6th cent. AD.
102. Vedībandha of Bhīmakicak temple, candraśālā on moulding, at Malhār, Bilaspur, c. 7th cent. AD.
103. Vedībandha and jaṅgha of Bhīmakīcak temple, candraśālā on moulding, Malhār, Bilaspur, c. 7th cent. AD.
104. Lakṣmaṇa temple, Sirpur, c. late 6th early 7th cent AD.
105. Lakṣmaṇa temple, second view.
106. Aśokalumbi on vedībandha, Siddheśvara temple, Palāri, c. 7th cent. AD.
107. Aśokalumbi and mouldings on vedībandha, Rāmacandra temple at Sirpur, c. 7th cent. AD.
108. Vedībandha with aśoka leaves and snake coming in and out of the crevices, Tīvaradeva Mahāvihāra, Sirpur, c. 7th cent. AD.
109. Aśokalumbi and snake emerging from cavity, vedībandha, Tīvaradeva Mahāvihāra at Sirpur.
110. Entrance gate of Suraṅgaṭilā, pañcāyatana Śiva temple, Sirpur, c. 7th cent. AD.
111. Sirpur, Tīvaradeva Mahāvihāra, Buddhist Monastery 3, SRP-5, c. 7th cent. AD.
112. Sirpur, mouldings, brick plinth, Suraṅgaṭilā temple, from southeast, before restoration, c. 7th cent. AD.
113. Sirpur, mouldings in brick plinth and stairs of Suraṅgaṭilā temple, from southwest, after restoration.
114. Sirpur, shops, ancient market 3, SRP-30, c. 7th cent. AD.
115. Sirpur, granaries, ancient market 3, SRP-30, c. 7th cent. AD.
116. Sirpur, underground drain, ancient market 3, SRP-30, c. 7th cent. AD.
117. Sirpur, Mañjuśrī in bronze, c. 7th-8th cent. AD.
118. Sirpur, votive boat in stone, c. 7th cent. AD.
119. Sirpur, stone mould for making gold ornament.
120. Sirpur, moulded bricks, c. 7th cent. AD.
121. Bhāravāhi gaṇas & candraśālā, śikhara, Citāvarī Devī, Śiva temple, Dhobin, Dāmākherā, Raipur, Chhattisgarh, c. early 8th cent. AD.
122. Citāvarī Devī Śiva temple, Dhobin, c. early 8th cent. AD.
123. Citāvarī Devī Śiva temple, Dhobin, Dāmākherā, elevation, Raipur, Chhattisgarh, c. early 8th cent. AD.
124. Śabarīnārāyaṇa temple, Khārod, Bilaspur, Chhattisgarh, c. mid 8th cent. AD.
125. Indal Deul temple, Khārod, front elevation, Bilaspur, Chhattisgarh, c. 7th cent. AD.

Architecture outside Chhattisgarh and Vidarbha: Temples

Architecture in Chhattisgarh: Door Jambs at Tala

157. Door jamb, Devarani, stambhaśākhā, flanked by patraśākhā, mālāśākhā, kalpalatā, pratiśākhā.
158. Sarasvatī, ardhamaṇḍapa, beside left door jamb, Devarani.
159. Left door jamb, Devarani, a close view.
160. Left door jamb, in the background of uttaraṅga and inner panels of door jamb, Devarani.
161. Left door jamb, stambhaśākhā, puṣpa and parṇapaṭṭis emerging from grāsamukhas, close view, Devarani.
162. Devarani, left door jamb, śākhāvibhakti, floral stands, including vallī, patra, puṣpa, parṇapaṭṭis, spiral mālāśākhā and allover kalpalatā, comprising half open, white lily/ lotus, kumudinī (Sans.), nymphaea stellata; small globular seeds of canna indica (Lat.), Indian shot (Eng.), vaijayantī (Sans.); close set kevaḍā (Hindi), screw pine (Eng.), P. Odoratissmus (Lat.); persistent calyx of dhaturā (Hindi) with fused sepals; butterfly-shaped butea monosperma (Lat.), kiṁśuka (Sans.), palāśa, dhāk (Hindi) threaded together; magnoliaceae (family), michelia champaka (genus), alba (specie); multi-coiled, under cut tendrils of saraca indica (Lat.), aśoka (Sans., Hindi). Also, pratiśākhā, framing kīrtimukha and mithunas on inner panels.
163. Left door jamb, śākhās, vallī, patra, puṣpa, parṇapaṭṭis.
164. Left door jamb, śākhās, including spiral mālāśākhā.
165. Left door jamb, śākhās, including kalpalatā.
166. Left door jamb, śākhās, including kalpalatā, mālāśākhā, stambhaśākhā.
167. Rūpaśākhā, framed by pratiśākhā, and vallī, padma, puṣpa and parṇapaṭṭi; Kubera; kīrtimukha, reproducing padma, nelumbo nucifera; mithunas; Gaṅgā being escorted, top down, inner side of left door jamb, Devarani.
168. Rūpaśākhā, Hara Gaurī at dalliance; Śiva gaṇas; kīrtimukha; Hara Gaurī at causar; Gaṅgā and Sagaraputras, top down, inner side of right door jamb, Devarani.
169. Kubera with attendants, inside panel, left door jamb, Devarani, Vallīpaṭṭi frame.
170. Mithunas, inside panel, left door jamb, Devarani. Parṁapaṭṭi frame.
171. Kubera, kīrtimukha, mithunas, inside panel, left door jamb, Devarani, Vallīpaṭṭi frame.
172. Lion head, inside panel, right door jamb, Devarani.
173. Gaṅgā with companion and Sagaraputras, frame of multipetalous flowers of genus jasminum pubescens, kund (Sans.), jūhi/cāmeli (Hindi), jasmine (Eng.), abraded bottom panel, right door jamb, Devarani.
174. Gaṅgā, Bhagīratha, Sagaraputras, right door jamb, Devarani, second view, Puṣpapaṭṭī frame on top.
175. Right door jamb with a view of inside panels, śākhāvibhakti including mālāśākhā, kalpalatā, pratiśākhā and pilaster with half-lotus medallion, ardhamaṇḍapa, Devarani.
176. Hara Gaurī in dalliance, gaṇas in various poses of stupefaction, top inside panel, right door jamb, Devarani. Puṣpa and vallīpaṭṭi frame.
177. Hara Gaurī at causar, Nandī being taken away as lost wager, middle inside panel, right door jamb, Devarani, Puṣpapaṭṭi frame.
178. Gajalakṣmī panel, saubhāgyapaṭṭa, uttaraṅga, door jamb, Devarani.

Architecture: Door Jambs in and outside Chhattisgarh

210. Fallen door jamb fragments, carved with Gaṅgā, Yamunā and lotus rhizome, near Bhīmakīcak temple, Malhār, Bilaspur, Chhattisgarh, c. late 6th cent. AD.
211. Door jamb fragment with male figure carried by load bearing gaṇa, Bhīmakīcak temple, Malhār, Bilaspur, c. late 6th-early 7th cent. AD.
212. Door jamb fragment, Bhīmakīcak temple premises, Malhār, c. late 6th-early 7th cent. AD.
213. Door jamb fragment, Bhīmakīcak temple premises, Malhār, c. late 6th early-7th cent. AD, second view.
214. Door jamb, Pātāleśvara Mahādeva temple, Malhār, c. 10th-11th cent. AD. (?)
215. Plinth mouldings, Pātāleśvara Māhādeva temple, Malhār, c. 10th-11th cent. AD.
216. Lotus medallion, soffit, door jamb, Lakṣmaṇa temple, Sirpur, c. 7th cent. AD.
217. Door jamb, Lakṣmaṇa temple, Sirpur, c. 7th cent. AD.
218. Lotus medallion, inner side panel, door jamb, Lakṣmaṇa temple, Sirpur, c. 7th cent. AD.
219. Door jamb, Svastika vihāra, Sirpur, c. 7th cent. AD.
220. Coiled Nāgarāja votaries on door jamb, Tīvaradeva Mahāvihāra, Sirpur, c. 7th cent. AD.
221. Figure twined with scroll, right door jamb, maṇḍapa, Rājīvalocana temple, Rajim, Raipur, c. 7th cent. AD.
222. Door jamb, inner face, south door, maṇḍapa, Rajīvalocana temple, Rajim, Raipur, c. 7th cent. AD.
223. Peacock on door jamb, maṇḍapa, Ānandaprabha kuṭi vihāra, Sirpur, c. 7th cent. AD.
224. Peacock on door jamb, maṇḍapa, Ānandaprabha kuṭi vihāra, Sirpur, c. 7th cent. AD.
225. Peacock on moulding of temple 2, Nalanda, Gaya, c. 6th cent. AD.
226. Peacock on moulding of later platform, Devarani, c. 7th cent. AD.
227. Door jamb with river goddesses and all over snake moulding, Śiva temple, Aḍbhār, from southeast, Raipur, Chhattisgarh, c. 8th cent. AD.
228. Door jamb, Nāga coils, entwined with figures, Śiva temple, Orāonṭolā, Deepadih, c. 8th cent. AD.
229. Door jamb fragment, stambhaśākhā, Sāmat Sarṇā, Deepadih, late 9th cent.-early 10th cent. AD.
230. Door jamb fragment with Kārtikeya, Sāmat Sarṇā, Deepadih, late 9th cent AD.
231. Door jamb with Nadī devīs and Gajalakṣmī on uttaraṅga, Sāmat Sarṇā, Deepadih, Surguja, late 9th-early 10th cent. AD.
232. Door jamb, Lakṣmaṇeśvara temple, Bhubaneswar, late 6th cent. AD.
233. Door jamb, Śiva temple, Bajrakoṭe, Ḍhenkānāl, Odisha, c. 8th cent. AD.
234. Door jamb, Kanakeśvara Mahādeva temple, Kuālo, Ḍhenkānāl, Odisha, c. 9th cent. AD.
235. Door jamb, Rājārāṇī temple, Bhubaneswar, c. 11th cent. AD.

Pillars & Pilasters at Tala

236. A pillar with prancing horses on ghaṭapallava base, ardhamaṇḍapa, south steps, Jethani, c. mid to late 5th cent. AD.
237. Prancing horses on ghaṭapallava base of pillar, south steps, Jethani, close view.
238. Prancing horses, ghaṭapallava base of pillar, south steps, Jethani, second view.
239. Pillar with prancing horses, makaras with human figures, elephant riders on leafy bracts on shaft, south steps, Jethani, c. 5th cent. AD.

268. Makaras, enmeshed with foliate forms, in frontal and profile view, fluted pillar, ardhamaṇḍapa, Devarani, c. late 5th cent. AD.
269. Makaras, enmeshed with foliate form, fluted pillar, ardhamaṇḍapa, Devarani, c. late 5th cent. AD.
270. Karimakaras, enmeshed in floriate frills, head turned back or front, fluted pillar, ardhamaṇḍapa, Devarani, late 5th cent. AD.
271. Gaṇa riding a swimming karimakara, fluted pillar, ardhamaṇḍapa, Devarani, late 5th cent. AD.
272. Gaṇa riding two affronted karimakaras, fluted pillar, ardhamaṇḍapa, Devarani, late 5th cent. AD.
273. Truncated pilaster, with lotus medallion, maṇḍapa, Devarani, c. late 5th cent. AD.

Pillars outside Tala

274. Pilaster with lotiform medallions, strung together, Sisdeori, Raipur, c. early 5th cent. AD.
275. Pilaster base with human heads and half lotus medallions at corners, Besnagar, c. early 5th cent. AD.
276. Pillars, Bhogārāma temple, Ramtek, c. 5th cent. AD.
277. Pillar with birds enmeshed in foliate forms, mithunas, worshipful lions, human beings and Kūrmajātaka, embedded in house wall, Malhār, Bilaspur, c. late 6th cent. AD.
278. Octagonal pillar with peacock, grāsakiṅkinikas and jewelled bands, Malhār, Bilaspur, MGM Museum, No. 2408, c. late 6th cent. AD.
279. Pillar with half lotus medallion, lions seated at corners, makaramukhas atop ghaṭapallava capital, Tīvaradeva Mahāvihāra, Sirpur, c. 7th cent. AD.
280. Jātaka tale, monkey and crocodile, owl, fruit and leaf cluster, door panel, Buddhist Monastery 3, Sirpur, c. 7th cent. AD.
281. Pillars with tall shafts and ghaṭapallava capital, Sirpur, Buddhist Monastery 2, SRP-4, c. 7th cent. AD.
282. Pillars with tall shafts, maṇḍapa, in front of double garbhagṛha, Suraṅgaṭilā, Sirpur, c. 7th cent. AD.
283. Pillars with tall shafts and ghaṭapallava capital, Sirpur, Buddhist monastary, c. 7th cent. AD.
284. Pillar with tall shaft, ghaṭapallava base and capital, Gandheśvara temple, Sirpur, c. 7th cent. AD.
285. Ānandaprabha kuṭi vihāra, Sirpur, c. 7th cent. AD.
286. Pillars, tall shafts, half-lotus medallions, lions at corners, ghaṭapallava capital, Rāmacandra temple, Rajim, Raipur, c. late 6th cent. AD.
287. Pillars, Gaṅgā on makara, tall shaft, vertical floral secions, half-lotus medallion, ghaṭapallava capital, maṇḍapa, Rāmacandra temple, Rajim, Raipur, c. late 6th cent. AD.
288. Pillars with lotus medallions, Rudra Narasiṁha temple, Ramtek, c. 5th cent. AD.
289. Pillar with lotus medallions, Rudra Narasiṁha temple, Ramtek, Nagpur, Maharashtra, c. 5th cent. AD.
290. Pillar with seated gaṇas at corners of tall shaft, Ellora, c. late 6th cent. AD.
291. Tetrafacial pillar with figures on all sides, cave 17, Ellora, Aurangabad, Maharashtra, c. late 6th cent. AD.

Female Figures at Tala

Female Figures outside Tala

317. Female figure, Rāmacandra temple Rajim, c. late 6th cent. AD.
318. Yamunā, Śiva temple, Sātmahallā, Kalcā Bhadvāhī, Surguja, c. 7th cent. AD.
319. Garland bearing lady, in tṛbhaṅga, Śiva temple, Sātmahallā, Kalcā Bhadvāhī, Surguja, Chhattisgarh, c. 7th cent. AD.
320. Vṛkṣakā, Malhār, Bhīmakīcak Temple, Bilaspur, c. 6th-7th cent. AD.
321. River goddess, built into west wall, Gandheśvara temple compound, Sirpur, Mahāsamund, Chhattisgarh, c. 7th cent. AD.
322. Āmrabhañjikā, door jamb of Buddhist temple, Kaṅṭhi Deul, Ratanpur, Sirpur, c. 8th cent. AD.
323. Gaṅgā, Sirpur, door jamb of temple, c. 7th cent. AD.
324. Ambikā, door jamb fragment, Sirpur, c. late 6th cent. AD.
325. Yamunā, door jamb fragment, Sirpur, M.G.M. Museum, Raipur, c. late 6th cent. AD.
326. Yamunā in tṛbhaṅga, door jamb, Sīddheśvara temple, Palāri, Raipur, c. 7th cent. AD.
327. Yamunā, door jamb, Kumrā Maṭh, Nācnā Kuṭhārā, Panna, Madhya Pradesh, early 6th cent. AD.
328. Lady carrying ghaṭa, in dvibhaṅga, Śiva temple, Orāonṭolā, Deepadih, c. 8th cent. AD.
329. Lady with child, Śiva temple, Orāonṭolā, Deepadih, c. 8th cent. AD.
330. Garland bearing lady, Sāmat Sarṇā, Deepadih, c. late 8th cent. AD.
331. Garland bearing lady, Sāmat Sarṇā, Deepadih, c. late 8th cent. AD.
332. Eight-armed Mahiṣāsuramardinī, stone, Sirpur, c. 7th cent. AD.
333. Mahiṣāsuramardinī, Sāmat Sarṇā, Deepadih, c. late 8th cent. AD.
334. Indrāṇī, Sāmat Sarṇā, Deepadih, c. 10th cent. AD.
335. Female figure, Sāmat Sarṇā, Deepadih, c. late 8th cent. AD.
336. Nadī Devī in profile, Aḍbhār, Raipur, c. 8th cent. AD.
337. Yamunā, door jamb, Aḍbhār, Bilaspur, Chhattisgarh, c. 8th cent. AD.
338. Gaṅgā, Indal Deul temple, Khārod, Raipur, c. 8th cent. AD.
339. Yamunā, Indal Deul temple, Khārod, Raipur, c. 8th cent. AD.
340. Darpaṇa Nāyikā, Maheshpur, Surguja, c. 10th-11th cent. AD.
341. Vṛkṣakā, Vaitāl Deul temple, Bhubaneswar, c. late 8th cent. AD.
342. Vṛkṣakā, Rājārāṇī temple, Bhubaneswar, c. 11th cent. AD.

Male Figures at Tala

343. Śiva Kṛttivāsa, in tigerskin, with broken trunk, northeast of Devarani, probably Jethani, c. 5th cent. AD.
344. Śaiva dvārapāla image, east of Jethani, c. 5th cent. AD.
345. Guardian figure, broken below waist, holding an image bearing gaṇa, south steps, Jethani, c. 5th cent. AD.
346. Varuṇa with rearing makaras, framed by pilasters with foliate carving, from its left, wall slab, south steps, Jethani, c. 5th cent. AD.
347. Varuṇa with lotus cap and halo, a close view, Jethani, c. 5th cent. AD.
348. Head of Varuṇa, with lotus crown, south steps, Jethani, c. 5th cent. AD.
349. Śiva Kṛttivāsa, ūrdhvaliṅga, in tigerskin, ithyphallic, with broken legs, arms and trunk, east steps, Jethani, c. 5th cent. AD.
350. Kārtikeya, wall slab, south steps, Jethani, Bilaspur Museum, c. 5th cent. AD.

Male Figures in Chhattisgarh

Male Figures outside Chhattisgarh

380. Dvārapāla, left of entrance door, east, cave 6, Udayagiri, Vidisha, Madhya Pradesh, c. 5th cent. AD.
381. Viṣṇu, Nāndchānd, Jabalpur, Madhya Pradesh, c. early 5th cent. AD.
382. Standing Viṣṇu with broken head and arms, from Guptārāma temple, Central Museum compound, Ramtek, Nagpur, c. late 5th cent. AD.
383. Dvārapāla, Bhūmarā, Madhya Pradesh, c. late 5th cent. AD.
384. Dvārapāla, Ramtek, c. mid 5th cent. AD.
385. Śiva, Soṅḍni, Māndāsor, Madhya Pradesh, c. 6th cent. AD.
386. Bodhisattva, Pavnār, Nagpur, Maharashtra, c. 5th cent. AD.
387. Sanchi, Bodhisattva, late 5th cent. AD.
388. Viṣṇu, Māndāsor, Madhya Pradesh, c. mid to late 5th cent. AD.
389. Buddha, wearing robe, covering both shoulders, ubhayāṁśikā saṁghāṭi, Pavnār, Nagpur, Maharashtra, c. 5th cent. AD.
390. Buddha, in abhaya mudrā, Sarnath, Uttar Pradesh, c. late 5th cent. AD.
391. Trivikrama, Trivikrama temple, Ramtek, Nagpur, Maharashtra, c. 5th cent. AD.
392. Vāsudeva Kṛṣṇa, Pavnār, Nagpur, Maharashtra, c. 5th cent. AD.
393. Kṛṣṇa, Śakaṭāsuravadha (execution of the cart-demon), Pavnār, c. 5th cent. AD.
394. Kṛṣṇa, Śakaṭāsuravadha, Pavnār, a second view.

Mithunas at Tala and outside Tala

395. Mithuna, inside panel, left door jamb, Devarani, c. late 5th cent. AD.
396. Escorts for Gaṅgā, inside panel, left door jamb, Devarani, c. late 5th cent. AD.
397. Mithuna, wearing scrolled, discal, grooved śīṣapatra earrings, catulatilakamaṇi crest jewel, male wearing bhramaraka trefoil hairdress, like bee with outspread wings, inside panel, left door jamb, Devarani, c. late 5th cent. AD.
398. Devarani, from east, mithuna on vedībandha of later platform, close view.
399. Mithuna, inside panel, left door jamb, Devarani, c. late 5th cent. AD.
400. Mithunas, inside panel, left door jamb, Devarani.
401. Umāsahita Śiva, at dalliance, flanked by gaṇas in various stages of stupefaction, at Kailāśa mountain, inside panel, right door jamb, Devarani, c. late 5th cent. AD.
402. Hara Gaurī at Causar, pillar 16, Gaḍhvā, Gwalior, Madhya Pradesh, c. 5th cent. AD.
403. Śiva and Pārvatī, pillar 15, Gaḍhvā, Gwalior, c. 5th cent. AD.
404. Rāma and Sītā in mango grove, Nācnā Kuṭhārā, Panna, Madhya Pradesh, late 5th cent. AD.
405. Umāsahita Śiva in paryaṅkāsana, snakehood spread out above Umā's śikhaṇḍa, hair crest, Sāmat Sarṇā, Deepadih, Surguja, Chhattisgarh, c. 9th cent. AD.
406. Hara Gaurī, Maheshpur, Surguja, c. 10th-11th cent. AD.
407. Mithuna, left door jamb, garbhagṛha, Rāmacandra temple, Rajim, Chhattisgarh, c. 6th cent. AD.
408. Mithuna, Paraśurāmeśvara temple, Bhubaneswar, c. 7th cent. AD.
409. Rāma and Sītā, Bhīmakīcak temple, Malhār, Madhya Pradesh, c. 7th cent. AD.
410. Rāma and Sītā, Nācnā Kuthāra, Panna, Madhya Pradesh, c. 6th cent. AD.

Male Heads in and outside Tala

441. Caturmukha Liṅga, Nācnā Kuṭhārā, Panna, Madhya Pradesh, c. 6th cent. AD.
442. Abraded head of Śiva, framed by cluster of mango leaves with bunch of fruits, Devarani, c. late 5th cent. AD.
443. Ekamukha Liṅga, Khoh, Satna, c. 5th cent. AD.
444. Head of Śiva, Nācnā Kuṭhārā, Panna, Madhya Pradesh, c. 6th cent. AD.
445. Head of Viṣṇu, right profile, Garh Dhanaurā, Kānker, Bastar, Chhattisgarh, c. 4th cent. AD.
446. Head of worshipful Sagaraputra, hair clustered in cūrṇakuntala, inside panel, right door jamb, Devarani, c. late 5th cent. AD.
447. Head of Sagaraputra, inside panel, right door jamb, Devarani.

Female Heads in and outside Tala

448. Female head and headdress, threaded with garbhaka, wreathed chaplets of flowers, hair plaited in spirally twisted vertical rows, valibhṛd alaka, left door jamb, Devarani.
449. Āmrabhañjikā, right profile, forehead ornament of kadamba flower leaf in center, flanked by leafy bracts of jack fruit (Eng.), Jethani.
450. Female head, Pavāyā, Gwalior, Madhya Pradesh, c. 5th cent. AD.
451. Female head, Khoh, Satna, Madhya Pradesh, c. 5th cent. AD.
452. Head of lady, Mānsar, Nagpur, Maharashtra, c. 5th cent. AD.
453. Gaṅgā, right profile, Pavnār, Nagpur, Maharashtra, c. 5th cent. AD.
454. Male and female heads, Khoh, Satna, Madhya Pradesh, c. 5th cent. AD.
455. Female head, Mānsar Museum, c. 5th cent. AD.

Sages in and outside Tala

456. Sage, Mānsar Museum, Nagpur, Maharashtra, c. 5th cent. AD.
457. Sage with broken head and legs, in gesture of benediction, Jethani, c. mid to late 5th cent. AD, Bilaspur Museum.
458. Sage with disciple, wall slab, Devarani, c. late 5th cent. AD.
459. Sage with broken trunk, carrying a pronged stick, wall slab, Devarani, c. late 5th cent. AD.
460. Right profile of sage, with drawn up knees, on nāgarāja base, recovered from front of threshold, Devarani ardhamaṇḍapa, c. late 5th cent. AD.
461. Sage with broken trunk, wall slab, Devarani ardhamaṇḍapa, c. late 5th cent. AD.
462. Sage on wall slab, from Devarani ardhamaṇḍapa, a frontal view of head, c. late 5th cent. AD.
463. Sage with disciple, wall slab, Devarani, c. late 5th cent. AD.

Hands, Feet, & Architectural Fragments in and outside Tala

464. Broken hand and small broken trunk, Jethani, c. 5th cent. AD.
465. Broken hand with upturned palm, Jethani, c. 5th cent. AD.
466. Broken hand with curled, downturned fingers, Jethani, c. 5th cent. AD.
467. Broken hand, holding sacred thread, Jethani, c. 5th cent. AD.
468. A broken foot, Jethani, c. 5th cent. AD.
469. Fingers of feet, upside down, on broken slab, Jethani, c. 5th cent. AD.

Gaṇas at Tala

495. Smiling load bearing gaṇa, legs tucked under belly, foot on head, south steps, Jethani, c. 5th cent. AD.
496. Gaṇa heads, recovered from south steps, Jethani, c. 5th cent. AD.
497. Gaṇas looking at game of chausar between Hara and Gaurī, right door jamb, Devarani.
498. Smiling Gaṇa head, above Sarasvatī image, left wall, ardhamaṇḍapa, Devarani, c. late 5th cent. AD.
499. Gaṇas at game of chausar between Hara and Gaurī, Nandī being dragged away as lost wager, inside panel, right door jamb, Devarani.
500. Gaṇas looking out from the slab with image of Mārtaṇḍa Bhairava, Devarani, c. late 5th cent. AD.
501. Gaṇa with Kubera, back turned to audience, inside panel, left door jamb, Devarani, c. late 5th cent. AD.
502. Gaṇa at entrance, Devarani, c. late 5th cent. AD.

Gaṇas outside Tala

503. Cluster of gaṇas, carrying a large ghaṭa, on bank of tank, Sisdeori, Raipur, c. 5th cent. AD.
504. Gaṇas in panels on left & right door jambs, Kevala Narasiṁha temple, Ramtek, Nagpur, Maharashtra, c. 5th cent. AD.
505. Paraśudhārī gaṇa, Buddhist vihāra, Sirpur.
506. Gaṇa with arms akimbo, Ramtek, c. 5th cent. AD.
507. Gaṇa raising load on shoulder, Ramtek, c. 5th cent. AD.
508. Agni on padmavedikā, lower part of door jamb, Sisdeori, Raipur, Chhattisgarh, c. 5th cent. AD.
509. Gaṇa holding daṇḍa, Nācnā, Panna, Rāmvan Musuem, c. 5th cent. AD.
510. Gaṇa running, looking back, Prince of Wales Museum, Khoh, Satna, Madhya Pradesh, c. 5th cent. AD.
511. Four-armed load bearing gaṇa, in the nude, with upraised head, hands on knees, Mānsar, c. 5th cent. AD.
512. Two load bearing gaṇas, one with moustache, the other with a cloth across shoulder, Mānsar, Mānsar museum, Nagpur, Maharashtra, c. 5th cent. AD.
513. Gaṇa with animal crest, open mouth, Mānsar, Mānsar museum, c. 5th cent. AD.
514. Kinnara, Mānsar, Mānsar Museum, c. 5th cent. AD.
515. Gaṇa, drunk, tilted over, Nāgardhan, Nagpur, Maharashtra, c. 5th cent. AD.
516. Śiva as gaṇa, Mānsar, National Museum, c. 5th cent. AD.
517. Gaṇas, jālavātāyana, south wall, garbhagṛha, Pārvatī temple, Nācnā, Panna, Madhya Pradesh, c. 5th cent. AD.
518. Garland bearing vidyādharas and vidyādharīs, jewelled band, yajñavarāha, Eran, Sagar, Madhya Pradesh, c. late 5th cent. AD.
519. Gaṇa, hands raised in explication, temple 2, Nalanda, c. 6th cent. AD.
520. Load bearing gaṇa, Nācnā, Teliyā Maṭh, c. early 6th cent. AD.
521. Two dancing gaṇas, cave 16, Ajāntā, c. 6th cent. AD.
522. Load bearing gaṇa with four arms, Bhīmakīcak temple, Malhār, c. 7th cent. AD.
523. Four-armed load bearing gaṇa, Bhīmakīcak temple, Malhār, c. 7th cent. AD.

553. Fragment of lion head, carrying figure, showing traces of foot on head, Sisdeori, c. 5th cent. AD.
554. Narasiṁha, Kevala Narasiṁha temple, Ramtek, c. 5th cent. AD.
555. Standing Narasiṁha with broken arms and legs, Eran, c. late 5th cent. AD.
556. Narasiṁha, Garh Dhanaurā, found in garbhagṛha of a temple, Kānker, Bastar, Chhattisgarh, c. 6th cent. AD.
557. Narasiṁha, Dev Dhanaurā, Kānker, Bastar, c. 6th cent. AD.
558. Four-armed, seated Kevala Narasiṁha, Sirpur, c. 7th-8th cent. AD.
559. Kīrtimukha, pillar capital, Pipariyā, Parasmaniyā plateau, Satna, Madhya Pradesh, c. 5th cent. AD.
560. Narasiṁha killing Hiraṇyakaśipu, Rājīvalocana temple, Rajim, c. 7th-8th cent. AD.

Meṣa, Varāha etc. in and outside Tala

561. Meṣamukha gaṇa, at entrance of Devarani, c. late 5th cent. AD.
562. Meṣamukha gaṇa, profile from its right, Devarani, c. late 5th cent. AD.
563. Prancing lions flanking lion head, emitting jewelled scrolls, Paraśurāmeśvara temple, Bhubaneswar, c. 7th cent AD.
564. Lions on elephants, Vaitāl Deul, Bhubaneswar, c. late 8th cent AD.
565. Nandī, its hind quarters embedded in stone, north of Jethani, c. 5th cent. AD.
566. Varāha head and architectural fragments, Jethani, c. 5th cent. AD.
567. Head of Varāha, Jethani c. late 5th cent. AD.
568. Hayagrīva, Nācnā Kuṭhārā, Panna Museum, Panna, Madhya Pradesh, c. 5th cent. AD.
569. Yajñavarāha, Eran, Sagar, Madhya Pradesh, c. late 5th cent. AD.
570. Varāha from Khoh, at Uceharā, municipal premises, Satna, Madhya Pradesh, c. 5th cent. AD.
571. Nṛvarāha, Excavation 5, Udayagiri, Vidisha, Madhya Pradesh, c. early 5th cent. AD.
572. Varāha, Varāha temple, Ramtek, Nagpur, Maharashtra, c. 5th cent. AD.
573. Nṛvaraha, Sāmat Sarṇā, Deepadih, Surguja, c. 8th-9th cent. AD.
574. Nṛvarāha, mound 3, Viṣṇu temple, Niśān Pākhnā, Maheshpur, Surguja, Chhattisgarh, c. 10th-11th cent. AD.

Rudra Śiva Paśupati at Tala

575. Prof. Pramod Chandra and V.K. Vajpeyi, Dy Director, State Archaeology, Madhya Pradesh, on find site of Paśupati.
576. Villagers waiting with bated breath for the Rudra Śiva imageslab, being brought out at the southeast corner of Devarani, c. 5th cent. AD.
577. Rudra Śiva image slab, on its back, after excavation, southeast of Devarani, probably from Jethani.
578. Rudra Śiva image slab, lying prone on its face, after clearance, southeast of Devarani.
579. Devarani temple, devotees assembled in fair, to gain view of Rudra Śiva.
580. Author with the Rudra Śiva image.
581. Rudra Śiva, from behind, left, author with Rahul Singh.
582. Rudra Śiva, right profile.

Śiva and Analogous Figures outside Tala

621. Sadāśiva, back, Māndhal, Nagpur, c. 5th cent. AD.
622. Sadāśiva, Māndhal, right profile.
623. Sadāśiva, Māndhal, left profile.
624. Śiva gaṇa, bearing flower, Māndhal, Nagpur, Maharashtra, c. 5th cent. AD.
625. Viśvarūpa Viṣṇu, Pārel, Maharashtra, c. 6th cent. AD.
626. Ūrdhvaliṅga, Śiva Kṛttivāsa, Māndhal, Nagpur, Maharashtra.
627. Gaṇa, with Kalāgni on belly, Bharmaur, Chamba, Himachal Pradesh, c. 6th cent. AD.
628. Udaremukha gaṇa.
629. Śiva with attendants, Citrakūṭ, Bastar, Chhattisgarh, c. 18th cent. AD.
630. Cāmuṇdā, Citrakūṭ, Bastar, Chhattisgarh, c. 18th cent. AD.
631. Pictish warrior with armour formed of animal heads, England, c. 12th cent. AD.
632. Demonic figure with animal heads on body, Poland, c. 16th cent. AD.
633. Aśokalumbī, later platform, Devarani, c. 7th cent. AD.
634. Hari Hara, four-armed, with upraised phallus, trident, conch,tiger skin garment, matted locks and crown, ayudhapuruṣas, akin to standing Lakulīśa. Worshipped as Bachrajkuanwar . Village Manpur, District Balarampur, Chhattisgarh, c. 6th cent. AD.
635. Standing Viṣṇu, Turturiyā, district Mahasamund, Chhattisgarh, c. 6th cent. AD.
636. Wooden mask, carved with snake, bird, crab. Collection from near Kondagaon, Bastar, Chhattisgarh, around 1980, reported by Mr. Niranjan Mahawar, Raipur, and given by him to Museum in Anthropology Deptt., Ravishankar University, Raipur. Comparable Bāiga pictographic mask from Pandpur, Mandla, Madhya Pradesh, illustrated by Elwin 1951 (Fig. 159).

Introduction

This volume seeks to correct marginalization and exclusion of Dakṣiṇa Kośala, of which the Indian state of Chhattisgarh has been a part, from the archaeological and art historical frame of contemporary interpreters. It counters the historicist characterization of dynastic, imperial, metropolitan, fine, conventionally natural art, as more valuable, of higher priority and originality than the popular, artisanal, suburban, seemingly non-natural art. It describes the itinerary of Śiva, who is credited with the origin of all arts, philosophy, sciences, and presides over the most radical and asocial cults. The itinerary bridges the divide between collective memory and orality, Āgama and Nigama traditions, transmitted through Śruti and Smṛti, votive and invocative inscriptions.

Despite the absence of texts that could provide ready explanation of the shape and meaning of the art in the region, there has been a logocentric obsession with exclusive iconographic identifications, on the basis of isolated textual canons. An inclusive and harmonious construction of texts and traditions shows that diverse identities and contrarieties, derived from many sources, coexist in the concepts and stylistic attributes of this art. Formal and conceptual approaches have, therefore, been combined to explain the roots and appreciate the fitness of this art for describing the idea and image of Śiva.

The Devarani temple at Tala in Bilaspur district of eastern Madhya Pradesh was already known to specialists for a most unusual plan and one of the finest door jambs with many inexplicable iconographic features. Attracted by these features, I visited Tala in October 1987, and was fascinated by the unique three door Jethani temple revealed in an earlier 1986 excavation. My curiosity and knowledge of Indian art were stretched to utmost by these two temples at Tala, and I was moved by a great desire to study and understand the unique remains. The prospect was a challenging one for the art of the region had been little studied, and the monuments of Tala even less so. Earlier studies had dismissed Tala art rather cavalierly as a tribal aberration from the ecumenical styles of India, and suggested that the temples had no relevance for the development of Indian art within or outside the region. The perception was readily explained by the fact that Tala was situated in the midst of a hilly, forested, inaccessible tribal hinterland, and its art could not be pinned down to any iconographic or architectural text, but this was difficult for me to accept. Instead, Tala suggested to me a classical power, naturalistic observation, volume and grace recalling 5th century Vidarbha art, and it also evoked in me memories of a medieval mannerism, that characterized the work of the other temples of the region, notably those of Malhār and Sirpur.

If a fascinating though baffling ambivalence between unconscious simplicity and conscious complexity was the fatal attraction of Tala art, it was also engrossing because of the overwhelming strength and opulence of its forms, replete with a sense of the sacred. This art was nothing like we had seen before in Indian art in its attempt to transcend all canonical boundaries for expressing the inexpressible and measuring the immeasurable. A quality of strange yearning, fervent energy and reaching for the unknown, latent in the sacred hymns of the early texts, seemed to inform this art. Its enormous vitality and creative zest incited in me a restless spirit of adventure, leading me to look for its stylistic and cognitive origins and to trace the influence, which I instinctively felt it to have exercised on the monuments that followed it in the Dakṣiṇa Kośala region of India. An assessment of the viability of art as a vehicle for attaining a knowledge of human life and destiny in the fathomless immensity of this universe appeared to depend on the feasibility of this enterprise. It was this quest which drove me to guide the clearance conducted by Govt. of Madhya Pradesh, on the mound surrounding the Devarani at Tala in 1987. The clearance revealed a colossal Paśupati image of brute power, iconographic features and experimental freedom, unprecedented in the history of Indian art. I followed up the Tala clearance by extensive surveys in Dakṣiṇa Kośala and located numerous mounds in Bilaspur, Raipur, Surguja and Bastar districts of Madhya Pradesh. I helped the Govt. organize successive clearances at Deepadih and Belsar in Surguja, and Bhoṅgāpāl and Garh Dhanaurā in Bastar and unearthed numerous temples, monasteries, and architectural fragments ranging from the fifth to the eleventh century AD. Many of these possessed remarkable correspondences to Tala art. As I extended the scope of my investigations to eastern, western and central India, I discovered distinct elements in these areas which seemed to be connected to the art of Tala and Dakṣiṇa Kośala. In fact, the unusual combination of ancient, tried elements, simultaneous preoccupation with overpowering scale or minutiae of ornament, interpenetration of meanings and forms, architecture and sculpture, use of processional, terraced access, punctuated by intrusive architectural members, the bold, playful, experimental concern with dynamic movement, created by asymmetrical arrangements, gestures and postures, diverse expressions, patterns, tones and hues of light and shade were elements of the art of Dakṣiṇa Kośala which were adapted in different mutations in later Indian art.

Since most the ground covered by me is fresh and untrodden, and the sites are new and virtually unpublished, I have been unable to assume prior information about these areas. Since I have suggested the formation of a new regional style of Dakṣiṇa Kośala which germinates at Tala, I have found it necessary to put Tala in the overall historical context by making an extensive discussion of its similarities and differences with other relevant sites. I could have excluded such details only at the risk of lending to Tala either an impossible isolation from or an all encompassing role in later Indian art. In the absence of relevant canonical texts, I have interpreted the iconography by going back to sacred texts, and by taking a holistic and eclectic rather than an orthodox or exclusivist view. Since I find the meaning or function of this collective art remarkably constant through the centuries inspite of its apparently individual expressions, I have harnessed references from different periods, looked for and found a firm and continuing core of meaning in them for the elucidation of this art. I have listed primary Sanskrit literary sources by categories, though my general references also include commentaries elicited from inscriptions, coins, foreign accounts edited by scholars, and texts on the theory and practice of arts the world over. I have grouped the illustrations by iconographic types in order to facilitate visual comparisons. References in the text to the illustrations, therefore, are not sequential. I have explained the unusual architecture by reference to the terminology used for approximately similar architectural segments or their modifications in Odisha and Central India. I have shown the irrelevance of southern terminology used for Tala art in certain earlier studies. Since the art of this period has to be understood, to the extent possible, in terms of its makers, and since the Sanskrit terms which give this art functional validity and meaning cannot be given in English translation alone without inpairing their integrity, I have used them as part and parcel of the text with diacriticals as is the growing practice. I have refrained from italicizing such terms and analogous terms in other languages not only for avoiding visual clutter but also because they have already passed into common scholarly use. Nevertheless, I have added a glossary of architectural terms from different regional vocabularies at the end, for the English reader's convenience. Otherwise, I have bracketed the translations with the literary and iconographic terms in the text itself. Diacriticals have been used only for less known names and place names (except for Tālā, Jethāni and Devarāni which are in frequent use) to induce a correct understanding of etymological derivation and pronunciation. I have put the footnotes and numbered them serially at the end of each individual chapter. However, I have numbered the illustrations serially through the volume. I have put Tala art in the background of the confluence of cults engendered by a surge of devotional faith and practice, using data from contemporary inscriptions and ethnoarchaeological studies. With new material pouring in from Dakṣiṇa Kośala, my conclusions are bound to undergo modifications. I have assigned approximate dates to temples and associated sculptures, on the basis of a comparative stylistic study bolstered by examples of dated structures. In the list of illustrations, I have indicated the period in general terms. My chronology is not to be taken as absolute, but only as a code for establishing a sequence of styles. This broad sequence, it is hoped, will survive.

The volume explores art history at the interface of archaeology, art history, cultural theory, ethnology, intellectual and religious history and philosophy, in the contested space of east-west cultural encounter and interaction in research. Those who lived and experienced the past in the art world of Dakṣiṇa Kośala, could not fully know or understand it. Those of us who are trying to know or understand this past, cannot experience it, and our knowledge is doomed to arrive too late on the scene of experience. Hence, my exercise in recapitulation, recollection and reconstruction of the past in the region, cannot but be imperfect. My attempt to move back and forth between cultural sites and the cultural landscape is not new. What is new in the art history of the region is the cross-disciplinary quest to locate the art in the backdrop of Indian ideological history and the global history of shape and meaning; to synthesize domains of thought, to induce understanding about the deep and simmering connection between the physical ingredients of style and the deep, incorporeal structures of meaning.

The volume begins with an analysis of the southeastern geographical and eco-cultural situation of Dakṣiṇa Kośala, on the north-south trade route. The hilly, forested topography, tribal demography, dynastic rule, respectful of local, institutional autonomy in Dakṣiṇa Kośala, and the rich artistic traditions nurtured in the adjacent cultural provinces in its neighbourhood, account for the autochthonous and complex artistic developments in the region. Since the boundaries of cultural provinces are not impermeable, such developments acknowledge and innovatively transform the ideological and stylistic influence of art in surrounding areas. The second chapter on history analyses the fusion of Gupta Vākāṭaka families and scripts, leavened by regional influences, to provide a historical background to the autonomous and experimental trends in the art of Dakṣiṇa Kośala. The third chapter on archaeology describes the tendency, in Dakṣiṇa Kośala, revealed through several excavations, towards growing rarification, ethnicization and experimentation in art and architecture, through successive structural and sculptural additions.

In the fourth chapter on historiography, reason for the limited scholarly attention received by Tala, the type site chosen for analysis, is analysed. It is shown that Tala art has tended to be misunderstood as a clumsy, idiosyncratic, xylographic tribal misinterpretation of the Gupta Vākāṭaka, Pallava or Cālukya dynastic art rather than as a bold local interpretation of pan-Indian traditions. The problem of understanding would appear to lie as much with the predilection for dynastic attribution of the motifs and patterns of Dakṣiṇa Kośala art as with the limited evidence accessible at the time of analysis.

The fifth chapter on architecture charts a transition, at Jethani and Devarani temples at Tala, from an additive, spread out, sculpturesque structure to a more integrated, architectonic, compact structure; from relative simplicity to complexity of forms; measured curvilinear rhythm to accelerated movement and sharp rectilinear accents; tactile and placid to visually mobile, chromatic surfaces. The stylistic transition is underwritten by the increasing refinement of the theme of emanation and resolution, in the multiplication, abstraction, interpenetration, merger of floral, faunal, geometric, figural patterns.

The sixth chapter on sculpture speaks of the coexistence of the volumetric and linear, heavy and slender, asymmetric and symmetric, simple and ornate, organic and geometric styles, unity and variation of iconographic elements, discontinuous and continuous narratives in the sculptures of Tala and analogous sites. Despite a simultaneity of 'classical' and 'medieval' features, or an internal movement towards greater stylization, linearization, geometricization, Tala sculpture remains integrally one in its central Indian preference for volume, naturalism and humanism. It is experimental, not demonstrative, expressive not expressionistic, large not ponderous, loyal to, not mimetic of nature, a complex whole, not a disparate sum of parts. This is explained through a comparison of Tala with earlier sites of Dakṣiṇa Kośala and Vidarbha and later sites of central India or rest of India. The study focuses on formal features of objects in the background of their epigraphic, numismatic, literary and epistemic associations.

The seventh chapter on iconography and iconology wrestles with problems of understanding path-breaking attempts at sites like Tala to integrate form with content, to realize the diversity and complexity of the idea of Śiva in concrete, physical form. It explains how scholars misinterpret the Paśupati image at Tala in two major ways. They fasten on one aspect of the image to the exclusion of all other aspects and support their preconceived identification by quoting some texts. Or, they misread the psychosomatic significance of Paśupati and associated images in biological terms. They appear to have a preconception about the tribal association of the art, and its instinctive, rather than rational inspiration. Such a preconception is corrected by a reading of the Indian tradition in the local context. This demonstrates the possibility of coexistence, in one image, of the features of Śiva as Paśupati, Aṣṭamūrti, Yogī, Lakulīśa, Agni and Yakṣa, and, of ambivalent benefic and malefic, logical and emotional aspects in associated images. This convergence of shapes and seemingly antithetical features in Śiva and his cohorts at Tala and associated sites, is induced by an idea of the cyclic interplay of Soma and Agni, fire and waters, eros and psyche, tapas and retas, in the microcosmic and macrocosmic body of the human and non-human beings and the universe. The idea is explained through a process of fecundation, germination, pollination, disintegration and integration of all anthropomorphic, zoomorphic, theoriomorphic forms. All organic and inorganic features of Tala, including the pillar, door leaf, flowers, creepers, dwarfs, river goddesses, couples, divinities, ascetics, ornament and dress play their roles individually and in unison, to narrate the theme of therapeutic rectification and transformation of nature through recycling of waters, ascent of consciousness, sacrifice of lower passions, interpenetration of forms. The temples act as the body, house, playground, stage for Śiva and his companions in this narrative. Dakṣiṇa Kośala, with all its temples, rivers, sacred landscapes, vibrates with the idea of Śiva. As Śiva walks in the terrain, all nature walks with him, seeking immersion in him.

The eighth chapter on ethnography confronts the suggestion of tribal roots of Tala art by exploring analogies between tribal art today and the ancient art of Tala and Dakṣiṇa Kośala. Continuity between the older and contemporary art of the region is conceded. Postulates of bioneurological constants or continuing oral traditions that may permit such continuity, are admitted. Priority, originality or superiority of one art over the other are denied. Instead, a constant exchange between the oral and visual, textual and contextual tradition is suggested. In the composite, synthetic imagery traditions of Tala and other contemporary sites, the snake, tiger, tortoise, crab, fish and plants, figure as identity markers, ritual and apotropaic symbols, ornament or armour, megalithic, architectural, technological or totemic designs. They also act as defining elements for time and space. Trees, plants, creepers, flowers and fruits, specially the lotus, are harnessed now, as then, to evoke images of marriage, pregnancy, water cosmology, fertility and communion. Naṅgā Baigā and Naṅgā Baigin are equated with Śiva and Pārvatī. Liṅgodev and Naṅgā Baigā are identified with Śiva in all his creative and procreative roles. Baigā guṇiās are assimilated to Pāśupata gurus. The older sacrificial, funerary, ancestral, residual or increase rituals, associated with Śiva, are comparable with current rituals of sacrifice and increase, practised by local communities. The sacred landscape continues to be vivified today, as in ancient Dakṣiṇa Kośala, with devotion for Śiva, mother goddesses, primordial couples and water cosmological principles, enshrined in temples situated on river confluences. Traditions of pantheism and heterodoxy continue to characterize the faith and practice of the region. The stage setting, identity building, primitivistic urban arts of the nascent state of Chhattisgarh consciously imitate the traditional narrative, decorative, iconographic repertoire of Dakṣiṇa Kośala. There is no reason to imagine that the tribal ritual, ceremonial or artistic expressions today, that hark back to older temple arts of Dakṣiṇa Kośala, do not coexist with or precede arts of Tala or corollary cultural sites. In fact, there is a fusion between the textual and contextual, local and universal canons of Indian art in the region, and, this is catalyzed by a network of patronage, that includes all sections of society.

Once the geographical, historical, archaeological, ethnographic, stylistic and ideological context of the Tala temples has been discussed, in the backdrop of the art of India and Dakṣiṇa Kośala, chapter nine on origins and influence of Tala architecture elicits the stylistic trends from this discussion and uses them as tools to unravel subsequent developments in the art and architecture of Dakṣiṇa Kośala and India. The discussion dispels the notion that Tala art is an orphan, isolated, inbred and sterile, without ancestors or progeny. It demonstrates that Tala nurtures in its bosom not one but three different stylistic trends, which bring Jethani closer to Gupta Vākāṭaka past; directly influence the subsequent art of Dakṣiṇa Kośala, indirectly, the art of Odisha; interact with the art of Vidarbha, and remains a vital impulse in the formation of the larger body of Indian art. The chapter analyses the manner in which Tala contributes, to harness and transform the legacy of earlier rock-cut architecture and structural temples into an innovative spatial plan; galvanize a fusion of architecture and sculpture; use older elements in new and unusual combinations; and reinterpret and recreate them, in the facades of the stone and brick temples of Chhattisgarh and Odisha. One can see the contribution of Tala and analogous sites in later artistic developments. Surprising and innovative mutations of the Tala style can be seen at later sites of Dakṣiṇa Kośala, in lean and heavy bodied figural forms; lateral and inward propulsion of door jamb figures; deep cut, restless, coloristic segmentation of door frames; terraced, processional access, moving and heaving with cyclopean sculptures; multiplication, miniaturization, amplification, stylization of elements, used sparingly at Tala. A seesaw, back and forth movement occurs between Kaliṅga and Dakṣiṇa Kośala, with intrusion of stylistic elements, emerging from territories, which may, for the sake of convenience, be considered to be under Nala, Pallava, Cālukya, Vākāṭaka, Pāṇḍuvaṁśi, Śarabhapurīya or Kalacurī control.

In chapter ten, in conclusion, a plea is made for resolving problems of understanding or misunderstanding. It is emphasized that in order to understand the art historical developments of this region and period, the art historian has to analyse the ways in which the form and function, sacred and profane, many and one, nature and culture have converged in this art. S/he has to accept a responsibility to combine sympathetic and critical, affective and rational approaches; dissolve artificial boundaries between subject and object; go back from the conceptual and perceptual, to the preconceptual and prerepresentational; and proceed, from the thought to the unthought. A homologic rather than hegemonic quest is advocated, to permit a perception of this art as cathartic rather than fetishistic. A formal, stylistic analysis is interwoven with an iconological analysis of the tradition, reflected in the catechistic, edificatory prescriptions in the epigraphic or religious texts. An appreciation of the mutually reinforcive relationship between figures of speech and figures of thought has been seen as necessary for explaining ramifications in the art of Tala, Dakṣiṇa Kośala and the neighbourhood.

These volumes try to make the visible legible. The art is legible in a universe of meaning, shared universally. It has been designed as a synthesis of discipline and enjoyment, yoga and bhoga, sāṁsāra and mokṣa, instrumental and moral action. It is based on the recollection of the first contract, a nexus, an exchange, a pot latch rite, which ties together the outcaste or avadhūta, ascetic or sannyāsī, householder officiant or yajamāna, and priest or purohita, through a material gift of land, in lieu of a spiritual gift of merit and deliverance. The patron priest sorcerer artist has dedicated the art, in an exchange of grace, in a religious rite, to bind the audience with the absolute.[1]

This exchange reflects a simultaneous awareness of ideas and forms, logical and historical order, causes and effects. Designed as memno technical theatres for presenting the relationship between nature and culture, the temples of the region in question are mythomorphic. They approximate the enunciative event, zeitgeist (spirit of the age), the kunstwollen (will to form), the idea, and the will to visualize the idea, in nonverbal correlates. They constitute a self reflective and autotelic (pregnant with purpose) activity, which is also representational and phatic (socially participative communication). They incorporate the idiolect (unique language), traces of their own 'funicity' (perpetual memory of origins), previous aesthetic problems and solutions, diachronic and diatropic (transverse to external stimulus) change, in the signifier and signified.[2] They provide an image of reality, which is also a sign for it. They substitute the image for writing, in which the letter is read allegorically, not literally, being created after the archetype, transmitted through memoria, as each man bears signature of God in his 'dei-formity'. The artist makes the whole thing, not small parts of things, acting analogously to the primordial act of creating the phenomenal from the noumenal. He articulates a universal dialect, a sophia perennis, a mimesis of the invisible paradeigma (archetype).[3]

Images like the Tala Paśupati have been created by the artist, to combine dispersion with integration, in imitation of the ceaseless creative cycles in the universe. Such images are composite, syncretistic, ambiguous, not because of his uncertainty about the tradition, but because of his continuous reinterpretation of the tradition, in every generation. The diversification of expression, exaggeration in gestures, distortion in natural appearances in art are governed by a coherent philosophy which shows the artist what this world is and should be.[4] The conscious and unconscious, are not two rooms connected by a doorkeeper in this philosophy of art, but two vessels whose contents mix by constant osmosis. This philosophical frame is not reified, fetishized as a superhistorical, natural or redemptive force in Marxian or Freudian terms. Rather, it is posed as a pre-reflective, anti-predicative (attributive) unity of world and life, speaking in terms of existential phenomenology.[5]

Because of conditions of under communication, not yet overcome by homogenization, the older society is fecund in producing variations, even as it retains fidelity to the thematic unity, projected in the philosophy of this art. The dynamic relation between form and content, part and the whole, perceived and developed in this art, permits such variations, every present having a different past, a new sense accruing with each new work. The apparently scattered elements of mythology converge to make a meaningful whole and the diachronic succession of events yields a synchronic order. To the extent the artist is able to reflect, through formal means, the concord between the form and content in this art, through all variations, it is lively and beautiful. Once this concord breaks down due to the slackening of the artist's attention, or, of the vision animating him, the art loses its plasticity and beauty. To the extent the idea of Śiva permeates the depiction of all communities, human and nonhuman, it gives life to such art. As soon as the idea loses its fervour, the art becomes desiccated and lifeless.[6]

Theory was not needed to explain the conjunction or disjunction of form and content, when it was not necessary to ask of this art what it said, because one knew what it did. Theory has come into sway with the voiding of meaning from form.[7] The interpreters may not, because of their newly gained authority, in this crisis of understanding, endow the idea or form with exclusive primacy. Instead, they may concede that their interpretation, being coloured by their time and location, is subject to critical evaluation, that they may be indulging in hypertrophy (unhealthy enlargement) of the intellect, to impoverish or deplete the pristine art world, to set up a shadowy world of meanings; and that they may be undertaking surveillance, from a Panoptic (station for encompassing view) tower, seeing without being seen, of the field of art. They may, instead, encode objects 'anaphorically' (in relation to other expressions), in terms of their metonymic contiguity, metaphoric similarity, relation with or distance from adjacent or absent others, in terms of given historical, social, cultural conditions. They may also read meaning 'anamorphically' (intentional distortion, as through magnification), as it unfolds dynamically through history, subject to displacement and migration, renarrativization or rereading. They may read the history of the work, in the work itself, composing itself, authorless, in the third person singular, as 'art history without names'. They may also return to origins, to detect, in the smallest features, the indexical and symbolic meaning of the work, without posing a divine artificer, absent from the work. To understand the diverse unity of the art, they have to act as coauthors, and walk backwards with the artist from the end to the beginning, from effect to cause, from background to foreground, to reinvent the method of artistic invention.[8]

The paronomasia or double meaning, the atiśayokti or overstatement, vakrokti or oblique allusion, the sthāyī (enduring) or vyābhicāri (transient) bhāvas (emotions) and bhaṅgīmās (postures), are not introduced as mere poetic conceits in the art of Dakṣiṇa Kośala. These devices are used to explain the cathartic process of emanation and resolution, through vyānjaña or suggestion rather than through literal explanation. These are used to present the infinite finitely, paint the passing tableaux against the perpetual void; reflect the indissoluble bond between parokṣa (invisible) and pratyakṣa (visible), adhidaivata (super being) and mānuṣi bimba (human prototypes), abidhā (denotation) and lakṣaṇa (connotation), mūrti (concept) and pratimā (percept), earth bound mortal and the immortal flame, in the smithy of the soul. The cosmology of release of waters is also an attempt to release śruti, the exalted intuitive understanding of yore, from smṛti, the routine of repetitive formulae. What is sought in this art is self renewal, in a hierophany, to make reality correspond with thought, in a homoisis, to repossess our true nature (after the concept of jalachāyā, shadow in water, the water retaining its nature irrespective of the shadow). In the process, the modernist claim to unity, identity and purity is bridged with the postmodernist claim of heterogeneity, hybridity, impurity. We walk the rainbow bridge between singular identities and diverse differences, with Śiva akliṣṭakarma, the effortless actor, to complete rather than deplete the beginnings of our creative adventure on this earth planet.[9]

NOTES

1. If the religious rite in India provides a sacred bond, religare in Latin also means, to bind together. The binding exchange is transacted through a mighty auto da fe (a public ceremony as an act of faith), auto sacramentale, a festival, in an effervescent environment. The exchange is accomplished in fulfillment of a socio economic order, which holds out promise of eternity or an everlasting renewal, a promise detected, in statu nascendi, in Vedic literature. Biardeau 1989: 2-4. One remembers that Brāhmins produced Pṛthu, the first consecrated king Pārthiva, from the body of Veṇa, after sacrificing him, as oblation, pārtha, to punish him for his hubris of identifying himself with the sacrifice and the Gods. Dumont 1968/1980: 192,269- 298, 373-374. The orthopraxy of Hinduism linked orthodoxy and heterodoxy in a relation of complementarity, consubstantiality, pure and impure, superior or inferior. Duvignaud 1967/72: 9, 29-34, 47, 57-63.
2. Preziosi 1989: 23,30,44-53.

3. "Archetype as letter form. The Dream of Edward Johnston", in Keeble 2005: 32-43. The art is comparable with a biological organism, in a state of mediated metabolism with the surrounding world. The means precede purpose, the purpose is revealed by the means. Seemingly forgotten things, preserved within us, come to the surface, and speak to us like the shadows of Odysseus, fed with his blood. Fischer 1963: 12,18; Mcluhan 1962: 135, 137. Also, "A K Coomaraswamy. The Art of Living", in Keeble 2005: 44-57. Such forms are not only of decorative, utilitarian or functional value, in Malinowski's terms, but are also of affective, mystic value, in Levy Bruhl's terms. They are animated by disinterested holistic appreciation of certain proportions and rhythms, inherent in the structure of the world, underlying the casual variations in forms, created in the stress of the world's evolution. Strauss 1978: 11-13; Read 1970: 368, 125. Nature is seen in such work as a garden house, not as a resource to be exploited. "W.R. Lethaby, Art and Labor", in Keeble 2005:17-13.
4. The art is in a state of suspended tension between vis centrifugal and vis centripetal, unrest and rest, in which only its becoming through interaction is real. This process helps the individual to assume, like Proteus, many forms and lead many lives, without being crushed by the multiplicity of his/her experience. This recreates for every individual the fullness of all that he/she is not but can be, the fullness of humanity at large. Fischer 1963: 129, 223.
5. The conception of art as expression of a forfeited life is not part of the mental horizon of the pre Romantic artist like that of Dakṣiṇa Kośala. For him, there is no choice between art and life, no renunciation of life as price of art, no obsession with his irrational faculties, no self pity, no discontent with civilization as raw material for his creativity. Freudian technical devices for analysis of dream work like displacement, elaboration, differentiation, condensation or over determination are not relevant to an art, the meaning of which is conventional, not personal. Hauser 1969: 33-34, 43-47, 54-63,95, 103. Man here is not a Kantian thinking subject, a behaviorist or Freudian homo natural, but dasein (being in the world), koinoia (celebration of God's presence in the world in Christian theology), a functional unity, an intentional projection and disclosure of the world as a being in the world through whom all things come to be and have meaning. Revelation, unveiling, alatheia of the hidden meaning of Being through human being takes place through its letting be. Gras, after Heidegger 1973: 2,5.
6. The fulfilling moments, highlights, peaks of excellence in the art of Dakṣiṇa Kośala embody an effortless mastery over formal techniques, and an easy familiarity with iconographic attributes and iconological perceptions. The visual perception is of a total and diversified field of collocation, a 'parataxis'(congregation without conjuction) of components, representing insight by carefully established ratios, all events in the foreground, with near uniform illumination. This questions idealist or materialist historicist perception of stylistic development in art, seen variously by Aristotle, Hegel, Marx, Husserl or Dvorak, as a romantic, organismic, teleological, genetic, gestalt unity and identity, prior to the forms, before they are thought, experienced or executed by anyone. Mcluhan 1962: 315-16; Read 1931/59: 204-15; Hauser 1969: 133-40, 168-71, 212, 252; Strauss 1978: 532-35. Interpretations given to forms are variable, and the same form may have different expressive values, not only for different peoples, but also for different periods of civilization. Read 1931/1959:20-21; Hauser 1969: 103-4. In the collaborative network of the art world, the conception, production and consumption influence one another. As problems in expressing ideas change, solutions change and the artistic tradition becomes a connected series of solutions to a commonly defined problem. The network of cooperation changes to accommodate innovations, which, in Dakṣiṇa Kośala, appear to have been generated by a melange of orthodox and heterodox cults. Becker 1989:1, 303-4. Read 1931/1959:165.
7. Heidegger speaks of us as tenants of a time of need, which lies under a double Lack and a double Not: The no more of the Gods that have fled and not yet of the God that is coming. Heidegger on Holderlin, in Gras 1973: 40. The perception of the idea that duality and individuation is an illusion of sphere of space and time, of Māyā, is difficult for modern man to attain, as the shadow falls between his conceptions and

creations, emotions and response, potency and existence. Poetic writing or art like Tala is like letting the word of such truth resound. Eliot 1936: 81-82, 91-92

8. Sontag 1966: 13, 17. The art historical readers of the message or its material traces may not walk, like 'active, transitive verbs, amidst a rabble of adverbs', prepositions and other insignificant parts of speech. Instead, they may see the interpretative act as operative in a discursive space, involved in a temporal spatial context, claiming no last or final word or knowledge, that is not subject to erasure or palimpsest. The interpreters have to look for telltale, minute, undeliberate details, le petit faits, that signify change. They may, on the one hand, look at art work as a lexical unit in a sentence, decomposable, like a morpheme (smallest meaningful unit) , into smaller phonemic (equivalent speech sounds) units, as a cumulative accumulation of solutions of different problems at different times. They may, on the other, adapt the role of sacerdotal semioticians, reflective of geist, wollen, istoria (learning through research), to divine authorial intention, on behalf of a lay congregation, in a temple of entelechy. Instead of adapting a deterministic, mechanistic, idealistic historicism, they need to decipher the meaning, unfolding through displacement and migration, as subject to constant rereading, as a cumulative, polysemous tally of notations, as multiply meaningful. They have to read the langue, collective language, the mother tongue of the race, in individual manifestations, parole, at a given moment. Preziosi 1989: 23, 27- 34, 48-53, 58-66, 76-79, 84-89, 118-19, 136, 155, 164, 169-171, 191. Hauser 1969: 33-34, 114, 125, 168-71 explains the autonomy of art history, rooted in both technique and meaning of the work. The modern interpreter has to embrace an open field method, excluding closure, and combine analogous perceptions of the universe, shared by scholastic grammatica and dialectica, scriptural exegesis, physics and mathematics. Mcluhan 1962: 42,72-73, 135, 155-156, 173,316,325-328.
9. S.N. Dasgupta 1922-55: 25-27, 33-35; Kaviraj 1983: 211; Balaram Srivastava 1985: 15-17, 39, 107-8, 117, 129-30, 163-9; D.C. Bhattacharya 1986: 43-8; J.L. Mehta 1990: 243; 285-7.

1

Ancient Geographical Situation of Tala

LOCATION

Tala (pronounced Tālā) is a site (Figs. 1, 2, 5) with two ancient temples, locally known as Devarani (Hindi, younger sister-in-law) and Jethani (Hindi, elder sister-in-law). It is situated at 21.50° latitude north and 82.05° longitude east, in village Amerikāpā in Sārgāon circle, Tehsil Bilhā of Bilaspur district, in the southeastern part of the state of Chhattisgarh in India. It is at a distance of 5 km from the nearest railway station Dagauri on the trunk railway line (Bombay to Calcutta via Nagpur). By road it is located at the end of 1 km long diversion from the 5th km of the Bhojpuri-Dagauri road, which branches off at Bhojpuri village, on the 24th km of the state highway from Bilaspur to Raipur.

The site is at an elevation of 264 to 266 metres above sea level, on an undulating plain, intersected by convergent tributaries of Mahānadī, which form watersheds and ridges, east to west. The rivers are subject to sudden raging floods known as bāihāpurā, which explain the raised embantment of the temples. The archaeological mound rises about 13 metres above the village in the east, and is located on the steep bank of the river Maniyāri which flows on its west. The river is joined at Tala by a rainfed stream called Vāsantī and meets river Seonāth (Śivanātha) near village Dagauri. Seonāth joins rivers Arpā and Līlāgar at about 10 km from Tala, and the ancient city of Malhār (Y) is situated at this confluence. Seonāth joins the great Mahānadī about 40 km from Tala. The Mahānadī, on its southwestern stretch, is dotted with 6th to 8th century AD temple sites including Palāri, Turturiyā, Sirpur, Āraṅg and Rajim, and, on its eastern stretch, with 7th to 9th century AD temples at Khārod, Śabarīnārāyaṇa, Pujārīpālī, before it turns southeast to enter Sambalpur district in the adjacent state of Odisha. As the crow flies, these temple sites and settlements are all within a distance of about 150 km from Tala.

The stone structure as well as the sculptures of the Tala temples are made of soft and friable sedimentary lameta sandstone. The sheer banks of the Maniyāri River are composed of this stone, which is still mined in the local quarries. Geologically, this stone is part of the narrow, discontinuous crop of Chandarpur sandstone, which forms a raised rim around the Chhattisgarh basin.[1]

NAME

The name Tala appears to have been associated in 6th-7th century AD inscriptions with the names of several important settlements as a prefix or a suffix.[2] It could also probably have been derived from a tradition of writing the land grants for such settlements on tāla (palm) leaves.[3] On the other hand, and with greater plausibility, the name may have derived from talapātaka, which denotes the sacred plot of land, that is the subject of such grant.[4] It is also likely, that, used in the early period as the name of a large territorial unit as Tārā, it was changed to Tālā in later Kalacurī inscriptions, Tārādaṁśakabhoga being changed to Talahārimaṇḍala.[5] The low-lying, water-logged cultivated fields to the east formed, according to local reports, a large tank (tālāv in Hindi), suggesting a further source for the name Tala.

DAKṢIṆA KOŚALA

Tala formed part of the ancient province of (Dakṣiṇa) Kośala (Map 2), which was always recognised as having a separate and independent identity, being part of neither Vidarbha nor Tosāli.[6] Kośala occurs well before the Gupta period in ancient literature, being qualified neither with a prefix Dakṣiṇa (South) nor Mahā (great).[7] In fact, Mahākośala is a misnomer, popularized by Cunningham and Hiralal. Dakṣiṇa Kośala is a nomenclature, which comes into circulation, in both a broad and a restricted sense, under the Kalacurīs of Tummān/Ratnapura.[8] From at least around AD 1497, it comes to be known as Chhattisgarh, the word being used in an eulogy for the first time.[9] Though the etymology of the word Chhattisgarh is variously understood, its physical extent is seen generally as more or less coterminous with the boundaries of Dakṣiṇa Kośala in eastern Madhya Pradesh and western Odisha.[10] The epics, Pāṇini in c. 6th century BC, the 6th century AD astronomer Varāhamihira, and the Viṣṇu Purāṇa of about the same date or a little earlier, distinguish Dakṣiṇa Kośala from Uttara Kośala, by either indicating the direction from which it is approached, or by clubbing it with the southeastern, mostly sea bordering states and towns like Kaliṅga, Vaṅga, Puṇḍra, Oḍra, Tāmralipta, or, with the forested southeastern territory Kāntāraka, rather than by specifying it as Dakṣiṇa.[11] The literary evidence about the southeastern location of (Dakṣiṇa) Kośala is reinforced by inscriptions from the 4th to the 10th century AD. In the Allahabad pillar inscription (known as Hariṣeṇa praśasti), Samudragupta claims to have defeated the kings of Dakṣiṇāpatha, including Mahendra of Kośala, Vyāghrarāja of Mahākāntāra, Manṭarāja of Kaurala.[12] Kośala is mentioned together with Mekala and Mālava, Kaliṅga, Utkala and Oḍra in the inscriptions of the Vākāṭakas, Cālukyas, Rāṣṭrakūṭas, Pāṇḍuvaṁśīs and Colas in the 5th, 7th and the 10th centuries as being within their sphere of influence.[13] The contiguity of Dakṣiṇa Kośala with Andhra further southeast is suggested by the existence there of a group of Brāhmins known as Kośalanātis, who probably migrated from Kośala.[14] Among early accounts, the Vāyu Purāṇa alone refers emphatically to Dakṣiṇa Kośala as one of the seven Kośalas, with the prefixes Kāśī, Pūrva, Kaliṅga, Krānti, Cedī, Mekala and Dakṣiṇa. It suggests, like the literary accounts and inscriptions, an wider cultural tradition, shared by Dakṣiṇa Kośala with eastern India.[15] This indicates the complex and interactive cultural heritage inherited by a place like Tala, situated in the heart of Dakṣiṇa Kośala in Bhāratvarṣa (Map 1).

While a vague reference is made by the Chinese pilgrim Yuan Chwang to the geographical extent of Dakṣiṇa Kośala in the 7th century AD,[16] its boundaries appear to have fluctuated with time. Nevertheless, a fairly precise map can be drawn for its boundaries between the 5th and the 10th century AD from literary and epigraphic allusions. In the northeast it is bounded by the Mekala range, which stretches from Amarkaṇṭak in Shahdol district across the borders of Bilaspur, Surguja and Raigarh districts. Beyond these lies Vatsa, and, further beyond, Uttara Kośala. In the southwest, it stretches, at its furthest, to the confluence of Indrāvatī and Godāvarī rivers, while, in the southeast it is separated from Andhra by the Tel River, which merges in the Mahānadī with its tributaries. Dakṣiṇa Kośala does not generally extend in this period in the south beyond the source of Mahānadī near Kānker in north Bastar, in what may have been the Śuktimat mountains of *Mahābhārata*.[17] Beyond these lies Mahākāntāra, later known as Cakrakoṭya or Bhramarakoṭya Maṇḍalas, and now as South Bastar.[18] To the west, the Wainagaṅgā River separates Kośala from Vidarbha, up to its confluence with Penagaṅgā and probably even up to the confluence of the latter river with the Godāvarī, the Āmāgāon state area of Bhāṇḍārā district and Sironcā and Warorā Tehsils of Chāndā district of present day Maharashtra being included in Kośala.[19] Beyond this lie Vidarbha, Vatsagulma and Ajanta. To the east, the ancient boundaries of Dakṣiṇa Kośala are not certain, but appear to have extended up to the upper valley of Mahānadī, including the Sambalpur, Bolaṅgir and Kālāhāṇḍi districts of Odisha, which comprise five earlier feudatory states, ruled by Somavaṁśīs.[20] Together with important towns like Bāndhavgaḍh, Śarabhapura, Mallālapaṭṭana, Śrīpura, Aṣṭabhāra, Prasannapura, Svarṇapura, Yayātinagara and Vinītapura, Ratnapura, Tummān, Śabarīnārāyaṇa, Tala appears to have stood on the ancient arterial route connecting Kauśāmbī in north India with the southeastern sea coast. Despite shifting dynastic boundaries, it appears to have been always part of Dakṣiṇa Kośala. The area of Dakṣiṇa Kośala probably extends between 17°50' and 13°10' N and 79°30' and 84°15' E, approximately covering an area of 68550 square miles.

Being hilly, heavily forested, inhabited mainly by economically backward tribal groups, Dakṣiṇa Kośala appears to have always escaped direct administrative control from major imperial dynasties and centres. The sequence of dynastic history, and the shifting, fusing boundaries of dynastic rule have been difficult to determine till the effective rise of Kalacurīs (Map 3) in the 11th century. The intractable political and physical geography, incapable of being subjected to convenient categorization, has led to a neglect of the art of the region. It has remained unsurveyed and unfamiliar, and has escaped, for a long time, denominational, racial or dynastic classifications, fondly cherished by earlier art historians. And yet, in recent years, this very lack of familiarity has led to forced and improbable suggestions classifying Dakṣiṇa Kośala and Tala as suburban, marginal outposts of sovereign cultural centres outside the core imperial region of Madhyadeśa and Vidarbha. A series of surveys and excavations, conducted in this area by the Directorate of Archaeology in the late 20th and early 21st century have shown that the very fact of geographical inaccessibility and political pluralism, which is considered responsible for the stunted and sterile growth of a partially 'provincial', 'tribal' art in Dakṣiṇa Kośala, may have accounted for the near autonomous development of an artistic style of tremendous inventive vigour and freshness at its different centres. Tala is the most sophisticated and nearly the earliest centre from where this style appears to have spread to other centres of the region.

NOTES

1. A.E Nelson, *C.P. District Gazetteers*, Bilaspur District, 1910: 9.
2. Variants of Tala found their way into names of settlements like Paṭṭanakhadirapadratala (identified with Khadirapadas in Kālāhāṇḍi district, Odisha), and Tārābhramaraka (identified with modern Tālbhanvarā on Tel River in Kālāhāṇḍi district), the 6th century AD capital of Parvatadvāraka kings and Telataṭa viṣaya on river Tel. See V.V. Mirashi and L.P. Pandey, *EI* 27, 1947-48: 321-25; D.C. Sircar, *EI* 30, 1953-54: 274-78; R.D. Banerji, 1930-31: 221.
3. A palm leaf charter is mentioned in the Kurud plates. A regrant was made necessary by a conflagration, which destroyed the charter. See M.G. Dikshit, *EI* 31, 1955-56: 264.
4. The same as tālavātaka or tālavṛtti of Kannāḍa inscriptions. Senākapāṭ inscription of the time of the 7th century AD. Paṅḍuvaṁśī king Mahāśivagupta Bālārjuna describes tālapātaka as a piece of land, granted for yāga (sacrifice), dīkṣā (initiation), samayasya vyākhyānam (exposition of Śaiva doctrine), annasya sattram (free feeding), used by Śaivācāryas. See M.G. Dikshit, *EI* 31, 1955-56: 31-37. Lodhiā plates also mention Khadirapadratala as the site of a donation made by Mahāśivagupta to a temple of Iśāneśvara Śiva.
5. The Malhār plates of Mahāśivagupta Bālārjuna refer to grant of village Kailāspur (identified, significantly enough, with Keslā near Malhār), to the vihārikā (monastery) of a bhikṣu saṁgha (community of monks) in the Tārādaṁśakabhoga. See V.V. Mirashi and L.P. Panday, *EI* 23, 1935: 120; Also D.R. Bhandarkar 1927-36: 1231, 1232 and 1240; *CII* 6: 134. For Talahāri Maṇḍala, see Hiralal 1916: 115-16. And, 1938: 48, 57-59.
6. K.D. Bajpai's opinion, according to which Kośala formed part of ancient Vidarbha, is countered not only by the independent mention of Vidarba and Kośala in *Mahābhārata*, but also by Vātsyāyana's mention of Kośala as bordering Strīrājya (kingdom of Amazons) identified with the western part of Chāndā district in Vidarbha. See K.D. Bajpai, *JKHRS* 1946. Hiralal, *Lists*, 1916/1932: 204 for identification of Strīrājya; *Mbh.*, Araṇya Parva, 58. 22, which mentions both Kośala and Vidarbha. N.L. Dey 1899/1971: 206 identifies Dakṣiṇa Kośala with Tosāli of the Dhauli inscription of Aśoka and Tosāle of Ptolemy. This is countered by the descriptions of Kośala by Rājaśekhara in his *Kāvyamīmāṁsā* in the 10th century AD as one of the eastern states, together with Kaliṅga, Tosala, Utkala and Magadha.
7. Dey 1899/1971: 103-4; D.C. Sircar 1971: 71, 78, 99, 106, 150, 212; L.P. Pandeya, *JKHRS*, 1946, 1.2.
8. Cunningam. *ASIAR*, 17, 1889:68; Hiralal 1933: 161. Sircar 1971:106 identifies Mahākośala mentioned in Śaktisaṁgama tantra as Uttara Kośala. Mirashi points out that, in the 20th century, the Mahākośala division of British India included ancient Ḍāhala (modern Tripurī) and part of Anūpa (southern part of Māhiṣmatī region). Dakṣiṇa Kośala is mentioned as a conquest of Kaliṅgarāja under King Kokalladeva of Tripuri in late 9th century AD. In an AD 1114 inscription of Jājalladeva, Dakṣiṇa Kośala is mentioned as one of smaller units of the larger territorial unit of the same name.
9. In AD 1497, the poet Dalarām Rāva of Khairāgarh used this nomenclature for the first time in an eulogy addressed to his King Lakṣmī Nidhi Rāva. See Pyarelal Gupta 1973: 40.
10. Cunningham 1889: 69-71 appears to derive the name Chhattisgarh from the title Cedīśvara, the king of Cedīs, assumed by Kalacurīs in medieval inscriptions, as well as from Ādiśāthra. Ādiśāthra is described by Ptolemy as the country bounded on the south by Ādiśāthron mountains (identified with ranges south of Sehoawā and Kānker in Bastar, in turn identified with Śuktimat mountain of *Mahābhārata*), with a fort in the northeast called Bālanti-purgon (identified with Bāndhogaḍh in Shahdol district). The opinion has also been expressed that the word is Chhattisghar, not Chhattisgarh, and refers to the thirty six houses of scheduled castes, which moved south from Bihār in the time of Jarāsandha of *Mahābhārata* fame. See Pyarelal Gupta 1973: 40 and further references therein. Literally, Chhattisgarh is taken today to refer to the thirty six mud forts that were supposedly built in the area, though there are remains of many more. During the British period, Chhattisgarh included fourteen states, five of which, namely, Kālāhāndi, Pātna, Rairākhol, Bāmrā and Sonpur were Oriya-speaking. E.A. de Brett 1909: I.

11. The discovery of a terracotta seal at Malhār with the legend 'Gāmasa Kosaliya' in 2nd century AD Brāhmi, has led to the speculation of Kauśalyā, the eldest wife of King Daśaratha being from village Kośala (Keslā), 16 km northeast of Malhār. See K.D. Bajpai and S.K. Pandey, *Malhār*, 1978: 4-5. References in the unpublished Kośala khaṇḍa, preserved in Gitā Press Library, Gorakhpur, have given rise to the suggestion that Kauśalyā was the only child of a king at Nāgapaṭṭam south of the Vindhyas. See J.P. Singhdeo 1979: 119-20. Pargiter feels that the long stay of Rāma in this area on his way south is responsible for its being named Dakṣiṇa Kośala. See Pargiter 1922: 278. *Rāmāyaṇa*, Uttarākhaṇḍa 7.107.7, 108.4, 5 and *Vāyu Purāṇa*, ślokas 80, 189, 200 mention installation of Kuśa in (Dakṣiṇa) Kośala, south of the Vindhyas, with Kuśāvatī as the capital, and of Lava in Uttara Kośala with Śrāvastī as his capital. *Raghuvaṁśam* 6.71, 16.31-32 mentions how Kuśa crosses the Vindhyas to reach Uttara Kośala. Kuśāvatī has been identified with Kānsil on Tel River in what was previously the feudatory state of Pātnā. See Kedarnath Mahapatra 1971: 65-71. Hiralal suggests the etymological derivation of Kośala from abundance of kuśa (grass), and of Vidarbha from the dearth of it, darbha being a synonym for kuśa. Hiralal 1938: 7, 25-26. The *Mbh.*, Sabhāparva 13.591-92, 31.11-16. lists (Dakṣiṇa) Kośala with Kāntāraka in Sahadeva's south Indian conquests and describes the southward migration of inhabitants of eastern Kośala for escaping Jarāsandha. In Aśvamedhaparva 82.29, it includes Kośala among southeastern kingdoms, with Vaṅga and Pundra, after Tripurī, in Karṇa's conquests. In Vanaparva 61.22 King Nala, while wandering in the Vindhyas, points the path to Dakṣiṇāpatha beyond Kośala. In the *Viṣṇu Purāṇa* 4.24: 64, the protection of Devarakṣita is extended to the southeastern territories of Kośala, Oḍra and Tāmralipta. Pāṇini, *Aṣṭādhyāyī* 4.1:171, mentions Kośala as one of the countries furthest to the south. Varāhamihira in *Br.S.*, 14.7:8, locates Kośala, together with Kaliṅga and Vaṅga in the āgneya diśi, the southeastern direction.
12. J.F. Fleet, 1888: *CII* 3. I, 7, 13 describes the extent of Kāntāraka from Prākkośala (east of Kośala) to Venātaṭa (bank of river Venā, a tributary of Godāvarī). Physically, Mahākāntāra comprised southern part of Kālāhāṇḍi, larger part of Korāpuṭ district of Odisha and Bastar district of Chhattisgarh. Kaurala included Sonpur in Bolaṅgir district of Odisha. See N. Senapati ed., Bolaṅgir, 1968.
13. F. Kielhorn, 1900-01; 1907-08: 229 ff; *ASIPRWI* 6: 92; *EI* 31, 219 ff.
14. B.V. Krishna Rao (ed.), *JAHRS*, quoted by L.P. Pandey 1946: *JKHRS* 1, 2.
15. *Vāy P*: 129-32.
16. Yuan Chwang describes his visit in AD 639. He says that he went 1800 *li* northwest of Kaliṅga to reach Kio-so-lo (Kośala), which stretched in a circuit, exceeding 6000 *li* (1000 miles). Watters, 2, 1904/1961: 200-209.
17. Cunningham, 1881-82: 69-70.
18. L.P. Pandey 1946, in *JKHRS* 2.4: 235, quotes Purāṇic sources to locate the southern boundary of Dakṣiṇa Kośala at Ṛṣitūlya river, stretching from Mahānadī to Svarṇarekhā, including Kaliṅga, Oḍra and Tosala, which were ostensibly independent most of the time. See L.S. Nigam 1984: 15.
19. Hiralal, *IA* 62,1933:162. V.S. Thakur 1965: 35, 44. Cunningham 1871/1963: 44; 1881-82: 68. The western boundaries stretch occasionally to the hilly regions of Māṇḍlā and Bālāghāṭ districts, specially the Sālheṭekri zamindari area of Bālāghaṭ district.
20. R.D. Banerji 1930-31, I: 7 would extend the eastern boundary of Dakṣiṇa Kośala to Kinjli, but the incidental references to Kinjli in Somavaṁśī or Kalacurī inscriptions do not support this conclusion. On the other hand, Cunningham 1881-82: 168, terminates the eastern limits at Jonk and Hasdo rivers, which does not take into account the extent of Somavaṁśī rule in Odisha. Nigam 1984: 14.

2

A Brief Political History of Dakṣiṇa Kośala and Tala

TALA FINDS AND HISTORY

The mounds at Tala are confined to those associated with the two temples, evidence of early human settlement in the vicinity having been destroyed. Successive excavations conducted in three seasons since 1978 have not yielded much that is useful in determining the history of the site, which seems to have begun with the construction of the temples. Two 7th century pilgrim records, a late 5th to early 6th century silver coin of the Śarabhapurīya king Prasannamātra, 12th and 13th century copper coins of Kalacurī king Ratnadeva (apparently Ratnadeva III) and Pratāpamalladeva are a few of the more useful finds. While they only provide indirect and circumstantial evidence about the occupation and use of the site from the late 5th to the early 13th century AD, they are of no particular help in fixing the date of the construction of the temples. And yet, these are helpful in providing a chronological context and in explaining the general political and religious environment of the settlement. There is some evidence for its contacts with Dakṣiṇa Kośala, particularly with Malhār, close to Tala, and with the political and cultural modes of the rest of India during the Maurya and Śuṅga period in the three centuries BC.[1] In the first three centuries AD, evidence of Sātavāhana influence on Malhār and adjacent areas is also available.[2]

VĀKĀṬAKAS

Vākāṭaka rule extended over Betul, Chindvārā, Seoni and Bālāghāṭ districts, south of Narmadā with occasional extension to Bundelkhanḍ and Bāghelkhanḍ in Madhya Pradesh, Vidarbha, Khāndesh, Mārāṭhvāḍā in Maharashtra, and Bidar in north Karnataka. Vākāṭakas had relations with Nāgas and Guptas in north, Viṣṇukuṇḍins in eastern Deccan, and Kadambas in western Deccan in Karnataka. Devices like conch shell, śrīvatsa, spotted wheel, bull Nandin before yūpa, running lions, legend vṛddhi or Śrī, box-headed Brāhmī characters link Vākāṭaka with Viṣṇukuṇḍin coins, found in Hamlāpuri, Mahurjhari, Mānḍhal in Nagpur, Arni in Yawatmal, Pauni in Bhānḍāra districts of Maharashtra. The northern Nandīvardhana Pravarapura branch and southern Bāsim branch of the Vākāṭakas were distinguished by the Bāsim grant of Vākāṭaka ruler Vindhyaśakti. Titles like Dharmamahārāja, exemptions, immunities and endowments are shared by records of both branches. Śaiva monasteries and Buddhist stūpas are found together in the region, resulting in a mingling of traditions.[3]

In the 4th century AD the relentless pressure of the Gupta emperor Samudragupta (c. AD 345-70) on his Nāga allies,[4] or on the neighbouring rulers of Kośala and Mahākāntāra appears to have induced the Vākāṭaka king of Nandīvardhana, Pṛthviṣeṇa I, to marry his son to Prabhāvatīgupta, daughter of the Gupta emperor Candragupta II (c. AD 380-415). Prabhāvatīgupta then serves as regent for their minor son. The Vākāṭaka alliance with the Bhāraśivas, who are devout Śaivas, and with the Guptas, who are Vaiṣṇavas, appears to have been of some consequence for Dakṣiṇa Kośala, which was then in the Vākāṭaka zone of influence. Except for Prabhāvatīgupta's husband Rudraṣeṇa II and her grandson Pravaraṣeṇa II, who transfer their loyalty to Vaiṣṇavism, the Vākāṭaka rulers style themselves as Paramamāheśvaras, or devout worshippers of Śiva.

Except for the combined use of 'Gupta' nail-headed characters together with 'Vākāṭaka' box-headed characters by Prabhāvatīgupta, the box-headed characters are in general use with the Vākāṭakas.[5] Following the Vākāṭakas, except for occasional spells of mixed use of nail and box-headed characters, the different dynasties of Dakṣiṇa Kośala in the 5th and the 6th centuries use the box-headed characters in their coins and inscriptions, and, except for occasional lapses into Bhāgavatism (worship of Viṣṇu), pursue the Śaiva faith. The strong southern leanings[6] of the Vākāṭaka script or nomenclatures appear to have had considerable influence on the characters used in inscriptions by its feudatories in Dakṣiṇa Kośala. Pravaraṣeṇa II's successor Narendraṣeṇa claims to make his writ run in Kośala and Mekala in Bālāghāṭ copperplates, a claim partially supported by the covert praise showered by the Pāṇḍu king Bharatabala of Mekala on Narendraṣeṇa in a copperplate grant from Amarkaṇṭaka, and by the Nācnā and Ganj inscriptions of Uccakalpa kings from Mekala region. All these inscriptions[7] use box-headed characters and nail-headed alphabet. After the death of Pṛthvīṣeṇa II (c. AD 470-90), the Vākāṭaka ruler Hariṣeṇa of the Vatsagulma branch appears to have captured effective power. He claims to have conquered Kośala, together with Kaliṅga and Andhra in the east, Lāṭa (Gujarat) and Trikūṭa (Nāsik) in the west, and Kuntala (southern Maharashtra) in the south. During Hariṣeṇa's time (c. AD 475-500), Dakṣiṇa Kośala seems to have been in the domain of Vākāṭaka influence.[8]

NALAS

The Vākāṭaka influence over Dakṣiṇa Kośala was seriously threatened by the Nala kings of Bastar-Gañjām-Korāpuṭ region, with an immediate impact on the Vākāṭaka script. From his capital at Puṣkarī in the Umarkoṭ tehsil of Korāpuṭ (Bārsur in Bastar), in the southeastern extremity of Dakṣiṇa Kośala, the Nala king Bhavadattavarman carried his arms into Vākāṭaka territory, ostensibly forcing Narendraṣeṇa to shift his capital to Padmapura, closer to the Vākāṭaka area of influence in Kośala and Mekala. He made a grant of land from the Vākāṭaka capital Nandīvardhana (Nāgardhan in Nagpur district) to honour Maheśvara and Mahāṣeṇa. The Riṭhapur copperplates, announcing this grant, have been found together with the copperplates of queen Prabhāvatīgupta, and show a distinct dilution of the box-headed southern characters by the nail-headed script.[9] Puṣkarī appears to have been devastated, however, in a retaliatory attack by Pṛthvīṣeṇa II. The deserted city was repeopled and provided with a Viṣṇu temple by the Nala king Skandavarman (c. AD 475-500). The Nalas were reduced once again by Hariṣeṇa around AD 500.[10] They suffered a complete eclipse after this at the hands of the Cālukyas.[11] They surfaced again in late 7th century with an inscription (recording the construction of a Viṣṇu temple by Vilāsatuṅga) on the Rājīvalocana temple at Rajim, and maintained a tenuous existence in their original nucleus till the 14th century AD.[12]

ŚARABHAPURĪYAS

In spite of incidental and isolated references to different dynasties of Rājarṣitulya (Sura) kula, Parivrājaka and Parvatadvāraka in early 6th century AD in Dakṣiṇa Kośala,[13] it is the Śarabhapurīyas, who seem to dominate the stage from the late 5th to the late 6th century. They are known from copperplate grants, most of which were issued from Śarabhapura, a few from Śrīpura, and at least one from a skandhāvāra (military camp). Written in box-headed characters, popularised by the Vākāṭakas, the plates are accompanied by seals with Vaiṣṇava symbols and refer to the kings as paramabhāgavatas (worshipper of Viṣṇu).[14] Inscribed in regnal eras, the plates refer to the town, and never to the family, which has been identified, on debatable evidence, as Amarajakula.[15] The town Śarabhapura remains unidentified, but the consensus is that it would not have been very far from Sirpur, Malhār, or, for that matter, Tala.[16] Though there has been controversy about whether the Śarabhapurīyas precede or follow the Soma or Pāṇḍuvaṁśīs, the consensus has gained ground that they precede the latter.[17] The sequence of rulers has been controversial, though it has been tentatively built up on the basis of the copperplates, reconciling, in one view, not generally accepted, the different birūdas (sobriquets), probably used by the same king,[18] and the different opinions about the exact relation among the kings. Though no Śarabhapurīya charter ever calls the donor kings lords of Kośala, the widespread distribution of their charters and coins in this area yield stronger evidence of their sway over it than mere, unsubstantiated claims of suzerainty.[19] Śarabhapurīyas appear to have begun in the second half of the 5th century AD as feudatories of the late Gupta kings[20] and contracted an alliance with the Pāṇḍuvaṁśī kings of Mekala.[21]

The third King Prasannamātra is the most mysterious and apparently the most powerful king of the dynasty. Two of his coins, one in silver, the other in copper, have been found, with the king's name and Vaiṣṇava symbols, at Tala.[22] These coins are similar to many other coins of Prasannamātra, mostly found in gold, made in repoussé technique.[23] The silver coin from Tala may have been used as legal tender, with gold polish.[24] Prasannamātra's gold coins have been found in Sirpur, western Odisha and Vidarbha, in association with the gold coins of Mahendrāditya and Kramāditya. His and Mahendrāditya's gold coins have been also found singly and independently. Mahendrāditya's gold coins have been found in association with those of Nala and other unknown kings of Bastar. Coins of Nala kings have been found independently at Durg. All these coins bear a mutual resemblance in the use of symbols and legends in similar box-headed characters.[25] The attempt to identify Mahendrāditya and Kramāditya as the 5th century AD Gupta emperors Kumāragupta and Skandagupta, to see these coins as their local issues, and, therefore, to virtually suggest a mid-to-late 5th century date on this ground alone for Prasannamātra, fails because of the differences in symbols and legends of these coins with those of 5th century Gupta coins.[26] Mahendrāditya and Kramāditya may well have been local rulers of an unknown dynasty like those they are found in association with.[27]

Prasannamātra appears to have founded a town called Prasannapura, in the Pūrvarāṣṭra (eastern country), on the bank of the Niḍilā River. While these places have not been incontrovertibly identified, these are mentioned in Vyāghrarāja's Malhār copperplates and should not have been far from Malhār and Tala.[28]

Though the lithic records of the Pāṇḍuvaṁśīs were in early Nāgarī characters of the Kuṭila variety, the palaeographical and linguistic affinity of the official Pāṇḍuvaṁśī copperplate groups with the Śarabhapurīya charters suggest that the Pāṇḍuvaṁśīs were political legatees of Śarabhapurīyas.[29] The Śarabhapurīya dynasty appears to have come to an end around mid to late 6th century with Pravararāja, who claims to have conquered the earth. In course of his conquests, he appears to have shifted his capital to Śrīpura (Sirpur), this being a more centrally situated place.[30] In his westward advance, he was confronted and halted probably by the Soma or Pāṇḍuvaṁśī king Tivaradeva.

PĀṆḌU/SOMAVAṀŚĪS

Already in the late 5th, early 6th century, the Pāṇḍu or Somavaṁśīs[31] appear to have been gaining ground in Dakṣiṇa Kośala by subordinate alliances with the Śarabhapurīyas, or by conducting campaigns against the Viṣṇukuṇḍin kings of Andhra from Dakṣiṇa Kośala to assist the Maukharī kings of Magadha. Tivaradeva, the first Pāṇḍuvaṁśī to be mentioned in association with his earlier capital Tivaranagara and Śrīpura, is considered by scholars to have ruled around the second quarter of the 6th century, and he may well have ruled somewhat later in the 6th century. He claimed to be lord of Kośala and Utkala, a claim supported partially by four copperplate charters found in the region, including that of his son Nannarāja.[32] He issued his charters from Śrīpura,[33] and was the first and the last Pāṇḍuvaṁśī ruler to use the box-headed characters of the Śarabhapurīyas, in a more angular and elongated manner, suggesting the possibility, that his was a transitional phase, in which Śarabhapurīyas were being replaced by Pāṇḍuvaṁśīs. Tivaradeva was followed in quick sequence by three rulers, of whom the third, Harṣagupta sealed the traditional friendship with the Maukharīs by a marriage with the Maukharī princess Vāsaṭā, daughter of Sūryavarmā of Magadha, who has been taken as the son of the Maukharī king Iśānavarmā of the Harahā inscription of AD 554.[34] Harṣagupta was followed by Mahāśivagupta Bālārjuna (c. AD 595-655), who, though a paramamāheśvara (worshipper of Śiva), patronised the construction or renovation of Śaiva, Vaiṣṇava and Buddhist temples or vihāras at Sirpur, Senākapāṭ and Kośalanagara near Malhār. The Sirpur Lakṣmaṇa temple stone inscription of Queen Vāsaṭā, dedicating a Viṣṇu temple, supposedly the Lakṣmaṇa temple itself, is palaeographically datable to the early 7th rather than to the early to mid-8th century AD.[35] This inscription, taken together with the copperplate grants and eleven other stone inscriptions of Mahāśivagupta,[36] provides a chronological confirmation of the stylistic developments in the art of Dakṣiṇa Kośala in the 7th century.

Mahāśivagupta's grants are the last dated records of the Pāṇḍu/Somavaṁśīs dynasty at Sirpur, and though Pāṇḍuvaṁśīs and Somavaṁśīs appear to have ruled in Mekala and Kaliṅga through the 7th century, their relation, if any, with the eponymous dynasty of Sirpur, is not quite clear.[37] The Somavaṁśīs appear to have ruled in Kaliṅga from the 9th to the 11th century AD and exercised influence in Dakṣiṇa Kośala, yielding ground gradually to the Kalacurīs, who established complete control over the entire area around Tala in Talahārimaṇḍala and Dakṣiṇa Kośala between 9th and mid-12th century AD.[38] Ratnadeva III and Pratāpamalla, whose copper coins have been found at Tala,[39] came in towards the end of the 12th century, Pratāpamalla ascending the throne around AD 1198. Kalacurīs continued till AD 1740, when the Bhonslās of Nagpur uprooted them.

It should be evident from this account that the area around Tala was a theatre for considerable interaction among Guptas, Vākāṭakas, Nalas, Śarabhapurīyas in the 5th and 6th centuries. The generally greater vogue enjoyed by box-headed characters preferred by Vākāṭakas in the inscriptions of regional dynasties of Dakṣiṇa Kośala in this period suggests a certain cultural influence exercised by Vākāṭakas, whatever the extent of their political control. However, the script of inscriptions or the alphabet of art are not written by kings, nor can any one to one relation exist between the two. The only appropriate suggestion is that Tala, together with Vidarbha and Dakṣiṇa Kośala, appears to have shared a more or less common language at this time.

NOTES

1. Maurya contacts are suggested by the reference in Aśoka's special Kaliṅga Rock Edict 2 about the recruitment of āṭavikas (forest dwellers) for his army from the wild uplands west of Kaliṅga; by the discovery of a large number of āṭavika dūrgas or mud forts in forests, very close to Tala; by the recovery of punchmarked coins, northern black polished (N.B.P) ware, and large sized 'Mauryan' period bricks from such forts, including the fort at Malhār. Two inscriptions in the Sītā Bengrā and Jogī Marhā caves of Rāmgarh hill in the 2nd century BC Pāli characters of the Śuṅga period suggest artistic and poetic gatherings in the forest retreats. See Bajpai and Pandey 1978: 4-5. Also Hiralal 1916/32, 'Rāmgarh hill cave inscription': 170-74. An inscribed Viṣṇu image in the Malhār Museum belongs to the 2nd century BC. D.C. Sircar 1942/1956: 529-30.
2. Gautamiputra Śātkarṇi claims suzerainty over the Central, Eastern and Western Vindhyas. See Sircar, in Majumdar 1968: 210. Terracotta, silver or copper coins of Sātavāhana kings have been found at Malhār, Gunji, Kirāri, Konār, Semarsāl, Bālod, Dūrg in Dakṣiṇa Kośala, Tarehalā and Akolā in Vidarbha. Roman coins of this period have been found from Chakarberā near Malhār. See Bajpai and Pandey 1978, *Malhār*: 2-13. A 1st-2nd cent. AD inscription has been found at Bhuji, Bilaspur about Sātavāhana prince Vardantavīra making a grant of cattle. Sātavāhana king Apilaka's coin has been found at Bālpur. Pandeya 2002: 39-40, 63-40. The matronymic names, titles Rāyo and Siri, elephant and tree railings used by Nāga rulers of Bāndhogaḍh in the 2nd and 3rd century AD in their inscriptions or coins, show Sātavāhana influence. For Purāṇic reference about the Maghas, see Pargiter 1913/1962: 51.
3. Shastri 1992: 47-49, 119-53, 284-94, 297-308.
4. The Bhāraśiva king Bhavanāga, whose copper coins have been found in Padmāvatī (Pavāyā in Gwalior), gave his daughter in marriage to Pravarasena I Vākāṭaka's son Gautamīputra. Gautamīputra's son Rudrasena I was a contemporary of Samudragupta. See Mirashi 1937, *EI* 24: 11-14.
5. See Pathak and Dikshit 1990-20, *EI* 15: 39-44; Mirashi, *CII* 5: 5 and n. 17. Also see Lakhāni copperplates issued by Prabhāvatīgupta from Bhāṇḍārā, in which she named Pravarasena II as her son, who issued the Pattan plates to honour Viṣṇu. Mirashi, 1935, *EI* 23: 81-86. Within this idiom, the earlier Vākāṭaka script is less stylized, angular and elongated than the Śarabhapurīya script. Shastri 1995, I: 8-22, 30. This is paralleled in the evolution of sculpture by the gradual replacement of the curves by angles.
6. The discovery of all early Vākāṭaka inscriptions south of Narmadā, the use of box-headed southern characters in their records, the use of words similar to those of Pallava grants in the Bāsim copperplate, the assumption of names like Hāritiputra or titles like Dharmamahārāja by the members of the Vatsagulma branch in common with southern dynasties like the Sātavāhanas, Kadambas or Cālukyas, the retention of the Maurya term Rājuka for a revenue officer, even after it fell into disuse in north India, are some of the factors which indicate the southern leanings of the Vākāṭakas. See Mirashi 1941, *EI* 26: 141,149; Sushil K. Bose 1937-38: 54; Shastri 1992: 5.

7. Kielhorn, 1907-08: 267 ff; Mirashi 1955, in *Shukla Abhinandan Grantha* 196: Mirashi 1963, *CII* 5: 89-93, specially his comments on p. 90; Sukthankar 1925-26: 12-14. Also Cunningham 1884-85, *ASIAR* 21, 91 ff. for Nācnā-kā-tālāi inscription.
8. Mirashi 1955 on Ajanta cave 16 inscription of Varāhadeva, minister of Hariṣeṇa. Also, *CII* 5: 103-12, and ns. 21 and 22.
9. Y.R. Gupte, 1927-28, *EI* 19: 100-04; Mirashi 1933-34, "An unfinished Vākāṭaka plate from Dūrg", *EI* 22. 210-11. For Puṣkarī's identification as Bārsur, see *EI* 22: 270. n. 5.
10. "Bālāghāṭ plates of Pṛthvīṣeṇa II", *EI* 9: 107-08: 271, in which the Vākāṭaka king claims to have raised his sunken family fortunes. Skandavarman celebrates the revival of Nala fortunes in the Poḍāgarh stone inscription in Jeypore on the borders of Bastar. Krishnamacharlu 1931-32, *EI* 21: 153-57. Also Ajanta inscription in *Hyderabad Archaeological series* 14. Sahu 1962, *OHRJ*, 11.2: 101.
11. The Āihole inscription (634 AD) of Pulakeśin II describes destruction of the Nalanilaya (residence of the Nalas) by Cālukya king Kīrtivarman I (AD 566-98). Pulakeśin II claims in this to have subdued Kośala and Kaliṅga. See Kielhorn 1900-01, *EI* 6: 1, 11. The Nalavādī viṣaya is mentioned as the southernmost province of Vikramāditya I (AD 655-80). Sircar 1954:241.
12. Mirashi 1941, *EI* 26: 49 ff; Also Sahu 1966: 47-48.
13. A copperplate grant of AD 501-02, issued by king Bhīmaseṇa from Suvarṇanadī, and found at Āraṅg in Raipur, names six rulers of the Rājarṣitūlya (Śūra) kula. Mirashi 1942, *EI* 26: 228; See also Hiralal 1907-08, "Āraṅg copperplates", *EI* 9: 342-45; Sircar, 1946, *IHQ* 22: 62-3; and Nisar Ahmad 1973, *JOIB* 23:339-41 for the Śūra dynasty, Bhīmaseṇa II's Ārang copperplates and his early 6th century AD date. Inscriptions of the Parivrājaka kings have been found from the same period at Ārang. Relations of the latter with the former are suggested by the mention of Suśarman, who lived like a Maharṣi. Fleet 1888/1963: 114 ff. The Terasiṅghā copperplate grants from Tārābhramaraka on bank of river Tel mention Parvatadvāraka kings, who occupied the upper Tel valley in early 6th century and worshipped Stambheśvarī. Sircar 1953-54: 274-78.
14. The seals of Śarabhapurīyas are inscribed with nimbate Lakṣmī on lotus, flanked by saṅkha (conch) and cakra (wheel), with pūrṇakumbha (full pitcher), accompanied by water lilies, and with crescents and pellets. Shastri 1977, *PRP* 5. 1: 2,6, 7,12-14.
15. In the Bāmhoni copperplate of Pāṇḍava king Bharatabala of Mekala, reference to Bharatabala's wife Lokaprakāśā, the princess of Kośala, as Amarajakulajā is accompanied by praise of king Narendra of this kula, suggesting Amarajakula to be the family name of Śarabhapurīyas. The Malhār copperplate of Vyāghrarāja, issued from Prasannapura, refers to the Amarāryakula. See *ASIPRWI*, 1904:54; Sircar and Bhattacharya 1961-62, *EI* 34: 50 and n. 2. The identity of Amaraja and Amarārya has been assumed, Amara being seen as the ancestor of the kula. Based on what may be an accidental similarity of names, this identification may well be a forced one.
16. Of the sixteen records referring to the place of issue of Śarabhapurīya charters, eleven were issued from Śarabhapura, the name of the issuing monarch being alone mentioned, not that of the family. Sten Konow 1915-16, *EI* 73: 275-82 improbably associates Śarabhapura with Śarabharam in the Godāvarī district of Andhra Pradesh, though none of the Śarabhapurīya charters has been found from there. Cunningham 1889: 57 ff. connects it with Sambalpur in Western Odisha and so does Lochan Prasad Pandeya 1930: 456-64. Pandeya 1939 identifies it alternatively as Śarabhagarh in the Sundergarh district (the ex-feudatory state of Gaṅgāpur), or, Śarabha near Śeorinārāyan or Śarbhar near Nāndaur in Bilaspur in *EI* 19: 144. Sahu and Behera 1971:15,27, agree with Pandeya. Bajpai and Pandey 1978:25,32 identify it as Malhār, seeing Sirpur as a second capital, though the foundation of Malhār appears to have long preceded that of Śarabhapura. Hiralal locates it as Śarabhapura at Sirpur, Śarabhapurīya plates having been found in sites surrounding Sirpur like Āraṅg, Raipur, Khariār and Sāraṅgarh. See *EI* 9, 1907-08: 283, and *EI* 11, 1911-12:186 and n. 5. Sircar, Pandeya and Dikshit support Hiralal's view respectively in *IHQ* 19, 1943: 144 and in *EI* 31, 1955-56: 254. Bhattacharya and Sivayya question this view in *EI* 34,1961-62: 39 because of the different names of the engravers, Droṇa and Golasiṁha, for the Sudevarāja plates,

issued from Śarabhapura and Śrīpura respectively. While pointing out that this is possible because of the existence of two Sudevarājas I and II among the Śarabhapurīyas, Singhdeo suggests location of Śarabhapura in the Mārāguḍā valley in the Navāpārā subdivision of Kālāhāṇḍi district, not very far from Sirpur. See Singhdeo 1987: 127.

17. Hiralal suggests that the Śarabhapurīyas had ousted the Somavaṁśīs from Sirpur and substituted the name Śarabhapura for Sirpur in order to associate themselves with the victory of the mythical creature Śarabha over Keśari or the lion, with which the Somavaṁśīs had linked themselves. See Hiralal 1916/32: 90-92. Hiralal himself points out the difficulty with this view, which is the chronological gap between the early Somavaṁśīs of Sirpur and the later Somavaṁśīs of Kaṭak, to which Fleet had drawn attention in 1888/1963: 327. However, he chooses to ignore this gap, making his view untenable. Indeed, a further objection to Hiralal's view is that the Soma or Pāṇḍuvaṁśīs rarely use Keśarin as the end of their title, and the characters of the Pāṇḍuvaṁśī records are more developed, elongated and angular, their description more elaborate and ornate, making it difficult to believe that they could have preceded the Śarabhapurīyas. Shastri 1977, *PRP* 5. 1:15,21.

    The discovery of a single Prasannamātra coin in the lowest stratum of Sirpur excavation by Dixit is not considered significant for identification of Sirpur as Śarabhapura. So far, Prasannamātra is the only Śarabhapurīya king known to have issued coins, and his successors may have continued to use his coin as legal tender. Moreover, except this solitary coin, all other remains from this site belong to the post-Śarabhapurīya period. Shastri 1995, *Inscriptions* 1: 93-94.

18. The tentative sequence proposed by Bal Chandra Jain is as follows.

Śarabha
↓
Narendra
↓
Prasanna
↓
Jayarāja/Mānamātra/Dūrgarāja
↓
Vyāghrarāja   Sudevarāja   Pravararāja

Jain 1962 assumes that Mānamātra and Dūrgarāja are birudas (sobriquets) of Jayarāja, no charters being issued by Mānamātra-Dūrgarāja, and the charters being silent about Jayarāja's relation to Mānamātra (Dūrgarāja). His views differ from those of Mirashi, Sircar and others. Pandeya 1943 places Prasannamātra earlier than Narendra. If Jayarāja is taken as an independent ruler, the unknown periods of Prasannamātra, Dūrgarāja and Mānamātra and the excess above the known periods of Narendra, Jayarāja, Sudevarāja and Pravararāja (41 yrs) take Śarabhapurīya rule to 590 AD. Shastri 1985, *Studies*, points out the radical differences in the characters of the alphabet, devices on the seals, or in Vyāghrarāja's charter, from those of Śarabhapurīyas, and concludes that the three persons of the Amarāryakula, mentioned in this charter, had nothing to do with Śarabhapurīyas, though they ruled from Prasannapura, without shifting their capital, after the Śarahapurīyas. Shastri accepts the reconstruction of the genealogy and the order of succession, proposed by Sircar and G. Bhattacharya as follows.

Śarabha Prasannamātra
↓
Narendra
↓
Jayarāja / Dūrgarāja / Mānamātra
↓
Pravararāja I   Vyāghrarāja Sudevarāja Pravararāja II

Also see Mirashi 1960-62, *Studies* I: 249; Shastri 1995, *Inscriptions I*: 97-98.

19. The area ruled over by Śarabhapurīyas is named as Pūrva or Tuṇḍaraka Rāṣṭra, Tuṇḍra being identified as a village near Śeorinārayaṇ or Śavarīnārāyaṇa. See *EI* 9: 281-85; *EI* 32: 15-23; *EI* 34: 45-50. Narendra's plates have been found from Pipardulā in Sāraṅgarh, and Kurud near Sirpur. See Sircar 1942/1965: 488-90; Sircar and Pandeya 1943: 140-45; Dikshit 1955-56, Kurud plates. Jayarāja's (and his birudas') plates have been found at Malhār, Aṅgura, Āraṅg. Sircar and Singhdeo. 1976. Vyāghrarāja's plates have been discovered at Malhār. See Sircar and Bhattacharya, 1961-62. Sudevarāja's plates have been recovered from Nanna, Āraṅg, Raipur, Kauvātāl, Khariār and Sāraṅgarh. See Fleet 1888/1963: 191 ff; *EI* 19 Hiralal: 281-85, 314-16. Pravararāja's plates have been traced at Malhār. See Bhattacharya 1961-62; Sten Konow 1907-08, Khariār plates. While Prasannamātra's plates have not been found anywhere, his coins have been found in Dakṣiṇa Kośala and outside in Kaliṅga and Vidarbha. From this evidence, Śarabhapurīya rule appears to have extended from Sirpur in the west to Sāraṅgarh in the east, and from Khariār in the south to Malhār in the north.
20. Śarabha, the earliest known Śarabhapurīya ruler, is identified with Śarabharāja, the maternal grandfather of Goparāja, who died fighting the Hūṇas for their common liege lord, the late Gupta emperor Bhānugupta, in a battle at Eran in AD 510. See Fleet 1888/1963: 191 ff. Also Sircar in Majumdar 1954, the *Classical Age*: 219. Śarabha is assigned to c. AD 460-80 by Mirashi 1946-47. Kurud plates of Narendra refer respectfully to the paramabhaṭṭārakapāda, which has been taken as a reference to the Gupta overlord. Sircar 1955-56, Kurud plates; Sircar and Pandey, 1943, Pipardulā plate. Again, the similarity of names of Śarabha and Śarabharāja may be coincidental.
21. Mirashi 1965, *Indica*.
22. The silver coin is larger, 1.6 cm, in diameter, 1 cm broad, weighing 1.211 grammes. The upper part shows Garuḍa, flanked by a crescent moon and a wheel, the sun and the conch shell. In the lower half, the name of Śrī Prasannamātra is given in box-headed characters in the Brāhmī script. The copper coin is smaller, with a weight of 0.561 grammes and shows only the first part of the name of the king.
23. More than 106 repoussé coins of Prasannamātra are known. His gold coins are preserved in the Nagpur and Sambalpur University Museums and the Bhuvaneśvara State Museum. The Tala coins are in the Bilaspur Museum.
24. A silver coin of Prasannamātra with faint traces of gilt was published by L.P.Pandeya 1930. Also see Rode 1950.
25. Prasannamātra's coins have been found together with those of Mahendrāditya and Kramāditya at Mārāguḍā valley of Odisha (Singhdeo 1987: 365), Pitāiband in Raipur district of M.P. (Jain 1966), Bhāṇḍārā in Chāndā district of Maharashtra (Jain 1954, pl.4). Mahendrāditya's coins have been found, together with coins of Nala kings Bhavadatta and Arthapati, and with coins of unknown rulers Nandanarāja and Stambha in village Kuliā, Police station Gurur, in Dūrg district. See Nigam 1977. Nala coins have been found at Eḍeṅgā in Koṇḍāgāon Tehsil of Bastar. Mirashi 1939. Prasannamātra's coins have been found singly at Berhampur in Quilābānki estates of the Cuttack district of Odisha (*ASIAR* 1926-27: 230), at Navannakagrāma or Nehnā near Khariār, also in Odisha (Singhdeo 1987: 115, 123-24). Mahendrāditya's gold coins have been found independently in the old fort of Madanpur Rāmpur in the Kālāhāṇḍi district of Odisha (*OHRJ* 1: 137), and in the Khairātāl hoard (Mirashi 1949, *JNSI* 11).
26. Rode 1948, 1950, makes the identification. Mahendrāditya's coins bear, on the obverse, Garuḍa, flanked by crescent, wheel, sun and conch, together with a cluster of encircling dots, and dots, accompanied by a letter ru below the royal legend. It has been pointed out that the legend Mahendrāditya never figures alone on any of the Kumāragupta coins, and the letter ru only occurs in the coins of later Gupta rulers like Prakaśāditya and Viṣṇugupta. Ajit Ghosh 1931-33.
27. It would not do, however, to suggest that Mahendrāditya is the birūda of king Mahendra of Kośala, defeated by Samudragupta. Nor would it be proper to identify, as Bajpai and Pandey do, king Mahendra, mentioned in Gupta Brāhmī characters, on two clay sealings, found at Malhār, as a Śarabhapurīya king,

and son of Narendra. Bajpai and Pandey 1978: 3,25. Even if the identification is taken as correct, there is no evidence of a Mahendra, son of Narendra. Shastri 1977, *PRP* 5.1: 22. If the Malhār sealings of Mahendra are inscribed in box-headed characters of Śarabhapurīyas, the Malhār copperplates of Vyāghrarāja are issued from Prasannapura, and are written in nail-headed characters of Gupta inscriptions. Jain 1954.

28. See Jain 1961. Utkīrṇa Lekh 174.
29. Shastri 1995, *Inscriptions* 1: 30, 91-93.
30. Śrīpura is named after Śrī (Goddess of wealth) who figures on Śarabhapurīya seals. About the vaunted claims of Pravararāja, see Mirashi 1933-34, *EI* 22: 17.
31. The first known Pāṇḍuvaṁśi ruler Udayana constructed a stone temple of Viṣṇu at Kālañjara on the border of Mekala. See Kālañjara stone inscription in Cunningham 1878-89, *ASIAR* 21:40 and pl. 9. His successor Indrabala is often identified with mahāsāmanta (the chief lieutenant) Indrabalarāja, a feudatory of the Śarabhapurīya ruler Sudevarāja. One of his sons, Iśānadeva, endowed the Lakṣmaṇeśvara temple with villages. Lakṣmaṇeśvara stone inscription in Bhandarkar 1927-36, *list:* no 1651. Another of his sons, Nannarāja, described as world conqueror, renovated a ruined Buddhist vihāra, according to an inscription found at Āraṅg. Mirashi 1955-56.
32. For Rajim plates of Tivaradeva, see Fleet 1888/1963: 291-99; Sircar 1961-62, *EI* 34; Hultzsch 1901-02; Jain 1955-56. The acceptance of the mid 6th century AD date, or even a date in the 2nd quarter of the century for Tivaradeva, does not appear to clash with the tentative chronology, in which Śarabhapurīya power appears to have crumbled very quickly after Prasannamātra.
33. Tivaradeva's capital Tivaranagara appears to have been attacked by the Viṣṇukuṇḍin king Mādhavavarmā (c. AD 520-60) in retaliation against Somavaṁśī attacks, forcing Tivaradeva to move to Śrīpura. Contemporaneity of Tivaradeva and Mādhavavarmā, assumed by Mirashi and Sircar, is not accepted by Shastri, who fixes c. 650 AD as the initial year of Tivaradeva's regime. See Jaunpur inscription, Fleet 1888/1963: 228 ff; Hirananda Shastri 1917-18. Mirashi 1979; Ajaya Mitra Shastri 1979, *JESI* 6; Also Ajaya Mitra Shastri 1976.
34. For a discussion of the Maukharī connection and Maukharī history, see Hirananda Shastri 1917-18; Majumdar 1954, ed., *The Classical Age:* 67-71.
35. For the bearing of a Viṣṇukuṇḍin plate on the history of the period, the late date for Lakṣmaṇa temple, Shastri 1966. Also Shastri 1985, *Studies*. Krishna Deva questions Shastri's dating of the Sirpur temple on palaeographic and stylistic grounds. Krishna Deva 1998:236.
36. For Mahāśivagupta's plates and inscriptions, see Mirashi 1934-35; Desai 1947-48 ; Mirashi and Pandeya 1947-48; Hiralal 1911-12, *EI* 11:184-201; Kielhorn 1889; Dikshit and Sircar, 1955-56, *EI*. 31. In 1987, 9 sets of copperplates (3 each in each set) of Mahāśivagupta were seized from an illegal dig at Sirpur by Nagaich, the then Registering officer, Raipur, of Madhya Pradesh State Archaeology. These have been edited by Shastri with the assistance of Rahul Singh, Curator, Bilaspur museum.
37. The Bāmhoni copperplate of Bharata (Indra) bala is almost the only evidence about the Pāṇḍuvaṁśīs of Mekala. It mentions the marriage of a princess of Kośala, who may have been the sister of the Śarabhapurīya king Narendra, with Bharatabala. It also mentions Jayabala, Vatsarāja, and Nāgabala as Bharatabala's predecessor and Śūrabala Udīrṇnavaira as his successor. See Jain 1961/2005: 10. The Śomavaṁśī rulers, named in the Kaṭak lists, are Śivagupta, Mahābhavagupta Janmejaya, Mahāśivagupta Yayāti, Mahābhāratagupta Bhīmaratha, who use the phrase, 'from the victorious camp', or from Kaṭaka, and who issue their charters from Vinītapura (Binkā on Mahānadī, 100 miles from Sirpur, 180 by river), Yayātinagara (probably an alternative name for Binkā, Murisiṅgā (in the ex-feudatory state of Patna), Suvarṇapura (Sonpur), both very close to Binkā. Hiralal suggests that these rulers may have been the successors of the Sirpur Śomavaṁśīs, who may have surfaced later. However, the palaeographic gap is too long to be satisfactorily explained, as Fleet had pointed out earlier. See Hiralal 1916/1932: 88-96; Fleet 1894-95, *EI* 3:327; Kielhorn 1889, *IA* 18: 179; B.C. Jain 1961/2005: 51.

38. In the late 6th century itself, the Kalacurīs under Kṛṣṇarāja of Māhiṣmati appear to have moved east, issuing copperplate grants from Amaravati and Betul, while his māṇḍalika issues charters, that have been found at Nāgardhan near Ramtek. In late 9th century, Lakṣmaṇarāja II appears to have advanced on Dakṣiṇa Kośala, recovering ground lost by Kalacurīs to Rāṣṭrakūṭa Govinda III, who had claimed conquest of Kośala, Kaliṅga, Ḍāhala. At the end of the 9th century, Śaṅkaragaṇa II, also called Mugdhatuṅga, seizes Pāli in Bilaspur from the Śomavaṁśīs, leaving his brother as the ruler, with Tummān as the capital. Probably ousted by the Śomavaṁśīs after this, the Kalacurīs of Tripurī, under prince Kaliṅgarāja, reestablish their rule in Tummān towards the end of the 10th and beginning of the 11th century. Kaliṅgarāja's successors in the 11th century appear to have ruled as feudatories of the Kalacurī branch. His son Kamalarāja assists king Gāṅgeyadeva of Tripuri in an assault on Utkala. King Ratnarāja shifts his capital to Ratnapura in mid 11th century. In late 11th to early 12th century, Jājalladeva acquires Talahāri maṇḍala and Utkala, defeats Chhindaka Nāgas of Cakrakoṭya and declares independence of Tripurī. Within the first three quarters of the 12th century, the Kalacurīs of Ratnapura beat back assaults of the jealous king of Tripurī and Kaliṅga and consolidate their rule. Brahmadeva, the Māṇḍalika of Talahāri maṇḍala, shows great bravery in the war with Gaṅgas of Kaliṅga, and Jājalladeva witnesses the construction of the Kedāreśvara temple at Malhār. Mirashi 1965, *Kalacurī Nareśa.*
39. Ratnadeva III's copper coin has a diameter of 1.7 cm., breadth of 0.15 cm, weight of 1.300 grammes. Pratāpamalla's copper coin has a diameter of 1.7 cm, breadth of 0.15 cm, weight of 1.400 grammes. Both are partly abraded, with the name of the king on obverse. Both the coins are in Bilaspur Museum, Chhattisgarh (Acquisition Nos 86 and 87).

3

The Archaeology of Tala

FIRST CLEARANCE 1977-78

The site of Tala in village Āmerikāpā has been known to archaeologists since at least 1878, when Beglar noticed the temple,[1] but did not visit it. The site was, however, left untouched till 1977-78, when a very limited clearance operation[2] was conducted at the entrance of the Devarani temple on the east. This led to the exposure of the steps leading to the temple, and of the two gaṇas on either side of the steps, the Sūrya image, and the anthropomorphic makara, adorned with a lotus cap. Two Nāgarī inscriptions, probably pilgrim records of 7th century AD, naming Śrī Hetukaraṇa and Śrī Bahukaraṇa, were found engraved at the base of the gaṇa on the left and a makara pedestal, lying in front on east. The plinth of the temple was only partially cleared, work being stopped when some brick and rubble debris was struck.[3] Enquiries from A.K. Risbud, the then registering officer, Bilaspur, who was present during these operations, revealed that the fragments of the huge abraded images of Śaiva dvārapālas, and other divinities like the Sūrya, with which the ground around the Jethani mound or in front of Devarani temple are still littered, were mostly shifted by him from different sides of the Jethani mound and east of Devarani, and placed on the ground near their respective locations in each direction, in 1978 (Figs. 10-11). Some crude attempts at restoration of the Devarani door jamb, a dancing gaṇa and other large heads, shifted inside Devarani (Fig. 89), with cement plaster, had been already made by villagers, even before 1978. Apart from these sculptures, several sculptures lying in front of Devarani (Fig. 356), had been shifted by the villagers before Risbud's arrival at the site.

SECOND CLEARANCE 1985-86

At the instance of the author, who was then the Director of Archaeology, Govt. of M.P., the Tala monuments were finally protected by the Govt in 1984. At that time, a few small images of Pārvatī and Viṣṇu (Figs. 304, 364), with short, squat legs, tall head and bust, of a somewhat cruder description than the general crop of images, were found near the temples.[4] Subsequently, a second clearance was undertaken in 1985-86 by the Directorate of Archaeology at the suggestion of Dr. Pramod Chandra, the Adviser to the Department of Culture, Government of Madhya

Pradesh.[5] This clearance was confined to the Jethani mound (Figs. 1-2), then measuring 30 m x 30 m x 6.3 m. All that was visible before the clearance, was the shaft of a large broken pillar, lying prone at the south entrance, the upper portion of two damaged and leaning stone slabs, carved with figures on the southeast, a siṁhagavākṣa on the southwest, the shafts of two slender pillars at the eastern entrance, embedded in the debris. A sixty year old imli tree and a wild galgalā tree had struck their roots deep into the mound in the northwest and southwest respectively, doing, as was evident later, considerable damage to the western segment of the temple. These were pruned carefully from top down before excavation.

Operations were commenced from the top of the mound and soon revealed a brick cladding (Figs. 67-68, 71-75) for the pīṭha, vedībandha and jaṅghā of the temple, the brick debris being the heaviest in concentration on the south. Brick ramparts extended up to 1.5 m on southeast and west, and 1.25 m on the north. A paved stone platform was found on east and west, and, long retaining walls of bricks and stones were found at a depth of about 0.10 m Brick buttresses, measuring 2.30 m tall and 0.80 to 1.6 m broad, strengthened by stone ramps, extended down the slope of the surrounding mound, binding it like forceps. No antiquities were found inside these brick and stone abutments, nor any fragments of a temple or a house. Coins, articles of daily use, and worship tools and implements of worship were, however, found on the southeast, on a raised brick revetment (Fig. 91). These deposits revealed occupation of the site from the 6th to the 12th century AD.[6]

The largest number of sculptures were found on the most extensive southern steps. Apart from the tetrafacial pillars, door jambs, lintels or wall slabs, a Gaurī plaque was found below the prone pillar at the entrance. A Kārtikeya image (Fig. 350) was found lying across the second to the fourth steps from below. The broken trunk of a lady wearing a blouse with fasteners and an Ardhanārīśvara image (Fig. 425), in three fragments, were found stretched across the fourth and the fifth steps. Heads of nāgapuruṣas (Figs. 434-35) and a headless vṛkṣakā (Fig. 295) were found on the seventh step. On the north, two elephant protomes, damaged by the trees, flanking a cell with a carved stone panel and pillars, were traced instead of an expected fourth entrance. A broken image of a Nandī and an architectural fragment, once part of a praṇālikā, were found near the cell. On the eastern steps, apart from the jambs or lintels, was found a four-armed Kārtikeya, with its rightside arms and attributes broken partially, while an image of Śiva in tiger skin (Figs. 343, 349) was found below the steps. On the western steps, apart from several pillar fragments, a Viṣṇu plaque was found on the fourth step from below, while a base carved with Hara Gaurī, holding gaṇas in snake noose, and seated on a rocky outcrop (Fig. 355), was found at the northwestern corner. At this point, no attempt was made to match the numerous architectural and sculptural fragments strewn all around the temples with the architectural segments.[7]

THIRD CLEARANCE 1988

The author visited Tala in October 1987, and checked out the fascinating finds on the site and in the Bilaspur museum. He found many unresolved questions posed by the most unusual structure and sculptures revealed at Jethani, and proposed a third clearance on the Devarani mound to the Directorate of Archaeology for resolving them. For one thing, there was the baffling question as to whether the brick cladding, ramparts or retaining walls around Jethani formed part of the original plan or were later additions. The author expected an answer somewhere below the large, sloping mounds (Fig. 5) to the north, south and west of Devarani since Risbud had struck brick to its southeast in 1977-78. He also expected intriguing finds specially to the north, where the mound stretched further than the south or west. Apart from expecting brick enclosures with minor antiquities like Jethani southeast, he also hoped to find contemporary clues to chronology like coins or inscriptions, and better preserved counterparts of the enormous, completely unrecognizable sculptures surrounding Jethani. A huge pillar, lying deeply embedded in the ground at the southeastern entrance of the temple, posed the possibility of discoveries below the layer of soil at southeast (Figs. 76, 78). A partial removal of the soil layer between the north facade of Jethani and the southeastern facade of Devarani was also considered necessary for finding out whether the Devarani jagatī was at the same level as the Jethani jagatī. Moreover, since the brick cladding on Jethani made it impossible to look at the original mouldings, if any, of its successive segments, it had become important, in order to get an idea of the pīṭha of the only adjacent temple, to complete the incomplete clearance, begun by Risbud on the southeast near the Devarani pīṭha. It was also felt that since, unlike Jethani, the Devarani temple still retained its jaṅghā walls, possessed pillars, rising high above the crowning moulding of the jaṅghā, and was enclosed by an extensive mound from three sides, the clearance might yield fragments of the missing Devarani śikhara. In any case, with the lesson of Jethani before us, which had lost even its jaṅghā walls, it had become very important to ensure that the Devarani temple and its huge maṇḍapa pillars, which had started showing visible signs of cracking up, were conserved by partially uncovering and stabilizing its foundations.

The third debris clearance operation at Tala began on 11th January 1988. The shallow accumulation of debris, which suggested no deep features, was removed in sections, to the south, north and west, (Fig. 4) revealing brick buttresses, about 0.35 m wide, that formed four trenches on the north, six on the south, and two on the west, including the corners. The trenches (Fig. 77) were all rectangular, measuring from around 2.38 m to 2.75 m in length, 1.25 m to 1.72 m in breadth, filled with brick and stone rubble. The edges were reinforced by stone blocks and the filling was covered by stone slabs. The brick buttresses were left standing everywhere as baulks, and the trenches were left more or less undisturbed except at the southeastern corner, where the filling was removed to look at the mouldings of the pīṭha (Fig. 80). The filling being of the same period, no cultural deposits from different periods were expected to be found. A brick enclosure measuring 2.30 m square was, however, found on the north, buried in the rubble, filled with articles of worship, and a similar enclosure was also found to the south, outside the brick chambers, on the ground.[8] On the north, the alignment of the broken fragments of the stone praṇālikā below the makaramukha on the vedībandha was followed up to reveal a square stone kuṇḍa (cistern) at a distance of 27 m. Retaining walls of brick and stone, similar to those to the north and south of Jethani, were found stretching from Devarani on the south, north and west, suggesting a similar purpose of binding and stabilizing the mound. The revelation of these brick cells and revetments around Devarani solved the riddle of the brick cladding on Jethani. The bricks measured 0.24 x 0.20 x 0.6 m, and were of the same size as Jethani, laid similarly in English bond, crosswise in headers and stretchers, moulded and offset to increase their load bearing capacity. Smaller and slimmer bricks were inserted in the gaps intervening between bigger bricks, plugging them. Bonded with clay and moorum, the bricks (Fig. 98) were smaller and lighter than the Maurya and Śuṅga bricks, cruder and plainer than, though roughly of similar size to the fine decorative Gupta bricks, but larger than later Kalacurī or Paramāra bricks.[9] That the brick cladding on Jethani was a later measure of restoration, became clear from the simultaneous use of boxed cells and low brick walls, riveted on the Devarani temple. The purpose was the same, to bolster the temples, by underpinning them, and by keeping the mound around them from sliding.

This was necessary because of the nature of the stone and construction. The structures were made of sedimentary lameta sandstone, which tended to peel off and come apart in slices, resulting in the shearing of the segments. The structure itself was made additively, without any bonding, out of vertically or horizontally laid slabs, without the iron clamps, used in later Pratihāra or Paramāra temples, to resist slippage. Slight recessing of the floor surface, and shallow chamfering of the pillars were the only means adapted to make the pillars or wall slabs stand up, no socketing or jointing, iron clamps and dowels being used at initial construction. The grooves cut on the side of the pillar or the large sculpted wall slabs, appear to have been emergency measures, adapted later to hold up an architecture, which was expected to stabilize itself with the weight and size of its own components. The problem was compounded by the nature of the bed on which the structures were constructed. It was sedimentary, laminated, soft, non-homogeneous and moisture absorbent. In fact, its instability was increased by the fact that it was artificially raised with moorum soil, full of humus and clinkers, cracks and fissures, which expanded in volume due to water seepage from the adjacent tanks and rivers.[10]

At Jethani, these problems were complicated further by the fact that it had three openings, while Devarani had only one. It was also a more extensive and unbalanced structure, with a disproportionately large south entrance, made of pillars of varying heights and immense vertical slabs. The insertion of brick bases to support the overburden of stone on the south shows that Jethani started crumbling down in the south, when wind pressure, combined with water percolation, resulted in the disturbance of the axial alignment of the temple, and in the unequal settlement of its segments. Once it started buckling down, one portion brought the other down in a domino effect, tearing off even the T-shaped iron clamps, which were used later to join the steps. While the vertical array of wall slabs on the steps of Devarani fell in a similar chain reaction, the Devarani temple itself, with its elongated, compact form, reinforced by the cellular boxes around it, absorbed the thrust and displacement effect of erosion more effectively. Yet, it started tilting towards the south as one structure, necessitating the present conservation measures.

The more extensive mound on the north, which became larger on the northeast, did not, contrary to hope, yield any evidence of a śikhara. The bricks, strewn all around, taken as evidence of a brick śikhara, are not moulded, and were obviously displaced from the brick buttresses and trenches. The displacement was caused by the disturbance of the covering slabs of the stone platform caused by the fall of the pillars, and probably, by the collapse of ceiling slabs of a larger platform at the northwest. The two staircases giving access to this larger northwestern platform (Fig. 81) from both north and east, did not appear to lead to any holy precinct. The Gaṇeśa image, backed up against the Devarani staircase wall, corresponded to a ruined elephant image placed against the south wall of the staircase. But, it was enclosed in a small cell (Fig. 94), approached from the east, and the platform was obviously not constructed for approaching this improvised shrine, the roof of which would have merged with the platform floor. Except for a damaged Gaurī plaque found on the outermost step of the northern staircase, no image was found on this platform.[11] However, the mouldings of the pīṭha of this broader section of the platform on the northwest are much more carefully carved than the mouldings on the rest of the platform on the north, west or south. Though the nibbling peacocks, kīrtimukhas, full or half candraśālās, mithunas (Figs. 92, 95), carved on a few mouldings recovered from the southwest, are accomplished works, no such sculpted fragment was found in situ on the platforms above the boxed trenches. In fact, the unusual motif of a snake chasing a mouse (Figs. 96-97), or aśokalumbī, or the mouldings on these platforms were executed much more crudely and cursorily than similar elements in the broader platform on the northwest. This suggested that this broader platform was no hasty patchwork made of covering slabs for trenches below. Thus, though it might not have been designed for occupation by a deity, it was probably intended for a sacred purpose like a gathering before the sacrificial platform, which had been found beyond its boundary on the north.

On the southeast of Devarani, a horizontal and continuous clearance was undertaken, widening out in a half circle from the moonstone of the temple staircase. At about four feet below the soil, accumulated against the ruined elephant image placed on the Devarani staircase wall, an enormous flat slab, about 9 feet tall, 4 feet broad, was found laid on the floor, as part of the stone paving. However, the strange, irregular profile of its carving (Figs. 577-78) was visible as soon as the soil, embedded in its cavities, was scooped out. We cushioned the slab below with old tyres, sacks and bamboos, tied with thick ropes, and gently lifted it by a chain pulley to face front (Fig. 576), on 17th January 1988, at its present location. The image of Paśupati Śiva (Pl. 48), with iconographic features virtually unparalleled in Indian and world art of that age, was found carved across the slab, in very high relief. The halo formed by the raised snake hood, its earlobe and earring formed by a peacock, the raised snake hood near its left foot, the crocodile constituting its right shoulder guard, the serpentine fingers of its two hands (Figs. 592-94) were found lying in the surrounding debris. These were matched, and fixed by using lameta stone powder. Parts of the club held in the right hand (Fig. 620), broken from above its base, the snake hood beside the right foot, could not be found. The toes were found (Fig. 469) but remained to be fixed after assessing the span of the intervening portion of the feet, which were missing. Though the base of a colossal image, about 3.5 ft. high, 2.5 ft. broad, was found close to the Paśupati image and it was carved with a rudragaṇa below, the surviving portion of the feet on the top did not match the broken portion of Paśupati's feet. The striking fact about the location of the image was the way it had been lowered carefully on its face, to save it from unknown hands, or to save the community from its apparently baleful glare. If it had fallen on its face instead of being laid out deliberately, it would have suffered far greater damage than was evident.

A similar purpose of concealment, or, as is more likely, a thoughtless later repair explained the positioning of a slab with a seated Śaivācārya on a nāgarāja base (Figs. 85-86, 461) with marks of the feet of a missing image on top. It was discovered lying on its face in ten splintered fragments on the ardhamaṇḍapa step.[12] In a similar secretive manner, a large slab, carved with Kārtikeya (Fig. 265), was found slid inside the debris behind the enormous maṇḍapa pillar on the right. As soon as it was released and turned, it revealed a Kārtikeya like the Jethani Kārtikeya, though its face, arms, attributes and its vehicle were all broken and virtually lost (Fig. 265). Since its original situation was not understood, it was shifted initially inside the Devarani temple maṇḍapa.

That the Paśupati, with its ostensibly malevolent aspect, was not the only form of Śiva worshipped at Tala, became evident from the further discovery in the southeast of a massive Śiva head (Figs. 432-33) of benign aspect and beatific calm, suggesting his yoga Dakṣiṇāmūrti. Its torso could not be traced or matched from the available fragments. A slab carved with a staff bearing Śaiva ascetic (Fig. 459), and a broken jamb, carved with the profile of the trunk of a river goddess (Fig. 311), were also recovered. The latter invites close comparison with a river goddess (Fig. 309) recovered earlier from the Devarani front.

The clearance, undertaken at Tala in three different seasons was most useful in demonstrating the brickwork and Devarani stone platforms as later restorations; in tentatively fixing, with the help of the inscriptions, coins, minor antiquities and brick sizes, lower and upper chronological limits for occupation of the site; in facilitating a imaginative reconstruction of the missing portions of the temples, by matching fragments in situ with detached fragments; and, in revealing a style, with unique and unprecedented features, which influenced subsequent developments in Indian art. Right at Tala, the clearance also revealed an evolution within the same broad framework of style, from Jethani to Devarani, and a co-existence of classical and medieval features, which made it a transitional site between the two periods. It also offered a demonstration of the ancient techniques of structural and site conservation, and lessons in the weaknesses of contemporary structural engineering around the time of construction.

NOTES

1. Cunningham, *ASIAR* 7, 1878: 8.
2. The removal of debris and overburden of soil from structures projecting above ground, from the same historic, cultural and chronological period, has been undertaken by the Archaeology Department of Madhya Bhārat/Pradesh on its monuments, from time to time.
3. The clearance was done by the then Registering officer A.K. Risbud. See G.K. Chandrol 1980: 9-10.
4. Archaeologist, Raipur, 1984.
5. This clearance was undertaken during the tenure of Shyam Bajpai and Vinay Shukla, successive Directors, and executed by G.L. Raikwar, the registering officer, Bilaspur, and Rahul Kumar Singh, Curator, Bilaspur museum.
6. Śarabhapurīya king Prasannamātra's silver coin, Kalacurī king Ratnadeva III's copper coin, varieties of earthen vessels, including pots with metal rings, arrow and axe heads, sickles, fish hooks and scissors, skin rubbers and iron back scratchers, stone sharpeners, storage jars, circular stone lamps, ear studs, pendants, blades, points, scrapers, borers, cores and flakes, made of flint, chert, quartz were found in the brick enclosure and around it. Raikwar. R.O. Bilaspur report (file No 39) 1985-86: 58, 64-67.
7. R.O. Bilaspur 1985-86:55,64.
8. The northern brick enclosure yielded ashes, earthen bowls, arrow heads made of iron; inadequately fired incense burners left in the green hard stage, equipped with outturned rim, and decorated with inverted loop patterns or triangles; bowls and inadequately sprigged pots or lamps, lamp stands and water jugs. The variety of articles was less than that on Jethani southeast, and, in a cursory view, the articles appeared to belong to one period, that of the later additions to the temple. A thorough comparative analysis of the antiquities found in the Jethani and Devarani brick altars is outside the scope of this study.
9. The brick sizes in the 4th - 5th century brick temples, excavated in the Bholāhuḍkī Tekḍi near Māṇḍhal, are 0.44 x 0.23 x 0.8 m and 0.40 x 0.24 m. Sharma in Shastri 1992: 221-22. The earlier Kauśāmbi ramparts are revetted externally with a battered facing of bricks measuring 0.48 x 0.30 x 0.5ms. Bhaṭṭiprolu, Guḍiāḍā stūpas are made on a solid core of kiln burnt bricks measuring 0.60 x 0.45 x 0.10ms. Satish

Grover 1980: 19, 47-48. Sirpur bricks are 52.5 cms x 22.3 cms x 7.5 cms, which are a bit smaller than Bhitargāon bricks. Longhurst, *ASIAR* 1909-10: 12.

10. For evidence of the artificial raising of the mound, see R.O.Bilaspur's Report 1985-86: 53, 61.
11. A broken image of Kārtikeya was found, before the clearance on the north, which was shifted inside the temple. A head and footless image of a lady was found on the northeast, outside the temple platform steps, after clearance.
12. Raikwar, R.O., must be credited with the hunch that the roughly packed slabs on the ardhamaṇḍapa step, apparently designed to bring it to a uniform level with the maṇḍapa, were not what they seemed. It was he who brought out the fragments and put them together. Raikwar 1987-88: 21-2 for details.

4

Historiography for Tala and Dakṣiṇa Kośala

INITIAL ACCOUNTS

Scholars in the 19th and most of the 20th century have generally confined themselves to a descriptive and epigraphic study of the monuments of Dakṣiṇa Kośala.[1] While it is possible to glean a dynastic history of this area from these accounts, a history of art, or, of the place of Tala or any other monument in that history has not really been their concern. Though the two temples at Tala have been known,[2] the initial, though incidental notice of their style and chronology, has been published for the first time, only in the Malhār excavation report in 1978, by Bajpai and Pandey.[3] In spite of the unresolved controversies surrounding the question of Śarabhapura, Bajpai has identified Malhār as the only possible capital of the Śarabhapurīyas, in view of its extensive habitational ruins and mud ramparts, and has identified Tala as the saṁgamagrāma (a village at confluence) mentioned in the Burhikhār copperplates, irrespective of the fact that Malhār itself is at the confluence of rivers Arpā, Lilāgar, and Śivanātha.[4] He attributes the Tala temples, together with the Deur temple at Malhār, the Indal Deul and Śavarīnārāyaṇa brick temples at Khārod and the Aḍbhār stone temple to Śarabhapurīyas, irrespective of the differences in their styles.[5] This is followed by a suggestion that Mahendra of Allahabad praśasti, identifiable with Mahendra of the Malhār clay seal, is a Śarabhapurīya ruler, and yet a contemporary of Samudragupta. This suggestion is accompanied by the further opinion that the Jethani temple is probably a Daśāvatāra temple of the 4th century AD, to be placed earlier than the Devarani temple, which can be placed around the end of 4th, beginning of 5th century AD.[6] Bajpai places other Malhār sculptures in the 4th or 5th century AD, without comparing them with the work at Tala or with Gupta art, and his iconographic identifications at Tala remain marginal and questionable.[7]

STADTNER AND THEORY OF EXTERNAL DYNASTIC INFLUENCE

It is, however, Donald Martin Stadtner who, for the first time in 1976, discusses the style and chronology of the Tala temples in relation to other 6th and 7th century sites of Dakṣiṇa Kośala. The Ph.D. dissertation for the University of California remains unpublished, but his observations on the Tala temples have appeared in an article published in the *Archives of Asian Art* in 1980. Yet another article by him is concerned with the 7th century brick temples of the area and has appeared in 1981. Stadtner's being the most extensive account to date, it is important to analyse his method and conclusions carefully before proceeding further.

In spite of his achievements,[8] Stadtner's understanding of the development of art in Dakṣiṇa Kośala and of Tala's place in it, is distorted by his view that powerful dynasties make for cultural accomplishment, and that Dakṣiṇa Kośala is a provincial backwater of great kingdoms, which hobbles the independent development of its art. In the absence of a strong stable dynasty in the area in the 6th century, the monuments built in this century reflect forces 'emanating from important imperial (Gupta and Vākāṭaka) centres' in north India and the Deccan. Though the area is not under direct Gupta or Vākāṭaka control, it is amenable to their influence. Acting on this presumption, Stadtner dates Tala, together with the Rāmacandra temple door jambs at Rajim to AD 530-50, broadly to the 1st half of the 6th century, on account of loose connections to late Gupta sites. He dates the Senākapāṭ, Turturiyā, Malhār, Rāmacandra temple (Rajim) pillars to AD 550-75 for treating the Gupta-Vākāṭaka motifs less inventively or efficiently than Tala. It is only in the 7th century when the Pāṇḍu or Somavaṁśīs give a strong government to Dakṣiṇa Kośala, that Dakṣiṇa Kośala overcomes Gupta and Vākāṭaka influences and develops a distinctive Nāgara style of north Indian temple architecture of its own, which breaks away from 6th century monuments like Tala. Unlike the 6th century, monuments can now be directly associated with royal patronage. Stadtner assigns the monuments at Sirpur therefore to the initial period of Mahāśivagupta Bālārjuna's reign (c. AD 595-650). In the later half of the 7th century and the first decade of the 8th, a second style, cruder than the Somavaṁśī style, popularized at Sirpur, emerges with Rajim as its centre, in response to the revival of the Nala dynasty and its patronage. Stadtner ascribes what he considers the crudity of Nala work to its origins in tribal Bastar, which is more backward even in backward Dakṣiṇa Kośala.[9] From the 8th century, there is dearth of art in Dakṣiṇa Kośala, again due to a political vacuum, which is filled only by the Kalacurīs around the 11th century AD. In this history of sporadic creativity, Tala is an isolated event in isolated Dakṣiṇa Kośala, being divorced both from other 6th century monuments, like those at Turturiyā and Malhār, which look to Ajanta and the Deccan, as well as from the 7th century developments, which seem inbred and autonomous. To him Tala takes nothing from, and gives nothing back to the art of Dakṣiṇa Kośala, being an anomalous example of southern architectural inspiration and tenuous northern Gupta affinities in sculpture.[10]

Stadtner, however, is not very successful in maintaining this position. In support of his views, he looks for monuments which would have acted as bridges between 6th century Tala and the south, 6th century Dakṣiṇa Kośala and the Deccan, 7th century Rajim and Nala works in Bastar or Andhra Pradesh. Unable to find any of them, he attributes their absence to the possibility of their being not yet discovered, or awaiting the excavator's spade, or having disappeared entirely due to the use of perishable material. Thus, the presence of the so called southern features at Tala,, in spite of their absence in contemporary south itself, is explained by the use of perishable material in the 6th century south, and the migration of a few south Indian Śaivas to Tala, who instruct its craftsmen in the use of some southern architectural elements, leaving them free to follow their own northern traditions in sculpture. What he considers to be the clumsy and massive rendering of Tala architecture is due to the inability of the Tala craftsmen to learn their lessons well. Similarly, according to him, the sophisticated features of the temple plan of 7th century Dakṣiṇa Kośala cannot really have been indigenous to the area. These must have originated in earlier north Indian examples, now missing. Since no monuments can be directly attributed to the patronage of Śarabhapurīyas and other rulers, or to their feudatories, it can be assumed that there is no active building programme in Dakṣiṇa Kośala in the 5th or 6th century.[11]

Stadtner's view of Tala and Dakṣiṇa Kośala monuments as existing in isolated stylistic compartments, or his chronology for them, is due to his tendency to rely on the unclear evidence of inscriptions, most of them undated or dated in regnal eras, as also on the impressive history of the Pāṇḍuvaṁśī and Nala dynasties, derived from such inscriptions.[12] He chooses to date Tala, working backward from the 'vantage point' of the 'securely dated' Lakṣmaṇa temple, though controversy continues about the inscription on which he relies for this date.[13] On the basis of an undated Rajim inscription, which, according to him, is the sole source of information about the Nalas, he works back to late 7th century dates for temples at Rajim, Palāri and Khārod.[14] Thus, the initial lack of art in 6th century Dakṣiṇa Kośala due to lack of dynastic patronage, the development of art in the later part of the century due to southern or Gupta influence, the presumed absence of influence of 6th century art, or the suggested originality of 7th century art, are assumed by Stadtner, as a matter of course, from the presence or absence of inscriptions.

With this reliance on inscriptions, not strictly associated with monuments, goes a reliance on motifs. The connection of Tala with Gupta sculpture or southern architecture, its isolation from 6th or 7th century sites in the area, and the association of these sites with the Deccan, are all established on the basis of a few isolated motifs. Though Stadtner claims to base his chronological sequence on a 'logical progression of architectural forms, motifs and sculptural style', he concerns himself primarily with motifs, negligent of the fact that, in Indian art, motifs are tenacious things, which tend to survive in different areas and periods, but are executed in different styles. He does not attempt a thorough or systematic analysis of motifs, either by building up a complete concordance of such elements, or by charting their simultaneous evolution through time, in a comparative context, at different sites. His attempts at stylistic analysis are also not very successful, not only because of his dependence on gestures, postures and surface patterns as stylistic criteria, but also because of his reliance on vague or abstract concepts of style outside a strict object specific spatial or temporal context. One is never sure with him, whether a feature is early or late, and why.[15]

While using motifs and stylistic criteria for this sequence, Stadtner is unsure of his conclusions and not free from contradictions in his assessments. Thus, he sees the 6th century monuments like Tala as 'isolated, somewhat idiosyncratic, and at times, masterful versions of the late Gupta' style, and at the same time, announces a general similarity of the sculpture at Tala and other 6th century Kośala sites with sculptures as diverse as those at Udayagiri, Eran, Bhūmarā, Sākor, Deogarh, Bhitargāon, Nācnā, Ajanta, Auraṅgābad and other allied Deccani sites, on the basis of their sharing of some isolated motif or its distant variation. Nor does he make any actual comparisons, content to make general assertions about a shared capacity for precision, miniaturization, or elaboration. Tala is thus linked with early as well as late 5th century Gupta sites, irrespective of the variations in the execution of the shared motifs within the 5th century AD at different sites and periods. The confusion that can be created by such an approach is demonstrated by the way he links motifs in the same door jambs with both early and late 5th century Gupta motifs.[16] Having thus affirmed the Gupta connections of Tala, however broadly, he proceeds to demonstrate its radical differences with its Gupta predecessors, albeit in a negative manner, by stressing the absence of certain Gupta architectural motifs, even as he points out that these recur in some Gupta examples as well.[17] On the one hand, he suggests that the 7th century temples of Dakṣiṇa Kośala use new motifs and physical features, which inaugurate a new and confident architectural style, under the aegis of Somavaṁśī rulers[18] by spurning the Gupta-Vākāṭaka heritage at Tala, at other 6th century sites, and even earlier, at Gupta sites. On the other hand, he speaks of the presence of such 7th century features in 5th and 6th century temples, and decries features he considers architecturally inappropriate, in 7th century temples, that have been ineptly borrowed from 6th century temples.[19]

Shuttling back and forth between motifs and what he considers as style, Stadtner is unable to spell out the elements which makes the 6th century style different from the 7th century style, or the Sirpur 'Somavaṁśī' style different from the Rajim 'Nalavaṁśī' style in the 7th century. He does not seem to be quite certain about whether three dimensional and deep carving, internal modelling or anatomical differentiation, clear definition of the underlying structure, 'refined' or 'accomplished' treatment are early, late or concomitant features. When in doubt, he tends to classify one style as a provincial and crude version of the other.[20] And, what essentially are motifs, tend to be taken by him as stylistic criteria, without being studied systematically. So, the type and weight of ornament, elaboration of architectural motifs and flexions are seen by him as chronological clues, without carrying out a rigorous analysis of their stylistic evolution.[21]

Because of his preoccupation with dynastic patronage, inscriptions and motifs, his preconception about Dakṣiṇa Kośala style being an appendage to more ecumenical and civilized styles, Stadtner has been unable to explain the legacy or influence of sixth century sites like Tala in the history of Indian art. He has, however, done considerable service in analysing the monuments themselves; in pointing to directions from which influence might have come; in establishing the presence of a trend towards the creation of bland facades, enlivened by recesses, facades or projections, and of plinth mouldings, relieved by animal heads; and, above all, in focusing attention on Tala and Dakṣiṇa Kośala as theatres of significant, if often inexplicable movements.

J.G. WILLIAMS AND THEORY OF TRIBAL LOCALISM

Joanna Williams comes back to the question of the chronology and stylistic origins of the Tala style in 1982. Given the nature of her study, in which the arts of imperial centres are assigned what seems to be excessive importance, it is not surprising that with her, as with Stadtner, the art of Dakṣiṇa Kośala is but a provincial version of a imperial style. If Stadtner finds the sculpture of Tala to be only loosely connected with late Gupta sites, she announces it as a legatee of the Gupta art in the third phase (c. AD 480-530). She continues to emphasize its folk aspect, stressing the tribal contribution, and what she describes as its deviation from and modification of the Sanskritik, Brāhmaṇical, Gupta tradition. While she does not accept Stadtner's theory of the derivation of Tala architecture from southern examples, she accounts for its features by the imitation of wooden forms no longer in existence, or by the misinterpretation of Gupta stone architecture. To her, Tala is but an isolated version of Gupta forms in a peripheral region, subsequent 7th century Dakṣiṇa Kośala moving further away from Gupta moorings.[22] At the same time, at Sirpur, she also allows for a greater continuity between the 6th and the 7th century Dakṣiṇa Kośala.[23]

Williams's entire analysis depends, more or less, upon an analysis of motifs.[24] She thus detects the Gupta heritage at Tala in some ornaments, figures and postures.[25] The Devarani door jambs, however, and their puzzling iconography, are attributed to tribal misinterpretations of orthodox Gupta motifs. The probability that we may here be confronted by a hitherto unknown local tradition is not considered.[26] The oblique cut, three dimensional treatment, the invasion of forms by foliate motifs, and the bland facade, carved with niches are seen by her as features appropriate to carving in wood. These, she speculates, are transmitted through a Gupta pattern book, which is not fully understood by the craftsmen. While conceding the speculative nature of these observations, she tries to establish a historical development through motifs, which, in the circumstances, is not easy.

Because of her preoccupation with motifs, her dynastic concern with empire and province, the complexities of the Tala style, instead of being confronted and explained, are dismissed by Joanna Williams as localisms. To her, it is an anomaly, not because it misrepresents, as Stadtner suggests, southern motifs, but because it misinterprets Gupta motifs, making its parentage doubtful.[27] Unusually, and contrary to her close dating of Gupta sites, she gives a broad date to Tala and brings it closer to the 5th century AD.

KRISHNA DEVA AND THEORY OF GUPTA-VĀKĀṬAKA ORIGINS

Krishna Deva has made an attempt (1988) to analyse and date the Tala style in the context of Dakṣiṇa Kośala and Gupta-Vākāṭaka art and with reference to the south.[28] He fixes the date of the Devarani temple to AD 550-75, moving away from the early 6th century date proposed by Stadtner and Joanna Williams, but he does not say why. He agrees with Stadtner in seeing a similarity of niches and makara toraṇas of the Devarani with those of Cālukya and Pallava temples further south. Unlike Stadtner or Joanna Williams, he emphasizes a strong Vākāṭaka rather than Gupta flavour in its figural relics. He finds the stone āmalakas at Jethani comparable both to those of the early 6th century Gupta temple of Deogarh and the mid-7th century Sabarī temple in Dakṣiṇa Kośala. He considers some of the ornamental motifs and figural types at Tala to be ancestors to slightly later forms of Dakṣiṇa Kośala, without citing examples. He agrees with Stadtner, that the Tala temples do not play an important role in the development of a regional style of architecture.[29] Though he renders a much more precise architectural account of Dakṣiṇa Kośala temples than any of the earlier authors, his failure to connect Tala with this style results in the site standing out in even more splendid isolation than before.[30]

About the relative date of Devarani and Jethani temples, all scholars except Bajpai and Pandey agree that they are roughly contemporary. Stadtner, on the basis of three stone āmalakas lying nearby, takes the Jethani temple, then covered with rubble, to possess forms more consistent with the north, but finds the sculptures of Jethani and Devarani similar enough to suggest a contemporary date. Williams and Krishna Deva agree with Stadtner.[31]

TALA CONSIDERED AN ISOLATED INCIDENT

None of the earlier commentators on Tala art and architecture except Stadtner, has had more than an incidental interest in it. They have been concerned with other areas and themes. Nor, when they have concerned themselves with Tala like Stadtner, have they had the advantage of the latest discoveries in survey, exploration and excavation in Dakṣiṇa Kośala, made in course of 1986-91, and till date. And yet, even considering their marginal interest or limited information, their remarks have been vitiated by certain preconceptions that occur frequently in earlier studies of Indian art. Thus, artistic style is equated with motifs, and there is an undue dependence on historical features, notably, unwarranted attempts to associate monuments with dynastic fortunes. Undue emphasis is placed on palaeography, and epigraphic evidence is forced. It is also surprising that the fascinating iconography has also been inconsequentially and perfunctorily discussed, being confined to unsubstantial identifications, to support the theory of external influence, or to assert tribal localism. The meaning of some of the unique and unusual forms has also been ignored. Tala has been more or less seen as an isolated incident in the history of Indian art, without ancestors, and without progenies. A need exists, therefore, to look at Tala more closely, examine its archaeology, iconography, architecture, the sources of its style, the impact of its art, its meaning, its unique and shared features, and its relevance in the development of medieval Indian art.

NOTES

1. Jenkins 1825, *ASR* describes the Rājīvalocana temple at Rajim. Beglar in *ASIAR* 7,1873-74, *ASIAR* 13, 1874-76, and Cunningham in *ASIAR* 17,1881-82 describe the monuments and inscriptions of Sirpur, Āraṅg and Rajim. Cousens 1897, 1904, and *1905*, provides a brief account of the antiquities, together with photographs, preserved now in the India Office library, London, and A.S.I. Delhi, in volumes on Central Provinces. Longhurst 1909-10 discusses the brick temples of Khārod and Pūjāripāli. A brief chronological account on Buddhist bronzes from Sirpur and Sirpur and Rajim temples has been presented by M.G. Dikshit 1955-56 and 1960 on the basis of excavations undertaken between 1953 and 1957, which have been separately and briefly noticed in *IAR* 1953-54: 12; *IAR* 1954-55: 24-25; 1955-56: 26-27. Among Indian scholars, Hiralal, Mirashi, L.P. Pandeya, B.C. Jain, Ajay Mitra Shastri, have rendered yeoman's service through the 20th century in numerous articles in Hindi, English or Marathi on the coins, inscriptions and history of this period. A list of 6th, 7th century AD inscriptions has been appended to the reprint of Fleet's *CII* 3, providing a summary of the work done till 1970.
2. Beglar was informed about this site at Raipur, though he never visited it. See *ASIAR* 7, 1873-4: 168. The temple of Devarani has been noticed by local scholars like V.S. Thakur and L.S. Nigam, and one may not really call it a recently discovered temple, as Stadtner does in Williams 1981: 137, 144, n. 4.
3. S.K. Pandey 1977; Bajpai and Pandey 1978.
4. The saṁgama-grāma is mentioned as a village donated in southern Mekala, in a set of three copperplates, by Pāṇḍuvaṁśī king Śūrabala, son of Bharatabala, to Jayeśvara Bhaṭṭāraka, or lord Śiva, at the confluence of rivers. See B. Sitaraman and M.T. Sharma 1977; Bajpai and Pandey 1978: 25-26.
5. Bajpai and Pandey 1978: 32.
6. *Ibid.*, 26, 27.
7. Bajpai places the Śiva and Ardhanārīśvara busts in the Malhār Deur temple campus in the 3rd and 4th century AD respectively. He assigns the pillar with Ulūka (owl) and Kacchapa (tortoise) jātakas (stories of Buddha's previous birth) in a Malhār house, to the 5th century AD, together with another pillar, carved with lotus and vase. However, elsewhere, he places the pillar with the jātakas in 500 AD. He does not quite see that the Deur temple busts are already informed by 'Gupta' experience, and the pillars have moved out of the Gupta period. His identification of the Śiva image on the Devarani door jamb lintel as kirāta (hunter), is not substantiated by a discussion of the iconographic attributes. *Ibid.*, 37, pls. 12-14.
8. Irrespective of the criticism that follows, Stadtner is a pioneer in bringing disparate material together, introducing a comparative perspective, establishing an analytical frame for a concordance of motifs, and, in posing a dynamic sequence of artistic patterns.
9. See Stadtner 1977: 30-31, 40, 47, 72, 94-95, 134-35, 149, 157, 177-78, 191-92, 195-96, 199-202; Stadtner 1980: 47; Stadtner 1981: 140,144 for the different dates. For Sirpur and allied works, his dates are as

follows: Svastika Vihāra (585-95 AD); Ānandaprabha Vihāra, Lakṣmaṇa temple, temples A & B (Rāma and another Lakṣmaṇa) and Gandheśvara temple (all 595-605 AD); allied sculptures in Sirpur Museum, Malhār, Turturiyā (AD 600-620); Indal Deul, Khārod (AD 650-60), Siddheśvara temple, Palāri (AD 675-85), Rāmacandra maṇḍapa pillars and pilasters (end of 7th century AD), and allied Sirpur sculptures (AD 710-30). For works deriving presumably from Rajim, Bastar and Andhra Pradesh, his dates are like this: Kuleśvara temple images, pillars and door jambs at Rajim (AD 685-95); the Rājīvalocana temple western gateway, four images in its corner shrines, the pillars and pilasters in its maṇḍapa at Rajim (AD 695-710), Śabarī temple at Khārod (700 AD).

10. Stadtner 1977: 12-13, 21,32, 183, 194-96, 200-02; 1980: 41, 47; 1981: 137,140, 144.
11. Stadtner 1977: 23; 1980: 41; 1981: 144.
12. *Ibid.*, 1977: 2.
13. Ajay Mitra Shastri. In Asher and Gai 1985: 105-9. The Lakṣmaṇa temple inscription was recovered, detached from the debris of the maṇḍapa.
14. Stadtner 1977: 157. M.G. Dikshit points out that the inscribed slabs in the Rājīvalocana temple walls may have little to do with the temple itself, being embedded in the walls haphazardly, in all probability, just to preserve them. Dikshit 1960: 18, 22, 28-32, relying on inscriptions, puts the Sirpur Lakṣmaṇa temple and vihāras, and the Rajim Rājīvalocana temple between 500-600 AD under the Śarabhapurīyas. He ascribes construction of the Rājīvalocana temple to four successive stages in this period. He attributes the Rāmacandra temple to the Paṇḍavas around 700 AD. On the other hand, the śikhara, the west gateway pillar of the Rājīvalocana temple or some of the columns and the passage of the Rāmacandra temple are assigned by him to the Kalacurī period. Dikshit does not distinguish these different stages by stylistic reasoning or comparisons.
15. Stadtner 1977: 97; Also Pramod Chandra, 1983: 28-29 for objections to the use of motifs as chronological guides.
16. Stadtner links up the Rāmacandra pillar door jamb (which he finds contemporary with Tala), and the Turturiyā pillar with Vākāṭaka Ajanta or later Deccani sites like Aurangābād cave 3 on the basis of the presence of various types of door band (like diamonds and indented ellipses, lotus petals or medallions, tubular floral bands etc), or the tapering, fluted, cushioned shape of the capital. He speaks of the capacity for precision as being common to Tala and late Gupta sites. He detects evidence of similar capacity in the depiction of the oversected legs of an amorous couple in the Rāmacandra temple door jamb, as well as in the twisted floral band framing a medallion on the Devarani soffit door jamb. In a more specific comparison, he speaks about the tendency at Tala as well as late Gupta site of Nācnā Kuthārā to reduce 'the cutting plane to a point beyond which planes are difficult to recognize'. He does not flesh out this observation by a careful comparison with a Nācnā scene. In view of the extreme clarity of the patterns at Tala, however minutely cut they may be, his observation needs clarification. According to him, the vertical, meandering lotus stalk and the tubular lotus band on the Senākapāṭ door jamb and the parallel, vertical rows of acanthus buds on the Rāmacandra door jamb are shared by the Devarani door jambs and pilasters, which divide antarāla and garbhagṛha. In the same Senākapāṭ and Rāmacandra door jambs, a vertical band of foliate merlons, and a hexagonal band, clasped by floral patterns, are declared by him to be like those on Udayagiri cave 6, the damaged door jamb on Udayagiri hilltop, and Eran Narasiṁha temple lintel. See Stadtner 1977: 13, 17-18, 23-31,41, 56-60, 200; 1980: 42.
17. The carving of figural sculpture on lateral sides rather than door jamb front; installation of the lintel on door jambs, with faces set obliquely; absence of indented door jambs, pilaster capitals uniting with miniature shrines on the lintel, or of mithunas in rectangular niches, are, according to Stadtner, significant departures from Gupta prototypes. Stadtner 1977: 22; 1980: 42. On the other hand, he notices the presence of figural sculpture on the inner door jamb in 5th century Gupta temple sites of Garhvā and Bilsad. *Ibid.*, 211, n. 13; Cunningham. *ASIAR* 10,1878-89: 9, 11, 19 ff.

18. Stadtner detects evidence of an assertion of the newly found political identity and stability under Somavaṁśīs in the use of the engaged corner āmalaka or octagonal cupolas in the śikhara; continuation of projections from wall to tower; adaption of tapered pūrṇaghaṭa pilasters to support cornices; use of khura kumbha mouldings with overhanging leaf; prominence of maṇḍapa antarāla, and introduction of the stellate plan in 7th century temples in Dakṣiṇa Kośala. Stadtner 1977: 62-64, 87, 125-26, 138, 180-181.
19. Stadtner acknowledges the presence of the so called seventh century features like āmalakas, pūrṇaghaṭa capital at 6th century Jethani (and the Deccan). He finds the vertical foliate band joining medallions at Devarani at Ānandaprabha vihāra porch door at Sirpur later, and, at Bilsad and Sarnath main temple door jambs earlier. He discusses the prominent use of maṇḍapa and antarāla at Devarani temple, at Bhūmarā earlier, and less prominently, at Tigavā, Sanchi, Udayagiri cave 19. The use of figural or floral sculpture on different sides of a pillar, is considered by Stadtner to be a 'mitigation of architectonic integrity'. Such pillars have been found in the Jethani temple maṇḍapa also, after clearance. These are not exclusive to 7th century AD or to Somavaṁśī sites like Ānandaprabha vihāra at Sirpur, Siddheśvara temple at Palāri, Rāmacandra and Kuleśvara temple at Rajim. Stadtner describes 7th century Rāmacandra maṇḍapa pillars as a pastiche of 6th century mouldings from Dakṣiṇa Kośala. One of these mouldings, a tubular acanthus, is shared also by Devarani temple. It is modified into a tubular floral band at the Sirpur Lakṣmaṇa temple. See Stadtner 1977: 26-28, 61, 64, 75-76, 90-91, 223, n.3.
20. In the 6th century, Stadtner seems to see the more deeply cut foliage and Śiva Pārvatī panel of the Devarani door jamb, as an early feature. On the other hand, in the 7th century, he explains the depth of the ornament at the Siddheśvara temple at Palāri as later than the flat treatment at Indal Deul, Khārod. He finds the individual differentiation of foliate members and clarity of underlying structure to be an early feature at Tala, and aligns it with late Gupta examples. However, the clarity of underlying structure in the foliage of 7th century Kuleśvara, Rājīvalocana and Śabarī temples is, according to him, a late and less refined feature. He does not explain how, the lack of anatomical differentiation (identified, apparently with lack of internal modelling), which affects the body in the Rajim style, does not affect the foliage, which is clearly defined. Tubular limbs of this style are, according to Stadtner, a definition of late age and crudity. He does not elucidate how the earlier modelling of limbs is different, or more refined. To him, Rajim is a provincial version of Sirpur, and the Śabarī temple at Khārod is a provincial version of Nala work at Rajim (though Khārod is connected by him with both Sirpur and Rajim tradition on account of shared motifs). See Stadtner 1977: 25, 78-81, 109-10, 122-23, 142-43, 151-53, 169-70, 186-91.
21. Stadtner finds the heavier jewellery of Indal Deul, Khārod as later than the jewellery of Lakṣmaṇa. He describes this as fluid, plastic and terracotta like, which is modified in Palāri later. He also speaks of the sparse ornament of the Rajim style Śabarī temple as a late and crude feature. In architecture, amplification of door jamb, increase in oblique vertical sections, divisions of wall, projections of kharaśilā are, according to him, late features, that put the Siddheśvara after the Indal Deul temple. But, the criterion of growing complexity is not used by him to chart architectural evolution through the 6th and 7th centuries. The tilted head, bent leg, chest and head thrown forward or backward, the crossed legs, stability or elegance of posture and pose are mentioned by him often as fine points of distinction. They do not, however, come through in his analysis as steady indicators of the stylistic evolution. See Stadtner 1977: 109, 112-14, 118-19, 122, 142-43, 149.
22. J.G. Williams,1982: 3-5, 128. She classifies the core period into three broad phases of inception (AD 370-415), maturity and crisis (AD 415-85), and Gupta art after the Guptas (AD 485-550). During this entire period, Gupta rule conditions artistic expression. Implicit in her assessment is the assumption that, in the post-Gupta period, the imperial style gives way to provincial deviations, of which Tala is an example. 'Tala', to her, 'is both at the outer periphery of Gupta influence and at the threshold of the use of the stone medium'. *Ibid.*, 125. Joanna Williams, however, agrees broadly with Stadtner when she says that the

Devarani temple seems to draw upon traditions of wooden architecture as did early Pallava shrines. Joanna Williams in Nigam 2000: 70.

23. Williams 1982: 160-63.
24. *Ibid.*, 6. where she avows her objective concern with style as a sum of parts rather than complex wholes.
25. To Williams, the maṇḍapa at Devarani, the river goddesses at the bottom and inner faces of its door jambs, its foliate bands, the complex postures of the figures in its lower lintel, the presence of a festooned vase in a Jethani fragment are 5th century Gupta motifs. The maṇḍapa reminds her of Bhūmarā and Sākor, the river goddesses of Bilsad and Bhitargāon, the foliate bands of Nācnā, the vase of Uparkot and Udayagiri 19, and the lintel figures of the Garhvā master. *Ibid.*, 125-28.
26. Williams finds the Tala features to be examples of the tribal localism of Chhattisgarh, 'outside the familiar Brāhmaṇical work of Sanskrit texts'. *Ibid.*, 127-28. Yet, she improbably suggests the fifteen crouching figures on the Devarani door jamb soffit as Brahmin teachers, who helped a local dynasty to expand Hinduism among forest dwelling tribals.
27. To Joanna Williams, Tala is a puzzle because it is 'like Athena sprung full grown with only half its parentage visible'. *Ibid.*, 5-6, 124-125. Joanna Williams in Nigam 2000: 71.
28. Krishna Deva, "Dakṣiṇa Kośala style", in Dhaky & Meister, ed., *Encyclopaedia* 2.1 (Text), 1988: 217-50.
29. *Ibid.*, 225, 227-30. According to him, the typically brick built idiom of AD 600-725 emerges only in the Rājīvalocana temple at Rajim.
30. Unlike Stadtner, Krishna Deva dates the two early pillars in Rāmacandra temple, two Turturiyā pillars (on account of general similarity to decorative and figural features on door frames and pillars of Ajanta caves 2 and 23) to AD 525-50, placing them earlier in his sequence, than Tala. His other dates are as follows: Rājīvalocana garbhagṛha, śikhara, kapili, some maṇḍapa pillars (600 AD); Rāma temple at Sirpur (AD 625-50), Sirpur vihāra and Lakṣmaṇa (AD 600-625), Śabarī temple, Khārod (AD 650), Indal Deul, Khārod (AD 650-75), Siddheśvara temple, Palāri (AD 675-700), Dhobini temple and Aḍbhār temple in Bilaspur district (AD 700), Rājīvalocana sanctum door frame (AD 700-725), Rājīvalocana temple prātoli (AD 750). He bases his dates on various grounds like growing complexity in plan and design, hardening of modelling, erotic intent, and frothy arabesque without explaining these general terms by concrete comparisons. As to why he puts Aḍbhār and Dhobini, placed by Stadtner in mid-9th century, in early 8th, or Rājīvalocana door or prātoli later than Aḍbhār, and, as to how these temples diverge from Tala or one another, he does not explain.
31. Stadtner 1977: 20; 1980: 38; Williams 1982: 125; Krishna Deva 1988: 229.

5

Architecture at Tala

SIGNIFICANCE OF THE STUDY

The earlier accounts[1] of the architecture of the two temples at Tala have been unable to take account of the clearances at Malhār in 1975-78, at Tala itself in 1978 and in 1986-89, in the adjacent area of Dakṣiṇa Kośala like Surguja and Bastar in 1987-91, or of the excavation at Sisdeori in Raipur in 2002. While some of the material is new and was not available to the earlier scholars, their general tendency to consider Tala as an isolated incident of no significance in the history of art, or as an unorthodox and provincial expression of the orthodox, ecumenical art of imperial centres in the north or south, was not justified even by the material they had at their disposal. They have been unable to see that the Tala temples are no sterile experiments of 'anthropological types' of people, but are instead important documents of a transitional period in art.

These temples demonstrate, on the one hand, the utmost degree of innovative flexibility, that could be brought to bear upon the execution of an available repertoire of physical motifs and constituents. On the other, they leave a legacy for the future, a legacy, not so much of the specific ingredients of a structure, but of a conception, larger, bolder, and more spirited and adventurous than ever before. The fact that these temples use conventional elements of contemporary architecture in combinations, paralleled never before nor since, does neither orphan them of parents, nor deprive them of progenies. To see this, one has to move beyond a mere recounting of the physical segments of the temples, to a consideration of the way these are made, and made differently, from before or after, even as they continue from the past, or influence the future of Indian architecture. Of the two temples of Devarani and Jethani, Devarani has been visible above the ground, in use, and long familiar to the scholarly world, which makes it possible to study earlier opinions about Tala vis-à-vis Indian art. It is also better preserved and its facade, unlike Jethani, has not been covered by later additions in brick, which makes the study of its plan and elevation easier. The original nucleus of Devarani consists, in plan, of steps, an ardhamaṇḍapa, maṇḍapa, antarāla and garbhagṛha (Fig. 6). Among later additions are a broad platform with two staircases on the northeast, and a narrow platform on north, west and south (Fig. 7). No śikhara or roof survive above the original or later portion and no walls, if any, survive on the later platforms.

DEVARANI: PLAN AND ELEVATION

The Devarani temple, which is quite unusual on plan (talacchanda) faces east, measuring externally about 14 m in length (excluding steps) from west to east, 9.55 m in maximum width to the west. It is divided into two almost equal chambers, the garbhagṛha measuring internally about 4 metres square, the antarāla being only a little smaller, measuring about 3.65 m in width, and 2.25 m in length. It is preceded by a narrow maṇḍapa, measuring about 3.65 m in breadth and 0.85 m in length, which in turn is fronted by a further space, preceding and virtually merging in the steps, serving as an ardhamaṇḍapa, measuring 4.2 m long, 2.2 m wide. Access to it is given by a sopāna of 6 steps, of the same width, at the base of which is a semicircular candraśilā, measuring 2.6 m at its longest, and 4 m at its broadest.

ELEVATION: DEVARANI, JAGATĪ AND MANḌOVARA

In elevation (ūrdhvachhanda), only the jagatī and maṇḍovara (consisting of vedībandha and jaṅghā) survive (Fig. 77), the śikhara, if any, being missing. The jagatī (Fig. 80) consists of a very narrow bhiṭṭa, an unusually vertical and broad kumbha, only slightly moulded on top, an even broader kandhara, and an equally sheer, rectilinear but heavy kapota, rising to a total height of almost 2.5 m. The vedībandha (Fig. 83), consists of a very broad kumbha, 1.08 m in height, a slender antarapaṭṭa, punctuated by very short galapāda projections, a series of flat paṭṭikās, culminating in a paṭṭikā with a median projecting band, acting as kapota. The kumbha is replaced by a wide kaṇṭha and kalaśa in the maṇḍapa.

At the corners, below the koṣṭha of the jaṅghā at the junction of the garbhagṛha and antarāla, antarāla and the maṇḍapa, there are vestigial, much eroded traces of small, flat nosed makaramukhas, projecting like a rudimentary tulāpīṭha from the kapota. At the junctions, they project in groups of two, facing front and the sides. Of the four larger makaramukhas (Figs. 79, 82), projecting from north and south of garbhagṛha and maṇḍapa, the makaramukha on the south side of the garbhagṛha functions also as a praṇālī. This praṇālī is connected by a vertical, grooved stone slab with a spill channel, which is joined in sections, and culminates in a kuṇḍa at a distance of 29 m to the north. The two makaramukhas on the maṇḍapa survive in a damaged condition.[2]

The vedībandha supports a jaṅghā (rising with the remaining part of the entablature to about 2.75 m) with oblong, framed koṣṭhas, two projected, two recessed, on north and south, two projected, and one recessed, in the west, and only two projected, on the east (Figs. 76-77, 81-82). The recessed koṣṭhas are provided with plain rucaka bhittistambhas crowned by makaramukha capitals. The makaras carry with their snouts toraṇas, consisting of two arches, which merge in a ghaṭapallava with a pendant mukula. The toraṇas resemble a convoluted pediment or illikāvalana, and apparently mark the line below the now missing vārāṇdikā. The corners of the garbhagṛha are also recessed, but these recesses are not provided with makaratoraṇas.

The visual impression of the jaṅghā of Devarani is of awesome simplicity. It emphasizes severe verticals and horizontals, which are varied ever so slightly by the shallow, curved toraṇas. It is enlivened by the few protruding makaramukhas that are made in varying sizes and face different directions, and are distributed with economy over the surface, without disturbing the clear outline. Since all the images found in the clearance operations have been retrieved from the east, it may be speculated that the devakoṣṭhas, without the devas today, were also originally empty. The bland and shallow projections and recesses, bathed in light, aureoled with thin, pencil like shadows, remain restful to the eye, in spite of their being part of a muscular and monumental facade.

ACCESS: STEPS, ARDHAMAṆḌAPA AND MAṆḌAPA

An idea of the elevation of the approach to the Devarani temple can be had only by matching the dimensions of the staircase steps with the many architectural fragments, which have been found in the debris near the staircase, to the southeast of the temple (Fig. 9). The present appearance of an open approach gives way, in this conceptual reconstruction, to a closed approach. The long, stepped kapiśīrṣakas or parapets of the sopāṇamālā at Devarani appear to have supported, on analogy with the Jethani, as we shall see later, several images carved in very high relief. These images faced in, the flat slabs at their back forming the walls of the steps, including a long step forming the ardhamaṇḍapa. Images appear to have been installed with their back against the outer walls of the parapet also. From the associated remains, it may be surmised that these carved slabs (Figs. 351-52, 356), representing various forms of Śiva,[3] stood on bases carved with Śaiva ascetics, nāgarājas, rudra or saumya bhāraputrakas. Sometimes, the main images and the base were monolithic, sometimes separately carved (Fig. 357).[4] Some of these slabs were carved on their top corners by flying garland bearing vidyādharas.[5] On either side, at the parapet fronts, a pot-bellied gaṇa stands (Fig. 84), with a damaged head. On either side of the parapet wall also stands a chāga or meṣamukha (goat or ramheaded) gaṇa (Figs. 85, 561-62).

A pillared porch or a tower (toraṇa) appears to have stood in front of the parapets. It seems to have possessed two enormous slabs of stone (Fig. 85), one of which presently lies prone on the ground on the left and measures 4.6 m in height (Figs. 255-56). The slab shows a tall rectangular base, and a recessed niche in the upper part, with the upper half of a miśraka pilaster, 1.9 m tall, with lotus petal mouldings, a ghaṭapallava capital, crowned by a narrow āmalaka. The neck of the ghaṭa is wrapped with knotted foliage emerging from either side. Another slab, lying to the right, in front of the parapet, is smaller, the surviving portion measuring 2.6 m in height. It has a tall square base, crowned by a narrow pilaster, serving as shaft, measuring 0.78 m high. The shaft is decorated upwards in successive segments of petals, decreasing in size, as they increase in number. Another slab, found in front of Devarani, has similar dimensions and decoration. In this, the narrow shaft is complete, measuring 1.60 m. If one matches the two slabs, their original height works out to be almost 2.5 m. The other surviving fragments, retrieved from southeast of Devarani[6] suggest the location, at intervals, on the sopāna flanks, of miśraka pillar shafts. These were carved either with vertical floral bands, emerging from kīrtimukhas (Figs. 250-51), or with a receding series of lotus petal mouldings, crowned by ghaṭa and a narrow āmalaka (Fig. 248). These were installed on a kumbha base. The bases were carved with a peacock, a siṁha (occasionally with a single head and two bodies), or human beings.

The ardhamaṇḍapa appears to have been separated from the maṇḍapa by a door. The door jambs were carved with river goddess Yamunā (Figs. 309, 311), standing below mayūrātapatras or peacock feather umbrellas (Fig. 308) and rock embedded proto-Śiva busts (Figs. 359-60), and framed with vertical floral bands on the side.[7] The entrance to the narrow maṇḍapa above is flanked, even today, by a pair of colossal, monolithic, engaged miśraka pilasters (Pl. 8; Figs. 85-86, 267). These tower well above the jaṅghā and the antarāla door lintel, rising, even with their crowning capital cut off, to a staggering height of 4.06 m. The pilasters possess a very tall, square base. The narrower shaft above measures 1.9 m, and has a short octagonal section, decorated with darpaṇas on the right side of the maṇḍapa. The darpaṇas are made of petals, and show makaras (Figs. 268-72) with flourishing foliate tails. The darpaṇas are succeeded by a sixteen sided section and a very tall thirty two sided section, decorated with petals, which create the impression of sharp faceting (dhārāvṛta). These sections are topped by the usual narrow āmalaka, compressed between two tāṭikās, and are finally crowned by a bhadraghaṭa, of which only the pallava survives.

The lateral walls of the maṇḍapa are formed by single tall slabs, divided vertically into two sections, one plain, facing towards the antarāla door jambs, the other carved, facing towards the ardhamaṇḍapa, the sections being framed by two floral bands. The carved section shows, in the upper part, what appear to be river goddess Sarasvatī holding a ghaṭa and padmalatā (Fig. 158). She stands with legs crossed, in a lotus pool. Clusters of lotus form a pedestal for her feet as well as a canopy over her head. Above her is a bhāravāhī gaṇa (Fig. 312). An attendant figure, now damaged beyond recognition, occupies the niche below the lotus pedestal of the river goddess.

DEVARANI: ANTARĀLA, DOOR JAMB

The door jamb (Fig. 157), giving access from the maṇḍapa to the antarāla, is one of the finest pieces of ornamental architecture in all of Indian art. Its śākhāvibhakti is a highly mobile sculptural composition, made unconventionally with door bands, laterally receding into the door aperture, which is penetrated, again most unusually, by the sculpture, bulging out from the panels on its inner flanks. The composition vibrates with the ebb and flow of proceeding and receding planes of the foliate carvings on the door bands. This restlessness is stilled in the circular stambhaśākhā (Figs. 166, 181), which projects the farthest out, from the centre of the bands outside the door. It is formed of four vertical floral bands and emerging grāsamukhas, and merges in maṅgalaghaṭas below. The grāsamukhas are crowned by a narrow āmalaka and a small ghaṭapallava capital. Two flower bands in front of the stambhaśākhā are raised slightly and executed with scintillating clarity. On the other hand, the patraśākhā (Fig. 157) which flanks the stambhaśākhā on either side, shows curling leaves, coiling and swirling like waves. The patraśākhā on the outer sides being also the bāhyaśākhā, is much broader than the narrow inner patraśākhā towards the opening of the door. It is a more dynamic and conspicuous composition, the petulant motion of the leaves on the inner patraśākhā being chastened by the firm and regular meander of a binding stem. One of the greatest glories of Tala architecture, however, is the mālāśākhā (Figs. 164, 175), which follows the inner patraśākhā. It is composed of three thick, braided, spiral floral strands, which are repeated endlessly, and are divided from one another by a thin, beaded floral band. The mālāśākhā whirls to the top, framing and responding to the dynamic rhythm imparted by the river goddesses and mālāvidyādharas to the Gajalakṣmī panel in the sur-lintel.

The door itself is framed by a bevelled band with an all over kalpalatā (Figs. 157, 166), which is breathtaking in the magnificence of its conception and execution. Though heavily damaged, it looks like the churning trough of a tumultuous whirlpool from a distance. Inspected from proximity, it yields the appearance of deeply and deftly cut floral scrolls, hung with parrots, squirrels, elephants, fishes and snakes, emerging from a karimakara, ridden by a gaṇa. This śākhā narrows at the top, dividing the lower lalāṭabimba from the upper saubhāgyapaṭṭa in the architrave, which rises from two trees behind the elephant protomes on the lalāṭabimba (Figs. 179-81). It is quickened to life by a turmoil of lights and shadows, which blend in a dark, overhanging mass above the shorter lalāṭabimba, withdrawing it into the background, and thrusting the longer saubhāgyapaṭṭa to the foreground.

The second band on the door is a pratiśākhā (Fig. 162), carved with a vallī, which is made, in deliberate contrast, in delicate and shallow relief, and terminates below the kalpalatā, framing the lalāṭabimba on the wings. The lower lintel on the lalāṭabimba in the uttaraṅga is framed below by a shallow puṣpapaṭṭi, and is divided into three rathikās (Fig. 179) by broad and shallow pilasters, which are carved with two sejant siṁhas and gaja protomes at the ends and in the middle respectively. The flexed figures of Gaṅgādhara Śiva as adhināyaka devatā (presiding deity), his companions Bhagīratha and Pārvatī, and his attendants, the two pratihārīs, create mutually counter pointed curves, which are accentuated in the upper lintel. The figures of river goddesses or vidyādharas converge to the centre, subsiding like a wave, and the elephants face both sides, above one another, forming a niche for Lakṣmī. The outspread limbs of seated Lakṣmī or her standing attendants, generate a fine-tuned play of rippling curves, which come to rest in the centre (Figs. 178-81).

On the inner wings of the door, a regular dialogue is established between the panels on either side (Figs. 167-68), which are framed by padma, puṣpa, valli or parṇapaṭṭis. These panels serve virtually like rūpaśākhās, that are placed most unusually inside rather than outside the door. The restless movement of the flowers and plants, and their softly modelled, winding contours are now communicated to the human figures. Even the two large kīrtimukhas (Pl. 17; Figs. 162, 167-68, 171-72), composed entirely of foliate elements, in a conception of surpassing grandeur, face each other, and are only seemingly still. Their faces are convulsed with the movement of the foliate forms pulsing out in divergent directions. The half-circular crowns of these kīrtimukhas, which are also the crowning panels, show Kubera (Fig. 169), whose body is framed by the precipitously inclined bodies of his ascetic attendants. Kubera is looking at an amorous Hara Gaurī (Fig. 176), who are flanked by a mass of agitated gaṇas. Below the kīrtimukhas, a group of sedate human mithunas retreat into the niches on the left, to witness the divine mithuna. Hara Gaurī, who are playing chausar, are also witnessed by their companions, who are also withdrawn into the recess of the niche. Below these, the two bottom panels heave and swell out again, becoming much larger, and occupied by river goddess Gaṅgā. On the right, Gaṅgā, escorted by Bhagīratha, awakens the Sagaraputras from their ashes to eager life, and on the left, she continues her procession under a festive pavilion of garlands, with the surging crowd of attendants milling around her (Figs. 173-74). Up above, the soffit of the door is carved with three lotus medallions, the central medallion being constituted by the upraised hands and folded legs of seated Pāśupata ascetics (Fig. 182), who are engaged in a ceremonial ritual at the threshold of the Śiva temple.

Juxtaposed against the rather stark and severe facade and antarabhitti of the Devarani temple, the walls on either side of its steps, the ardha and mukhamaṇḍapa, and the door jambs to the maṇḍapa and antarāla, appear to have offered a sharp contrast, in the splendour, variety and scale of the figures, and in the extraordinary range of floral ornament. The enormous carved slabs faced one another across the steps, showing a dominant central figure, which was jostled on all sides by a mass of small figures, flying, tumbling, flexing their limbs in different directions.

The river goddesses (Figs. 307-09, 311-12) were placed alternately, now at the bottom of the ardhamaṇḍapa door jamb, now up above on the lateral maṇḍapa walls, and finally, on the laterally placed rūpaśākhā of the antarāla door jamb. They were crowned by the projecting canopy of peacock feathers, lotus leaves, rocky outcrops and proto-Śiva busts (Figs. 359-60), framed by flowers and foliage, and surrounded by a mass of worshippers, rising from all directions. The projected and obliquely recessed vertical segments of the antarāla door jamb give way to panels containing diagonally inclined figures, framed by curves, spirals, circles and ellipses of the floral bands, carved at different depths (Figs. 157-74, 176-77). The shallow carvings become flat and almost indistinguishable in the light. The deeper carvings flicker in varying combinations of light and shadow. If one could imagine it all intact and in place, this heaving, pulsating group of sculpted, architectural segments would create an inexorable visual propulsion to the door of the antarāla and beyond.

DEVARANI: ŚIKHARA DOUBTFUL

Much of the visual impact would have depended, however, on the existence and nature of the śikhara, if any. The considerable height to which the pilasters of the maṇḍapa rise beyond the jaṅghā, the visible traces of the missing ghaṭa, which would have taken these even higher, the size of the pillars, lying around, speak of a roof, coming down in graduated steps, at least above and beyond the maṇḍapa. The earlier speculation about a brick śikhara cannot be sustained any longer merely from the bricks strewn around (Fig. 98), because these bricks have been revealed in the clearance of 1987-88 to be part of the buttresses and filling of the later platform at Derarani and curtain walls (Figs. 73, 81, 94). There are square sockets on the plain inside corners of the two bhāratulās, that would have been used as lintels of the antarāla door jamb. There also are square cuts on the bhittistambha of the kapili wall, that separates the antarāla from the garbhagṛha (Fig. 87). These sockets suggest the use of bhārapaṭṭas to span the space between the antarāla door and garbhagṛha. If one could imagine the arrangement of the garbhagṛha and antarāla to be similar to that of the garbhagṛha maṇḍapa (without the catuṣkis) inside Rudra-Narasiṁha and Kevala-Narasiṁha temples (Figs. 288-89) of the not too distant Ramtek,[8] one would, on such analogy, come up with a flat roof (Fig. 276) for this temple. To imagine the alternative of a śikhara as in the 7th and 8th century in Karnataka, built under Cālukyas of Bādāmi[9] is, on the other hand, much more difficult, in the absence of any moulded fragment from the śikhara in brick, or in stone, even in the early debris filling. There is an obvious gain in the height of the sur-lintel of antarāla over the cornice level of the jaṅghā. Moreover, a broken and incomplete shaft with lotus medallions survives above the square base of the right bhittistambha, which separates the garbhagṛha from the antarāla. In view of this, one may speculate that a recessed prastara could have intervened between the cornice of the jaṅghā and a flat roof. On the available evidence, it is not possible to be certain.

DEVARANI: LATER ADDITIONS

The vertically placed figured slabs on the Devarani steps that formed the walls, appear to have given way, like those at Jethani, inducing the patrons to reinforce the Devarani temple from three sides. Because of the greater stability of the structure of Devarani, they seem to have decided to build a platform (Figs. 81-82, 91) against the pīṭha, rather than provide brick cladding all the way up to the jaṅghā, as at Jethani. The platform also performs two functions, that of a pseudo-jagatī, and that of an apron, used as pradakṣiṇāpatha around the Devarani. It extends for 20 m to the south, 18.8 m to the west, and 15.5 m to the north. Its length is shorter at the north, to accommodate a broader platform, which measures, at its broadest, 10 m x 10.3 m on the northeast. The platform is aligned with the maṇḍapa, and projects well beyond the steps. It is equipped with two staircases on the north (5 m broad), and the east (4.2 m broad). North of the main Devarani staircase, at the level of the ardhamaṇḍapa, inside a flat topped devakulikā, a large slab was placed, carved with a seated Gaṇeśa (Fig. 528). Its counterpart on the south, now completely ruined, is an elephant rather than Gaṇeśa. The installation of Gaṇeśa appears to have preceded the construction of the platform on the northeast, because a devakulikā, housing it, has survived with a garbhagṛha (1.5 x 1.2 m) and maṇḍapa (1.4 x 1.3 m), separating the platform from the staircase (Figs. 91-93). An independent covered access was provided for the north facing Gaṇeśa from the east, to allow construction of the platform, without disturbing Gaṇeśa. The platform terminates outside before the door jamb, dividing the maṇḍapa from the antarāla, to give way to a narrower (only 4 m broad) platform on the north, which goes around the temple on the west, and terminates after the ardhamaṇḍapa on the south. The platforms, both broad and narrow, appear to have been built approximately at the same time, though the generally rough work on the narrow platform suggests a slightly later date for it. The pīṭha of the broader platform has survived more or less intact. It shows khura, a broad jāḍyakumbha with padmadalas at corners, a shorter kalaśa, an antarapaṭṭa carved with recessed caitya doors and ghaṭapallava pilasters and kapota.

In spite of excessive dislocation and disturbance of the filling in the narrow platform, the mouldings (Figs. 95-97, 226) appear to have partially continued on its pīṭha, all around the temple. This is suggested by the most unusual motif of a snake gliding in and out of the jāḍyakumbha and kalaśa in pursuit of a mouse. The suggestion is reinforced by the aśokalumbī, which adorns the kalaśa at regular intervals on the broad platform after its northern steps, and also adorns the chamfered khura on the narrow platform. The execution of the snake, mouse or aśokalumbī is cruder and more perfunctory on the narrow platform, suggesting a slightly later packing. A few other fragments recovered at the southeastern corner of the narrow platform are carved with recessed central bands, which show, in high relief, mithunas sharing a cup; a man dragging a woman; peacocks with flourishing and stylized tails, moving and nibbling on the ground, often back to back (suggested by the remains of a tail on the edge); candraśālās, with doves climbing on roof, with kīrtimukhas in shallow relief, or with ghaṭapallavas on nāgapāśa bases, spilling over with foliage and lotus petals. The carvings run out over the slope into the flat vertical base. These appear to have been inserted as kapota on the pīṭha or superstructure of the broad platform.[10] The extremely rough packing and complete lack of continuity of these mouldings in the narrow platform, suggest a reuse of these elements for the foundation at a later date. From available (Figs. 106-08) examples in Dakṣiṇa Kośala,[11] the kapota may have been followed by antarapaṭṭa, at least on the broader section of the platform.

The recovery of several pillar fragments from the broad platform, also suggests the existence of a roof, covering a holy precinct, the narrow platform being left open to the sky as a perambulatory.[12] The short, squat pillars share a tall, square base, with variations in the design of the upper shaft and the capital (Fig. 266). Thus, in one pillar, the shaft has four recessed corners, occupied by seated flower bearing gaṇas, followed by a narrow octagonal, recessed segment, with petals at corners, a ghaṭa, almost squared off by flat pendant foliage at the edges, a square cushion, and a square impost block. Another pillar resorts to greater ornament and modelling on the shaft. It shows a plain octagonal segment, followed by a sixteen sided segment with ardhapadmas on eight projections, and gaṇa busts or foliage on eight recesses, a sixteen-sided ghaṭa with minuscule ardhapadmas at the base on all the sixteen sides, a projecting square cushion, indented at the corners, and a bracket with an incurved base. The incurved base and the ghaṭa are overhung by a harness of rope of four and eight loops respectively, mutually connected below the cushion. The ghaṭa itself is tightly clasped by a band, hung by pearled chains on eight sides from the loops above. Apart from these two, the surviving portion of a third pillar shows lotus medallions on four sides of the square shaft and a sixteen faceted ghaṭa with foliate hoods at the corners above a flat square base. In the disposition of the pillars in the broad platform, an exact symmetry of design was not aimed at.

While, on the available evidence, these conclusions must remain tentative, a radical change in the architectural style is evident in the later additions. The figured and ornate mouldings of the pīṭha are more closely set. The shorter and more squat pillars go up in segments, without becoming circular. The earlier all over floral ornament with its variety and complexity is banished from pillars or jambs. There is a visible lack of architectural slabs, sculpted inside or outside with figures. The cyclopean and monumental is abdicated in architecture or sculpture. All this shows a change in perception and age. At the same time, the twin passages to the broad platform, so close to each other, on the north and east, the readiness for novelty and experiment in the motifs of the mouldings and pillars, the heavy, ponderous kalaśa in the pīṭha, or the soft plastic modelling of the foliage or birds on the kapota, betray links with the earlier Tala style, so that the two cannot be far off in date.

DEVARANI: THEORIES OF EXTERNAL INFLUENCES

Though known to scholars since late 12th century, Devarani has been overlooked by them for detailed analysis. However, among earlier scholars, it is Stadtner, who has offered the most detailed comments to date on the Devarani temple and Jethani fragments in site in 1976 at Tala. Therefore, his suggestion that Tala architecture reflects influence of southern architecture, has tended to receive continuing consideration, and has to be dealt with on its merits.

Stadtner's conclusion about southern influence suffers from several problems. Thus, he incorrectly announces a similarity in the sequence of Devarani mouldings above the wide sloping khura, kumbha of the foundation cornice, with the sequence of such mouldings in certain Pallava Cālukya temples in the south, from the 7th century onwards.[13] In fact, the sequence of mouldings in Stadtner's example is replicated neither in the Devarani vedībandha, nor in the pīṭha, which was not seen by Stadtner in 1976.[14] He wrongly brackets the Devarani and some southern mouldings as constituting pratibandha adhiṣṭhānas. He emphasizes the common presence of makaras on the Devarani and southern mouldings, though the makara is neither the only creature found in pratibandha adhiṣṭhānas, nor an exclusive monopoly of the south. Nor are such adhiṣṭhānas an attribute, only of southern foundation mouldings.[15]

Stadtner also finds the alternation of recessed and projecting niches on the jaṅghā walls of Devarani, with makaratoraṇas above the recessed niches, as being of southern affiliation. He compares them to their counterparts at Arjuna and Valaiyankuṭṭai rathas at Māmallapuram and at Mālegitti Śivālaya at Bādāmi in the 7th century, and elsewhere in the south later. It is easily noticed however, that alternation of projected and recessed niches is not a general feature of the southern temple of an early date, even at Māmallapuram or at Bādāmi. Also, at the

Arjunaratha, load bearing vyālas rather than makaras appear above the phalakas of the jaṅghā pilasters. At the unfinished Valaiyankuṭṭāi, makaratoraṇas do not really appear above the central recessed koṣṭha on the south, and can only be inferred on the north. When the makaratoraṇa does clearly appear, as at Mālegiṭṭi or Upper Śivālaya at Bādāmi, it is flat, low and recessed, its central mukula pendant touches the crown of the niches, and it does not, as at Devarani, soar up and free.[16] The emphasis placed by Stadtner on makaratoraṇa as a southern feature thus seems to be somewhat misplaced.

In fact, it is much more rational to look for a common ancestor in existing examples for the makaratoraṇa or praṇāla both at Tala and in the south, than to postulate southern influence on Tala, as Stadtner does, by saying that non-existent southern examples anticipate these elements at Tala. Indeed, makaratoraṇas are found above the pillars in the facade of the early 7th century AD Palavanur cave of the Pallavas even before they appear in their structural temples. They make their appearance, long before this, above the mukhamaṇḍapa door of the Jogeśvarī cave in Kuṅkanadeśa under Mauryas of Puri in c. AD 525, above the door of cave 6 at Ajanta or cave 4 at Bāgh in the late 5th century, and even earlier, in the candraśālā of the mid-5th century Gupta temple at Darrā. In the 7th and 8th century, makaratoraṇa appears not only in Pallava caves and temples, but also at Ellora in caves 6, 15, above figured niches and windows at Kailāsa, and even at Kārlā, above the later Buddha image.[17] If the makaratoraṇa is generally adapted above the jaṅghā niches in the south from the 7th century onwards, and is not used in the north except as gateway to the interior of the temple or in the śūkanāsās of the śikhara,[18] this becomes an argument of the Tala makaratoraṇa being an ancestral prototype for such toraṇas on jaṅghās of southern temples, rather than the other way around. The use of projected and sunk niches is not exclusive to the medieval south. It is anticipated already in the surviving facade of the 5th century northern temple at Nāgarī and can be seen also in the medieval north, from the 7th century onwards, in the śilāmaṇḍapikā shrines of Daśārṇadeśa.[19] Closer to Tala, in 5th century Vidarbha temples at Ramtek like a tall kumbha, flat bands, crowned by plain paṭṭikā. The 1st-2nd century AD Kuṣāṇa monuments at Rājghāṭ or Mathura, the 5th century Gupta temples of Deogarh (U.P.), Nāgarī (Rajasthan), Bhūmarā, Tigavā, Marhiā (all in Madhya Pradesh) have already used makarapraṇāla on the vedībandha mouldings.[20] Such praṇālas continue to appear in the medieval period at different places and times.[21]

If Stadtner looks for origins of the Devarani architectural forms in southern motifs, he relates Devarani sculpture loosely to Gupta motifs. Oblivious of the integration of the architectural and the sculptural style in Tala art, or of the way Devarani architecture is treated as a sculpted form, he makes the inappropriate suggestion that the massiveness of the vertical niches of Devarani jaṅghā is due to the inept execution by Dakṣiṇa Kośala craftsmen of forms imported by southern immigrants.[22] In fact, the unadorned, simply outlined, freely soaring makaratoraṇas, the weighty makaramukhas, praṇālas and mouldings in the Devarani vedībandha display an even more vigorous and muscular style, than is revealed by the flat, constricted, ornate toraṇas, mouldings, choked as they are with rows of small, stylised makaras or vyālas, and jostled by other heterogeneous elements in the later southern temples. The tall, rather overbearingly heavy Devarani kumbha, slightly moulded at the top, is quite different from the shorter, bulbous, vṛtta or kaṭakāvṛta kumuda in the pratibandha mouldings of the south in the later period. A swelling, three dimenstional treatment, and the surging, dynamic movement created by projecting and receding planes, are the hallmark of the architectural facade of Devarani. These are characteristic also of the ornately sculpted door frame of its antarāla, or of the crowded composition of its sculpted side slabs, like the slab with the image of Mārtaṇḍa Bhairava. The lack of ornament on the external walls of Devarani and the presence of such ornament inside, does not hide the fact that the Devarani architecture, and the sculpture on it, are modelled with the same sturdy, bold and firm hands. This overriding sense for volume, combined with an impeccable feeling for decorative fitness, links Devarani with the 5th century AD style (described conveniently as Gupta-Vākāṭaka) of Vidarbha and the Deccan, rather than with examples of contemporary south, of which, in any case, no examples have survived.

While this Gupta-Vākāṭaka connection will be dealt with later, the existence of this connection does not, per se, make the Devarani style a provincial or inferior version of the imperial, and superior modes of the Gupta sculpture, as Stadtner or Joanna Williams thinks, or of the Vākāṭaka style as Krishna Deva seems to think. While Krishna Deva accepts Stadtner's version of Pallava and Cālukya connections (retrospective) of Devarani architecture, Williams reads the deep, oblique cut in the Devarani door bands, the intermesh of foliate, human, or animal forms, the projected and sunk niches, the very deviations from Gupta architectural forms, pointed out by Stadtner, the 'bizarre' iconography, elements alike of sculpture and architecture, as unorthodox tribal misinterpretations, rooted in local myths and wooden techniques, of orthodox, lithic, Gupta vocabulary.[23] She does not base this suggestion on comparison with any example of contemporary architecture in the area, because, according to her, none exists, to which it can be significantly related. Nor does she enter into a careful discussion of the wood carving techniques transferred to stone.[24] According to her presumption, the regional adaptation of imperial Gupta forms at Tala should have left a lasting impact on the development of the regional style. However, in a somewhat contradictory fashion, she describes this event as an isolated one, of no real significance to the development of 7th century architecture of Dakṣiṇa Kośala.[25]

JETHANI: PROBLEMS OF RECONSTRUCTION

Before we can establish the significance of Tala art for the development of a regional style, we have to render an account of the newly revealed temple of Jethani, since this is the only other temple which, though made on a different ground plan, uses combinations of elements and style similar to Devarani. The task of reconstructing the plan or elevation of Jethani is not easy. The superstructure, if any, and its walls have crumbled down. None of its individual pillars or figured slabs survive either in one piece or uneroded. The architect has not paid too close an attention to the symmetry of proportions among the different internal segments of the pillars or wall slabs even in similar contexts. Nor has he tried to maintain a mirror image in the combinations of elements in the original mouldings of the pīṭha and vedībandha. A plan has been found incised on the top western step. While some remote affinity exists between this plan and the Jethani plan, it is not easy to imagine it to be an accurate, contemporary representation of the present shape of either of the two Tala temples.[26]

And yet, an attempt has been made here to get some idea of the main features of the temple from what has survived. For one thing, the huge, vertically placed, carved slabs of the wall, which have fallen mainly on the east and the west, mostly with their face up, are very useful in ascertaining the nature of the wall. For another, the pillars, door jambs or lintels, which have collapsed on the steps of the temple in the east, west and the south, can be grouped logically according to their designs, and permit suggestions about their original location. Measurements have been matched, as far as the broken and abraded architectural fragments permit it. Portions of the ceilings have been made out from the collapsed remains on the garbhagṛha, antarāla, and, behind the temple, on the north. Assuming that the brick cladding follows the original plan closely, a plan has been made.

JETHANI: PLAN

With this, what we have is a rectangular stone temple (Fig. 6), facing south, and clad in bricks, consisting of a series of halls or architectural segments, rising in steps (Fig. 9), from south, east, and west, to a relatively small garbhagṛha on the top, backed up by three cells facing north (Figs. 63, 65). The temple stretches externally to about 24 m from north to south, and to 20 m from east to west.

The approach to the garbhagṛha is direct from all three sides, consisting of seven steps each on east and west, eight steps on the south. The main southern approach (Figs. 42-43), consisting of much broader steps, rising at a more graduated and easier gradient, is the most extensive and most impressive, measuring approximately up to 16 m east to west and 12.5 m north to south. It is flanked by huge sculpted wall slabs, and penetrated by a group of towering pillars on the steps with figural and foliate ornament. The eastern and western (Figs. 69-70) approaches are relatively narrow and short, being approximately 7.5 m long and 9 m broad externally. They possess sculpted wall slabs and pillars on the flanks, but not on the steps.

On all the three approaches, there is an antarāla. However, on the south, the first step from the garbhagṛha creates an antarāla (Figs. 44, 61), which is nearly as broad east to west (2.6 m) as the garbhagṛha is from north to south (2.5 m), and as long north to south (4 m) as the garbhagṛha is from east to west (3.9 m). The garbhagṛha (Figs. 60, 65), though nearly equal in size, looks relatively narrow and constricted, being accomodated to the narrow approaches from east and west. The antarāla on the east to west approaches (Figs. 69-70) is created by the first three steps from the garbhagṛha, the third step being the broadest, measurements internally being 3.1 x 0.85 m, 3.1 x 0.55 m for the first two, 3.1 x 2.3 m for the third.

The second step from the garbhagṛha on the south, (6 x 1 m) appears to have carried the door jambs on makara bases (Fig. 56), the third (6 x 0.8 m) and the fourth steps (10.5 x 0.8 m) being empty of pillars and forming a clear approach. The fifth to the eighth steps, going further down (9.8 x 1.05 m for the fifth and sixth steps, 8.00 x 2.5 m and 7.5 x 1.1 m for the seventh and eighth steps are the measurements), create the most magnificent space of a proto-maṇḍapa, pierced by figured blocks which rise in successive tiers, to build up two enormous tetradic rucaka pillars, which occupy all the four steps, and form a proto-catuṣki with the pillars below (Fig. 52, 61).

The figured slabs forming the walls also rise in tiers on the south wings, facing in, over slabs with seat backs on the lower steps. There appear to have stood large slabs with yakṣa images on the fourth (3.05 x 0.55 m), fifth (4 x 0.4 m) and sixth (3.5 x 0.4 m) steps on the east and west. The impressive tiered array of sculptures, occasional parikaras (as in Varuṇa) on the south, and the dwarfs of great iconographic variety, seem to have been excluded on the east and west.

On the lowest, the seventh step (2.5 x 0.95 m) on both east and west, miśraka pillars (Figs. 59, 69-70, 74) stood on either side. The existence of two towering miśraka pillars also on the level platform (7.5 x 3.1 m) giving access to the southern steps (Pl. 2; Figs. 53, 61), may have been parallelled by the existence of pillars on the candraśilās, which give access to the eastern and western stairs. This may be surmised from the miśraka pillar fragments recovered from these directions (Figs. 67, 351). Combined with some ghaṭa-āmalaka pillars (Figs. 65, 254), these may well have given access to a proto-maṇḍapa on all three sides from prototypes of mukhamaṇḍapas.

The temple is abruptly cut off behind the garbhagṛha on the north, to which is attached a pillared central cell (1.2 x 1.3 m). It is flanked by two elephant protomes (2 m broad), both rising to the level of the garbhagṛha at a height of about 2 m (Figs. 64-65).

JETHANI: SOUTH APPROACH, MUKHAMAṆḌAPA, FRONT PILLARS

Having set up a general image of the temple, I shall now proceed to a detailed description of different parts, trying to visualise the original shape of the temple, with the help of the architectural fragments revealed in the excavation.

The level platform in front of the southern steps may have formed a kind of mukhamaṇḍapa. The smaller and relatively frail pillars, made of ghaṭa-pallava-āmalaka segments, crowning one another, may have belonged to it. These pillars have been found strewn around the entrances and at the back of the temple, and do not seem to have been capable of performing a major load bearing function, like the other gigantic pillars inside the temple. This suggests their possible use at all the entrances for holding up a low and modest porch.[27] (Figs. 59, 61)

The southern steps, around which most of the Jethani structure arranges itself, are fronted right at the entrance, by two enormous miśraka pillars (Figs. 42-44, 236-40). These are separated from one another by a distance of about 2.2 m and from the side pilasters by around 1.1 m. They give access to a stepped maṇḍapa with a central catuṣki made monolithically out of a single stone block. The pillar on the left has fallen, with its base still resting on the kumbhaka, the carvings on the kumbhaka being highly eroded. The corners of the kumbhakas in both pillars are formed by small, crouching gaṇas, while the centre on all four sides is occupied by large gaṇas with pendulous, fleshy chest and belly and hunched shoulders. These fleshy forms are matched, with evident deliberation above, in the square base of the main pillar shaft, by the swelling belly and curved shoulders of the bhadraghaṭas on all four sides.

The bhadraghaṭas are overhung with vandanamālikās interspersed with muktāgrāsas, emitting pearled festoons. The shoulder curves of the ghaṭas are answered by the highly accentuated curve of the foliate forms, which surge out of the mouths of the ghaṭas to form, at the same time, two springing addorsed lions and a kīrtimukha. The lion tails culminate in upturned flowers, forming the kīrtimukha's eyes. A floral rhizome soars up and spreads out between the lions, forming the eyebrows, ears, and forehead of the kīrtimukha, the rootstalk of the rhizome serving as its nose. The lions hold, in their upraised paws, floral stalks, like so many maces, worshipfully (Figs. 237-38). Flowers come out from the corners of the ghaṭa, constituting the whiskers of kīrtimukha. A small grāsamukha appears on the ghaṭa below on a plain, blank background. It is naturalistically rendered. The grāsamukha is also rendered in an ornate and stylized manner, and made larger, to fill the background with a network of symmetrical curves. The ghaṭa itself is anthropomorphized, looking like the neck and bust of the kīrtimukha. At the corners, two lion heads merge in one, and spout mukulas and leaves, which also assume the shape of a nāgapāśa, with a diagonal array of scales on either side, and a central rib, terminating, at the corners of bases, in a poised, hooked snake hood. The crown of the kīrtimukha is formed by a puṣpapaṭṭi.

Above this ghaṭa-pallava-kīrtimukha base in both the pillars, on a narrow moulding of padmalatā on the main pillar shaft, rise five rows of padmadalas (Fig. 236). The first four of these diminish in size as they increase in number, arithmetically, from eight to sixty four. The fifth, almost one and a half time taller than all of the other four rows put together, go up in thirty two segments. The central spines of these lotus leaves reduce the pillar from an octagonal to a circular one, making it dhārāvṛta.

As they go up, the curved top profile of the leaves becomes more and more angular, generating the impression of serrated arrises, acentuated by the angular tips of petals peeping between the broader petals. The first two rows of peeping petals are darpaṇas in which yakṣas stand between makaras, to prise their jaws open, ride an elephant, prodding it with a raised hand, sit astride a horse, guiding it by the bit in its mouth, or on a padmalatā, holding it in their hands (Fig. 239). The darpaṇas are also filled with descriptions of standing Śiva Pārvatī and bull Nandī, padmalatās, intertwined with theriomorphic or anthropomorphic elements, as well as with foliate motifs enclosing a peacock or a jewelled central clasp. The third row has petals incised with regular rows of diagonal lines, subduing the highly diversified, complex compositions in the darpaṇas below. The leaves in the fourth row, and the top mahāpaṭṭi of petals are stark and plain, so abstracted as to be hardly recognizable. They merge, mutate and interchange foliate, human, and animal forms, to arrive at a surface, which is blank except for the flutes.

Fragments of a few large āmalakas, with flat base and a relatively constricted shape, measuring about 1.07 x 0.88 x 0.12 m or 1.16 x 0.60 x 0.16 m appear to have crowned these pillars (measuring at present, 0.90 x 0.90 x 0.25 m on the top), above the missing ghaṭapallava capital. This would seem likely from the general Tala practice, of putting an āmalaka or a grooved cushion on the ghaṭa atop the pillar, as in the stambhaśākhā of the maṇḍapa door jambs, in the recessed pillar shaft at Devarani entrance, pillars at Jethani east and west or pilasters in the Varuṇa parikara at Jethani south. However, unlike the āmalakas in the other pillars of Tala, which are carved from the same block, the āmalakas above the free-standing pillars at Jethani south appear to have been carved separately (Fig. 241).

The bhittistambhas on either side of these principal stambhas rose on separate blocks, carved on three sides with siṁhasaṁghātas (Fig. 42). Two lions, sharing one head, occupy the front and the corners, their tails curled and swishing behind. A lion is shown on each flank, seated behind the composite lion at the corner, putting up and resting its paws on the back of the lion in front. The crowning ornament of the lion bases is a puṣpapaṭṭi. While the portion above the lion base at the left is missing, the highly eroded fragment surviving above the lion base at the right suggests a further, plain square section, carved with a nidhi kalaśa, with an emerging kīrtimukha. The shaft of the pilaster above this may have been made out of a figured slab. A slab, carved with a slender, headless male image, with uttarīya, tied across the chest and thigh (measuring 2 x 0.60 x 0.30 m), was moved out from the southeast of the mound, and is now lying in the same direction (Fig. 352). It has proportions roughly matching the lion base, or the kalaśa above it, and it is likely that a similar figure stood on the other side too.

The details of the lintel above these pillars and pilasters can be gained from fragments[28], lying to their north, and south (Figs. 58, 63). These fragments are characterised, by roughly similar proportions, in spite of having, in their broken state, different sizes (1.48 x 1.05 x 0.04 m, 3.10 x 1.10 x 0.40 m, 1.16 x 0.70 x 0.35 m). They are partitioned by panels created by pilasters with square capitals and tall rectangular bases with octagonal shafts. They are framed by bands with diagonal lines above, and geometrical criss-cross lines below. The fragment to the north, found at the foot of the Varuṇa image on the next step shows, in pillared panels, a four-armed Śaivite deity with jaṭā, accompanied by two women, a two-armed, single-headed Kārtikeya seated on a peacock and holding śakti (Fig. 199).

A second fragment (Fig. 198) lying in front of the south steps shows an elephant advancing towards a yogī seated with folded legs. The yogī's arms are placed on his thighs, and are intertwined with the arms of the lady standing on either side. A second male figure is shown seated in rājalīlāsana. A third fragment, also lying in front of the south steps, shows slender figures seated in pralambapādāsana, with hands placed on thighs, and flanked by ladies. A fourth fragment shows two yajnayūpas or sacrificial stakes, one of them complete with a ghaṭa-pallava base, a slender shaft, and a fluttering dhvaja at the top. Other fragments in the south show a broken seated Gaṇeśa, kīrtimukhas, flying mālādhārī vidyādharas, lotus medallions and flowers (Fig. 200).

JETHANI: SOUTH APPROACH, PROTO MAṆḌAPA, PILLARS

Two tetrafacial pillars are raised on the first succeeding four steps, going up in three separate tiers and creating a proto-catuṣki, together with the two miśraka pillars at the entrance. Separated from one another by about 3 metres, they are separated from the pilasters at the flanks by 1.5 metres. In the third and uppermost tier, figured slabs (Figs. 43-46, 51, 62), positioned against the main shafts in both the pillars, have collapsed. Even the gaṇa bases for these figures have crumbled in the second tier on the left. However, the carved fragments, recovered from the south, together with the surviving portion of the pillar on the right, enable us to reconstruct the shape and segments of the pillars. Out of all the steps, the least space is occupied on the first, the broadest step, by a rectangular block, moulded on three sides by a crowning padmapaṭṭi, as also by the bulging chests and bellies of the gaṇas, three of them being carved in front, one each being carved on the sides.

The second and the third step are occupied by a separate stone block (Figs. 56, 61), from which four karimakara heads are hewn on four sides. Two of these project east and west on the second step. A third juts out to the south on the first, broadest step. The fourth, carved from the snout rather than the chin, to maintain level, looks out to the north from above the third step, spilling on to the fourth. The large flipped back ears of the karimakaras, the incised or ridged curved lines of their jaws and mouths, visible from the sides, their diminutive, rolled up trunks in the front, offset the accents of the rectangular gaṇa base on the steps. Their large, semicircular, lolling tongue, the segmented gums of their mandible, their sidefangs, vary the profile in the front, like the padmapaṭṭi above the gaṇa base. The corners of the stone block, from which these makaras are carved out, protrude like sharp karṇaka offsets.

The pillar shaft, which stood on the second step, was square all the way up and served as the support, on all the four sides, for the flat backed slabs carved with figures in high relief, or directly, for figures made in the round. These figures stood on a semicircular base, carved with three bhāraputrakas on three sides. Unlike the lowermost rectangular gaṇa base, the visual continuity in these semicircular bases is not interrupted by vertical partitions in the corners. The curve in the profile, which is gradually enhanced in the padmapaṭṭi and makara trunk below, is now rounded off, completing the transition. The bhāraputrakas in the lower and upper tiers sit, crouch, tumble in diverse postures, creating a lively play in light and shadow, counterpointing the blunt, bland, sunlit surfaces of the shaft of the karimakaras or of the single figures on the plain, flat slabs. Several gaṇa heads and busts, attached to fragments of halfcircular or rectangular slabs, and a dancing gaṇa panel, suggest other variations of their posture in the pillar on the left.

The shorn bust and head of an āmrabhañjikā (Fig. 306), with an inclined head, the headless and legless body of a woman in short, thigh length dhotī, tucked up behind (Fig. 296), the body of another woman, truncated from the chest, with a blouse, strung together by threads, the image of a vṛkṣakā, a dryad, her legs missing from below the knees (Fig. 295), two other female heads and busts, broken from below the waist (Fig. 305), indicate the installation of such female images in subtle flexion, in the round, in the third tier, around the shaft, on semicircular bases. Some other fragments of worshipful nāgarājas (Figs. 434-35), Ardhanārīśvara (Fig. 425), a varāha head (Fig. 567) should have belonged to images arranged around the pillar shafts, while other smaller images may have functioned as attendant figures, or gaṇas on the bases (Figs. 457, 493, 495).

On one pillar base, displaced from the back of the mound to the north, gaṇas or nāgapuruṣas are replaced by two divine couples, probably Hara Gaurī, canopied by irregularly formed cubical chunks of overhanging rock (Figs. 193, 355). While Gaurī is seated on Hara's lap, human figures are shown milling around below, bound by coils of a nāgapāśa wielded by one of Hara's hands, while, with another hand, he clutches a human being by hair. This base is deliberately roughhewn, irregularly scooped, crowded with tumbling figures. It shows the variety and range of experiment in the making of an architectural component like a base. Obviously, the architect was not content with conventional groupings of gaṇas, nāgapuruṣas or a Kārtikeya.[29]

JETHANI: SOUTH APPROACH, PROTO MAṆḌAPA, PLATFORMS & SEATBACKS

On either side of the first broad step, which provided room, in its middle, for the catuṣki pillars of a proto-maṇḍapa in the south, there are platforms and seatbacks serving as āsanapaṭṭas and kakṣāsanas. On the left, the āsanapaṭṭa appears to have carried an enormous image, befitting the height and size of the pillars of the proto-catuṣki (Fig. 351). Fragments of a similar abraded image (2.26 x 1.08 x 0.36 m) of a base (2.26 x 1.10 x 0.45 m), and of a base fragment (0.67 x 1.10 x 1.33 m), have been recovered from the southwest (Fig. 67). These figures were accompanied by a diminutive attendant on either side. The rest of the āsanapaṭṭa on the left was occupied, as is evident from the huge, eroded, now headless gaṇa image seated on a slab, by a gaṇa base, supporting a figured slab above (Figs. 42, 45).

The similar space on the āsanapaṭṭa on the right, on the other hand, is occupied by a siṁhagavākṣa (Fig. 54), with the remains of the feet of a figure above. The base of the gavākṣa is carved with what appear to be recesses and pilasters of a kaṇṭha moulding. The round siṁhavaktra projects out of an elliptical cavernous cella mouth, which itself is framed by pilasters with a kumbha-kalaśa-āmalaka base, square shaft, and, what may have been a double ghaṭapallava capital. The pilasters are connected by a lintel of square bosses, alternately recessed and projected. Though the corresponding place on the left does not show a siṁhagavākṣa today, a moulded slab with two lion paws placed casually one upon the other, in a posture similar to that of the lion on the right, has been recovered from the southwest. This might suggest replacement of the siṁhagavākṣa on the left by the gaṇa base at the time of later restoration, or placement of the gaṇa base above the gavākṣa.

A certain correspondence of elements might have also been observed between figured slabs on the extreme flanks of the third step. On both left and right, the base remains. It is formed by a siṁhavaktra, virtually crushed between rolling cakras with Kaṅkanapatrapaṭṭi in the rims of the wheels framed by tulāsaṁgrahas at the sides (Fig. 43). Smaller siṁhavaktras, heavily damaged now, are carved on the flanks of the wheels. A carved side slab with a standing female figure (Fig. 299), measuring 2.25 x 0.60 x 0.32 m found in the southeast, seems to have stood on a semicircular gaṇa base above the siṁhavaktra, which still survives on the left.

In between the tetrafacial pillars of the proto-catuṣki, on the step above the broadest step, a reinforced brick-plinth has been found, ostensibly constructed at the time of the later restoration (Fig. 52). Above this plinth was installed an independent devaprakoṣṭha. It apparently faced the garbhagṛha to the north, having fallen on its back, facing the north. It is framed by vṛttadaṇḍikās, carved with spiral padmavallī in very high relief, crowned by square phalaka, cogged āmalaka, circular kalaśa, and a gradually stepped up square phalaka. The round pillarets were spanned by a lintel, the remains of which are apparently missing. A very unusual four-handed image of what seems to be Varuṇa (Fig. 346), is framed by these pillarets. Varuṇa is shown with padmamukuṭa and padmaprabhāvalī, holding pāśa. Two surging makaras with curved tails look worshipfully up, covering the lower part of what may have been Varuṇa's swimming body. Three figures, one in the middle, above the padmaprabhāvalī, facing front, two on the flanks, facing in, crown Varuṇa. The round kalaśa, cogged, round āmalaka, the winding curves of the lotus rhizome on the shaft of the pillars, the multiple closed lotus buds, the circular lotus halo, semicircular outline of the Varuṇa head, the bulging globes of female bust above it, the tortuous curves of the lashing, upturned tail and bared jaws of the makaras, create a lively correspondence of answering rhythms, comprehending the images and the pillars into one harmonious architectural composition.

The location of the Varuṇa prakoṣṭha between the tetrafacial inner catuṣki pillars, blocking the passage, and facing the garbhagṛha, is an illogical one. Its position could more logically be postulated on the flanks, as part of the side walls. The suggestion that deities like Varuṇa found their place in the side walls, is substantiated by the discovery of a fourhanded Kārtikeya image (Fig. 350) outside the eastern wall of the temple. In view of the footmarks atop the siṁhagavākṣa on the left, and in view of its semi-circular base, the Kārtikeya could not have stood on the siṁhagavākṣa. It could, however, have been on the top of a gaṇa (in view of the general convention of a slab, semicircular both at top and bottom of a gaṇa base) or a makara base, occupying the empty portion of the kakṣāsana slab, its flat back forming a segment of the wall in this portion on the east.

JETHANI: SOUTH APPROACH, ANTARĀLA, PILLARS

On the next, the fifth and sixth steps, there are no pillars on the steps. These form a transitional space for gaining entry to the antarāla above. An idea of the arrangement can be derived from the surviving fragments on the right flank of the fifth step. On the outer side, behind the tetrafacial pillar of the catuṣki, stands a rucaka pillarslab (Figs. 48, 50, 57). It is plain on three sides, and carved with lotus medallions, a lotus rhizome and a floral frame, only on its western face. Right on its front, on a semi circular block, projected out as an independent entity on the lower step, three gaṇas were placed. These, instead of carrying a figured slab above, like the gaṇas in the catuṣki pillars, directly carried standing figures on their shoulder, head or hands. Of these, the central gaṇa, with the remains of a foot on its head, remains in situ (Fig. 495). The gaṇa on its right retains only a truncated head, (Fig. 475) carrying the fragmented feet of a lady, both held by a damaged guardian image. Between the gaṇa base and the pillar behind, another slab with two standing figures was placed, of which the remains of an ascetic type bust and standing legs have alone survived. The ascetic bust (Fig. 457) has been removed to the Bilaspur museum. Apart from this congregation of figures, a flying load bearing gaṇa (Figs. 488-89), enclosed within a square base, is placed below, to the right of the main semicircular gaṇa base and block, on the lower step.

Right beside the lotus medallion pillar, to its left, on the inner side, at the same level, another pillar slab, now virtually destroyed except for its carved lower shaft, stands. The carving is damaged almost beyond recognition. It seems to show a sack, apparently of treasures, held with its mouth open, by the hands of a gaṇa, from either side (Figs. 48, 51). This may have been part of a base, with a standing figure on the top. There are no remains from which one could imagine a similar arrangement on the left. Several fragments of a rucaka pillar with lotus medallions, recovered from the west[30] do suggest, that at least part of the arrangement may have been duplicated on the other approaches. That the flying gaṇa on the lower step, or the sackholding gaṇas might have carried figures, seems plausible from the moustachioed head of a an Ardhanārīśvara with jaṭāmukuṭa (Figs. 192, 427), accompanied by a bust with tiger skin uttarīya, and a Bhairava head (Fig. 428) with skulls adorning its jaṭā, recovered from behind the brick base of the Varuṇa image, where they may have rolled down in the fall. The door jamb (Fig. 57) of the garbhagṛha has also fallen on these steps, pushing down and covering these fragments.

A large, broken, flatbacked figured slab, of which only two fragments can be put together, was found lying overturned on the top of the wall, outside the pillar slabs on the right. This shows a large male figure (Fig. 473), which holds a small female figure by cupping his left hand below the left breast of the figure, and by clutching its stretched right arm by his right hand. The left hand of a this female figure is raised to its head to hold the left foot of another small figure, standing on its head, only traces of the latter's feet being visible. A tapering, scalloped trunk of what looks like a palm tree, and may actually be a cornucopia of coins, dangles from its necklace. While no corresponding image has been found from the remains in the west, a hand, holding a tall fragment of a similar tapering, scalloped palm tree trunk, or column of treasures has been recovered from the west, and is now preserved in the site museum at Tala (Fig. 474). These slabs formed the side walls outside the antarāla in the south.

It is noticeable that in this portion, unlike the catuṣki, the figures are arranged in tiers, one holding, carrying or standing on the other, without intervening slabs. The makara disappears. Instead of miśraka pillar shafts with a diminishing or growing number of padmadalas, organized in increasingly shorter or taller segments, moving from square to circular shape, and, instead of plain, square shafts, we have now rectangular pillar slabs, plain on three sides, with large lotus medallions covering one side entirely. The scaly, scalloped palm tree trunk or cornucopia comes in as an iconographic attribute, varying the architectural profile of the inside wall. While the gaṇas are now all equally small, the place of the larger central gaṇa on the entrance step is now taken by an open sack, probably of treasures. Altogether, the harmoniously and sedately organized elements of architecture on the lower steps are now infected by a restless impulse of experiment.

JETHANI: SOUTH APPROACH, ANTARĀLA, DOOR JAMB

We reach the sixth step now, which gives access to the antarāla. The door jamb of the antarāla rested on a rectangular slab on either side. It is carved into the shape of an anthropomorphic karimakara (Figs. 57-58, 532). The elephant trunks emerge from either side of the human mouth, to be raised and joined in a devotional salute. The human face has thick, dilated nostrils, lips, slightly parted, as if chanting a prayer, and half-closed meditative eyes. The makara wears large, circular karṇakuṇḍalas (ear rings), and its forelegs rest on the ground in the devotional posture of prostration. Its tail has foliate tips, and is curled up to lie still below its body. Its face and trunk protrude beyond the slab, offering a profile of deep contemplation, with shadows nestling in the cavernous corners of the mouth, and above the deep sunk eyes.

The antarāla door jamb has crumbled down and broken into three major fragments (Figs. 52, 57, 59, 61), and lies north to south across the middle of the southern steps. The conception of the śākhāvibhakti is obviously similar to that of the door jamb of Devarani antarāla, anticipating it. It is however simpler, less elaborate, and carved in lower relief, with a softer touch. Though it is cut obliquely like Devarani, the rūpaśākhā, carved on the inner lateral face of the jamb at Devarani is missing. The narrow pratiśākhā, carved with a padmavallī, is the first śakhā at Jethani. The mālāśakhā, being a garland of spirally twisted floral strands, follows, preceding rather than following, unlike Devarani, the kalpavallī. It is thus not closely aligned with the laterally carved rūpastambha, which is unlike Devarani. The third śākhā, like its Devarani counterpart, is the bevelled kalpavallī, though its undercut scrolls are now completely destroyed, except for vanishing vestiges, which show the undercutting to have been shallower than Devarani. The fourth is a stambhaśākhā, architecturally modelled with the same slenderness as the stambhaśākhā at Devarani, treated as a similar focus for converging forms, with similar narrow, constricted āmalaka, and presumably, with a similar ghaṭapallava capital on the top. The sharply, precisely, volumetrically cut vertical rows of tightly bound or intertwined flowers or rhizomes, emerging from a regular row of grāsamukhas, seen at Devarani, are, however conspicuous by their absence. Instead, the stambha comes alive with curvilinear designs of stems, leaves, flowers of different kinds, spun more lightly and gliding more leisurely across the less crowded surface. They are outlined by much thinner and irregular shadows than the deeply chiselled, rectilinear rows of floral motifs at Devarani, which are further separated from one another by straight, grooved channels all the way up. The fifth bāhya or pratiśākhā is not made like the broad, prominent band of Devarani. Instead, a narrow band of diagonally arranged leaves at the base of the stambhaśākhā is followed by the flat, plain, empty section of the door jamb slab itself.

The uttaraṅga of the door jamb may have been composed of two slabs like Devarani. The lower slab, which is lying on the east, not very far from the door jamb, is carved with swelling and weighty lotus medallions with clustered petals on the soffit. These are joined by short twin bands of petals and framed by rhizomes, weighted down by heavy leaves. No attempt is made like Devarani to form lotus medallions out of the hands and legs of human beings. On the front, the lintel (Figs. 353-54, 485) is carved into niches, partitioned by pillars, square at base and capital, octagonal in the central shaft. One niche shows three women. One of them is probably Pārvatī, holding up a padma. Another shows Śiva, with one hand raised in abhaya, the other lowered in kaṭyāvalambita, standing together with Pārvatī, who has one hand resting on Śiva's shoulder, the other hanging low, holding a padma. A third niche shows Śiva as Bhairava in dhotī and a broad uttarīya, wearing skulls in his jaṭā, and touching the breast of Pārvatī, who appears as a Bhairavī in a short jaṅghikā, nude above the waist. She has skulls in her jaṭā, and one of her hands is draped around Bhairava's shoulder, the other hanging down at the side. The other niches show a peacock with outspread wings, a flying mālādhārī vidyādhara and a kīrtimukha. Atop this lintel, which may be taken to display in its lalāṭabimba Śiva Pārvatī in their ascetic forms, may have sat the sur-lintel (Figs. 49-50, 197), that lies prone near the tetrafacial pillar on the west. It is partitioned into square panels by the usual pillars, with a tall square base, octagonal shaft, and square capital. The panels show three siṁhavaktras, with bulging eyes, framed by arched and joined eyebrows; protruding tongue, shown in one piece, or forked into three segments; regular teeth below curving mouth, deeply carved and lined cheeks; and, paws looking out from below the corners of the mouth. These fill their panels, and alternate with a dancing gaṇa, a siṁha, mounted on a bull with a shower of coins, looking like scalloped palm tree coming out of its mouth, and Paraśudharī Śiva or Paraśurāma. Bands of alternating round and petalled flowers frame the panels above and below.

JETHANI: SOUTH APPROACH COMPARED WITH DEVARANI APPROACH – ICONOGRAPHIC PROGRAMME

The sharply undercut, all-over design of the kalpavallī, dividing the lower from the upper lintel at Devarani, and overhanging the lower lintel, is not found at Jethani. The vyālapāda or gajapāda partitions of Devarani are also not in evidence. The rush of figures converging from the sides to the centre in the upper lintel of Devarani, creating varying pools of light and shadow, is also missing in the Jethani lintels, where no centre is really established among the equal sized panels. The experimental variation and alternation of large animal figures filling the panels, with gaṇa or Śiva figures, the display of Śiva and Pārvatī as figures of equal size and value at Jethani, are conceptions different from those at Devarani, where Śiva is flanked by a diminutive Pārvatī figure and the animals act as atlantes figures for the trees, or as attendants for bathing Lakṣmī.

The result of this different iconographic programme is the greater clarity and tactile differentiability of the Jethani panels as against Devarani, where the human figures in the lower lintel seem to retire into deep recesses, and the figures in the upper lintel fuse into a more incorporeal, visually mobile, indistinct mass, enlivened by light and shade. The difference in the impact of the Jethani door jamb and lintel, less crowded in composition, carved in low relief, and the Devarani door jamb and the lintel (Fig. 157), more congested with ornament, with planar and recessional elements, is obvious. The difference, could not have been intended at Devarani, because a vitāna was there, and because, the closed, sculpted side walls of Devarani would have blocked off the sunlight and the chiaroscuro. However, an artistic intention can well be imagined at Devarani, to refine the Jethani door jamb forms into more ornate and playful configurations, as a demonstration of virtuosity, or as a display of the capacity to establish standards, and then, to move into myriad variations on them.

JETHANI: ANTARĀLA, PILLAR SLABS

On either side of the Jethani antarāla door jamb with its karimakara base, stood a sculpted pillarslab (Figs. 48, 55). Its shape can be inferred from the remains lying on the east. The slab is carved into a niche, divided into two sections. The lower section is smaller, framed by a shorter puṣpapaṭṭi above and a larger padmapaṭṭikā below, both the sections beginning as straight, horizontal bands, to turn into semicircular edges at the end. Between these two bands, carved in the lower section of the niche, is a crouching gaṇa (Figs. 491-92). The flaring mass of his hair is flattened by the shorter band above. His legs are spread out to span the recess above the longer band below. The surviving portion of a left foot above the shorter band indicates the existence of a figure, most probably standing (judging from the height of the door jamb), carved into the upper recess of the niche. The longer band below acts as chādya overhanging a plain, narrow pedestal, which curves in at the outer end, imitating the curve of the longer band above.

The slab itself is not framed on the eastern semicircular end of the floral bands, but left open. It is framed only on the western, straight, inner end of the bands by a jamb (Figs. 48, 52). This jamb is plain on all sides except the front, facing south, along with the crouching gaṇa. It is carved with a vertical row of lotus medallions (Figs. 55, 57), enclosed in squares, partitioned from one another by a parṇapaṭṭi, made of a serried row of triangular leaves. The corners inside the squares are also filled with lotus petals. A variation is thus introduced from the design of the lotus medallions on the corner pilaster of the fifth step, in which medallions almost touch one another, and are separated only by the joined stems of the lotus petals, filling the corners (Fig. 258). The blank frame on the side of the medallions in the antarāla wall slab is also a deviation from the doorjamb fragment on the fifth step, which vibrates with the full, swelling forms of an ascending array of flowers and petals (Fig. 262). The greater geometricization of the lotus medallions, disposed in overtly partitioned squares on the architectural slabs of the antarāla, appears to be intended, to substitute austerity, for a luxurious surfeit of ornament, near the sanctum sanctorum.

JETHANI: ANTARĀLA, DOOR JAMBS

The lateral arrangement of the figures on the inner side of the antarāla door jamb and the side walls of Devarani, as against the frontal placement of figures at Jethani, on the door jamb flanks of the antarāla, or on the corner pillars of the approach steps to the antarāla, all were in place, would have built up a more vibrant programme of visual access to the garbhagṛha at Devarani (Figs. 52, 85). However, while at Devarani, the access is halted and regulated by the relatively closed cubes of the ardhamaṇḍapa, maṇḍapa and the antarāla, the access to the Jethani garbhagṛha through the maṇḍapa is ostensibly more free, open and flowing (Figs. 8-9). The worshipper or the art historian at Devarani has, however, to look only right, left or up front to absorb the vision of the artist. At Jethani, he also has to stop, go around the pillars, and walk from one wall to the next. Unlike Devarani, the pace of his visual access is punctuated and varied by the arrangement of the gaṇas, lions or makaras at the pillar bases. Sometimes, all the three gaṇas at the base look out in one direction, hands stretched, legs flailing, charging the air with tension and forcing the gaze to follow their movements. Sometimes, they look out in different directions, compelling the eye to flicker around. Or, they seem to gasp and groan with their effort, communicating their agony to the empathetic visitor. Or, they sit, stolid, columnar and still, with dogged, dour or glowering miens, below the impassive masks of the makaras, confronting and outstaring the visiter. The lions, on the other hand, being at the foot of the stairs, as well as the makaras above, being more heraldically conceived, seem to move in, hemming the spectator in. The larger figures on the pillars or on the flank are aloof and olympian, looking down on the visitor from a remote height.

MOVEMENT IN ACCESS

At Devarani, the visitor is not detained by all these in ascent to the temple. Yet, the huge maṇḍapa pillars and the ardhamaṇḍapa door jamb with Yamunā, would have loomed over him, obscuring the view of the antarāla door jamb. The sculptures at Devarani seem to organically grow far out of the architecture, instead of being carved on it. A mass of attending figures sprouts around the principal figures, milling in helter-skelter movements. A new accent is placed on the visually unstable, plastic substance of flowers and plants, which surround the figures with their irregular, swaying shapes (Figs. 356, 360-61). This dynamic phalanx replaces the sedate columns of figures, arrayed like sphinxes at Jethani, with their relatively austere, empty background (Figs. 295-301, 351-52).

The visitor has a feeling of being buffeted around in the large space of south Jethani. At Devarani he has instead, a claustrophobic feeling of being hemmed in by a procession through a narrow tunnel, made narrower by the agitated sculptures, intruding upon it from the sidewalls or jambs. The space in Jethani south envelops the visitor, and makes visual transitions more difficult than the space to Devarani east, which segments itself, permitting a visual breathing spell from one segment to another. At Devarani, the ornament on the door jamb, the sculptures on the flanks, create elements of visual tension by projection and recession (Figs. 157, 160, 175, 185-86). At Jethani, the architecture itself, with its four sided, seemingly rotating pillars, its dynamic arrangement of diverse figures at different levels, seems to heave and move, cleaving and electrifying the space between them with pulsing tension (Figs. 45-46, 52).

JETHANI: GARBHAGṚHA, ICON

The antarāla and the garbhagṛha, succeeding the vibrant space at Jethani south, appear to be something of an anti-climax, being small, flat and empty. The floor of both is plain and the circular perforation in their floor slabs, probably scoured out by rain, does not necessarily suggest socketing for the base of a Śivaliṅga, or for the bull Nandī in front. The single corner of a flat slab, equipped with a kapota profile and a karimakara head, recovered from below the mound top, may suggest the existence of a slab, equipped with makaras at all the four corners. However, even if its location on the garbhagṛha floor is assumed, it offers no clue to the identity of the image on its top. The speculation, whether the only large intact image of Paśupati, found southeast of Devarani, was the main image in either Devarani or Jethani, is idle. Its flat back and its missing, probably a gaṇa base, may suggest its installation on the side as a wall slab as well. Indeed, these figured wall slabs with carved bases appear to have stood so large and tall, that the available room, at least in the Jethani garbhagṛha, could have accommodated them with considerable difficulty. It is, indeed, not unlikely that the garbhagṛha contained a smaller image of Śiva, or a Śivaliṅga, no trace of which has, however, been found. A small block, carved into a Nandī, measuring 0.60 x 0.42 x 0.04 m, recovered from the foot of the mound at the north (Fig. 565), lends some plausibility to the suggestion for the existence of a liṅga, with this Nandī seated in front.

JETHANI: GARBHAGṚHA, VITĀNA

We are more certain about the shape of the vitāna of the garbhagṛha. Fragments of a bhārapaṭṭa (Figs. 59-60), plain on the sides, carved with a lotus medallion, with three rows of petals, (the first row covering the stamen, the third row peeping from below the second), enclosed in a square with foliate boundaries, suggest the use of such bhārapaṭṭas to construct the vitāna. The centre of the vitāna might have been constituted by a fragment (Fig. 59), measuring 2.56 x 1.13 x 0.42 m, shifted from the mound top at north. It is carved with a sahasradala padma (thousand petalled lotus), which radiates out from the stamen and corolla, and is rimmed by a circular garland of spiral strands.

The outermost beam (Fig. 60), facing the south, now seems to be lying atop the northern wall of the garbhagṛha. It is carved on one side with a series of lotus medallions, threaded together by a floral string, the intervening spaces being filled with lotus petals. The medallions are framed by a narrow spiral garland all the way across its length. The inevitable lotus medallion appears on the underside of this beam, set in a square foliate frame. The rhythm built up by the lotus medallions on the corner pillars of the proto-maṇḍapa, and the pillars outside the garbhagṛha door jamb, is fulfilled by this arrangement, suggesting the provision of a padmavitāna, with the token provision of a short padmavaravedikā, as we approach the garbhagṛha.

JETHANI: EASTERN APPROACH, SIDEWALLS

The space of the eastern and western approaches to the garbhagṛha (Figs. 69-70), appears to have been organized much more simply than the southern approach. The much eroded or broken fragments of door jambs standing on the topmost western step, or lying across the length of the eastern steps, suggest presence of door jambs much simpler in design than Devarani or Jethani south door jambs. The fragments appear to have been broad plain slabs, carved on either side of the height by a deeply cut band of floral and geometric scrolls, interwoven into basket patterns. An āmalaka, crowned by a ghaṭapallava, has been found on the eastern edge of the garbhagṛha. This indicates the possible existence of a stambhaśākhā, which was probably carved separately, and placed up against the door jamb. The architrave is not traceable on either east or west.

The continuing presence of carved slabs on the inner side of the eastern steps, bears evidence to the earlier presence of similar slabs on the outer side of the steps, now empty. One of these slabs lies prone on its face beyond the inner door jamb. It hides an image, which would have stood on the step outside the door jamb. On the third step from below, on the inner side on the east, the vestigious shape of a colossal dvārapāla in kaṭyāvalambitahasta, with massed flowing locks, can still be made out. A bust, measuring 0.85 x 0.95 x 0.30 m, has been recovered at the foot of the eastern steps. Inclined in the manner of the dvārapāla, broken from the chest, with an abraded head, it may have stood on the outer side of the steps. The inclined feet, carved on a pedestal, measuring 0.57 x 0.97 x 0.43 m, would have belonged to an image of similar proportions and stance. Other fragments of flatbacked slabs carved with remains of large images, found outside the eastern steps, reinforce this suggestion about their installation on the eastern steps.[31] The organization of the western steps, with raised but empty side walls, is similar to that of the eastern steps, and these side walls may have had similar flatbacked figured slabs raised above them. However, the relative dearth of such slabs found in the west, creates doubts about this.

JETHANI: EASTERN APPROACH, PILLARS

While the eastern sidewalls are slightly different from the western side walls, the two pillars at the eastern entrance (Figs. 70, 257-58) are not replicated anywhere else at the Tala temples. Though both are miśraka pillars, and show broadly similar segments, they use combinations of different floral designs. Much more slender, much less massive than the entrance pillars to the south (Fig. 236), these are also chamfered on one side, and backed up by a slab. The tall, slim kumbhaka in these pillars is stark, austere and flat as compared with the squat, heavy kumbhakas below the southern pillars with their square, ponderous and bulging sections. An architectural continuity is created by the five successive rows of padmadalas on the southern pillar shafts, the fifth row going all the way up, to wrap the pillars with flutes. This continuous row, found on the southern pillars, is interrupted on the eastern pillars by two raised grāsapaṭṭīs, one narrow, one broad, that are separated by a plain portion, and by a chequerboard design. Three successive rows of padmadalas erupt abruptly into sight on the shaft of the eastern pillars. Unlike the south pillar, these padmadalas diminish in size and relief as they increase in number, from eight through sixteen to thirty two. The lowest row of the padmadalas also functions, as on the south pillars, as darpaṇas, enclosing winding lotus rhizomes, and fantastic, fluid, springing, rearing creatures. The harmony in size or rhythm is maintained among the bold shapes of the padmadalas, or grāsamukhas spitting puṣpavallī. The narrow āmalaka, special to Tala, comes next, completing the syncopated rhythm generated by the sequence of raised paṭṭis going around the pillar.

One of the eastern pillars, with a similar tall, slender kumbhaka at the base, and the chequerboard design and ghaṭa-pallava-āmalaka in the capital, has its shaft sliced in half. A fragment of this shaft (Fig. 253) has been found on the east. This fragment shaft shares, with the shaft of its opposite number, one padmapaṭṭi functioning as darpaṇa enclosing floral rhizomes, two padmapaṭṭīs enclosing grāsamukhas spouting vandanamālikā, which drapes itself around the shaft. Unlike the opposite pillar, the broad paṭṭikā now precedes the narrow paṭṭikā in the upward ascent. A new motif of roundels, formed by composite makara-foliate-human forms, inserts itself between the padmapaṭṭis.

Apart from these two pillars, a third, flatbacked pillar slab (Fig. 245) of similar proportions has been recovered from the eastern part of the mound. Above the tall kumbhaka, and rows of padmadalas, its shaft is decorated by sixteen spiral bands of floral and geometric designs, partitioned by thin, grooved channels. Unlike the spiral floral bands in the mālāśākhā of the Devarani door jamb, these bands are carved in soft and shallow relief, in the manner of the stambhaśākhā on the Jethani south door jamb. A muktādāma is hung above these bands from the base of the ghaṭapallava capital, which is draped around its neck by aśokalumbīs, crowned by a cluster of young fruits and an āmalaka.

Fragments of pillars, carved with padmadalas, floral bands, geometric motifs, muktāgrāsas, ghaṭapallavas, āmalakas, retrieved from the eastern part of the mound, yield an idea of the decorative repertoire used in the other displaced pillars in the east.[32]

A smaller figure of ūrdhvaliṅga Śiva wearing tiger skin, standing in tribhaṅga, carved on a wall slab, in high relief, has been recovered from the foot of the eastern steps (Fig. 349). It demonstrates the probable use of such smaller Śiva or proto-Śiva attendant figures, alongside the huge dvārapālas, at the entrance of the eastern staircase. Whether or not the candraśilā and two initial steps, served as a prototype of an ardhamaṇḍapa, one cannot be quite sure. However, some credence is lent to this inference by the breadth of these steps, by the positioning of the flat backed pillar slabs, and, by the retrieval of several pillar fragments in the east. These indicate that figured or plain slabs may have been used to back up the flat backed pillar slabs, forming the walls, pillar slabs without a bevelled back being used independently up front.

JETHANI: WESTERN APPROACH, SIDEWALLS & PILLARS

The western entrance to Jethani is equipped with steps similar in proportions to the eastern steps and with similar broad shouldered side walls. It does not show in situ any counterpart of the larger dvārapāla or smaller Śiva image of the east. However, the fragments of pillars and pilasters (Figs. 243-44, 246-47, 252) found on outside the western steps, are larger, sturdier, in size more impressive, and more organically and satisfactorily built than the slender eastern pillars, with their broken rhythms. They share spiral floral bands, grāsapaṭṭi, vandanamālikā, successive rows of padmadalas on the shaft, or the aśokalumbī on the kalaśa capital, with the eastern pillars. At the same time, they adapt the robust shape of the square kumbhaka base of the southern pillars, rather than the tall, over elongated base of the eastern pillars. The padmadalas in the lowest row of the shaft are used as darpaṇas like the pillars at south and east. However, enclosed in these darpaṇas, the swimming karimakaras carrying foliate stems and leaves in their mouth, the seated, front facing, garland-bearing lion worshippers, the luxuriant flourish of the lotus rhizome, are carved much more boldly and vigorously, and in higher relief than the darpaṇas of the eastern or southern pillars.

The carving on the shafts comes close to the volumetric rendering of the composite ghaṭa-pallava-siṁha-kīrtimukha motif on the base of south pillars. The rows of padmadalas are executed with a more pronounced curvilinear profile, a more emphatic delineation of the upper edges, or of the peeping petal tips between the broader petals, than at the east. On the other hand, unlike the south pillars, the surface of these upper rows of petals is left stark and empty of decorative or structural description. In the south pillars, the ornate rows of petals finally give way to an austere, rectilinear, plain row of very tall petals. In the west, the plain petals make way for spiral rows of stylized floral bands (Figs. 246-47) in pilaster. In another pillar, the process of pollination from the stamens is presented in spiral rows. The insertion of a mouse or a mole, climbing down in the midst of the spiral floral bands (Fig. 252), flaunts an artistic conceit,[33] which is not found in the eastern or southern pillars. The juxtaposition of the verticals and diagonals in these pillars somewhat modifies the impression of the convergent rush of lines, jetting upwards, which the southern pillars so powerfully convey. One can thus see, how, at Jethani, an experimental play is undertaken by the artist with different forms and designs at different entrances.

COMPARISON OF JETHANI AND DEVARANI PILLARS

It is indeed the pillars which emphatically distinguish the Jethani entrances from one another, and the Devarani entrance from the Jethani entrances, and give them their individual character and identity. Some pillars also establish continuities and linkages between the two temples, which serve as chronological clues.

At Devarani, in the flatbacked maṇḍapa pillars, the tall, slender kumbhaka of the flatbacked eastern pillars of Jethani is rendered in a more muscular and powerful style. The diagonal accents of the western pillar shafts of Jethani, are given up in the Devarani maṇḍapa pillar shafts, in favour of the tall, vertical, petal flutes, used so effectively in the south pillars of Jethani. The simplicity and plainness of the padmadalas on the western pillars of Jethani, are also discarded at Devarani in favour of the more ornate petals in Jethani south pillars. At the same time, the rows of petals, including the darpaṇa, are brought down from up to five in Jethani south to only three. However, while the frank protrusion of peeping petals from between the bigger padmadalas on Jethani south and west is accepted at Devarani, the peeping petal tips lose the vigorous naturalistic rendering of Jethani, and become harsh, spiky and angular. The soft, fluid plastic rendering of the makaras in the darpaṇas of Jethani pillars, with more simply and naturalistically rendered tails or rhizomes, and a smaller number of loops, indicates the pristine architectural tradition, involving less of an impression of effort. In the Devarani maṇḍapa pillar darpaṇas (Figs. 268-72), the makara body and rhizome become stylized into many more loops, and stray into the use of ridged outlines. The interpenetration of the foliate and animal forms becomes much more emphatic in these. The few spaces left empty at Jethani are filled up to the point of congestion. The play of light and shade, much more softly contrasted around the simple curves of the makara body at Jethani, is now accentuated and galvanized by being channeled into sharp crevices and crests. The softly modelled spines of the petal flutes at Jethani now became razor sharp, culminating in a knife edge at the top.

The tall base, used on the eastern steps of Jethani, is adapted in the pillars, lying at the foot of the Devarani stairs, and made disproportionately massive and tall in relation to the shaft above, giving a rather naked appearance to the pillars (Figs. 255-56). The rows of padmadalas, including darpaṇas, on one of the Devarani maṇḍapa pillars, indicate incorporation and reuse of similar arrangements at Jethani. But, the recessing of the upper portion in the shaft of the principal pillar at Devarani entrance shows a novel experiment, not tried at Jethani. The deliberate asymmetry in the decoration of the pillars continues from Jethani. The diagonal bands of floral or geometric bands above vertically arranged rows, used at both east and west of Jethani, are, however, not adapted at Devarani. Instead, the vertical accent, stressed in Jethani south pillars, is preferred, by letting down the floral bands in vertical rows from grāsamukhas on the Devarani antarāla door jamb or on the pillar fragments recovered from east.

Using the pillars as a clue, we can see how, at Devarani, out of the two styles at Jethani, one prettified, internally disharmonious, rather slender and feminine, the other massive, organically formed, rugged and masculine, the latter is preferred. However, the robust strength of this style is somewhat misunderstood. It is minimized either by exaggeration of the bulk of the base, distorting proportion, by the sharpening of contours, or by the geometrization and stylization of natural forms.

JETHANI: NOTHERN FAÇADE, SHRINE

The three entrances to Jethani have thus offered to us a unique variety of ambivalent features, combining both volumetric and linear, simple and complex patterns. The deep, complex relief at the Devarani entrance is thus anticipated at Jethani.

The northern side of Jethani (Fig. 65) is the only side without an entrance to the garbhagṛha. However, we are not, on this account, confronted with a blank, faceless facade. Instead, it is provided in the centre with a small projected niche, which functions as a devakulikā. It has a standing image, carved on a wall slab, in a cell. The cell is in ruins, and has a miniature pillared maṇḍapa in front. From the surviving decoration, it appears that the pillars were provided with vertical flutes composed of small, raised squares, floral side bands, and lotus medallions. The devakulikā is flanked, on either side, by the protruding forefront of a seated gaja, faithfully described with beady eyes, padded nails in feet and swelling protruberances on the side of the head. The extension of the brick rampart on either side of the gajas suggests that they may have been housed in roofed cells of their own in later 7th cent. AD restoration.

The height of the pillars of the central cella being evidently at the same level as the floor of the garbhagṛha, the gajapīṭha could not have had pillars taller than the extant brick ramparts beside them. The general impression therefore, would be of a platform projecting behind the backwall of the garbhagṛha at its floor level, as against the huge pillared passage on the other three sides. Such a projection, with an access and an existence, completely independent of the temple, would appear to be something of an afterthought. It could have been intended to compensate for the impression of visual inadequacy of the Jethani temple, which the architect may have had, after completion of its three approaches. The long, wide processional approach from the south, appearing already to be much longer and wider than the eastern and western approaches, may have made the sharp cut-off on the north look a bit abrupt, as an insistent pointer to the anti-climatically small garbhagṛha. This may have demanded a projection, as wide, if not as tall and long, as the southern approach.

JETHANI: ŚIKHARA DOUBTFUL

Having established a general idea of the original walls of the Tala temples, and having eliminated the possibility of the existence of a śikhara above Devarani, I shall now examine the probability of the existence of a śikhara above Jethani.

I have suggested earlier, from the remains in situ, the near certainty of the existence of a padmavitāna above the Jethani garbhagṛha. The bhārapaṭṭas lying at location being flat, this might have been flat too, though this cannot be vouched for. Other fragments of bhārapaṭṭas, both plain and carved with lotus medallions, have been found in different directions.[34] Even if the slabs, firmly associated with a vitāna, are not sufficient in number to cover the entire temple, the existence of a flat padmavitāna could be assumed over its approaches as well. However, if we could imagine the four huge catuṣki pillars, complete with ghaṭapallava, āmalaka and an architrave, drawn up to their full height and in place, the fallen door jambs at the south or the east would not, on being set up, have been much higher. The gain in height at the transitional points could well be bridged by stepping up the vitāna with vertically connecting slabs.

While a regular nāgara or lātina śikhara spanning the vast spread of space on the south does not appear to have been viable, a lātina śikhara only above the small garbhagṛha would have been aesthetically undesirable. Nor is it possible to imagine a brick-clad śikhara of this type, because not a single brick, moulded to such a formation, has been found. Since the later restorers took care to mould the pīṭha and vedībandha of Jethani on the brick-cladding (Fig. 73), they would not have refrained from suggesting the moulded outline of the brick śikhara, if it really existed. Also, the absence of any fragment of such a śikhara at Devarani is an argument against its presence at Jethani, because Devarani is ostensibly a slightly later construction, which learnt from the structural weaknesses of Jethani. A śikhara would have been a major area of continuing linkages or divergences between the two.

The biggest argument in favour of a śikhara above Jethani is the existence of a few āmalakas at Jethani south (Figs. 59, 61). Lying close to the damaged or fallen southern pillars, conforming to their gigantic proportions, these āmalakas may have, however, got detached from the pillars. If these had belonged to the śikhara, we should have found other such āmalakas buried under the debris on the southern stairs or above the garbhagṛha, or on the three other sides of the temple. We have found none. The suggestion will, of course, remain tentative till we find fragments or evidence of a superstructure, which uses such āmalakas exclusively at a corner of one of its entrances, or, assuming that the āmalakas were pulled down from the top of the mound, above the flat padmavitāna over the garbhagṛha.

JETHANI: LATER REINFORCEMENTS

If the original nucleus of the Jethani temple differs radically in its plan from the Devarani temple, the reinforcement measures adapted for the two temples are also different. Unlike Devarani, Jethani is sheathed by bricks. This brick envelope is fairly thick (Figs. 67-68, 71-72), extending from some 1.5 m to about 2.6 m, but the huge stone slabs have nevertheless fallen, crushing the bricks with them. A brick platform on the east, aligned with the south steps, approaching the antarāla, served as a location for a sacrificial altar. The addition of this brick dyke was apparently undertaken later to conserve the temple, and not as part of it or contemporaneously with it. Apart from the way the bricks are used to completely clad the plinth or walls of the temple as an obvious measure of protection, the strongest argument against the contemporaneity of this measure with the original construction is the illogical and unaesthetic use of a brick plinth on a southern step for bolstering up the Varuṇa image, which does not belong there. That protection is the primary motive becomes clear also from the low brick walls which radiate out across the sloping ground from the cladding of the temple on the north, south or the west, stabilizing the base, in a pincer movement from different directions.

And yet, unlike Devarani, this later brick construction is not hidden below as a series of ramps, creating boxes for brick and rubble infill (Fig. 77). Devarani being constructed with self stabilizing horizontal slabs, these ramps were hidden by a circumambulatory platform, concealing the pīṭha from view (Figs. 90-91, 94). Jethani walls being constructed with unstable vertical slabs, the use of a surrounding platform may have been ruled out, and cladding was used all the way up on the plinth and the walls. Faced with this compulsion, the architect would appear to have decided not only to reveal the brick cladding, but integrate it as part of the overall architectural design the pīṭha and mould it (Fig. 73).

Though the brick mouldings of the pīṭha are heavily damaged, enough survives on the east to help us make out the existence of a khura, a tall kumbha, a kandhara with projected galapāda partitions, and recesses with a slightly swelling centre, framed by slender pilasters, a heavy kalaśa and a kapota. Whether the mouldings were consistently wound around the temple on all sides, or whether variations were introduced, is however not quite clear. It is also not clear if the brick cladding replicated the moulding of the stone pīṭha beneath it. The mouldings are shared by Devarani pīṭha, though the kandhara with projections and recesses or a kalaśa are missing from Devarani. Since the Jethani pīṭha rises directly to the jaṅghā, formed by the figured slabs, it acts as the vedībandha too. At Devarani the segments of the vedībandha are separately articulated.

The flat, unrecessed backs of the figured slabs suggest that the jaṅghā walls of Jethani, unlike Devarani, were left plain, and not enlivened with projections, recesses or makaratoraṇas. Nor would this have been structurally feasible, in view of the high relief carvings on the inside face of the slabs. Thus, from the outside, the Jethani, in spite of the much greater wealth of sculpture inside vis-à-vis Devarani, would have tended to look even more austere than Devarani. However, this apparently solid mass would have been relieved by three big voids of doors piercing its three sides, and probably three small, parallel lowlying doors at the back. As against this, the Devarani temple, with its single door, would have presented, despite its tall, arcuate niches, a closed and impenetrable volume to the world.

DEVARANI & JETHANI: STRUCTURAL COMPARISON

The differences in the plan, elevation and construction of the two temples (Figs. 6-9; Pls. 1-2) account not only for the difference in their general outlook but also for the greater durability of the Devarani structure.

The walls of Devarani are made of plain horizontal slabs except on the steps, whereas, in the Jethani walls and steps, enormous sculpted vertical slabs stood, to crumble down because of the inherent instabiliy of their disposition, and the unequal settlement of the foundation. The walls of the Devarani temple were surrounded, unlike Jethani, by a pillared platform on the ramps, to serve as a pradakṣiṇā patha, probably in the 7th century AD. While this platform further stablized the structure, the Devarani temple survived better, being also a more compact and tight knit structure, with but a single door to the east, unlike Jethani, which was a large, sprawling temple, with a very broad main entrance to the south, and two narrow constricted entrances to the east and west.

Moreover, the steps to the east of Devarani temple were shorter, designed mainly for access for the much longer temple platform. The steps to the south of Jethani were longer, larger, broader, integrated into the temple as its integral parts, spanning the temple from wall to wall, and penetrating deep into it, up to the disproportionately small platform of the garbhagṛha. The Devarani temple dispensed with the huge pillars on its only eastern access, which were used so liberally on the southern steps of Jethani, to only topple against one another, bringing themselves down. The pillars of Devarani were also more monolithic, excluding, at least on the temple platform, the additive arrangement of blocks and figured slabs on the Jethani south pillars.

Devarani was indeed conceived more architectonically, making it possible to vary its external profile by projections, recesses, toraṇas, makara mukhas and praṇālas, leaving the large garbhagṛha and antarāla more or less empty of a clutter of sculptures. Jethani was more like a congregation of enormous sculptures, which made it difficult to carve on the flat back of the figured slabs, used all the way for its walls. The Devarani temple, therefore, has remained in use and worship to this day, unlike Jethani, which was covered by rubble, ruined further by being overgrown with a colossal tree on the west.

The greater stability of construction in the Devarani temple is not necessarily an argument for its later date, unless one assumes that Devarani was built upon the experience of the failure of the techniques adapted at Jethani. Apart from the fact that clearance has revealed the level of the ground for construction to be the same for both temples, the size and texture of bricks used in the boxed chambers below the platform around Devarani and in the cladding or tunnels around Jethani is similar. The decorative repertoire, specially of the pillars or door jambs, the grandeur and scale of the sculpted architectural slabs used in the walls, are also similar in both. And yet, a detailed comparison of the two temples reveals a greater attention to decorative detail at Devarani, an intensification of the common tendency to intermesh foliate, geometric, theriomorphic and anthropomorphic elements, a stiffening in the modelling, and a definite rearrangement of the Jethani elements in the architecture of Devarani, which suggest a familiarity with conventions initiated at Jethani. Sharing a common corpus with Jethani, and broadly the same period, the Devarani may yet be slightly later than Jethani.

NOTES

1. See the chapter on Historiography for the notices of Devarani by Pandey (1977), Bajpai and Pandey (1978), Stadtner (1976, 1980, 1981), Joanna Williams (1982).
2. The makaramukha on the south of the garbhagṛha is no longer there in situ. However, an architectural fragment, carved with a makaramukha, measuring 1.47 x 0.98 x 0.52 m and a second fragment with only part of the head and snout, measuring 0.46 x 0.39 x 0.16 m have been recovered from the debris to the south, having apparently been shifted there before the 1978 excavation.
3. An enormous head, carved with matted locks, measuring 1.04 x 0.50 x 0.26 m, the crown of a head, measuring 0.36 x 0.50 x 0.40 m, carved with matted locks or skulls, portions of busts, measuring 0.60 x

0.64 x 0.20 m and 1.44 x 1.65 x 0.44 m adorned with tiger skin or claws, a larger head, measuring 0.66 x 0.45 x 0.25 m, equipped with a third eye and crescent, are some of the examples.

4. Several pillar bases, with traces of feet surviving on the top, have been recovered. One, measuring 0.64 x 0.43 x 0.39 m, is carved with a bearded ascetic holding lotus stalk and staff. A second, measuring 1.33 x 0.71 x 0.41 m has two ascetics, master and disciple, facing each other, standing in profile. A third is carved, on the upper level, with a crouching ascetic, and, on the lower, with an abraded nāgarāja. It measures 1.12 x 0.73 x 0.30 m in the upper part, 2.13 x 0.86 x 0.43 m in the lower part. A fourth is carved with a bhāraputraka with ekāvalī (single string necklace) and sarpamālā (garland of snakes), and measures 1.12 x 0.74 x 0.38 m. A fifth, recovered from inside the Devarani temple (1.10 x 1.40 x 0.23 m), is carved with feet on a padmapīṭha, with three dancing gaṇas below. Often the base is an independent slab. Instances are, a base (0.68 x 0.37 x 0.37 m) carved with bhāraputrakas on four sides, another base (1.09 x 0.53 x 0.31 m), carved with Kārtikeya, seated astride a peacock.
5. Several fragments, measuring 0.20 x 0.41 x 0.55 m, 0.97 x 1.08 x 0.25 m and 0.17 x 0.33 x 0.13 m have been recovered, with garland-bearing vidyādharas.
6. Some pillar fragments (sizes 0.70 x 0.70 x 0.27 m, 0.69 x 0.57 x 0.23 m, 0.86 x 0.55 x 0.40 m) show ghaṭapallava and āmalaka, while others (1.64 x 0.55 x 0.52 m, 1.44 x 0.57 x 0.39 m, 1.22 x 0.39 x 0.23 m, 1.84 x 0.53 x 0.22 m) show a siṁha, or a single-headed, double bodied siṁha above the kumbha. One (1.57 x 0.66 x 0.62 m) shows depiction of a peacock and two human beings at the base, and lotus petal mouldings on the shaft.
7. The figure of a river goddess was recovered from the 1978 excavation at the southeast of Devarani, and is kept at the Bilaspur muesum. Several fragments have been recovered in 87-88, matching its proportions and ornament, near the earlier location. One, apparently the top of a river goddess jamb, shows garland bearing vidyādharas and vestiges of peacock feathers. It measures 1.40 x 0.63 x 0.44 m. A second (0.19 x 0.69 x 0.64 m) shows peacock feathers and curled human feet. A third (0.52 x 0.68 x 0.13 m) shows two feet, ostensibly of Gaṅgā on makara. A fourth (1.65 x 0.67 x 0.47 m) shows the mekhalā, incised right side of the dress of the goddess, as also the twin vertical floral mouldings on the side of the jamb. A fifth image of a dwarf female attendant, now in the Bilaspur museum, may also have belonged to one of the river goddesses.
8. *Encyclopaedia*, 2. I. (text): 66, 68, Figs. 27, 28, 66, 68.
9. *Ibid.*, 295, 297, 303, Figs. 116-117, 120.
10. The śikhara of the Devgarh Gupta temple, Dhānk Sūrya temple, bhūmiāmalaka of the Rāmgarh Muṇḍeśvari temple, the door lintel of the Rāmgarh (Vidisha) maṇḍapikā shrine, the toraṇa cross beam in Nāgarī temple, the udgamas above rathikās in the jaṅghās of maṇḍapikā temples at Baḍoh, Pāṭhāri, Kuchdon, or in the jaṅghā of Odishan temples like Paraśurāmeśvara, do tend to show candraśālās, spread over a band with a central recess. See Dhaky & Meister 1988, 2.2: pls., 81, 258, 272, 306, 316, 320, 474, 520.
11. Sirpur Lakṣmaṇa temple, Khārod Āndal or Śavarīnārāyaṇa temple, Palāri Siddheśvara temple, Dhobini Śiva temple show kapota mouldings with full or half candraśālās. See Dhaky & Meister 1988, 2. I; pls. 466, 477, 480, 487, 503. At Sirpur and Dhobini, kaṇṭhas with recesses and projections occur both above and below this moulding.
12. The debris of the narrow platform, specially on the northeastern side, has yielded a large number of plain stone slabs, used either in the packing above the brick and rubble filling of the trenches, or in the roof of the broad platform.
13. Stadtner finds Devarani foundation mouldings similar to those of the Jambuliṅga temple (as the earliest dated type, of AD 694) at Paṭṭadakal, of the Dharmarāja Ratha temple of Māmallapuram, and of 8th century Cālukyān and Tamil temples, the Pallava temples lacking the makara on a moulding, the Cālukyān temples possessing it. Stadtner 1977: 22-23, 211 n. 14-15; 1980: 41, n. 7-8.
14. In fact, the sequential profile of pādabandha (spelt as pīḍabandha by Stadtner) is as different from the Devarani temple mouldings as the pratibandha. The pādabandha does not, it is true, often show a makara or vyāla like the pratibandha, and usually has a tripaṭṭa kumuda. On the other hand, in sheer,

unadorned simplicity, the pādabandha mouldings come closer to the Devarani vedībandha. The Jambuliṅga and Dharmarājarāja temple, quoted as comparable by Stadtner, have, contrary to what he thought, kapotabandha rather than pratibandha adhiṣṭhānas. At Devarani one can see neither the sequence of vājana, pratimukha, gala, kapota or tripaṭṭa kumuda, usual in kapotabandha mouldings, in the actual examples of Stadtner, nor the sequence of ūparikampa, prativājana, pratimukha, kaṇṭha etc. appropriate to pratibanda mouldings. See Dhaky & Meister 1988 (South India), II (text): 32, 37, 74-75, Figs. 17, 18, 27-29; 2.I (text), 296; 2.I (plates): pl. 611.

15. For vyālas, faceted or prismatic bosses in place of makaras in pratibandha mouldings see *ibid.*, I, I (text): 137, Fig. 63 A; II (plates): pls, 75, 76. *Ibid.* (text): Figs. 31 a-c, 80-83, 94 show vyālas and makaras on other types of adhiṣṭhānas. For comparison, see Devarani mouldings in *ibid.* 2.I (plates): pls. 444-45 and southern mouldings in II (plates): pls, 76, 91, 134, 163, 167.
16. See *ibid.*, II, (plates), pls. 4,15. Stadtner refers to Zimmer 1955, 2: pl. 141 of the Mālegitti Śivālaya temple as that of the Upper Śivālaya temple, which is a different temple. See Stadtner1977: 211, N. 14. For Upper Śivālaya see K.R. Srinivasan1972: 131-32. For the makaratoraṇa in Mālegiṭṭi Śivālaya, see Lippe 1978: 204, pl. 116.
17. For Dalavānur and Ellora, see Philippe Stern 1972: Figs. 170-72, 174-76. Also Gupte and Mahajan 1962: pl. 75. For Ajanta, Odette Viennot 1964: pl. 5. For Jogeśvarī cave, Spink 1967: 10, 13, 52, 66. For Dārrā, Dhaky & Meister 1988, 2.I (plates): pl, 29.
18. See Pramod Chandra 1975: pls, 16, 59.
19. The śilāmaṇḍapikā shrines are shrines with a sanctum and a porch, with simple slab superstructures, with pilasters and recesses on the broad slabs of the sanctum walls. See Dhaky, Meister 1988, 2. I(text): 126-27; 132-32, 151-55, 158; 2. I (plates), pls. 275-77, 305, 318, for such shrines at Mahuā, Kuchdon, Badoh.
20. See *Ibid.*, 2.I (plates): pls, 9, 100, 106, 120; *ibid.* (text), Figs. 30a and c. Also Dhaky. in Bettina Baumer 1982: 135-37, Figs. 1-3.
21. Dhaky, Baumer 1982: 123, 125, Figs. 5, 6 for examples in Rajasthan, Gujarat or Madhya Pradesh from the 7th to the 11th century.
22. Stadtner 1977: 23; 1980: 41.
23. The straight-edged base mouldings above khura, lacking a round or reverse curve, the shallow, pilastered niches, and the makaratoraṇa remind Joanna Williams of a common wooden ancestry for such elements at both Tala and in the South. She derives such elements from an open pavilion, made of arches of pliable material. The diagonally cut door jamb slabs recall, for her, a wooden veneer. The three dimensionally treated, deeply undercut foliage of the door bands, the leafy treatment of the kīrtimukha and his crown, also seem characteristic to her, of wood rather than stone. Joanna Williams 1982: 125-28, 152, ns. 81, 82. The Tala woodworking traditions are shared, according to her, by Mukundarā rather than Garhvā, though she alludes to Garhvā style carving in the Devarani lintel.
24. Colored, lacquered, chamfered, lathe-turned, wooden columns, with an inward rake, supporting portable pavilions, have been seen earlier as origins of Indian lithic forms. Williams, however, does not substantiate her suggestion by comparison with relevant prototypes in early bas-reliefs or painting. For illustrations of wooden prototypes, Percy Brown 1965: 3, 11, 21, 45, 50, 59, 75.
25. To Williams, the stellate plan, breaking up of the wall plane, use of candraśālās on the upper cornice and base mouldings, of a leaf on the plinth moulding, of a porch, supported by columns, or the door, with a strong inward pull, are innovations at Lakṣmaṇa temple, not visualized at Devarani, with its cellular structure, lacking in columns, or with its laterally set back doorband, used as a 'discrete' unit. She traces the heritage of the columns, porch or false door at Lakṣmaṇa to individual features of Gupta or 6th century western cave architecture. She does not try, logically pursuing her own method, to trace such elements at Lakṣmaṇa to individual features at Tala. Williams 1982: 160-63, ns. 14, 15.
26. The plan is in the shape of a cross, made of squares. One vertical arm is crossed in the middle by an equally long horizontal arm. The two arms touch and enclose a square. The horizontal arm, in turn, is flanked by one shorter horizontal arm on either side. One could try and imagine this, with some difficulty,

as a distorted plan of the temple itself, with three side entrances and one mocked up back entrance. To make this plausible, we have to cut off its extended vertical arms, and imagine the squares to be not as equal to one another as they are shown in the incised such elements drawing. On the other hand, this could be the drawing of the brick encasement and brick ramparts planned in all directions, or, even, for that matter, a scrawled game board. Though the plan is apparently ancient, found only after clearance, its contemporaneity with either the construction of the temple or its later reinforcement cannot be vouched for.

27. Thus, the proportions of the āmalakas atop the ghaṭas in the pillars generally remain within about 0.60 m in diameter, 0.25 m in breadth, the height of the pillars going up to 1.72 m in a pillar lying on the north. On the north, pillar fragments with ghaṭa-āmalaka segments measure 1.72 x 0.48 x 0.31 m, 0.61 x 0.70 x 0.30 m, 0.47 x 0.54 x 0.15 m. On the east, such fragments measure 0.71 x 0.23 x 0.34 m, 0.62 x 0.57 x 0.35 m. On the west, these measure 1.45 x 0.45 x 0.20 m, 1.27 x 0.62 x 0.28 m, 0.66 x 0.60 x 0.19 m, or 0.68 x 0.64 x 0.47 m. On the south, a vertical array of āmalakas and ghaṭas ranging from 0.11 to 0.26 m in width, have been found.
28. Measurements and carved edges of some of these fragments, found in the south, show kīrtimukhas (0.97 x 0.47 x 0.23 m, and 0.75 and 0.39 x 0.20 m), Gaja (0.87 x 0.34 x 0.27 m), or seated figures (1.40 x 0.70 x 0.25 m). When matched and put together, they appear to have been lintels for spanning the intercolumniations, at the flanks.
29. Most of these images have been removed to the Bilaspur State Museum. An Ardhanārīśvara head with skull (0.45 x 0.35 x 16 m), a head with kīriṭamukuṭa, with kīrtimukha decoration, (0.53 x 0.26 x 0.12 m), a male head (0.54 x 0.36 x 0.9 m), a truncated rudragaṇa head with thick lips (0.38 x 0.28 x 0.9 m), head of a varāha (0.36 x 0.20 x 0.10 m), a moustachioed Śivagaṇa with large and protruding eyes (0.44 x 0.24 x 0.15 m) would have belonged to images either on the pillar shaft or to figured slabs on the side. Smaller portions, of a nāgapuruṣa with folded hands, human bust and reptilian trunk (0.48 x 0.24 x 0.15 m), the upper portion of a nāgapuruṣa with a snakehood and broken arms, an abraded and damaged bust of a nāgapuruṣa with folded hands (0.19 x 0.16 x 0.10 m), a truncated nāgapuruṣa head with snake hood (0.19 x 0.16 x 0.10 m), and a female bust (0.20 x 0.20 x 0.14 m) would have belonged to attendant figures on the pillars or side slabs. The Hara-Gaurī base with figures bound in nāgapāśa measures 1.20 x 0.56 x 0.35 m.
30. Fragments of pillar shafts, adorned with full lotus medallions (1 x 0.6 x 0.33 m, 0.41 x 0.59 x 0.24 m, 1.44, 0.55 x 0.35 m) have been recovered from the west.
31. The lower half of images (2.80 x 1.25 x 0.45 m, 1.32, 1.15 x 0.39 m), the right thigh of an image (1.58 x 0.50 x 0.47 m) have been found to the east.
32. Thus, fragments (0.95 x 0.60x 0.22 m, 0.73 x 0.50 x 0.12 m 0.40 x 0.28 x 0.8 m, 0.62 x 0.62 x 0.25 m) with lotus and floral bands have been found. Other fragments (0.38 x 0.29 x 0.11 m, 0.61 x 0.38 x 0.26 m, 0.54 x 0.40 x 0.25 m, 0.45 x 0.42 x 0.15 m) show lotus petals, jewelled festoons, geometric designs, and grāsamukhas. Still others (0.62 x 0.57 x 0.35 m, 0.71 x 0.41 x 0.25 m, 0.48 x 0.38 x 0.13 m, 0.71 x 0.23 x 0.34 m, 0.95 x 0.30 x 0.32 m) have ghaṭas, āmalakas, muktāgrāsas. One fragment (2.39 x 0.52 x 0.41 m) has a gaṇa riding a makara.
33. The pillar with sixteen fioral bands and a climbing mouse is broken into several fragments measuring 2.32 x 0.65 x 0.42 m, 1.88 x 0.65 x 0.40 m, 0.84 x 0.51 x 0.21 m. Another pillar with beaded spiral bands, probably suggesting pollination, has fragments measuring 1.44 x 0.70 x 0.38 m, 1 x 0.64 x 0.34 m, 1 x 0.69 x 0.33 m and 1 x 0.71 x 0.23 m. Several fragments also show ghaṭapallava and āmalaka.
34. In the north itself, another beam fragment with a lotus medallion (1.95 x 1.13 x 0.42 m) has been found. In the east, a plain fragment (0.60 x 0.55 x 0.18 m) has been recovered. In the south, a fragment measuring 0.69 x 0.50 x 0.20 m has been traced. In the west, a plain fragment (0.87 x 0.85 x 0.32 m) has been located. Apart from these, many plain slab fragments, which may or may not have belonged to the ceiling, have been pushed out from above the mound, to be arranged on the ground.

6

The Style of Tala Sculpture

A discussion of the Tala sculpture has already been made in the context of Tala architecture. It was unavoidable because in Indian art the two are inseparable. This is all the more true at this early period when unimaginative repetition of sculpted motifs to merely fill the space is not considered essential, and when rhythm is created more by numerous transformations of the same motifs or patterns than by their symmetrical arrangements. It has not, however, been possible in the earlier discussion, to look at the Tala sculptures either in their entirety or in distinctive groups, to gauge the manifold universe they create, or their unifying bonds. The living, moving patterns of Tala sculpture can be felt more kinesthetically by a human observer than the relatively inert facades or mouldings of Tala architecture. Once the style of Tala sculpture is understood, it furnishes a better chronological clue than architecture to the transitional character of a janus-headed art, which stands at the threshold of the medieval style, without losing its 'classical' flavour, and which looks early in spite of its late features, or vice versa.

COEXISTENCE OF STYLES AT JETHANI AND DEVARANI

Our attempt, therefore, will be to understand the sculpture on its own terms first, and in terms of its relations with other sculpture later. A detailed discussion of iconography or meaning of sculpture will be excluded from this analysis for reasons of clarity, and for focussing attention on the broad identity of Tala style, in spite of subtle differences between Jethani and Devarani. In doing so, the variations introduced within the same broad style to fulfil the iconographic theme, will, however, be considered. A coexistence of traits and trends, memories and anticipations will be found within the style at Tala, which follows from its ambivalence as a site bridging early classical with medieval art.

Two styles coexist at Jethani. One stresses large size and volume, girth, height and square proportions. The other emphasizes smaller, slender figures and elongated proportions. In the same sculpture, the two styles often combine, as do contrary preferences for organic and stylized forms. At Devarani, in spite of a continuing sense for volume or natural form, the slender or stylized form begins to be preferred. The charming asymmetry and innovative vigour of Jethani ornament begins to give way to a more rigorous regularity and over refined elegance at Devarani. As such, Jethani is closer to the classical style as Devarani is closer to the early medieval, and Tala serves as a source of inspiration for competing classical and medieval trends in the later Dakṣiṇa Kośala or Indian art.

AMBIVALENCE BETWEEN STYLES AT JETHANI

Generally, the Jethani figural style is distinguished from the Devarani style by more massive proportions, an impression of greater and overpowering strength, chastened by an expression of more intense solemnity. The heads are more rounded in contour, the forehead lower and more sloping, the face and body fuller and fleshier, the nose broader and thicker, lips more pouting, eyelids more hooded at Jethani. Compared with Devarani, the shoulders are wider, the neck stronger and thicker, sunk deeper in the trunk, the arms and legs more powerfully formed and laterally spread. The description of the ornament or garment is simpler at Jethani, which draws greater attention to the modelled surface of the body they adorn than to themselves. The hāra is broader in Jethani figures, the hairdress more elaborate, and the cloth gathered near their waist or thighs is heavier, enhancing the breadth of their body.

The Varuṇa, Kārtikeya, the truncated gaṇa or Bhairava heads, load bearing gaṇa (Fig. 478) recovered from Jethani south (Figs. 346, 350, 416, 428), a slab in Devarani garbhagṛha, carved with Pārvatī with jaṭāmukuṭa (Fig. 302), are examples of this style. The Tala Paśupati image (Fig. 584-85) with the huge, round heads on its body, its barrel shoulders and short, thick, grounded neck, its squarish trunk, its pent-up power or quiet menace, appears to belong to the Jethani rather than the Devarani idiom. The intact head of a colossal image was crudely restored with cement by villagers and kept inside the Devarani garbhagṛha. When entire, it would have stood taller than the Paśupati image. It shows the same rounded contours, thick nose, fleshy lower lip in vogue at Jethani, and does not seem to belong to Devarani (Figs. 89, 420). The same observation would appear to be true about a rudragaṇa on a detached base found at Devarani southeast. While the rounded limbs of the rudragaṇa with sarpahāra conform with the Jethani style, no image with proportions answering the footmarks carved on this gaṇabase has been found at Devarani. The sculpted wall slabs found at Devarani (Figs. 167-68, 196, 360-61) seem to prefer an arrangement in tiers (e.g. Sūrya, Yamunā, Sarasvatī sculptures) to the monolithic sculptures of Jethani. They also appear to have been scaled down and tailored to the relatively narrow Devarani staircase. Though damaged almost beyond recognition, the huge dvārapāla images on Jethani east (Figs. 351-52), with broad shoulders enhanced by massed hairlocks, the two fragments of a Jethani west slab, carved with the profile of an image, with its hand raised in abhaya, the two fragments of a head and legless image, carrying an image bearing lady, found on the Jethani southeast wall (Fig. 395), and a samabhaṅga image with two defaced attendants, on Jethani southeast, stand ten to fourteen feet tall (Figs. 70, 72), and belong to the same idiom. Among the smaller Jethani images, the Bhairava Bhairavī, Hara Gaurī mithunas (Figs. 353-54), and dancing gaṇa or paraśu bearing figures on the south lintels show a preference for the round heads, powerful, heavy bodies, squared off proportions of the larger group of Jethani images.

However, at Jethani itself, this impression of overwhelming size, strength or monumentality is modified by a burgeoning tendency towards attenuation, elongation and verticalization, which goes with a certain flattening and hardening of the body (Figs. 295-301). Slightly smaller in size, these images from Jethani south walls and pillars stand in dvibhaṅga. While the waist is usually curved above their straight leg, it is steepened above their flexed leg. Their chest and waist are slender, and their legs long, tapering, separated by a paryastaka, which clings to the straight leg. Of these, one female image, still standing on Jethani southeast wall (Fig. 301), and a corresponding female image, lying prone on Jethani southeast (Figs. 299-300), display heavy breasts and hips on their long body, and have oval heads, with peaked jaṭā. Of the two male images, one with, the other without a head, recovered also from Jethani south, the headless image retains a uttarīya crossed at the waist, in straight diagonals, which point to the sharp, sheer contours of the body. Among other small, fragmentary sculptures recovered from Jethani south (Figs. 295-99, 343, 349), the broken head and abraded bust of an āmrabhañjikā (Fig. 305-06), four images of female attendants (one of them carrying a flower) in tribhaṅga or dvibhaṅga, without legs, arms or heads, a crowned head with a kīrtimukha crest (Fig. 429), two nāga heads, one of which is equipped also with a bust, two gaṇa heads, of which one has a bust and shows traces of female feet on its shoulder (Figs. 434-35), show a similar preference for the slender, streamlined proportions of the pillar or slab images mentioned above. They have slightly inclined, long oval heads, peaked jaṭā, āmralumbī or crest jewel, drooping eyes, and half parted lips. In women, the chest, though narrow, is burdened with heavy breasts above a sensitively modelled, swelling navel and a small, constricted waist, while the slender bust bends slightly under the weight of blossoming youth. The tapering, broad hipped thighs are hugged by a close clinging dhotī and one end of the kacchā is now pulled in between the legs and tucked behind.

MIDDLE MEAN BETWEEN STYLES AT DEVARANI

The Devarani figures, in general, adapt a mean between the massive, broad proportions and the trimmed down, slender proportions used at Jethani. The Śiva in samabhaṅga or the rock embedded proto-Śiva bust in Bilaspur museum (Fig. 360), the tribhaṅga Śiva with arms and legs missing (Fig. 357) and the defaced Mārtaṇḍa Bhairava, both lying in front of Devarani (Figs. 356, 362), retain the broad, powerful frame of Jethani. However, once these Devarani figures are compared with the large, standing male images of Jethani or the seated Kārtikeya, they betray a different idiom in the steepening of the curve, outlining their chest, a more abrupt, horizontal division of their waist, thighs and legs, a greater elongation of their heads, and a suppression of the pulsing breath, which seems to dilate the chest of Jethani images. The flexed lower trunk of a large Devarani image in the Bilaspur museum (Fig. 363), and the trunk of the small Gaṅgādhara Śiva image on Devarani door lintel (Fig. 179) demonstrate similar proportions, slimmer than the Jethani colossi but broader than the smaller pillar or side wall figures of Jethani. When we compare the headless body of an atibhaṅga Śiva in tiger skin in front of Devarani (Fig. 343), with a tribhaṅga, ūrdhvaliṅga Śiva in tiger skin at Jethani east (Fig. 349), we find that the Śiva from Devarani front has a sharper, more rectilinear contour at the transition from the waist to the legs, or around the thighs, and is rendered in a harder, drier style.

The narrow, heavy breasted bust, and the tapering, heavy hipped trunk of Jethani female images (Figs. 302, 353-54) seems to have inspired the hourglass torso of Lakṣmī or the river goddesses (Figs. 307, 309, 312) on Devarani maṇḍapa wall, and on antarāla or maṇḍapa door jambs. The waist, wilting under the burden of the breasts, the clinging substance of the cloth revealing the curves of the limbs, are also similar. However, as in the male, so in these female images, Devarani adapts a middle way. It does not make its figures either as squat or square as the Bhairava Bhairavī or Hara Gaurī couples on Jethani south lintels, or as slender and girlish as the Jethani ladies occupying the south pillars or their attendants. The smooth envelope of flesh on the waist, belly or navel of the Jethani figures is interrupted by occasional horizontal creases (as in the figure lying southeast of Jethani). It is now modulated by several creases moving in different directions. A softly incised line of the nīvibandha bifurcates the upper and the lower trunk of the Jethani (in tiger skin) Śiva or Kārtikeya. It survives in the river goddesses or attendants of Devarani antarāla door jamb. However, in the Devarani (Jethani) Śiva in tiger skin, this bifurcation is made sharper and more emphatically visible by the broad cincture, and by the bulging flesh of the belly. The roughly incised, regular rows of diagonal lines in the dhotīs of the Jethani images survive in the dhotīs of the river goddesses in Devarani maṇḍapa walls, or in the upper garments of the rock embedded Śiva bust in Bilaspur museum. However, in the uttarīyas or dhotis of the river goddesses or their attendants on the Devarani door jambs, the lines meander, radiate, curve in and out, marching in step with the curves of the body. The broad, rectangular sheet of the uttarīya, carved with parallel lines, on the Bhairava of the Jethani south lintel, or the heavier swags of uttarīya, wrapped around the arms of the prone Jethani southeast female figure, give way to thinner, more transparent and delicate pieces of cloth on the river goddesses, Gaurī or Lakṣmī at Devarani. This preference for finer cloth at Devarani is not without precedent at Jethani, being anticipated by the gossamer fine substance of the jacket, threaded together across the bust, or by the cloth, lapping across the thighs of the Jethani goddess or Vṛkṣakā (Figs. 297-98) in Bilaspur museum. The raised, curved lines of flying uttarīya, described behind images at Jethani, are given up at Devarani for incised, stiff and schematic lines. The kacchā, tightly wound between the legs and tied at the back, or hanging in heavy folds at Jethani, is replaced at Jethani by meticulously looped, daintily formed tab ends at the edge of the waist, from which fine lines spread out in a ripple.

Gaṇas

The gaṇas at Jethani occupy pillars on slab bases (Figs. 494-95), while gaṇas at Devarani (Figs. 196, 497, 499) occupy narrative panels in the door jamb or the parikara of carved figure slabs. The Jethani gaṇas generally have large, round, heavy heads, pushed deep into the trunk. A low forehead, short chin, thick, broad dilated nostrils, large bulging eyes, a downward gaze and low sunk tear ducts, deep dug corners of mouth, set off by full and fleshy lips, distinguish their faces (Figs. 417, 421-22) . Their pursed lips part occasionally in a smile when the burden, being a beautiful woman, is pleasant (Figs. 493, 495). When the burden is heavy and a drudgery, their mouths open in a grimace with turned down corners and bared teeth (Figs. 476-77, 491). Sometimes their lips are open, panting in exertion, and sometimes their lips close over clenched teeth. The heavy line of their eyebrows is puckered into an occasional frown, while the muscle is corded over the nose between the eyebrows (Fig. 486). The flabby chest or belly swing like a tapering pitcher in standing images, and, in seated images, the chest is folded in layers above the pendulous belly, which flops and spreads itself on the ground between the legs (Figs. 476-81, 487) . The thick sash of cloth, tied below the chest, the single heavy bangle, the intertwined coils of the snake on the chest, huge animal ears or earlobes, elongated by large kuṇḍalas, frilly curls and cascading locks of hair, adorn the heaving, gyrating gaṇas (Figs. 487, 490, 494). Their jutting heads, mounted on bodies thrown out of plumb, furnish stable anchors in the bewildering variety of gestures and postures. The flying swags of the uttarīyas, legs of the flying gaṇas and the profiles of the gaṇa heads are often curved like bows in answering rhythms (Figs. 200, 479-80, 485) .

Unlike the Jethani gaṇas, Devarani gaṇas appear as dwarfish participants and witnesses in the drama unfolding in front of them in the narrative panels. They move towards, look at or attend upon Hara Gaurī gaming or at dalliance (Figs. 176-77, 497-99), mill around the river goddesses as sagaraputras (Figs. 173-74, 446-47), crowd around rock embedded Hara Gaurī (Figs. 193, 355) and Mārtaṇḍa Bhairava as vidyādharas, carrying flower baskets, (Figs. 196, 500) and accompany Kubera as nidhis (Fig. 168). They are usually shown wearing an incised drawer, and though their belly hangs out over it and their arms and legs are still plump and their faces round, the rippling or corded flesh fold of Jethani, separating the belly from the chest, are no longer in evidence. In the flower bearing or dwarfish figures, looking out from behind the principal deity, the body remains chubby without being flabby. The mithunas (Fig. 170), installed on the Devarani door jamb opposite the Hara Gaurī mithuna, are overtaken by a thinning and elongation of arms and legs, and a straightening of the curved, bowlike profiles, so usual at Jethani. The heads of the mithunas become positively oval, losing the rounded contours of the Jethani gaṇas.

Ascetics

The striking feature about the Tala gaṇas is their distinctive, individual personalities and almost portraitlike qualities. The same disregard for uniformity and convention is expressed in the modelling of the ascetic heads. A Jethani ascetic head (Pl. 33) shows a master's unerring instinct for capturing the relentless character of an ascetic, unsparing to himself or to others. It is very different from the olympian aloofness of the Jethani colossi, and is forcefully direct. The head of the ascetic is a cadaverous mask, in which the flesh has all but dissolved due to wasting penance. The bony rectangles of the forehead, the cheeks and the chin, come down in steps. The deep sunk sockets of eyes are overhung by cliff like eyebrows. The cheeks are hollow, triangular. The depressed chin is flanked by two bony bumps. The glare of the wide open, seemingly sightless eyes is accentuated by the sharp curves of the eyebrows. The cruel, thin line of the compressed lips is emphasized by the fine honed edge of the whiskers. The out thrust bone of the throat is aligned with the steep, precipitous incline of the nose and the vertical parting of the jaṭā. The thin, incised strands of the angular beard hang like a flesh fold over the throat. The firmly and deftly cut volumes of the cylindrical, tightly bound jaṭā create a frame which forcefully thrust the rectangular death skull into view. Altogether, it is an image of searing severity and rugged strength, which are mollified by an expression of intense and poignant suffering.

None of the Devarani ascetics matches the stark perfection of this deathless image of asceticism. The seated ascetic with drawn up knees, on a polycephalous nāga base (Figs. 460-63), recovered in fragments from the Devarani doorsteps, has a fulness of body which, but for the kaupīna (loin cloth), would not quite go with the conically formed head of an ascetic, supposedly stript of flesh by ceaseless penance. The gentle slope of the forehead contrasts with the sudden drop of the Jethani ascetic's forehead. The voluminous knot of its beard is very different from the stabbing edge of the Jethani ascetic's beard. The horizontal strips of its whiskers, outlined against full cheeks, fail to capture the gaunt angularity of the Jethani ascetic head. The garland bearing ascetic, accompanied by a disciple, carved on another Devarani slab (Figs. 458-

59, 463) also has a head modelled like the Devarani door step ascetic. Its long forehead and chin, short and flat nose muster an expression of crude hauteur, and misunderstand the ascetic fervour of the Jethani head. The fifteen ascetics in the Devarani door jamb soffit (Fig. 182) also adapt the crouching posture and fulness of limbs of the ascetic recovered from the Devarani doorsteps. Interestingly enough, a potbellied, headless, legless, smoothly modelled Jethani figure, with both hands raised in abhaya (Fig. 457), may offer an alternative model of an ascetic, which does not find an echo at Devarani.

The utterance of the word aum svasti or siddham as benediction, in Pāṇḍuvaṁśī inscriptions issued from Sirpur, use of the word udakapūrvam for gift provide a context for the svastivācana by ascetics in the circular medallion in the soffit of the door jamb in Devarani temple, opposite the panel, showing rejuvenation of his ancestors by Sāgara, using udakapūrvam tarpaṇa, with the waters of Gaṅgā in her descent.

Lions

The Tala sculptor delights in the depiction of animals, and, of all animals, the lion is his favourite. The lion appears in its full fledged form only at the pillar bases of Jethani (Fig. 544). Its round head, mantled by waves of mane, and equipped with hollow, drooping globular eyes, jutting cheekbones, curved jaws, parted in a growl, furrowed forehead, eyebrows joined in a horizontal bridge over the nose, look natural enough. However, the frozen quality of its bulging chest, its column like forelegs, its crudely shaped paws, or its weak hind quarters do not meet the expectation roused by its head. On the other hand, when the lion prances out of the ghaṭa on a Jethani south pillar (Figs. 236-38) and holds a floral rhizome or a pearl chain, its body is curved, contoured or modelled with greater sensitivity to the tactile life of its flesh. The lion heads, compressed between pillars or wheels, on Jethani south stair flanks (Fig. 54), show the hollows and bulges as faithfully as the heads of the lions at pillar base. The forelegs and paws of lions in siṁhagavākṣas are loosely and naturally draped over one another, and are provided with creased muscles and sharp claws, with an eye for the natural form. Yet, one can notice the artificial curve given to the lion heads, to accommodate them between the rotating wheels. On the other hand, the siṁhagavākṣa design is abbreviated to insert two lion heads on a Jethani south lintel, to suppress their forelegs, to place their heads directly over their paws, and to flatten out their heads, for artificially adapting them to the shallow space of the panels. In a dilution of the organic form, the bulging globes of the eyes of the siṁhagavākṣa lions, are flattened and interminably stretched out in the lintel lions. In these lintel lions, their jutting cheekbones are reduced to curved incisions. The hollow of the gaping jaws is replaced in them by a mere indication of the teeth, gums or a tongue, forked out in three parts. In spite of the partial negation of the natural form, the sense of volume is captured even in the low relief lintel lions (Fig. 197). Volume is prominent also in the foliate lion head on another Jethani south lintel fragment (Fig. 547). In this head, the leaves are arranged with deliberate asymmetry, acknowledging their movement, irregular sizes and shapes in nature, but the hollows and bulges of the lion head are now artificially organized by subtly manipulating the life of the leaves. The loosely draped mane on the shoulders on a Narasiṁha on the same lintel fragment, the tiered locks and lotus boss on another Narasiṁha head, architectural fragments recovered from Jethani stupa (Figs. 544-47), are treated with sensitivity to their organic shape, while the locks of a broken, horned muktāgrāsa are artificially rendered as serried rows of triangles. Though stylization is the order of the day in the description of the lions at Jethani, it is modified in diverse degrees, by a commitment to the natural form.

The lion is a less prominent feature at Devarani. It is rendered consistently in a more stylized manner. A small architectural fragment, for example, shows a seated image, with its feet borne up by a lion with human hands and a mane less head (Fig. 548), in which the undulations are shown without respecting the underlying structure of the bone. It has unnaturally bulging eyes, ringed by muscular cords, and looks more monstrous than human or leonine. The heads of the horned lions, forming the flanks of the siṁhāsana are also unduly elongated, giving them a comical look. In fact, they almost look like the fish, flanking the lion head, in the seat of Kubera in Devarani door jamb (Fig. 169). The kīrtimukhas spouting the floral strands on the Devarani stambhaśākhā (Fig. 161) are also much less natural than Jethani. Stylized, trefoil floral designs spring from between their ridged eyebrows. Their cheeks are puffed up into balloons rather than fleshy bulges, and a horizontal ridge marks their cheekbones. With the two magnificent foliate kīrtimukhas on the door jamb surrounds (Figs. 167-68, 171-72), stylization reaches its culmination at Devarani. The rigorously symmetrical organization of these faces using similar leaves, flowers and buds is quite a departure from the Jethani practice. The variety of elements, shapes and combinations, used in the kīrtimukha on the left surround, is much greater, and the rendering of volume much more accomplished than in the kīrtimukha on the right surround. However extraordinary the impact of such artificially suggested volumes, the impression of geometric regularity is not negated.

Varāhas and Gajas

Though these are heads of dissimilar animals, a comparison of the similarly tapering head of the elephant and bull Nandī (Fig. 565) on Jethani north, or of the varāha head from Jethani in the Bilaspur museum (Fig. 567) with the ram head of the gaṇa (Figs. 561-62) on Devarani step front, or the Gaṇeśa head on Devarani west (Fig. 528), shows the slight elongation and hardening that has come over the Devarani heads, subduing the soft, swelling planes around the eyes. In the Jethani varāha, the dilated nostrils are executed with a delicacy and softness, which are not captured in the Devarani ram head. The curved top of the elephant head at Jethani (Fig. 66) is given up for a flat-topped head in the Devarani Gaṇeśa (Fig. 528).

Makaras

The makaras are the most frequent at Tala after the lions. At Jethani, experiments are made with several types, apparently according to the architectural context. In the tetrafacial pillar bases (Figs. 46-47, 56, 249), a deliberate archaism is the logical corollary of the use of the makara as a basal element. It is modelled with a flat precipitous forehead, almost flat sides, and slightly moulded front. The curled elephant trunk, or the division of jaws are described by harsh, linear incisions, radiating out from the centre, and only occasionally by a rolled moulding. The bevelled eyes jut out near the top of the blunt head like powerful headlights of a sinister looking submarine. And yet, the softly rendered, flipped back ears, the careful alignment of the down curving horns with upward curving fangs, the relaxed, easy contour of the moulded front, or of the tongue hanging out, announce mastery over the techniques of modelling, and an intentional use of rectilinear accents.

Another type is seen in the makaras with human heads (Pl. 24; Figs. 57-58, 532) at the Jethani south door jamb. The makara has now a fully developed body, with a gently and delicately modelled human arm and hand, earring, and a pensive, meditative, fleshy human face with a divided chin, canopied by the makara snout. In spite of these concessions to modelled form, the eyes nudging close to the flat crown of the head, the sharply outlined foliate tail and the compressed rectangular block of the body suggest, once again, a tendency for the use of the makara as a basal slab.

It is only in the Jethani south and west pillars that the makara is allowed to develop more or less fully with a curved body, foliate tail, fins, curled elephant trunk, and swimming legs (Figs. 239-40). Though liberation from the necessity to serve as an architectural base has enabled it now to float free, the freedom is again carefully restricted by the enclosing boundary of the darpaṇa on the pillar.

A fourth type is represented by the two makaras below Varuṇa (Fig. 346). No trace of the deliberate archaism remains in the single, sweeping, dynamic movement, with which these makaras have flung themselves on their back, and twisted around to look up to Varuṇa; in the thick fleshy folds which have formed below their jaws or on their throat as a result of this violent movement; or in their thick, curled elephant snouts or softly modelled upturned flats of feet, which emphasize the tremendous, upward urgency of their movement. Joined into a single, tightstrung bowlike curve, and yet equipped with irregular bulging muscles, appropriate to two bodies rising successively from the sea at different moments, these makaras are executed with a knowledge of the behaviour and movement of such marine creatures, which was deliberately suppressed while using them at pillar bases.

At Devarani also the makaras are not made in one uniform style. The change from Jethani pillar base makaras is evident in the makara praṇālas (Figs. 536, 539) used in Devarani. The headlight eyes, the divided human chin of Jethani makara remain. However, the moulded and rolled snout of the Devarani makara is marked inside by incisions or by irregular curves. The snout is raised, prolonged and brought in line with the long, sliding slope of the makara's throat, giving it a more angular and awkward look than Jethani.

Another type of makaras can be seen in the darpaṇas of the Devarani maṇḍapa pillars (Figs. 268-72). Unlike the Jethani makaras, which show some incipient and minimal foliate elements in their tails, the Devarani makaras sprout foliate elements all over and around themselves, virtually choking their background. The sweeping and gliding motion of a makara is created at Jethani by carefully modelled postures. At Devarani motion is communicated to the frilly vegetal flourishes springing from all parts of the makara, turning it into a dynamic decorative design. From deliberate 'archaism', we thus arrive at deliberate 'mannerism'.

Flora

In the description of flowers, leaves and plants, as in human or animal figures, Jethani stresses clarity of natural shape, tangible volume and movement in response to the wind or water. Even while using these as decorative designs, Jethani shows them in large and distinctive sizes, and does not intermesh or merge them in such a way as to make them indistinguishable from one another. The fulness of the lotus buds above Varuṇa (Figs. 347-48), or of the mango fruits clustered above an āmrabhañjikā (Fig. 306), show an unmistakable feeling for volume. The lotus petals in the medallions, or the pillar slabs beside the crouching gaṇa at the south door, in the sahasradala padma of the vitāna fragment, lying to the north, swell and dip, buffeted, as it were, by water. A rippling, simmering line goes vibrating through the spines of these petals, visibly ruffling their entire surface (Fig. 258). The distinct shapes of flowers and leaves are delineated without much distortion in the Jethani south pillar darpaṇas, or in the several spiral garlands wound around the Jethani west or east pillars (Figs. 243, 247, 252). The lotus petals covering the head of Varuṇa (Fig. 348), āmrabhañjikā (Fig. 306), Narasiṁha or lion (Fig. 546-47), the padmapṛṣṭha moulding above the gaṇa bases of Jethani south pillars (Figs. 477, 479, 484), are accommodated to the shape of the head of the figures, or to the sloping side of the slab. The lotus leaves invading the face, head or hair of a kīrtimukha on a Jethani south lintel, the tail of makaras on Jethani west pillars, or the armlets, wristlets or crowns of Jethani figures (Figs. 470, 547) retain their natural sway and life. The lotus rhizome expresses its urge for luscious, abundant growth through thick winding stems and substantial flowers, carved in high relief on the Varuṇa image pillars (Figs. 259-60). It expresses the same urge in shallow relief in the meander on the stambhaśākhā of Jethani south door jamb (Fig. 262). The floral tips of the tails of the udyata siṁhas on the Jethani south pillars offer their inside for inspection in a natural perspective. Everywhere, the fruits, leaves, buds, petals or creepers show curvilinear contours, created by their own weight or direction of movement. Nowhere, even in the flowers of the garlands, offered in symmetrical rows on pillars for frontal view, symmetrization has been allowed to stifle the prolific life of the plant world.

At Devarani, a continuing commitment to the volume, clarity, distinguishability of the floral elements can be discerned in their descriptions on the door jamb, pillar fragments, canopy, ornament or headdress of human figures, in fluttering lotus petals above and below the maṇḍapa wall river goddesses (Figs. 158, 191, 312). However, at Jethani, in both shallow and high relief, the sway of fruits, full of sap, the natural layers of petals or movement of a creeper are sought more effectively. At Devarani, the floral bands ejected from grāsamukhas show vertical rows of flowers and vegetal loops, hanging rigid and lifeless, schematically uniform in size and shape, without any variation in pace or direction (Figs. 248, 250-51). The leaves in these bands are more conical, and the edges of petals are raised higher and made sharper than Jethani. Because of the greater miniaturization and angularization of every constituent element, the floral designs at Devarani give out a more metallic, glittering sheen than Jethani. The leafy forms of the door jamb kīrtimukhas (Figs. 171-72) insist on a stricter clarity and regularity of pattern than in the Jethani lintel kīrtimukha (Fig. 197). These are thus reduced from more organic, live shapes evenly bathed in light, to stylized masks, infested with valleys and ridges, full of light and shadow. A comparison of the āmralumbī above the Jethani āmrabhañjikā and the rockembedded Devarani proto-Śiva bust (Figs. 359-60) reveals how the leaves and fruits at Jethani are slightly separated from one another, and animated with individual life and movement, and, how at Devarani, the fruits are clustered and leaves are joined by incised lines, to hang down in motionless masses. Even in the use of floral elements for ornament, large lotus petals or flowers form independent caps for Jethani heads. But Devarani figures have a mass of flowers woven into the hair like ornamental patterns.

Narration

At Jethani, the sculpture is larger in scale, heavier in volume, and the figures are displayed graphically, singly or in twos and threes, on the surface plane, without any attempt to reach after depth effect or chiaroscuro. The narration is not continuous in the figural panels (Figs. 197-200). The gaṇas, makaras and figures, arranged on different sides of the tetrafacial pillars and wall slabs establish a lively discourse among themselves with a variety of gestures, postures and expressions (Figs. 42-52). However, this discourse is broken and syncopated by mutually asymmetrical postures of gaṇas or principal figures, and is not continuous from one pillar or wallslab to the next. In the Devarani door jamb, the Gaṅgādhara Śiva panels on the lower lintel are also arranged like the Jethani south lintel panels to offer graphic descriptions (Figs. 178-81). However, these panels are thematically linked with the abhiṣeka of Lakṣmī on the upper lintel, and with the descent of Ganges on the lower lintels. The figures of Bhagīratha or Gaṅgā are repeated in this continuous narration, sometime in the same panel. Moreover, in the Devarani door jamb panels, including the panels on the upper lintel, the figures are organized in crowded compositions, graded in successive planes, the larger and more important figures being disposed in front, the smaller and less important ones being oversected and foreshortened behind. The convergent movement towards the centre in the Gajalakṣmī lintel, the divergent degrees of diagonal movement, rising and subsiding in waves in the lateral surrounds, force some figures out, withdraw others inside, and show some fully, others only partially (Figs. 173-74). This introduces a variety of volumes and shapes, rhythmically interknit, and modelled in varying degrees of light and shade, unlike the fewer shapes displayed on the shallow, frontal plane in Jethani lintels. The continuous, flowing narrative is thus substituted at Devarani for the selfcontained, closed descriptions of Jethani.

THEORIES OF EXTERNAL INFLUENCE

A correct understanding of the context for the development of the style of sculpture at Tala is bound up with a correct understanding of the development of Central Indian sculpture in the late 5th and 6th century AD. Such understanding can be acquired by reference to the sculpture itself, rather than by reference to dynastic, patriotic, literary or iconographic considerations external to the sculpture. It is not possible, for example, to fit the Tala style into R.D. Banerji's theory of a national revival in Central India under the influence of the Eastern Indian school of Banaras, which is supposed to have adapted linear and abstract forms by late 5th century in rejection of the 'foreign' preference of Kuṣāṇa (late 1st to 3rd century AD) Mathura for physical volume.[1] Thus, though he discovers a climax at Bhūmarā in the progress to the Banaras ideal, he finds the Central Indian preference for full, overdeveloped busts of the aboriginal type as contradictory of the slender Sarnath type.[2] Nor, for that matter, is it possible to fix the late 5th early 6th century Central Indian sculpture as a stage in the progressive linearisation of the plastic urge in Gupta sculpture from Mathura to Sarnath, seen by Kramrisch. She does suggest that Central India experiences in this period shares the same broad Indian development, in which 'innervation', confined to pre-classical Mathura to plants and animals, is 'inflected' into the human body at classical Sarnath, 'transsubstantiating' it.[3] However, she finds Central Indian sculpture dragging behind in the general development, to remain close to Mathura.[4]

The corollary thesis of a socio-economic development, corresponding to, and mirrored in developments in literature or sculpture, also does not fit the situation of Tala. Goetz, for example, notices a gradual degeneration of the Gupta 'nāgarika' idiom into effeminacy, mannerism or passive melancholy, due to a substitution of aristocratic and priestly ideals for middle class ideals. However, while he finds evidence of this in the 6th century in the ornate 'Gauḍa' literary style or 'tired', 'overrefined' sculpture of the east, he detects influence of the 'Vidarbha' style in the simplicity of western Indian sculpture. Assuming that Tala sculpture is simple, which it is not, Goetz does not really use his theory to explain his long sequence of Gupta art from AD 320 to AD 800, in which Tala could have found its place.[5] Harle, like Goetz, finds the 'late Gupta' style as being characterised by attenuation and idiosyncrasies, and quotes Fahien and the language of kāvya (poetry) in inscriptions, to reflect on the 'euphuism' and 'mannerism' of late Gupta sculpture at Māndāsor, Deogarh and eastern Madhya Pradesh.[6]

Behind this view has been the steady preconception that art of the late 5th, early 6th century in Central India, including sculpture, is really a later aberration of Gupta art, and that this aftermath of Gupta art, like Gupta art itself, is conditioned by Gupta dynastic influence on art. Occasionally, Vākāṭaka influence has been substituted for Gupta influence in this perception, denying any autonomous regional development, or, when conceding such development, denying it independent artistic merit or validity. This is evident from Joanna Williams's characterisation of much of Central Indian art, including that of Tala, as Gupta art after the Guptas, and of Tala art per se as a provincial, tribal formulation of the imperial, oecumenical style. She fortifies the prevailing theory of growing abstraction in Central Indian art at the end of the 5th century by suggesting a replacement of 'martial' or 'power' images by ascetic images, and displacement of the ascendancy of Mathura style by that of Sarnath, with change in royal preoccupations. She therefore finds a declining naturalism and growing stylization to be the hallmark of the later or post-Gupta style, establishing a pattern which does not fit Tala. In fact, the wasted, cadaverous ascetic skull from Jethani exudes, if anything, an impression of superhuman power.[7]

In an indirect manner, Walter Spink links the late 5th century developments in Central India at places like Bāgh, Deogarh, Nācnā or Bhūmarā with a shift of Vākāṭaka dynastic patronage from Ajanta to these places. For this he uses uncertain literary evidence, isolated inscriptions, and what he sees as the development of architectural motifs at Ajanta.[8] He asserts a pattern of increasing compositional complexity on the model of what appears to him to be the metropolition Ajanta style, a pattern which is not worked out by him from one site to the next in Central India.

No doubt, an understandng of Tala sculpture has suffered because of this. Scholars like Krishna Deva and Stadtner have suggested Gupta, Vākāṭaka or south Indian influence on Tala sculpture without comparing objects and without explaining the unique elements at Tala. The mere absence of a strong local dynasty to which works of art can be directly attributed, is no evidence of external inspiration for Tala sculpture. We cannot confuse extent of dynastic rule with depth of aesthetic experience, which, in the case of Tala, may be the result of deeper empathy than in other contemporary sites.[9] Nor, because of this intense individual expression, can we forget that the essential aspect of this art is a function of its own space and time, rather than an imperfect memory of more accomplished dynastic styles.[10] In assessing Tala as a progeny of its space and time, it is more useful to use the style of making motifs as our guides, rather than the motifs themselves, which, as we shall see in our comparative study of Tala architecture, are constant in Indian art and reappear in unique configurations.[11]

SIMULTANEOUS MEMORIES OF VOLUMETRIC AND LINEAR STYLES

A comparison of the Tala sculpture with 5th and 6th century sculpture in north Indian sites quickly reveals the inadequacy of theories which would see in Central Indian or Tala art a unilinear development towards linearisation, elongation, attenuation, abstraction, breakdown of proportions, exaggeration or distortion, effeminacy or over-refinement, or a vulgar surfeit of ornament, gestures and postures, choking form and expression. In its ambivalence between the volumetric and linear, Tala recalls both Mathura and Sarnath, often in the same figures. The ambivalence is greater at Jethani than at Devarani, and, when it comes to a choice, both the temples share the Central Indian preference for massed volume over linear angles. On the other hand, in Central India itself, Tala sculpture, in spite of being informed by the Sarnath experience which affects sites like Nācnā, Bhūmarā (Figs. 204, 207-08, 383, 410, 440-41, 444), Marhiā, harks back emphatically to the early fifth century accent of Udayagiri, Māndāsor, Khoh (Figs. 380, 388, 439, 443) on powerfully rendered volumes. As such, the Tala style continues to be characterised by a careful observation, secular temper and humanism, undimmed by the lofty spiritualism of late fifth century Sarnath, or by the increasing schematization or symmetrization, which overtakes sixth century sites outside Central India, including the great centres of Mathura and Sarnath. And, then, as our study of the situation of Tala in the evolution of subsequent architecture will demonstrate, its ambivalence becomes part of the idiom of Dakṣiṇa Kośala sculpture, with the same continuing predilection for volume. Imperceptibly, the Tala style contributes its share to the formation of the powerful, plastic modelling of Odisha, and becomes part of the heritage of the cave sculpture in the Deccan or western India.

The elongation of the bust, legs and head of some of the pillar and side slab figures of Jethani reminds us of late fifth century Sarnath Buddhas (Fig. 390) and Bodhisattvas.[12] A similar elongation characterises the figures at Nācnā, Bhūmarā (Fig. 383), Marhiā, Khoh (Fig. 443), and some figures at Deogarh and Sindursi.[13] The use of magnāṁśuka, or clinging 'wet drapery', cleft by hard, sharply outlined legs, indicated by a faint outline at the waist, or keen, jagged edges on the legs, in the Buddhas in Sarnath Museum or Kṛṣṇa Govardhana in the Vārānasi Kalā Bhavan Museum,[14] find reflection in a headless Devarani (Jethani) Śiva in tiger skin, and in the trunk of a Śaiva dvārapāla, truncated from the waist (Figs. 343, 357). The fine, simmering lines of semi transparent cloth across the chest or thighs of a Sarnath Maitreya or a Kauśāmbī museum Buddha in bhūmisparśamudrā[15] parallel use of similar conventions in the cloth of the Tala river goddesses, Lakṣmī or their attendants. The soft, smooth, accentless modelling of Sarnath, negates the irregular surface of the flesh, dissolves it to near nothingness on the frame, and dissimulates sex. It is parallelled not only in the *Rāmāyaṇa* figures, Hara-Gaurī or a seated couple from Nācnā, the seated Hara Gaurī in dalliance or at chausar in a Gaḍhvā pillar (Figs. 401-02, 404), a Hara Gaurī in Kailāsa panel from the Bhitargāon temple,[16] but also by the amorous Hara Gaurī in the Devarani door jamb or the head and bustless figure of a girl from Jethani holding a filmy uttarīya across her thighs in the Bilaspur museum (Fig. 401). The low, finespun foliate relief on the Jethani south door jamb, the fastidious exactitude of the foliate designs on Jethani pillars (Figs. 243, 258) also convey memories of the organic and sophisticated lotus designs in the haloes of Sarnath Buddhas (Fig. 390).[17] The elongation, hardening of flesh, the more rectilinear descent of contour, the compression of frame and suppression of the sense of arrested breath that overtake Tala modelling are evident from a comparison of the Jethani head crowned by a kīrtimukha crest (Figs. 429, 443) with a fifth century Ekamukha liṅga from Khoh or a Cleveland Museum head with a similar crest. The growing abstraction is seen in the eyes, which, at Jethani, are no longer outlined by fleshy, subtly curved, hooded eyelids, or, in the cheeks, which are afflicted by desiccation.[18] A similar change is also visible in the head of the Jethani āmrabhañjikā, when it is compared with a 5th century female head, with a leafy and floral crown from Mathura and the head of a lady from Mānsar[19] (Figs. 306, 452). In this case, the rhythmic correspondence of down dipping curves in the butterfly curls, eyebrows, eyes, nose bridge or lips, so carefully organized in the Mathura head, is given up at Jethani for a more vertical slope.

On the other hand, the complete dematerialisation, abstraction, linearization, attenuation and elongation which are the hall-mark of the Sarnath style (Fig. 390) in the late phase, are never fully accepted in Central India and are accepted even less at Tala. The relatively pallid forms of Nācnā with a delicate, wan grace, and a quiet, subdued mood of introspection (Figs. 404, 410), or the squat, lumpy shape of Garuḍa of Eran capital are both renounced at Tala for mighty dvārapāla and Śiva figures, full of pent up power and vehemence. Though the implacable frontality of Mathura Buddha figures has given way to a 'praxitilean dehanchement' at Tala, the lithe, soaring, weightless quality of the Sarnath stance is held in check by heavy, somewhat sluggish, though firmly planted legs. The attenuation and elongation in some of the Tala figures are offset by wide shoulders and hips. The robe, though more transparent and bodyhugging than before, expresses its volume in the raised edge of cloth, the bunched up or flying uttarīya, paryastaka or kaccha. The huge heads, cascading locks, broad torque, wide shoulders of the abraded Jethani east dvārapāla or Jethani south Kārtikeya still remind us of the 5th century standing Narasiṁha (Figs. 350, 555) from Eran.[20] The round fleshy form of a truncated Jethani gaṇa head, or the large male head, probably from Jethani (Figs. 417, 420), recovered from inside Devarani temple, not only offer a drier, harder and more abstracted version of the fifth century Mathura head in the Cleveland Museum or the 5th century Gosnāwell, Mathura Ardhanāriśvara, but, at least in terms of powerfully expressed volumes, evoke faint memories of 2nd and 3rd century Mathura heads.[21]

Similarly, the flexed figure from Devarani, cut off from the waist and the torso of Jethani Śivas in tiger skin (Figs. 343, 349) not only give a dry and still version of the dvārapāla with paraśu in the Udayagiri Sanakānika Cave No. 6, or of the headless Mathura image in Los Angeles County Museum, but also offer faint memories of a second century AD headless male torso from Timulgiri, Andhra Pradesh.[22] The subtle modulation of flesh, specially of the balls of the knees in the Udayagiri or Mathura image, the soft rendering of their paryastaka, or of the curved edges of their cloth, the restlessness of the body planes or the frilly robe of the Timulgiri image have made way for a harder, more rarefied surface, stiffer cloth folds and sharper outlines at Tala, but the overpowering sense of volume never leaves Tala.

In terms of lateral expansion, emphasized by broad flaring arms, dilated chest, spread out legs of the main image, and by the expanded wings and chest of the bird vehicle, the Jethani Kārtikeya is comparable with the early fifth century Mathura image of the anointing of Kumāra. It recalls the forceful, spread out forms of the late fourth century Vidisha Jinas, Baḍoh Pāṭhāri Vīrabhadra, 5th century AD. Nāndchānd Viṣṇu, some of the seated male figures representing zodiacal signs in the Udayagiri hilltop lotus ceiling fragment, and the Vidisha lion capital abacus in Gwalior museum, or second century Mathura Buddhas much more effectively than the relatively constricted forms of the late fifth century Bhūmarā (Figs. 381, 383). Kārtikeya, Marhiā Garūḍāsina Viṣṇu, or the Nācnā Jinas.[23] The Saumya Śiva head recovered from Devarani southeast is closer in its volumetrically rendered face and jaṭā, or in its frontality, to the Khoh ekamukhaliṅga, and to miniature sculptures, recovered in a 1987-88 excavation, than to the Bhūmarā ekamukhaliṅga head with its stringy, fussy locks, or the more drooping, prettified, rarified, slender profile of its face[24] (Figs. 432, 440, 443). In fact, if the modelling of the Khoh heads is softer, more delicate and relaxed than Tala, the feeling for plastic volume is more prominent at Tala than Bhūmarā.

Some of the enormous, damaged Jethani dvārapālas (Figs. 345, 351-52), or the sturdy Hara on the Jethani south lintel recall the transformation of the Buddha from yakṣa in a monk's clothing to a transcendant master of the law in mid-fifth century. They are robust figures in dvibhaṅga, with one hand raised, the other clutching the uttarīya below. The round head of Hara on Jethani lintel, enhanced by the jaṭāmukuṭa, resembles the round head of the early fifth century Sanchi Padmapāni (Figs. 353-54, 387).[25] It is, however, the numerous gaṇas, with their tumbling bellies, chubby, flabby arms and legs, adorned with broad and heavy uttarīyas, hāras, kuṇḍalas or graiveyakas, large heads and an amplitude of flowing locks, which provide an emphatic contrast with the late fifth century figures of Nācnā, Bhūmarā, Marhiā, Khoh on 7th century (Figs. 404, 409, 454), with their elongated busts and somewhat flat features.[26] The makaras, which are modelled with different degrees of archaism, with flat head or snout on Jethani south maṇḍapa or Devarani vedībandha are throwbacks to some Soṅkh and Jānkhāt type architectural fragments, which were sculpted with linearized makaras in the first to third centuries AD.[27] These are offered as a deliberate contrast to some of the fluently modelled makaras with Jethani Varuṇa or on Devarani pillars. The decorative preciosity of these Devarani makaras distances them equally from the stark but eloquent simplicity, naturalism or pulsing vitality of makaras at Jethani Sisdeori, Ramtek or Bhūmarā or the heavier hand at draughtsmanship of Sirpur or in later Chhattisgarh and Odisha (Pls. 23-25; Figs. 532-40, 542).

STYLE MORE 'CLASSICAL' THAN LATE-GUPTA SITES

That Tala is informed by the experience of the high Gupta phase of fifth century art is clear from the Devarani river goddesses, Hara Gaurī couple, Jethani Kārtikeya or Varuṇa. Their bodies are youthful and pliant, relaxed into placid, gently breathing expanses of robe and flesh, full of quiet power and grace. The volume and physical tension of the early fifth century has been harmonised in them with internal spiritual repose. Graceful, effortless flexion, fluid curvilinear contour, spare ornament, reticent mood, softly defined hairlocks, eyebrows or eyelids, gestures and postures, vivified with life, characterise these figures. In spite of the enlargement in the size of its figures, Tala is never quite overcome, because of its vivid sense of the 'classical' legacy, by the loss of balance or proportion which over take Mathura or Sarnath in the 6th century. Nor does Tala show phenomena like the bloated, ponderous dvārapālas or mātṛkās of 6th century Central Indian sites like Nāndchānd, or the manneristically reticulated fingers, 'vermicular' headdress, explosive drapery lines, accentuated breasts, depressed groins of 6th century Māndāsor (Figs. 385).[28] The variety in ornament or hairstyle grows, specially in the Devarani mithunas or river goddesses, but these do not ever become too coarse or too abundant, and never hide or distort the body. Gesture and scale are never substituted completely for modelling or expression. The swell of the toe, the raised edges of nails, the lines on the palms, the pulsations of flesh on the belly, the impact of breeze or wave on leaves floating in water, the simmer of movement galvanizing ornament and drapery, are reproduced infallibly and described meticulously. However, this is never done with a repetitive, fussy surfeit of detail. The gradation of planes, layering of light and shadow, ascent and descent of the compositional lines, the scintillating array of boldly cut floral ornament in the Devarani door jamb show great virtuosity, but no vulgar search for meretricious effect. The compositions are vibrant, without being restless and uncontrolled. The artistry is sophisticated and self-conscious. It avoids a blind emulation either of the dainty, fluttering belts, sashes, tab ends of drapery, or of the carefully orchestrated rhythm of poses, gestures and postures of the figural sculpture at Udayagiri and later fifth century Gupta sites like Nācnā or Bhūmarā. And, yet it remains experimental and playful without being frivolous.

The style of Tala sculpture appears to emerge directly out of developments, local to Dakṣiṇa Kośala, though it evokes memories of the shared Gupta Vākāṭaka idiom, outside Dakṣiṇa Kośala. This becomes obvious from a study of the sculptures found at Sisdeori in the 2002-3 excavation, carried out by the Directorate of Archaeology in Chhattisgarh. The stirrings of the innovative spirit of experimentation, characteristic of Tala, are evident in the iconography of Ardhanārīśvara (Fig. 426). The triple string girdle, swirls, ringing bells in the lower garment, the leafy curls in the floral clasp and jewelled band on the head on the female side, the upraised phallus, lion tail and paw, wrapped around the lower garment, the truncated moustache, matted locks on the head on the male side, the seated bull and lion heads below, the beaded garland coming out of the nostrils of the lions, are features that show deft and imaginative handling of the concept of the biune God. It anticipates the Ardhanārīśvara at Tala (Fig. 425). A figure of Kārtikeya, seated on Garuḍa, has been found, flanked by human attendants, foretelling the broad shouldered Kārtikeya figure at Tala.

The gaṇa head on leonine body, a smiling gaṇa with streaming hair, a gaṇa, head bent, hands on knees, straining forward under the load above; presages the greatly enlarged variety of gaṇas at Tala. The double or triple flexed female figures (Figs. 295-98, 307, 309) cross their feet, holding one leg straight, the other turned, wear flowers in their cascading locks, necklaces with circular pendants, garlands, made of rudrākṣa seeds, circular tāṭaṅka cakras as earrings, jewelled and conchshell girdles. Their clothes are tightly wrapped around shoulders, taken out below armpits, tucked in between legs, to be tied behind, and to fall in multiple triangular folds in front. Many of them stood on gaṇas, held by guardian figures or on horned lion heads, on one of which are visible remnants of the broken feet of a lady, adorned with serpentine foot rings, that show snakes biting and gobbling their own tails, and of Gaṅga (Figs. 475, 493, 495, 551-53). While many of these female figures, framed by mango or aśoka leaves, anticipate the dryads of Tala, one of them, framed by mayūrātapatra, anticipates the river goddess Yamunā at Tala.

If the iconography of Sisdeori (Figs. 424, 426, 503, 508, 551-53) is as daring and innovative as Tala, it also anticipates the careful observation of nature in Tala. The curled fingers, distinctly delineated nails in the feet, the emphatic clarity of the lines described on the big finger of a hand, the radiating lines of cloth folds, the minute hair strands shown below the tear ducts of the eyes, the swelling and dipping planes of thighs, cheeks, under lips, bellies, or, of the lotus petals, speak of a meticulous attention to natural detail, with which we are familiar at Tala, specially at Jethani. The attention to nature does not restrain the Sisdeori artist, as it does not restrain the Tala artist, from accentuating natural details for enhancing their impact. So, the Sisdeori lions are rendered with curved fangs, swelling chins and cheeks, bumpy foreheads, globular eyes. The male and female halves of Ardhanārīśvara are balanced and contrasted with an unabashed boldness of detail.

Despite the shared spirit of innovation and natural observation, Sisdeori comes immediately before Tala in mid-5th century in its relative restraint, and in what may be seen as an even greater fidelity to nature. The casual elegance and insouciance of the postures of the female figures is stultified in most of the Jethani figures, which gain in size, what they lose in ease. The expression and movement of gaṇas are more restrained at Sisdeori. The lion hair, the cloth folds are described at Sisdeori with cursory striations, rather than with the opulent detail of Tala. The body, the cloth, the ornament merge more easily at Sisdeori, and loud definitions of joints or under cutting are avoided. The body is smoother than Tala, with no muscular emphasis except for triple dents below breasts. It is rendered with broad, sweeping strokes, with a lighter, feathery touch. The style of Sisdeori is yet to harden into the incipient mannerism, monumentalism and verticalism of the figural sculpture of Jethani.

MEMORIES OF VIDARBHA STYLE

The surviving simplicity and strength of the Sisdeori style in mid-5th century or the Tala style in late fifth-early sixth century do, however, hark back to a manly and vigorous style in some of the fifth century Vidarbha sites nearby. The coexistence of the heavy and the lean, often in the same body, of the principal figures; the general preference for the massive and monumental in these figures; the extraordinary skill in executing the fleshy bodies of gaṇas, simultaneously filling them with power and grace; the capacity for electrifying narrative panels, and every actor in them, with surging power and movement; the sensitive and soft modelling of large volumes, never allowing them to become torpid or ponderous, are features of the Tala style, which appear to be partially a legacy of Vidarbha. The primeval force of this style has been somewhat chastened by the refining influence of the 'Gupta' classical style in Central India. However, the fullness, manly strength and vitality, secular temper and humanism, earthly joy and careful observation are never quite overcome at Tala by the etherealization, the mood of implacable austerity and spiritualism, which overtake the later Gupta style. If this is true of Central India as a whole, it is true of Tala, much more than of other late fifth-early sixth century Central Indian sites. For this reason, Tala could well be considered as a late florescence, and culmination, in an autochthonous transformation, of many of the features in early fifth century 'Gupta' style in Central India, specially in Daśārṇa, and in mid-fifth century 'Vākāṭaka' style in Vidarbha.

Three, four, eight and twelve-headed Śivas, a club-bearing ūrdhvaliṅga goat-headed Nāigameśa, a ūrdhvaliṅga gaṇādhyakṣa, a ūrdhvaliṅga, skull bearing Śiva in tiger skin, a four-headed Brahmā seated on lotus pedestal, a standing Pārvatī and a mother goddess seated on siṁhāsana (Pl. 47; Figs. 621-24, 626), recovered from Māndhal excavations[29] presage the square and heavy bodied, round-headed, laterally spread images of Tala like the Paśupati, Bhairavī, Hara Gaurī couples and a flying vidyādhara in Jethani south lintels, the Bhairava head, Varuṇa and Kārtikeya, recovered from Jethani south, a Pārvatī image found in Devarani garbhagṛha and the dwarf gaṇas, or Kubera in Jethani and Devarani (Pls. 20, 40-41; Fig. 169). The multiheaded Śivas reproduce the use of sarpa, udara and kaṭibandhas of Tala Paśupati as flesh or cloth bands, and use extra heads to push the body out into fleshy bulges. Almost all the images use multiplied human heads and bhālapaṭṭas or head bands, ekāvalī or single tier necklace, thick hair, cascading down on shoulders, or spread around the head, in diagonal strands, arrays of concentric curls or, as in the mother goddess, in heavy triangular braids, threaded with floral bands, in place of the Tala human animal combination, to enhance the broad shoulders and outspread arms, which terminate in hands, hooked at the waist like Tala. The tiered arrangement of heads in the twelve-headed Mānḍhal Śiva, used to enhance the height, is replaced in the Tala Paśupati by tiered snake locks for similar effect. The single-headed club bearing Nāigameśa or gaṇādhyakṣa share with the multiheaded Mānḍhal Śivas, Tala Paśupati or Jethani gaṇas, huge, round heads, sunk deep in wide shoulders, a low, sloping forehead, short chin, broad nose, thick lips, an wide and pendulous belly, spilling over the constricting cloth. The Pārvatī image from Mānḍhal, apart from anticipating the stocky and sturdy Pārvatī, Gaurī or Bhairavī at Tala, also shows the fine, filmy uttarīya, gliding across the breast and the waist, establishing a convention for modelling the cloth, which becomes pervasive at Tala.

Of course, because of the passage of time since Mānḍhal, the Tala style does show changes. The Tala Paśupati with its flat slab back is no longer made in the round like its Mānḍhal ancestors. No Tala image has the heavy, squared off body, emphatically delineated curves or cleft at the back, the soft, fluid, mellifluous contour dipping in and out like the Mānḍhal images. The growing complexity of Tala conception, which fuses various iconographic elements in one image, is also obvious. All the Mānḍhal bodies, in spite of their protruding bellies, are modelled more tightly, and are electric with a contained tension, which is somewhat dissipated in the slightly more amorphous modelling of Tala. The bellies of the dwarfs in Devarani door jamb panels hang out with a more angular edge, and at Jethani, the fleshfolds are often allowed to flop around with greater slackness. Compared with their Mānḍhal counterparts, some of the Tala dwarfs appear attenuated and flaccid, while others, though equally monumental and powerful, are drier and flatter.

Specific comparisons of Vidarbha and Tala gaṇas will make this point clearer. A corpulent dwarf from Nāgardhan or Mānsar,[30] and a now headless fat dwarf on a Jethani south pillar base (Figs. 481, 511), crouch in a similar manner, with hands on knees, heads sunk in chest, carrying their own weight, and the immense burden above them. The rippling curving rings and folds of flesh, which form around the tensed arms, and below the seemingly crumbling chest of the Nāgardhan gaṇa, the irregular creases in his jaṅghikā, his popping eyes, the huge mass of dishevelled hair, spilling over his shoulders, and his buckling knees, facing front, convey the strain of carrying the stupendous burden more emphatically than the Tala gaṇa, with its chubby, comparatively limp arms and body, or with its awkwardly splayed feet. Another Nāgardhan gaṇa (Fig. 515),[31] comparable with a Jethani south pillar gaṇa (Fig. 494), has tumbled over, with a leg flung in the air, and a hand clutching the ground for support, as he lifts the other hand to carry the burden above. The huge, round, tipped back head, the enormous globe of the belly, are harmonised to create an impression of overwhelming obesity, which is deliberately offset by the relatively thin, short legs, tucked below the belly, and, by the arms, stiffened to lever the body up. The Tala gaṇa is relatively flat, and does not establish a similar rhythm of bulging forms.

The early 5th century AD sculptures, excavated at Mānsar since 1977,[32] have rendered the living, pulsating, breathing body more empathetically than Tala. The kinnaras play veeṇā (Fig. 514). Gaṇas bear loads, bare (karāla) mouth, dilate eyes, and contract brows in strain. They are equipped with curved fangs, leonine mane (āyāla), ear ring, large sloping forehead, diagonal tiers or ringlets of hair, honey comb, corkscrew or snail shell curls (Pl. 21; Figs. 509-13).

Women are crowned with mango leaves, five petalled floral clasps and cascades and waves of curled tresses of hair (Figs. 452, 455). All such figures anticipate analogous figures in Tala and Dakṣiṇa Kośala. However, the swelling planes of their cheeks, rolls, folds and marks on their stomach are more emphatic at Mānsar; their out thrust lower lips and dilated nose are more vibrant with life breath; their gestures and postures are more vivid and picturesque, and characterized by greater intimacy, effortlessness and exaltation.

An instructive comparison is possible between the dwarf Śiva from Mānsar (Fig. 516)[33] and the dwarf Kubera in the Devarani door jamb. While the slight sharpening of features establishes the Mānsar dwarf as a conception later than the Nāgardhan gaṇas, it still retains the earlier skill in showing overlapping folds of flesh, cloth and jewelled strands, and conveys an impression of easier mastery over the idiom than the Devarani Kubera, which is deliberately built up of rather symmetrically superimposed volumes of flesh, as part of the crown of the kīrtimukha below.

Finally, the three dancing Jethani gaṇas and other standing gaṇas in the Devarani panels or at Devarani entrance, offer a contrast to the aṣṭanidhi gaṇas in Kevala-Narasiṁha temple door jamb (Fig. 504), weaponbearing, walking gaṇas in the Trivikrama temple vedībandha, two standing staffbearing gaṇas at the Rudra-Narasiṁha temple door, or the gaṇas dancing or playing musical instruments on the Bhogārāma temple vedībandha at Ramtek. The fleshy bodies of these Ramtek gaṇas are creased into many more natural curves and folds in response to their movement (Figs. 506-07) than the prototypically smooth, unmuscled bodies of the Tala gaṇas. The longish legs of Tala gaṇas are also less convincing as a characteristic feature in the dwarf companions of Śiva than the short, thick, bowed legs of the Ramtek gaṇas.[34]

If the stockier or heavier Tala forms are anticipated at Māṇḍhal, Nāgardhan or Mānsar in Vidarbha, the more elongated forms are anticipated at Pavnār (Figs. 386, 389, 392-94).[35] Some of these images, specially the Buddha, offer, unlike Jethani south pillar and slab figures, a disproportionately small head, planted on huge shoulders, powerful flaring arms, long tapering bust and legs, and sizeable hips.

The Tala images do not retain the feeling for arrested movement, which charge the racing contours of the Gaṅgā image at Pavnār. The inscribed Gaṅgā image (Figs. 315, 453)[36] is free from all traces of archaism, though it combines heavy, close set breasts and thighs with slender legs, waist and a long oval head. The Tala Jethani female figures on side slabs (Figs. 299-301), the āmrabhañjikā, lotus bearing nāyikā, the nāyikā cut off above her waist, holding the end of her uttarīya, the river goddesses and their attendants in Devarani door jambs look back to images like this Gaṅgā image. However, except for the Jethani sideslab figures, the Tala figures are not as tall and as slender as the Pavnār Gaṅgā. The pleats of the dresses of Tala ladies do radiate out from the kaccha or from the hips like the Pavnār Gaṅgā. However, in the Pavnār Gaṅgā, the pleats are rendered as rippling and raised lines, descending and contracting in size, in a finetuned rhythm, synchronized with the subtle frills and folds of the kaccha. At Tala, these pleats are reduced to diagonally and somewhat roughly incised crinkled lines, which do not convey the simmering cobweb like substance of the garment as effectively. And yet, the slight stoop given to the nubile female body by the youthful burden of the breasts, the high slope given to the shoulders, the diving and swelling planes of the navel, subtly emphasized and demarcated by clinging drapery, kaccha or mekhalā, are features in the Gaṅgā image, which continue in the Tala images.

Generally, the Devarani freestanding slab images adapt a via media, with a stress on volume, evident in the Devarani samabhaṅga Śiva image (in the Bilaspur museum) or the dvibhaṅga

Śiva image, cut off from the thighs in front of Devarani (Figs. 357-58). The headless and armless Viṣṇu from Ramtek (Fig. 382) Guptārāma temple in the Nagpur museum[37] is a precursor of these images. The uttarīya, bunched against the thighs and floating down on either side of the Ramtek image, possesses greater volume and animation than the similar uttarīya of the Tala Śiva in the Bilaspur museum. The flow of planes in the Ramtek bust is more kinetic than the Devarani Śiva busts, in which this flow is slowed down, and interrupted by numerous strands of cloth and ornament.

The comparison of some of the single figures with the participants in the narrative panels at Tala and Vidarbha, and a comparison of the composition of the panels is also instructive. The Trivikrama image in Ramtek, three Kṛṣṇalīlā panels from Pavnār, Kṛṣṇa heaving upwards in pratyālīḍha to seize Kaṁsa by his hair, Kṛṣṇa advancing, also in pratyālīḍha, after dhenukā or śakaṭāsura-vadha (execution of the ass or cart demon),[38] Vāsudeva moving ahead, holding Kṛṣṇa in arms, in a graphic narration (Figs. 391-94), Trivikrama image of Ramtek[39], are all modelled with a similar posture. The head is thrown backwards, and the chest is thrown forwards, in an aggressive challenge. The tall body is stretched and tautened like a bowstring, brittle with tension. In the legless Śiva outside Devarani, the head is thrown back and the chest stiffened in a similar incipient movement. The ascetics advancing with garland behind Kubera, or a gaṇa looking out from the lowest tier behind Gaṅgā, led by Bhagīratha (Figs. 169, 174), adapt similar postures. Though the forward movement is never expressed at Tala as eloquently as Ramtek or Pavnār, broken images of the tribhaṅga Śiva in tiger skin and the ūrdhvaliṅga dvibhaṅga Kṛttivāsa Śiva (Figs. 343, 349) respectively at Devarani and Jethani east, depict a reverse movement with great elan. However, the crackling tension of the Vidarbha figures is no longer captured so effectively.

Rows of smaller figures rise and subside on sequential planes, above and behind one another, to frame and thrust out the principal figures to the forefront of the stage at Tala, specially at Devarani. This arrangement seems to be a complex amplification of a device used in the Pavnār narrative panels. In the quiet scene showing Rāma, Sītā and Lakṣmaṇa, meeting Bharata, in the slightly more animated panel of Kṛṣṇa janma (birth of Kṛṣṇa), or in the action filled drama of Kaṁsavadha (execution of Kaṁsa), the figures and actions are organized in different, successive planes, behind or above one another, at Pavnār. When the figures are put on the same plane, as in the meeting with Bharata, their heights are regulated in a gradual ascent to the centre. The result is the same as at Tala, to focus attention on the central action and the principal protagonists in the drama. However, the means adapted at Pavnār are simpler, the stage is less crowded, and the relentless diagonal pull and propulsion of the Tala river goddess panels is not anticipated. When one compares the seated Rāma Sītā panel from Pavnār with the Hara Gaurī panel at Devarani, one notices, in spite of their mutual link in the fluent contour and slender modelling (specially of the similarly placed hand of Rāma or Śiva), the more complex torsion of Pārvatī, and the greater tumult and confusion, in the background of the Tala panel. A comparison of the Pañcāyatana Śivaliṅga panel of Pavnār[40] with the Mārtaṇḍa Bhairava panel in Devarani, betrays a similar disregard for the tectonic frame, in both Pavnār and Tala.

The ancestry of the style of Tala animal heads can also be traced to Vidarbha. Though very little prominence is given to Narasiṁha at Tala, the seated Narasiṁhas in rājalīlāsana in the Kevala[41] and Rudra-Narasiṁha temples at Ramtek provide a sturdier, more fully modelled version of the Jethani lintel Narasiṁha (Figs. 547, 554). Of the two Ramtek images, the Kevala-

Narasiṁha temple image trembles with arrested breath and movement, and it is further removed in the past from the Jethani image than its heavier, harder counterpart in the Rudra-Narasiṁha temple. A broken Jethani Narasiṁha head with a lotus crest (Fig. 546) shows the drier, bonier, thinner version of the Ramtek Narasiṁha heads. Though a fullfledged varāha has not been found at Tala, the varāha head, recovered from Jethani, also shows a similar change from the varāha of the Ramtekgarh Varāha temple. The fleshy head of the Ramtek varāha, with its rounded, bulging snout, with double, irregular fleshfolds in its throat, gives way at Tala to a linearized, though a very sensitive head of varāha (Figs. 567, 572). The abraded makara in the makara praṇāla of the Rudra-Narasiṁha temple, the makara relief in the Bhogārāma temple at Ramtek, and the makara, putting a fish in its gaping mouth in a makara praṇāla from Nāgrā,[42] offer less stylized, more energetic and fleshier counterparts of the animals of Devarani. Jethani doorjamb makaras retain stronger memories of their naturalism and volume (Figs. 533-39, 543, 268-72). A comparison of the slow curving, heavier foliate tail of the Bhogārāma makara, or the bulging cheeks, nose or huge, curving horns of the Nāgrā makara, or the less rectilinear contours of the vestigial makara of the Rudra-Narasiṁha praṇāla, show a phase preceding the work at Tala, which increases the size of such makaras, without modelling them with the fullness of Ramtek.

Sites like Ramtek and Nāgardhan speak of the birth and nurture of an artistic idiom, which appears to have flowered in several other Vidarbha sites.[43] In spite of its strong, individual expression and unique elements, the art of Tala evidently draws on the art of Vidarbha, which is a near contemporary theatre of art activity, closest to its idiom.

INFLUENCE OF TALA

In examining the influence of Tala on later Indian art, we shall examine the continuing ambivalence between the plastic and linear styles in the sculpture of Dakṣiṇa Kośala and the roots of such ambivalence in Tala sculpture itself. In spite of the coexistence of the two styles of modelling at major Dakṣiṇa Kośala sites like Sirpur, Rajim, Garh Dhanaurā and Deepadih, and in spite of the adaption, at such sites, of certain conventions of the linear eastern Indian style, bred at Sarnath, Dakṣiṇa Kośala remains, by and large, committed to the volume and plasticity, characteristic of Central and western India. This continuing commitment is, to no small extent, due to the extraordinary elan vital and feeling for plastic mass, stressed by Tala at a moment, when this feeling is considerably diluted in the art of the eastern centres of Central India. It is through Dakṣiṇa Kośala art that Tala transmits its overriding concern for volume to the art of Odisha, which is never overcome by the linearization of much of medieval eastern Indian art. On the other hand, the almost flawless, if somewhat fastidious execution of sculptural embellishment, the fascination for colossal figural scale, scrupulous description of detail, bichromatic use of solids and voids, light and shadow are bequeathed by Tala, with its own reinterpretations, to Odishan art and to Pratihāra and later medieval Kalacurī art of Central India.

NOTES

1. R.D. Banerji 1933: 164, 168, 70, 173, 181-82, feels that the Banaras school returns to the normal in human figure, and shows 'an uncommon devotion to real naturalism and symmetry' in rejection of the Kuṣāṇa mannerism of Mathura.

2. *Ibid.*, 122-54, 161-62, 170-71, 174-75, 203-5 for discussion of Bhūmarā, Khoh, Deogarh, Māndāsor and early Bheḍāghāt.
3. Stella Kramrisch, *Indian Sculpture*, 1933: 15-39: 5-7, 17, 55. As the language of Kramrisch is highly individual, a few words of explanation are necessary. 'Innervation' is the 'plastic urge to swell into form from within', the 'principle of the flowing sap of life'. 'Inflection' is the immigration of this fluid rhythm, confined to pre-classical sculpture to plants and animals, into the human body, in classical sculpture. 'Transsubstantiation' is the transformation of round, three-dimensional modelling into a flatter surface, mastered by linear angles.
4. Kramrisch 1933: 60. 'Central India keeps pace with Sarnath, but though its measure is the same, experience is different, nearer to the earth and the past'.
5. Goetz 1963: 253-54, 259, 261.
6. Harle 1974: 3-4, 27-28.
7. Williams 1982: 4-5, 26, 40-41, 60-61, 64-67, 76, 79, 99.
8. Spink 1971: 168-69, 172, 197; *Ibid.* 1975: 143-66; *Ibid.* 1975; *Ibid.* 1976: 55, 63.
9. Coomaraswamy 1927: 35, 72, who points out that in Indian art, 'when we perceive increased reality or truth, we must ascribe this, not to a change of habit, but to a heightened consciousness, a more complete identification with the theme itself... a more profound empathy'. The misunderstanding created by dynastic predilections about the chronology of Dakṣiṇa Kośala sculpture in general, and about Tala in particular is evident in some of the suggestions in Nigam 2000. P.K. Agrawala in Nigam 2000: 111, finds the Tala Paśupati image as imbued with early Vākāṭaka concepts of gross physical energy, before such concepts were permeated by typical Gupta classicism. Yet, he assigns the image to mid-6th century AD. Nigam 2000: 43, classifies Dakṣiṇa Kośala art as a regional variation of Gupta art. He describes it as 'xylographic' with regard to the designs on the Lakṣmaṇa temple door.
10. Fleet 1888: 163-4 deals with such misunderstanding by saying that 'alphabets varied, not according to dynasties, but according to localities, and in establishing any system of comparative paleography, we must select territorial not dynastic names'. Fleet's remarks about inscriptions apply, mutatis mutandis, to style. For objections to dynastic classification, see Chandra 1983: 69-72.
11. Indeed, the concern with style as a sum of parts rather than as a complex whole has often led to misleading conclusions about Central Indian development, or about Tala. See Williams 1982: 6 for the statement of this approach. Chandra 1983: 66 for problems with this approach.
12. Williams 1982: pls. 87, 97.
13. *Ibid.*, pls. 148 (Pārśvanātha from Nācnā), 154 (Pārvatī temple, door, Nācnā), 169 (Rāma shooting at Vālin, Nācnā), 185 (guardian at Bhūmarā), 188 (Vāmana temple door, Marhiā); PC neg. 92-27 (Viṣṇu from Khoh at Rāmvan Museum); Also compare the Jethani south lintel Kevala-Narasiṁha with his counterparts at Sindursī (AAB neg. 80-43) and Deogarh (AAB neg. 90-17). The elongation is less at Jethani, due to the constriction of space and the loadbearing function of an image like this in the lintel. The flowing, irregular locks, with a floral boss, is a link between the Narasiṁha figures in the three sites. Also see Pramod Chandra, 1985: pl. 35 (Ardhanārīśvara, Feroze Mistry Collection, Bombay, from Nācnā) or PC neg. 103-53, 103-55 (Marhiā).
14. Harle 1974: pls. 63, 66-9.
15. Williams 1982: pl. 96; DGASI neg., 1014/61, 1016/61 (Bodhisattva, Kauśāmbī Museum, Allahabad university).
16. Williams 1982: 89-92 (Sarnath); 165-66, (Nācnā): 243 (Gaḍhvā) PC neg. 7-80 (Rāma Sītā at Rāmvan from Nācnā), 56-4 (Musical couples from Nācnā): 71 a) b) (Gaḍhvā); Harle, pl. 132 (Bhitargāon).
17. Harle 1974: pls. 69, 70.
18. PC neg. C. 6. (Cleveland Museum head).
19. Mathura Museum No. 261, AAB neg. 19.65.
20. Harle 1974: pl. 25.

21. Cleveland Museum No. C-5 (Mathura head); Chandra 1985: pl. 25 (Gosnā well); Czuma 1985: pls. 4-5 (heads in Cleveland Museum of Art and Virginia Museum of Fine Arts, Richmond).
22. PC neg. 4013, (Udayagiri), PC neg. C. 29 (Los Angles Museum head); Chandra 1985: pl. 20 (Timulgiri torso).
23. Williams 1982: pl. 76; V.S. Agrawala, Catalogue, No. 22, 1949: 140-41 (Kumāra at Mathura); Williams 1982: pls. 12-13 (Jinas from Durjanpura), Vidisha (decans on Udayagiri hilltop fragment), 146-48 (Nācnā Jinas), Harle 1974: pl. 28; (Baḍoh Pāṭhāri), 37 (Vidisha lion capital); Czuma 1985: pl. 13. (Buddha, Mathura); *ASI*. Western Circle (1920-21), serial No. 5482 (Bhūmarā); AAB neg. 103-53 (Marhiā); AAB neg. 101-30 (Nācnā Pārśvanātha, Rāmvan Museum).
24. Williams 1982: pls. 171 (Khoh), 182 (Bhūmarā); AAB neg. 90-54 (Bhūmarā); PC neg. A.3-22 (Khoh); *ASI* Western Circle 1920, serial no. 5152 (Khoh).
25. Williams 1982: pl. 111.
26. Chandra 1970: pls. 58-59.
27. Williams 1982: pl. 7 (Jānkhāt, door jamb); Czuma, 1985: pl. 10 (Toraṇa architrave from Soṅkh).
28. Czuma 1985: pls. 227 (Govardhanadharī Kṛṣṇa from Gataśramanārāin Ṭilā, Mathura), 230-31 (Ṛṣabhanātha, Mathura), 235 (Buddha, Māradharṣaṇa, Sarnath); Williams 1982: pls. 173 (Nāndchānd guardian), 219 (Guardian from Sondni, Māndāsor), 220 (River goddesses on toraṇa post from Khilchipurā, Māndāsor); Also Harle 1974: pls. 98, 99 (for Māndāsor); AAB neg. 103-37 (Nāndchānd mātṛkā), A-6-31 32 (Nāndchānd dvārapālas).
29. Mānḍhal, 73 km to the northeast of Nagpur, was excavated in 1975-76. by Nagpur University. All the images, found in the excavation at the site called Bholāhuḍki are in the Nagpur University Museum except the four and eight-headed Śiva and the ūrdhvaliṅga Śiva in ordinary adhovastra (lower cloth), which are in the Nagpur Central Museum. Shastri 1977. Sculptures recovered from Bholāpuḍkī Tekḍi and Bāṇgī Huḍkī in Mānḍhal, preserved in the Nagpur University Museum, include also the frontally posed bust of Vāsudeva (Kṛṣṇa), the principal object of śātvatavidhi worship, Vṛṣṇivīra saṁkarṣaṇa (Balarāma), in dhenukāsuravadha pose, with a snake wrapped at back, and a lotus bearing Vṛṣṇivīra, presumably Sāmba. As regards the Śaiva sculptures, the two-armed eight-headed Śiva is identified as Maheśvara comprising three tiers of heads, representing, from top, yogin (ascetic), brahmacārī muṇḍin (celibate aspirant with shaven head) and uṣṇīṣin (turbaned) forms. The four-armed, four-headed image, is identified as Nandīśvara though he does not satisfy all the criteria. The twelve-headed image with two tiers of four heads on shoulder, two heads each on twin arms and thighs, is identified as Sadāśiva. The two-armed ithyphallic skull bearing image is identified as Rudra in Andhakāsuravadhamūrti, though the necessary features are not distinguishable.
30. It is in the Central Museum, Nagpur. See Chandra 1985: No. 41a, 104-5.
31. Also in Nagpur Central Museum, Chandra 1985: 41b, 104.
32. Mānsar, in Nagpur, Maharashtra, excavated between 1998 and 2005, has yielded sculptures, from the 3rd to 2nd century BC, the largest yield being from early 5th century AD. The sculptures are made of rough grained sandstone and schist in the Maurya Śuṅga period, rough grained grey sandstone or shale type limestone in the Sātavāhana period, and fine grained red sandstone in the Vākāṭaka period. Finds of a three eyed Pārvatī, Śiva Pārvatī with bull from late Maurya early Śuṅga levels, Lajjā Gaurī from Sātavāhana level, and, of Śiva and his pantheon from the Vākāṭaka period provide a backdrop to the innovative vitality of the sculpture of Tala and Dakṣiṇa Kośala.
33. National Museum, New Delhi, L 77/2, Chandra 1985: No. 40, 102-3. The Mānsar Śiva is identified variously as Baṭuka Bhairava, Yakṣa, Kubera, Hrasvavāmana, Vāmadeva, Soma, or Kapardin. He wears kapāla (skull), aṣṭapuṣpikā (eight flower ornament), taṭaṅka (circular earring), nāgavalaya (serpentine bangle), candrakalā (lunar crescent), nāganūpura (serpentine foot ring). He displays feminine grace in the left half of the body and performs dāna (gift) of an ornament.
34. AIIS negs. 580-53, 580-54, 580-92.

35. Pavnār has yielded images of a scholar in savyaparyaṅkāsana, holding a book, a Narasiṁha in rājalīlāsana, a Mahiṣamardinī, with truncated trunk, a standing Śiva Buddha, Vāsudeva, a mithuna, river Gaṅgā, and a seated lady squeezing her breast and thighs. The Pavnār images are now housed in a hut on the bank of river Dhām near the Paramadhāma āśrama of the well known follower of Mahātmā Gandhi, Śrī Vinobāji. These were found, from time to time, in the diggings in the surrounding fields and discussed for the first time by Mirashi. See Mirashi 1963: 60-61. Also Deo and Dhavalikar 1967. And, Shastri 1992: pls. 74-77.
36. The image is inscribed on the proper right side of her legs, as Gaṅgā Bhagavatī. The characters of the inscriptions resemble those of the Paṭṭa plates of Vākāṭaka king Pravarasena. Mirashi 1963: 62, 63, pl. 6.
37. *Encyclopaedia* 2.1: pl. 128, AIIS neg. 581-9.
38. Mirashi identifies this as killing of Vāli by Rāma but he is unable to identify the dangling dhenukā (ass) held by Saṁkarṣaṇa (Balarāma). See Mirashi 1963: 5, 62, pl. C. For Trivikrama image, Dhaky & Meister, 2.1: pls. 108-9.
39. As a matter of detail, the carving of the long, slim lotus petals on the halo, or the perforations on the back of the halo of the Ramtek Trivikrama image are similar to such features in the halo of the Devarani Śiva and a Jethani eastern dvārapāla.
40. Shastri 1992: pl. 22.
41. *Encyclopedia* 2.1: pls 120 After removal of vermilion paint and restoration, pl. 14 in the album of Asstt. Director, State Archaeology, Nagpur.
42. *Enclclopedia* 2.1: pls. 120 (makarapraṇāla, Rudra Narasiṁha), 126 (makara relief), Bhogārāma, PC neg. 7 (makarapraṇāla, Nagpur Central Museum).
43. A seated Gaṇeśa from Hāmlāpurī, a Viṣṇu head from Nandapurī in Ramtek Tehsil, Nagpur, a few female heads from Nandpur in Pārāseoni Tehsil, Nagpur, some mother goddess heads and busts from Ghuggusgarh (ancient Nandpur), including a Mahiṣamardinī, a Pārvatī pañcāgnitapas (holding penance of five fires) from Akolā in the Nagpur Central Museum, have the fulness of volume, energy of lines, suggesting variations of the fifth century Vidarbha idiom. Several other sites like Repanpalli in Garhchiroli district, Bhibhākuṇḍa, Dhesurerā, and Kolitmārā (near Ghugghusgarh) in Nagpur district, suggest Gupta-Vākāṭaka heritage, and await thorough exploration and excavation. At least three bronze images of Buddha in the Nagpur Central Museum, one larger and earlier, two smaller and later, with long arms, bowed, somewhat attenuated and stunted legs, show the gradual leavening of the sturdy Vidarbha idiom by the contemplative abstraction of Sarnath. For these bronzes, see A.P. Jamkhedkar 1985, *LK* 22: 13-19. For Mānḍhal excavations, see Ajay Mitra Shastri, *VSMV* 20, 1977: 42-43. The Hāmlāpuri and Nāgrā excavation reports remain unpublished.

7

Iconography and Iconology of Tala Art

In any study of ancient Indian art, the investigations of form and content cannot really be separated. If we have separately discussed the formal arrangements which go to make the Tala style, we have done so in the interest of clarity, and for establishing a relative and chronological sequence of architecture and sculpture, which are not firmly anchored in time by archaeological or historic evidence. While an exclusive study of form is reasonably subject to criticism for ignoring the impact of content on the form, formalism itself has not excluded the study of content, which provides the unifying principle underlying and explaining both the visible event and its intelligible significance, and requires synthesis rather than analysis.[1]

PROBLEMS OF UNDERSTANDING

A total appreciation of form and content in the art of Tala is fraught with problems. The iconography of the image that has been identified as Paśupati, Varuṇa, Kubera or Sūrya is not described by any known iconographic text. Plant, animal and human forms are often seen to combine; and, in the body of Paśupati, unique antithetical elements find their home. Gaṇas, makaras, human figures adorning pillars and walls in Jethani serve no obvious architectural function, nor provide any evident cosmological meaning. In a casual reading of their features, they seem to live in isolation in their individual world, apparently unrelated to one another. The relation of the numerous floral bands with the surging figures of Devarani door jamb, or connection of the composite Paśupati image with Sūrya, Varuṇa, Kubera or Gajalakṣmī is not apparent in a physical enumeration of their features. The shape of Jethani with three direct accesses to the sanctum, and a disproportionately large access from the south, its huge sarvatobhadrikā pillars, seemingly rotating in all directions, the enormous figured wall slabs, facing one another across the steps of both Jethani and Devarani, are also baffling, with no exact known precedent, or support in the architectural canons.

The problems of understanding Tala are, however, essentially problems of alienation from the specific iconological context of Indian art,[2] which can make the seemingly unique or strange features of Tala appear familiar or intelligible. This alienation can be bridged by a realization that the juxtaposition of apparently dissimilar floral or faunal elements in the same images, the composition of different limbs of Paśupati's body with heads, human and non-human, the use of flowers to constitute the kīrtimukhas, the hands of Kubera or the limbs of makaras are obviously not borrowed from any original in nature in a servile manner, but are executed in the free manner of the artist, as adequate symbols or reminders, equal or akin to the images conceived in meditation, in mantras or metrical formulae. As such, the floral and figural alaṁkāra (ornament) on pillars, wall slabs or door jambs of Tala are not 'meaningless decoration', designed to entertain senses, but meant for proper communication of an idea. Stript of such ornament, the Tala icons become unqualified, unconditioned, nirguṇa (without attributes), incapable of communication. The extent of success of the Tala artist depends on the extent he has successfully assimilated himself to the image conceived in meditation, and on the fervour with which he has executed his vision. It is this integration of form and content, which we have to look for at Tala.[3]

Here then is the crux of the problem of understanding a site like Tala. The spectators or critics like us, like the artist before us, can only make an imperfect attempt to recapitulate the initial process of creation of Tala art, or repeat the steps of identifying ourselves, the knowers, with the known, by a process of 'self-naughting' and transformation of nature. We can try to step back to the earliest texts, put the right questions to them to incite the right answers, unlock the meaning of Tala art from the words of the past, making their half said, implicit meaning explicit, for the object of art made in the future. We shall thus try not to read meanings into the symbols at Tala, but reconstruct, to the extent possible, their original meaning, which has been forgotten because of our alienation from our ancient world of symbols.[4] In our attempt to do this, we shall discover that the single myth of the descent of Gaṅgā forms a unifying link in the different panels of the Devarani door jamb; that the image of Paśupati comprehends several mythological and philosophical meanings, and that the same participant in the Tala artistic programme, be this a siṁha, a makara, a lotus flower, or a gaṇa, performs a multiplicity of roles in different locations and contexts. The interpretation of the myths and philosophical exegeses suggests an interpenetration, simultaneity and ambiguity of meanings rather than alternative, or mutually exclusive explanations. In reading the myths or the philosophy, an attempt will be made to understand this congruence of meanings, by reading forwards from earlier texts, but, it will also be necessary to reassemble, even from later texts, the evidence fragmented by culture in time and space, through different retellings of the original. Such a reading becomes plausible, in a collective art without personal signatures, in which, however individual the expressions, the same melange of meanings for the myths of Śiva continues through all the layers in time.[5]

It would follow from this continuing validity of Śaiva mythology or its philosophical parameters, that the metaphysical content of Tala art, which is involved in its physical surface, can be recovered by a rereading of mythological texts, through their perpetual interweavings. In modern discourse on such texts, the distinction between signifiers and the signified is seen as invalid, and the text tends to be read as a multiplicity of layered forms rather than as a binary structure of a content and a form. Indian mythological and philosophical texts do have such formal strata, accumulated through time, but, through all these strata, the figures of speech or thought, remain inextricably interwoven.[6] Once we go back in time through these strata, we discover that the iconic signs of Tala are culturally but not arbitrarily coded; that, in their polyvalence of meanings, these are like verbal signs, subject to a multiple articulation; and that, these are still analyzable into pertinent coded units of an internally coherent philosophy of a many dimensioned Śaivism,[7] in which the Vedic image of sacrifice is completed, inter alia, by the epic image of devotion.

This attempt to see in Tala objects a philosophical world view, which remains internally consistent, in spite of its diverse shades and hues, is not in conflict with our attempt to analyze the diverse stylistic impulses, affecting the evolution of Tala or Dakṣiṇa Kośala art, or released by its impact. When we see, in Gupta Vākāṭaka or Tala art, a realization of the 'classical' and ecstatic harmony of swelling volume and chastening line, strength and grace, we propose no revolutionary change in the philosophy behind it, but a more intense identification with its meaning.[8] On the other hand, when we detect in this art medieval features like growing scale, ornament, chiaroscuro, preciosity of description, display of virtuosity, elongation and hardening, features which fulfil themselves differently in different medieval Daksina Kośala sites, Odishan, or western Indian caves in succeeding centuries, we do not suggest a radical volte face in the evolution of Śaivism or Indian philosophy per se. Instead, we see a slackening of fervour, a less intense identification with the theme.[9] The changes or variations in the individual styles or capabilities do not necessarily involve outright changes in the collective philosophy.[10] This philosophy remains like a perennial fountain, in the area around Tala, to which individual streams of art, feeding sites like 5th century Mānḍhal, Mānsar or Kevalanarasiṁha temple, Ramtek, Sisdeori, late-5th early 6th century Tala, early 7th century Sirpur, and 9th century Deepadih, return from time to time, to renew and refresh themselves.[11] In this journey, Tala provides a landmark, standing in the middle, pointing to a communion with the source in the 'classical' period, and to a gradual separation from it in the 'medieval' period.

FERMENT OF DEVOTIONALISM

Though the Tala temples themselves are not associated with any Śaiva ruler by epigraphic or numismatic evidence, the contemporary religious milieu, in which the temples are rooted, is permeated by Śaivism, often coexisting with Vaiṣṇavism, and, to some extent, with Buddhism.[12] A reading of the fifth century Vākāṭaka inscriptions, or of the inscriptions of various dynasties of Dakṣiṇa Kośala, from the fifth to the seventh centuries, reveal the consistent claims of kings to be devotees of Viṣṇu or Śiva, ruling by his grace, carrying his insignia or weapons, and finally, to be even assimilated with him.[13]

The kings of Dakṣiṇa Kośala and Vidarbha appear to be closely associated with their Gods. They connect the increase in their moral, spiritual and political well-being with the construction, maintenance and use of temple sites as royal as well as divine sanctuaries, for performance of Vedic sacrificial rituals to their Gods, in a manner appropriate to the status of sovereign and powerful kings. The kings call themselves Gṛhapatis after Śiva, Vāstospati, Lord of the House, and treat sites dedicated to Gods as royal sites, claim to uphold royal virtues and divine grace, both regnum and sacerdotium.[14] Vākāṭaka and Pāṇḍuvaṁśī copperplates, mention grants to Brahmins of different Vedic affiliations and performance of Vedic yajñas by kings. Remnants of sacrificial ceremonies have been found at Mānsar in Vidarbha and Dakṣiṇa Kośala, reminding us of vāstupūjā and puruṣamedha tradition of Somayāga, mentioned in Śatapatha Brāhmaṇa, performed at the foundation ceremony of a palace or a house.[15]

The Śarabhapurīya or Pāṇḍuvaṁśī kings are paramabhāgavatas. They share the devotional approach to pūjā with paramamāheśvara Vākāṭaka kings. Ritualistic offerings, or grants are made by Śarabhapurīya king Sudevarāja to residents of village Śivaliṅgikā, or by Mahāśivagupta Bālārjuna to Śiva Iśāneśvara.[16] While several Dakṣiṇa Kośala kings now boast of being from a lineage of royal ascetics, several ascetics and Brāhmiṇs assume names, which establish their affiliations with Śiva or Śivaparivāra (family of Śiva). Many Vākāṭaka grants are made to teachers or noble individuals, upādhyāyas and mahāpuruṣas, who are described as belonging to a lineage of apratigrāhaka, those who spurn gifts. Various copperplate grants provide information about the guruśiṣya-paramparā, the teacher disciple lineage of Śaivite, specially Somaparamparā affiliation,[17] dedicated to the mastery of the principles of fire and water. This would suggest influence of Somasiddhāntin cults[18] on the iconography of Tala and Dakṣiṇa Kośala.

Commenting on the contemporary Bṛhatsaṁhitā, Bhaṭṭotpala speaks of Śiva images, consecrated according to the Vātulatantra (the crazy, unconventional way), which was apparently preached by Pāśupata ascetics and was no longer extant. Bāṇabhaṭṭa describes the worship of Śiva with leaves and flowers, by mahāvratin kāpālikas (ascetics with skull cap, devoted to the great, left hand way), who carry khaṭvāṅgas, skull capped lances. He also mentions the respectful greeting offered by the Maukharī king Puṣpabhūti Paramamāheśvara, to Bhairavācārya. Contemporary inscriptions of Dakṣiṇa Kośala and Vidarbha unfold the numerous ramifications of Śaiva Bhāgavatism. They mention the sixtysix forms of Rudra, name him as Bhairava, Bhūtapati, Lord of animals, and describe him as carrying Gaṅgā, trident, riding bull, framed by rearing snakes, wearing matted locks and tiger skin, as protector and destroyer, and as being associated with Kārtikeya, Nāigameśa and Lajjā Gaurī. The art of the region in general, of Tala in particular, mirrors all these diverse forms and associations of Śiva.[19]

That the devotional approach is shared by Buddhists equally with Śaivas or Vaiṣṇavas in this area and period, is demonstrated by the explicit use of Śaiva or Vaiṣṇava terminology in Buddhist inscriptions. The words of the Pāṇḍuvaṁśī inscriptions in Dakṣiṇa Kośala, the Vākāṭaka inscriptions in Ajanta, the Buddha images, sealings, stamped with dhāraṇī mantras (meditative incantations), jātaka panels, recovered from Sirpur or Jaitpur, Malhār panels and village names show the influence of bhaktivāda (devotionalism) in Buddhism on the area surrounding Tala at this time. The image of a Padmapāṇi (lotus bearing) Śiva from Māndhal, the image of Padmapāṇi Avalokiteśvara in Sirpur Ānandaprabhavihāra or Sanchi (Fig. 387), and the plaques of Śiva Pārvatī, Gaṇeśa, Mahiṣamardanī, found in the same vihāra, the huge, broken Bodhisattva like Śiva dvārapāla image (displaying flowing locks, saṁghāṭi, and what looks like abhaya mudrā), recovered from Devarani east or lying on Jethani west (Figs. 352, 356-58) and Bodhisattva at Pavnār (Fig. 386), suggest the confluence of Buddhism and Śaivism on the common platform of devotionalism.[20] This is a trend in Indian religious history, which appears to have influenced the theological, political and artistic developments in Asia. That this trend towards devotionalism caused a wider ferment is proved by mention of Buddhist teachers and pilgrims in the surrounding regions, which point to a commerce in ideas between Dakṣiṇa Kośala and other areas of the world, particularly China.[21]

Tala art appears to have been born in this ferment of ideas. The artist at Tala may well have been performing a priestly or ministerial function, translating the ardent perceptions of the original exemplars into concrete images. His patrons, like the patrons of the art in the surrounding areas, would appear to have undergone the rectification of their personality, evidenced by claims of assimilation to divine nature, through extraordinary devotion. The coexistence of works from different cults, often mentioned together impartially in the inscriptions, indicates a convergence in modes of expression, arising out of an all pervasive wave of devotionalism, and a receptivity to mutual modes. Tala appears to have served, in consequence of this reciprocity, as a meeting place for samājas or communities and mahas or festive gatherings (some of which continue till today), dedicated to Rudra and Śiva, nāga (snake), nadī (river), vṛkṣa (tree), yakṣa, Kubera, Skanda, prāsāda (palace, temple), kīrti or dari (excavation or cavern). All these mahas are mentioned in the Mahābhārata and contemporary Pāli literature.[22] It is this festive devotion, permeating patron and artist alike, which must have woven form and content together in Tala art.

DEVOTION FOR FORMS OF ŚIVA

In view of this background, the numerous human, animal, vegetal or geometric forms of Tala art should not be seen as isolated images, existing by themselves, but as names and shapes (nāmarūpa, forma and figura) of Śiva himself. The Atharvaśiras Upaniṣad shows Rudras as immanent in, and transcending each deity singly and collectively. The beauty of the entire and essential form of Śiva at Tala is greater than the sum of his actual or partial manifestations, and the representations of his many likenesses are meant to serve also as their denials, and as participants in the perfection of the universal form. Thus, at Tala, the emanations of Śiva's universal form are, to begin with, shown individually, and are then brought together in the composite form of Rudra Śiva/Paśupati (Pl. 48). It will be demonstrated how, like a forest with many trees, Paśupati is many things in one, which are mutually complementary rather than exclusive. He thus becomes at once Viśvarūpa, Agni, Aṣṭamūrti, Yogīśvara, Lakulīśa, or a great yakṣa. Varuṇa, Sūrya or Kubera imitate his acts, purging, releasing waters, to make wealth and well-being. Lakṣmī, yakṣas, gaṇas, river goddesses, nāgas, gajas, siṁhas, kīrtimukhas, makaras are the hosts assisting Paśupati in his regenerative role, and Gaṇeśa and Kārtikeya provide leadership to most of these hosts. Nandīśa, the bull, Vighneśvara, the elephant-headed God, Rāvaṇa, the demon king, even Viṣṇu appear as recipients of Paśupati's anugraha (grace). Loving couples, the dress, hairdress and ornament equip and complete Paśupati and his consorts. The ghora (malignant) is chastened to become śānta (benignant), and the destructive heat of tapas (penance) is mollified by its creative heat. The temple becomes the house, the body, the altar of Paśupati, where the paśu (individual being) merges gradually in pati (supreme being), and the transitional stages in his progress towards this fulfilment, attainment of adequacy and sufficiency, are facilitated, punctuated and celebrated by floral and figural ornament, alaṁkāra (marker of adequacy).

Śiva emerges at Tala as lord of both creation and destruction. He is seen as gross and subtle, as both saguṇa (with attributes) and nirguṇa, the divider and dividend, sacrificer and sacrificed, being and becoming, perceiver and perceived, one and many, as coincidentum oppositorum, of one essence and two natures. The temple itself becomes his mantramūrti (body made of invocatory syllables), a cosmic mountain, choreographed in space and time, and built up by hymns,[23] a suggestion, buttressed by stellar symbolism of an astronomically conceived universe. The different identities of Śiva merge into one another, in a harmonious construction and reading of ancient texts. It would seem that in this period of Indian art, formal canons and rigid conventions of religious art had not yet overtaken the bold spirit of experiment, which expressed itself at Tala in an attempt to capture the surpassing grandeur of the idea of Paśupati or of the Lord of Being in early religious texts. Our inability to find a contemporary iconographic text with a one to one relation to Tala art, would not, therefore, be a ground for dismissing this art as tribal localism, or a provincial variation of a metropolitan art, the physical or literary evidence of which awaits discovery.

Paśupati

We shall begin by a discussion of what we have chosen to call the Rudra Śiva or Paśupati image. This image (Pls. 20, 22, 48), virtually unparallelled in Indian or world art, has features, discussed by no iconographic text. It seems to be among the very few comprehensive attempts in Indian art to make an all inclusive icon, which would surpass all its individual connotations, to denote the idea of universal God, ardently discussed and sought from the earliest sacred texts.

Physical Details

The Rudra Śiva/Paśupati image stands, even without its missing base, 2.60 m tall, 2.80 m in diameter at its maximum girth, with its head alone being 1.65 m in diameter and 0.67 m in height. Nude, in samabhaṅga (equal flexion) carved in very high relief on a stele, its right hand swings free to hold the broken shaft of a lakuṭa, a club, while its left hand and thumb are hooked into the kaṭibandha (waistband) (Pl. 48; Figs. 619-20). The jaṭā (matted locks) consists of two snakes in seven coils, their hoods protruding at the top (Figs. 584-89). Two larger snake hoods rise as high as the head to frame it from either side, forming a sarpaprabhāvali (snake halo) (Figs. 583-91). The hāra (necklace), valaya (wristlet) udara and kaṭibandha are snake coils and the fingernails are snake heads (Figs. 592-94, 600-01, 619). In addition, two snakes raise their hoods from either side of the feet, forming a kind of parikara (frame) for the image with their body (Pl. 48; Figs. 586, 588, 603). Other poisonous and demonic creatures compose the face. The thick tail of a descending kṛkalāśa (lizard) spans the four lower coils of the jaṭā, forms the third eye on the forehead, while its sharply dented, outspread legs and toes skew up the eyebrows into a bhṛkuṭi (frown). The upper part of its body dilates into the nose and nostrils, swollen with passion. Its twin short, sharply clawed forelegs clutch a pair of affronted mīnas (fish) reproduced with fluttering fins, protruding eyeballs and sloping mouth, to create flaring whiskers with a menacing upward flourish (Figs. 595, 598-99). Below the thin, pursed, cruel line of the mouth, and the thick lower lip, the short, round chin is made up of the round, sloping body of a kulīraḥ (crab) with four tapering tentacles, curving in and out on either side, to grip the cheeks (Figs. 595, 598-99). The glowering eyes, overhung by the frowning eyebrows, are made of expanded eyelids, engraved with the eyeballs, downgazing, circular pupils, and bulging nose of a demon, while the eyeballs are transformed into gaping demonic jaws with lolling tongue and fangs (Fig. 598). The head is deeply embedded between the shoulders, which are constituted by the gaping, sharp toothed, indented jaws of karimakaras (crocodilian creature of the sea with elephantine trunk), equipped with staring, globular eyes, set above curled trunks (Pls. 23, 48; Figs. 606-08). The poisonous creatures in the face are set off by the ears of the image, which are formed by two mayūras (peacocks). The alert head of the peacocks touches their tensed, swelling chests. Their toes tightly clutch the perch of Paśupati's earlobe, while their wings flap back to frame their fanned out tail, which forms the ear itself (Pl. 20; Figs. 595-96, 604-06, 608-09).

The chest, the thighs on the front and on the sides, are covered with two gaṇa (attendant of Śiva) heads each, the belly being made of one large gaṇa head (Figs. 580, 582). The terrifying expression of the Paśupati head changes to sombre expression in the heads on the chest (Figs. 600, 610-11, 616-17), a gracious, if unsmiling expression in the gaṇa on the belly

(Fig. 601), a slight smile in the gaṇas on the thigh front (Fig. 612), and, to loud, menacing laughter in the gaṇas on either side of the thighs. The gaṇas on thigh front are provided with hands, folded in namaskāramudrā (posture of salute), while the gaṇas on the chest and belly are alone equipped with whiskers. While the ears of the gaṇas are pulled down by earrings, the gaṇa on the belly does not have ears (Pl. 22; Figs. 582, 600, 610-17). In between the two gaṇas on the thigh front, rises the erect liṅga, the testicles being formed like two bells, and the phallus being made into a kūrma (tortoise) head with parted mouth (Fig. 602). The knees are carved with two grinning siṁha (lion) heads with small ears, overlapping hair locks, deeply socketed eyes, overhung by curved eyebrows, and with sharply incised jaws (Pl. 48; Figs. 603, 618).

The enormous girth of the image, enhanced by the outspread arms, makaras, and snake hoods, is poised lightly and easily on the huge legs (Fig. 582). The uncompromising frontality of the stance is varied subtly by the outward swing of the snake hoods and peacock tails above the shoulder, or the placement of the gaṇas, slightly off centre on the chest (Figs. 583-74). The verticalism of the image, stressed by the alignment of the lizard nose with the tortoise phallus, is offset by counterplay of curves created by the folded hands of gaṇas on the thighs, the snake bands girdling waist, chest, throat and head, and by the raised makara snout. The protruding heads on the body give immense vitality to the undulating body surface. The ferocious calm of the head (Fig. 595) and the still posture, compressed by the frame of the open, leering jaws of snakes (Figs. 589-94), is relieved by the surpassing dignity and gravity of bearing, and the lively expression of gaṇas and lions (Pl. 48; Fig. 580).

ATTEMPTS AT IDENTIFICATION

An attempt has been made, in a volume compiled at the turn of the millennium[24] by a few scholars from different parts of the world, to understand and explain this unique sculpture from Tala. A sense of bafflement has characterized the nature of the various conclusions. Faced with the difficulty of finding any textual reference that provides a comprehensive explanation for the various features of this image, the scholars have characterized it as a riddle, deliberately posed to succeeding generations as a generalized expression of the variety of shapes in the world, lacking any theological or cosmological scheme; as a regional aberration from Gupta or Vākāṭaka forms; as a crude, ethnic tribal artefact, devoid of normative concepts of classical sculptures; and, as a subordinate deity, found in its original location, which would have had a replica, on the other side of Devarani steps. Though some of them have acknowledged the impropriety of adapting a monolinear view of this complex sculpture, they have generally refused to recognize this image as that of Śiva himself, or to accept the possibility of its being simultaneously representative of the various aspects of Śiva. They have chosen, instead, to select a few textual references, isolate these from iconological history, and, to fasten on exclusive nomenclatures. In the process, they have concentrated on certain characteristics of the sculpture, which they have tried to explain. They have, however, contradicted, by their postulates, the evidence they have themselves assembled, the evidence that suggests the polyvalent character of the image, its many dimensioned cosmology, or its cognizance as Śiva, in his diverse manifestations.

And yet, the scholars have, in various ways, offered vital clues to the composite nature of the sculpture, to the confluence of Śaiva and Buddhist ideas in it, to the fusion of what they see as 'elite' and 'non-elite', 'tribal' and 'classical' world views, and, to its ritual, ceremonial, sacrificial symbolism.

Joanna Williams describes the image as a visual conundrum inviting surprise and awe, and, as the inscrutable Brahman, who appeared as the Yakṣa before the Gods.[25] L.S. Nigam agrees and identifies it as the Yakṣa who posed a riddle to the Gods in the Kenopaniṣad.[26] Michael Meister also accepts this image as an illustration of the Yakṣapraśna or a rebus, and approvingly quotes the story of Yakṣa Mudgarapāṇi, doorkeeper in the service of Śiva.[27]

A variation is introduced in this argument by Doris Meth Srinivasan, who assumes, in view of its size and weight, that the Tala image was found in its original location to the right of the Devarani temple stairs, and could be identified as the Rūpayakṣa, and that its counterpart, the Nāmayakṣa, could be found to the left of the Devarani stairs, if it was cleared. She says that the idea of the Mahāyakṣa was prominent in the late BC and early AD centuries, and had declined by the time the Tala image was made. Yet, she assumes that the image is one of two Mahāyakṣas, representing name and form, or intellectual and sensitive cognition, whereby the Mahāyakṣa, Mahāpuruṣa or Brahman, mentioned in the Vedas, Brāhmaṇas, Upaniṣads and the *Mahābhārata*, descends into the world.[28] It should be pointed out here that the right side of the stairs was cleared, to reveal a large seated Gaṇeśa, contrary to Srinivasan's presumption. Moreover, just as this image appears to have been carefully laid on its face, rather than fallen where it stood, the image of a sage was also concealed at the top of the Devarani stairs.

I.K. Sharma, Chandrasekhar Gupta and R.C. Agrawala agree with Srinivasan that the massive size and volume of the sculpture suggest that it has been found in its original location. In view of its demonic and fierce features, Sharma classifies it as a subordinate Āvaraṇa devatā (a deity in the outer temple facade), and identifies it as Kiṅkara Kumbhodara, the potbellied doorkeeper of Śiva, who is accompanied by Nikumbha on the opposite side. He is also willing to accept the image as that of Bhairava Kṣetrapāla, installed in the āgneya (southeastern) aṅgālaya (side shrine) of the temple. He offers no textual support or iconographic parallels for his position or explanation for the absence of a statue of Nikumbha. B.N. Mukherjee, in an allusion in his analysis of numismatic arts in India, identifies the image as Vīrabhadra and compares it with a mask on a punchmarked Kāśī or Kośala coin. The comparison is based on some physical details of the mask. The eyes and mouth of the mask emulate broad leaves, nose imitates radish, and the moustache imitates lobsters and fishes. The comparison is not supported by necessary illustrations or iconographic analogies.[29]

Chandrasekhar Gupta identifies the Tala image as a subordinate 'Parivāradevatā' or a family deity, though he is baffled by the absence of āyudhas or weapons, and vāhanas or vehicles, associated with such deities. He quotes from the *Suśruta* and *Kāśyapa saṁhitās*, from the Bālagrahacikitsā or the pediatrics section of *Āyurveda*, to characterize it as one of the forms of Kārtikeya, named Skandāpasmāra, which embodies and personifies the fearful, ghoulish shapes of children's diseases. He does not, however, match specific diseases with the specific shapes in the Tala sculpture, or provide relevant textual allusions.[30] R.C. Agrawala describes the sculpture as a subsidiary figure of Mahāyakṣa. He associates it with a bigger statue in the sanctum, but does not try to explain the absence of any surviving evidence for such a statue in the sanctum or the low height of the sanctum, which does not appear to have been constructed to house such a statue.[31]

In an amplification of such suggestions, Hans Bakker refers to the Mahābhārata, to nagna (nude), ghoṇāsāvaraṇa (clothed by snakes), anekaprāṇirūpin Śivagaṇa (a servant of Śiva, who combines the shapes of many creatures), who performs protective functions, and characterizes the Tala image as a composite apotropaic Śivagaṇa.[32] Bakker's description of the Tala image as 'gaṇa', or as 'weird' should be read with his admission that this is an 'elusive' identification, which conceals the fact that the meaning of the image is not understood.

P.K. Agarwala also describes the Tala image as that of a club bearing Śivagaṇa, guarding the door. He quotes from the *Prapañcasāra Tantra*, Kriyā and Mantrapāda of the *Iśānaśivagurudevapaddhati*, and the *Uttarāgama* to identify this gaṇa as Aghorāstra, or a personification of the weapon of Aghora Śiva. Its limbs are fashioned out of snakes (ahipravaraghaṭitagātra). Its body is decorated by a garland of spiders and scorpions (lūṭavṛścikamālā) and by serpentine ornaments.[33] This identification isolates a few and does not explain all the shapes in the sculpture.

In a further ramification of this argument, L.S. Rao quotes from the *Ṛgveda, Arthaśāstra, Gautama* and *Āpastambha Dharmasūtras* and Jaina literature to identify the Tala image as that of Varuṇa, the Māyin, the great illusionist. He finds it to be dominated by aquatic creatures. He associates these creatures with mahākacchavardhana rites, that help increase oceanic waters, overcome pestilences, and cleanse oneself. He links the tortoise and crab, represented in the image, with magical spells, witchcraft and wizardry. He identifies the seven staring human heads in the image as watchful spies and the glowering eyes in its head as indicative of the argus eyed vigilance of Varuṇa.[34] He does not explain the absence of conventional iconographic features, characteristic of Varuṇa and does not relate the image to the proto-Varuṇa image in the Jethani temple.

The scholars reject identification of the Tala image as that of Śiva in any of his major forms, not only because of its location, which they assume as original, but also because of what they consider to be a lack of familiar iconographic features. Srinivasan refuses to recognize the image as that of Viśvarūpa Śiva, as it lacks the ascending hierarchical order of aquatic, earthly, atmospheric and heavenly beings, found conventionally in the 6th century Viṣṇu Viśvarūpa image from Samālāji. She refuses to acknowledge it as Paśupati, Mukhaliṅga, Maheśa or Śiva, as she finds the image to be devoid of major Śaivite symbols and iconographic traits, including the third eye. She dismisses the upraised phallus of the image to be a startling composition, supported by no known Śaivite iconography. She adds that the aspects of the Paśupati image had not been concretized by the 5th or 6th century and when they were, the Tala image did not anticipate them.[35] Srinivasan agrees that the image does not conform to the iconography of Paśupati as the Paśupati aspect was not one of the aspects of Śiva, concretized by the 5th/6th century AD. Kalyan Kumar Dasgupta spurns its identification as Lakulīśa on the incorrect assumption that it lacks a Lakuṭa or rod. Nor would he accept its naming as Rudra.[36] I.K. Sharma also finds it to be devoid of the features of Vedic Rudra or Purāṇic Śiva. Nigam rejects its identification as Pañcamukha, Ekādaśa or Dvādaśa Rudra as it is not polycephalous.[37] L.S. Rao rejects its designation as Paśupati, as it does not represent the entire animal world, or as Aṣṭamūrti, as it does not conform to well known forms of Aṣṭamūrti. Srinivasan also asserts that the Tala image, unlike the Aṣṭamūrti Māndhal Śiva image, with its four conventional faces of caturmukhaliṅga, does not conform to basic Śaiva religious iconography.[38]

The scholars are quick to attribute what they incorrectly see as the lack of familiar Śaivite features in the Tala Śiva, to unknown, indigenous, tribal, local, sui generis ideas and traits. K.K. Dasgupta[39] and Hans Bakker describe such traits in the Tala Śiva as animistic, on a surface physical level; suggesting, either respect for animals represented; or, knots, used at body joints, to confine soul sources, on the pattern of joint markings on human bodies in Oceania, Far East, and pre-Columbian America.[40] L.S. Rao characterises the Tala Śiva as an aberrant and enigmatic regional interpretation of a Tāntric God of magic.[41] Michael Meister describes the multiple shapes in the Tala Śiva as contradictory features that form part of the anti-canonical layers of alternative belief systems and oral mythologies. He does not offer to unravel these strands, as it is too late in the day to make such an attempt successfully.[42] R.C. Agrawala, Hans Bakker, J.P. Singhdio, P.K. Agrawala variously misunderstand the extraordinary blend of power and grace in the Tala Śiva as a local tribal style[43], characterised by parṇavastra, or leaf garment, and, by cyclopean size;[44] a crowded and cumbersome style, characteristic of early medieval Vindhya and M.P. region;[45] and, a style afflicted by gross roundness, muscular build, naive mannerism and awkward imagination, characteristic of the early Kuṣāṇa art of Mānḍhal and Mathura.[46]

Joanna Williams explains the deep cut, three-dimensional carvings with their puzzling iconography as evidence of a transition from wood to stone technology, from tribal to Brāhmaṇical ideas, and, as evidence of the work of artists, used by a local dynasty, to extend Hinduism among forest dwellers, with the help of learned Brāhmins. According to her, the work shows gouging of the friable stone by an wood carver's chisel, rather than rough, ridged channels, created by blows of a heavy mallet of a stone mason. Bakker describes the Tala image as hybrid, spectacular and slightly obscure and explains this resemblance, like Joanna Williams, as indicative of the tribal ideological environment evolving towards Hinduism.[47] Joanna Willams and Bakker do not illustrate this transition by any local example in wood or in stone.

Since the inspiration behind the Tala image is thus considered to be tribal, the corollary argument follows, as Srinivasan or Bakker suggest, that it lacks any rational theological cosmogony, and that there is nothing more than a desire for comprehensive representation or ingenuity in the use in this image of the device of symmetrical placement of shapes to mimic anatomical forms.[48] Bakker finds a metaphysical hierarchy in four tiers of diminishing subtlety ranging from yogin 1, yogin 2, muṇḍin (brahmacārin with shorn head) and uṣṇīṣin (turbaned), from sakalaniṣkala to sakala, from absence to presence of attributes, in the four tiers of heads arranged on the body of the Mānḍhal Śiva image, found at Bholāhuḍki Tekḍī. He does not find any such metaphysical hierarchy or organizational structure in the five vertical tiers of heads on the Tala Śiva, and offers symmetry, numerical convenience and representation of various aspects for the initiate or layman as reasons for grouping of heads on Tala and Mānḍhal images. Bakker misses the metaphysical hierarchy in the Tala Śiva image, which he finds in the twelve-headed Śiva image from Mānḍhal, because his attention is diverted from its convergent meaning by the divergent physical detail.[49]

Doris Meth Srinivasan's attempt to establish the biological nature of the concept of cosmic parturition, or explain the Tala image biologically as a parturient or pregnant male God, or Yakṣa, follows as a logical consequence of her argument, about the image lacking any theological rationale or cosmogenic scheme. According to her, the variety of forms covering the surface of the Tala Yakṣa are forms he had contained in his large belly before pushing them out. At the same time, she adds that the Tala Yakṣa's full belly proclaims the rich store house of forms still contained within it.[50] Her description of the emergence of the Rūpa and Nāmayakṣas should be read, in the light of her eloquent characterization of the Vedic sacrificial fire piling rites or Agnicayana, as rites designed to reimpregnate Brahmaṇ, Prajāpati or Mahāyakṣa, after he had emptied his womb of forms and given them names, in expression of his primordial will to create. Srinivasan quotes the *Brāhmaṇas* and *Saṁhitās* to show that the different parts of the sacrificial rites and oblations are identifiable with the different limbs of Prajāpati. She explains that the Agnicayana fire altar is made in five layers, of which the first layer is retassik, or semen discharging, and the last layer has the bull brick, symbolic of potency. She concludes that the sacrifice is made pregnant with all beings through dīkṣā or initiation, a condition reinduced in Prajāpati, after he has evacuated all forms, by the making of the fire altar.[51] If the ramifications of Srinivasan's argument are to be accepted and extended to Tala, the crouching gaṇas at Tala, being provided with large, pendant bellies or parted legs, should be explained as figures, bowed by womb chambers, replete with forms, that show intense exertion before giving birth. The making of the Tala temple may be interpreted as an exercise in the reimpregnation of the Mahāyakṣa through the piling of the fire altar. The stambhas or pillars, the kalaśas or pitchers at Tala can be seen as interchangeable with Rudra and Brahmaṇ for performing a biological role in the creation of multiple forms. Finally, the Tala Paśupati and its companions can be taken to illustrate the transition in iconographic history, suggested by Srinivasan, from Veda or theological statement about Godhead, to līlā, divine play or labour, undertaken by God for the edification of worshippers.[52]

It is true that the cosmology of fire and waters underlies the postulate of coincidence of creation and procreation at Tala. However, it is a coincidence with a psychosomatic rather than biological meaning. Srinivasan herself has assembled overwhelming evidence in her seminal work *Many Heads* etc., which emphatically demonstrates that the meanings attributed to the multiple body parts of Prajāpati are symbolic rather than literal in content. She describes and accepts the Vedic homology of human and cosmic creation, the agnihotra sacrificial ritual being equated in it with a mental sacrifice of the lower self for the constitution of a higher self. She narrates the psychological rather than biological process, enacted by the devotee, to reconstruct what has been dismembered, for transforming his earthly into a heavenly body.[53] Unlike the images illustrated in her book, the Tala Paśupati does not multiply its limbs but contains and transcends diverse shapes in its body. More than any image illustrated by her, the Tala image thus exemplifies her theory of residual power, inherent in Rudra as the extra element in the numerical cycle. It is a power of engendering by remaindering, a power which creates by transcending, by sacrificing the elements, and ensures the continuity and renewal of the cycle.[54] The names and forms of nature, which she finds personified in two Tala yakṣas, one extant, the other imagined, have to be shattered in order to understand the nature of the Tala Paśupati and its iconological context. The Tala Paśupati powerfully illustrates the composite nature of the divine, which can function in different ways at the same time, not only to offer a theological statement to illumine the nature of God, but, also to narrate graphically the story of the multiplicity of phenomena emanating from and merging in the unity of noumen. The linear sequence suggested by Srinivasan from theological to narrative concerns[55] is not substantiated at Tala in view of the simultaneous presence and blend of the concept and percept, the denotative and the connotative in its iconographic programme. The tight muscular, and what Srinivasan herself describes as the 'pneumatic' body of the Mahāyakṣa of Tala[56] neither suggests the labour of creation, nor the post partum state of relaxation after emptying the belly of forms. Instead, it combines relaxation with tension, appropriate to a yogic body of arrested breath. To interpret the Tala image biologically rather than psychosomatically, after Srinivasan, in the teeth of the evidence, which she has herself adduced to the contrary, would be an act of sensationalism, if not fetishism.[57]

J.P. Singhdeo identifies the three faces with moustache on the chest and stomach as male faces, representing tripura or three cities of āṇava mala (egoism), karma (deeds and their binding consequence), and māyā (illusion). In view of the lion head on the knees, he identifies the four faces without moustache on the thighs as female faces of śakti, that represent four methods of awakening śakti or energy, latent in mūlādhāra, through dhyāna, bhāva, japa and mantra, or through meditation, emotional identification, repetition of the name and incantation. He thus characterizes the image as a composite Aghori Tāntric Yogic figure of Mahākāla and Mahākālī, made under the guidance of a Tāntric Aghori. He suggests vogue of the Aghori cult at Tala, in which Mahākāla was the fulcrum, connecting infinity and zero.[58] While one may not discount Singhdeo's suggestion of the presence of Aghori Tāntric elements at Tala, it is difficult to accept his inference, based as it is on an isolated physical feature, rather than on any iconographic parallel or textual evidence. Nor does his suggestion help us explain the absence of bisexual features in the head, trunk or the genital organ of Paśupati.

P.K. Agrawala is close to the truth when he opines that the image was not a freak of the artist's imagination, but had evolved within the iconoreligious, mythical and Āgamic traditions of Śaiva teachers.[59] Meister is also close to the mark when he says that no simplistic, canonical linearity of interpretation of the complex tradition is feasible at Tala, and argues that we have come too late to Tala to understand the immense philosophical speculation and meditation of several millennia, which were compressed in the Tala images.[60] Pramod Chandra, while discussing the contributions of scholars in analysing the Tala image, has pertinently warned against the random matching of text and image, and, against the import of current social and historical conditions, as understood by modern scholarship, into an ancient context. He has correctly emphasized the fact that even though every individual feature of the Tala image may be explained by reference to conventional Hindu thought, imagery and practice, it is the unique juxtaposition of these features in a single image that requires understanding and explanation. He adds that suggestions about borrowing and lending between Hindu and tribal ideas with regard to the Tala image have to be established with specific evidence. He concludes that presentation of such evidence requires vast learning, knowledge and experience of languages and culture, both high and low (mārgī and deśī), which involves a pooling of scholarly resources.[61]

The Multivalence of Meaning: Paśu and Pati

The quintessential idea behind this great Śiva image seems to be the relation between paśu and pati. The paśu is shown on the body of his pati in his independent, individual existence. In terms of later non-dualistic Kashmir Śaivism, this suggests the spanda (throb) of its separation from the ocean of awareness. The spanda seems to be symbolically represented by the twin bells of Śiva's testicles. At the same time, the paśus are collectively involved in the composite body of Śiva, suggesting yamala (togetherness) with him.[62] According to the Śaiva Siddhānta philosophy, the paśus play an active role in this nexus. The graduation of expression in the gaṇas, ranging from wild laughter to overbearing gravity, may suggest a growing realization of unity with Śiva by kṣetrajña (cognizant of the field) jīva (individual creature). The gaṇas would seem to correlate to different categories of bhaktas (devotees), who respectively attain, by virtue of caryā (service), kriyā (purificatory rite), yoga (union of friendship) and jñāna (wisdom), sālokya (residence in the region of God), sāmīpya (proximity to God), sārūpya (assumption of God's form) and sāyujya (union with God). They would undertake these padas (methods) in order to snap the pāśas (bonds) of guṇas (attributes), malas (impurities) or kleśas (afflictions), which create an unreal duality between them and their lord, and reduce human beings and animals to the same level in Paśupati's body. These different bonds would appear to be embodied by the nature of the different paśus.

The pañcakleśas (the five afflictions), for example, would be strongly suggested by the five categories of creatures in the head of Paśupati, where the battle with the passions would seem to be the fiercest. The aim of the Pāśupata way, celebrated by the gaṇas, presumably by dancing, chanting, laughing, drumming on the mouth or meditating, at Tala, is duḥkhānta, end of suffering.[63] In non-dualistic Kashmir Śaivism, the pāśakṣaya (snapping of bonds) or Śivatvayojana (attainment of Śivahood) does not depend on individual exertion like this. It comes to persons, who are pierced by the sharp, stabbing rain of grace (dṛḍha-śaktinipāta-viddha), God pouring himself into those who are ready for him. Yet, laughing loudly, uttering auspicious sounds, offering namaskāra (salute) with folded hands, or silent meditation, in which the gaṇas on Śiva's body are engaged, are all acts of pure devotion, called upahāra (offering), which would seem designed to seek the descent of such grace. The very fact of the merger of the individual creatures in the body of Śiva, would appear to indicate the creative movement of sphoṭa (explosion), in which the individuals merge with their archetype, with the pratyabhijñā (realization) of their mutual unity, and this is synonymous with the restitution of their original state of grace.[64]

In terms of later Kannāḍa Vīraśaivism, this would be seen as liṅgāṅgasāmarasya (the assimilation of the flavour of the sign and the signifier), the image of Paśupati appearing as an anthropomorphized liṅga (literally, phallic sign), the creatures on his body appearing as aṅgas (literally, limbs or facets). The image is frozen, as it were, in an arrested moment of duḥkhānta (end of sorrow), the summum bonum of Paśupata Śaivism. In terms of later tantra, it would seem frozen as a mantramūrti, or a body made of sacred, sacrificial formulae, in which the individual creatures act like varṇas (letters) of the formulae. These help the bhakta (devotee) to identify himself with the mūrti by a contemplative ascent and descent, through vyāpakanyāsa (comprehension by mentally touching every part of the image) and bhūta śuddhi (harmonization of the five elements of earth, water, air, fire and ether).[65]

Merger a Sacrifice

In the *Vedas*, *Upaniṣads*, *Brāhmaṇas* and the *Mahābhārata*, the Tala image of Paśupati finds direct inspiration in the recurring theme of sacrifice of paśus to Rudra as Paśupati. Sometimes, in the *Brāhmaṇas*, the gods create him with their most dreadful shapes, and endow him with overlordship of cattle, so that he pierces the incestuous Prajāpati, who himself represents the sacrifice, dislodged from its true end of burning of lower passions. Elsewhere, in sūtras and saṁhitās, Rudra spares the cattle, or Prajāpati, being either favored with the cattle, or with the remnants of sacrifice. The *Mahābhārata* not only mentions sacrifice in Paśupati's temple, but also sarvamedha (a total sacrifice) of paśus by Paśupati, who further assumes most of the shapes and features found in the Tala Paśupati. *Āraṇyakas* explain the sacrifice as internal rather than external, mental rather than physical. The *Upaniṣads* clarify this, speaking of the pāśas which can be snapped by knowing Paśupati, the pāśas thus becoming objects of the sacrifice.[66]

The Tala Paśupati goes far beyond the conventional description of the Paśupati image in later texts, by giving a vivid and concrete shape to this idea of immolation of the lower selves of paśus in the body of Paśupati, in order to secure union of their higher nature with their lord. Sometimes, the gods themselves assume the shape of paśus. Viṣṇu assumes the shapes of kūrma or matsya. The Ahirbudhnyas, the divinities of the middle region, become the snakes. The vrātyas (the uninitiated), creatures of pātāla (infernal region), pitṛs (manes) or marūts (storm winds) become the seven gaṇas on the body of Ekavrātya or Rudra.[67]

Viśvarūpa

The Tala Paśupati image can be perceived also as the Viśvarūpa (omniform) of Śiva, almost as a logical corollary of the idea of Jīva Śiva union, implicit in the nexus between paśu and pati. The image virtually becomes jagaccittra (mirror of the universe) being both viśvamaya (immanent) and viśvottīrṇa (transcendant). It offers an illustration of the Vedic sūtrātman (thread soul) doctrine, in which the multiplicity of things is strung together by the single thread of the spirit. It creates, as it were, a circumference and a centre, in which the gati (motion) of individual beings is pravṛtta (centrifugal) initially, nivṛtta (centripetal) finally, in which the differentiated world of śakti (energy) comes back to its source, the puruṣa (principle), by annulling its finite, mutilated personality. It fulfils the inspired words of *Śvetāśvatara Upaniṣad*, which speaks of Rudra as one who spins out many forms, gross and subtle, from within himself, conceals himself under their different shapes and limbs, creating, protecting, pervading and absorbing them. Bahu or kāmarūpitva (power to acquire forms at will) is an attribute of his vibhūti (glory), illustrated in the Tala Paśupati, and the raudrīgāyatrī or śatarudrīya is a vāgyajña (a sacrifice in sacred words) to the myriad forms, high and low, from the regions of earth, air and sky, selectively represented in the Paśupati.[68]

The Tala Paśupati also illustrates the other aspect of the sūtrātman doctrine, the unity and integrity of the supreme person being unaffected by the multiplicity of forms, that emerge from it or return to it. It is a symbol of the ananta (both zero and the plenum), which is unaffected by the emanation from or resolution in its body, of individual creatures. In fact, if the individual beings are withdrawn from its body, it is reduced virtually to an abstract outline. It is the 'actuator' and 'spectator' rather than the 'doer', passing from body to body, without being affected by the bright or dark fruits of their actions. It is the measuring out of the measurer, himself remaining unmeasured, to be worshipped by the bhakta (devotee, etymologically, divided) in different interchangeable shapes, while itself remaining undivided.[69]

The Tala image mirrors the eloquent description of Mahādeva Viśvarūpa in *Mahābhārata*. In this description he is the fount of time and space, all things, animate and inanimate, all creatures, human and non-human whom he marks with his sign or the sign of his spouse. He assumes, among others, forms of yakṣas, gandharvas, snakes, lions, birds, peacocks, lizards, goats, panther, Aśvins, Rudras, ṛṣis, yogīs, siddhas, Kirātas, Śavaras and, is adored by them. He makes rain, gives heat. He has empty space for his covering, and he covers all things. He has large and terrible eyes. Lord of all creatures, he is one and many, and assumes many heads, faces and sides. Endowed with all attributes, he is divested of them. Formless, he assumes all forms.[70]

Therefore, the mortal pleasure with which individuals cling to the tangible, physical shapes on the Tala Paśupati's body, will remain a hindrance to the realization of its universal, ideal form. The pañcakṛtyas (the five activities) may or may not be represented by the creatures on his body. The characteristics of the sacred trinity, or the apex, middle, and bottom of the universe, or the specific physical attributes, which later Purāṇas propose to see in Śiva's Viśvarūpa may or may not be fully embodied in it. The presence of non-human creatures on the body of divine and semi-divine persons is a continuing feature, common to all denominations, in different periods. However, the Tala Paśupati remains almost the only image in Indian art to give complete physical shape to the idea of Śiva's Viśvarūpa by incorporating the limbs of individual beings as integral parts of its body, rather than by sprouting or multiplying these as external appendages.

It has incorporated aspects and activities of the Trinity, principles of life and death, creation, preservation and destruction or significant signs of the helio planetary universe, in its encompassing form. It is a convincing example of the doctrine that the omnipresence of Śiva's form is an act of grace, since he assumes the shapes desired by his votary. The recognition of this enables the jīva to abandon his individual being, and yoke himself to the source of his being.[71]

Lakulīśa

Ithyphallic, standing heroically with a club, like a defender of faith, the Tala Paśupati is also a foremost leader of hosts, and a sovereign presence at the centre of the universe, which demonstrates the ultimate possibility of a jīva becoming incarnate as Śiva. As such, it satisfies the description of Lakulīśa, the great Śaiva teacher, considered to be the twenty eighth incarnation of Śiva in early inscriptions and texts. Śiva has assumed the body of Sadguru, Deśika or the true teacher to perform his mission of giving dīkṣā or initiation to the jīva or paśu, to release him from his bonds, and to make him fit for redemption through union with Śiva or Pati. It is at once an ascetic and a regal figure, which reminds us of the association and assimilation of the identity of Śaiva tribes, teachers and kings with the tremendous presence and nature of the club bearing Śiva in early historical accounts, inscriptions and coins. The Lakulīśa aspect of Tala Paśupati finds its antecedents in ascetic or tribal dress, royal homonyms, weapons and banners.[72]

By integrating the vyūha (group) of jīvas with Śiva himself, and by demonstrating Iśvara (the puissant God) as the instrumental as well as material cause of the universe, the Lakulīśa image at Tala goes not only beyond the vyūha of Vṛṣṇivīras (Vṛṣṇi heroes), which keeps Viṣṇu out of the vyūha, but also beyond Paśupata Siddhānta dualism, which sees Śiva as only the instrumental cause. It not only conveys a suggestion of the diverse incarnations of Paśupati being directly integrated in his body, but also seems to illustrate the five avasthās (situations) of the Paśupati's devotee, in the paśus arrayed in different tiers on Paśupati's body. It would appear to be deliberately dressed wildly like a lunatic, in the manner required by Pāśupata practices, to demonstrate rejection of conventional social norms.[73]

Though the Tala Paśupati does not satisfy the textual traits of Lakulīśa being seated, or holding mātuluṅga (citron fruit), or displaying a preaching mudrā, Pāśupata ascetics at Tala do show the occasionally prescribed utkuṭikāsana, and hold mātuluṅga, while a large Śaiva dvārapāla or attendant at Jethani seems to display an abhaya or vyākhyāna mudrā with its raised, though abraded hand.[74] Many archaeological precedents (and successors) for a standing club bearing Śiva or proto-Śiva image exist, which makes the identification of the Lakulīśa aspect of Tala Paśupati plausible.[75]

Yogī

The image of Paśupati at Tala ipso facto becomes the image of a Yogīśvara, an archetypal yogī. It offers, in its body, a demonstration of the technique of yoga, union of paśu with pati. It appears to illustrate this technique by symbolically recalling the role of Śiva in samudramanthana, churning of the ocean, and the birth of Skanda, the son of Śiva Pārvatī and the general of the Gods. The ocean is kṣīrasāgara, kṣīra (milk) being equated with the retas, semen, the cerebro spinal fluid in the body. The upright shaft of the Tala Paśupati image appears to represent the mount Mandara, the pole used for churning this ocean. The pole can be also seen as the trikāṇḍa iṣus (three pronged spear) of Śiva in his role as Piṇākapāṇi (bow bearing), lubdhaka or mṛgavyādha (deer hunter, star Sirius). The spear pierces and joins the pṛthivī (earth, spinal cord), antarīkṣa (sky, medula oblongata, bulb), dyūloka (heaven, the brain) in the body of a yogī. The tortoise on Śiva's body (a symbol of immortality and vitality, life animating its limbs even after mutilation and decapitation) acts as the pivotal rest for this pole, while the nāgas wrapped around him act as the churning ropes, or, as waist and arm bands.[76] Śiva fulfils the Ṛgvedic idea of a divine physician,[77] who effects all healing by using the therapeutic potency of water in the body. Water acquires the rejuvenating influence of amṛtam, or ambrosia, only when it is purged of its viṣam, or toxic elements.[78] The kṣīrasāgara in the body yields viṣam as well as amṛtam when it is churned by Gods and demons or virtues and vices. The amṛtam becomes fit for use only when it is purged of the halāhala or poison, known as kālakūṭa, which springs from the ocean, to be absorbed in small drops by the snake, crab and the peacock, which find home on the body of the Paśupati. Appropriately in this context, the peacock is born of the feathers in the wings of Garuḍa, which fetches the amṛtaghaṭa, the pot of nectar, from the heavens.[79]

The homeopathic use of poison to counter poison, passion to regulate passion, is suggested by the ambivalent associations of the paśus on Paśupati's body. Kāma consecrates the image of Śiva's fish form on the Maṇikūṭa mountain in Assam. The mīnas and makaras, as insignia and vehicles of Kāmadeva, speak of creation permeated by passion, while the mayūras, as banners of Skanda, speak of its control. The kūrma represents, on the one hand, withdrawal from sense objects, and, on the other, it makes (akarot) offspring, and saves Vaivasvata Manu, the progenitor of the human race, from the deluge. The lizard is poisonous, but it constitutes here, the anti-erotic frown burning Kāma. The snakes remind us of Āḍi, who interrupts penance, and, with his power to cast off slough, embodies force of rejuvenation and metempsychosis. The lions recall their use by Śiva to control vṛṣa or varṣaṇaśīla retas (the incontinent flow of semen).[80]

Similarly, tapas (penance) burns and channelizes creative passion. Skanda's birth is a result of intense tapas, of which one aspect is the heat of anger, indicated by the bhṛkuṭi (frown) of the Tala Śiva. His incandescent frown burns Kāma, or Smara, the God of love and recollection. The idea of Kāma is suggested by the memory of six kāmāvacāra lokas (passion ridden regions). The memory is evoked by six creatures, namely, the pair of fish, a crab, two demons and a lizard, occupying the face of Śiva. Another aspect of tapas is the creative heat of metabolic fire, which burns retas or semen through six cakras in the suṣumṇā (an artery, probably the carotid), and distils it into the purest essence of the fluid in the somapūrita kalaśa or nectar filled pitcher of the mastiṣka or brain. This is the purest essence or skanna, from which the name of Skanda or suṣumṇāputra (progeny of suṣumṇā) is derived.[81]

If the descending lizard may suggest the yogic practice of nāsikāgra dṛṣṭi, or of gazing at the nose tip for achieving concentration, the pair of fish between the nose and the lips may represent the yogic practice of eating the fish. Together, these may represent kevalakumbhaka or the yogic control of breath, which swims through the right and left nostrils, and are equated with rivers Gaṅgā and Yamunā.[82]

The ascent of jīva to Śiva from dormancy, takes place through successive stages of awakening. The yogī harnesses Kālāgni, embodied in the guṇa on the belly to burn the pāśas through sādadhva dāha, tremendous heat and burning sensation, which probably may be represented by the creatures shown in the face of the Tala Śiva. The yogī moves to complete fulfilment and consecration or pūrṇākhāta and pūrṇābhiṣeka, to become śodhita adhva, or a person of purified passions, and turn into a benefactor for the entire world. The paśus on Paśupati's body move through the sthūla, sūkṣma, kāraṇa, mahākāraṇa and kaivalya dehas, and through the annamaya, prāṇamaya, manomaya, vijñānamaya koṣas, or the faculties of ingestion, breathing, meditation and knowledge, dominated by three guṇas, tamas, sattva, rajo, to reach their true self or svarūpa, ānandamaya koṣa or joyous state of purṇahanta or total fulfilment.[83]

Thus, in the body of Yogīśvara Paśupati at Tala, the mūlādhāra (coccygal) at the lower end of the vertical column is related to elements of earth and may be represented by the tortoise phallus. The svādhiṣṭhāna (sacrum at the lower end of spinal column) is related to the element of water and may be linked with the snake serving as waistband. The maṇipūra (the lumbar in the navel, controlling the digestive system) is probably presided over by kālāgni, the element of fire. The anāhata (dorsal) is related to the element of air, and the circulation of blood, pumped by the rhythmic systole (contraction) and diastole (expansion) of the heart. This may be embodied in the two gaṇas on the chest, representing prāṇa and apāna. The iḍā on the left and piṅgalā on the right above, are represented probably by the makaras or the snakes. They flank the viśuddhi cakra (cervical region), which is centred on the throat, is possibly equated with the element of akāśa or space, and produces sound. The combined sound of the six cakras, the saḍja or udgītha svara, supposedly synthesized in the voice of the mayūra, is represented by peacocks on Śiva's shoulders, between the fifth and the sixth cakras. The ājñācakra is represented here, between the eyebrows, by the third eye, formed by the lizard tail. The krauñca dvāra, or the curved door, by which the kuṭila or curved spinal cord is supposed to enter the brain, is the magnum foramen, suggested ostensibly by the curved snake tail above the forehead. The serpents unfold their vibrant and buoyant hoods in massive, upward sweeps, and coil themselves around Śiva's head. These may also represent the unfolding of the vital energy, prāṇa, the trikoṇikā śakti (three pointed energy) or kuṇḍalinī. Coiled in the mūlādhāra or śaktipīṭha, this energy surges upwards, after lighting up the six plexi, and enters the sahasrāra (crown of head, supposed to resemble thousand petalled, reversed lotus cap) or Kailāsa, for a marriage with Śiva. In Pāśupata or Kāpālika Kaula, this stage is described as Uttarakaula in which Śiva is reduced to his elements and is draped by śakti as Ādhāra kuṇḍalinī. With the loss of the sense of 'I' and 'this', the yogī reaches the turīya state or the state of communion, in the full unfolding of kuṇḍalinī shown by radiating snake hoods above Paśupati. The adho and ūrdhvagati, down and upward movement, prasāra and saṅkoca, expansion and contraction of the kuṇḍala or coils of the snakes is equivalent to the saṁvatsaracakra or annual cycle, comprising uttarāyaṇa or devayāna, the upward movement of Gods, and dakṣiṇāyāna or pitṛyāna, the downward movement, of ancestors. The kālacakra, the inexorable march of time, the cyclic process of emanation and dissolution, is witnessed by the Yogī as udāsīna sākṣī, detached observer.[84]

The seven gaṇas and the mayūras also recall the symbolic *Mahābhārata* story of Agni's flirtations with the wives of the seven sages, who are identified with vital airs or prāṇas. Svāhā, the daughter of Dakṣa, takes the form of the gāruḍi bird after cohabiting with Agni in the form of the wives of sages, and throws the seed in the golden lake, on the peak of the white mountain, guarded by Rudra's hosts.[85] The seven gaṇas may represent the sages or Rudra's hosts, while the gāruḍi bird could have changed itself into peacocks.

The legend of the birth of Skanda becomes an allegory for the ṣaṭcakrasādhanā (the penance of six wheels). The image of Tala Śiva turns, in this formulation, into a representation of the psychomachy of virtues and vices, reason and passion, poisonous and beneficent forces, life and death, within the body. From the birth of Skanda follows the victory of Devasenā, the militia of the commons, over Tārakāsura, the demon of the subconscious, for the attainment of ṛtambharā prajñā, or the faculty of the highest spiritual intelligence, and restoration of the body to health and good odour.[86] The image thus becomes a celebration of the attainment of svarāja or autonomy as against anyarāja or heteronomy, because man becomes a free man by actively mastering passions, and not by passively submitting to them.[87] And, it is thus, that the Tala Śiva image becomes the image of a yogī, who has stilled the turbulence of conflicting emotions in his body, and looks like a showerless cloud, rippleless lake, flickerless lamp, in a windless place.[88]

Agni

The Viśvarūpa or Yogīśvara form of Tala Paśupati is interchangeable with his form as Agniskandha or a pillar of fire. In the *Ṛgveda, Śatapatha Brāhmaṇa* or *Taittirīya Saṁhitā*, Agni, Prāṇāgni, Sahasramuṣka Agni are seen as names of Rudra or Paśupati; different animals are seen as his aspects as much as Paśupati's; and, as lord of the Soma plants, Agni becomes annada, and converts Soma or food into prāṇāgni or the radiant flame of life.[89]

The Tala Paśupati represents both Agni and Soma as sacrificial partners and displays on its body agnisomīya paśus.[90] It is simultaneously a symbol of the primeval Puruṣa, Prajāpati, Agni and Yajamāna. It is a symbol of the creation of the world by the sacrifice and dismemberment of Puruṣa, and, of the reintegration of the world by a reassemblage of his dispersed members.[91] The restoration is effected by the symbolic offering of the paśupuroḍāśa, or the sacrificial cake of animal heads. This offering is substituted for sacrificial burial of animal heads under the altar, the heads being suggestively represented on the body of Tala Paśupati.[92] In fact, the actual burial of a live tortoise used to be done earlier, to sprinkle Agni with its blood, rasa or life sap, to imitate the primordial creative act of Prajāpati. Mentioned in *Taittirīya Saṁhitā,* this act was designed to induce rain and fertilize the soil. The presence of the tortoise on Paśupati's body may well be explained as a celebration of this pristine divine act.[93] In the *Taittirīya Saṁhitā*, snakes are seen as guardians of the quarters, and, in the sarpāhuti, the Yajamāna renounces oblations, offered by the adhvaryu (officiating priest) to the snake. This may account for the snakes draped around Śiva.[94]

The sacrifice, in fact, is initiation, which is both a death and a rebirth for the initiate, who is himself the oblation. The Tala Paśupati becomes the prototype of kiṁpuruṣa, man, ānaddhapuruṣa, or a mockman, made to represent Agni. The pouring (siñcana) of the paśus in his body, represented by the creatures carved on him, is an internal agnihotra, a burnt offering of inferior, elemental, psychophysical selves. It is an ātmayajña, or self-immolation, conducted by the devotee, for identifying himself with his immortal self. It is a sacrifice of the eros to psyche, vāk to om, le noi to le soi, of the little self of the puppet to the great self of the puppeteer.[95]

The body of Tala Paśupati can be compared, on this analogy, with the Vedic fire altar with three ring stones, serving as self-perforated bricks. The altar is known as svayamātṛṇṇa, and the three bricks correspond to earth, air and sky, Agni, Vāyu and Āditya, apāna (outer breath, aspiration), vyāna (inbreath, transpiration) and prāṇa (central vital air), gārhapatya (household), āhavanīya (sacrificial) and dakṣiṇāgni (crematory fire), are represented by creatures of different regions. The kṣobhaṇa (vibration), manifested as saṁkoca (contraction) and vikāsa (expansion) in the pillar of fire, is probably symbolized by the two bells serving as the forelegs of the tortoise. The varying expressions of gaṇas may well recall the kṛlumat (playful), lelihyamānān (flickering) seven flames of Agni, devouring oblation, suggesting the krīḍā or līlā (sport), in which the lord participates without being moved or divided. The different perforates of the altar, quickened to life by the sun, serve as yonis (birth places) for passage from inferior to higher stages of being (represented by the paśus on Paśupati) in the agnerāroha (ascent after Agni), to assume the form of Agni. Skanda, symbolized by the peacocks on the Tala Paśupati's shoulders, framed by their sun eye plumage, is the culmination in this ascent, being seen as a result of Soma, burnt to its purest essence by Agni, in the skull of the cosmic man, pierced at the chine, foramen, the dvāra of mount Krauñca. He is, therefore, called Agnibhū, born of Agni, while Agni is called Kumārasū and Rudragarbha, progenitor of Kumāra, womb for Rudra. The seven heads on Paśupati's body can well be the seven Maruts, who are fellow initiates, gṛhamedhina (household sacrificers), assisting gṛhapati (Lord of the household) Rudra or Agni. They participate in the sacrifice, and attain divinity as Rudras by self-control. Skanda is the leader of this host by virtue of mastering and harnessing the passions.[96] The Tala Paśupati image thus symbolically demonstrates the process of sacrifice of lower instincts in the fire of self-restraint and its fruition.

Aṣṭamūrti

As an image of Agni and Viśvarūpa, the Tala Paśupati acquires the trait also of the Aṣṭamūrti. In the absence of any anthropomorphic representation of Aṣṭamūrti like the Tala Paśupati in Indian art, or a text establishing the iconography of Aṣṭamūrti, one has to relate literary evidence to the features of the Tala image. Interpreted in the light of such evidence, the seven gaṇa heads, together with the principal head, can be variously identified as the heads sacrificed in agnicayana, or the heads of Lokapālas (guardians of directions), Ādityas, Vasus, Bhairavas, or heads of Vīrabhadra. The categories of creatures, represented on Paśupati's body, are also eight in number, if we exclude mayūra or peacock, which is recognized as the ninth product, representing Kumāra (Skanda). The image may even suggest an eight sided sacrificial pole, with the śukrapātram (pot of semen) being represented by the phallus. Ultimately, these categories are perceived in the Gītā as the eight forms of lower nature, designed for sacrifice.[97]

According to the *Śatapatha Brāhmaṇa*, Rudra, born from the incestuous union of Prajāpati and Uṣas, is so-called, because he cries (arodīt) for names to rid himself of the memory of the primordial evil. The crying does not stop until eight names are given to him, represented by the eight categories of creatures on Tala Paśupati, and Kumāra, having received the eight names, one by one, becomes the ninth, represented by the peacocks. The eight names are presided over by the sun and moon, and mind of the initiate. In the late *Mārkaṇḍeya Purāṇa*, these elements are identified as bhūtamātra (matter), prāṇamātra (life), and cinmātra (mind), equated with the tripura or three guṇas, pierced by the bāṇa (arrow) of Śiva, to create Kumāra.[98] This recalls our earlier postulate of the Paśupati body being the shaft of the arrow or spear, penetrating different forms of the universe. The eightfold form of Śiva is developed in *Liṅgapurāṇa* later as complementary to the Pañca Brahmā (five Brahmā) doctrine, which suggests five temperaments. Of these, the austere ṛṣi (sage) type is probably represented by the principal head of Śiva; the deva (God) type, detached and yet interested in the world, by the two heads on the chest; the pitṛ (ancestor) type, engrossed in worldly life and welfare, by the head on the belly; the merry gandharva (genie, guarding Soma) type, by laughing gaṇas on the side thighs; the manuṣya (human) type with volatile temperament, by the gaṇas on the thigh fronts.[99] With this assimilation to different temperamental types and as yogādhyakṣa (lord of yoga), the Aṣṭamūrti at Tala may well preside over the aṣṭāṅga yoga (the eight limbed process of union). It can also be worshipped as a Mantreśvara (lord of mantras), by utterance of the eight syllabled mantra, a/u/m/na/maḥ/Śi/vā/ya, which can be associated with its eight concrete manifestations in meditation. Finally, one may refer to the eight flowers in the aṣṭapuṣpikā pūjā (worship with eight flowers), which may well have inspired the diverse floral representations on the Tala pillars and jambs. In this manner, the Tala Aṣṭamūrti becomes an instrument of contemplation for a Śiva bhāgavata.[100]

Yakṣa

Conceived as an embodiment of such diverse qualities of God, the image of Tala Paśupati also becomes the image of Apūrvayakṣa (the unparalleled yakṣa), whose body is veritably Brahmapura (the city of Brahmā), in which the qualities of a vīra (hero), and a mahāpuruṣa (a great being), come together.[101] He fulfils the *Mahābhārata* description of a wondrous yakṣa as mahākāya (colossal), tāla samucchṛta (tall like a palm tree), parvatopama (towering like a mountain), mahābala (of great strength).[102] He has lakṣaṇas of a mahāpuruṣa like the uṣṇīṣa (crown), śiraścakra (halo for head) and elliptical prabhāvalī (aureole at flanks), formed by snakes, pṛthukarṇatā (huge ears), created by peacocks, daksiṇāvartakeśa (hair turned to the right), and a topknot, made up of snake coils, viśāla vakṣa (broad chest), and, nyagrodhaparimaṇḍala (with the dimension of a banyan tree) body of great beings.[103] The pururūpaḥ (many-formed) Rudra of *Ṛgveda* is also the expert shape shifter yakṣa, attached to the site of Tala in village Āmerikāpā like a tutelary and guardian deity. The club bearing Śiva recalls the description in Buddhist literature of the huge, wooden, iron mace bearing jakkha Moggarapāṇi (Mudgarapāṇi or club-bearer), installed in Rājagṛha.[104] The nāmas and rūpas (names and shapes) of agnīṣomīya paśus on the body of the great heroic yakṣa (yakṣāmaḥ, we eat) serve as rakṣābhūṣaṇa (apotropaic amulets) and āhāra (nourishment) to equip, protect and nourish the image for working as an adequate dhiyālamba (support of contemplation).[105]

PARALLELS AND PRECEDENTS

The dynamic relation of the gross and subtle (sthūla and sūkṣma), explicit and implicit (nirukta and anirukta), finite and infinite (diti and aditi), void and plenum (śūnya and pūrṇa), immanent and transcendant (adhyātman and adhidaivatam), usufruct and essence (bhojyam and bhoktṛ), many and one, emerges as the theme of the Tala Paśupati image from the preceding discussion.

Though many of the ideas, which could have propelled an image like this into existence, have been traced to literary sources, no exact parallel can be found for this image among earlier sculptures, including those of the Kuṣāṇa and Gupta period. However, seeds of the idea can be found in several examples, given by Maxwell, of images replicated around a central phallic column, tree or a cluster of columns; columns, populated by a vertical array of figures; or, of an anthropomorphic axis, surrounded by human or animal figures or heads, arranged pyramidally or obliquely in a circular or elliptical formation, imitating a halo (Fig. 625).[106]

The juxtaposition of matsya and kūrma, with sarpa, siṁha or mayūra in the body of Tala Paśupati suggests a convergence of Vaiṣṇava Pañcarātra (of five nights) and Śaiva Pāśupata ideas. As a corollary, the integration of heads on front or sides of a central anthropomorphic axis, formed like an engaged column, in the body of Tala Paśupati, suggests the fusion of the ideas of emanations and mergers of vyūhas (groups of beings) in a viśākha yūpa (sacrificial stake), or śaktikoṣa (sheath for female cosmogenic forces), with ideas of such emanations and mergers in a principal deity, or pradhānapuruṣeśvara.[107] The Tala image is different from these omnidirectional, caturvyūha (carved on four sides with different appearances) representations in having a flat slab for its back. Though it unites iconic and aniconic forms, and is theroretically polycephalous, it comprises the heads within the outline of its body, and, unlike the Kuṣāṇa or Gupta images, mentioned by Maxwell, does not put them forth directly from its trunk, or as independent attachments on the sides or the back.

It is in fact in neighbouring Vidarbha, during Vākāṭaka rule, at Mānḍhal, that a few images are made in the 5th century, anticipating features of the Tala Paśupati. One of these is a standing eight-headed Śiva (Figs. 621-23). Though it does not have animal heads like Tala and its principal four heads face all the four directions unlike Tala, it does have muṇḍin (a shaven head) on its left arm, obviously replicated on the missing right arm, as well as uṣṇīṣins (turbaned heads) on its thighs like Tala. This is the first time known in Indian art that a Śiva image uses such heads to form its limbs. A second twelve-headed Mānḍhal Śiva (Pl. 47) from 5th century shares human heads on shoulders and thighs with Tala Paśupati apart from displaying a second tier of four heads facing the upadiśās (the intermediate directions). Standing,[108] club bearing, ithyphallic Lakulīśas anticipating the Tala Paśupati have been reported from pre-Kuṣāṇa, Kuṣāṇa, Gupta and Vākāṭaka days.[109] Individual elements of the image like udaremukha gaṇa (head on belly), or head dress of Nāgarāja, Bhairava, intertwined or threaded with snake, are found in isolation (Pls. 19, 39, 42; Figs. 627-28).

It is however, not in India but further afield, in China, that closer correspondences have been found for the Tala Paśupati, of these, the closest in date and iconography is an extraordinary image of a dvārapāla (Pls. 36, 38), carved in relief on the south side carridor of the main entrance in the middle Pin Yang Jung (Binyangzhongdong) cave of the Long Man grottoes in the Honan province of China.[110] Vertically cut by an abrasion, the image probably had four moustachioed heads, with two each on chest and stomach, paralleling similar heads on the Tala Paśupati. Of these, two heads survive on the left stomach and breast. Two smaller heads appear to have emerged from the sides of the principal head in a more conventional manner. Of these, only the head on the right survives. An exact parallel with the Tala Paśupati is offered by the two makaras, from which the arms emerge. Of these, the makara on the left survives. A further similarity is the insertion of tusked elephant heads in place of the Tala siṁhas on the knees, and in part of the legs below knees. A yakṣa, cut in half, survives on the left, to hold up the left foot of the image. It is comparable to the Jethani gaṇas, directly holding up the figures above. The image is generally identified as Brahmā, though the grounds for this identification remain unclear.[111] A AD 517 inscription in the Ku Yang cave of Longman appears to echo the ideas behind the Tala Paśupati. It says, "the divine pattern is a sublime emptiness, but if one did not use the visible likeness of art to make manifest a divine likeness,... how could anyone... imitate the divine achievements ?"[112] Examples given by Soper speak of the influence that was wrought by forms like Tala Paśupati on the development of the idea of Bodhisattva in China.[113] As ideas of Śiva and Avalokiteśvara converge in India, Avalokiteśvara is feminized into Kuān-yin, in an accentuation of the aspect of karuṇā, which is described by Mādhava in *Sarvadarśanasaṅgraha* as synonymous with Paśupati. This speaks of the earlier ferment of ideas in places like Vidarbha, resulting in integration of ideas of both śūnyatā, emptiness, and transience of the world (suggested by the abstract outline of Paśupati), and karuṇā or commiseration, incited by human suffering in this ephemeral existence (suggested by the acknowledgement of the physical presence of paśus in the body of Paśupati).[114] Like Buddhism, Paśupatism is seen as the road to duḥkhānta, end of suffering.[115] In the centuries following immediately, in medieval Europe and the Americas, the iconographic features of the Tala Paśupati or Longmen cave 'Brahmā' surface again and again in guardian armour, totem poles, masks, portrait heads, trees of life, semimonstrous, composite, organic figures (Pl. 18; Figs. 631-32),[116] suggesting independent development of kindred prototypes, based on cognate myths, rather than direct influence or identical ideas. The intensity and depth of the symbolic imagination, which inspire the Tala Paśupati at this early period, does not, from the available evidence, appear to have been captured in these later images.

AMBIVALENT MANIFESTATIONS: RUDRA AND SAUMYA ŚIVAS

The benignant and malignant, creative and destructive forces have made their common home in the body of Tala Paśupati, and then, they have migrated into the Saumya (gracious) and Bhairava (fearful) Śiva forms at Tala. Except for the proto-Bhairava head of Paśupati (Fig. 595) himself with his glowering eyes, frowning eyebrows, dilated nostrils, cruel compressed lips or a Bhairava on Jethani lintel, fondling the breast of a Bhairavī, all other Bhairava images at Tala are united with Saumya Śiva images by an expression of deep, contemplative fervour. In fact, the headdress of a Bhairava, and a huge Saumya Śiva from Devarani are similar. In both, a central band of hair holds in place the locks, which rise from below, and fan out from the top. While the proto-Bhairava head of Paśupati shares whiskers with two Saumya Śiva heads from Devarani and Jethani, all other Bhairava and Saumya heads lack moustaches (Figs. 353-54, 357-58, 416, 425, 427, 435, 462, 533). However, unlike Saumya heads which lack any decoration except a floral boss, the Bhairava heads are generally equipped with pearl strands, floral bands, a triangular crown, a semi-circular lotus crest, or a diadem of skulls, rising in number, from one to three, above a complex interlocked jaṭā. Only two Jethani Bhairava heads, including the Bhairava in the Jethani lintel, have simple flowing locks or wear a lotus crest, like the Saumya heads. The heads of all the Śiva images show the same fulness of cheeks, lips, eyelids, a similar droop to the half-closed eyes, identical soft, gradual and easy transitions in planes, and an equally grave, pensive calm, occasionally emphasized by a slightly downturned or creased corner of the lips, which light up the face with a gracious smile.

Irrespective of their affiliation to the specifically benefic or malefic aspect of Paśupati, the Saumya and Bhairava images of Tala are united with the Paśupati by the theme of sacrifice of animal instincts in the fire of self-restraint. Thus, while a specific feature like the head on Paśupati's stomach may represent Bhairava as Kālāgni (the devouring fire of time), the skulls adorning the Bhairava heads (Fig. 428) are portions of Brahmā's fifth head, cut off by Bhairava in Brahmāśiraśchedakamūrti. The fifth head of Brahmā is an outgrowth of unregulated passion, roused by his claim to be the originator of the universe. The location of the decapitated skull on the head becomes the symbol of paśumedha (animal sacrifice) on mount Meru, which is another name for the crowning cakra in the yogaśarīra (the body of yoga). The Paśupati himself is a prototype of the Bhairava, who has been freed from the skull (the sin of Brahmahatyā, slaughter of a Brāhmiṇ, being a result of unregulated anger) at Kapālamocana (release of skull at Vārānasi). The several Pāśupata ascetics appear to be beneficiaries of instruction imparted by him about the Pāśupata vrata as a sacrament of fire and ashes. In his Rudra form, Paśupati appears at Tala also as the great kirāta (hunter), the nude mahākāla, who hunts the elephants and tigers, uses their skin, to sheathe himself, as a symbol constituting the force for harnessing the wild, uncontrolled prakṛti or prāṇic energy for creative purposes.[117] The Saumya heads, on the other hand, display the jaṭā of kapardin (with matted locks) Śiva as the symbol of the womb of prāṇic vibrations. Their third vertical eye, together with the other two eyes, are equated with the sun, moon and fire, the three breaths, arteries, mental states or metres which combine to conjure up the image of an internal sacrifice of lower self or ātmayajña. Thus, though the Bhairava and Saumya images equally symbolize the sacrifice of passion, the Bhairavas at Tala assume Saumya, rather than the usual rākṣasa (demonic) characteristics.[118]

YAKṢAS AND YAKṢARĀJA KUBERA

Paśupati Śiva demonstrates his ambivalence also as yakṣādhyakṣa (the head of yakṣas), which is the alternative name given to his Agnivaiśvānara form. The Tala temples are like yakṣāyatanas (houses of yakṣas), presided over by Śiva and his yakṣas, who appear as colossal dvārapālas at the entrances (Figs. 351-52), on wall slabs, or on the tetrafacial Jethani south pillars, recalling the caturmahārājikalokapālas (guardians of cardinal directions) of Pāli literature, who guard the quarters of the universe, or the pañcavīragoṣṭhī (host of five heroes) of Daṇḍin's *Daśakumāracarita* (6th century AD), who guard the Avadhya Brahmapura (the impregnable precinct of Brahmā).[119] Two other images, both head, foot and armless, from Jethani and Devarani, wear the tiger skin (Figs. 343, 349). The Jethani Śiva in tiger skin is shown as ūrdhvaliṅga, the tail, the skin over the paws and head of the tiger being rendered with greater volume than its Devarani counterpart. The dvārapālas and guardian figures (Figs. 344-45, 351-52, 357-58, 363) stand huge and tall on bases, carved with animals or ascetics, gaṇas or makaras in dvi, tri or samabhaṅga, accompanied by diminutive attendants, equipped with a plain, circular or elliptical lotus halo, broad and thick floral hāra, or yajñopavīta (sacred thread with floral clasps), urūjālaka (thigh band), uttarīya (scarf, bunched in heavy folds beside the thighs), semi-transparent dhotī with delicately turned, small folds of sūtranaddha (cloth band). A huge hand from Jethani holding a scalloped, scaly, tapering column, a base on Jethani east with two abraded gaṇas, holding a striated, sacklike shape open, with a scaly outpour from its mouth, and fragments of an enormous male figure on (Figs. 345, 473-75) Jethani east wall, holding a lady with a similar scalloped trunk dangling from her hāra, suggest the presence of very large yakṣas guarding treasures. The scalloped shapes, resembling kharjūra (date palm, phoenix sylvestris) trees, should, if this identification is correct, suggest coin trees, and the sack may suggest a nakulaka (mongoose), whose neck is being squeezed to make it vomit jewels. Above the river goddesses, associated with the Devarani ardhamaṇḍapa, proto-Śiva busts (Figs. 359-60), embedded in rock, overhung by foliate canopies, indicate their yakṣa like character, associated with sthalavṛkṣas (trees connected with a sacred precinct), and guardianship of the vegetative source of life.

The yakṣas appear at Tala as vyāntara devatā (intermediate divinity), provided with both terrifying and protective presence, to whom a sacrifice of expiation or propitiation can be made, to avert their wrath or attract their goodwill. The projecting pedestals, adorned with flowers, where worshippers sprinkle coins, rice grain or flowers to this day, may have served notionally, as balipīṭha (sacrificial altars) for their offerings. The volumetric modelling of the yakṣas is in conformity with their protective function, inspiring terror, mixed with devotion. In the inimitable words of Coomaraswamy, "the type is massive and voluminous, and altogether plastically conceived, not bounded by outlines; the essential quality is one of energy, without introspection or spiritual aspiration".[120]

It is no accident therefore, that Kubera (Fig. 169), who is endowed by Śiva with the overlordsip of yakṣas, and who was assisted by Śiva in finding and protecting his wealth, and then befriended and sheltered by him, should also occupy a panel on the inner surround of the Devarani door jamb. The shaft of the liṅga above Kubera's head explains his devotion for Śiva. His position in the crowning panel, viewing the topmost panel, carved with Kailāsa, on the opposite side, fixes his residence in the Chaitraratha grove, replete with lotus and dense vegetation in Nandan forests near lake Alakā and river Mandākinī, in Alakāpurī near Kailāsa mountain. It is not fortuitous that he occupies the left surround, facing north, and directly looks at the panel of amorous Hara Gaurī on the opposite surround, because he is the guardian of the north, and is reported to have been punished by Gaurī for looking at her lustfully.[121]

Lacking his purse, pots, mace, spear, a northern dress or a spouse, this figure does not satisfy the conventional description of iconographic texts, or answer the traits of actual icons for Kubera. However, the lotus flowers, leaves or rhizome, which he holds like ṛddhiśṛṅgas (cornucopias) in his hands, and which adorn, probably form his ears, crown his head, and frame his panel like a kalpalatā (wish-fulfilling creeper), associate him with fertility and plenty. His rotund, chubby head and body, made of three bulging, superimposed globes, strengthen this association. Five of the eight treasures or aṣṭanidhis are numerically suggested by the three figures, which, their heads thrown back, advance from either side from behind Kubera, and by the two crouching figures, which flank Kubera, and offer their back for view to the spectator. Of the remaining three treasures, the two makaras flanking Kubera's vehicle may be associated with the padma or lotus, while the sthūṇārāja (the great pillar) may well be represented by the liṅga.

The installation of Kubera at a location directly below the Gajalakṣmī lintel (Fig. 160), also puts us in mind of the *Mārkaṇḍeya Purāṇa* passage, that identifies eight treasures as the ādhāras (basis) of padminī vidyā, and their presiding deity as Lakṣmī. Alternatively, the figures behind, in their ascetic dress and headdress, would resemble the jambha-sādhakas, who worship Jāmbhāla (Kubera prototype) and offer the immortal drink of yellow honey. If this suggestion is correct, the tapering, jarlike shapes of the figures flanking Kubera would suggest droṇameyas (jars) containing the yellow honey, which resembles paipīlika (granular gold). In a further alternative interpretation, the six figures behind could be identified as six yakṣas associated with Kubera, and the flanking figures as the two sons of Kubera. The deliberate concealment of the two flanking figures, also reminds us of Kubera's other name guhyakapati (lord of the hidden ones), the guhyakas being chthonic spirits guarding treasures like minerals, hidden in the earth. The piśāca (demon) like nara (human) head below Kubera recalls his aspect as naravāhana (with human vehicle).[122] Kubera is thus represented at the threshold, personifying both devotion for Śiva and attraction for Pārvatī, both acknowledgement of wealth as well as its renunciation.

SŪRYA AND VARUṆA

If the yakṣas and their lord Kubera illustrate Paśupati's aspect as a great yakṣa, inspiring both fear and devotion, the images of Sūrya and Varuṇa demonstrate his simultaneous aspects of both Agni and Soma, and link him up with a pervasive ideology of water cosmology, complementing the theory of fiery sacrifice and redemption. In this theory, the consubstantiality of Śiva with Sūrya and Varuṇa is established by their common function in releasing, purging and stimulating the flow of water in all its forms in the universe. At Tala, the bhakta identifies himself with his God, by imitating this divine act, by purging the psychosomatic flow of retas in his body of its toxic elements, by treating it therapeutically in the fires of breath. The iconographic representations at Tala of Sūrya and Varuṇa, which are unique in all of Indian art, seem to have for their model the Tala Paśupati, who, as Jalāśa, or Yogīśvara, presents the world with Skanda, the purest product of metamorphosed nature, by inundating and fecundating the cakras with retas burnt in tapas, for a rectification of consciousness.

In fact, the damaged fragments of the Sūrya image (Figs. 194-96, 361-62), recovered east of Devarani, do not have the attributes listed in iconographic texts or displayed in known images of Mārtaṇḍa Bhairava. But they satisfy the criteria listed in early religious literature for suggesting the form of Mārtaṇḍa Bhairava or Rudra Bhāskara, a form that shares the traits of both Sūrya or Agni and Śiva or Bhairava.[123] The jaṭāmukuṭa in this image, is threaded together by skulls and bones on either side of the head. The Pāśupata Śaiva attendant, stationed on its right, wears kaupīna, jaṭā and beard, and holds an akṣamālā (garland of beads). These iconographic elements associate the image with Śiva and Bhairava. On the other hand, the fluttering array of petals in the lotus halo and the seven flying garland bearing female figures (of whom four survive, three on the right, one on the left), suggest, respectively, the flickering flames of Agni, and the most unusual personifications of the seven rays or colours of the sun, seven threads of the solar spider, seven metres, or the seven rivers.[124] Though the display of two horses with Sūrya is not unprecedented, their location here behind Sūrya, flanking his shoulders and head at different heights (the horse on the left is carved higher), is too unusual to enable us to identify them as horses for the solar chariot. They appear instead to suggest the two Aśvins who agitate the cosmic tree in opposite directions to liberate Agni from the ocean. The headless female attendent, bearing the lotus stalk on the left of the image may be identified as Sūrya's spouse Uṣas. She archaistically recalls an earlier phase of solar worship, when the number of consorts or daughters of Sūrya had not yet multiplied. The lower portion of the fragmented slab is abraded beyond recognition. Yet, traces of what may have been a third ruined figure in the centre between the ascetic and Uṣas, would indicate that the lower portion of this image was appropriately concealed.[125]

From the allusions in early sacred texts, it becomes possible to reconstruct the theme of this Mārtaṇḍa Bhairava image. It becomes the pivot, used by the Aśvins to create the diurnal, annual solar movement from one station to the next; or the hiraṇyavetasa (the golden reed of the body), driven by prāṇa and apāna (anabolism and ketabolism), presided over by Aśvins. The systolic and diastolic movement of contraction and expansion becomes the heart beat of the universe, and the lotus wheel behind Sūrya and the seven female shapes above the wheel would seem to vibrate with its rhythm. The image anticipates the use of the term suvarṇaretas (of the golden semen) for both Śiva and Sūrya, who galvanize their energies or the waters from potentiality to actuality, freeing them from fetters fastened by demon to incarcerate them. The circular halo, formed by the petals and female shapes, becomes the prototype of the circular path of the sky crossed by solar rays, or traversed by madhunāḍīs (luminous rivers of honey), described in *Chāndogya Upaniṣad*. Incitement of rain, ripening of corn, or abundance are thus directly related to the bursting of the solar reservoir of the firmament. In a further ramification of the concept of release of waters, the body of Sūrya is assimilated to the body of Yajamāna, as the arena for sātcakrasādhanā (the yogic ascent of retas through seven centres). The Aśvins (pervaders), supposedly pervade everything with moisture or light, and fulfil their role as divine physicians, to assist in the sādhanā. Sūrya himself performs his function as a healer of diseases, using the prophylactic properties of water.[126]

The unique Varuṇa (Figs. 346-48), unparalleled in Indian art, recovered from Jethani south steps, directly complements the ideas of the image of Paśupati and Mārtaṇḍa Bhairava at Tala. The image is flanked by a lotus pillar and crowned by a lotus cap and halo. Three figures rise, half-hidden behind the lotus halo, and include a headless female figure in the centre. The lower portion of the Varuṇa image is hidden by two makaras that rise to its chest from the sea. Not unexpectedly at Tala, it fails to conform to most of the criteria, listed in iconographic texts, except for the fact that its only surviving hand does hold a pāśa (noose). One can only assume, from the position of the abraded, upraised right hand, that it might have been in abhaya, while the upraised left hand may have held a lotus in the conventional manner. Varuṇa is shown rising above two makaras, instead of the usual number of one, indirectly prescribed in the *Agni Purāṇa*. With its lower part concealed by makaras, the image gives a vague premonition of a later Pāla sculpture found at Gaya, in which the divinity appears to swim, or rise from the sea, recalling his description as an aquatic bird. Inspite of these apparently conventional traits, the image is different from all the Varuṇa sculptures in Indian art. Instead of being conventionally placed below him, the makaras heave up to his chest, covering part of his bust. The lotus cap and halo, which looks like an inverted canopy, possess substantial volume and are most unusual. The three figures above Varuṇa also do not have any precedent or progeny.[127]

The iconography of the image, however, establishes it as Varuṇa and links it with that of Paśupati of the waters, who offers aquatic paśus to Skanda at his birth. In a sense, the birth of Bhṛgu (from bhṛj, burning of retas) from the sacrificial fire of Varuṇa, can be seen as equivalent to the birth of Skanda. In this formulation, the seven priests of Varuṇa are equated with the seven gaṇas on Paśupati's body (and both with seven flames of sacrificial fire), and Bhṛgu is identified as a form of both Śiva and Varuṇa. Whether the headless ascetic image, shown in profile behind Varuṇa's halo at the right, holding an akṣamālā, is Bhṛgu himself, cannot however be stated with certainty. This is because we are not certain either about Bhṛgu's iconographic features or about the sex or identity of his missing counterpart on the left.[128]

What seems to be more probable is the association of the image, on a parallel plane, with Sūrya, Agni, and pari passu, with Paśupati Śiva. The circular lotus halo or canopy on its head, with many buds, imitates a rayed wheel, and an inverted cask, and reminds us of the solar disc and the downpour of water from the heavens, at Varuṇa's instance. The padmastambhaparikara (lotus pillar frame), crowned by ghaṭa āmalaka, recalls the inverted world tree. It pillars the paired spheres of earth and heaven apart. Varuṇa exists at its base and upholds its crest. Together, the lotus pillars, umbrella and cap covering Varuṇa's head, suggest the yaśas (sovereignty) of Varuṇa. Like Paśupati and Sūrya, he oversees and governs all things at once, in their diversity and coincidence. The traditional association of Sūrya or Agni is, in this manner, established with Varuṇa. They are installed by Varuṇa, and represented as the eye, emissary, other face, brother of Varuṇa, Varuṇa himself. They turn Varuṇa's menacing face away from humanity. Together, they become guardians of the order of the universe.[129]

Like Paśupati and Sūrya, the Tala Varuṇa would seem to function in the role of a physician, using the waters for restoring creation to health and well being. The image recalls samudramanthana, in which Varuṇa represents the ocean, and rises with Dhanvantarī, the divine physician and Vāruṇī, Surā, or Soma, the divine drink. The ascetic image behind Varuṇa's halo could be considered as Dhanvantarī. The headless female image, half-hidden behind the centre of the lotus halo, would lend itself to identification as Vāruṇī. The lotus halo and lotus cap, with Vāruṇī or Soma behind them, would suggest assimilation of Varuṇa's head with the sahasrāra and the somapūrita kalaśa (the pitcher, full of soma) in a yogaśarīra (the body of yoga). The profound, contemplative gravity of Varuṇa's expression, lends force to this suggestion. This suggestion is reinforced by the association of Varuṇa with Bhṛgu or Agni (and his role in the rectification of the personality of man), and, by the notion of sacrifice and redemption of the lower self, suggested by the pāśas and makaras. The pāśas are designed to bind and afflict the sinners with, or release them from, the knots of diseases, death and evil. They ensure the state of nirvaruṇatva (freedom from Varuṇa). Such a state is analogous to the release of waters, available to those who ritually sacrifice their lower selves in the maws of Varuṇa, symbolized by the gaping jaws of makaras. The image thus becomes a symbol of healing the agnisomīya paśu, made of principles of fire and water, homoeopathetically, with its own elements of fire and water. It is also a symbol of fertility, coolth and truth, ṛta or order.[130]

GAṄGĀDHARA ŚIVA AND GAṄGĀ TRIPATHAGĀ

Sūrya and Varuṇa, therefore, restore celestial order (Ṛta), rhythmic succession of seasons and fertility by releasing and purging the waters. In doing so, they imitate the original act of Gaṅgādhara (Gaṅgā bearing) Śiva, who, by acting as a catalytic agent in Gaṅgāvataraṇa (descent of the Ganges), stimulates abundance and well-being.

The descent of Gaṅgā[131] is shown in various stages on the lower lintel and the two large lower panels of the Devarani door jamb (Figs. 173-75). Gaṅgā appears in the heaven, which may be represented on the door lintel (Figs. 180-81), as Mandākinī. She appears on the earth as Bhāgīrathī. She emerges from the Bindu Sarovara in seven streams, three (Hlādinī, Plāvinī, Nalinī) on the east, three (Sītā, Sindhu and Kucakṣu) on the west, and one behind Bhagīratha, to meet Sāgara or ocean. On the way, the sage Jahnu swallows Gaṅgā and then releases it at the prayer of Bhagīratha. Gaṅgā then enters the subterranean region as Bhogavatī. Her passage through the earth is represented in the abraded Devarani door jamb by showing several streams three dimensionally, and by repeating her anthropomorphic form in a continuous narration. The four handed Gaṅgādhara Śiva (Fig. 179) is conventionally shown in the central panel of the lower lintel as Dakṣiṇanāyaka, as a lover with equal affection for Gaṅgā and Pārvatī, who are represented as sisters competing for his exclusive attention. Śiva releases Gaṅgā, shown as a column of water, as his pratyakṣa or jalamayī mūrti (alter ego, in liquid form) from his jaṭā, with his raised left hand, at the entreaty of Bhagīratha on his right, and quells the jealousy of Pārvatī on his left, by placing his forearm around her, as a mark of rāja nīti (sovereign policy).

Bhagīratha is shown in the diminutive form of an ascetic with kaupīna (loin cloth), upavīta (sacred thread), rudrākṣamālā (beads), and a pointed staff. Pārvatī turns away in a huff. Two staff bearing, kapālin (adorned with a headdress of skulls) Pratihārīs stand in two side panels. They are separated from the Gaṅgāvisarjanamūrti (image releasing Gaṅgā) of Śiva by two shallow pilasters, unusually carved with elephant protomes, carrying tree trunks. In a manner unprecedented, they are flanked by two more shallow pilasters with makara protomes. Śiva appears here as Tīrthya, presiding over tīrthas, or places of pilgrimage, where Gaṅgā mingles its streams.[132]

The lower most panels on the inner lateral sides of the door jamb (Figs. 167-68) are iconographically unique. The panel on the right shows Gaṅgā inundating and reviving the Sagaraputra's sons and Sagara from the ashes. Gaṅgā is shown first, jetting upwards, in a widening column from the open hands of Bhagīratha, which are gathered together to offer tarpaṇa (libation).[133] Gaṅgā is then shown, personified as a river goddess, leaning with her left arm on the shoulder of Bhagīratha, who is shown again, as a diminutive ascetic, holding a crooked staff with both his hands, to carry the weight of Gaṅgā and guiding her forward. Revived by the tarpaṇa, the Sagaraputras now tumble over one another and eagerly surround Gaṅgā and Bhagīratha, joining the procession. The lowest panel on the left surround shows a continuation of the procession. Gaṅgā passes through a celebratory vandanamālikā, garland of pendant streamers. Her progress is heralded by flying, garland bearing vidyādharas above, and is eagerly witnessed by Sagaraputras from the side.

The river goddesses appear not only on the Devarani antarāla door jamb, but also on the side walls of the maṇḍapa and the detached jambs of the ruined ardhamaṇḍapa. In a most innovative presentation, the defaced river goddess Sarasvatī stands on the leftside maṇḍapa wall (Fig. 312) inside a lotus lake, on a lotus pedestal, and under a lotus canopy, holding a lotus stalk in one hand, a pot and a lamp in the other, framed by winding lotus rhizome and stem. Her vehicle, Haṁsa, is missing here, but it appears on the later jagatī mouldings. The half-sunk bust of a load bearing gaṇa is visible above the canopy. A female attendant, which appears below the relatively unfinished river goddess on the opposite wall, appears to have stood below the pedestal. Buffeted by the waters into cuplike folds, the leaves of the lotus pedestal and canopy suggest the presence of the river Sarasvatī (river of the lake) in the womb of the earth, ready to rise through its crust, upheld by the gaṇa. Sarasvatī performs an ameliorative and curative role, similar to that of Paśupati, Varuṇa, Sūrya, by purifying the water in the paśu, and by enlightening his mind.[134]

Apart from Gaṅgā and Sarasvatī, fragments of jambs (Fig. 309), recovered from Devarani, help us reconstruct the images of three fascinating figures, one of Gaṅgā and two of Yamunā, which stood at the opening of the ardhamaṇḍapa. The jambs are chamfered on one side, and moulded with two vertical rows of flowers and fruits, separated by a ridge, on the other. Yamunā is shown holding a large lotus flower in her lowered left hand, wearing a pleated dhotī, a four strand muktā mekhalā (pearl girdle), hung with tassels, a ruffled uttarīya, draped around her left arm, and a head dress, woven with multi strand floral garlands. She is flanked by two diminutive attendants, one of whom might have held the shaft of the mayūratapatra (Fig. 308) above her head. Iconographically, Yamunā with a similar mayūratapatra is very much in vogue in later Dakṣiṇa Kośala, but the arrangement of figures above the umbrella is unparalleled before or since. The bull Nandī appears to have sat atop this peacock feather umbrella. A curved nāgarāja figure seems to have spanned the slab above this, and two flying vidyādharas appear to have framed the slab, with the head of a third protruding from the top. Above all these, embedded in irregular, projected chunks of rocks, should have sat the bust of a proto-Śiva image (Fig. 442). Its head is crowned by a flower embossed jaṭāmukuṭa and framed by thickly clustered mango fruits and leaves.[135] A makara has also been found at Jethani, with the traces of the feet of a missing Gaṅgā on its back. It encloses a gaṇa head, with a moustache, parted lips, thick nose, a crown and eyebrows, made of lotus leaves (Fig. 533).

Together, these representations of the river goddesses at Devarani, present a further demonstration at Tala of the resuscitative properties of water, as also of the simultaneously creative and destructive aspect of the heat of fire, generated by tapas or penance. They symbolize tīrthas (literally crossings, pilgrimage places), where the bhakta, like Sagaraputras before him, has to sacrifice his lower selves in the fire, and regenerate himself by a ritual ablution. The sixty thousand Sagaraputras, who symbolize the diurnal movement of the earth, are reduced to ashes through the fire of the penance of ascetic Kapila, a name of the sun. They are cleansed and restored by Gaṅgā, the river of life, which follows the wheels of the chariot of ascetic prince Bhagīratha (bhagin ratha, having a glorious chariot), another symbol of the sun. As a result of Bhagīratha's penance, Gaṅgā descends from Kailāsa, the abode of Śiva, as the ambumayī mūrti (liquid form) of Śiva. It is endowed with Siva's purifying power in its āloka, avagāha and ācamana (sight, ablution and sip). It divides itself into three streams, including Yamunā and Sarasvatī. Sarasvatī rises from the Mānasa Sarovara (lake of the mind) near Kailāsa. The Kailāsa and Mānasa Sarovara are displayed respectively on the door jamb and maṇḍapa walls of Devarani. Having separated from one another at the source as triveṇi (triple braided), the streams come together at the threshold of Devarani. This movement of Gaṅgā, symbolizing the rhythmic vibration of prāṇa, and coming to rest at its immutable source, is presented in the most inventive iconographic programme of three rivers at three successive entrances of Devarani. In this programme, we have a dramatic presentation of the self-cleansing/treatment of the agnisomīya paśu, using elements of fire and water in his body, to cross the threshold, meet God face to face, and assume a new birth in the garbhagṛha, facilitated by germination rites.[136]

GAJALAKṢMĪ

Paśupati, Gaṅgādhara Śiva, Sūrya and Varuṇa help in purging and releasing the waters. The waters yield abundance and well-being, which are personified by Lakṣmī in the upper lintel of (Figs. 178-81) Devarani. Conventionally, as anapagāminī acañcalā (stable, unmoving) Lakṣmī, she is seated in padmāsana (lotus posture), on the double petalled viśvapadma (the universal lotus), which has petals pointing both up and down. Quite unconventionally, she does not show any of the prescribed attributes. Her curved arms, placed on her thighs, her interlocked legs, and her straight frame, therefore, offer an authentic imitation of the auspicious śrīvatsa symbol (a motif with double arms, curved around a central stem, literally, the favorite of śrī), and an effective integration of iconic and aniconic features. In an original adaptation, the śrīvatsa is reduced to a central stem and enclosed in a further, larger śrīvatsa, described by the double curved arms of the four diggajas (elephants of the quarters).[137] Lakṣmī is shown as Padminī, a prototype of female beauty and radiant motherhood, with full breasts, hips and narrow waist. One of her breasts is crossed by the fine, transparent uttarīya, in vogue at Tala, rather than by the prescribed channavīra (sash).

Lakṣmī is lustrated by elephants from either side, but, instead of two, we have the unprecedented number of four elephants. Of these, two stand below, facing Lakṣmī, and pour water over her from downturned jars, while two stand above, facing away from Lakṣmī, in an inventive variation, to pick up pūrṇaghaṭas (full pitchers), to keep up an incessant supply of water. The text supports the identification of the two elephants, bathing Lakṣmī, as śaṅkha (conchshell) and padma (lotus) nidhis (treasures). These are two of the treasures of Kubera, and ādhāras (foundations) of padminīvidyā. The unusual location of Kubera on the door jamb, near his consort Lakṣmī, is also explained by their relation, as are the lotus flowers in his hands, ears or cap.[138] The two elephants above may, on the other hand, be the unique representations of Airāvata (born of Irāvatī, who is in possession of irā or fluid) and Abhramū (the fabricator, mū, of the clouds, abhra), who emerge, like Lakṣmī, from the churning of the ocean. They pick up pūrṇakalaśas from the Samudradevatā (the god of the ocean) for consecrating Lakṣmī, who is also kalaśābdhiputrī (daughter of the ocean, represented in the pitcher). The representation of Samudradevatā, submerged to his chest in the invisible ocean, holding up the kalaśa, is unprecedented. Unprecedented also are the representations of three river goddesses on either side, of whom two stand behind the sea god, holding up kalaśas, and one glides in below, holding trays, which are carved with rippling streams, filled with aquatic creatures. They are engaged in replenishing the sea constantly, to keep up an unfailing supply of water for the abhiṣeka (lustration). Three flying vidyādharas and vidyādharīs, converge from either end of the frame, to worship Lakṣmī, in a carefully orchestrated rhythm of gradual descent from the sky. They recall similar convergence of figures to the centre in Gupta door lintels. Unlike general representations of such flying figures in Gupta panels, the garlands, carried by the figures here would, be also identified as Lakṣmī, who is called Puṇyagandhā (of sacred fragrance) in the *Śrīsūkta*.[139]

The unique element in the iconography of Lakṣmī at Tala lies not only in this picturesque representation of her abhiṣeka, but in the all encompassing sense of endowment and bounty, which the entire Devarani door jamb and Tala architecture convey overwhelmingly. The ornate door jamb, filled with floral festoons, garlands and rhizomes, resembles the splendrous form of Lakṣmī, conceived as hemamālinī suvarṇayaṣṭi (a golden central rod, encircled by a golden necklace, hung in strands on either side). The lotus medallions, adorning pillars, pilasters, lintels and ceilings, are akin to śrīcakra, in which Lakṣmī is situated, encircled by hiraṇyaprākāra (golden ramparts). Within its precincts are ṛddhi (abundance), dhana (wealth), dhānya (corn), prajāḥ (progeny), bhāgya (luck), rājya (royalty), and āyuḥ (longevity). The lotus wheel, formed by limbs of ascetics on the Devarani door jamb soffit, would appear to form a bhāgya cakra (wheel of destiny). It fluctuates according to good or bad deeds of beings at the instance of the Goddess of fortune. The saubhāgyapaṭṭa of the door jamb lintel, in which Lakṣmī is anointed as the subhagā (of excellent fortune), thus becomes the personified apex of her many-hued personality. It becomes, so to speak, the forehead, described in *Ṛgveda*, where the gods reside, and with which Lakṣmī touches heaven. It becomes the fount, described in *Śatapatha Brāhmaṇa*, from which the gods, including Agni and Soma, Mitra and Varuṇa, draw their essential qualities, and, to which they then return these qualities. In order to meet this grand conception of Lakṣmī, the simple representations in early Indian sculpture, of Gajalakṣmī on lotus flowers, emerging from bhadraghaṭas, in abbreviated panels and small medallions, are given up at Tala for an elaborate narrative panel, which concludes the all inclusive, bounteous mission of Lakṣmī.[140]

MITHUNAS

The celebration of the release of the waters by Śiva, on the Devarani door jamb, is accompanied by the depiction of mithunas (Figs. 176, 179, 193, 198-99, 395-401). Their curved, yielding shapes, assimilated to the winding forms of the plants or river goddesses, are animated by a similar water cosmological inspiration. The dammed up water, released by Sūrya, Varuṇa or Śiva, carried by tripathagā (three forked) Gaṅgā for ablution or lustration, exists in plants and flowers as sap or honey, and in human bodies as blood or seminal fluid. The union of Paśu and Pati, Agni and Soma, Puruṣa and Prakṛti, effected in the divine mithunas of Hara Gaurī at Devarani, Bhairava Bhairavī or Ardhanārīśvara at Jethani are primordial acts, imitated by the secular mithunas. The heat of yogabhogātmaka tapas (the penance for enjoyment and union) burns animal desire, to create Skanda symbolically, from the body of Paśupati. The generative, nutritive powers of the universe are mirrored in divine and human pairs, and juxtaposed on opposite surrounds of the Devarani door jamb, as auspicious symbols. It is no accident that this is done at the threshold of the garbhagṛha, where the laying of the womb or seed takes place.[141]

Ahorātra, day and night, ghraṁsa and hima, heat and cold, are children of the union, the up and down, udgrābha and nigrābha movement of the wheel, the Saṁvatsara, the year, set in motion by Varuṇa (Figs. 346-48). The creative union, maithunī sṛṣṭī, is the result of the ṛta, the ordinance of Varuṇa, binding heaven and earth, through the fusion of passive and kinetic, male and female, fire and water principles.[142]

The two Hara Gaurī mithunas have been presented in a drama of mounting passion, stepped up from mere play, to passionate love play. Śiva Pārvatī play chausar (game of squares), accompanied by five of their attendants on either side (Fig. 177). The male gaṇas on the left carry flywhisks or small boxes, or just wait, a hand raised in concern. The female attendants on the right are more eager. One of them rests her chin and hands on the shoulder of her companion in front, keenly watching the victorious moves made by Pārvatī, while a third attendant takes away Nandī, who reluctantly clutches the ground with his hooves, from a Śivagaṇa.

In the panel above this, Pārvatī, as Bhogeśvarī and Śivakāmī (lady of enjoyment, desiring Śiva), is seated on Śiva's right lap (Figs. 176, 401). Her robe has slid down her thighs. One of her arms is wrapped around Śiva's shoulder. Śiva draws her coy but yielding body close, turning her towards himself. The gaṇas on the left modestly turn their faces away from the scene, and one of them seeks shelter in a desperate hurry, with his back towards the spectator. The gaṇas on the right are in various stages of stupefaction. One of them places his hand over his eyes in embarrassment. Another places his finger on his lips, enjoining silence, and raises the other hand in astonishment. A third raises his hand to his head in dismay, while a fourth and a fifth look from top and below with ill concealed anxiety. A sixth vyāghramukha (tiger-headed) gaṇa, and a seventh gaṇa with huge, curved ears, try to gain a view from the sidelines. Abraded heads peep out from behind the other damaged arms and āyudhas (weapons) of Śiva. The agitated manner of the gaṇas and the impatient movements of the divine couple remind us of the story in which Gods beseech Śiva to abandon mahāmaithuna (the immense drama of passion), and to adapt ratimātra (mere love play). It also warns us of the imminent arrival of Agni, to interrupt Śiva's amours, which provokes him into spurting his semen into the mouth of Agni. Unable to carry the burning seed, Agni consigns it to Gaṅgā, who, also unable to bear it, hides it among bulrushes (or reeds), where kṛttikās rear it into Skanda. The Gaṅgādhara Śiva on the Devarani lintel takes the drama a step further. He has allowed Gaṅgā to move in the forest of his locks long enough to make Pārvatī jealous. With a precise economy of action, and minimal physical contect, he simultaneously lets Gaṅgā go, and brings the jealous Pārvatī around. The standing Hara Gaurī on the Jethani lintel play no amorous role, though the Bhairava on the same lintel fondles the breast of Bhairavī.

The secular mithunas on the Devarani door jamb are less explicit in their amours than their divine counterparts. They are seated side by side, or behind each other, holding one another by the wrist or by the waist. Occasionally, the woman clutches the hāra of the man or holds up and admires a bangle, a gift from her friend. Some of the stocky couples on a later Devarani pīṭha moulding (Fig. 92) are shown in closer amorous embrace, or engaged in passionate mutual pursuit. Generally, however, at Tala, the display of sexual passion is muted, and nudity is not stressed as in early or mediaeval Indian sculpture. In partial undress, Pārvatī's body is offered in a three quarter profile view, rather than for blatant frontal inspection. The curvaceous and alluring female shape, the soft bulges of the pelvis, hips or thighs are however brought out suggestively by clinging garments, which hug and dig into the flesh. The slender but heavy hipped and heavy breasted figures are always shown, with a slight stoop created by the burden of their blossoming youth. In fact, the Tala mithunas, like the river goddesses or the flora, evoke an erotic interest in the creative abundance of nature, as a bridge for transcending it, rather than as an end in itself.

FLOWERS AND PLANTS

A discussion of the assimilation of human, mithuna, or female forms with vegetal forms brings us back to the fundamental role of Paśupati in the water cosmology at Tala. He is seen as the indwelling chthonic spirit or energy of the vegetation world, animating floral, faunal and human beings, which does not die with the physical death of its recipient, but only changes form, regenerating itself. In the *Śatapatha Brāhmaṇa* and *Śatarudrīya*, he is praised as ruling the waters and plants in all their forms, while the marūts or storms are seen as his children.[143] While many of the plants or flowers shown at Tala are perennial herbs, some are also dear to Śiva, used till today in Śiva worship. He is praised as the first physician in *Śvetāśvatara Upaniṣad*, and, in the *Ṛgveda*, he is beseeched as Agni, to resuscitate the dead and diseased, drawing, it would seem, on the restorative and curative properties of waters and plants. The same therapeutic power of Paśupati is evoked when herbs and plants are assembled and addressed to act in close accord, while consecrating the field of Agni, so that Agni is raised from the earth, to restore the diseased limbs of sacred architecture, to create an abode of order. At Devarani, Agni is so raised to help, cure and restore the Sagaraputras, and, with them, the diseased or mutilated selves of the bhaktas, who worship him in the dynamic force field, created by the cascading columns of waters and plants.[144] It is in the light of these beliefs that we should see Paśupati as the actuator behind the intermesh, interchange, and mutual mimesis of all shapes and forms. The plant, human and animal beings tend to look more and more like one another, and freely undergo mutations to assume each other's shape, movement and life.

The different segments of the door jambs, the frames of the panels in the doors, carved slabs and pillars, head dress, ornament and halo (Figs. 157-201, 236-73, 306, 311-12, 346-48, 359-60, 395-401, 473-85, 546-47) show many variations on the same standard designs of flowers, creepers and fruits. Though these are stylized, for being integrated into the vertical, horizontal or diagonal rows of ornament, their natural shape is more or less recognizable. They are also shown in different stages of flowering, fruition and organic growth, in consonance with the thematic scenes of regeneration, plenty and beauty, to which they provide a celebratory background. The rotary cycle of rain is suggested by the river goddesses and dryads. The symbolic abhiṣeka of Lakṣmī in the sap of waters and plants, ensures virtue, success and wealth. The lotus cap or bosses on the heads of Varuṇa, Kubera, mithunas or yakṣas, signify attainment of suzerainty or flowering of the soul, and indicate the tremendous significance attached to the bounteous life of the plants.

An identification[145] of the flowers and fruits, or of the state in which they are shown, points to the careful deliberation which went into the making of the vegetal life and aspect of iconology at Tala. The small, beaded, fully ripened subglobose seeds, which propagate the perennial Vaijayantī (Indian shot),[146] have been used to form a series of diagonal bands in a fallen west pillar at Jethani, the dividing bands between each spiral strand in the mālāśākhā of the Devarani door jamb, or between the floral bands in a fallen Jethani pillar on the north, or some of the lion or gaṇa bases or at Jethani south.

The dhaturā, dear to Śiva, is usually shown at Tala without a stem, and with a persistent calyx of fused sepals or petals, which are retained even after pollination and fertilization, unlike other species. Seeds, carved with regular squarish patterns, stand revealed above, the pericarp (wall of the fruit) being ruptured on maturation.[147] The dhaturā is visible in this shape, not only as a spiral strand in the mālāśākhā at Devarani, but also as a vertical row on the moulded side of the river goddess slabs at the entry to the Devarani ardhamaṇḍapa. In the stambhaśākhā of the Devarani door jamb, on the other hand, the multipetalous dhaturā, instead of being seen in profile, is seen from above. Its ten spirally arranged petals surround the pollen producing stamens, which are known in Sanskrit as puṁkeśara, an equivalent of the male reproductive organ.

On the Devarani stambhaśākhā again, the sweet scented, five petalled campā flowers are offered for frontal inspection, pyramidally arranged above one another. The flowers are linked, as the Dhaturā in the adjacent band is linked, by their fruits, split into two valves, both of which display small, round seeds. In order to form this pattern, revealing abundant fruition, the fruits have been isolated from their usual clusters, and the seeds have been arranged with stylized regularity.[148] The campā is also in evidence, without the linking chains of fruits, on the Devarani door panel frames and on some of the lion and gaṇa bases at Jethani.

One of the spiral strands in the mālāśākhā at Devarani, and the second vertical row beside the row of dhaturās on the river goddess slabs of Devarani ardhamaṇḍapa, a spiral floral band on a Jethani north pillar, are composed of the orbicular (disk-shaped) kumudinīs, or white lilies, known, appropriately enough in Sanskrit, as Indu, a synonym for moon.[149] A further spiral strand of the Devarani mālāśākhā is constituted by closeset young kevadā (screwpine) flowers, which are revealed, by deliberately excluding the spaths (leafy parts), which sheathe their individual bracts.[150] On the Devarani door jamb is also displayed the evergreen vine, known as white camelī or kuṇda, a special variety of jasmine. Its petals are shown raised a bit, rotating clockwise like a wheel, and fusing at the centre, to form the throat of the corolla tube.[151]

Apart from the more regular floral designs, found on the Devarani maṇḍapa door jamb, and their variations, Tala also has other floral designs of similar geometrical regularity, as well as winding plants, with unequal leaves. One of the diagonal floral bands in the Jethani west pillar (Fig. 243), which is also repeated in the Jethani pillar base frames, is, for example, formed by the vakul (in Marathi or Bengali), maulsiri (in Hindi), or Spanish cherry. It is fragrant, and rotate.[152] On the same pillar, another diagonal band is constituted by a design born of jhumkā (Hindi), kṛṣṇakamal (Sanskrit), or the passion flower. Though it is a climber with palmately (with deep, finger like lobes) divided into three to five leaves, it is displayed here with overlapping leaves, the flowers being ranged side by side.[153] On the slab with the river goddesses, on the Devarani maṇḍapa side walls, another ornamental evergreen climber is shown. Known as amarphal (Hindi), it is shown with closeset pennate (feather like) leaves, which are divided from the petiole (midrib, stock of leaf), and become widely and palmately divided at the apex.[154]

Carved on a fragment found near the Saumya Śiva head, at the southeast of Devarani, are flowers, known as palāsh or dhāk (Hindi and Bengali) or kiṁśuka (Sanskrit), that have unequal petals, with curled tips, and look like butterflies (Fig. 251). On a broken pillar on Jethani east, the same flower has been threaded together and given a regular shape in a vertical row, with stamens and anthers protruding on top, and at Devarani, it has been shown in an artificial meander, without being strung together.[155] On the Devarani door jamb, only a variant of kiṁśuka is shown in a top view of the corona (the outer circle), the stigmatic head in the centre being also displayed.[156] Another fragment, found at the southeast of Devarani, demonstrates a serrated five petalled design, known as kanaka campā or bullbay magnolia, in juxtaposition with leaves of other varieties.[157] A similar juxtaposition of dissimilar elements like a lotus and lotus rhizome, and a variation of the magnolia, leaves and flowers, can be detected on the stambhaśākhā of the fallen Jethani south door jamb as well (Figs. 61, 192). One multicoiled tendril on the Devarani door jamb shows the aśoka flowers in profile, at the same level, rising in unequal sizes, on unequal pedicils (stalk of flower).[158]

Among leaves with fruits, what has generally been recognized as aśokalumbī on the later Devarani mouldings and the Jethani pillar ghaṭas, is identified by botanists as bargad (Hindi), nyagrodha (Sanskrit), or banyan leaves with reticulated veins and veinlets, crowned by a bunch of fruitlike inflorescence, each fruit being round in shape, with a micropyle (an opening on its top), through which insects enter for pollination.[159] The canopy of āmralumbīs, the āmrabhañjikā and the rock embedded bust (Figs. 306, 360) in the Bilaspur museum show mango seedlings with bunched leaves, hung with unnaturally and uniformly aggregated fruits.[160] The Āmrabhañjikā also wears ornaments, that imitate plant and floral designs. She wears a central silver clasp on her forehead, shaped like a cluster of ball like kadamba flowers with globose heads.[161] On either side of this central clasp, the Āmrabhañjikā wears a silver ornament made of a cylindrical, tubercled panasa (Sanskrit) or jackfruit flower, the thick, leafy bract, covering the inflorescence above, being opened up to reveal this to be a female flower.[162] Above many of the pillars at Tala, the fleshy, globose, grooved āmalaka fruit is in evidence.[163]

Finally, we have the lotus (Figs. 59-60, 188-91, 258-62, 268-73), symbolic of the Ādityamaṇḍala or solar circle, everywhere at Tala, which seems to be floating and trembling in the waters, an impression conveyed most effectively above and below the Devarani maṇḍapa river goddesses. The lotus at Tala is usually shown in sideview on pillars. The sahasradala (thousand petalled) padma on Jethani south ceiling is shown in front view. Its thalamos is in the centre and is raised on sunk carpels (ovule bearing part of flower). Its location and its downward turned petals suggest its identification as the sahasrāra cakra, symbolic of flowering of consciousness through seven cakras, the uncoiling of the kuṇḍalinī.[164] The petals in the Devarani door jamb soffit are reproduced as seated ascetics. The prancing lions on Jethani south pillar, kīrtimukha heads on the Devarani door, makara tails or snouts on Tala pillars, are made of lotus petals.[165] The shivering frame of lotus leaves anticipates the śiśirita or shivered frame of later tāntric conception.[166]

Agni, beseeched to create, hides from gods as a mole or a mouse,[167] which is offered in the *Śatarudrīya* as Śiva's share, and later becomes Gaṇeśa's mount. At Tala, the mole plods down the diagonal row of kumudinī flowers on a Jethani west pillar, emphasizing its attachment to the subterranean world of plants and waters. The plants are actually called guhyakas or the hidden ones in the Mahābhārata, and are thus associated also with Kubera, who is their chief.[168] So, the scalloped date palm trunks seem to serve as substitutes for coin trees, associated with Kubera. The plants at Tala are thus related, in different ways, to the forces of fertility and abundance, which well from the earth, to be personified as Sūrya or Agni, Soma or Varuṇa, Kubera or Śiva.

GAṆAS

If Śiva pervades the water cosmology of Tala art, he also presides over the gaṇas and different animals as Paśupati or Bhūtanātha. Though gaṇas have appeared in early Indian sculpture at railing pillar bases, or in Gupta art in śikharas or window frames, they present themselves at Tala in an unprecedented role, by entering the temple, and by preempting all the vantage points of the accesses. Because of this deliberate location, the gaṇas at Tala, specially Jethani south (Figs. 475-95), personify the elements of creation, and act as pāriṣadas (courtiers) of Śiva and as bhāraputrakas (load bearers). They carry the pillars in the temple of Śiva, which is his house and body. The pillars carried by them are like so many sacrificial stakes (yūpas) with pedestals (balipīṭha). These are raised often on pūrṇakumbhas, which serve as śukrapātras (pitchers full of life-fluid), that are guarded from all directions. The puffed up bodies of these gaṇas are like so many fiery breaths, which bring tribute to the imperial breath (viśvarūpa prāṇādhipaḥ) of Śiva, which, in turn, animates the Tala temple. Awaiting the union of Agni and Soma in the garbhagṛha, they await also their share of the Soma. Hence, as aberrations of the prāṇic principle,[169] they still remain deformed, and out of plumb. As pramathas (churners)[170] they would seem to assist their lord in the churning of the life fluid, to make it yield its purest essence, Soma.

The gestures, postures and expressions of the Jethani gaṇas[171] vary, suggesting different names, shapes (nāmarūpa) and natures (ātmaka). They satisfy descriptions of gaṇas in the *Mahābhārata*, Purāṇas or in actual sculpture, but offer a variety of permutations and combinations, unparalleled in Indian art, in their load bearing function. They conventionally possess dwarfish bodies with big nose, ears, heavy lips and belly, short necks and long arms, matted mane like hair (vāmana, mahānāsa, lambakarṇa, sthūloṣṭha, kumbhodara, hrasvagrīva, mahābhuja, jaṭila). They are also addorsed or affronted (pṛṣṭhagāmita or sammukhīkṛta), and their heads are thrown up, forward, backward (utkṣipta, āvṛtta, parivṛttaśiras). They exploit an entire range of postures and gestures, to express manifold reactions to their assigned task. Some of them give an impression of back breaking exertion, sit or stand in a crouch, or tumble over, with outstretched arms, hunched shoulders, dilated eyes, furrowed eyebrows, pursed or panting lips, swollen toes or fingers. They look bhīṣaṇa (formidable), caṇḍa (wrathful), virūpina (bizarre), cipiṭānana (flat faced), jvālāsya (flaming face), vyāditāsya (gaping mouth). Others carry the load with one hand, in an attitude of boredom, or nonchalance, or an expression of long suffering, patient resignation. A few even seem to beam with joy (smitavadana or dīptimanta). Some run or fly with their cloth streaming behind them, with effortless speed. Some others are saumya (placid), with drooping, meditative eyes and an absorbed expression.

Tala does not display many of the animal-headed gaṇas seen in Gupta temples. However, unlike any other image before or since, the Paśupati image absorbs in its body animal heads or heads on different parts of the body, prescribed for individual gaṇas. Thus, the descriptions of gaṇas as skandhamukha (mukha or head on shoulder), hanumukha (head on chin), udaremukha (head on stomach), pārśvānana (head on laterals), jaṅghāmukha (head on thigh), or as mayūravadana (with face of peacock), bhujaṅgabhogavadana (with face of cobra hood), kṛkalāsamukha (with chameleon face), nakravaktra (crocodile face), as digvāsasa (nude), vṛhacchepāṇḍapiṇḍika (megalophallic), vyāghracarmaparidhāna (adorned with tiger hide), ghaṇṭājālapinaddhāṅga (wearing knotted bells), āśiviṣacīradhara (dressed in poisonous serpents) seem to be descriptions, of each one of the many aspects, combined in the Paśupati image. The Paśupati seems to thus make the incomplete, deformed gaṇas complete and whole, by uniting them, as agnisomīya paśus, in Paśupati, with himself.

The gaṇas also appear on Jethani and Devarani pillars as heroic riders (Figs. 239, 271-72), controlling creatures, aquatic or otherwise, prising the mouth of makaras open, or grabbing them by their head, prodding an elephant or a horse into movement, or clutching an encircling lotus rhizome. They appear as bhaktas on Paśupati's body with samputāñjali (hands folded in worship); on base of pillars and pilasters, as prototypes of Saumya Śiva, displaying rudrākṣamālā, abhaya and cinmudrā; or on Paśupati, wearing sarpahāra (garland of snakes) and a tripaṭākā bhṛkuṭi (a three forked frown). A Jethani lintel panel shows three dancing gaṇas, fulfilling their description as nānāsthānanartaka (dancers of myriad postures). Two of them also appear in front of Devarani as daṇḍa or muṣalahasta (holding staff or pestle), and perform the role of door guardians. The gaṇas appear to sing, chant, dance, laugh boisterously, meditate, drum on the mouth in huḍḍukāra, recalling the apparently wayward practices of Pāśupatas, and, of Śiva Mahādeva himself.[172]

The identification of the goat or ram-headed (chāga or ajānana), staff bearing gaṇa (Figs. 502, 561-62) at the entrance of Devarani staircase, lends itself to the most interesting and varied speculations. Traditionally viewed as a symbol of inordinate lust in different stories, he becomes both the progeny and victim, protege and sacrifice of Agni or Rudra, both a harmful and benign influence. At Tala, he is a prototype par excellence of the Agnisomīya Paśu who is purged of his benighted, deformed self, and endowed with a new, satisfying, fulfilling life and personality, in intimate association with Paśupati. He represents ucchhiṣṭa, the residue, of nāmarūpa, pravargya, the surplus of yajña, the detached ego head, replaced by Śiva with the horse head.[173] He epitomizes the ambivalence of the relation of Paśu with Pati. Pati both punishes and cherishes the Paśu, giving him his due according to his nature. He is thus variously identified as the tamas (darkness) in Andhakāsuravadhamūrti (slayer of demonic blindness); as progeny of Agni; as Agni himself; as head of Skanda (spurt of semen); of Nāigameya (head of the guild), who attends or soothes Skanda, or his afflicting spirits; the demon created by śukra (semen); or as Dakṣa Prajāpati (the skilful progenitor). Either as demon or as Dakṣa, the goat-headed gaṇa is slain and then revived, instructed and allotted a station by Śiva as vāstupa (guardian of the house) in the Tala vāstumaṇḍala at the entrance, close to bhogya, identifiable as Kailāsa on Devarani door jamb, where Śiva sports with Pārvatī on the peak of delights. The stories present simultaneous evidence of the Rudra and Saumya aspect of Paśupati, who extracts sacrifice of the unregulated passions of a Paśu in an internal agnihotra, in order to bind the Paśu to his gracious, rejuvenating presence.[174] The vṛṣabha or bull Nandin appears as the four footed sacrificial animal, seated in the deva-vīkṣaṇa-tatpara stance (engaged in looking at his lord constantly). He represents dharma, appearing as the bull vehicle of Rudra. Dakṣa represents offering of a bull vehicle to Rudra, to head his gaṇas, or Rudra himself. He optimizes the bounty of the rain cloud, fertility and reproductivity.[175]

The standing gaṇas from Ramtek (Figs. 504, 506) anticipate the flexion and sedate posture of the Devarani gaṇas. However, it is the standing or seated gaṇas from Sisdeori (Figs. 503, 508) which provide precursors to the supple modelling of Jethani gaṇas. On the other hand, the shouting, running, tilted, animal crested, bird footed gaṇas from Mānsar and Nāgardhan (Figs. 510-12) provide, in their vibrant movement, expression, elegant stance and crouch, dilated eyes and lips, luxuriant, curved moustache, curved fangs, floating hair and ruffled, flaring cloth, circular earrings and single strand necklaces, the closest, if a superior parallel, anticipating the diversity and polyvocality of Jethani gaṇas. The Jethani gaṇas, in turn, provide a livelier version of the gaṇas at Nācnā, Sirpur or Malhār (Figs. 517-24), and impart inspiration to the gaṇas at Deepadih or Maheshpur (Figs. 525-27).

KĪRTIMUKHAS

In a role analogous to that of the gaṇas, kīrtimukhas (faces of glory or of an excavation), made of plant or foliate elements, appear on the crown and armlets of figures, kalaśas or śobhāpaṭṭikās (decorative frames) of pillars and pilasters, or on the door jambs (Pl. 17; Figs. 161, 167-69, 171-72, 429), spouting and absorbing pearls or floral festoons. They are associated with Paśupati as a symbol of lower passions and lust, which devour a person, and have to be sacrificed at the threshold, as insignia of vanaspati (king of vegetation), death and the relentless march of time. They look like mukhakośas (masks), simultaneously inflated with arrested breath, and hollowed by the blight of death. According to legends, they represent, at the same time, the Narasiṁha head, cut off by Śarabha, to restrain his violence; the leonine head, created by a spark, released from the third eye of Śiva, to devour Jālandhara lusting after Pārvatī, Jālandhara, who was condemned to eat himself as a punishment, until he was reduced to his face; and also, the greedy jaws of Vṛtra, smashed by Indra, to release the waters. Śiva stations him at the threshold, here at Tala, as a doorkeeper, who will at once embody the lower self and its devourer, the sacrifice and sacrificer.[176]

SIṀHA

The siṁha appears at Tala as one of the indispensable Paśus associated with Paśupati, appearing not only as stylized kīrtimukha, but also as a load-bearer, vehicle, attendant, worshipper of Śiva (Figs. 197, 252-53, 257, 485, 544-45). In fact, the lions are presented generally as worshippers of Śiva, holding garland, wearing a small lotus cap on the head, suggesting the sahasrāra, or the thousand petalled lotus, symbolic of the crown of the head, and occasionally, as Kevala Narasiṁha, who is supposed to have worshipped Śiva's Śarabha incarnation. The depiction of lions on Paśupati's knees (Figs. 603, 618) reminds us of the description of lion in the *Mahābhārata* as Śiva among animals, and of Śiva as Siṁhaga (of the leonine gait). The siṁhamukha appears on the lintels of Jethani, without floral frills.

The siṁhas appear at the pillar bases, compressed between wheels, and at the bases of the side wall slabs of Jethani, as load-bearers, carrying the vimāna (chariot) of Śiva's temple (Fig. 54). This image of a lion as a vehicle of Śiva is reinforced by an iconographically unique, small figure of Śiva, cut off from the breast, carved on a caitya or a kapota moulding, recovered from Devarani. He is seated in pralambapādāsana (Fig. 548). Two of his hands rest on the eroded heads of two lions, while his feet rest on the palms of the upraised hands of a siṁha. Two horned lion heads adorn the sides of the slab he is seated on. Together, these representations remind us of the *Mahābhārata* and *Harivaṁśa* definitions of Śiva as Siṁhavāhana, and of his lion drawn chariot. It has been noticed how, on a Jethani south lintel, a siṁha sits on a bull, reminding us of gaṇa Kumbhodara (potbellied), who represents the lust for food, and on whom Yogīśvara Śiva places his foot, to mount vṛṣa (varṣaṇaśila retas or incontinent flow of semen).

Some of the lions at the corners of Jethani pillar bases appear with a single head and two bodies, or in pairs, prancing away in opposite directions, after emerging from the pūrṇaghaṭa (Fig. 237). These composite or conjoint pairs may suggest one essence, with two natures, of the gṛhamedhina and gṛhapati (the sacrificer and owner of the house), the two selves, one eating poison, the other ambrosia, one burning the body, the other withholding fuel from the fire of life, by mortifying hunger.[177]

MAKARA

Apart from the siṁha, the makara, which also appears on Paśupati Śiva's shoulders, is present at transitions from one segment to another on Jethani south steps and pillar bases inside (Figs. 46-47, 56-58, 532-33, 535), and on the Devarani vedībandha (Figs. 536, 539) outside. It also appears with gaṇa or without riders on pillar shafts (Figs. 268-72) at maṇḍapa entrance. Surging from foaming surf, cutting it in twain, pinions held high, the makaras flanking Varuna at Jethani (Fig. 396) recall the composite, half-elephantine, half-equine, half-piscine creatures, described in classical literature as Mātaṅganakra, or Vājīmīṇas. The makara represents the śiṁśumāra, literally, the devourer of śiśu, the babe, the moon, or the lower self of the ritually dead Yajamāna. It suggests Varuṇagrāha (seizure by Varuṇa, paralysis), in which the lower self is offered in sacrifice to Varuṇa's maws, to ransom and release the higher self, and facilitate its maturation in the womb chamber. As the floriate crown or mouth of a brimming vessel on a Jethani south pillar (Fig. 239), it is also conceived as the uppermost self-perforate or svayamātṛṇṇa in a sacrificial altar, through which the symbolic passage of the initiated Paśu takes place, for union with its Pati (Figs. 606-08). Thus, the makara, like kīrtimukha, symbolizes the passage of the Agnisomīya Paśu to Paśupati through several stations.[178]

GAJA

The two elephants (Figs. 65-66) on the Jethani pīṭha are caryatids like siṁha and makara, identifiable probably with Airāvata and his consort Abhramū, who emerge from the churning of the ocean, as śrīgajas, or diggajas, and symbolise royal authority, fertility and abundance. They appear on the Devarani as subhagas (highly favoured), or masculine clouds, consecrating Lakṣmī, and on the lower lintel, as veritable gajapādapas or elephant trees (Bignonia Suavelens)

(Figs. 178-81), to form a projected architectural or stage segment, akin to niryyūha mattavāraṇa, nāgadantaka, or wall projection with projected elephant tusks.[179]

GAṆEŚA

The Tala artist not only shows Paśupati's gaṇas, but also Gaṇeśa (Fig. 528), the lord of all gaṇas or categories, backed up against the Devarani staircase on northeast. The Devarani Gaṇeśa does not have the conventional sacred thread, made of snake or mouse vehicle, four arms, attributes of noose and hook, or usual gestures of abhaya or varada. The Tala sculpture stresses his aspect of gaja head, planted by Śiva to replace his human head (ga being goal, and ja origin), replacing illusion by wisdom. His trunk, bent to the left, suggests vāmamārga (the left hand way of destroying obstacles), his large winnowing ears (which removes the impurities) serving the same goal. He shows his single tusk (suggesting union of māyā or illusion and māyin or ilusion maker). His other tusk has been allowed by him to be cut off by the paraśu, the weapon of Śiva, thrown by Paraśūrāma, and it is held in his right hand. His left hand thrusts the modaka (sweet meat, literally, the gladdening thing) into his trunk, acknowledging enjoyment, and he is shown pralambajaṭharaḥ (with hanging belly), like yakṣas.

Thus, the image of Gaṇeśa, being placed quite unusually beside the staircase, becomes an image of vighnarāja and vighneśvara, the creator and remover of obstacles, who stops entry of Śiva into Pārvatī's apartments at the instance of Pārvatī (nature), and then permits Śiva's passage on the destruction of his own illusion. In order to gain entry to Tala Śivālaya, the bhakta has to utter the puṇyāha vacana (the sacred chant), invoking Gaṇeśa, preliminary to sacrifice. The sacrifice is conceived as equivalent to the sacrifice done by Gaṇeśa himself, the sacrifice of the limited human nature (he is born of Pārvatī's scurf) and dualism, represented by his original human head and twin tusks.[180] Though the mouse is not shown with Gaṇeśa, it is shown on the pillars, like his master, with fan ears, full belly, short and conical head. Gaṇeśa, with his big elephant trunk, is dependent, as it were, on the small mouse, which epitomizes the secrecy required for success or siddhi in work, the secrecy which has been described as mantra, ātmā, sādhanā or vibhūti gupti, or reticence with regard to letters of incantation, soul search, penance or pursuit of grace.[181]

The later Ganeśas at Sirpur, Dantevāḍā and Bārsur in bastar demonstrate diminution in the tremendous volume of the head at Tala, elongation of their body, an increase in accoutrements or ornament (Figs. 229-31). The dignity and gravity of mien, demeanour and pose, firm, clear, rounded contours of the animal heads of Tala, Ramtek or Sisdeori or Udayagiri give way to sharp, rectilinear angles of the body, infestation of the body with ornament, manneristic exaggeration, repetitive beading, distorted proportions, desiccation and a certain commonness (Figs. 231, 235, 540-74).

KĀRTIKEYA

Kārtikeya, the other son of Hara Gaurī, is also represented as the leader of Paśupati's hosts, against the enemies of gods at Tala. Of his images recovered at Tala, two are from Devarani and are much more heavily damaged than the magnificent figure in the round from Jethani, which is preserved in Bilaspur museum, or the casually carved relief on a south step lintel (Figs. 199, 265, 350). After being represented only by his vehicle on Paśupati's shoulders (Figs. 595, 597, 604-05), he is now personified as Skanda or the leaping spurt of semen, emitted from the fire of Śiva's tapas (penance), which is incited to flaming desire by Pārvatī's tapas. He is represented as frontally posed, seated astride the peacock, whose name Paravani is logically translated as the year, since Kārtikeya is identified with the saṁvatsara-agni (the solar cycle of the year), and as such, with the nīlalohita (blue red) form of Rudra.[182] The four broken arms of Skanda are clasped by a nāgarāja valaya or armlets, made of four snake coils.

Kartikeya's image at Tala demonstrates the victory of prāṇic fires, symbolized by the encircling halo of the sun eye plumage of the peacock, over the poison of passions, symbolized by the snakes. Nursed through the six centres of the suṣumṇā, he is born as the quintessence of the purest life energy of a yogī. A remnant of the thunderbolt, shown in his only surviving hand, is the counterpart of the solar lance, the abraded tip of which is visible above one of his broken hands. He is presented as a heroic yogī, absorbed in meditative calm, as one who has pierced the krauñcadvāra (the foramen magnum, or the door of the spinal cord in the lower brain); and, as an everchaste adolescent Kumāra, with triśikhā (three locks of hair). As a yogī, he becomes the equivalent of Śiva. As Skanda Viśākha (a many jointed branch, spinal column), which is used as one of the titles of Śiva in the epics, he becomes the ninth integrated form of Rudra, who continues to cry even as eight names are given to him successively. Kārtikeya at Tala thus becomes a symbol of the integration of the Agnisomīya elements in the paśu.[183]

ARDHANĀRĪŚVARA

The integration of Agni and Soma, sun and moon, is also discernible in the androgynous Ardhanāriśvara image (Figs. 425-26) of Śiva at Tala. It is broken in two parts, consisting of the legs and the headless bust, preserved in the Bilaspur museum. It is an integer of man and woman, precluded from sexual union by its bilateral frontality. The left portion is Pārvatī, carved with a female breast and longer dhotī. The right portion is Śiva, carved with a shorter tiger skin drawer, and a tiger head lapping on the thigh. An ascetic attendant of Śiva, cut off from the waist, is visible against his leg.[184]

The hermaphrodite becomes an image of the cosmic sacrifice of Soma in Agni, of the union of (male) time and (female) space, vimarśa (deliberation) and prakāśa (manifestation). It represents the ābhāsa (reflection) of the perfect beauty, which can see itself only in itself.[185] The features of a bisexual image have been clearly and conventionally appreciated at Tala. In view of this, the stridently male Paśupati image appears to have been incorrectly identified as bisexual, on the strength of presence or absence of moustache on gaṇa heads on his body.

ASCETICS

The erotic merges in the ascetic, Śakti in Śiva[186], and the image of Śiva as an ascetic, burning Soma in Agni, becomes paramount at Tala. All his images, be they Saumya or Rudra, have jaṭā, tiger skin garment, short drawers or no garment (Figs. 177, 179, 343, 349, 353-54, 358-60). He himself appears as Paramaguru, the greatest ascetic teacher of all, incarnate as Lakulīśa, and offers instruction in paśupāśavimokṣaṇa (the snapping of the bonds of animals) (Pl. 48). Paraśurāma, an incarnation of Viṣṇu, born of Jamadagni (consuming fire), consort and master of Reṇukā (semen particle), also appears on a Jethani south lintel, holding paraśu, as an ascetic worshipper of Śiva (Fig. 197). The five hooded nāgarāja including one below the crouching ascetic, recovered from Devarani steps (Figs. 434-35), and the tiger/lion head on Paśupati's knees (Fig. 603), probably anticipate the later representation of serpent hooded, tiger footed (vyāghrapāda) sage Pātañjali. A ṛṣi stands holding a garland and a shaven-headed brahmacārī in a kaupīna, offers a coconut to him (Fig. 458), while an ascetic displays a gesture of benediction (Fig. 457) illustrating the relation between ācārya (teacher) and śiṣya (disciple).[187] The fifteen seated ascetics on the Devarani door jamb soffit (Fig. 182) create a counterclockwise wheel like motion with their hands raised above one another, recalling, interestingly enough, the lions on Jethani south pillar bases (Pl. 2; Figs. 42-43), with their paws raised above the head of the lion in front. They generate a cakra or a yantra, framed by a circular mālā of spiral strands, tied at the top by what may well be nāga coils, presumably performing maṅgalācaraṇa (invocatory rites) with the auspicious word siddham or aum svasti. They may also represent sagaraputras performing udakapūrva tarpaṇa or ancestral rites by pouring water.[188] Ascetics accompany Kubera, Sūrya, Varuṇa, Ardhanāriśvara, or Jethani pillar figures (Figs. 169, 194, 348, 356) as attendants. On the Devarani door jamb, Bhagīratha appears as a staff bearing ascetic beside Śiva or Gaṅgā (Figs. 168, 173-74). Ascetics appear as sabhasmadvījas, besmeared with ash, as Keśins, wearing long, matted hair, and short garments, and as Śivabhāgavatas of the Pāśupata faith, holding staff, lotus stalk, or spiral garlands (Figs. 457, 459-63). Physically wasted but luminous (Pl. 33), they demonstrate the efficacy of sacrifice of flesh in the fire of penance, of Soma in Agni. They thus model themselves on Rudra Paśupati, who, as Agni, acts in the capacity of a purohita and a ṛtvik (priest and sacrificer) in the Ṛgveda.[189]

ORNAMENT AND EQUIPMENT

In the iconographic programme of Tala, each image thus plays a role as a member of Śiva's pantheon, to fulfil his roles and present his aspects. The attributes of dress, ornament or equipment serve as alaṁkāra, providing nourishment, empowerment, and protection to the images (Pls. 17, 20, 40-41, 48; Figs. 305-09, 350, 395-97, 426-29, 449, 470, 488-91, 493), to make them sufficient for and capable of performing their assigned tasks in the overall design. The paśus adorn Paśupati Śiva's body, or his house, in the Tala temples, where he resides as the vāstospati (lord of the house), and serve to equip and manifest him as saguṇa (qualified). Stript of the paśus, he becomes nirguṇa (unconditioned) and invisible. The paśus are made of the elements of sun and moon, Agni and Soma, who are called Śiva's āhārya (nourishment) in the *Abhinaya Darpaṇa*. The alaṁkāra is provided at Tala to display the agnisomīya paśus and their lord, to communicate their qualities, rather than merely to please.[190]

CLOTH

The ornament and dress at Tala are permeated by the concept of śṛṅgāra or the erotic, in which creation and procreation become one. If Agni and Soma are the stuff of the sacramental rites of Pāśupata Śaivism, they also form the stuff of the cloth worn by Śiva. The form of the yajña is called the saptatāntava, woven by seven threads of the cosmic loom. It is also the combined form of the agnisomīya paśu, sustained by Agni, assimilating soma or food, by the power of prāṇa. The river goddesses Lakṣmī, Pārvatī, Bhairavī, the female door keepers or their female attendants, are all shown with a bare bust (Figs. 295-309, 311-12, 353-55), with full, proud breasts, and occasionally (as with Pārvatī in the Kailāsa scene), with bare thighs, the bareness being stressed rather than concealed by an ekāṁśika cīvara (a scarf passing over a shoulder and breast), serving as a nirmokapaṭṭa (a piece of transparent cloth resembling serpent slough). The partial nudity of Pārvatī is stressed by the piece of cloth, flung casually across her thighs. Occasionally, even this is missing on the bare bust, and a lady wears only an ardhorūka (a cloth covering half the thighs), wound deeply and tightly (nibiḍanipīḍita) between her legs and her hips by a uccaya (a twisted knot), revealing the soft, alluring curves of her body (Fig. 401).

The Devarani river goddesses, displaced from the ardhamaṇḍapa, display the amplitude of their youth, by wearing diaphanous muktāṁśuka or kṣauma (fine pearl studded silk, or linen). It is tied at the waist by a fluttering netrasūtra (a silken waist band), stretched tightly across the legs with rippling folds and creases (taraṅgita, ūrmika). More often than not, the lower garment clings to the female body like magnāṁśuka (wet drapery), extending up to the feet (āprapādina). Its presence is indicated only by a thin line, described by Bāṇabhaṭṭa as the patrānta-tanu-tāmra-lekhā (the fringe of a thin copper streak, inset in silver). A sūtranaddha (a strip of fastening cord) or paryastaka (a fold of cloth) falls between the legs of the ladies on Jethani wall slabs, enhancing the impression of their long, slender, nubile frame. Ūrujālakas, made of pearl or gem strings, hug the hips of the women, accentuating their width. One woman, cut off from her chest, wears an aṅgikā (blouse, tied by cross threads), with phundnās (Hindi, fasteners) streaking down her bare navel.[191]

JEWELLERY

The female headdress or ornament for the upper bust at Tala is also evocative of erotic sentiment. Many of them hold a līlākamala (a sportive lotus).[192] One woman wears a snake, coiled above her breasts like a balikā (string). Most of the women wear the mandākinī or ghanamuktā ekāvalī (a single wreath, densely woven with numerous pearls), with a nāyakamaṇi (a central gem).[193] While one woman wears a twisted string or snake as her keyūra, the river goddesses wear keyūras made of muktāgrāsas, framed by gold leaves, suggesting plenitude. The ear lobes of the women are extended, hung with karṇaveṣṭanas, or karṇapūras (ear clasps made of danta or kanakapatra, ivory or gold leaf), entwining or filling the earlobe, and circular cabochons, associated with the lotus and the sun, with the cult of Lakṣmī and the Vedic agnicayana rite.[194] The lotus-bearing ladies wear sīmānta-cumbī catulatilakamaṇi (an ornament, suspended by a golden chain, over the dividing line of hair)[195] in their jaṭā, which suggests their ascetic associations. In the āmrabhañjikā or the mithunas, this ornament takes the shape of a floral or metal boss. Apart from this, the women wear haṭakakaṭaka (a loose bracelet) or a cluster of valayas (bangles), and large nūpuras (anklets). In the Āliṅgana Umāmaheśvaramūrti (the divine couple Umā and Maheśa in embrace), the scanty dress, combined with the presence of ornament, becomes uddīpana vibhāva (factor fanning flame of love) and generates madanarasamahaugha (the gushing stream of love), which infects the other mithunas on the door jamb with śṛṅgāra rasa.[196]

HEADDRESS

The hair of women (Figs. 170, 298, 397-99, 446-49) is curled into alaka, massed and gathered into a topknot as dhammilla-keśa-racanā, falls on the shoulders in ringlets, as cūrṇakuntala, and is made wavy or taraṅgita. It is also tightly braided in chains, or veṇīs and praveṇīs, and twisted together as vardhara, to form a juḍā or chignon. Occasionally, garbhakas or wreathed chaplets of flower are woven into the hair, or a variant of a maulimālatimālikā or jasmine diadem is tied around the head. One female partner in a Devarani mithuna wears her hair like a raised wing, which frames a crest jewel with fluttering leaves (Fig. 397). This hairstyle, imitating a bee with outspread wings, is appropriately called bhramaraka keśapāśa, evoking associations of honeysucking, pollination and love.

As against this, Tala displays figures of Śiva in different forms above gaṇas, whose dress or ornament appear to emphasize their more austere or functional roles. Śiva images usually wear intertwined hair knots (vardhara) enclosing a peak. The locks of Ardhanārīśvara, Saumya Śiva and Bhairava (Figs. 177, 353, 358, 425) escape on the shoulder as aṁsāvalambinī jaṭā (shoulder hugging locks). The jaṭā is tied on a Bhairava head (Fig. 428) by a floral lalāṭapaṭṭa (head band) with a lotus śikhaṇḍa (crest), the śikhaṇḍa-khaṇḍikā (crest jewel) being formed by a deeply hollowed jewel skull. The central crest is embossed with a muktāgrāsa above another head. In an Ardhanārīśvara head, the taller mass of cascading jaṭā, coming down on one side, distinguishes the Śiva half of the head, together with a moustache.

The gaṇas (Pl. 35; Figs. 418, 479, 484-85), attending the precincts of Śiva as his load bearers, most frequently display semicircular, parasol (chattrākāra) hair, made of a mass of thickly clustered curls, looking like crosses between commas and interrogation marks. Sometimes, such hair has a central parting hairline (keśavīthi), sometimes none, and usually, it is adorned with a circular floral boss in the centre. The heavy, broad bodies of the gaṇas, with outstretched limbs, look heavier and broader with this canopy of hair, which also makes the head appear larger and better capable of bearing the tremendous load above. The standing Śiva on a Jethani lintel, several nāgarājas from Jethani and attendants of Kubera, Bhagīratha, Gaṅgā or Sūrya at Devarani have the same umbrella like hair (Figs. 169-70, 435). Some of the other Jethani gaṇas, as well as the gaṇas attending Śiva Pārvatī playing chausar, and other gaṇas including a moustachioed gaṇa behind the heavily damaged river goddesses on the left surround of Devarani door jamb, have valibhṛd alaka (Figs. 177, 312, 483, 486, 498), which consists of one or more vertically arrayed rows of thick, spiral side braids, which, in turn, are, sometimes threaded through a further cluster of plaits, on the crown of the head. The rows of spiral locks spread out in an arc, and are galvanized by the sideways movement of the head of a dancer or a load-bearer. The hair of Jethani Kārtikeya, of two small gaṇas flanking a bigger Jethani gaṇa, or, of a male touching the chin of his female partner, in a Devarani door jamb mithuna, comes down in one long, heavy cascade over the shoulder or the back, like massed peacock feathers, and is called the barhabhārakeśa (Fig. 170). Some gaṇas and Śaiva figures (Figs. 360-61, 430) wear hair piled in tiers, occasionally diminishing in size, suggesting karaṇḍamukuṭa.[197]

KUṆḌALAS, HĀRAS

Sarpa or kūrma hāras (necklace made of snakes or tortoise), sarpakuṇḍala (snake earring), sarpa yajñopavīta (sacred thread made of snake), worn by several gaṇas (Figs. 483-88, 490, 495), speak of their association with Paśupati. Most of them wear in their ears tāṭaṅka-cakras (Figs. 421, 423, 480, 488, 496), shaped as perforated, annular discs, or discs compressed between two flat, round flans, or a disc with a central depression, or a rondella with granular dots on the encircling barrel. Some other figures seem to wear rectangular or square metal bars, bent to a double loop, attached to a block, which, not being cubical, offers an approximation to the prākāravapra kuṇḍala (rampart like earring) (Figs. 297, 306, 422, 478, 489, 498). Lord bearing gaṇas (Figs. 482, 486) the two gaṇas on the Paśupati Śiva's chest, and the other two on his thighs, have in their right-ear kuṇḍalas made of bells, which, also form testicles of Paśupati. Some of the Jethani gaṇas seem to wear a sliced conch shell with a spiral line, which probably is a śaṅkhakuṇḍala. While with some, kuṇḍalas are the same in the two ears, in others they are different in size, shape and design. The crouching Jethani gaṇa wears a heart shaped pendant (Fig. 491) made of śīśa, tāla or dantapatra (leaf, bone or ivory strips). The hāras, valayas are simpler studded with gems, made like flowers and leaves, and hung, as in case of the hāra of Varuṇa, with vandanamālā like pendants (Fig. 347, 450, 470).[198]

GESTURES

Together with ornament, goes gesture and posture. The lower lips dangle occasionally, a feature known as adhararucaka, being a mark of beauty (Figs. 429, 435, 488). The bhaṅgura (creased) uttarīya, phalli paṭṭa (cloth fold dangling between legs), aṁśuka (silken or costly cloth) go with frizzled looks, lola (swaying) kuṇḍala, unmatta bhrūvīkṣita (quickened brow movements), or bhaṅgura bhrūkuṭivibhrama (frowning eye brows) (Figs. 419, 486, 491). The still volumes of clustered leaves, fruits, locks of jaṭā, or the arrested moment of love, go with mantharita-pakṣman-cakṣu or motionless eyelashes.[199] (Figs. 306, 395, 400)

AGNIKṢETRA: TEMPLE AS ALTAR

The Tala temples are themselves probably conceived as agnikṣetras (fields of fire), as areas where the fire qua man is reassembled (saṁdhā), and reconstructed (saṁskṛ), after being dispersed and dismembered, in the shapes of many paśus. The sacrifice of all paśus, the sarvamedha, takes place in the composite body of the Tala temples, in what may be seen as the agnyādheya rites. The temples, thus conceived, become citis, funeral cairns, to hold the ashes of the psychophysical selves of the śyenaciti, shaped like a bird with outspread wings, made of seven squares, a shape closely recalled by the Jethani temple (Figs. 6, 63). Its pakṣadvāras or side doors may be seen as the aratnis, or wings, its front as pradeśa, on the main trunk, the cella at the north being its puccha or tail. The temple is a fire altar, and is also synonymous with the all encompassing all engendering form of Rudra.[200] The yūpa forms the pivot in the altar, with a śukrapātra at the base. It is seen twice in the panels of a Jethani south lintel, crowned by fluttering canopies of cloth. It provides a model for the massive pillars of the temples, which may themselves hark back to the Vedic concept of reproductive pillar, tree of life and death, sacrificial stake, Viśvarūpa, Agni, Rudra or Prajāpati.[201] The Kalaśa at the base and crown of the pillars and pilasters, is variously seen as both male and female, in the *Vedas*, as a great hero, a seed pot, generative of Rudra, as Viśvarūpa, comprehending all forms, and, as an object of worship in fire ritual.[202] (Pl. 2; Figs. 44, 157, 237, 249, 252, 256)

Śiva, as the presiding architect of this agnikṣetra, stations himself at the cross roads[203] at Tala. He is offered worship in the *Śatarudrīya* as the Vāstupya and Vāstuvya, guard and protector of the house. He lays out a sketch plan and allots the deities their particular stations in the Tala vāstumaṇḍala. In this, the sacerdotium is established in the regnum, Agni in the Soma, and the Paśupati is established as an aggregate of the agnisomīya paśus, who participate in the sacrifice of lower selves, and attain divinity by self control. The residual part of the sacrifice, pierced by Paśupati, is now given to him, turning him into Vāstoṣpati, and inducing him to rise towards the heaven as Agni.[204] The Tala vāstu, specially the Jethani temple, becomes the chariot, the fort, the palace of Śiva. It is carried by the vimānapāla (chariot carrying) siṁhasaṁghātas (lion groups), gaṇas and makaras, and held up on the caturbhṛṣṭi (facing all the four directions) sthūṇārājas (great pillars). It simultaneously recalls the design of great skandhāvāras (royal camps) of that time. In these, elephants function like sañcārī giridūrga (moving hill forts), from which arrows can be showered. Bāhyapratihāras (guards of the outer precincts), āsannasevakas (confidential servants, like the gaṇas of Tala), and the birds or animals (like the pañjarasiṁha), act as royal companions in udyānakṛḍā or ṛtucaryā (garden and seasonal sports). They are always at the beck and call of the lord of the house, at a prāsāda (palace, temple) like Jethani. A kṛḍāparvata (mountain of dalliance), made of gaṇḍaśīlā (stone blocks) is present in the Kailāsa of Devarani door jamb. Opposite this are the apāna, līlālāsya or madanotsava maṇḍapas, pavilions for drinking, frolic and fun, occupied at Devarani by the mithunas. The divine and human mithunas or water cosmological patterns act as śṛṅgārasaṁketacitra or the love inducing signs. Māṅgalika cihnas (auspicious signs) like pañcāsyakalaśa (vessel with five wide mouths), fishes, tortoises and crocodiles are present, as are the river goddesses, which replace Rati and Prīti, painted on either side of the bridal chamber door in a palace. In the centre of a palace is a vitardikā (covered platform), supported on a suvīthi (arcade of pillars), which is equivalent to the catuṣṭikā at Jethani. Altogether, the Tala temple precinct conjures up the impression of the camp, the chariot, the citadel, the palace, occupied by Rudra or Agni, after the sacrificial upasada (siege) rites. The siege is of the Tripura, the demonic city of tṛguṇa, three attributes, iron, silver and gold, pierced by the bāṇa (arrow), with Agni as its point, Soma as its socket. This city becomes synonymous with the body of the paśu, and the rites become the rites of consignment of the lower selves of the paśu to paśupati.[205]

Jethani can thus be visualized as analogous to the agnicayana altar, in which the seven prāṇas or vital airs are combined in the seven squares to reconstitute the shape of the Puruṣa, as the Śyena, the eagle.[206] In the body of Paśupati, the seven breaths are brought together. By stages, the distance to God diminishes. The gaṇas, siṁhas, makaras are shown initially at the outer periphery, and are then put together on the body of Paśupati. Some of the Śiva Pratihāras assume the aspect of Śiva himself. Ultimately, the temples establish a sequence, a progression, in which the paśus gradually become one with Paśupati. If the Paśupati image is the anthropomorphic iconostasis of this sequence, the temples, specially the Jethani temple premises, epitomize its architectural form.

NOTES

1. As Wölfflin, the pioneer in the study of form, points out, 'Beholding is just not a mirror, which always remains the same, but a living power of apprehension which has its own inner history and has passed through many stages.' Also, 'It is true, we only see what we look for, but we also look for what we can see.' Wölfflin 1915: 226, 230-31. As against this, Panofsky, explaining the primacy of content, points out that '...the connection of the eye to the world is in truth a connection of the mind to the world of the eye', in Holly 1984: 61. Analysing the somewhat artificial distinction, set up between the two points of view, Holly, *ibid.*, 62-66, points out that Wölfflin does see content as more than subject matter in his discussion of the double root of style, in which the subject matter becomes content through both its formal arrangement and its historical ethos, and in which the formal arrangements are no mere modes of representation, but are also expressively significant. Panofsky 1955: 28, 32, 40-41, sees the study of content as the unifying principle underlying factual, expressional, pre-iconographic description of primary subject matter, literary, iconographic description of secondary subject matter, synthetic, intuitive, iconological description of cultural symptoms or symbolic values. Moreover, opposition of res and verba, research (quaestio) and verbalization (elocutio) is breaking down, and the ideological can no longer be so easily separated from the phraseological. Barthes 1986: 66-67.

2. 'The hermeneutic act of understanding comes into operation with a sense of alienation from tradition, with a sense of its otherness from our present and remoteness from it.' J.L. Mehta 1985: 156.
3. Dealing with this question of integration of form and content, with the help of medieval scholastic texts, Coomaraswamy explains that the success of the artist depends on the coming together of mantraśakti or theoretical power of visualization, with utsāhaśakti or practical power of execution. He quotes *Abhilāṣitārthacintāmaṇi* 1.3.158, 'Cintayet pramāṇam; tad-dhyātam bhittau niveśayet', 'Realize the visualization; then put it into execution'; Or, the *Aitareya Brāhmaṇa* 6.97, which speaks of an anukaraṇa (mimesis) of divine forms to achieve metrical self integration (chandobhirātmanām saṁskaraṇa). A properly visualized and executed image, combining form and content, thus becomes alam (sufficient) kāra (made), or ornament, which is an adequate expression of its model, and hence an effective instrument for meditation. See "The Intellectual Operation in Indian Art", Coomaraswamy, I, ed. Lipsey, 1983: 131; "Figures of Speech or Thought", *ibid.*, 21, 34-5; "Buddhist Art", *ibid.*, 165; 'Ornament', *ibid.*, 243; "Literary Symbolism", *ibid.*, 323-24; "The Part of Art in Indian life", *ibid.*, 71: 85, 88; "Art of Eastern Asia", *ibid.*, 116. The Tala artist is to be considered free and original in his capacity to personally conceive and execute an ideal. He is not to be seen as a servile imitator, obediently copying a biological copy of the original ideal. "Imitation, Expression and Participation", *ibid.*, 277, n. 9.
4. J.L.Mehta speaks with Heidegger about the need for stepping back, for reiteration, for beginning the beginning once again, more radically than ever before, for recovering the sense of the sacred, as a key to the interpretation of ancient texts like the Vedas, for understanding tradition. He speaks of the need for unlocking the hidden meaning of the Vedas, by quoting *Ṛgveda* 10.5.2. "The poets hide the paths of truth; they keep secret their hidden names. To be able to retrieve these forgotten meanings, we must exorcise the desacralization, which has overtaken our life and our understanding. Only then we can perceive the unified play of the fourfold of earth and heaven, gods and mortals, in which man dwells on earth as his home, under the heavens, in friendly commerce with the gods, with his fellowmen, and with things, building and making untiringly, with thoughts and words and things "Heidegger, Indian and Western Philosophy," J.L. Mehta 1990: 8-10; "Hindu Tradition", *ibid.*, 3; "The *Ṛgveda*, Text and Interpretation", *ibid.*, 288; "Life worlds, Sacrality, and Interpretative Thinking", *ibid.*, 237. Coomaraswamy has already spoken about the need for transforming our own nature to be able to read meanings back into forms, ignorantly left out of them. In "Aesthetic Shock", Lipsay, ed., *Coomaraswamy*: 184; "Rape of a Nagi", *ibid.*, 337-8, 340; "Loathly Bride", *ibid.*, 368; "Akiñcana, Self naughting", *ibid.*, 102.
5. Thus, O' Flaherty suggests that the Śaiva corpus resembles a piece of chain mail in fabric rather than the brachiated, family tree structure, sought by text historical analysts. O' Flaherty 1973: 20-21. Good and evil are inseparable in the mythical universe. Like a kaleidoscope, the myths contain and constantly rearrange vivid episodes like bits of coloured glass, through which one sees one's own personal history. O'Flaherty 1976: 375-77. Different creator Gods like Tvaṣṭṛ or vivifier, Viśvakarman or maker of the world, Mitra, Varuṇa, Indra, Soma, Agni, Puruṣa, Prajāpati, Rudra, Skambha and Yūpa (cosmic and sacrificial pillar), Rohita (the ascending Sun), Tat (the one), mentioned in the *Vedas*, *Śatapatha Brāhmaṇa*, *Maitrāyaṇī* and *Vājasaneyī Saṁhitās*, or in the *Śvetāśvatara Upaniṣad* are interchangeable with regard to the source, nature and expression of their creative powers. Valuable evidence has been brought together about the interpermeability of such forms by Doris Meth Srinivasan 1997: 6 to 9, 25 to 36, 43 to 49, 60 to 128.
6. What Kālidāsa in *Raghuvaṁśam* calls 'vāgarthāviva sampṛktau Pārvatī-Parameśvarau'. 'Pārvatī and Parameśvara are assimilated like the word and its meaning'. For a contrary modern western view, see "Mythology today", in Barthes 1986: 66. Also, "Style and its image", *ibid.*, 90-91, 93, 99, where he says that the text consists only of layered forms, without a content. "It is neither melodic nor harmonic, but contrapuntal, mingling voices in a volume, not in a line, not even a double one." If hitherto we have seen the text as a fruit with its pit (an apricot, for instance), the flesh being the form and the pit the content, it would be better to see it as an onion, a superimposed construction of skins (or layers of levels, of systems)

whose volume contains, finally no heart, no core, no secret, no irreducible principle, nothing but the very infinity of its envelopes, which envelop nothing other than the totality of surfaces. In their application to Indian art, however, the ancient and medieval texts of India appear to retain, through all the successive reformulations, forms which do constitute the appearance or garment of content, which, in turn, is its truth. In this context, see, "Imitation, Expression, Participation", *Coomaraswamy* 1, 1983: 282, where he says 'symbols are projections or shadows of their forms, in the same way that the body is an image of the soul, which is called its form, and as words are images of things'. Instead of using the analogy of the fruit, we might here use the example of the finger pointing to the moon, which may not be confused with the moon, though the other images evoked by the moon, may well be assimilated to its shape and its soothing radiance. The imagery of Indian art shows neither binary opposition between form and content, nor layers of forms, but a blend of both.

7. See Umberto Eco 1979:191-92, where he points out that it is possible to assert that the iconic signs are culturally coded without saying that they are arbitrarily correlated to their content, thereby restoring to the category of conventionality a more flexible sense.
8. The 'Gupta Vākāṭaka' art and some of the Tala art (like the foliate relief on Jethani door jambs, the Hara Gaurī panel in the Devarani door jamb, the āmrabhañjikā or Kārtikeya at Jethani, the art of Mānsar or Sisdeori, Mānḍhal or Sirpur) is classical in this union of form and content, 'ethos' and 'pathos'. Coomaraswamy 1927: 35, says that in Indian art 'when we perceive increased reality or truth, we must ascribe this, not to a change of habit, but to a heightened consciousness, a more complete identification with the theme itself .... a more profound empathy'.
9. What Coomaraswamy would call 'śithila samādhitvam', a slackening in both 'mantraśakti' and 'utsāha-śakti', the power of conception or of execution, which affects the saṁvega or the 'aesthetic shock', experienced by the spectator or critic. Excessive ornament or exaggerated accents restrict the efficiency or adequacy of the symbols in reminding us of their referents. These indicate a fault, not necessarily in the artist, but most probably in the patron, who has more to say, less to mean. One might notice the onset of such trends at Tala itself in the foliate relief of Devarani door jamb, or in the obsession with superhuman height or size at Jethani. See "Art in Indian life", in *Coomaraswamy* 1, 1983: 84; "Aesthetic shock", *ibid.*, 183; "Imitation, Expression, Participation", *ibid.*, 278; "Rape of a Nāgi", *ibid.*, 340; "Ornament", *ibid.*, 252.
10. Donald Preziosi 1989: 90, explains that the perspectives brought together in the study of cultural signs involve a study of the social, collective language in a given state, and a study of individual features in time and change. Saussure 1959: 157, points out two sides of the linguistic sign, namely, the collective langue and the individual manifestation in parole. In Indian art of this period, however, the study of the collective langue cannot feasibly be separated from the study of individual parole, or confined, in Saussurean terms, to a given moment ('a un moment donne'), in which it forms a structure au tout se tient.
11. In this connection, see the quotation of a Longman cave inscription in China in "Buddhist Art", *Coomaraswamy* 1, 1983: 168. "It is as if the summit of the mountain has been reached and the river traced to it's source: The fruition is accomplished, and one rests upon the principle". It is interesting for students of iconography and iconology, that this inscription is carved near a guardian image, hewn out of the rock near the grotto gate of Binyangzhongdong at Longman caves, that offers the closest analogy to the Paśupati image from Tala.
12. The Mānḍhal copperplates of the 5th regnal year of Vākāṭaka king Rudraṣeṇa II refers to the instruction of anantaśāyī Viṣṇu for the construction of a temple near Mānḍhal, and the existence of sātvata adhivāsare, a devotional Vaiṣṇava community, dedicated to the worship of four Vṛṣṇivīras. The śātvata pāncarātra Vaiṣṇavism appears to have migrated from Vatsagulma Bāsim to Nandīvardhana Pravarapura region and shaped the iconography of Mānḍhal and Rāmagiri. The Nala King celebrated reestablishment of Visṇu's footprints at Puṣkarī, after the Vaiṣṇava Prabhāvatīgupta celebrated Viṣṇu's footprints at

Rāmagiri. Prabhāvatigupta's Māheśvara successors at Pravarapura fought a seesaw battle with Nalas, with the help of the Vaiṣṇava Viṣṇukuṇḍins, in late 5th and early 6th Century. Bakker 1997: 55-56; Shastri 1992. Prasannamātra's coins at Tala, a Śaiva site, show Vaiṣṇava symbols.

13. See Mirashi 1963: 7, 12, 18, 23-4, 27-28, 30, 44, 50. In Jāmb, Belorā, Chammak, Dudiā, Pattan, Pāṇḍurṇā plates, the Vākāṭaka king Pravarasena II proclaims himself a Paramamāheśvara, a Mahābhairava bhakta, a Bhāraśiva, carrying Śivaliṅga on head; as a progeny of ancestors, whose heads are consecrated by Ganges waters, obtained by their valour (parākramādhigata bhāgīrathyāmalajalamūrdhābhiṣiktānām), or, as one who has established the kṛtayuga or the golden age on earth by the grace of Śambhu. In the Bāmhoni plates of Mekala Pāṇḍu king Bharatabala, queen Lokaprakāśā is compared with river Ganges for her peerless character (suralokādāgatā Jāhnavīva), and king Nāgabala, a devotee of Śiva, is declared to be a venerated teacher, a God, a supreme deity, paramaguru devatādhidaivataviśeṣa(ḥ).

14. The 2nd century AD Kirāri wooden pillar inscription in Bilaspur mentions gahapati *(gṛhapati)* and the mid 3rd Century AD. Amaravati inscription mentions the Vākāṭaka king as gṛhapatī, Lord of the house. The Vākāṭaka king Rudrasena II (375-60 AD), in his inscription, recut on Aśoka's inscription at Deoṭek, Chandrapur, Maharashtra, mentions Śiva temple as svadharmasthāna, his own religious site. King Pravarasena II, in a 435 AD charter from Pāṇḍurṇā, mentions Pravareśvara devakulasthānam, the place of the pantheon of the Lord of Pravara, and vaijayaka dharmasthāna, or the sacred site of victory, dedicated to God. In his Pattan plates he refers to the temple site as mahāpuruṣa pādamūlasattropayojyam, used for the worship of the feet of the Great Being. In his Yawatmal and Pauni plates, Pravarasena II makes grants of land and house sites by rājamānaka mānena, by royal measurement. Prabhāvatīgupta, in her 456-7 AD inscription in the Kevala Narasiṁha temple at Ramtek, designates the Kevala Narasiṁha image, seated in mahārājalīlāsana, the sovereign royal pose, as Prabhāvatīsvāmin, Lord of Prabhāvatī. The image is supposedly made in conscious reminiscence of Rudrasena II, whose rule was installed by one whose emblem was a cakra. The Riddhapurī copperplates of Prabhāvatīgupta are given from the footprints of Rāmagirisvāmin. The words, śāsanam ripuśasanam, governance, in chastisement of enemies, are used in Miregāon plates of Pravarasena II, year 29, to describe the rule of the regent Prabhāvatīgupta. Rudrasena II's Mānsar inscription makes a grant to Monḍasvāmin, Śeṣaśāyī Viṣṇu, probably in allusion to Prabhāvatīgupta's earlier name Muṇḍā. Nine copperplates of Pāṇḍuvaṁśī Kings found at Nandpur, Sirpur, mention devasthalas, the presiding Śiva being identified as the Lord of founder queens like Āmmādevī, Amaradevī, Abbānibbaḍḍi. They provide for offering of sacrifice, dance, music, incense, oblation, and daily provisions at maṭhikās or monasteries. These are consecrated as tapovanas, places of penance for teachers in the spiritual lineage of Vyāpa (Vyoma) Śiva or Śrīghoraśiva.

Naya, vinaya, śaurya, prajñā, prabhāva, tyāga or logic, discipline, courage, wisdom, power and renunciation, are praised as virtues of the King in the Malhār copperplates of Bālārjuna and in the Aḍbhār copperplates of Mahānannarāja issued from Sirpur. Satya, ārjava, kāruṇya, vikrama or rectitude, energy, compassion, heroism, are praised as royal attributes in the copperplate grants of Pravarasena II and his grandson, Pṛthvīṣeṇa II, issued from Nandīvardhana. This catalogue of royal virtues should be read in the background of the Lakṣmaṇa temple maṇḍapa debris inscription of Queen mother Vāsaṭā. It exhorts Kings to refrain from sins. It asks them to compare the temple flag in the sky, dipping up and down in the breeze, with royal fortunes (kṣaṇamadhaḥ kṣaṇamutpatitairnabhaḥ pavanalolatāyā dhvajapallavaiḥ). It prompts them to look at the high and low states of existence, obtained by creatures, with their cage like bodies, through their diverse actions, depicted on the temple (uccāvachaiḥ karmāṇām vaicitryād... vahuvidhāvasthāyirvapupañjaraiḥ), Jain 1961: 3-5,6-10, 175, 193-4, 196-2174; Shastri 1997: 143-74.

15. Vākāṭaka kings of Vidarbha made land grants to exponents of the Vedas. Pravarasena I (c. 275 – 335 AD) uses the words, 'agniṣṭomāptoryā .... vājapeyavṛhaspati savasādyaskra' (184, line 1). His tradition appears to have been followed by Pravarasena II at Pravarapura, after he shifted his capital there in c. 435 AD. Pravararāja's Malhār copperplate grant is made to the son of Ṛgvedi bahvṛcā of Bharadvāja

gotra. King Hariṣeṇa of Vatsagulma branch makes grant in year 3 to Brāhmin Sāmavedi students. Sudevarāja's Khariyār and Ārang copperplates grants are made to Vājasaneya Brāhmins of mādhyandīna branch. The Māṇḍhal plates, Yawatmal and Pauni plates of year 32 of Pravarasena II, Māṇḍhal and Māsod plates of years 2, 17 and 19 of Pṛthivīseṇa II, Riddhapuri plates of Prabhāvatīgupta are made out in favour of Brāhmins of Taittirīya śākhā of the black Yajurveda. The Pauni plates of year 30 of Pravarasena II make grant to a student of *Ṛgveda*, a bahvṛcā.

The Pāṇḍuvaṁśis of Dakṣina Kośala made similar land grants to Vedic scholars. The Lakṣmaṇa temple stone inscription of Queen mother Vāsaṭā at Sirpur, makes the grant to Brāhmins of four Vedas conditional on their being agnihotṛs, Vāsatā herself being compared to the Vedas, for those living in faith, as varṇāśraminām trayība. Jain 1961: 15-27. 10-14, 81-21. Arrangements for initiation of ascetics into sacrificial rites and the cult of time, i.e., yāga, dīkṣā, samayasya vyākhyāna, are mentioned in Senākapāṭ inscription of Mahaśivagupta's time. Dikshit and Sircar 1955-56: 33. Remnants of sacrificial ceremonies have been found under the brick platform added to the Devarāni temple at Tala. While no firm conclusion is possible about direct association of royal patronage with the Tala temples on the basis of available archaeological evidence, Śiva appears to be performing the role of the Lord Sovereign of the House at Tala.

Mānsar in Nagpur, Maharashtra, has been identified as a royal site in the light of the discovery of remnants of sacrificial ceremonies behoving a Cakravartī, at Hiḍimbā Tekḍi, from the 2nd 3rd c. AD, at the juncture of Sātavāhana and Vākāṭaka periods, continuing the vogue of the Vedic sacrificial tradition. The remnants include hawana kuṇḍas, vedis, and balipīṭhas, sacrificial pits, altars and platforms. The altars are made of fired bricks in the shape of śyena and kūrmaciti, a flying eagle and a tortoise. A crouching male, in loin cloth and anklets, made of lime, lies with folded legs, severed forehead, smashed chest. A square brick platform, pierced by an oval hole for fixing a wooden yūpa, or stake, is mounted on him. An iron snake, with raised hood, and a mollusc shell wheel, lie close by. Adjoining stairs give access to another sacrificial pit and a square brick shrine, with outlet for water. Joshi and Sharma 2005: 3, 10-14, 21.

16. For Sudevarāja's Āraṅg copperplate, see Jain 1961/2005: 20. 4. Also the allusion to sacrificials offerings, including music, at restoration of temple ruins, Bali-caru-naivedya sattra-nṛtta-vāditra-khaṇḍa-sphutita-saṁskāra in verse II in Lodhiā plates of Mahāśivagupta in Mirashi and Pandey 1947-48: 321. Reference to provision of garlands by mālākāras or gardeners in Śrīpura to the Gandharveśvara Śiva temple, is found in several Gandheśvara temple inscriptions of Mahāśivagupta at Sirpur. Hiralal 1916/1932: 86-88.
17. See Āraṅg plates of Bhīmaseṇa in Hiralal, *EI* 9, 1907-08: 342 ff. for the Rājarṣitūlyakula, the dynasty of ascetic like kings. Examples of names of grantees, showing Śaiva affiliations, are Rudrārya, Somārya, Skandārya, mentioned in Chammal plate of Pravarasena II, Mirashi 1963: 5, 25. Rudrasoma, Tejaḥsoma and Bhīmasoma are trained by a disciple of Lakulīśa himself (Mahāvraten dīkṣita) according to verses 16-19, in Junavāni (Malhār) copperplate of the 57th year of Mahāśivagupta, tentatively read by G.L. Raikwar and R.K. Singh at Bilaspur. Sadyahśivācārya, Sadāśivācārya and Āmardakatīrthanātha, are mentioned in Senākapāṭ inscription, which is discussed by Mirashi and Sircar in *EI* 33, 1959-60: 251, 255-56, and in Ranod inscription, *IA* 1: 352. Rāśirudra is mentioned as a great tapasvin in the 'Gandheśvara Temple Pillar Inscription of Ambullaka', edited by B.C. Jain in *EI* 28 1954-55: 2-3. Agnicandrasvāmin is mentioned in 'Malhār plates of Vyāghrarāja', edited by Sircar and Bhattacharya *EI* 34, 1961-62: 45-52. King Pravarasena's stone inscription, dedicated at Śaṅkhacakrabhoga village found at Māṭiā village near Malhār, makes a grant to Śubhacandrasvāmin of Bharatagotra and Ṛgvedic branch. Pandey 2002:012. Two of Śivagupta Bālārjuna's grants, namely, the Lodhiā and Malhār plates are respectively made at the request of an unnamed Śaiva teacher and Śivanandin. Shastri 1995, 2: 132, 140.
18. In view of the mention of ascetics with the suffix Soma and the use of Pāśupata terminology in Sirpur inscriptions, late V.S. Pathak has suggested influence of Somasiddhāntin ascetics on Tala iconography in a discussion with me. He points out that Somanaya is extensively mentioned as Na-ya-su-mo in now

lost Sanskrit Buddhist texts compiled by Tucci from Chinese translations. Tucci notes the influence of this school on Gautama Sūtra. Kaulajñānanirṇaya calls Somasiddhāntavādins Bauddhas. See Pathak 1960: 23-28; Chakravarti 1932: 220 ; G.Tucci 1930: 28-29. While this suggests esoteric ideas at work around Tala, confirms the mingling of Śaiva and Buddhist ideas and the transfer of such ideas to China, one has to point out that the Tala Paśupati image precedes the Sirpur inscriptions by nearly a century, and no such image has yet been found at Sirpur itself.

19. See *Bṛhat Saṁhitā* for Paśupata worship and V.S. Agrawala 1969, for Kāpālika worship. The inscriptions of Dakṣiṇa Kośala and Vidarbha provide description of the various forms in which Rudra Śiva is invoked by worshippers and depicted in art. Rudrasatṣaṣṭianugrāhaka or Rudra in sixty six incarnations are mentioned in Junavāni Copperplate Inscription of Mahāśivagupta, in Jain 1961: 190, verses 14-16, p.190. Queen Vaśatā's Lakṣmaṇa temple maṇḍapa debris inscription speaks of an ancestor, who has influence like Bhūtapati, Udbhūta Bhūtapati samaprabhāva. Jain 1961: verse 4. He is described as Mahābhairava and Maheśvara in the copperplates of Vākāṭaka kings Pravarașeṇa II and Pṛthīviṣeṇa II. Shastri, *Māṇḍhal Utkhanan* 1977: 143-76. The Senākapāṭ inscription mentions Āmardaka, a form of Kālabhairava. Somavaṁśī king Mahābhavagupta Janmejaya's copperplates, and Kudopāli copperplates of Mahābhavagupta II speak of the donor being praised by Āditya, Varuṇa, Soma, Hutāśana, Brahmā, Viṣṇu and Śūlapāṇi. Jain 1961/2005: 42, 47.

    Malhār copperplates of Mahaśivagupta Bālarjuna equate his father with Kṛttivāsas, the one robed in tiger skin. His Junavani inscription names Śiva as Aṣṭamūrti and Lakulīśa. In his Gandheśvara temple inscription, Śiva is described as Lord of Gandharvas, and worshipped as Gaṅgādhara, in the words, dhāritam yena Gaṅgāyām śṛṅgoccam patanādbhūṣin jaṭāvīṭapasaksthena saḥ haraḥ pātu bo .... Let Śiva, who has received the surging columns of Gaṅgā waters in his matted locks, protect us. In a broken inscription in the same temple, Śiva is described as jvālākalāpakapilākuladehidehamāhāra (vahni) bhārani or bhāravahnimeva; with matted locks, looking like all consuming flames. Jain 1961: 194, verse line 3; 195, verse line 4. The Gandheśvara temple inscription of Ambullaka names Śiva as Bhavabhedin, the world destroyer. Śūravala Udīrṇṇavaira's copperplates, regnal year 8, offer praise to Śiva as Vṛṣabhavāhana, Śūlapāṇi and Bhujagaparikara; bearing trident, riding bull and framed by an aureole of rearing snakes. Jain 1961: 185, verse lines 1-2.

    Śivaparivāra, or the immediate family of Śiva and the family of his companions, is also worshipped. Cults of Nāigameśa, Kārtikeya and Lajjā Gaurī are found in mutual association. King Bālārjuna's Malhār copperplates from Thākur Gulāb Singh collection and Suraṅgatilā compare him to Mahābhyūdayaḥ Kārtikeyaḥ. Jain 1961: 193-4. verse lines 5, 7-9; 197. Nāigameśa is installed on either side of the entrance of a Uttānapāda Lajjā Gaurī shrine at Siddhānakollā, Karnataka, while Lajjā Gaurī plaques have been found at Pavnār, Nāgardhan and Māhurjhari in the Vākāṭaka kingdom of Nandīvardhana. Pṛthīvīṣeṇa's (460-73 AD) copperplates have been issued from Māhurjhari. In the sīmantonnayana marriage ceremony, prescribed in Gṛhyasūtra, offerings are made to Nāigameśa, and, in the context of the Somaparamparā in Dakṣina Kośala, also to Soma, for the birth of a child, and, for the safety of a male child. A pregnant mother is compared, in a Ṛgvedic hymn, with Mahīuttāna, the earth mother. Jamkhedkar: 23-40.

20. The confluence between Buddhism and Brahminism appears to have been underway since the Upāsaka (devotee) king Aśoka, 'devānām piya', beloved of Gods, claimed, in the Rūpnāth rock edict near Jabalpur, to have mixed the Gods, that did not mix, through his exertions. Amisā devā husu te dāni misā katā pahamasi hi esa phule. Jain 1961/2005: 171-2. Memorial stone inscriptions found from the region are dedicated to the citā, the funeral bed of Isikāga, an expert in Majjhima Nikāya and Nyāya, and to Nisa, an expert in Śivanegama, both of whom had disintegrated (chaya or kṣaya) into elements. *Ibid.*, 181-3. The inscriptions often speak of Buddha or his precincts in terms similar to those used for Śiva and Śiva temples. See Hiralal 1911-12: 192. Also, Jain 1961/2005: 38. The Bhāṇḍak copperplates of Bhavadeva Raṇakeśarin during the reign of Nannadeva I celebrate the synthesis of fervid contemplation and

redemptive action in both Buddha and Śiva. These invoke protection of Buddha as 'tāyī, sugata, a terror to Smara, God and passion, one on the right track, dedicated to sakalajanābhyudaya, upliftment of all, inanimate, yet animated with consciousness, nirjīvasaltanārān, despirated, yet luminous, dīpto nirvaṇa, traits shared by Buddha with Śiva. They praise Bhavadeva, who constructs a temple to (Śākya) muni, and is dedicated to the people's welfare like Bhava, Śiva. *Ibid.*, 28-36. A resident of Padmabu (Bhavabhūti ki kāriyā near Āmgaon, Bhāṇḍāra, Maharashtra), describes how parivrājaka Kamangati encourages Mālatī to worship Śiva, while his disciple Saudāminī gives up Buddhism to become a disciple of Aghori Tāntrik Aghoraghaṇṭa. Muni Kāntisāgar 1953: 284-87. Kielhorn 1905: 617-33. The Ajanta cave inscription and the Ghaṭotkaca cave inscription of Varāhadeva and an inscription in cave 17, describe Buddha as an extinguisher of worldly flames, a teacher of teachers (gururguruṇām) a thunderbolt to the tree of worldly existence (bhavadrūmāśanim) in terms similar to the description of Śiva and Lakulīśa in Gandheśvara temple inscription and Junawāni copperplates. Katare 1957: 229-39. Apart from epigraphic allusions to the pervasive devotional mood in Buddhism, there is abundant evidence of Buddhist monuments and images adapting Tāntrik modes of worship, and transferring plans for monastic architecture from inside the caves to urban settlements.

For mention of construction of Buddhist vihāras under Pāṇḍuvaṁśī king Mahāśivagupta Bālārjuna, see *EI* 3: 197-98. The Bhāṇḍak inscription, mentioned above, also speaks of the restoration of a derelict temple of Buddha constructed by Sūryaghoṣa, under Nanna I. Donation of a village to a Buddhist vihāra by Mahāśivagupta, at the request of his uncle Bhāskaravarman, is recorded in a Malhār copperplate. See Mirashi and Pandeya 1935:13-22. A 7th century temple complex of Hevajra of Buddhist tantrayāna, his image and clay sealings inscribed with mantras, a perforated amulet inscribed with the impression of a seal and the legend Kalyāṇarciya in 7th century characters have been recovered in Malhār excavations. See Bajpai and Pandey, 1978: 21ff. The pillar with Kūrma and Ulūka jātakas in a Malhār house, burnt brick stūpas and a Buddha image from Bhoṅgāpāl, Bastar have been discussed in chapters on sculpture and architecture. The Kauni (Bilaspur) stone inscription mentions, in 1st- 2nd century AD Prākṛt, a teacher and his five disciples, and a memorial pillar being raised on their corporeal remains. It shows familiarity of the writer with Buddhist āgamas. See B.N. Mishra 1984: 115-18. That the monastic faith is undergoing popularization under this surge in devotionalism is best evident from village names like Saramana, Sirimā khoh, Buddhasāgara, Jogīmārā in Raipur and Bilaspur divisions, which further demonstrate the assimilation of faiths on the basis of common cults like Śrī or practices like yoga. Finally, it is a point of some interest, in view of the Vidarbha connections of Tala art, and in view of the impact Tala itself appears to have had on the Buddhist art of Sirpur, that Nāgārjuna, one of the greatest Mahāyāna Buddhist teachers, is assigned by the author of the *Laṅkāvatāra Sūtra* to an unspecified place Vedālo which may have belonged to Vidarbha. Mention of Nāgārjunagupta at Ramtek is suggested as a memory of this contact. See G.C.Pandey 1976: 369.

For syncretic images of Śiva and Buddha in Ceylon, in Caṇḍi Jāvī, representation of Majāpāhit emperor Kṛtanagara as Śiva-Buddha after his death, identification of Śiva-Buddha as the national deity of Java in the Siṅgasari inscription, or of Buddha as the younger brother of Śiva in Bali, see Majumdar 1957: 763.

21. Yuan Chwang's route has been charted from Kaliṅga through (Dakṣiṇa) Kośala, K.N. Mohapatra 1971: 65-71. For the many pilgrimages between China and India through Central Asia, and by South China Sea, see l-Ching, trans, Lahiri 1986: 19 ff. Upaśūnya and Paramārtha went from Ujjayinī to China in the 6th century AD. P.C. Bagchi 1951: 21. A constant exchange of missions from the 4th to the 6th centuries resulted in the copying of texts, construction of monasteries and erection of statues in China. Three Indian painters Śākya Buddha, Buddhakīrti and Kumāra Bodhi worked in China in the Wei period, helping translate fresco paintings to the Chinese landscape. See Majumdar, *Classical Age*: 611-26. A small, circular Chinese copper coin with a square central hole, attributed to Kāi (AD 713-41) and the word Pāo tung, suggest the popularity of Sirpur as a pilgrimage destination among Chinese Buddhist pilgrims in the 8th century AD.

22. Sacrificial altars appear to coexist at Tala with worship by bhaktas or vratikas of the vibhūti or special manifestations of roceśas or Gods of popular choice. The widespread use of kīrtimukhas, used as

mukhakoṣas (masks) by dancers in the worship of Śiva, the pillars and door jambs, hung with myriad floral and pearl festoons, the huge yakṣalike dvārapālas, the prevalence of nāga, Skanda, Kubera, vṛkṣakā and river goddess figures at Tala, the presence of a host of gaṇas, laboriously, playfully, watchfully attending their lord, seem to suggest a vogue enjoyed by popular festivals, associated with such divine and semidivine figures, at Tala. For the considerable amount of contemporary literary evidence for such festivals, see V.S. Agrawala 1970.

23. Kramrisch, *The Presence of Śiva*, 1981: 88-97.
24. Nigam. Ed., *Riddle of Indian Iconography*, 2000.
25. Joanna Williams, "Thoughts about a Remarkable Sculpture from Tala," in Nigam 2000: 69-72.
26. Nigam, "The Image of Śiva from Tala", in Nigam 2000: 65-66.
27. Michael W. Meister, "Too Late to Tala", in Nigam 2000: 83-88.
28. Doris Meth Srinivasan, "Rūpa yakṣa," in Nigam 2000: 89-96.
29. K. Sharma, "A Polycephalous Image from Tala: Analysis and Identification" in Nigam 2000: 98-99: Chandrashekhar Gupta, "Identity of a Unique Sculpture from Tala," in Nigam 2000: 118; R. C. Agrawala, "An Enigmatic Statue from Tala," in Nigam 2000: 108; B.N. Mukherjee 2007: 15. C, 52, No 106, 4. 16-18
30. Gupta, in Nigam 2000: 117-20.
31. Agrawala, *ibid.*, 107-9.
32. Hans Bakker, "An Enigmatic Giant from Tala," *ibid.*, 101-5.
33. P.K. Agrawala, "A Mysterious Sculpture from Tala: A Rare form of Varuṇa", *Ibid.*, 111-16.
34. L.S. Rao, *ibid.*, 121-26.
35. Doris Meth Srinivasan, "An Enigmatic Image of Śiva", *ibid.*, 89-96.
36. Kalyan Kumar Dasgupta, *ibid.*, 73—81.
37. Sharma, *ibid.*, 97-100; Nigam, *ibid.*, 63.
38. Rao, *ibid.*, 122 ; Srinivasan, *ibid.*, 90.
39. Dasgupta, *ibid.*, 79
40. Bakker 1997: 105-7; In Nigam 2000: 105, note 6.
41. Rao, in Nigam 2000: 122-24.
42. Michael Meister, in Nigam 2000: 82-86.
43. R.C. Agrawala, *ibid.*, 46; Bakker, *ibid.*, 105. R. C. Agrawala recalls, in this context, the pre - Kuṣāṇa image of what he calls Kṛṣṇa, a village hero, draped in leaf garment, from Burhikhār, Malhār, Bilaspur, in Chhattisgarh; the double faced Śiva liṅga from Gāmri, near Bharatpur, in Rajasthan; the colossal 10th century Viṣṇu incarnation images from Bāndhavgarh fort in Shahdol in M. P., and the huge Vidisha Yakṣa.
44. Hans Bakker, *ibid.*, 101.
45. J.P. Singhdeo, "Composite Tāntric Yogic Figure of Mahākāla and Mahākāli", *ibid.*, 127.
46. P.K. Agrawala, *ibid.*, 111.
47. Joanna Williams, *ibid.*, 71-72; Hans Bakker 1997: 105-7.
48. Srinivasan, in Nigam 2000: 94 suggests a desire to represent life in all its variety through animal forms. Bakker *ibid.*, 101; 1997: 105.
49. Bakker 1995: 637, 639, 644; 1997: 105-7.
50. Srinivasan in Nigam 2000: 94.
51. Srinivasan 1997: 20-23, 60-69,150,194.
52. Srinivasan, *ibid.*, 7-8, 14, 35-36, 41-44, 50-69, 89. She quotes *Śatapatha Brāhmaṇa*, *Āpastambha* and *Baudhāyana śrauta sūtra*, as well as *Atharvaveda*, to suggest analogy between ūkhā vessels in Agnicayana, equipped with a girdle, breast or udders and yakṣas with swollen bellies, tied by the girdle. *ibid.*, 201-2.
53. For the textual evidence, amassed to demonstrate the dynamic process of reconstruction of the identity of the psychic and cosmic self, see Srinivasan 1997:25-27, 92-100, 162-75, 196, 250-52, 280-81.
54. Srinivasan 1997: 52-54, 80, 162-75, 250-52, 280-81. She offers a penetrating discussion, based on Vedic texts, about the germinating, propagating power of the remnant, the uccheṣanabhāga, in a Soma sacrificial oblation. She speaks about Rudra being offered (as vāstavya) the animals, created from the charred

residue of the fire, left at the site (vāstu). The residue protects the fecundating seed, and ensures renewal and continuity of the creative cycle.

55. Srinivasan 1997: 186-7.
56. Srinivasan, in Nigam 2000: 93.
57. The application of biological symbolism is evident in Srinivasan's characterization of the upraised phallus in the Russet collection Maheśa, as an indication of creative power rather than as containment of the capacity for creation. See Srinivasan 1997: 277. The numerous Vedic references quoted by Srinivasan demonstrate the equation, interchangeability and assimilation of stambha and yūpa (cosmic pillar), Rohita (ascending Sun), Mitra Varuṇa, Agni Soma, Tvaṣṭṛi (the vivifier), Viśvakarman (the all maker), Puruṣa, Prajāpati, Rudra, Śiva, Indra and Nārāyaṇa with regard to the source, nature and expression of their creative power, in nonbiological rather than biological terms. Srinivasan 1997: 6, 20, 25-30, 35-8, 40-49, 60-128. One may recall, in this context, the description that Prajāpati, unhappy alone (sa ekāki reme), depletes himself as one of multiple progeny (bahuprajāḥ). Unhappy fragmented, he then creates death (nirṛti), and replenishes himself. The mind, breath and speech (manas, prāṇaḥ, vāk), contained in the jewel chest (vasudāna koṣa), are exhausted and replenished in this process. Prajāpatiḥ prajāḥ sṛṣṭvā vyāsraṅsata *SB*. 6.1.2.12. V.S. Agrawala 1963: 117,193.
58. J.P. Singhdeo, in Nigam 2000: 127-34.
59. P.K. Agrawala, *ibid.*, 115.
60. Meister, *ibid.*, 83, 86.
61. Pramod Chandra, Foreword, *ibid.*, 6-7.
62. B. Bhattacharya 1975, 2: 605-11, 639-42, 674-75.
63. In Śaiva Siddhānta formulation, the pāśas are due to the three evolutes of ahaṁkāra (ego), corresponding to three guṇas, which reduce men and animals to one through their common activities of ahāra-nidrā-bhaya-maithunam, eating, sleeping, fearing and fornicating. The pañcakleśas are avidyā (ignorance), asmitā (ego), rāga (attachment), dveṣa (aversion), abhiniveśa (clinging to life), together known as puṁstva mala. Bhattacharya 1975: 570-2, 577-9, 583-4, 600; K.C.Pandey 1986: 64-5; Majumdar, *Age of Imperial Kanauj*, 1964: 300-4.
64. Bhattacharya 1975: 605-11, 639-42, 674-75. In Kashmir Śaivism, Śiva, Śakti and aṇu replace Pati, Pāśa and Paśu. Paśutva or animality is explained as a state of asvātantrya or thraldom, or of bondage to bodies of kārya and kāraṇa, of cause and effect, of matter and faculties, a state of sañjana, or of being tainted by colouring elements of passions . The aim of Pāśupatism is the destruction of this state of animality and the restoration of Śivatva or divinity, or, recovery of the state of nirañjana, or of freedom from colouring elements, which is the true nature of souls. Gopinath Kaviraj 1984: 131-34. An outcaste and heretic himself, Śiva Pāśupati deludes and makes heretics of people, to reveal their beastly nature, and to release them from that nature. O' Flaherty 1976: 286-87, 319.
65. Bhūtasiddhi is attempted by Aghori Tāntriks through the pañcamakāras or five Ms of meat (earth) of silence, fish (water) of breath control, grain (air) of concentration, wine (fire) of God intoxication, and coitus (ether) of ego with the absolute in Sāttvika consciousness. With the five elements brought into equilibrium, and, with the emotions transferred to a cosmic deity personifying these elements, a state of health and well-being is attained. R.E. Svovoda 1993:13-14. *Śivāṅka,* Saṁvat 1990/1933: 24-29; Bhattacharya 1975: 744.
66. *Vājasaneyī Saṁhitā* III & IV recites the formula of Agnihotra or fire sacrifice and asks for the well-being of every limb in the body. The *Śatapatha Brāhmaṇa* speaks of Prajāpati consecrating himself, to create everything out of himself. Winternitz 1963, vol. I: 155-7, 172. *RV* 1.114.1; *AV* 2.34, 11.2.24-25 address Paśupati or associate him with protection of Paśus. *AB* 3.33.1, *KB and SB, Mbh,* Sauptikaparva, 10.188; *ASS* 12.23.11. speak of Rudra sparing the Paśus in exchange of being included in the sacrifice. See Hillebrandt 1927, vol. 2, trans. 1981: notes 8, 13, 77, 82, 98 for the legends. See *MS* 4.2 for Prajāpati

offering the overlordship of cattle to Paśupati, when Rudra appoaches howling (arodit), aiming arrow at Prajāpati's loins. Sṛṣṭikṛt rite in Aśvamedha, Śūlagava sacrifice, and oblation to vāstavya fire are intended to stop Rudra from slaying cattle. Sukumari Bhattacharji 1970: 115-16.

The insistence of *Āraṇyakas* on the internal nature of this sacrifice is designed to bridge karmamārga (way of action) of the *Brāhmaṇas* with jñānamārga (way of knowledge) of the *Upaniṣads*. Majumdar 1951, the *Vedic Age*: 448. *Asup, Sup and Jab*, and the later *ŚiP* speak of the knowlege of Paśupati as a termination of *pāśas*. *Śup* 4.16 or *Śip, Vāys*, Pūrva Khaṇḍa, 5.62. *Mbh.*, 12. 8.36 speaks of the sarvamedha (the universal sacrifice) before Paśupati. Jarāsandha designates imprisoned kings to be offered for sacrifice as paśus in Paśupater gṛhe (temple of Paśupati).

Mbh., Anuśāsanaparva 14. 141-50 lists kūrma, matsya, siṁha, mayūra, kṛkalāsa as some of the shapes assumed by Rudra, who is also called ūrdhvakeśa (of peaked locks), mahāśepha (megalophallic), nagna (nude), and vikṛtalocana (with glowering eyes), and is endowed with the attributes of a Brahmin, being called a Daṇḍī (club bearing), and chattrī (canopied). All these characteristics belong to the Tala Paśupati. Pāśupatas are, in fact, the earliest Śiva bhāgavatas mentioned in Nārāyaṇīya chapter of the *Mahābhārata*.

67. Sivaramamurti, *Śatarudrīya* 1976: 62 for Śiva as fisherman; for creatures of pātāla and pitṛs, Dawson 1961: 233, 236; For Ahirbudhnyas, Monier Williams 1899: 125. The *AV* 15.5.1-21 lists the seven attendants of Ekavrātya as Bhava in east, Śarva in south, Paśupati in west, Ugra in north, Rudra, Mahādeva and Iśāna in the nether, upper and intermediate regions. The *YV*, *Vās* 30.8 and *TB* 3.4, 5, 1 designate vrātyas as sacrificial victims in the Puruṣamedha (human sacrifice). The Marūts, born of Diti and Kāśyapa, constitute the Saptavātaskandha, the seven wind cluster, comprising āvaha, pravāha, udvaha, suvaha, vivaha, parivaha. Winternitz 1963.1: 365-8 The *BrP* 22.53-5 mentions four beautiful offsprings (kumārakaḥ) emerging from Śiva's sides, namely, Jāti, Muṇḍi, Śikhaṇḍī and Ardhamuṇḍaḥ. At least two are visible on the sides of the thighs.

68. Thus, the dual aspect of Viśvarūpa is announced as viśvam garbham (the germ of all) in *RV* 10. 121.7; bahudhā vyāviṣṭi (multiply distributed) in *SB* 10.5.2.16. The pervasive presence of Viśvarūpa Śiva is explained in *Sup* 3.11 and 16.

   Sarvānanaśirogrīvaḥ sarvabhūtaguhāśayaḥ I.
   Sarvavyāpi sa bhagavān tasmāt sarvagataḥ Śivaḥ II.
   Sarvataḥ pāṇipādam tat sarvatoakṣiśiromukham I.
   Sarvataḥ śrutimalloke sarvamāvṛtya tiṣṭhati II.

   In sum, the eyes, ears, face, head, hands and legs of everyone being his, Śiva is everywhere, in everyone. In *ibid.*, 3.2. Śiva reabsorbs what he creates at the end of time (saṁcukopāntakāle). For invocation of Rudra as lord of sthāvara and jaṅgama, śānta and ghora (mobile and immobile, benignant and malignant), as architect of war and peace, earth and heaven, see Sivaramamurti, 1976. Anthropomorphization and apotheosization of universal forces is due to the simultaneous accommodation of terrestrial (pṛthvīsthāna), aerial (antarikṣasthāna), and celestial (dyausthāna) beings (as classified in *RV* 1. 139.11, followed by Yāska) in Paśupati's body. The dome like shape of the tortoise is suggested as the representation of the three worlds. P.E. Dumont, 1957: 15-18. The *PS* 1.13.17, 2.20, 5.25 advocates chanting of raudrīgāyatrī and the name vahurūpī (manyformed, like a chameleon).

69. This immutable aspect of Paśupati, overriding his mutable forms, is explained in *Vyāsa Gītā* 18.20 as avibhakta vibhakteṣu (undivided among the divided); as kārayitrī and prekṣaka (actuator and spectator) in *Mup* 2.6.3. In *Śup 4.* it is explained thus:

   Sa eko varṇo bahudhā śaktiyogād I
   Varṇān anekān nihitārtho dadhāti II

   Freely translated, he remains of one color, even as he assumes many colors through his dormant power. In 'kha'; *Coomaraswamy* 2: 220-30, Coomaraswamy explains how the zero and infinity, śūnya and pūrṇa are one in bījagaṇita (algebra). Also 'Traditional psychology', in *Coomaraswamy* 1: 353, 370-74: 'Measures of fire', *ibid.* 2: 163. The Tala image gives iconic form to the Vedic and post-Vedic formulations about Viśvarūpa and its various emanations.

70. *Mbh*, Anuśāsana Parva.
71. The sakala body of graces, characterized by animal attributes, is assumed out of compassion or karuṇā for edification and redemption of suffering beings. It is variously characterized as nirmāṇakāya in Mahāyāna Buddhism, nirmāṇacitta in Sāṁkhya yoga, Svabhāvanirmitaśarīra in Nyāya, māyā, prasāda or līlā deha in Vaiṣṇava philosophy. Kaviraj 1984: 139-45. The niṣkala body, the mantra, kaivalya or vaindava deha is the nature of Śiva, without attributes. Kaviraj 1963:26; 1983:54-55. Kalyan Kumar Dasgupta alludes, in the context of the presence of non-human creatures in the body of the Tala image, to Varāhi Mahiṣāsuramardinī in the Archeological Museum of Mahāsthān in Bogrā, Bangla Desh; the composite Buddhist deity, Nīlakaṇṭha; the Viśvarūpa form of Lord Kṛṣṇa, described in *Gītā*; to 18th century Kāngrā paintings that show Śiva with multiple faces, hands and legs, the sun and moon, and Padmanābha Viṣṇu on his body. See Dasgupta in Nigam 2000: 73-81. *BrP* 23: *IGP* 4.36.67 offers obeisance to Śiva's Viśvarūpa. The sixth and seventh chapters of Śivagītā, which is part of *Padmapurāṇa*, are captioned vibhūtiyogaḥ and viśvarūpadarśanaḥ (the way to glory and vision of the omniform) on lines similar to the tenth and eleventh chapters of the *BhP*. The *LP* 2.18. 1-4. finds everything at the apex, middle or bottom of the universe in Śiva's Viśvarūpa, and mentions gods like Skanda, stellar shapes like planets, concepts like death and immortality as part of his body. It calls Śiva Viṣṇu in his sāttvika (pure, virtuous) aspect, Brahmā in his rājasa (regal) aspect, Kālarudra in the tāmasa (dark, malignant) aspect, and Maheśvara in his aspect comprehending and surpassing all these. The makara (capricornus), mīna (pisces), siṁha (leo) and kṛkalāsa (cancer) represent zodiacal signs, it not planets, and the mayūra and nāga juxtapose life and death giving forces. The Tala Paśūpati has been compared with the Zodiac man, made by fusing with animal signs, in medieval Europe. Dasgupta, in Nigam 2000: 79.
    The pañcakṛtyas associated with the supreme being do appear to find reflection in the Viśvarūpa aspect of Tala Paśupati. The liṅga may represent sṛṣṭi (creation); the nāgas and kūrma (the churning rope and rod in samudra manthana) sthiti (stability or preservation); the zoomorphic helmet, earpiece, shoulder, thigh, knee, stomach guards and breastplate illustrating the saṁhāra (destruction) aspect. Rudra is addressed by Arjuna, in an invocation of his secret weapons, in *SR*, as namo varmine ca, varuthine ca, namo vilmine ca, kavacine ca, ātatāyine ca, or, salute to the armoured, helmeted, corsleted... aggressor, Sivaramamurti 1976: 16.35, 29-32. The absorption and concealment of human members in animal form, including the sarpaprabhāvalī (tiruvasi in Tamil) suggest, finally, pralaya and tirobhāva (absorption and obscuration). The aspect of anugraha (grace), activating these various revelations, is explained in *SB* 10.5.2.20 as 'yathopāsate tadeva bhavati'. He becomes whatever he is worshipped as.
    Finally, the vision which penetrates to the one behind these many aspects, is recognized in *Munup* 5 as ekībhūta prajñānaghana (the unified density of cognition) or as ādarśe pratirūpaḥ (mirror reflection) in *Ka up* 4.2.
72. Thus, the Mathura pillar inscription of Chandragupta II of Gupta era or 61 / AD 380, calls the standing club bearing Śiva, carved on the pillar, variously as Bhagavān daṇḍaḥ, Rudra-daṇḍaḥ, and Agranāyakaḥ, lord of the club, of the terrible club, and the foremost leader. The daṇḍa of Śiva is identificed as kāla or bilva daṇḍa in *Mbh.*, Anuśāśasnaparva, 14. 314. 549: Aśvamedha parva, 8.17.6112: Śāntiparva 284.126.5173, and as Brahma daṇḍa in *HvP*, Viṣṇuparva 126.46.724. The Siboi tribe, which lived near the junction of the Jhelum and the Chenab, claimed descent from Dionysios, a Śiva prototype, held club, and dressed themselves in the skin of wild beasts. See Sudhakar Chattopadhyaya 1970: 128. The name of the Kuṣāṇa king Wema Kadphises reads as a homonym for Bhīma Kharparīśa, the terrible lord of the skull cap. Bhattacharya 1975: 753 ff.
    Ist century BC Audumbara coins from the upper Sutlej and Ravi region mention King Śivadāsa, the servant of Śiva, and his title, Mahādeva, the great God. Allan 1914/1967: 86. The Mathura pillar inscription of AD 380 is also relevant, as it mentions the installation of Śivaliṅgas, together with portraits

of teachers, who are Lakulīśa's disciples, in the temple of the teacher (Gurvāyatana). The liṅgas are named after the teachers, emphatically suggesting their assimilation as Bhāgavatas (devotees) with the Iśvara. This event is announced as a result of their passage through the brahmarandhra (magnum foramen). Bhandarkar 1931: 8.

In this connection, it has to be recalled that Śiva incarnates himself as brahmacārī Lakulin in the corpse of a Brahmin at a cemetery at Kāyārohaṇa, identified with Kārohaṇa, Dābhoi taluk, Barodā district, Gujarat. The name Kāyārohaṇa, or ascent of the body, is suggestive of the metamorphosis in the constitution of a Paśu, caused by association with his Pati. Bhandarkar 1913: 165 ff.

73. The vyuha is not formed here by only four disciples of Lakulīśa, like the four Vṛṣṇivīras (heroes of the Vṛṣṇi clan, in the vyuhavāda (theory of congregation) of Vaiṣṇava *Prapañcasāra tantra*. The criticism of Māheśvara Śaivas by Śaṅkara in the 8th century (in his Śārīrika-Bhāṣya on the *BS* 2.2) as Iśvara-kāraṇin (those who see God as instrumental cause), is apparently anticipated by the Tala Lakulīśa-Paśupati by involving Śiva in the universe both conceptually and physically. K.C. Pandey 1986: 64-65; Pranavananda Jash 1974: 52. The *BrP* 23 lists the twenty eight incarnations of Śiva, in groups of fours.

A late version of Kāravana Māhātmya is of relevance, as it gives an account of Śiva, born a Brahmin, dying at seven months, to be taken by tortoises, through an initiatory journey in the underworld, to the Jaleśvara liṅga. This suggests an allusion to the liṅga of Tala Paśupati, formed by the tortoise, at the very base of the spinal cord. David N. Lorenzen, 1972: 180-82. For versions of the legend, Kāravana Māhātmya in *Gaṇakārikā* 37-57; *LP* 1.24: 124-34; *Vāp* 23: 219-24; Bhandarkar, 'Lakulīśa', *ASIAR* 1906-07: 180-83.

For the five avasthās (situations), and practices appropriate to them, See Gaṇakārikā, quoted by Sāyana-Mādhava in Nakuliśa-Pāśupata-darśana in *Sarvadarśanasaṁgraha*. *IHQ* 2: 12-32. For Paśupati's lunatic like dress, unmatta-veśa prachchannaḥ, Sukumari Bhattarcharji 1970: 144-45.

74. For conventional attributes of Lakuliśa like ūrdhvameḍhra (raised phallus), daṇḍa, mātuluṅga (citrus), utkuṭikāsana, vyākhyāna mudrā, *Viśvakarmā- vāstuśāstra* in Bhandarkar 1904- 7: 151- 66; 1906-7: 179-92; 1914: 57-64; *VdP* 48.2.2 for mātuluṅga and daṇḍa, which represent, respectively, paramāṇava or atoms of the universe, in small citrus seeds, and death (in daṇḍa). Devala Mitra 1984: 112 reports Lakuliśa without erect phallus in Odisha, suggesting variations.

75. Standing, club bearing, ithyphallic proto Lakuliśa images are seen in the 3rd-2nd century B.C. tribal kāḍā coins (A.K.Narain 1968: 73-4) or in Ujjain coins (J.N. Banerjea 1956: 117, pl, 1, figs 7, 8, 13), in pre Kuṣāṇa period at Ṛṣikeśa, U.P. (W.H. Siddiqui 1978: 76-80; Meister, *Discourses*, 1984: pl. 23); in the Kuṣāṇa period in Saozma kala (Rosenfield 1967: 93-94, fig. 126); in the Mathura pillar of Gupta period (Bhandarkar 1931-32: 1-9); and, in Māṇḍhal from Vākāṭaka period (Ajaya Mitra Shastri 1977. *Māṇḍhal Utkhanan:* 142-74). Later, from the 7th to the 9th century, standing Lakulīśa images are found in abundance in Andhra Pradesh, Rajasthan, Karnataka, and a gaṇa is displayed at the base below him (Meister, *Discourses*, 1984: pls. 100, 104).

76. Stella Kramrisch connects this with the Vedic perception of the motion of the vernal equinox form Orion to Aldebaraṇ. Prajāpati, pierced by Rudra's bāṇa becomes the constellation Rohiṇi (Aldebaran), the arrow, the constellation Trikāṇḍa (the belt of Orion), and Rudra, the constellation Mṛgavyādha (Sirius). *Aitareya Brāhmaṇa* 3.33; Kramrisch, *Presence* 1981 40-3. *Kalyāṇ* 1933: 502-03. To kill Andhakāsura, Śiva creates mahāsarpas like Vāsuki, Takṣaka and Dhanañjaya and uses them as his waist and armbands. *Varāha Purāṇa* in *Sivāṅka*: 596.

77. *YS* 16.5 addresses Śiva as prathamo daivyo bhiṣak, the first divine physician. Mantra 16.49 invokes his healing powers.

Yā te rudra Śivā tanuḥ
Śivā viśvahā bheṣajī I
Śiva rujasya bheṣaji
tayā no mṛda jīvāse II

78. It is noticed in this context that in the Nighaṇṭu, jalam or water has one hundred and one names, of which viṣam and amṛtam are two. Kalyāṇ 1990/1933: 495-96. Rudra, Śiva-Pañcānana later, is a physician, whose healing prescriptions, mentioned in *RV* 1.43.4, 2.33 or in Atharvan ritual in *AV* 2.27.6, are based on Jalāśa, cow's urine, and anticipated by gāomaezā in the Āvestā. See Mahadev Chakravarti 1994: 57, n. 240 and N.P Joshi 1969 for Śiva as Jalāśa.

79. Mentioned in the *RV* 2.292.24, these peacocks are equivalent to twentyone śirās or arteries and they drink from the navanavati nāḍis or nadīs, or ninetynine entrails or rivers, mentioned in later sūktas. They are also equivalent to flames of fire or prāṇa. Kalyāṇ 1933: 502-3, which quotes and interprets this śloka.

   Trisapta mayūryaḥ sapta svasāro agruvaḥ I
   tāste viṣam vijabhrira udakaiḥ kumbhiniriva II

   Translated freely, these are the twenty one peacocks, which purge the poison through seven fiery breaths, like water purged through a sieve. For Garuḍa's role, *Kalyan* 1993: 502-3.

80. The contribution of Kāma in fish form of Śiva is described in *KaP*, 82: 50-52. For samudramanthana, *VP*, Dawson 1961: 14. Kacchapa (tortoise) is identified as philological recension of Kāśyapa (Prajāpati), who adapted this form to make offspring. See *SB* 7.5.2.5-10. The *Gītā* gives the analogy of kūrma withdrawing into shell, as from sense objects. Dawson, for the story of Kūrma rescuing Vedas and Manu, according to legends culled from *Bhāgavata Purāṇa* and *Śatapatha Brāhmaṇa*. The *Haṭhayogapradīpikā* describes the practice of drawing the penis back into the abdomen in the manner of a tortoise contracting its head inside its shell, as equivalent to the Aghori Yogic practice of Vajroli Mudrā, Śvovoda 1993. The snake's rejuvenative powers are discussed in Bhattacharji 1970: 148-50, 176-77 and are associated with Cyavana restoring his sexual powers through tapas, in O'Flaherty 1973: 56-57, 59. Mīna and Makaraketana are names of Kāma, as Mayūraketu is a name of Skanda. Monier Williams 1899: 771, 789, 818. *Raghuvaṁśam* 2.35 speaks of Śiva using Siṁha Kumbhodara as footstool to mount his vṛṣa. Kalyāṇ 1933: 500 discusses the meaning of vṛṣa. Śiva becomes Mṛtyuñjaya (conquerer of death) by this process of internal cleansing. Kramrisch 1981: 128-29.

81. *Śivāṅka* 1990 1993: 13-14, 495-96. Suṣumṇaḥ is one of the principal rays of the sun.

82. J.P. Singdeo makes the suggestion about nāsikāgra dṛṣṭi and kevalakumbhaka in Nigam 2000: 128-30.

83. Kaviraj 1983, 1: 33-34, 45, 54-57 61-63.

84. Kaviraj 1983, 1: 197-98, 228-9, for Kuṇḍalinī symbolizing the samvatsaracakra. Winternitz 1963.1: 34-36, 72-76. For Iḍā and Piṅgalā, *Chup*. 8.6.1. Irāpada and Piṅgalā are names of snakes. Monier Williams 1899: 170, 1625. Also, Gopinath Kaviraj, Liṅga Rahasya, in *Kalyāṇ* 1993: 473-77. V.S. Agarwala, *Śiva Mahādeva*, 1966 5-8, 12. Kaviraj 1984: 1 - 11, for uttarakaula.

85. *Mbh*. 3.213.41-52; O'flaherty 1969: 74-95.

86. *Kalyāṇ* 1933: 500 ff; *RV* 10.5.7; Agrawala 1966: 13.

87. "Bhakta aspects of the Ātman doctrine", Lipsey, *Coomaraswamy* 2, 1983: 393.

88. Kumārasambhavam 3. 48.

   Avṛṣṭisamārambhamivāmbuvāham
   Apāṁ ivādhāraṁ anuttaraṅgam I
   Antaścarāṇāmmarutāmnirodhān
   Nivātaniṣkampaṁ iva pradīpam II

89. *RV* 1.115.1; 2. 1. 6 ; 3. 19. 4; 3.20.3 ; 5.81.2 ; 8.93.17; 10.45.7; *SB* 1.22; 2.2.2.15; 4.8.4.11-48; 6.3.2.7; 9.1.2.22; *TS 4.5.10; VS* 16.3.61; "Vedic Monotheism", *Coomaraswamy* 2, 1983: 171; "Vedic Exemplarism", *ibid.*, 180, fn. 3; Sudhakar Chattopadhyaya 1970: 99.

90. Agni as satya, prāṇa or bala, truth, life breath, force, Soma as ṛta, rāyi, rasa, moral order, bliss, savour, combine as brothers and sisters, in sacrifice. Agni consumes Soma in brahmodana or injection of food, for poṣa, nutrition; Agni and Soma combine in gharma or boiling milkpot; Soma is sacrificed in Agni in kāmarūpa or Sarvahuta yajña, a total wish fulfilling sacrifice, in the universe. Out of this emerge Veda

and Paśu, idea and form, mind and matter, as sabandhu, sayoni, of conjoint origin. V.S. Agrawala 1981: 4-26, 38-39, 45-46, 55-56 illustrates these convergent ideas from the *RV*, the Puruṣasukta, and the Yama Yamī sūkta. *TS* 4.5.10, *VS* 16.3.61 invoke Rudra to go beyond the Mujāvat mountains, which are associated in *Mbh* 14.8.1 with Soma, and, in *AV* 5.22.5, with Mahāvṛṣas, the bull people. The Malhār plates of Vyāghrarāja, issued from Prasannapura, record a grant in Pūrva-rāṣṭra in favour of the Brāhmaṇa Dīkṣita, Agnicandrasvāmin, the Lord of fire and water. The nail-headed alphabet, ornate style or devices of these plates are different from Śarabhapurīya charters. Shastri, *Inscriptions*, 1995: 99-100.

91. The heads of the Paśus, displayed on the body of Śiva, are the wombs of prāṇic vibrations. Śiro vai praṇānām yoni. *SB* 7.5.1.22. Agrawala, *Śiva Mahādeva*: 1966, 42. For Vedic sacrificial ritual of *agnicayana*, *RV* 10.90. *Maiup*: 6.3. For agnyādheya rites, *TB* 1.1. 1-3. Also, Staal 1983. *Agni* I: 65; *Agni* 2: 78, 91.
92. Staal 1983. *Agni* 1: 119; *Agni* 2: 144.
93. *TS* 5.2.8.5. Biardau and Malamoud 1976: 18, explain how Prajāpati creates the earth and throws it into the water, the juice flowing from it becoming the tortoise. Kaśyapa is the name for both tortoise and Prajāpati, suggesting assimilation of sacrifice and sacrificed, the Yajamāna and Paśu. Dyavāpṛthvī, heaven and earth, are two shells of a single egg, together identified with the primal Kūrma, tortoise or Kāśyapa Prajāpati in the Purāṇas. V.S. Agrawala 1981: 98.
94. *TS* 4.6.1.5; Staal 1983, *Agni* 2: 458, 535.
95. *TS* 6.1.4. 5 declares, havirvai dīkṣitaḥ, the initiate is the oblation. Also, "Measures of fire," *Coomaraswamy* 1, 1983: 162-63, fn 15; "Ātmayajña: selfsacrifice", *ibid.* 2:108-11, 10, 13, 15, 16, 126-32; *ibid.* 2: 137, where he quotes Buddha, 'I pile no wood for the fire altar. I kindle the flame within me, in the heart'.
96. *VP* 1.2. 31; *Prup 4.3; Ags*, discussed by B.Bhattacharya 1975, 2: 852, 875, n 65; 'Svayamātṛnna. Janua Coeli', *Coomaraswamy* 2, 1983: 470-72 for the selfperforates and kṣobhaṇa; For Agni's līlā, *Mup*, analysed in 'Līlā', *ibid.*, 151-52; For ascent after Agni, *SB* 5.2.1.5; *TS* 6.6.4.2.; Hopkins, 1915: 227-29, for legend of Skanda and Maruts; Dowson 1961: 135, 152, for Agni's tongues. For the seven vital airs, combined in the body of Agni, with mantras for ritual preparation of ukhā pots *TS* 4.1.32; Staal 1983, 1: 65,293.
97. In the sacrificial ritual of *agnicayana*, a cake of black rice (kṛṣṇavrīhi) is offered to Agni on eight pot shards (aṣṭakapāla purodāśa). For this and the octagonal pole, see *TS* 1.8.10. For the eight Ādityas, Iṅdra, Agni, Mitra, Varuṇa, Bhaga, Āryamān, Puṣan and Mārtaṇḍa, nursed into two fold rhythm of life and death, *RV* 10. 72. 9. The eight Bhairavas are Asitāṅga, Ruru, Caṇḍa, Kruddha, Unmatta, Kapāli, Bhīṣaṇa, Saṁhāra in *VP* 1.8. For the eight regions of lokapālas, including Purajyoti of Agni, Dowson 1961: 7. For Vīrabhadra's heads, eight Vasus and elements *SB* 2.6.3.6. and 6.1.310-17. Finally, *Gītā* mentions aṣṭadhā aparā prakṛti, the eightfold lower nature.
98. A tabulation of the eight names of Vasus, together with those mentioned by Bāṇabhaṭṭa, or Purāṇas, is made on V.S.Agrawala's model below:-

NAME OF VASU	CONSTITUENTS	BĀṆABHAṬṬA	PURĀṆAS
1. Śarva	Pṛithivīmūrti (earth)	Avani	Sadyojāta
2. Bhava	Jalamūrti (water)	Vana	Vāmadeva
3. Rudra	Agnimūrti (fire)	Dahana	Aghora
4. Ugra	Vāyumūrti (wind)	Pavana	Tatpuruṣa
5. Bhīma	Akāśamūrti (sky)	Gagana	Iśāna
6. Iśāna	Sūryamūrti (sun)	Tapana	Sun
7. Mahādeva	Candramūrti (moon)	Tuhina kirana	Moon
8. Paśupati	Yajamānamūrti (sacrificer)	Yajamāna Ātmā	Sacrificer

See V.S. Agrawala *Śiva Mahādeva,* 1966: 10, 21, 25-6, 45. V.S. Agrawala, 1960: 22-25. *SB* 6.1.3.18-19 mentions the ninth product as Kumāra 'Tanvetāni aṣṭau agnirūpāṇi, kumāraḥ navamaḥ'. Also see Kramrisch, *Presence* 1981: 109-10. The *SB* 6.1.3.7-8; *KB* 6.1.9. also list these eight names.

99. On the body of Paśupati, the change from gravity to loud laughter in the gaṇas may suggest a growing distinction of knower and known, the gravity suggesting amānībhāva (feeling of self effacement). "Bhakta aspects of Ātman doctrine", *Coomaraswamy* 2, 1983: 388; *LP*: 2.14.1-64; V.S.Agrawala, *Śiva Mahādeva,* 1966: 19-20.

100. B. Bhattacharya 1975, 2: 574, 700-1 for Patañjali's system. J.N. Banerjea 1956:479 explains the Parel Viśvarūpa as eight mantreśvaras. The eight Bhairavas, namely, Svacchanda, Krodha, Unmatta, Ugra, Kapālin, Jhaṅkāra, Śekhara and Vijaya could have been combined in this form. The God is lambodaraḥ, pot-bellied, vṛttapiṅgalalocana, round and tawny eyed, sarvataḥ sarpabhūṣaṇaḥ, bedecked with serpents, and abode of parivāra and gaṇas, or, of his family and lieutenants. Pramod Chandra quoting D.C. Bhattacharya's opinion, based on *Vdp,* in foreword in Nigam 2000: 7. For aṣṭapuṣpikā pūjā, see Agrawala 1960: 122-25.

101. Agrawala 1966: 39. Meister quotes *BhP*, *SB*, and R.C. Agrawala refers to large Yakṣa statues and Śivaliṅgas from Chhattisgarh, Malhār and Rajasthan (Gāmri near Bharatpur), to identify the Tala image as one of Puruṣa, Mahāpuruṣa, Mahāyakṣa. In Nigam 2000: 85, 91-93, 107-8.

102. *Mbh.*, Āraṇyaka parva: 297.20-21; Agrawala, *Indian Art*, 1965: 113, 116-17.

103. Such features are mentioned for Buddha by Aśvāghoṣa, *Buddha Carita* 1.60, *Pratimālakṣaṇa:* 21-24; *BrS*: 68. 7; Banerjea 1956: 288, 311. These terms may be interchangeably used for the Tala Śiva.

104. *RV* 2.33; Coomaraswamy, *Yakṣas* I, 1928: 14-16,21-22.

105. *Suśruta* 54.13. Kālidāsa, *Mālavikāgnimitram* 1.14 for the use of auspicious ornament. Invocatory introduction of *Abhinaya Darpaṇa* for āhārya.

106. T.S. Maxwell 1988: pls. 1-9, 19-22, 24-25 for four sculptures from Mathura and Ajmer, Rajasthan, with heads around column or cluster of columns. Pls. 17, 28 and 30 for heads arrayed around central busts or figures from Mathura and Rangmahal, Rajasthan. Pls. 31-45, 47-57, 61, 63-64 for Gupta images from Deogarh (U.P), Mirpurkhās (Karachi), Pavāyā (Gwalior), Bhānkari (Mathura), Sāmalāji (Gujarat), Kanheri (Maharashtra), Parel (Bombay), with heads clustered around central figures like halo (Chaumābaṇdapura).

107. *Ibid.*, 3-16, 33-35, 46-52, 87. In this context, Maxwell uses Pañcarātra texts like *Sāttvata Saṁhitā*, the Lakṣmītantra 28-30, as also *Maiup.* 4.6, which says that a man can approach the exalted forms of Brahman by first meditating on them, and then, by discarding them.

108. N.P.Joshi 1984: 53. It is No A. 93 in the Nagpur Museum, and is identified by Joshi as Aṣṭamūrti Śiva.

109. See n. 75.

110. *Chuggoku Sekkutsu: Ryumon Sekkutsu (The Grotto art of China: The LongMen grottoes)*, 1987: 7,I, pls. 29, 31. The image was brought to my notice by Junghee Lee of Cambridge, Massachusetts, to whom many thanks.

111. This particular cave is assigned to AD 508-24. The Long Men cave temples were made first during the T'ai-Ho era of the emperor Hsiao(Xiao) Wenti of the northern Wei dynasty in late 5th century AD and continued to be constructed through the 6th and 7th century till the middle of the Tang period. See Ta Chung Kung 1981.

112. Soper 1956: 138.

113. In order to bring the Buddhist paradise on earth, Soper says, Buddhism had to reconstitute the idea of Buddha, using Śaivite myths. So, like Śiva, Avalokiteśvara or Kuan-Tzu-Tsai sprouts many arms and heads, and widens his personality to include terrible and benign forms. Bodhisattva Bhaiṣajasamudgata (who parallels the perception of Tala Paśupati as a healer of diseases) has light streaming in simulacra from his body in the forms of Māra, lokapālas, asuras, gandharvas, mahoragas (great serpents), human and non-human beings. Seven Buddhas, like the seven gaṇas or marūts on Tala Paśupati, is a favourite

number in Buddhism. In the *lotus sūtra*, Buddha's phallus emerges to entwine mount Sumeru seven times, which is a Śaiva manifestation (and a reminder of the samudramanthana myth). The polymorphic representation of Long Men falls in place as an attempt to concretize the sublime, on the model of Śiva. See Soper, *ibid.*, 146-49, 178-79, 188, 205.

114. Nāgārjuna, reputed to have flourished around Vidarbha in the lst-2nd century AD, sought to unify śūnyatā and karuṇā in his *Mādhyamika kārikā*, ostensibly on the model of the life and precepts of Buddha, who preached śūnyatā, but practised karuṇā, and postponed his nirvāṇa (despiration), even after sambodhi (enlightenment), out of compassion for human suffering. Bodhicitta is described in the following words: Bhinnāpi-bhinna, śūnyatādvaya lakṣaṇa, Kaviraj 1984: 52-58, 70-76. The Mahāyāna text *Vajracchedikā* and Nāgārjuna's *Mādhyamika Sūtra*, have the following explanation:

    śūnyam iti nā vaktavyam
    Aśūnyam iti vā bhavet,
    Ubhayam nobhayam ceti
    Prajñaptyārtham tu kathyate

This cannot be called void or non-void, as both or neither, but, in order to indicate it, it is (called void). Max Müller, *Sacred Books* 50. 2:114.

115. This perception is equally evident in Śaṅkara's theory of Vivartavāda (illusory manifestation), the theory of Nirvikalpa Samādhi (non-dual absorption) in Hinduism, in Nirālambavāda (manifold reality, existing without any support, except that of the creative principle) in Mahāyāna Buddhism, in the theory of Kaivalya (isolation) from Upādhis (conditioning, limiting attributes) in Jainism, or, in the theory of Yoga (communion), impartially adapted by orthodox and heterodox faiths.

Parallel Confucian and Taoist ideas of combining Yin (concentration) with Yāng (expansion), action with repose, emerge in 5th and 6th centuries BC Images like the Tala Paśupati or the Long Men 'Brahmā' would result from the coincidence of opposites, the individual and collective, sought in such ideas. For the many pilgrimages from India to China, from the 4th to the 6th century, which account for the meeting of such ideas, see P.C. Bagchi 1951: 21, 34, 43, 101-3, 115; Majumdar, ed., *Classical Age*, 1954: 611, 626.

Svabhāvavāda, Kālavāda, Yadṛcchāvāda, Niyativāda are the non-theistic, deterministic, collateral assumptions in Indian philosophy, which complement the idea of heroic exertion by the Yogī in Sāṅkhya Yoga. Mahāyāna Buddhist philosophy parallels Śaiva, Nyāya Vaiśeṣika philosophy in its perception of the reality as one and many.

116. The *Śatarudrīya* harps on the idea of Rudra as an armoured warrior, and it is interesting to note that many of the creatures on Tala Paśupati are found in the armour of later guardian figures in other parts of the world. A guardian figure from Anyāng in Honān, dated AD 589, shows a panther or tiger on its left shoulder, human faces on its breast and stomach, elephants on its knees. Many of the later guardians from the Tāng period, like those on the lower portion of the great (gander) pagoda, Dā-yen-tā, Chāng-ān, datable to AD 653, and a tomb figure from the Xiān museum, dated AD 664, show animal masks on their armour, the pagoda figures showing makaras and the Xiān statue showing panthers on their shoulders. Okada's article in *Bukkyo Geijutsu*, 177 with this information has been reported very kindly by Cynthea Bogel, a scholar of Japanese art.

A water colour by John White of Ca. AD 1590 shows a naked Pictish warrior from northern Britain, painted all over the body with leonine heads on the shoulders, bust and knees. The Picts shared the tradition of body painting with other Celtic tribes and used it for their naked shock troops. See John Sharkey 1975, repr, 1979: 50, pl. 29.

Totem poles, trees or masks have been associated in different parts of the world with creation myths. The Roman statue of Artemis of Ephesus shows figures on her body as the great mother. In the apocalyptic myth in Alaska of the deluge at the end of the world, a totem pole with a vertical array of animal images has been reported near Sitkā. World trees, from which the world takes its birth, are also reported. A

Polynesian creation myth shows the nude sea God Tāngāroā with creatures detaching themselves from his various limbs. Joseph Campbell 1976: pls. on 21, 36, 84, 110-11, 201, 267.

Among monstrous figures, we have the figures of a demonic child, born in Cracow, Poland. E. Rosslin 1553. Its head is porcine. Goat or jackal heads replace the gaṇa heads of Tala Paśupati on the chest. Dog heads replace the Tala makaras or lions on its arms or knees. Its claws become animal like and only eyes appear in its stomach. Another image appears on the capital of a twelfth century manuscript Bulgakov. It has snakelike hair, animal ears, eye on stomach, hydraheaded dogs below its legs and tailed men emerging from its mouth.

Bakker illustrates motifs of gaping makara mouths sprouting arms or legs and faces on limbs and belly, on Māra's host on the walls of the ancient Buddhist temple of Iwang in central Tibet, and, on the devil in a wooden panel in the choir stalls of the 15th century Martini Church of a 13th century Franciscan monastery in Bolsward, Frisia, Netherlands. Courtesy, the Liturgical Institute, University of Groningen. Bakker 1995: 644-46, Fig. 5.

Kalyan Kumar Dasgupta quotes *Vāmana Purāṇa*, verses 28-43 and describes Śiva as Kāla or time, with a body made of different rāśis or zodiac signs in the context of the manuscript from the Viennese Shepherd's Calender of 1503, that shows a Zodiac man, with his body formed by different animals. See Dasgupta in Nigam 2000: 75-80.

117. *ShP, Pp, VaP, KuP, VarP* give the story of Rudra cutting off the fifth head of Brahmā and making atonement by observing the life of a Kāpālika. The tiger represents the vanam or the universe, in which the forest and the tree embody the universal and the individual. See *RV* 10.82.4. For Mahākāla as the Kirāta, *AV* 20: 136.11. The *Suprabhedāgama* reports how wives of ascetics near the slopes of Mount Meru fell in love with Śiva, who was passing by in the nude; how the ascetics sent their incantations after him as tiger, lion, snakes, paraśu, apasmārapuruṣa (the demon of oblivion), and black deer; how Śiva killed the tiger and lion and put on their shapes, trampled apasmāra under his feet, and used him as a footstool, and, took up the black deer, paraśu and snakes in his hand. Rao, 1914-16, 2.1: 113-14. For the significance of the use of animal skin V.S. Agrawala, *Śiva Mahādeva,* 1966: 45.

118. Dve tanū tasya devasya...

Ghorām anyām, Śivām anyām... *Mbh.* 3.41.7-8, 13; The *KuP* 2. 31.3. 61-73; *BrP* 11.3.1-18; *LP* 1.80. 1-2, 54-6 describe the various facets of the legend of Bhairava. For the saumya form of Śiva, Agrawala 1966: 2-3, 17-18, 21-23, 26, 32, 41. He speaks of the three breaths (prāṇa, apāna, vyāna), three arteries (piṅgalā, iḍā, suṣumṇā), three states of mind (jāgrat-waking, svapna-dreaming, suṣupti-sleeping), and three metres (Gāyatrī, triṣṭubh, jagatī), correlated to right, left and central eye of Śiva. For the head as the origin of breath vibrations (prāṇānām yoniḥ). *SB* 7.5.1.22. See *RV* 6.11.2 for the invocation of Agni for self sacrifice. Yajasva tanvān tava svām. Sacrifice your own body. The ātmayājī is his own sacrificial priest.'ātmayājña', *Coomaraswamy* 2, 108-9, 126-27. Bhairava, Mahākāla, or Saṁhāra Paśupati, like Agni, have rākṣasa characteristics like kravyāda (corpse eater), to whom oblation is offered on blood red palāśa (flesh eater), and for whom a hekatomb of human sacrifices is prepared. See Hopkins 1915: 2-3, 44, 75, 83-84, 173; Sukumari Bhattacharji 1970: 145-46, 187 for evidence on this score from epics, *RV* and *SB*. The Tala Bhairavas do not have the conventional fangs or weapons, and except for the proto-Bhairava Paśupati, they are not nude. None of them seems also to be associated with ophiolatry.

119. For Agni as yakṣa *RV* 10.88. 13; For yakṣāyatana and its guardians, Agrawala 1970: 169, 173-74, 189.

120. Coomaraswamy 1927. The attributes of the Tala yakṣas are generalized from the available fragments. For equipments and association with trees and mongoose spouting jewels, Banerjea 1956: 33-41. The attributes of the Tala yakṣas are generalized from the available fragments. An intact proto-Śiva dvārapāla image with damaged legs and a further image without a bust from Devarani are in Bilaspur Museum, while two Devarani dvārapālas, without legs or the upper trunk, lie in situ in front of Devarani. Only one dvārapāla, sliced virtually in half, survives in situ on Jethani east steps, while attendants can be traced beside a Jethani east dvārapāla, and ascetic figures can be made out on the base of the Jethani west

dvārapala, both lying outside the temple. The lady wearing a hāra with a dangling coin tree, is held by the yakṣa on the Jethani east wall by her hand, and by her breast, which is cupped in the yakṣa's hand. The traces of the feet of a figure are found directly on her head. For the description of the great size, strength and splendour of yakṣas, *Mbh.*, Āraṇyaka parva 258,15. The ambivalence of *Atharvaveda* calling yakṣas both puṇya and itarajanaḥ (sacred and other folk) reflects the simultaneous respect and fear for yakṣas. Banerjea 1956: 337.

121. Śiva makes Kubera lord of yakṣas, in *pp* 26; helps him unearth his wealth through Śivagaṇas, and punishes Uśanas for stealing it in *Mbh.* 12.278 and 14.64.65, gives shelter to Kubera, a half brother of Rāvaṇa, from Rāvaṇa in Kailāsa in *Rāmāyaṇa* 3. 44. 28, 4. 44. 4, 7.11.25-50. Kubera is called a friend of Rudra, in *HvP*, 13.13. For loss of his left eye due to Pārvatī's curse, Chitrav 1964: 148; Bhattacharji 1970: 185; *Br.S.* 3.22.
122. For Kubera's attributes, *VdP* 3.53. 1-7. Piśācas are associated with Vaiśrāvaṇa (Kubera) by Patañjali, while commenting on Pānini's *Sūtra* 5.2. 129. and the nara vehicle, not being shown as an ordinary man, is probably shown here like a piśāca. See *Br.S:* 57, Banerjea, 1956: 338-39. Jambhasādhakas and Droṇameyas are mentioned in *Mbh.*, Udyogaparva 62. 25 and in Agrawala 1970: 175. Aṣṭanidhis are listed in Dowson 74. and discussed in Agrawala, *Indian Art*, 1965 81, 325. Ṛddhiśṛṅgas, like cornucopia, are held by Demeter (Greek), or Hārīti (Buddhist), akin to Kauberī. A.V. Agrawala, 1970: 274. *Ibid.*, 247, for identification of a vine wreath around Kubera head (replaced by the lotus wreath here), as a baccanalian symbol of drunkenness and lassitude. The names of six yakṣas, Maṇibhadra, Pūrṇabhadra, Maṇikandhara, Maṇibhūva, Maṇisragvin, Maṇikārmukadhāraka are listed in *Chitrav* 1964: 148. Kubera's sons, Maṇigrīva and Nalakubera, are mentioned in Dowson 1961: 74. Guhyaka in *AV* is suggestive of concealment. See Banerjea 1956: 337. They conceal themselves, using their power of antardhyāna or disappearance.
123. *Mbh* Śāntiparvan: 298.86 *KuP*, Pūrvabhāga 10, *Pp* 24: 68-69, *GaP*, Ācāra Khaṇḍa 23.6 describes Śiva and Sūrya as identical. Śiva is identified with Sūrya in the saṁhāriṇi mantra of the *AgP* 73: 16-17. Puṣan (nourisher for paśus), Mārtaṇḍa, Savitā are names of Rudras as well as Ādityas in *MarP* 5: 29-30. The compound Ravi-Śankaran appears in *MarP* 68: 35. Suvarṇaretas is name of both Śiva and Sūrya in *SkP* and Hemādri, Caturvarga 11.2: 535, 553. *SamP* 53 prescribes aṣṭapuṣpikā and samvatsara maṇḍala for worship of Sūrya, identifying him with Śiva.
124. The two fragments, the upper (1.05 m x 0.75 m) and lower (1.25 m x 0.75 m) match. The breast is defaced, as is the trunk, and arms are cut off, but the head, halo and attendants are intact. The image of Mārtaṇḍa Bhairava at Tala does not resemble any actual image, and does not satisfy the criteria in texts like *Br.S.* 58: 46-48. *AgP* 300-1, *VdP* 3: 67 for Sūrya or the Śaradātilaka commentary on *Nārāyaṇīya tantra* for Mārtaṇḍa Bhairava. Mallman 1963: 98, 104, 107, tableau u. For hundreds of examples of sun images, see L.P. Pandey 1971. For saptaraśmiḥ, or sapta tantu āvaraṇa (seven thread cover of prāṇic vibrations) of Sūrya, or the Mahānagna Puruṣa (the great nude) wearing it, see *RV* 1.146.1. 'Traditional Psychology', *Coomaraswamy* 2, 183: 350-51, n. 5; 'Līlā', *ibid.*, 151; and 'Vedic examplarism', *ibid.*, 180, n 3, discuss the playful Agni, who, as kavi, wears the forms of all things in their kind, frees them from Varuṇa's pāśas, bringing their latent possibility to fruition. For seven rays, drawing up juice, and seven names for a one horse chariot, Yāska, *Nirūkta* 4.27. The seven metres are suggested as substitutes for the seven horses in the *VdP*.
125. The lower portion is abraded. The absence of specific features, but for vague traces of an image, suggest concealment (gūḍhagātra) of this portion. This, according to the Purāṇas, is the result of the lower portion of his body being pared off partially up to the knee by Tvaṣṭṛ (Viśvakarman), father of Sāranyū, to make his son in law's unbearable tejas (light) bearable to his daughter. *BhaP* 55-59. For other textual evidence, Pandey 1971: 183.
126. Aśvins, derived from aśvas, literally, the pervader, are mentioned frequently in *Ṛgveda*, and are born of Sāranyū and Vivasvat (sun). The Aśvins act as match makers at the marriage of Sūrya with Soma or Moon. They receive the Sun as a milk cauldron in the Pravargya sacrifice to the Sun. They receive Soma

in a sacrifice by Cyavana in exchange for rejuvenation. They are described variously as born of Mārtaṇḍa, from one of the Ādityas, or from the tears of Agni. They are relatable to the Greek Dioskuri, and appear in corollary forms in German and Lettish mythology. Sūrya Sūkta in *RV* 10: 85. Keith 1917: 30-31, 66-7, 131-2, 153.

The Aśvins assume shape of mare and horse, and suggest opposite and complementary forces like heaven and earth, day and night, sun and moon. Yāska, *Nirūkta*: 12.1.11. The *BhP:* 76 prescribes their display on either side of Sūrya. Supposedly horse-headed, they are shown as horses. In the absence of any representation of Aśvins from this period, this representation is unique. Named Dasra and Nāsatya (destroyer and truthful), they herald the dawn. Dowson 1961: 29-31. Agrawala, *Śiva Mahādeva* 1966: 5, 30-1, 150 mentions the rhythmic oscillation, suggested by Aśvins. Like Tala, two horses alone flank Sūrya as vehicles for his chariot in a catulacūḍamāṇi on a lady's forehead (Lucknow Museum), and in a marble sun image from Khair Khāneh, Afghanistan (Kabul Museum). However, unlike Tala, they are shown in front of the chariot, not behind it. Pandey 1971: 171, pls. 6. (2) and 7(1).

Uṣas is described as Sūrya's wife in *RV* 7. 75.3, and Sūrya is the healer of leprosy in *Śāmba Purāṇa* and of skin diseases (takman) in inscriptions. See *EI* 27: 25-26. Aśvins are also mentioned as divine physicians, specially for leprosy in *RV* 1.17. 2.7. This makes them appropriate assistants for Sūrya. They nibble every moment at the sweet cake or apūpa of prāṇa, breath. *Chup* 3.1.1-5 speaks of solar rays as madhunāḍīs and *SB* 3.8.2-5 describes the same concept. *RV* 1.32.2, 8,9: 4.28.1. Dowson 1961: 124-26 further reinforces this concept by inducing the reflection that the Tala Sūrya may be seen interchangeably as Indra, who rides a chariot of two horses, and smites Ahi or Vṛtra to release the seven rivers and to fertilize the parched earth, thereby performing a curative and restorative role, like Sūrya. However, the difficulty with the position of the horses behind the Tala image will have to be resolved for this simultaneous identification. Sūrya has been identified as the horse in the cosmic aśvamedha in *SB* 10.6.5.8., as the horse yoked to kāla, samvatsara or time in *AV* 19.53.1, as the horse qua prāṇa in the fire chariot, treated by the Ṛbhus, three brother architects in the *RV*. V.S. Agrawala 1981: 45-6.

127. The Varuṇa image does not have Varuṇa's iconographic characteristics, described in *Br S* 57.57, or the *Vdp* 3.52.1-21. Neither the consort on his lap, nor the river goddesses at his flanks, required in the texts, are visible The missing conch shell or jewel box might or might not have been traced in the broken hands. For a conventional Varuṇa sculpture, see Banerjea 1956: pl. 46(1). *AgP* 51. 15, however, forms the lower part of Varuṇa with fish or crocodile, which supports the location of the Makaras at Tala. Varuṇa from the Pāla Period is shown on Viṣṇupada temple at Gaya on a mound. It is treated in its hind parts like a pair of swimming human legs, folded at the knees. *Umesh Mishra Commemoration Volume*: 712, pl. 149. The treatment of the lower part of Tala Varuṇa does anticipate similar notions.

128. For birth of Bhṛgu and Varuṇa's presents to Skanda, see *Rāmāyaṇa* 1.5.7; Hopkins 1915: 13, 36, 85, 88, 118, 151. *RV* 8. 41.8 assigns the role to Varuṇa of sundering and joining worlds, presumably as a world pillar. *Mbh* 5.96.6 puts Varuṇa at the base, supporting the tree of life. The crest of this tree is vanasya stūpam, the tumulus of the forest in *RV* 1.24.7. *SB* 13.3-6, which mentions the bald head of Varuṇa, indirectly suggests to us the presence of his lotus cap as a physical cover, irrespective of the metaphysical implications of lotus as a life tree or its crest. *RV* 1.24.7, 2.35.8, 7.65.2, *AV*.10.7.38, 11.2.24 describe Varuṇa as a great yakṣa acting on behalf of Paśupati, reclining in tapas in the waters, and supporting the inverted tree, with its base above, and branches below. The tree represents an inverted man, to be set upright by a transformation in his nature. 'Inverted Tree', Coomaraswamy 2, 1983: 398, 52, 403, n. 65. Both Bhṛgu and Skanda are types symbolizing such transformation in the lower nature of the paśu.

129. The lotus wheel behind the head of Tala Varuṇa is, traditionally a solar symbol (Macdonnel 1897: 155), and is found in coins, seals and hands of sun images. *RV* 5.85. 3 and Kuiper 1983: 114-16, provide description of Varuṇa pouring from nīcīna-bāra, the inverted bowl, over the universe. The inverted lotus cap or wheel on Varuṇa reminds us of this description. Varuṇa is called Sūryanetrī (sun eyed) in *RV* 5.85.5, 7.66, sun faced in *RV* 7.34.88. Sūrya is Varuṇa's ambassador in *RV* 10.123: 20. 223. Agni is Varuṇa's

brother in *RV* 4.1.2., which asks Agni to turn Varuṇa around (vyāvṛtasva). Together with Mitra, Agni and Soma, Varuṇa is called ṛtarsya gopa (guardian of order) and dhṛtavrata (of fixed ondinances). See Macdonell 1897: 26. *RV* 5.85, speaks of Varuṇa establishing Agni in water, Sūrya in sky, Soma on the rocks. For extensive references to Varuṇa's role as the solar eye, activated by Sāvitrī and Agni (identified with mṛtyupāśa, bond of death, as release from Varuṇa's pāśa or vāruṇya, see 'Symbolism of the dome', Coomaraswamy 2, 1983; 'Ātmayajña: self sacrifice', *ibid.*, 115-16, n. 229; 'Vedic Monotheism', *ibid.*, 172. In cryptic language, these allusions refer to the interchangeability of Varuṇa's role with that of Agni or Sūrya.

130. For birth of Varuṇa, Dhanvantarī, together with Apsarasas (Apsu rasa, the essence of waters, rivers) *Rāmāyaṇa* 1.45.30: 1.46.26; Coomaraswamy 1928, *Yakṣas* 1,: 50-52; Sukumari Bhattacharji, 1970: 39. For description of vāruṇya as death, varuṇagrāha as paralysis or dropsy and Varuṇa's pāśa as granthavistāraḥ or net of knots, from which release can be secured through sacrificial rituals like Varuṇapraghāsa or Varuṇa sava, *RV* 1.2: 7.59.12: 10.92.14; *TB*, 1.5.9.7: 2.6.17.7: *AV* 7.83.88. Sukumari Bhattacharji 1970: 32-33; 'Vedic exemplarism, *Coomaraswamy* 2, 1983: 180-2, 90, ns 5, 11, 31: 'Manas', *ibid.*, 211. The twofold nature of pāśa is explained in *MS* 3.7.8 For release of streams from Varuṇa's pāśa, *Rāmāyaṇa* 3.102.1: 3.99.334; *Mbh.* 5. 96.12: 9.6.93; 2.3.14; Hopkins 1915: 118. *RV* 7.64.2 calls Varuṇa sindhupati, lord of sea or streams, together with Mitra. Role of makaras as siṁśumāraśiraḥ, gobblers of the passion ridden selves, is explained in "Svayamātṛṇṇa, Janua Coeli", *Coomaraswamy* 2, 1983: 485-92, 517-18. Varuṇa chooses (Ver, to choose) the king, fertilizes the earth with rain, milk, rivers and floods, and punishes sinners, for violation of Ṛta, norms, with thirst. Keith equates Ṛta with the Aśā of the Āvestā and distinguishes its opposition to Anṛta, from the conflict of Greek Moirā or fate with divine will. Keith 1917: 70-71

131. Queen Lokaprakāśā of Amaraja-kula, wedded to Mekala Pāṇḍava king Bharatabala, is compared to sacred Jāhṇavī, in the purity of her character, Malhār plates of Śūrabala, Shastri I, 1995: 121. *RV* 3. 58.6 and 10.57 for mention of Jāhṇavī or Gaṇgā, as the one who comes to the earth (Gam+GA+Ap). For her three fold movement, see Winternitz 1963, 1: 318—40.

132. Śiva's rājanīti in acknowledging both Gaṅga and Pārvatī is mentioned in *Śivotkarṣamañjarī*. Sivaramamurti 1979: 32-33. The identification of this panel by K.D. Bajpai in 1978: 75-78 as Kirātārjuna, or by Stadtner as Kaṅkālamūrti, is incorrect. Though the figure on the left is Gaurī, the figure on the right is not Arjuna, and the heavy, slanted protruberance above Śiva's head is no represention of Pāśupatāstra, required in a Kirātārjunīya image. On the other hand, the rod, placed by Stadtner in the right hand of the socalled Kaṅkālamūrti, has no resemblance to a kaṅkāladaṇḍa and is really the staff in the left hand of the ascetic figure of Bhagīratha, whose association with Gaṅgādharamūrti is recognized in iconographic texts. The slanted protruberance above Śiva's head on the left is no drum, as Stadtner would have it, but Gaṅgā, shown conventionally as a pouring column of water, being released from his matted locks by Śiva, with his uplifted hands. The figure on Śiva's left is a woman, and no man, as Stadtner seems to think, and her position on Śiva's left, the fact that she has turned away in a huff, and that Śiva holds her with his left hand, are established as attributes of Gaṅgādhara Śiva in iconographic texts. The suggestion that this is Gaṅgādharamūrti was made by Chandrashekhar Gupta of Nagpur university in a spot visit, and I agree with him. For the attributes of Kirātārjunamūrti, Kaṅkālamūrti and Gaṅgādharamūrti, Rao 1916, 2.1: 214-17, 293-309, 313-21. Gaṅgā is the eldest daughter of Himavat and Menā, and is hence both a sister and a rival of Pārvatī. *Rāmāyaṇa* 1.35.14; 1.36.15.

133. The Aṁguda and Āraṅg copperplate grants of Śarabhapurīya King Jayarāja, Pāṇḍuvaṁśī king Mahāśivagupta Balārjuna's Malhār copperplate grants are dedicated, in the name of deceased ancestors, udakapūrvam, with offering of waters. In the Devarani panel, gift of life is being made through rejuvenation by waters. Jain 1961/2005: 10-15, 45-46.

134. Sarasvatī is addressed as Sarasvatī in Sky, Bhāratī in heaven, and, as Ilā on Earth. The role of Sarasvatī is explained in *RV* 1.3.10-12, 3.10.12 as Vājinivatī and Thiyāvasuḥ, the giver of food and desires, the holder of sacrifices and inciter of good sense. She is the Vākdevī or Goddess of sound and speech.

Possessed of water or saras, she signifies the installation of luminous Agni in rasa or water and vice versa. *Bhṛgūpaniṣad* elucidates this as apsu jyotiḥ pratiṣṭhitam, jyotiṣvāpaḥ pratiṣṭhitaḥ. In *VS* 19 of *YV*, sacrifice is made to Aśvins as well as Sarasvatī, and, Indra is cured of indisposition, caused by excessive intake of the intoxicant Soma, by Aśvins and Sarasvatī. Haṁsa symbolizes the words so aham, I am He, uttered with intake and expulsion of breath. Ham and Saḥ are also equated with Puruṣa and Prakṛti. Kaviraj 1983: 222-3; Winternitz 1963: 46-66 .

135. Of the four slabs used in the ardhamaṇḍapa jambs, the two lower parts were carved with Yamunā. Of these, one, found in the 1978 excavation, and preserved in Bilaspur museum, shows a defaced Yamunā, shorn of its right leg, arm and its left arm, below the elbow. A similar slab, found in the '89-90 excavation, shows similar ornament on the moulded side or the lower right trunk of Yamunā, and traces of attendants. Of the two upper parts of the jambs, one is in Bilaspur museum and shows the defaced head and bust of a proto-Śiva figure embedded in rocks. The other fragments, still lying on site, show similar moulding and ornament on the sides, the defaced head and bust of Śiva as well as a curved, defaced shape below, resembling the nāgarāja profile on the base of the Devarani ascetic image, assembled from fragments on ardhamaṇḍapa steps. The shape of a bull with horns is faintly discernible. The mayūrātapātra is in evidence above Yamunā at many Dakṣiṇa Kośala sites like Surguja temples at Deepadih, Siddheśvar temple, Palāri, Indal Deul, Khārod, Aḍbhār or Pūjaripāli.

136. The creative and destructive heat of penance is explained in O'Flaherty 1963: 36, 43-44; Chauncy Blair 1961: *AoSP* 83. Tapas, according to *Chup* 5.10. 3-6 generates rain, vegetation, food, sperm and body. *AV* 11.5.5, and 7.10.26 speak of the one born of tapas, and of the Brahmacārin creating by tapas in the ocean. Rites of garbhādhāna and aṅkurārpaṇa (germination and seedlaying), performed to help in a new birth in the womb chamber, are discussed by Kramrisch 1946 1: 13: 126, ns 85a and 86. Kapila, with his destructive anger, is a name of the sun in *Mbh.* 3.154, a form of fire. Monier Williams 1899: 744. Bhagīratha, who has a regenerative goal for his penance, is also a symbol of the sun. Agrawala, *Śiva Mahādeva* 1966: 37-38 explains the etymology of his name, linking him with the sun. The sixty thousand Sagaraputras represent the product of the multiplication of thirty days and nights, resulting from the diurnal movement of the earth around its axis and its movement around the sun from month to month. They are thus indissolubly connected with the solar course, be it destructive or creative.

    Gaṅgā is visualized as the liquid form of Śiva in Kālidāsa, *Kumārasambhavam*: 10.26. No wonder, her representations as three rivers at the threshold of Devarani take the place of actual tīrthas, where the Sagaraputras can substitute new, purer selves for their old, unclean, mutilated selves. The process, mediated through dīkṣā (initiation), is explained as a homeward journey of Jīva towards Śiva, through ātmasamarpaṇa (self-surrender) and upasaṁhāra (merger in Godhead). Kramrisch 1946. 1: 3; Zimmer 1929/1984: 42-46, 209-12. The river goddesses assist the bhakta to metamorphose his nature, attain the nature of Śiva and assume a new embryo in the garbhagṛha. The transforming nature of the descent of Gaṅgā is described in *Rāmāyaṇa* 1.38-44, and in *Purāṇa*s including *MarP* 55.

137. For Lakṣmī, as a symbol of stability, see Sivaramurti 1955. The effective integration of iconic and aniconic in the double Srīvatsa of Devarani can be compared with the conventional representations at Kāveripakkam and Madras Museums. Banerjea 1956: pl. 19, figs 1-3. Also Pramod Chandra 1971: 1475. Lakṣmī, Gaṅgā and Sarasvatī, who are all displayed in Devarani, are three wives of Viṣṇu. See Nirmalananda 1981: 46-56.

138. *Mbh* 3. 1683. describes Lakṣmī as Kubera's consort. For analysis of their association, on the basis of nidhis shared in Lakṣmī's padminīvidyā, and Kubera's aṣṭanidhis, see Banerjea *1941:* 141-46. For personified or physical representations of treasures of Lakṣmī on early seals or sculptures. Banerjea 1956: 193-98, 376, 396, 560.

139. *VdP* 1.9, 3.82.7 10; *Mbh*.1.17ff. for identification of the elephants. Kalaśa is seen as Viśvarūpa, ākāśa (space) and praṇava (*aum*), and is worshipped independently before it is associated with Lakṣmī as abhiṣekapātra (the anointing bowl). Lakṣmī has his residence in flowers, oṣadhis, vanaspatis, kalpavṛkṣas

(medicinal plants, trees, wish fulfilling creepers) as Puṇyagandhā (of sacred fragrance) or Araṇyāni (the sylvan deity). See Sivaramamurti 1970: 34-35, 61, 80-81, fig. 127. Samudrasubhagā (favourite of ocean) is a name of Gaṅgā. Monier Williams 1899: 1167.

140. Śrīcakra and Suvarṇayaṣṭi are discussed in Śrīsūkta, khila in *RV* 1.165. Agrawala 1965: 81. *RV* 10.1-5 for the forehead of Lakṣmī touching heaven. *Tup* 1.4. sees her as the fount of all coveted things. Her association with lotus is explained in Zimmer 1955, 1: 158-60.

141. The impregnation rites of temple, transacted to symbolize the coupling of earth and heaven Puruṣa and Prakṛti, Śiva and Śakti, are explained by Kramrisch 1946, 1: 134, n. 96. The Cappadocian Teshu and Mā mentioned by Raychaudhuri, 1958, 201-2 or the Oesho and Nānā on a quarter stater of Huviṣka in the Punjab Museum, described by Banerjea 1956: 126, bear close affinity to the idea of the primordial pair of Hara Gaurī. Ānanda Bhairava and Ānanda Bhairavī are the forms of Śiva and Śakti in Kaulācāra.

142. Dyāvā Pṛthvī Varuṇasya dharmanā Viṣkambhite. *RV*. 6.70.1. Also, mantra 11 of Aśva-vāmīya sūkta. Agrawala, *The Thousand Syllabled Speech*, 1963: 42, 52, 55.

143. *SB* 6.1.3. The Śatarudrīya 16.31 offers worship to Śiva as namaḥ (salute) urmyāya (waves) ca, vasvanyāya (floods) ca, varṣyāya (rain) ca, namaḥ meghyāya (clouds) ca, vidyutyāya (lightning) ca, vatyāya (storm),... namaḥ saśyāya (grass) ca, phenyāya (foam). It also worships him as vṛkṣebhyaḥ harikeśebhyaḥ (trees with green crests),... auṣadhinām pataye (guardian of herbs),... śuśkyāya ca, harityāya ca (of the tender, green shoot and the withered leave)... lopyāya cālopyāya ca (the barren ground and verdant growth). Sivaramamurti 1976: In the *Śatapatha Brāhmaṇa* 6.1.3 Paśupati is equated with plants because the Paśu (cattle) acts as the master (Pati), when it gets plants. *RV* 5.57 calls the Marūts, the storm clouds, thrice seven in number (reminding us of the seven gaṇas on Paśupati's body) Rudraputras. Like Rudra himself, they are seen as destructive but also as bountiful and propitious. They are like the howling winds, which cleave mountains, uproot trees, whirl dust, but also make rain, renew the forest and the landscape and provide the healing calm after the storm. Keith and Carnoy 1917: 38. For a terracotta seal showing a Śivaliṅga described as Pādapeśvara in Gupta characters, see Banerjea 1956: 114; B. Bhattacharya 1973: 963-64.

144. *RV* 10. 45 addresses Agni as Somagopā (protector of soma) and Apsurāja (king of waters). *TS* 4.2.6 1a-c, 1d-5, 1g and *BŚS* 10.13: 13. 13-14 propitiate Agni in the plants, and ask the plants to cure diseased limbs. Soma has been identified variously with the Ephedra Pachyclada, a tall western Himalayan shrub and the hallucinogenic mushroom amanita muscarita, or fly agaric. Stein 1931. Wasson 1971. A sarvauṣadhapātram (a bowl mixing all medicinal herbs) is handed over to the Adhvaryū (priest), while preparing the field for Agni. Staal 1983: 392-94. In his role as a physician and yogī, which has been noticed earlier, Paśupati or Agni uses the waters and the plants. *RV* 10.16.3-4 beseeches Agni to carry the ancestors to sky, earth, waters or plants according to their works, while *RV* 10.16.6. requests Agni and Soma to restore their limbs, gnawed by beasts. For similar connections between harvesting and ancestral rites, see Sukumari Bhattacharji 1970: 128-29, 152-56. These are the traditions which provide a backdrop to the cleansing of the ashes and rejuvenation of the sons of King Sagara in the Devarani door jamb panels.

145. In the discussion that follows, I have been briefed by Ramlal Kashyapa and his team of botanists at Bilaspur who visited the site and studied the flora with me.

146. These are black, known as Canna Orientalis in Latin, perforated to form necklaces of Cannaceae family.

147. Pinkish white fruit, called Dhaturā metel (pink) or alba (white); of the Solanaceae family. The wall of the Dhaturā fruit is green and full of spiked and scattered spines, and hides the seeds inside. The flowers are musk scented and trumpet shaped. Unlike other families, the sepals or petals do not fall out after fertilization. This lends special importance to Dhaturā as an ever bountiful kind.

148. The Campā is white, of the Magnoliaceae family, Michelia Champaka specie. The pyramidal arrangement for frontal view is apocarpous, and the splitting is called dehiscence.

149. Also known as white lotus, of the family Nymphaeaceae, species Nymphaea Stellata.
150. Kevḍā of Pandanaceae family, Podoratissimus specie. Its leaves are acuminate (with pointed tips), and have spiny margins.
151. Jasmine is of the family Oleaceae, and the genus is Jasminum Pubescens.
152. The family of Vakul is Sapotaceae, and the specie Mimusops Elengi.
153. Jhumkā, also know as Kaurava Pāṇḍava, is of the Passifloraceae family, Passiflora Edulis specie, seen here in an artistic distortion.
154. The Amarphal is of Araceae family and of the Monstera Deliciosa specie. Has bright, polished, green leaves.
155. The Kiṁśuka is of a bright, orange red color, and belongs to the family Leguminosae Pepilionaceae, and specie Butea Monosperma.
156. This is of the family Asdepiadaceae and specie Calotropis Procera.
157. Family Magnoliaceae, specie Magnolia Grandiflora. It has yellow, scented flowers. Tree is tall and evergreen.
158. These are scarlet flowers of Caesalpiaceae family, Saraca Indica specie.
159. An evergreen tree, spreading laterally by sending down aerial roots. Of the Moralceae family, Ficus Benghalensis specie.
160. The leaves are linear, lanceolate (lancelike) and natural in shape. However, there are never as many fruits as flowers like here or the twig would break, nor are they so systematically stacked in nature. The impression of a cluster could be an impression in a distant view. The family is Aancardiaceae, the specie Mangifera Indica.
161. The Kadamba is yellow of Rubiaceae family, Cadamba Indicus specie. Has a spreading crown, but is a deciduous (leaves shed annually) ornamental tree, and undergoes complete defoliation.
162. The jackfruit is of Moraceae or Verticaceae family, and of the Artocarpous Heterophylous subspecie. The reniform (kidney shaped) seeds are not visible here, because the flower is still to turn into fruit.
163. A schizo (split) carpic (carpel) fruit with stonehard seeds, the Āmalaka is of the Euphorbiaceae family and Emblica Officialis specie.
164. The Śaiva Kuṇḍalinī Sādhaka contemplates the four-petalled lotus in mūlādhāra, the six-petalled lotus in svādhiṣṭhāna, ten-petalled lotus of Viṣṇu in maṇipura, the twelve-petalled lotus in anāhata, sixteen-petalled lotus in viśuddhi cakra, the two-petalled lotus of Sadāśiva in ājñācakra, and none in Bindu Śiva, in the Sahasrāra or thousand-petalled lotus above the eye brows, which is a state of Nādānta or end of sound, and Unmani, beyond mental faculties. See description of vādhamayī dīkṣā in the *Śaradā Tilaka*, quoted by Gopīnath Kāviraj 1983, 1: 114-44; Campbell 1974: 390-91. The union of Candra, Sūrya and Agni is described in Tantra, in a luminous expression, as ākāsā candra bheda, piercing of the moon in the sky. In this union, the down turned thousand petalled lotus is turned upwards in the sahasrāra, in a flowering of understanding. Gopinath Kaviraj 1983: 127-8, 160-61. Installation of bīja or seed of a temple through the evocation of its causal creative image from the lotus heart of the devotee is also the remaking of the universe by the original architect, Brahmā. Kramrisch 1983: 65-6.
165. The lotus leaves are shown peltate, compressed into bowlike shapes by the presssure of water. It is the padma, or Nelumbo Nucifera.
166. The shivered frame is a square sanctuary with concentric circles and interpenetrating triangles, equipped with the pīṭha (seat) of the iṣṭadevatā (chosen deity) of the devotee. Zimmer 1946: 143.
167. *TB* 1.1.3.3.
168. *Mbh.* 1.66.40.
169. The Gaṇas, designated Nāga, Kūrma, Kara, Devadatta, Dhanañjaya, Vāyu are associated with udgāra, kṣudhā, jmṛmbhana, burp, stupor, hunger or yawn, which indicates chronic disturbance in the wind or breath. (The figure of hunch backed lady suggests probable identification of a princess of Kānyakubja, who was reduced to her deformity by her frustrated Yavu lover. Keith 1928 1, 365-7.) Gaṇas are equated with prāṇic aberrations, and Soma with Pārvatī, V.S. Agrawala, *Śiva Mahādeva*, 1966: 4. Gaṇas and their

lord are equated with breaths and the imperial breath. *AV*. 11. 4.1.10 ; *Prup* 3.3.4. ; *Kaup* 2.1: 3.3; *SB* 6.1.1.7. 'One and only transmigrant', *Coomaraswamy* 1983, 2: 67-9.

170. The name pramatha (churner) for a gaṇa is derived from the common Indo-European root of the Greek name Prometheos (fire fetcher), suggesting a further connection between Agni and Rudra. Sukumari Bhattacharji 1970: 134.

171. For the characteristic features, gestures and postures of gaṇas, described in this and the next paragraph, see *Mbh.*, Śalyaparva 9.44. 74-108: *MatP* 53. 531-46: 182. 64-6; V.S. Agrawala, *Indian Art*, 1965: 73, 317; Dhaky 1984: 243-48. Dancing, chanting, boisterous laughter, drumming on the mouth or huḍḍukāra, and silent meditation are mannerisms observed by Pāśupatas, and characteristic of the gaṇas, who are bred in the tradition, promulgated by Śrīkaṇṭha Santatbrahmā, consort of Umā and Lord of bhūtas. *Mbh.* 12.337.62;13.14.

172. Dhaky 1984. The mercurial and unpredictable shifts in Mahādeva's behaviour are described in the *Mbh*, Anuśāsana parva. He yawns, sleeps, cries, laughs, sings, dances, plays music, rejoices, shouts loudly, acts mad or intoxicated.

173. See V.S. Agrawala, *The Thousand Syllabled Speech*, 1963: 117, 163, 166-68 for discussion, in this regard, of mantra 6 of Aśva-vāmīya and Ucchhiṣṭa Sūkta of *AV*.

174. *TS*. 4.3.5.1a. Bricks of a sacrificial altar are consecrated by comparing the goat and ram together with the tiger, lion and bull, with different metres. Their heads are buried under the Agnicayana altar, identifying the sacrificer with the sacrifice, in a process of death and regeneration. *TS*. 4.2, 10.4. The goat is born of Agni's embryo. Staal 1983, 1: 113-17, 119, 458. What is sacrificed is excessive lust, symbolized by the ram or goat in Hindu mythology. Supposedly a symbol of lecherous nature, the goat head of Dakṣa is also the result of a curse of bull Nandin. Further, when Indra takes the form of a ram to rape a Brāhmin woman, he is castrated and his testicles are replaced by those of a ram or a goat. Prajāpati's seed turns into a billy goat. Rudra / Agni supplies, as goat or ram, their testicles as food of matṛkās (mother goddesses). *PP* 5.2, 91-125; *LP* 100. 1-27; O'Flaherty 1973: 128, 285.

As a force of darkness, the goat-headed gaṇa is created from the sweat drop of Rudra, the Andhaka slayer. The goat-headed demon is created by the sacrifice of a goat, in order to fight gods through the instrumentality of Śukra (semen), which generates poisonous passion. The goat head of Dakṣa is planted on him by Rudra after decapitating him for refusing him sacrifice. He is then instructed by him in the Pāśupata vow (of enjoyment without attachment), which equips him for staying close to bhogya (Śiva's city of enjoyment), as head of Śivagaṇas. Śiva ordains that whoever builds a house for God or man has to worship the goat-headed one as vāstupa first. For the story of Andhaka and the goat demon. *VaP* 43. 26 44; *MatP* 12. 252.5-7, 13-14. For Dakṣa's story, *LP* 1.80.54-56; *ŚiP*, 2.2.37. 49-61: 42. 30-32; *BhāP*, 4.7. 2-3; Kramrisch 1981, 68-70, 331.

Association of Skanda and Nāigameya is explained in *Mbh.*, Vanaparva 217.12; Agrawala 1970: 72, 78, 80. The inscription below the goat-headed gaṇa suggests visit of a merchant from a guild (nigama) to worship Nāigameya (of the guild). Skanda is reported to have sprouted the sixth goat head when Indra, frightened by his loud cry, hit him with a thunderbolt. On the other hand, the goat-headed Nāigameya is identified at Tala as Agni, who soothes and amuses Skanda, as one of the twelve attendants of Skanda, produced by Śiva, or as a benignant spirit, who soothes bālagrahas or spirits of Skanda, afflicting children.

175. *Mbh*, Anuśāśanaparva for Dakṣa's offering. *RV* for zoological mythology of bull. *Mbh*, Droṇa parvan for description as Śṛṅgin and Vīṣāṇin. *MatP* for the bull's constant gaze. *Gṛhyasūtras* for Śūlagava sacrifice. The signs of the bull and goat, in the Zodiac, mark the spring equinox and are responsible for the origin of the phallic cult in parts of the world. Dulaure 1934: 222. Coins of Vākāṭaka king Pṛthviṣeṇa show bull Nandin standing before sacrificial post or yūpa. See Shastri, 'Vākāṭaka Coins', in Shastri 1992: 290.

176. For the meaning of legends associated with kīrtimukha, *SkP* 2.1.17; Hopkins 1915: 229 -30; Coomaraswamy, n. in Zimmer, *Myths*, 1946: 184. The kīrtimukha is comparable with the Greek

Gorgoneion, Green man, in the English church arch, the Chinese Tao Tieh or glutton, the Odishan virāla and South Indian vyāla. Stella Kramrisch 1946. 1: 322-34.

177. *Mbh.*, Anuśāśanaparva 17.11. 5523: Śāntiparva, 284.30.3166; Vanaparva, 231.29.1610; *HvP*, Viṣṇuparva 124. 18. 718 mention comparisons of lion and Śiva, creation of lion by Śiva to destroy Dakṣa's sacrifice, and Śiva's chariot, drawn by a thousand lions, to carry Pārvatī and Skanda, or to protect Bāṇāsura. Kālidāsa, *Raghuvaṁśam* 2.35 38, mentions Siṁhagaṇa Kumbhodara as being in the service of Śiva Aṣṭamūrti. He is used by Śiva as a footstool to mount vṛṣa, varṣaṇa śīla retas, flow of semen, to enact regulation of senses. Monier Williams 1899: 1213 lists Siṁhavāhana as one of Śiva's names. The principle of one essence, two natures, is represented by birds in *RV* 1. 164. 20 or *Mup* 1.3.1. It is discussed also in 'Traditional psychology', *Coomaraswamy* 2, 1983. 2: 340, fn. 29. For Śarabheśa, Rao 1916: 2.1. 171-72.

178. For Makara's role, explained in Kāmadhenu Tantra, Winternitz I, 1963: 318-40. 'Svayamātṛṇṇa', *Coomaraswamy* 2, 1983: 485-92, n. 3, 517-18. ns. 89 and 90 for discussion of makara as the uppermost self-perforate. Makarasaṁkramaṇa (the transit of makara) is the passage of the sun from Sagittarius into Capricornus, which vindicates its location at points of transition. Monier Williams 1899: 771, 1213.

179. Elephants were shorn of wings by the curse of Dīrghapatas, and induced their celestial winged companions to descend, bringing rain. See *Mbh.*: 1017 ff; *VP*, 1.9; Zimmer 1946: 102-9. *Meghadūtam* 1.38 uses the word subhaga for masculine cloud; For gajapādapa, see Monier Williams 1899: 342. Tiwari in Shastri 1992: 282-3. Sātavāhana coins found at Malhār are engraved with elephants. Pandey 2002: 37, 63. The elephant caryatids at Jethani remind us of the practice of tying elephants at Sirpur temple permises, evident from stones with circular holes near Suraṅgaṭilā steps, Bālesvara temple and plinth of Tivaradeva Mahāvihāra. Sharma 2012: 15.

180. Winternitz 1963: 270-92. *Gup* 11-14 describes Gaṇeśa's conventional attributes. For the legends of Gaṇeśa opposing Paraśurāma's entry to the sleeping apartment of Śiva on Kailāsa and losing his tusk; of Gaṇeśa opposing Śiva's entry to Pārvatī's apartment, when she is at her bath and losing his head; or of the child Gaṇeśa's head being burnt by Śani's glance, in *Śip* and *BvP*, Dowson 1961: 106-8. For some of the meanings, Alain Danielou 1964: 291-97. For an elephant-headed, tuṇḍila (pot bellied) yakṣa on Amaravati coping, Coomaraswamy 1928, *Yakṣas* I: 7.

181. Winternitz 1963: 270-92.

182. The Mekala Pāṇḍava king Bharatavala's birth from queen Indrabhaṭṭārikā is equated with that of Kārtikeya from Pārvatī in Malhār plates of Śūrabala. Shastri 1980.

183. *SB*, Brahmā Kāṇḍa, 6.1.3. 8-18. for Kārtikeya and Agni. *Rāmāyaṇa* 13.17.72 for Viśākha. Viśākha is perceived as merudaṇḍa (spinal column), equated with the Vedic hiraṇyavetasa (golden reed), swung to and fro by two Aśvins (prāṇa and apāna). Agrawala, *Śiva Mahādeva* 1966: 5, 7-10. explains this in course of his description of Kārtikeya's achievement as a Yogī.

184. The *MāP* 50.10 sees this as Virāj created by Brahman, possessing characteristics of both sexes, and split into two halves as Manu and Śatarūpā. For the discussion of the hermaphrodite form, *LP* 1.99, 6-11. The bisexual form of Ardhanārīśvara is mentioned in *LP* 19.8, *PP* 1, Sṛṣṭikāṇḍa. *Prapañcasāra Tantra* 28, harks back to the Ṛgvedic twins, Yama and Yamī (*RV* 1.66.8), to Prajāpati's form in *Kup* 8.7, and, to the form of Ātman in *Brup* 1.4. The *SB* 6.4.4.2 and *AB* would see this as the image of Roḍāsi dyāvāprithivī, or, of the Brahmāṇḍa itself.

185. Kaviraj 1983: 317 for Ardhanārīśvara as Guru. Kulasādhaka in *Kulārṇava Tantra* 9. *BuP* 1.4.3; Karapatri 1941-42: 114, 153-54; Danielou 1964: 203. V.S. Agrawala *Śiva Mahādeva*, 1966: 8.

186. Having identified the Tala image as Aghora Śiva, J.P. Singhdeo identifies the four faces without moustaches on the front and side of his thighs as female faces of Śakti, and assumes that the lion heads depicted on his knees symbolize the vehicles of Śakti. He also suggests that the sculpture was guided by an advanced Tāntric Aghori and conceived as a composite yogic figure of Mahākāla and Mahākālī. At the same time, he concedes that no Śaiva mythology may be found to give his suggestion iconographic support. Singhdeo in Nigam 2000: 130-32. Ardhanārīśvara was created, according to Kāmikāgama, to

induce ṛṣi Bhṛṅgī to circumambulate both Śiva and Pārvatī. Rao 1914-16, 2.1:322-23. It represents a confluence of Śaiva and Śākta ideas.

187. Sivaramamurti 1981: 148-68, figs. 71, 72, about Patañjali and relation between ācārya and śiṣya. Aṅgirā Ṛṣi, literally, a cluster of live coals, was Agni himself, a friend of Śiva. *RV* 1.31.1.

188. Pāṇḍuvaṁśi inscriptions, issued from Sirpur, use the work Udakapūrvam for gift and provide a context for this giftt of blessings. Sixteen filaments of a lotus are drawn in pairs in a yantrarāja (king of instruments). One wonders if the fifteen ascetics, who fall short of this number by one, and complete the number only by repeating the end number from either side, do not anticipate this yantra. Shastri 1. 1995: 19. The words 'aum svasti' are used as prefatory in Bālārjuna's Malhār copperplate grants and in Suraṅgaṭilā copperplate grants. The word 'siddham' replaces the word 'svasti' in Bālārjuna's Gandheśvara temple inscription and in the older Gunji stone inscription of Kumāravaradatta. B.C. Jain 1961/2005.

The auspicious, invocatory, celebratory narrative of the worshipful ascetics and lions in the circular medallions of Devarani door jamb soffit may be read in the background of similar medallions in European art. In the third or fourth century AD orphic sacramental bowls, sixteen figures of neophytes are shown in the outer circle, in various stages of mystery initiations, whereby the initiate is made cognizant of the portion within him of the ever living god, who dies to himself to live manifold in us all. In the central circle are shown creatures of the wild, driven by a hunter. A medallion surrounds the winged serpent, covering the sun door, through which initiates ascend, through clashing rocks or simplegades, which open and close constantly, to admit them into communion with eternity. In a 13th century AD eucharistic bowl from Mt. Athos, standing and seated figures, sixteen each, surround the virgin mother, who has the Christ child in her womb. In this manner, each person's fate is linked with that of every other in a harmonia praestabilita, in which every person is the hero in his own drama, and an actor in that of the rest. Campbell 1968: Fig. 3, pp. 9-17, fig. 11, pp. 97-99, fig. 24, pp. 167-64, 344.

189. The Paśupatas were mentioned by various names and Pāśupata philosophy was known as pañcārthakulāmnāya. They are mentioned in Akulavīratantra and described as Somasiddhāntins in Śrī Harṣa's *Naiṣadhacaritam* 10.88. Kaviraj 1983: 40-44. Patañjali, *Mahābhāṣya* 5.2.76 on *Pāṇini Sūtra* 2. 36. mentions 'āyaḥ śūlikaḥ' and 'daṇḍājinikaṇ', or Śiva bhāgavatas holding iron lances and wearing animal hide. This a description answers that of the Punjab tribe Siboi, subdued by Alexander, and, of Herakles and Dionysios in Greek writing and mythology. Arrian, *Indica* 5.12 in McCrindle 1901: 34. For Keśin, ascetics drinking viṣa, see Keśī-Sūkta. *RV* 10.136. For Keśin as Rudra, *AV* 11.2.18. For sabhasmadvijas, *BS* 59,5.19. For their association with Pāśupatism, Banerjea 1956: 449. *RV* 1.1.1-2. and *Mbh.* 1.5.8. for the role of *ṛṣis* in sacrifice. Ṛṣis are described as bhadrapramāṇa (of auspicious mien) in *VdP* 3.42. 3-4.

190. Alaṁ, sufficient, kṛ, to make. *RV* 8. 24. 26 has the expression sumbhāni, I furnish. In this case, Agni or Paśupati is being furnished with prayers. *Suśrūta* 54.13 speaks of rakṣābhūṣaṇa, apotropaic amulet. 'Ornament', *Coomaraswamy* 1, 1983: 243- 44, 249; *Abhinaya Darpaṇa*, Invocatory Introduction.

191. For terms used, V.S. Agrawala, *AinD*, 4, 1947-48: 149; V.S. Agrawala, 1960: 26, 5, 125; Moti Chandra 1973: 127.

192. For sportive lotus called parihāsaprahāramṛṇāla (the lotus meant for hitting in sport) of the women of Śrīkaṇṭha Janapada, described by Bāṇa, see V.S. Agrawala 1969: 78. Also līlākamala to make bees buzz, *Raghuvaṁśam* 6.13: *Meghadūtam* 2.2.

193. V.S. Agrawala, *Indian Art*, 1965: 234-35.

194. M. Postel 1989: 40-41, 173, 202-6, for illustrations and symbolism of earrings.

195. Bāṇa, *Harṣacaritam* 1.32; V.S. Agrawala 1947-48: 139, figs. 66, 104.

196. Sivaramamurti, *Sanskrit Literature and Art*, 1955: 54-55.

197. For the terms and plates relevant to headdress of Tala images, see V.S. Agrawala, *AinD* 4, 1947-48: 142, pl.49, fig. 154 (chattrākāra), p.134. pl. 47, fig. 123, pl. 49, figs. 139, 140, 144, 147 (valibhṛd alaka), p. 131, pl. 43, fig. 108 & pl. 50 (bhramaraka), etc.

198. For terms and prototypes of ornament. Postel. 1989: 55-68. Moti Chandra 1973: 217; Sivaramamurti, *Sanskrit Literature and Art*, 1955: 54-55; V.S. Agrawala, *Indian Art*, 1965: 20-21, 24.
199. Agrawal 1969: 65, 187-88, 194-95.
200. The shape of the fire altars is discussed by the *Sulvasūtra*s of Baudhāyana, Āpastambha, and Kātyāyana. The *TB* 1.1.6, 1-3 speaks of the tanuhaviṁśi or reassemblage of Agni's body by offering different kinds of earth. For dispersion and recuperation of Ānaddha puruṣa and Agni by the Agnyādheya rite in the Agnikṣetra, shaped like a bird of seven squares, see Seidemberg 1983: 65, 78, 91, 7, fig. 2; N. Tsuji 1983: 149. For the altar, shaped like a bird, which will carry the yajña to heaven, with the largest square in the centre forming the Ātman, and the three projections, wings and tail, Staal 2, 1983: 66, figs. 6 & 7, 67, 120-21. For a śyenaciti outside the ancient city of Kauśāmbī in mid-1st millenium BC G.R. Sharma 1960: 87 ff. Also, at sites at Jagatgrām near Kalsi, Staal 2, 1983: 34.
201. It is the yūpa, sacrificial pillar, Skambha, the axis muṇḍi, Brahmasūtra, or Viśvarūpa, a breathing self with human limbs, senses and voice, which mirrors all elements, spheres, time and space. Wooden yūpas, inscribed in 2nd century AD Prākṛt, found in Hirābandh tank at Kirāri village in Bilaspur district, Chhattisgarh in 1931, show the vogue of the cult of installing the pillar in the tank, for filling it with waters. The cult continues to this day. Jain 1961/2005: 1-3. *KB* 6.1.9. *AV* 10.7 offers hymns to the Skambha, which becomes the altar ego of Prajāpati, Agni or Rudra, and at the seven layered āhavanīya fire altar in the Agnicayana rites. *RV* 10.1-10 describe the blazing pillar of light, (jyotir) stambhas, which can beget Hiraṇyagarbha or Purāṇapuruṣa, the God of reproduction. It may be identified as 'valsa vanaspati' of *Ṛgveda*, the symbol of the ūrdhvamūlam adhaḥśākham tree, with its root, immortal source above, branches, material manifestation, below. This is the tree of *Kaṭhopaniṣad*, the Sahasra Udumbara, to which each paśu is bound as to a stake, atop which is the God of death, who is to be appeased by every Naciketas or organism. *RV* 7. 33.9, *RV* X.135.1, V.S. Agrawala 1981: 73, 75, 78, 130.
202. Kalaśas, encircled by floral and faunal forms, are analogous to the pot bellied, girdled yakśas or siṁhas, stationed at the base of pillars. The Hiraṇmayam camasam, the golden jar, was created by Prajāpati, in which Prajāpati poured his seed, to give birth to Rudra, who demanded to be named, and was named in eight ways. The male pots, buried at the foundation of the altar in the Agnicayana ritual, were left unmarked, while the female ones and the ukhā vessel were marked with breasts, girdles or udders. F. Staal 1983, I: 404-9. *ŚB* 6.5.2. 2.2. Prajāpati was identified as the Droṇa Kalaśa, which, when full, was also the Viśvarūpa. See. *AV* 10.8.9. In the Pravargya ritual, the pot was worshipped as Māhavīra or a great Hero enthroned. Buitenen 1968. The Śaiva Kumbha is mentioned in Śaivāgama. Brunner 1968. In the Sūryasoma fire ritual, Vedas were represented as vessels, to which oblations were offered. Clothey 1983, 129 ff. Also, discussion in Srinivasan1997: 201-5.
203. The *SB* 2.6.2.7 speaks of offerings made to Rudra at his favourite haunt at the cross roads. In West Bengal, worship is offered at the cross roads to Dharmarāja, who is identified with Yama or Śiva.
204. See Sivaramamurti, Śatarudrīya, 1976: 79-80. Śiva is responsible for the plan by scattering ashes (sūtrapāta) in his dance and for the execution of the work (bhuvana; sthāpanasūtradhāra), for the sacrifice and establishment of Agni in Soma. Indeed, as architect (sthapati) of the universe, he is recognized as yajamāna, one of the aṣṭamūrtis, *ibid.*, 50. 'Traditional psychology', Coomaraswamy 2, 1983: 360-2, ns. 84-89. See *RV* 1.87.5. Kaviraj 1983: 176-79. SB III 3.4.1.22 describes the sacrifice as being produced from the union of the upper stick, male Pururavā, with the lower stick, the female Urvaśi. Also, Srinivasan 1997: 69, for the image of Paśupati turning into Vāstoṣpati; *AB*. 3.33; Kramrisch 1981: 65-66.
205. For possible associations of such architecture with a royal camp, palace or fort, see Agrawala 1969: 45-53, 88-99, 95-98, 108-10, 117-19, 123, 248. For upasada rites of siege and burning of Tripurā. *TS* 6.2.3.1-2; *SB* 3.4.4, 23-5. Also Kramrisch 1981, *Presence*: 413-15. Śiva's regime at Tala, in such analysis, becomes the prototype of the prosperous and victorious reign of the Śarabhapurīya king (pravarddhamāna vijaya rājya). See Kurud plate of Narendra, who is a Viṣṇu Bhāgavata, for analogous vision. Jain 1961/2005.
206. Staal 1983: 65-7, 113-17. The Puruṣasūkta of *RV* 10. 90 is a celebration of the creation of the world by the sacrifice and dismemberment of the Puruṣa. The sacrifice of the yajamāna is in the nature of this original act, and recreates the same cyclic process of death and regeneration.

8

On Ethnography

SPEECH AND ECHOES

Parallels for the art of Tala and Dakṣiṇa Kośala are traceable today in oral narratives, in customary or ritualistic arts, and in primitivist movements in modern art. The search for such parallels may be questioned on the ground that contemporary motifs, patterns or imagery may serve purposes and convey meanings different from those of the past, and, may represent a different response to the changed ideological and physical environment. A question may arise whether the flawed and subjective human understanding of the interpreter is adequate for negotiating the instinctive or cognitive gulf separating him/her from the past artist.

The venture acquires validity when we consider the fact that the imagery of Tala and Dakṣiṇa Kośala, like contemporary or near contemporary folk and tribal imagery, is backed up by an oral, recitative, visual and contextual tradition, which continues unbroken among rural communities; and that, these communities have lived as ecological isolates in bio cultural habitats, which have remained substantially unchanged till recent days. A continuity of pantheistic responses in traditional arts to the surrounding world has been consciously acknowledged by primitivism in modern urban arts.[1] Primitivism in modern art, however, makes a programmatic and conscious presentation, by formal simplification and symbolic generalization, of the quality of organic and universal unity, intuitively appreciated in the older art. The narcissistic preoccupation with form or with transient anxieties in primitivistic modern art has no distant kinship with the functional, ritual, ceremonial relation between the symbol and its representation in the earlier art. And yet, the immersive experience of unity of organic and inorganic forms, the unexpected congregation and dematerialization of forms, found in modern art as well as in the art of Dakṣiṇa Kośala, point to the raison d'etre of such primitivistic art.

A hermeneutic reconstructive movement between art of the past and present may not be considered fruitless. Art and speech tend to pass into each other and offer a lexis, based on a relation between a signifier and a signified, constituted by a constantly moving turnstile, which uses an ambiguous signifier, at once intellective and imaginary, arbitrary and natural. The ultra signification of the speech of Dakṣiṇa Kośala may lapse back to pre semiological infrasignification of oral poetry today. The comparison may not appear arbitrary when we recognize echoes of the pristine speech in oral traditions, within the 'isoglosses' or ideographic limits of the mythological province of Dakṣiṇa Kośala, and, detect in them allusions, however distant, to the shared universe of narrative art of India and Asia.[2]

In tracing a commonality or continuity of motifs, patterns or themes, no suggestion is being made that an unknown aboriginal tradition of art has converged with Brahmanical traditions, and, has been transplanted into the Brahmanical core, or, has survived or evolved as an explant or a fragment in contemporary adaptations. However, it should be possible to build bridges among various domains of arts, by tracing the commonality among constraining neuro mental structures, conceptions of the world, systems of truth, grammar or syntax in mythology shared by audience in different art worlds. These may be mutually translated in terms of dialectical contacts and correlations. Such translation is possible because mythology and visual arts, on analogy of music, adjust the internal or natural grid with the external or cultural grid, to achieve conscious approximations of unconscious truth. Once the entire range of the mythic story or musical scores is surveyed, it is possible to grasp length of directions, recurrence of themes, back references or parallels. The science of myth has been understood as anaclastic which studies both reflected and broken rays, and measures directions and angles in order to postulate their common origin. Just as their elements can be disentangled and separated, they can be knit together in response to unexpected affinities.[3] Mythology, like music, takes a direct leap from sonemes or tonemes, notes, and phonemes or letters, to musical scores or sentences, through a conjugation of opposed principles. Like music, it is to be read not line after line, left to right, but as a whole page, stave after stave. The diachronic succession of events yields a synchronic order, which is to be appreciated holistically, as a shared patrimony.[4]

It may also be suggested that similarities in non-iconic, geometric motifs of art in different times, places and artistic realms are induced through recurrent entoptic constants of phosphene images, which are generated bio-neurologically by deliberately altered or aberrant states of body and mind. One may, on such a presumption, pose the thesis of biological or phylogenetic longevity of certain universal types and patterns in human art and a certain continuity of behaviour, belief systems and material conditions among isolated forest and hill based demographic groups of Dakṣiṇa Kośala, Chhattisgarh and outside.

However, we may not, on this presumption, adapt a confirmationist approach, to identify a convention, by assembling similar images from different periods and places and assert the convention to be statistically homogenous. Nor can we harness 19th and 20th century theories of utilization ethnography and sympathetic magic, to see essentially similar forms from different cultures as ongones, which change external shapes to mediate between this world and the other. It is also not plausible, after Freud and Jung, to see similar patterns from different times and places as being inspired by identical sexual or psychological drives, increase or fertility rituals. Nor is it possible to ignore the taphonomic logic that the available evidence, on which we base our suggestions, for similarity or continuity between the art in Dakṣiṇa Kośala and elsewhere, represents a fraction of the evidence, that has been destroyed or discovered.

Having said all this, we have to yet accept the continuing and vital links, textual and contextual, written and oral, in Dakṣiṇa Kośala, between magic, religious and social organization and creative activity of the past and present, in India and the World. Contemporary tribal art in

India carries a freight of symbolic meaning, akin to that of ancient Dakṣiṇa Kośala or the world of local communities outside. They share a theory of the congeneric nature of the micro and macro systems, creation and procreation. Even if we do not assert a one to one relationship between Indian and global art in this respect, if is necessary to try and read pristine meanings back into forms, left out of them, rather than embrace nihilistic solipsism about the fruitlessness of such an effort. An empathetic approach needs to be adapted, to move from appropriative understanding, to visit the garden behind the window, to understand the other as one's own self. This may offer a clue for the appreciation of human sameness, as it appears in human difference, reflecting similar impulses in different forms.[5]

Many of the geometric patterns in the art of Tala and Dakṣiṇa Kośala have been essentialized and abstracted out of anthromorphic, zoomorphic, theriomorphic forms like griffins, tritons, centaurs, or from bead and reel, lotus and bell, rosette and petal, tree and mountain, umbrellas and banners, frets and spirals, volutes and swastikās. These forms have been carried through centuries, in ceramic, textile and pictorial scroll designs, by nomadic balladeers, reciters, picture showmen, rope walkers in art worlds all over Asia. The narrative art in portable scrolls, temple cloth hangings, leather puppets, paṭas on paper or cloth, carried by paṭuās, citrakārs and citrakathis, puppeteers of Eastern India, Andhra Pradesh and Karnataka, are anticipated by the frozen tableaux in the temples of India, including Dakṣiṇa Kośala. They have entered Indian Art at its inception, as part of a common, shared vocabulary.[6]

PAŚUS AS TRIBAL MARKS OF ATTRIBUTES

Forest and hill based tribal communities of Chhattisgarh, Odisha and Madhya Pradesh apply tattoos of animal images to their body joints to acquire powers and qualities of such animals. Paśus have been carved on various body joints of Tala Paśupati also to appropriate their strength and quality. The Paśupati is preceded and followed by images, which also include various organic forms in their body. However, no other known image would appear to be as composite, syncretic or comprehensive in its iconographic features. The depiction of animals on the Paśupati image anticipates, or, probably reflects, the continuing traditions among Kols, Āgārias and Orāons in north, Korwās, Orāons and Pānḍos in east, Kanwars, Bhīls, Gonḍs and Baigās in southeast Dakṣiṇa Kośala, of tattooing their bodies with animal designs. They etch designs of fish and snakes as symbols of water, love and fertility. Tribal surnames are connected with totemic animals and plants to provide taboos and prescriptions, surnames like Ekka (tortoise), Tirkey (bird), Minz (eel fish), Lakra (lion), Kujur (creeper plant), Kispotha (pork) and so on. The elephant God (Gajakarandev) design is a mark of power, horse design (Ghorā dev) is a symbol of speed. Monkey God (Hanumān dev) and Earth mother (Dhartimātā) are marks of strength, patience and bounty. Peacocks and parrots are suggestive of beauty and romance. Bhīl women inscribe their bodies with Āmbam, or peacock, drinking mango juice from flowering trees, scorpions, honey bees and butter flies, to suggest fertility and passion, and, with trees and birds, to epitomize life. Tattoos are used as ornamental identity markers, which can be carried beyond death. Triangles, squares, swastikās, hexagons, zigzags, loops, wheels and circles are used in body decoration and folk and tribal arts in Dakṣiṇa Kośala to describe attributes of Pārvatī's motherhood, union of Śiva and Pārvati, sun and moon, knowledge, mind and eternity. Remarkably, these signs appear in the prehistoric rock art of Raigarh, Sundargarh, Jharsuguḍā,

Sambalpur, Kālāhāṇḍi in the bordering areas of Chattisgarh and western Odisha and suggest an intense concern with generation and nutritive patterns.[7] The name of Jogī Magaradhwaja, the ascetic with crocodile as his insignia, is inscribed in many places, including Kaṅkāli temple at Kavardhā, to remind us of the all pervasive makara at Tala, including the makara on Paśupati's shoulders.[8]

GAṆAS, BHŪTAS AND THEIR MASTERS

The gaṇas at Tala are deformed, and are engaged in a ceaseless effort to recover their form by assimilation to Paśupati. They correspond to protective grāmadevatās or tutelary deities, as also peygel or piśācas, who represent lust, delusion, malice and cruelty, and to bhūtas with lion and elephant heads, in the army of Subrahmanya, in rural India today. Among Gonḍs of Bilhā, Bilaspur, Barādeo lives in a sacred Sājā tree along with a bull and is worshipped by five men, named Uikā, Śyām, Naitām, Tāndro and Mārāvi. They request Bhagvān to make a Barāpen for Barādev.[9] They remind us of five gaṇas carved on Tala Paśupati, and, of the disciples of Lakulīśa.

PAŚUS ASSOCIATED IN TRIBAL LORE WITH ŚIVA AND PĀRVATI

The idea at Tala of emanation of various Paśus from the body of Paśupati, or the association of paśus with Śiva and Pārvatī, as their companions, ornament, armour or equipment find echo in tribal oral traditions and art of Central India. The Gonḍ myth of Pākhāri in Mānḍlā describes how, on his marriage with Pārvatī, Mahādev adorned Pārvatī with ornaments made of all the poisonous things in the world, and took her to Madhuban, the forest of honey. It describes how Mahādev made for Pārvatī snake armlets from his thigh dirt, a hornet nose stud from chest dirt, a scorpion ear ring from eye dirt, and a toad spangle for her forehead from the dirt of his penis.[10] Among the Āhirs of Upri Mānḍlā, the hair or body dirt of Pārvatī, turns into a krait or a tiger, while the chips of wood, hurled by Mahādev at these creatures, become mongoose or wild dogs to chase them back. In a Baigā variant of this story, Pārvatī makes stripes on the coat of the tiger, by stroking it with her hands, that are black with soot from cleaning an old earthen pot. Pārvatī thus reassures the tiger, as it runs up to her, on being chased by the wild dogs of Mahādev.[11]

PAŚUS IN TRIBAL TECHNOLOGY AND ARCHITECTURE

Living and non living elements metamorphose into one another in dress, domestic and temple architecture, resource management and subsistence implements, and folklore of Chhattisgarh as in ancient Dakṣiṇa Kośala. In the songs of Hirākhān Khattri of Rājneṅgi Pardhāns of Mānḍlā District, the Mahāṅgu Mahilā puts on python skin pāyjāmā, a leopard skin coat, a peacock feather cap and a turban, made out of the shiny gunsi gādāin snake. The Dhanuār Basor caught two tigers to serve as bullocks and tied them up with snakes. He fixed a scorpion at the end of his goad, made his ploughshare out of a krait, and his yoke from a python.[12] In Northeast Konḍāgāon, the hero Usārāmgipalli is hailed for making a house with a Dadāi fish door, lizard door frame, Chipā fish walls, Bāni and prawn fish bone cross beams and peacock feather roof thatch.[13] In Gonḍ marriage posts from Mānḍlā, Madhya Pradesh, or Muriā Ghoṭuls made by Tullur Muttāi and her husband Kādreṅgāl, in Bison horn Mariā memorial pillars, dedicated to ancestors, or poles supporting swings of Sirāhās, temple priests from Bastar, Chhattisgarh, in Sānthāl marriage litters from Sānthāl Parganās, Bihar, and, in Kuṭiā Konḍ house doors from

Gañjām, Odisha, geometric designs jostle with totemic designs of cattle, stags, fish, crabs, tortoise, tigers, elephants, horses, crocodile, lizards, peacocks, serpents, birds and pots. They betray an inspiration similar to the door jambs and mouldings of Devarani, Deepadih or early medieval temples of Odisha, in which animal and human motifs were intertwined.[14] There is a tradition in Raipur of making Bāghmuā (tiger mouth) house, broader in front than at the back, and, of avoiding construction of a house, facing south, the direction of Yama, God of Death, or North, the direction of Gaṅgā.[15] At Tala, the tradition is recalled, in breach rather than in observance.

PAŚUS AND THEIR LORDS IN TRIBAL LIFE AND DEATH

The tribals of Bastar identify themselves, in death and after life, with various paśus, and remind us of paśus, mirrored in the body of Paśupati. Megalithic memorial posts of stone and wood, called Uraskal and Koṭakkal, have been and are being erected by Goṇḍ tribals at Kilepāl, Lālāguḍā, Tārāgāon, Gānḍā in South Bastar. These are carved with their totems like tortoise and crocodile, iguana and tiger.[16] The Muriā clan God, Buḍhā Pen, Āṅgādev or Pāṭdeo, who occupies the Penravār or Penkarār, the spiritual capital of the Muriā guild or Pen, is represented by parallel Sājā or bamboo log poles, decorated with snake, bird, peacock, jungle cock, feathers, sun, moon and bell motifs. An intermesh of such forms occurs in the door jambs of Dakṣiṇa Kośala, beginning with Devarani temple at Tala. In the Muriā world of dream, the Jīva or soul has adventures after leaving the body, in which animals play a prominent role.[17]

THE SNAKE IN TRIBAL LORE AND ARTS

The pervasive presence of the snake in door frames, mouldings and sculptures is another continuing feature in Dakṣiṇa Kośala temples. Images, worshipped by Bastar tribals today, are formed, equipped, adorned, supported and framed by snakes. Features of nature are personified as, or inhabited by snakes in tribal folklore. An 18th century black schist group of images is installed in the ledge, cut out of the hill slope, facing Chitrakūṭ falls near Jagdalpur in Bastar. In this group, snakes are engraved on the arms and chest of a three-headed image, designated as Brahmā Viṣṇu; constitute the lower body of a Nāgadevī, and rise, double-headed, from its flanks to form a seven hooded canopy above her. Alongside this Brahmā Viṣṇu panel, is an image of a deity locally called Hanumān Pānḍe and Prahtam. Akin to Goddess Mahīṣamardinī, killer of the buffalo demon, the deity stands on twin lions and is accompanied by a lion head and tail (Fig. 629).[18] Snakes wrap themselves around an 18th century black schist image of Teliṅgin Mātā at Narāyaṇpāl in Bastar; emerge out of the seat and head dress of a four-armed goddess at Mārāguḍi, at Ektāguḍā near Jagdalpur; coil up jhulās or swings; and form pillars and beams of the Māriā Ghoṭul.[19] The Śavaras worship two serpent deities Asorām and Jayandeneusun. Mariās speak of a great serpent, haunting river rapids and water falls.[20] The rainbow is seen as Dhawan gotā, a polychrome snake, by aboriginals of Betul; as the raised head of Bāsuk, supporting the world, by Pardhāns of Mānḍlā; and, as the snake Bhūmtaras, rising from ant hills, to stop rain, by Muriās of Bastar.[21]

Tiger in Tribal Ritual

The tiger or lion adorns or forms the seat slab or the pillar base, or crowns the door jamb panel or window niche at Tala and in Dakṣiṇa Kośala, and continues to dominate people's imagination till date in the area. Sāorās are connected with Sheorinārāyaṇ temples, and, chant Śabarī mantra, for appeasing spirits of people killed violently by tigers. In death in a tiger maul, the Baigā Guru goes into a trance and invokes Ṭhākur Dev and Dharti Mātā, in the māṭi uṭhāvanā or earth raising ceremony, to exorcise the presence of a tiger, by addressing him as tiger of nail, rocks or horns, as Āgibāgh, Tājibāgh, Āṭāriābāgh or Lāṭāriābāgh.[22] A Dhanvār sept called Manākhi, christens a man, killed by a tiger, as Bāghiā Māsān or tiger imp, whose spirit can be laid by an efficient Guṇiā, Parghaniā or sorcerer. Basrākhān Gāzi or Dakṣin Rāi in Bengal, riding a tiger, recalls Siṁhavāhana Śiva at Jethani.

PAŚUS AND ŚIVA IN TRIBAL CREATION MYTHS

The intermesh of linear and volumetric, abstract and realistic forms, visible at Tala or Dakṣiṇa Kośala, continues in the tribal art and mythology of the region, to symbolize creation and procreation on the earth. The organic and inorganic shapes of nature appearing in tribal arts continue to be pregnant with a creative and procreative impulse, vibration, meaning and purpose, imparted by the mythology of Śiva. If the abundance and profusion of animals, flowers and plants in Dakṣiṇa Kośala art is incited by water and fire cosmology, associated with Śiva, the creative efflorescence in the tribal art of the region is sparked off by Śiva in various mutations, as Mahādev, Barādeo, Liṅgodev, Āṅgādev. The various animals that congregate in the body of Tala Paśupati or in the temple mouldings of Dakṣiṇa Kośala, continue to be associated with Birhor, Chero or Sānthāl legends of creation. The crab appears on Paśupati's chin at Tala. The Kākarmal Khattri or the crab fetches earth from the bottom of the waters at the command of Ṭhākur Jiu in Sānthāl legend, in Sānthāl Parganās; at the instance of Singboṅgā in Birhor legend in Chhattisgarh; and, on the instruction of Bhagavān in Āgāriyā myth in Mānḍlā, Madhya Pradesh. He stops the theft of the earth in Devār stories of Tendu Bhāṭā in Raipur.[23] The tortoise forms the liṅga of Paśupati at Tala. In a Kayāvarohaṇa Māhātmya story, Śiva is transported by tortoises by subterranean routes to the Jaleśvara Liṅga, or the liṅga, presiding over waters. Born out of a miscarried foetus of Pārvatī, thrown in a stream, in a Goṇḍ story in Bañjar Mānḍlā, the Barasmār Marrādeo as fish brings disease to seven daughters of Jalandhar Guru (the water bearing preceptor).[24] Kāchim Kuār or the tortoise, Solehāo or the Sole fish perform the function of bringing up the earth, from under the waters, at Ṭhākur Jiu's command, in Sānthāl legend. In an Asur Āgāriyā legend, father of mankind comes out of the valley of the fish Raghurāman. Like the mole in a Jethani pillar, a rat climbs down the stalk of Ḍepi grass to bring earth to Kiṭṭung Mahāprabhu and the Mahendra mountain, according to a Lānjiyā Sāorā story of Gañjām.[25] In a Goṇḍ myth in Binḍrānavāgarh, Mahādev replaces Ganeśa's head with a crab head, unlike the elephant head of Tala, and then revives the crab, without its head, leaving sword marks around its neck.[26] According to a story of Rājnengi Pardhāns of Pāṭangarh, Mānḍlā, the creation of earth is celebrated by Naṅgā Baigā and Naṅgā Baigin, who are treated as equivalent to Śiva and Pārvatī in tribal lore. They dance and embrace at Bhoramdev in Kavardhā in Dakṣiṇa Kośala with their twelve sons, twelve daughters, and with Gods and Goddesses. The tiger beats the Māndar drum. The panther beats the timky. The peacocks dance.[27] The temples at Tala and in Dakṣiṇa Kośala are also treated as stages in which the Śiva, his gaṇas, and his nonhuman companions, enact a drama of passion, exertion and fulfilment, to celebrate the reintegration of paśus in the body of Paśupati.

FLORA IN TEMPLE ART AND TRIBAL FERTILITY MYTHS

The fusion of floral, faunal, human and geometric forms in Devarani door jambs or in the art of Dakṣiṇa Kośala suggests the pantheistic imagination of tribal art today and evokes images of marriage, pregnancy, water cosmology and fertility. In a Gonḍ tale, God makes a bird out of gold mohur leaves and uses its bright red flowers for the bird beak.[28] Flowers and trees, shrubs and creepers come out of the body of cows and horses in the legends of Dhuliās of Mānḍlā and Pardhāns of Seoni.[29] In a Gonḍ myth from Barlātolā, Mānḍlā, the flowers elect Jasmine as their King, to solicit Mahādev to impregnate them through a bee born from his body ash.[30] Among the Rājnengi Pardhāns of Mānḍlā, who sow seven herbs in seven seed beds, Mahādev is associated with herbs and plants.[31] The colour and texture of Tinsā, Sājā and Ebony trees (Qugenia dalbergioides, Terminalia tomentosa, Diospyros melanoxyion) are linked by Muriās with the touch of the God Liṅgo.[32] Āṅgādev is adorned with grass and corn stalks, bean and pulse pods. In a Gonḍ story of Bañjar Mānḍlā, Mahādeo makes trees and hangs them with flowers and fruits, while Pārvatī conceives after receiving their pregnancy scent, reminding us of dohada of classical literature, in which vṛkṣakās (dryads) and vṛkṣas (trees) quicken each other to fruition by touch or glance.[33] A Halbā girl is married to a Mahuā tree when no suitable match is found for her on attaining puberty.[34] A Binjhvār Baigā story from Baihār, Bālāghāṭ describes how the Baigā, dressed in Mohlāin leaves, is chosen by the earth maiden as her consort, over Gods, bedecked in jewelry and finery. A description follows, of the Baigā making a wedding hall of śal and ḍumar branches, clothing the earth in bark, feeding bears and tigers with spear grass grains and sājā flower paste. The Baigā and the earth maiden circle around the marriage pole. Finally, the Baigā goes to the earth maiden and blood comes to her for the first time.[35]

The integrating imagination, fusing forms for a creative explosion, appears in folk and tribal traditions, in Dakṣiṇa Kośala, and elsewhere in India. The lotus limbed Kubera on Devarani door jamb, the leafy, leonine, equine form sprouting from kumbha at Jethani pillar base, the proto Śiva heads or female heads framed by massed mango leaf clusters, the multiform, ithyphallic form of Paśupati, find cognate, analogical response in Wārli art in Maharashtra. In Wārli Art, Pañcasūryadeva is shown as a figure on a horse, with five human and animal heads and an upraised phallus, at Gaurī festival, after rains. Gaurī's head is aureoled by a creeper orb, and corns sprout from her head. Pregnant fish and progeny are shown inside her body in the X ray style. Pālghāṭa and Kānsāri are goddesses of trees, plants and corns in Wārli marriage paintings. The groom of Kānsāri devī is Banadeva, represented as a paddy sheaf. Mahādeva and Gaṅgā Gaurī are the original self generated Wārli couple, who use mud to make elements, animals and plants, and then, submerge the universe in flood, to destroy and recreate it.[36]

LOTUS AS A PSYCHIC AND FERTILITY SYMBOL IN TEMPLE AND TRIBAL ART

The lotus at Tala is a symbol of the seven ways ascent of consciousness from dormancy to wakefulness. It is also symbolic of the cyclic, centripetal and centrifugal process of emanation and merger, procession and recession, ascent and descent of prāṇic forces in the living world. The tribal deities Singboṅgā (among the Munḍā and Birhor), Dharmā, Bhuiyā, Bhagvān, Otebaran, Sirmā Ṭhākoor or Sun (among the Kol, Baigā and Chero), or Ṭhākur Jiu (among the Sānthāl), live on and brood over the lotus.[37] Sātcakra or seven wheel diagrams, depicted in Madhubanī paintings of Bihar, show figures with psychic centers, symbolized by lotus petals.[38] The lotus and lotiform medallions and diagrammatic, geometric forms in Tala find response in Āripans in Bihar, Ālpanās in Bengal, Osā in Odisha, Chowkā in U.P., Māṇḍnā in Rajasthan, Sāthiā in Gujarat, Raṅgoli in Maharashtra, Kolam in Tamil Nadu. These are inscribed as bhūmi śobhās, or auspicious writing, in life ways rituals. Some designs show a lotus with feet and hands, holding leaves and shoots, to represent fertility and child birth. Others show lotus, joined by bamboo shaft, as symbol of the union of Hara Gauri.[39] Serpents or Nāgas are intertwined with lotus leaves, plants and foliage in these, as in Rajim, Tala or Odisha door jambs. Kukeśvara, Bhūteśvara, Pañceśvara Śiva at Rajim, Pateśvara, Champakeśvara, Kopeśvara, Bhamneśvara and Fingeśvara is situated in the Kamalakṣetra, lotus zone. Lotus fibre was used, according to tradition, for making garments, when there was no cotton thread in Chhattisgarh.[40]

PAŚUS DEFINE TRIBAL TIME AND SPACE

As in the art of Dakṣiṇa Kośala, so in folk and tribal art and philosophy today, worship of nature becomes the source of affinity, consanguinity, kinship and names, and defines landscape, space and time. Gods of forests, hills and hunting are worshipped as Banjāri Deo, Doṅgar Pāṭ and Māsvāsipāṭ in Bilaspur. The Bison horn Māriās deify spirits of mountain passes and precipices as rou, spirits of forest as Vandevī, and spirits of river as Jalkāmāṇi.[41] Names of villages, tanks, streams of Dakṣiṇa Kośala are taken from trees, animals, birds, insects, rocks, soils and sounds. Bailāḍilā range of Bastar derives its name from the hump of the bull. Villages are called Āmlidiḥ or Āmgāon after mango, Bhainsādiḥ or Hāthi Bāri after buffalo or elephant, Kekrādiḥ after crabs, while village tanks are called Bāgh Ḍābri and Sāras Tāl after tigers and cranes.[42] Kamal Baṅśīs or people of the lotus (Kanwars) derive their origin from Brahmā, who was born on the lotus. Halbās name their gotras after animals and fruits, and worship a grown up tree as Kolo. Hill Māriā phratries are named after Bakrā (goat), Nāg (snake), Kādiāri (cuckoo), Kāchchin (tortoise). The rhythm of hours is linked with the rhythm in floral or faunal behavior through the dawning or waning day. In Halbi, pharpharberā describes the flight of the night at 5.00 A.M. In Gonḍi, hirriporrā describes the invasion of green parrots in the field at 4 p.m., when crops are green, and zhulpulberā characterizes the hour 7.30 p.m., when flowers have shed their best fragrance, an hour also described as bhainsāndhiyār or the buffalo night.[43]

ANALOGOUS ROLES OF ŚIVA AND LIṄGODEV

A close correspondence exists between the mythology of Śiva at Tala and Dakṣiṇa Kośala and that of Liṅgodev, Liṅgopen, Ḍherāpen, Buḍhādev or Barādev, among the Gonḍs of Bastar, or, of Liṅgopinnu among the Kuṭiā Konds of Odisha.[44] Like Tala Paśupati, he is the creator of all paśus, teacher of all arts, pastoral and agricultural skills, including techniques of slash and burn cultivation. He creates sun, moon and other heavenly bodies. Liṅgo, like Vāstupa Śiva at Tala, provides foundation, as the Ghoṭul Māñjhi, for the Ghoṭul, Ḍinḍāmahal, or the youth dormitory, occupied by the Muriā Chelik and Motiyāri, boy and girl.[45] Liṅgo approaches the earth as Bhimul, in heat, generates rain, discovers fire and liquor, and recalls Paśupati's role in the cyclic interaction of fire and water, operative in the creation, procreation and dissolution of agnisomīya paśus. Like Yogī Śiva of Tala, he is a celibate. His legend, like that of the all pervasive Śiva in Dakṣiṇa Kośala, incorporates the story of Kirāta or hunter, who defeats a tiger; of Piṇākī or bowman, who shoots an Āginbāṇa, arrow of fire or a rainbow into the sky; of a nude buffalo rider, who, like Śiva in the nude, tempting wives of sages, tempts the wives of his brothers, by playing musical instruments.[46] He pervades and comprehends all worlds like Paśupati. His hair goes up to Porobhūm or Uparpur above, his tail to Thārbhūm or Māñjhpur in the middle.[47] In one legend, he is created by Mahādev and Pārvatī, and is liberated by Gonḍs from a cave in Kāchikopā Lohāgaḍh, or from an iron fort on a red hill. His birth and release are accompanied by bursting of flowers and opening of clouds. This recalls Śiva's act of releasing waters, imprisoned by Vṛtya, which has been depicted in the Devarani door jamb, in the release of Gaṅgā from Śiva's locks.[48] Muriās of Bastar speak about Liṅgo and his brothers, driving their harrow across the sea, to bring out land.[49] Many Gonḍs of Bijāpur and Bhopālpatnam in Dantevārā district have continued till recently to wear Śiva liṅgams or silver boxes, containing rudrākṣas or beads, sacred to Śiva, reminding us of Bhāraśivas, who carried the phallic symbol on their head.[50]

PROTECTIVE ROLE OF ŚIVA AND TRIBAL HEROES, LIKE NAṄGA BAIGĀ

Mahādev and Pārvatī, the primordial couple, are acknowledged by the Baigā tribe in Dakṣiṇa Kośala, as Baigās. Naṅgā Baigā commands the animals and tigers after outwitting Mahādev in negotiations, like Pārvatī, who takes away bull Nandī after defeating Śiva at a board game.[51] In a role similar to that of Śiva Kṣetrapāla, or Vāstupa at Tala, he protects the village boundaries, crops, life and property from wild animals and encroachments, and repairs the magical boundaries by driving a nail into the earth. He is capable, like Tala Paśupati, of turning himself into wild animals. He is characterized as the true Paśupati, who lives in poverty, close to the earth, in spite of being Bhumāi Rājā or Lord of the earth.[52] Vīra or Kṣetrapāla appears among Wārlis of Maharashtra and the Rāṭhvās of Gujarat and Western Madhya Pradesh as guardian of the field, riding snake, carrying spear and a liquor vessel.[53] He reminds us of Śiva as guardian of the house at Tala.

PĀŚUPATA, GONḌ AND BAIGĀ GURUS

The legend of Lakulīśa of Tala and his four disciples is recalled by the fact that Baigā Gurus or Guṇiās have borne names like Gorakhnāth, Bhasmāsur, and, that four famous Baigā Gurus, Daugun, Nindhān, Danāntar, Madhakawār are brothers. Wild and wayward Pāśupata mannerisms are practiced by these Gurus. Thin and cadaverous, they have hollow, deep sunk eyes, carry a bottle gourd, hung with charms and simples, and wear a necklace of curved forest fruit kernels. They are associated with witches, who, in turn, adopt Bīrs or familiars from the graves of the four Baigā brothers.[54] They resemble the images of ascetics at Tala. In Baigā lore, the Jīva or soul, goes to Bhagvān, Chāyā, shadow of death. It is reincarnated as fish, frog, Bhūt or the evil ghostly self, and must not be permitted to come back from the burial ground. The magical pantheon of Baigā Gods and demi Gods reminds us of the bhūtas and gaṇas, who accompany Paśupati, Gonḍ God Barādeo and his disciples.[55]

ŚIVA, PRIMAL TRIBAL CULTURAL HEROES, AND AGRICULTURE

The myth of fertility and bounty is associated with the Śiva, the first God, the primal cultural hero, among tribals. Twelve kinds of seed are yielded by an old serpent, or by the knotted and hollow bamboo tube body of Bāsin Kanniyā, at the instance of Naṅgā Baigā. The Naṅgā Baigā pleases Ṭhākurdev and is allowed to bless the seeds. Ānnā Dāi or Kuṭki Dāi is worshipped by the Baigā as the goddess of food, born with sprouting leaves and grains, in Bevār or shifting cultivation.[56] The art of agriculture is imparted by Liṅgo to the Muriā, by Naṅgā Baīgā to the Baīgā in Bastar, by Rusi to the Juāng, Boramguḍhā to the Bhuiyā in Odisha, by Dharmes to the Orāons and by Ponomosor to the Khariās of Chhoṭā Nagpur, and by Nārānbarambhā to the Wārlis.[57] The Gonḍs of Pākhri Mānḍlā have a story about Kavā Lavā, the Koyal, the Rāj Pānḍā or head of flying birds, who left jungle along with birds, ants, butterflies and insects, so that the Gonḍs could turn the jungle into cultivated fields, by sowing Kodon, which they had secured from the Basors.[58]

SACRIFICE OF PAŚUS IN PĀŚUPATA AND TRIBAL CEREMONIES

The theme of sacrifice, in remembrance of ancestors, and their resuscitation, or metempsychosis, which is at the background of the art in Tala and Dakṣiṇa Kośala, is very much in vogue in the Gonḍ lore of Bastar. The children of Pārvatī are killed and buried by Mahādev, to be reborn as Barādeo, with seven heads and thirteen eyes, as Liṅgodev on Liṅgo hills, as Samduriā dev in river bank burials, and, as Marrādeo at the cows' resting place.[59] They remind us of the various universe of Tala or Deepadih, peopled by Śiva and his companions, in many shapes and forms.

Bison horn Māriā pillars are dedicated to ancestors.[60] The Muriās preserve an earthen pot, Hānāl Kunḍā, dedicated to the departed, in the Hānāl Kholi, room of the departed. They offer sacrifice at the ancestral clan shrine or Hānāl Koṭ. They invoke ancestors by offering grain and liquor in life ways and subsistence ceremonies, at birth and death, sowing and harvesting, winnowing and bringing of crops to the granary, hunting or fishing, to seek protection against hazards. They ask ancestors to go to Gods, and become like them.[61] These prayers and practices put us in mind about the prayers that are offered to effect union of paśus with their pati, or of the pots, carved, entwined with flora and fauna, at the edge of pillars in Dakṣiṇa Kośala.

The burial graves have Hānāl Guṭṭā, wooden posts, which are set up like a series of pots, crowning one another, like some pillars at Tala. Hānāl Garyā is a cromlech, set up as a ghost throne at the base of the Hānāl Guṭṭā. At the Pānḍums, hunting rituals, Hānāl Gāytā is the priest, who uses pots and rice plants, and sacrifices mangoes and mahuā fruits to the deceased Hānāl to keep it pacified. The Dāniyākāl or the stone platform, placed on four boulders, is supposed to increase in size, if the Hānāl commemorated is happy.[62] This reminds us of the balipīṭhas or pillar platforms of Tala, presumably used for ceremonial offerings.

In the practice of Pāñclakariyā, five sticks or five small earth balls are placed in a heap at the head of a grave, with an exhortation to the soul to incarnate itself in another human being.[63] Among Baigās, a Bhiri or a stone circle is made above a grave, covered with thorns and bushes, surmounted by carved posts, which, in turn, are crowned by a trident. The Koṭakkal, Uraskal or stone Menhir, the Uras Gaṭṭā or wooden Sājā posts, commemorating the dead, are carved with scenes of hunt and chase. The dead man's Hasiā, Sūpā, Ṭumā, Khantā, tobacco thaili and Chākmā, i.e., articles of daily use in agriculture or household, are put near the grave, and his bow and arrows are hung on a tree nearby, as in bordering areas of Nāgāland and Arunāchal Pradesh.[64]

Terracotta and metal icons of snakes, horses, bulls and elephants are symbolically sacrificed to wooden posts and effigies, in memory of ancestors, in Bastar Guḍis or temples. Terracotta bulls and elephants are offered to Bhāṅgārām and Māolimātā tribal shrines at Keshkāl. Sacrificial scenes are depicted in tribal shrines.[65] The Āṅgādevs or Pātdeos, made of sājā logs and bamboo cross pieces, peacock quills and jungle cock feathers, grass or corn stalks, bean and pulse pods, silver and rupees, are sprinkled with the blood of sacrificial victims in rites of nourishment and reproduction.[66] The display of aquatic, aerial, subterranean creatures, in the body of temple, in its pillars, on Paśupati, or in ornament and equipment, in Dakṣiṇa Kośala and Vidarbha, provides background to such symbolic sacrificial practices of unknown antiquity surviving in monumental arts of the area.

RESIDUAL SHARE IN SACRIFICIAL RITUAL

The theme of Paśupati at Tala as the recipient of residual offerings, inducing and overseeing a bounteous profusion of organic growth, is paralleled by the continuing practice of Barhonā or increase ritual, in Chhattisgarh, in which the last sheaves of grain are left standing in the field, with the belief that the corn spirit takes refuge in them.[67] The Naṅgā Baigā or Baigā Guṇiā makes rain and induces fertility by chanting Mohinīmantra, the hypnotic chant, or by invoking Ṭhākurdev, Anna Kuaṅrī, virgin goddess of food, and Baḍhāunādev, the lord of increase.[68] The Pardhān, Khariā and Muṇḍā stories mention the predicament of Ponomosor, who found none left to offer him sacrifical food after he destroyed the human race by a rain of fire. In these stories, Ḍākāirāṇī shows Ponomosor the surviving human beings on condition that, after death of one of the remaining human beings, Ḍākāirāṇi would have seven shares of the body of the deceased, while Ponomosor could claim the single share of the human soul and would never destroy humankind again. These stories remind us of the destruction wrought by Mahādeva's hosts at the sacrifice, organized by Dakṣa, in which Mahādeva was excluded from the offering, and invite allusions to the incorporation of the agnisomīya paśu in the body of Paśupati.[69] At the first fruit or new eating ceremony after death, the villagers are invited, among the Mariā Gonḍs of Bastar, to a feast called Harā Tānḍānā or eating of the remains.[70]

SHARED AMBIVALENCE

Bhagvān resides east of Maikal on an island, ringed by Āgnadī and Dāgnadī, two rivers of fire, in half life and goodness and half death and disease,[71] recalling ambivalent tendencies, benefic and malefic, associated with Tāntrik Śaivism, and the images of Rudra and Saumya Śiva, in Dakṣiṇa Kośala art.

WORSHIP OF MOTHER GODDESS

The worship of Śakti as the animating principle behind Śiva, which was in vogue in all of Dakṣiṇa Kośala, continues in the entire region till this day. Śiva presides at the convergence of Narmadā, Sonbhadrā and Johillā on the Amarkaṇṭak plateau, overlapping Chhattisgarh and Madhya Pradesh, which is known as the Śrīkṣetra. It is the triangular zone of the Goddess, ringed by three mountain ranges, Mekala, Satpuḍhā and Vindhya. Rajim is known as Padmāvatīpura or the City of the Lotus Goddess. The Danteśvarī temple is situated at the confluence of Shankhinī and Dānkinī rivers in Dantevāḍā. Sambaleśvarī or Samlāidevī is worshipped in Sambalpur in Odisha as well as in Sāraṅgarh in Chhattisgarh with the recitation of Devī Bhāgavata. Māolimātā is worshipped at Chitrakūṭ, Bastar as well as at Fiṅgeśvar, Raipur. Khameśvari is the Kula devī of Mainā Kings at Basnā in Mahāsamund. Chitāvarī Devī is installed at Dhobin near Raipur. Bamleśvari or Bamlāidevī presides over Doṅgargarh. At Ratanpur and Lāfāgarh, a fair takes place in honour of Mahāmāyā. Ambikādevī is worshipped at Ambikāpur in Surguja. Dhamtari has Bilāimātā as protective Goddess. Close to the junction of Bālamdināllā with Mahānadī, Sursuri Gaṅgā rises at Turturiā, in a constant susurrus of water, bubbling out of rock interstices, and is supposed to bring in waters of fifty two pilgrimage stations of the Ganges. It has been the place of a nunnery, both Buddhist and Brāhmiṇical, serviced by women priests.[72]

The Mother Goddess in general, seven Mother Goddesses in particular, found at Dakṣiṇa Kośala sites, are celebrated in contemporary folk art today. In Chhattisgarh and Eastern India, seven virgin women are shown going around a terracotta sculpture of Hara Gaurī in the Gaurī vrata or ceremony. In this vrata, the virgins pound rice and offer it to Gaurī before Diwāli and desire mango seeds and children. The Kuānvarī Bhanwar, the virgin circle, and the Suhāgin Bhanwar or the bride circle are created after the pattern of a marriage bower, with four pitchers at the four corners.[73] The Vṛhad Gaurī Vrata in Maharashtra conceives Gaurī as a bundle of nine wild flowering plants. Māriāyī in Maharashtra is the mother of Kannimārās or seven virgins and buffaloes are sacrificed to her as the earth mother.[74] Andhra Pradesh has Pochāmmā and Satāmmā, the elephant and tigress mother goddess.

The Yakṣīs, Apsarases, river and mother goddesses which adorn the temples at the cross roads of Dakṣiṇakośala, Kaliṅga and Vidarbha, remind us of the continuity of the practice of crossroad sacrifices or bali from Vedic till current times. Rudra and Ambikā are invited to accept such sacrifice in the *Śatapatha Brāhmaṇa*. Two of the companion mothers of Skanda are mentioned in *Mahābhārata*, Śalyaparva as catuṣpathaniketanā and catuṣpatharatā, housed at and fond of crossways. Māri-Āi, Śītalā Devī, Gaurābā are workshipped to avoid cholera, smallpox and measles in villages of Maharashtra. Mothers or their consorts like Āi and Bāī, Jogurāi or Jogeśvari, Mhālsā, Vīr, Mhāsobā or Khāṇḍobā, are offered gāmvā sai, ceremonial worship or sacrifice, at Cācchārā Rācchā or crossways, outside such villages, in the shape of double stones. Seven mother goddesses are worshipped as Sāti Āsarā, seven apsarases. Māvaelā Devī or water godesses are worshipped in Māval or Māmalahāra region of Maharashtra. They are mentioned in Kārle, in Sātavāhana inscriptions. This reminds us of the Māolimātā cult in the Raīpur region of Chhattisgarh. We are also reminded of worship and sacrifices, offered to Ṭhākurāin in south Bastar, Danteshvarī in Dantevārā, Bamlāi Devī in Khairāgarh, Kasikalī Devī near Boriā, Khuriā Rāṇi near Sannā, Sāt Bahinī Devī of Korwās, Kosgāin Devī of Kosgāingarh in Korbā.[75]

PRIMORDIAL DIVINE AND TRIBAL COUPLES

The interaction of Agni and Soma, fire and water, Sūrya and Varuṇa, and mithunas, is an active principle in the art of Tala and Dakṣiṇa Kośala. It is inspired by a view of universe, in which every element, every creative and procreative impulse is born out of the interaction of static and kinetic, of seemingly contrary but mutually dialogical principles. Pairs of apparent opposites continue to inspire the art of tribals of Dakṣiṇa Kośala till this day. The primordial couple is variously described by Goṇḍs as Siṅgāmāli birds, male and female, living in the midst of waters; as clay images, animated by Ponomosor into man and woman, by the Khariārs; as Singh Chāndo, the Sun, and Nindo Chāndo, the moon, by the Sānthāls; as Mulā and Mulāin, brother and sister, among Korkus; as Parhir Buḍhā and Baḍāmani Burhi, made of mud, by

Dharmā, among Bhuiyās; as Pilchurām and Pilchubuḍhi, hatched by birds, or as Hās and Hāsin, created at the command of Ṭhākur Jiu among Sānthāls, as Kavāchi and Kuhrāṃi, brother and sister, placed in a gourd in waters by Gajbhimul; as Tallur Muttāi and Kadreṅgāl, brother and sister, incited to desire by sago palm juice, or, as Bhūdeo and Bhūdevī, among Bison horn Māriās.[76]

Nāṅgā Baigā and Nāṅgā Baigin are the first couple, born in a state of nature on Kājli Van Pāhār or the collyrium dark elephant hill, through the instrumentality of Bābā Vaśiṣṭha Mooni or sage Vaśiṣṭha and Bāsmatī Kanniyā or bamboo grove damsel. The description goes like this. "The blood of all women in the world was in the well. That blood was like the sea; it was alive, it stirred with waves. When Naṅgā Baigin saw it, she laughed at the sport, and at her laughter the sea of blood fell calm. Then the blood sank down, down to the bottom of the sea that is below the world. When the blood was shut down there in the darkness, it began to ask, Who has imprisoned us here? It was living blood; it awoke; it rushed up through the earth; it spouted up in the well. It covered Naṅgā Baīgin's face, her nose, her arms, her belly, her legs."[77]

The Bhuiyā legend of Keonjhar in Odisha speaks of a demonstration by Gandhinidhi and Nighi to their Mātis or Bhuiyā children about how the iron ploughshare and wood could be treated as the penis and vagina, and the earth could be penetrated by yoking a bullock and cow to the plough.[78] Among the Kuntichokes in Ponḍi and Lāfā in Chhattisgarh, the mortar and pestle have been treated as a sexual pair, while, among the Lānjhiā Sāorās of Tarāb in Gañjām, Odisha, the hearth, made of baked earth, has been seen as vaginal in shape, with a small tip at top like the tip of the clitoris.[79] The Chelik boy and Motiyāri girl, at the Muriā Ghoṭul and Bhindiā boys and Dhāngri girls in the Juāng Durbār on Mānḍāgharh in Odisha undergo ritual of post puberty co-education. These Bachelor dormitories and club houses are carved with phallic and vaginal symbols, harking back to fertility symbols in Dakṣiṇa Kośala art. Jhoriās of Bastar have practiced ceremonial cross- dressing, reminding us of the blend of features in Ardhanāriśvara in the older art.[80] River Shivnath is associated with the story of the marriage of Gond girl Śivā with a Gond boy, by Gāndhāri or abduction mode.

COSMOLOGY OF WATERS IN TRIBAL LORE AND TEMPLES

Dakṣiṇa Kośala is still permeated by the idea of water cosmology, worship of all organic and inorganic elements in nature, associated with sacred waters. Tala temples were created at the confluence of rivers Sheonāth, Līlāgarh and Maṇiyāri. Between the 6th and 12th century, Śeorinārāyaṇ temples were installed at the confluence of Sheonāth, Jonk and Mahānadī; Rajim temples at the junction of rivers Mahānadī, Pairi and Sondhur; Deepadih at the meeting of rivers Suryā, Kānher and Galphullā; Harrāṭolā at the convergence of Kerākāchār and Mahānadī; Karṇesar Mahādeo at the union of rivers Mahānadī and Balkā. The Bhairamgarh Śiva temple is sited on Indrāvatī. The Ekādaśa Rudra Temple of Deogarh is situated on Rihānd or Reṇukā river. There are Śiva temples, sited close to waters, at Kalāri at Ghaṭiyāri, at Ganḍāi in Khairāgarh, at Tumbān in Kaṭghorā, at Gaṇiyāri in Bilaspur, at Nanesar in Bāgicā, at Ghāgrā and Sitāmaḍhi in Koriā, in Shaṇkar Khol Gufā on Chaiturgarh fort in Bilaspur, at Basesarā near Pendrā, at Lakṣmaṇeswara at Khārod, on Son river.

The cosmology of waters has been traditionally associated with the rotary cycle of creation and dissolution, and has continued from the older Dakṣiṇa Kośala art into contemporary tribal conceptions. The myth of Naṅgā Baigā and Naṅgā Baigin of Naṅgā Pāhār, Pāndpur, Mānḍlā, links waters in the human body with waters in the body of the earth. It speaks of days when no blood flowed from women during their period, and started flowing only when the Naṅgā Baigin cleaned the deep well hidden in the jungle, which would appear to symbolize female vulva.

The theme, described on Devarani door jamb, of resuscitation of the Sagaraputras by Gaṅgā at the instance of Bhagīratha, is parallelled by the Bhuiyā story of Kumbakarṇa Ruṣi, son of Bāghrāti. He is reduced to ashes by Gods for the sin of marrying Kanniyās or girls. He brings up Gaṅgā from the lower world on a Siyāri leaf cup at the suggestion of Mahāpurub. He is revived by Gaṅgā. The Kalpalatā, generated by the regenerative waters, along the temple door jambs, is recalled by the myth of Gaṅgā becoming seven great oceans of passions, elements and treasures, as fire, water, salt, milk, grain and wealth.[81]

THE COSMIC THEATRE IN TRIBAL LORE AND TEMPLE ART

The various elements of nature and heavenly bodies play out their act in the art of Tala and Dakṣiṇa Kośala as dramatis personae in the theatre of the universe. In the temples of the area, the drama of interaction of sun and moon, fire and water, is played out in the body of human being and universe. The waters are imprisoned and released, polluted and purified, channelized or released into flood. The fire burns, to destroy and fructify. Śiva, in his various manifestations, presides over this drama.

The vivid story of Rudra chasing Brahmā across the sky, to pierce him for his incest, is found in a mutated version among the Goṇḍs of Pāṇḍāriā, Rājneṅgi Pardhāns and Baigās of Pāṭangarh Māṇḍlā, in which Laxman is shown rushing, armed with a grass bow and arrow, in hot pursuit of Bijaldev Kanyā or lightning, the daughter of Meghrājā and Meghrāṇī, thunder being the noise of the pursuit. Laxman is replaced by Belkuar in the Devār legend in Donḍi Lohārā, while Bijaldev Kanyā becomes a shower of sparks, emanating from the full red moon, in the Dhanvār legend in Uprorā.[82]

The Uttarāyana or the northern ascent of the sun into the Makara or Capricorn constellation is accompanied in Bihar by bhūmipūjā or earth worship, bhitti śobhās or decorative painting, to celebrate the fecundity of the earth. The southern Dakṣiṇāyana movement of the sun into the Karka or tortoise constellation takes place at the time of dormancy of this creative urgency in the womb of the earth. It is accompanied by propitiation of mountain and forest spirits. These equinoctial and solstitial movements provide the back ground to the madhubanī paintings of vrata and utsava maṇḍalas, of celebratory geometric diagrams, equipped with gates and Kṣetrapālas.[83]

In Muriā myth, thunder is the noise made by Indra playing tipitcat with the clouds, or by Bhagvān rushing across the sky in his chariot.[84] Muriās explain thunder as the sound of the hammer, and lightning as the flash, which emerges from the anvil of the Lohār, the heavenly blacksmith, forging iron in Parrobhum, the upper world.[85]

HETERODOXY IN FOLK, TRIBAL AND ŚAIVA SECTS

The tradition of nature worship, heterodoxy and dissidence, evident in Pāśupata or Somasiddhāntin concepts and iconography of Tala, continues in tribal Chhattisgarh. Kādāmārā Sārṇā, Mahādevi Sārṇā are sacred precincts, full of Śāl groves. Temples, dedicated to Kādā or buffalo, are part of the Sāri Dharam of Orāons, Munḍās and Sānthāls in Chhoṭānāgpur plateau. Ṭhākurdev, Dulhādev, Bañjāridev, Doṅgarpāt, Masvāsipāt are tutelary gods of crops, household hearths, pastoralism, hills and hunting. Chithrāidevī is the Goddess of rags.[86] Kudarmal and Kavardhā are important to Kabir panthīs, who anathematize animal slaughter and sectarian distinctions. Gosāins or Śaiva ascetics have monasteries. Bairāgīs of Rājnandgāon wander begging for eight months outside rains. Nātha Siddha cult, Bhīmā Bhoi, Sahajiā Śūnyavād, Piṇḍa Brahmāṇḍvād and Satnām have prospered in Chhattisgarh and Western Odisha. At Kāleśvarnāth at Pithampur, nude Nāgā sages stage unique bridegroom procession in honour of Pañcamukhī (five faced) Śiva.The mahimā dharma of Odisha, which celebrates the alekh, anādi, ananta, nirguṇa, nirañjana, indescribable God, without beginning, end, attributes or colors, continues the tradition of Vāssā Bhānnā tribe of Utkala Janapada, described as ahetuvādīs, akriyāvādis, preachers of causelessness and actionlessness in Majjhima Nikāya. Shaṅkara Daśanāmī, Rāmānandī, Nimbārka Vairāgins continue to live in traditions, deviating from established religions.[87]

At Tala, one of Śiva's roles is presumably, to delude enemies of God, as an outcaste and heretic, before enlightening them; to subject them to their beastly nature before releasing them; to permit both Vedic and Tānrik approaches to theodicy; and to give room to both good and evil simultaneously. A role model for Naṅgā Baīgā, Liṅgodev, Barā Deo, Āṅgā Deo, Śiva Paśupati would appear to have contributed to the pantheistic and unorthodox character of sectarian persuasions.

THE PATRONAGE NETWORK

A study of the ethnography of the art of the region can not be completed without exploring the network of patronage. Acquisition of merit, promotion of religion, public welfare and development of natural resources figure prominently in royal charters of Dakṣiṇa Kośala and Vidarbha, which provide for the maintenance of monastic establishments. The charters of maṇḍala kingdoms of Odisha see villagers in the neighbourhood as kith and kin (pratinivāsi kuṭumba janapadāḥ), and announce the objective of promoting their happiness and welfare (sukhena prativāstavyamiti).[88] Noble or royal women patronize arts, in partnership with their consorts. They dedicate images of iṣṭadevatās, personal deities, offer them music and dance, accompany their preceptors on pilgrimage and construct monasteries to house the faithful. Names of temples and tanks announce autonomy of women. Vākāṭaka and Bhaumakāra grants are made to promote agriculture, by providing house to cultivators, reclaiming land, and nurturing biological, aquatic and natural resources.[89]

Patronage is given to public works not only by the aristocracy, but also by people at large. The suffix karaṇa and prefix Śrī in the names of Śrī Hetu karaṇa and Śrī Bahu karaṇa, inscribed in 7th century AD characters at the base of the gaṇa and makara pedestals at the access of Devarani temple, suggest their association as scribes, civil servants or merchants, with the enlargement of and installations at the Tala temples.[90] The honorific Śrī signifies their homage to Gaja Lakṣmī on the Devarani door jamb for causing and increasing abundance. The inscribed gaṇa may be an attendant of the Rudra Śiva on its left, Rudra Śiva being identified as Gaṇapā Diṇḍi or gaṇādhyakṣa. In later medieval inscriptions of Odisha, gaṇadaṇḍa is prefixed to Vīrabhadra, the chief deity of the republican Bhañjas, reminding us of the identification of the daṇḍa bearing Rudra Śiva as gaṇa Vīrabhadra. The Ganeśa in the sub shrine on the right of the access to the Devarani temple may have been installed as a patron deity by Śrī Hetu karaṇa and Śrī Bahu karaṇa, for blessing the renovation carried out by them as representatives of a guild or gaṇa, and, for invoking vāstospati, guardian of the house, at the inauguration of the work. The collective nature of the performance of Vedic sacrificial rites, management of Buddhist monasteries or the discharge of duties by chieftains of republics have also been signified by the word gaṇa.[91] All these circumstances suggest association of guilds of merchants, artists and religious orders with the construction of temples and monasteries in the region.

THE PATRONAGE INFRASTRUCTURE

Developed for their Gods by traders, priests and kings, the religious establishments are sustained by an extensive land and sea trade in Dakṣiṇa Kośala and Kaliṅga from 6th to 12th century AD. This trade is transacted through fortified mud, hill, river sea ports and dock yards, equipped with kulyās or canals. Remains of laterite ramparts, ditches, tanks, punchmarked Maurya, Sātavāhana, Magha, Mitra, Kuṣāṇa, Nala and Śarabhapurīya dynasties have been found at numerous sites in the region from the 3rd century BC till 14th century AD, in association with N.B.P. and rouletted ware, Roman coins, amphorae, Chinese celadon ware and coins, ring wells and brick temples.[92] Excavations have revealed the alliance of governance, trade, art and religion in the organization of market, storage, manufacture of trade goods and a commercially efficient urban infrastructure, at Sirpur in Chhattisgarh (Figs. 114-20).[93] Mason marks and names of engravers, goldsmiths and architects have been inscribed on foundation stones, images, pillars and copperplates at Sirpur. They tell us about the master craftsmen who gave shape to the ferment of ideas, catalysed by an alliance of the different sections of society.[94] Names of Buddha's disciples prove the existence of an established mercantile community in Odisha in 6th c. BC Rivers like Māhānadī have integrated Dakṣiṇa Kośala with Odisha on long standing mercantile routes. Temples have been shaped and named in Odisha after boats. Temple scenes attest the practice of using boats to transport trade articles, including elephants and mobile icons like Mārtaṇḍa Bhairava; worshipping Tārā and Maṅgalā and inscribing boats with names of near and dear ones, for protection on sea. Large boats continue to be made for trade on river Mahānadi.[95]

STATE CHURCH ALLIANCE IN CULT CONVERGENCE

Goods, skills, materials and ideas flow through trade arteries and contribute to a confluence of Buddhism and Śaivism in Dakṣiṇa Kośala. Such confluence is catalysed through a surge of devotionalism which unites cults like sāttvata, pāñcarātra Vaiṣṇavism, Bhāgavata, Pāśupata Śaivism and proselytizing, Mahāyāna Buddhism. Aśoka, in Rūpnāth edict near Jabalpur, speaks of his exertions to mix Gods, unmixed before. The Mahāmeghavāhana ruler Khāravela declares himself, in the Hāthigumphā inscription, to be a votary of all denominations, savapāsāṇḍapūjaka. He constructs and dedicates a dwelling for śramaṇas, yatis, tāpasas, ṛṣis, saṁghayānas, ascetics of diverse religious persuasions, hailing from all directions. Xuan Zang is criticized by Hīnayānīs of Oḍra for his inclination to Mahāyāna Buddhism, a sky flower doctrine like the Kāpālika sect. The Buddhist deity, Bhagavān Lokeśa, is worshipped in regions like Bonāi. Vaisṇava and Śaiva deities serve as roceśa devatās, objects of ekāntikā bhakti, single minded personal devotion, for vratikas or celebrants.[96]

The convergence of Śaivism and Buddhism is catalyzed by the spread, from Gujarat, of the Kaulākāpālikā, Mattamayūra Śaivasiddhānta system of Matsyendranātha, in Dakṣiṇa Kośala and Kaliṅga. Spiritual successors of Rudrasoma, sthānaguru of Bālesvar temple at Sirpur, propagate it by incorporating Mausula Rudra incarnations of Lakulīśa in the Lakula Pāśupata order, to enlarge their number. So strengthened, they contribute to the assimilation of Śaiva and

Buddhist features in temples. Lakulīśa comes to be shown, like Buddha, seated on full blown lotus, with disciples, in dharmacakrapravartanamudrā, turning the wheel of order, in Śiśireśvara, Śatrughneśvara, Paraśurameśvāra and Vaitāl deul temples in Bhuvaneśvara. Lord Jagannātha is seen as Buddha by King Indrabhūti, through jñānasiddhi, the Vajrayāna road of enlightenment through knowledge.[97]

STATE COMMUNITY ALLIANCE IN CULT CONVERGENCE

The fusion of Buddhism and Śaivism in Dakṣiṇa Kośala and Kaliṅga is further facilitated by the influence of local cults of hill and forest people, whose existence is attested by inscriptions issued between 3rd c. BC to 13th c. AD by Aśoka, Samudragupta, king Tuṣṭīkāra of Kālāhāṇḍi, Baudh and Ghumusura region, and maṇḍala chiefs. The ambivalent, generative, nutritive, zoomorphic symbols, geometric triangles and circles, hand prints painted in pre historic rock shelters of Raigarh and Sundargarh in bordering areas of Chhattisgarh and Odisha, are taken to be associated with fertility cults and Śābara tantra.[98] Āṭavika or forest people are mentioned by Aśoka in the 13th Rock Edict after Kaliṅga war in 3rd century BC. Local chiefs of Mahākāntāra, the great forests of Kaliṅga and Dakṣiṇa Kośala, are listed by Samudragupta in Allahabad pillar inscription in 4th century AD. Mahārājā Tuṣṭīkāra issues his 5th Century AD copper plates from Parvatadvāraka, the hill gateway to the forests of western Odisha, near Asurgarh, the hill fort. The association with hill and forest people is acknowledged in these areas in animal symbols like bull, lion, elephant, horse, snake, fish, scorpion, inscribed or punch marked on Maurya, post Maurya and maṇḍala coins. Peacock is the emblem of the Mayūravarāhas of Bonāi. Peacock and cobra are emblems of Bhañja kings of Mayūrbhānj. Śiva is worshipped as Baneśvara Mahādeva, lord of forests and adhisṭhāna devatā, presiding over Bonāigarh. Adbhesthumārī, Kicakeśvarī, Kāntakumārī, Daṇḍadevī, Dvārashuni are worshipped by tribals and Brāhmins. There has been a continuing, formal association of ritual jajmāni payments and purity pollution rites linking Garhjāt tributary chiefs, tribal sāmantas and upasāmantas, with Jāti or Kulabeherā Brāhmins from Śāsana villages and tribal headmen. Early medieval inscriptions of Sūlkis, eastern Gaṅgas, Tuṅgas, Śailodbhavas, Bhaumas, Bhañjas, Somavaṁśis of Kaliṅga, Chhindaka Nāgas, Nalodbhavas, Śarabhapurīyas of Dakṣiṇa Kośala bear evidence to the worship of diverse mutations of Śiva and Śakti as grāma devatās and grāma devatis, by Śabaras, Pulindas and Kirātas living in forests and hills.[99] The Śabaras of Śabarāimaṇḍala in Korāpuṭ have been associated with the worship of Mukhāliṅgam, Jagannātha and Liṅgāraja in Odisha, and Śabarīnārāyaṇa in Chhattisgarh. Muṇḍās and Orāons have been worshipping Bhairava as bhoktās, as both God and Goddess, during caitrapūjā.[100] Śabara, Kondh and Bhuiyān headmen have been consecrating kings. The kings, so consecrated, become regents for God, Rāuta, Devarāja, Ṭhākurrāja or Mahāprabhu, while deities of tribal association guard their palaces, at Bonāigarh, Keonjhar, as rāṣṭradevatās.[101]

NATURE IN ART

In consequence of its interaction with local cults, the art of Dakṣiṇa Kośala, Kaliṅga and Vidarbha shows a close intimacy and empathy with the creatures and features of hilly and wooded habitats. In this art, the snake chases a mouse or swallows a frog. Rams or wrestlers fight. A cow licks its calf. A mouse or squirrel climbs or descends a pillar. A bee sucks honey. A crab turns tables on a stork. Ascetics, deities and animals emerge from caverns in forests. Śyena and Kūrma citis appear at sacrificial sites. River and mother goddesses epitomize elemental forces. Wet bricks in Sirpur excavations carry pug marks of bears and lions. Male and female priests worship rivers, caves, palaces, gardens, mother goddesses and natural forces in osā, vrata, maha festivals. Śabaras worship icons in ittal māran or iditāl paintings. Brāhmin ladies honor Lakṣmī in Jhoṭi wall paintings. Sārhul processions are taken to places like Sāmat Sarṇā in Deepadih for sympathetic transcreation of vegetation and crops. Sarṇā Burhi is still worshipped by Sānthāls in Jhārkhand as Jahirā Erā, and by Bhuinyās as Ṭhākurāṇi Mā.[102]

The unique ethos of the art and architecture in Dakṣiṇa Kośala can thus be appreciated when we move back and forth from the textuality of iconology to the contextuality of ethnography. This can be done by trying to see how kings, queens, priests and merchants join hands to serve the people, riverine and sea trade, urbanization and agriculture. This alliance contributes to the interpenetration of sectarian persuasions with community based cults of nature and fertility. It gives the art of the region its innovative, experimental zest, and a non-hieratic concern with a complexity of imagery, drawn from diverse sources. It does not choke the wellspring of life and imagination by superstitious, analogical, magical theories about the universe. Instead, it reduces the seeming chaos to cosmos, by seeing and mirroring a regular succession of laws in nature and art.[103]

NOTES

1. The tendency in the medieval art of Dakṣiṇa Kośala to see all elements at once instead of seeing them as a sum of parts; to link each individual to the things that surround and happen to catch her/his eye; to merge the identity of individual units in an inanimate, patterned, orderly world of nature; to understand the equilibrium of pure relations, required by natural appearance; to clothe the idea of emanation and merger in concrete form; to enclose plants, animals and the universe in a deeply felt unity; to juxtapose familiar and unexpected objects, forms and impressions in ambiguous, startling and double images; to arrange figures in a hierarchy of relative importance rather than proportions; to use art to render visible rather than render the visible, find their echoes in modern art.

   The Blaue Rieter group, the Purists, Gauguin, or the Child Cult artists have moved towards a pantheistic style, intended to express emotions of flora and fauna, which we also notice in the art of Dakṣiṇa Kośala. The dense flora and fauna around Christ on the Cross by Gauguin, the lush, thick foliage in his South Sea painting, the leaf by leaf rendering of luxuriant vegetation in the Dream, painted by Henri Rousseau, evoke a respect for the volume, substance and unity of life, which we also find in the Proto Śiva panel or the Kalpalatā on the Devarani door jamb at Tala. The ambiguous and double images in Dadaism and Surrealism find their echoes in the art of Dakṣiṇa Kośala. A comparison is worthwhile between the concrete expression of abstract thoughts in the art of Dakṣiṇa Kośala and the definition of abstraction by Neoplasticists like Mondrian, as inwardness, brought to its clearest definition, as externality interiorized to the highest degree. As in Tanguay's dream perspectives, so in the art in Dakṣiṇa Kośala, the subject of meditation becomes the subject of art and one moves away from the direct emotional plane to the allusive and literary plane. Goldwater 1967: 309-10, Also, p. XXIII, figs. 7, 10, 42 for paintings of Gauguin and Rousseau. Chipp. 1968: 127, 132, 138, 170-71, 197, 201, 212, 252-3, 256, for quotations from Franz Marc, Kandinsky, Dubuffet, Tanguay, Klee and relevant discussion.
2. Roland Barthes 1957: 123-133, 149.
3. Strauss 1975: 5-18, 26-28.
4. Strauss 1978: 33-35, 39-40, 44-47.
5. Redfield 1953: 46-47, 56, 64-65.
6. Coomaraswamy 1927; Jayakar 1990.

7. Chakravarty and Bednarik 1997.
8. Debrett 1909: 140.
9. Elwin 1949: 433.
10. *Ibid.*, 159.
11. *Ibid.*, 402, 431.
12. Elwin 1949/91: 317, Elwin 1954: 200.
13. Elwin 1947/92: 249.
14. Elwin 1951: figs. 83-85, 98, 101-2; Postel and Cooper 1999: Figs. 132, 193-40, 256-9, 264-5, 269, 273.
15. Nelson 1909: 117.
16. Elwin 1951: Figs. 73, 75, 83-5, 95.
17. Elwin 1947/1992: 59, 189.
18. Postel and Cooper 1999: Figs. 130-35, pp. 70-72.
19. *Ibid.*, Figs. 100, 194, 196, pp. 57, 122, 124.
20. Elwin 1949/91: 163-64.
21. *Ibid.*, 102–3.
22. Elwin . 1940/86: 298-304.
23. Elwin 1949/91: 4-27,45, 153; *Ibid.*, 1940, 1986: 308-10.
24. Elwin 1949/91: 349.
25. *Ibid.*, 45, 174.
26. *Ibid.*, 154.
27. *Ibid.*, 485-86.
28. *Ibid.*, 182.
29. *Ibid.*, 144-6.
30. *Ibid.*, 149-50.
31. *Ibid.*, 49.
32. *Ibid.*, 129.
33. *Ibid.*, 349.
34. Debrett 1909: 45-50.
35. Elwin 1949/91: 273-4.
36. Dalmia 1988:41-49.
37. Elwin 1949/91: 7-8; Chapter 17, n. 120.
38. Jayakar 1990: 129-30.
39. *Ibid.*, 137.
40. Nelson 1909: 115.
41. Grigson 1938- 49: 193; Elwin 1947/92: 59, 189.
42. Nelson 1909 – 10: 108-9.
43. Grigson 1938/49: 188-89; Nelson 1909-10: 87; Debrett 1909: 45-50.
44. Elwin 1947/92: 119, 228-9, 258-60.
45. *Ibid.*, 252-8.
46. *Ibid.*, 240-43, 261-3.
47. *Ibid.*, 244-5.
48. *Ibid.*, 230-31, n. 6, 230.
49. Elwin 1949/91: 47.
50. Debrett 1909: 42.
51. Elwin 1940/86: 324-27.
52. *Ibid.*, 306-7, 339.
53. Kosambi 1962/83: 103.
54. Elwin 1940/86: 340-43.

55. Elwin 1949: 433.
56. Elwin 1940/86: 318-23.
57. *Ibid.*, 303, 312-13.
58. Elwin 1949/91: 317-18.
59. *Ibid.*, 431.
60. Elwin 1951: Fig. 98 on page 93, Fig. 192, pages 92-7.
61. Elwin 1947/92: 146, 153, 158, 173; Grigson 1938/49: 111-14.
62. *Ibid.*, 208 – 21, 225, 274, pl. 20, 280– 82.
63. Nelson 1909-10: 86-87, 90, 103.
64. Elwin 1940/86: 293- 204; Elwin 1947/92: 244-45.
65. Postel and Cooper 1999: page 56, fig. 103, page 59.
66. Grigson 1938/49: 197-204.
67. Nelson 1909-10: 78.
68. Elwin 1940/86: 349-50, 354-57.
69. Elwin 1954: 411.
70. Grigson 1938/49: 392.
71. Elwin 1940/86: 293-7.
72. Nelson 1909: 350 - 51.
73. Debrett 1909: 235.
74. Jayakar 1990: 228-47.
75. For discussion and representation, see Kosambi 1962/83: 84-94, 103-9, 131, Debrett 1909: 45, 93, 148, 209, 235.
76. Elwin 1949/91: 4-26, 61-2, 85, 181-83.
77. Elwin 1940/86: 283, 315.
78. Elwin 1954: 303.
79. *Ibid.*, 309-10.
80. Elwin 1947/92: 301-2, 330-31, 441-42, Varma 2012: 3 for Śivnath.
81. Elwin 1949/91: 96-7.
82. Elwin 1949/91: 61-2, 65-6, 91-3.
83. Jayakar 1990: 121-23.
84. Elwin 1949/91: 88-9.
85. Elwin 1947/92: 260-1.
86. Nelson 1909-10: 73-77.
87. *Ibid.*, 79, 85-87: O' Flaherty 1976: 26-7, 319, 375; P.K. Mishra 1997, in Mishra and Samal 1.1:XXV.
88. D.C. Sircar 1965: 387; *EI* 7: 141.
89. Bharadwāji, wife of Parṇadatta, gets a stone image of Viṣnu carved in the round and inscribed in second century BC Brāhmī Script at Malhār. Pandeya 2002: 6, 14, 33, 74. Alhā, wife of Koradeva of Tārādaṁśaka bhoga constructs vihārikā of Kailāshpur near Malhār to house Buddhist monks, āryabhikṣusaṁgha. The name Ḍiḍin is used for 10th-11th cent. Ḍiḍineśvarī temple, Ḍiḍin Āgeti and Diḍin Pāchati at Malhār. This Chhattisgārhi word is used for a wife living away from her husband as Pārvatī lived away from Śiva to do penance for a child. Queens Āmmādevī and Ābbānibbaḍḍi make grants to maintain devasthalas and maṭhikās at Sirpur, with offering of dance and music. Jain 1961/2005: 46,196-217; Shastri 1992: 37-45. Finds, including polychrome shell and glass bangles, suggest use of Ānandaprabhakuṭi vihāra, Sirpur, and Turturiyā near Bārnavāpārā sanctuary, as nunneries, and by women votaries. *IAR* 1955: 24-27. Raipur, Sāraṅgarh plates of Śarabhapurīya king Sudevarāja confirm donation by queen Rājyamahādevī to Brāhmins. Jain 1961/2005: 34; J.K. Sahu in Mishra and Samal 1.1:140. Vākāṭaka royal grants are made for the benefit of mātṛbhaṭṭārikā, mother and wife, at the instance of bhāryāmahādevī. Queen Rājallā Devi, wife of Prithvī Deva of Ratanpur, constructs Śiva temple at

Tummān in late 11th century. Vāchhallā Devi, wife of Jājalladeva, has Rudra Śiva Dignāga as Guru, and goes away on pilgrimage with Makaradhvaja Yogī, never to return, in 12th century AD Pandey 2002: 121, 126. Depictions in the arts of the region show that women use head gear, hair dress, jewellery, cosmetics, clothes of elegance, sophistication and complexity, and associate with men as equals in ceremonies. Construction of farmhouse or residence of ploughmen, abhyantaraniveśana or karṣaṇaniveśaṇa, is promoted by Vakāṭaka grants. Shastri 1999: 19. Bhaumakāra kings of Odisha issue copperplate charters in 8th and 9th century AD for making permanent endowments on principles of akṣayanivīdharma, laws of perpetuity. They give out land with forest, fish, waters, land, tortoise, mango, mahuā trees and marshes, and, as rent free holdings, Devadāya or Brahmadāya, to reclaim fallow or waste land, on the principle of bhūmichhidrapiḍhānanyāya. Umakanta Subuddhi, in Mishra & Samal 1.1:189.

90. Scribes in medieval Odisha inscriptions are described as karaṇa, karaṇika, kāyastha, dharmalekhin. Akṣapāṭalika or karaṇa are conferred as caste titles by kings of Odisha to bless marriages. Early medieval inscriptions and coins of Odisha mention hereditary vaṇikas, merchants and puraśreṣṭhins, custodians of properties of urban mercantile negamas, guilds. S. Tripathy, in Mishra & Samal 2:432; S.K. Panda, *Ibid.*, 468.
91. Bakker 1997: 99-101, 105-7 for identification of Rudra Śiva as head of gaṇas. Keśarī copperplate of Khijjingakoṭṭa for gaṇa prefix to Vīrabhadra. Jadumani Mahapatra,in Mishra and Samal 1.1: 250. For identification of the Rudra Śiva image as Vīrabhadra, see B.N. Mukherjee 2007: 15. For the use of the term gaṇa for the Buddhist saṁgha by Varāhadeva in Ghatoṭkaca cave inscription, or the collective performance of sacrifices, gaṇahoma or Śreṇiyāga by gaṇayāji, in Jāmb copperplates of Pravarasena, Shastri 1997: 3, 40. Excavation at Sirpur has yielded a white lime stone block, inscribed with the king's name, Śrī Mahāśivaguptarājadevasya in Kuṭila Brāhmī characters. It is engraved with the rectangular insignia of a traders' guild, and associated with the iauguration of a hall on boxed cell foundation and performance of sacrificial rites at a burnt brick altar. This strengthens the presumption of the performance of similar rites at the construction of a perambulatory platform on boxed cells by a traders' guild in 7th century AD at Devarani. Sharma 2012: 12, 14-15, pl. 213.
92. Rivers Arpā, Ib, Maini, Mānd, Mahānadī, Sheonāth, Hasdo appear to have served as arteries of trade, art, religion and administration. 6th – 7th century brick temple foundations and canals cut in the granite bed for a fort, have been found at Sirkaṭṭi on river Pairi, a tributary of Mahānadī. 12th century remains of a port have been discovered at Pālur, on Ṛṣitūlya river in Gañjām. Ancient river ports have been explored in Prāchi, Dayā, and Bhārgavī river valleys. Marine ports have been found at Khalkāṭṭapaṭṭana on Kuśabhadrā near Konāraka estuary or Mānikapatna on Chilkā Lake. Forts at Ārod near Dhamtari on Mahānadī, Jaugaḍā, Mārāguḍā in Nuāpārā, Asurgarh in Kālāhāṇḍi, provide relics of trade. See K.K. Basa, in Mishra and Samal 1.1.: 29-33; A.K. Pattanayak, in Mishra and Samal 1.11: 697-704 for coins found at Malhār, Barhiphar, Jaitpur, Chakarberā.
93. Trade and manufacturing equipments with use marks, from 6th – 7th century AD, have been found at S.R.P 10, S.R. P. 31, and from the south verandah of the Lakṣmaṇa temple at Sirpur, and at Malhār, Rajim, Turturiyā, Kabir chaurā and Jogimārā. Ancient mining pits, shafts and inclines have been found in acid volcanic belts of Sonādehi hill. Slag heaps are scattered on river bank of Pairi in Bindrā Navāgarh. Old gemstone workings and beryl, gold, diamond deposits have been traced in hill ranges around Sonākhān, Deobhog, Mainpur, Rāoghāṭ, Tel and Indrāvatī rivers. Ancient quarries nearby have provided materials for the construction of Sirpur. Sirpur excavation has yielded evidence of 80 ft wide roads, dotted with watch towers, wells, tanks, drainage channels connected with rivers, underground granaries, medicine shops, liquor stores, gold testing equipments, bronze plures used for Buddhist images, iron and copper ingots, shale, laterite, basalt, sandstone, wood and brick used in architecture and sculpture, moulds, querns, crucibles and various modeling and manufacturing equipments. Areas have been demarcated for various trades. Remains have been found, of a small bazaar, haṭṭa, inside, and a bigger

bazaar, penṭhā, outside the town. See A.K. Sharma 2009: 79-80; Sharma and Singh 2010: 19-21; *IAR* 1955-6:24.

94. Engravers Droṇa and Golasiṁha are mentioned in Sudevarāja's. Śarabhapura plates. Engravers Boppanāga, Gotranāga and architect Viṣṇudatta are mentioned in S.R. P. 5, Tivaradevamahāvihāra, and mason marks are found on its foundation stones. Name of Droṇāditya has been inscribed on the images of Tārā and Avalokiteśvara in Ānandaprabhavihāra. Kumārāditya and Droṇāditya have been mentioned on the sandstone pillar at the entrance of Suraṅgaṭila Śiva temple. 7th century AD Nāgari inscription of Śrī Vitṭhala on toraṇa gataway pillar of SRP 18 A, Shri Dhrūva Bala on Śiva temple SRP 24 pilaster, 10th-th century AD inscription of Viṭṭpāla and Tikam bang, on pilasters of reconstructed Śiva temple SRP 24, inscription of King Mahāśivagupta Bālārjuna donating 160 iron fans, 3 fire wood piles and paddy to Bāleśvar temple for feeding worshippers and Brāhmin priests, demonstrate the patterns of patronage at Sirpur, that cut across ethnic and class divides, stretching across a vast territory between Gujarat to Dakṣiṇa Kośala, from 7th to 11th century AD. Sharma 2012: 113, 122, 129. Expertise in metallurgy, in polishing and gilding bronze, is highly prized and carries personal signatures. A. K. Sharma 2009: 116-18. 19-21. 9th and 10th century AD Nala charters have been engraved by Padmanātha, son of goldsmith and trader Panḍi. Jadumani Mahapatra, in Mishra and Samal 1.1, 1997: 285.

95. Tāpassa and Bhalluka, merchant disciples of Buddha, are from Okkalata, Utkala, Odisha. Brahmeśvara temple frieze shows elephants being transported on boat. The jagamohana parapet at the Konārak temple shows a dancing Mārtaṇḍa Bhairava being carried on boat. At Jagannāth Purī, the calanti pratimā has been carried by boat in candana yātrā, the sandal wood journey. Names of semi-cylindrical, gourd shaped Khākharu temples like Vaitāl Deul remind us of boitā bandhanā, boat worship. Tārā, the Buddhist Goddess of protection, is seen in relief carvings of ship wreck scenes at Ratnagiri. Overseas traders, known as sādhavas, sārthavāhas, have been traditionally welcomed back through festive Khuderul Kuni Oshā rites of worship of Goddess Maṅgalā. Banana stem boats are still floated with candles in tanks, rivers and sea, on kārtik pūrṇimā or akṣaya tṛtīyā day, with the names of aā- kā-mā-bhāi, kith and kin, for their safety. Kaivarta fishermen continue to make large boats, called kusli, to float forest produce, salt, semi precious stones, on Mahānadī. P.K. Mishra, in Mishra and Samal 1.2: 641; A.K. Pattanayak, *Ibid.*, 698-99, 704-6; 713 PP. Mishra, *Ibid.*, 718-20.

96. For Aśoka's inscription, Jain 1961/2005: 171-2. For Khāravela's statement, C.R. Mishra, in Mishra and Samal 1.1: 116, 128, For comment on Xuan Zang, J.K. Sahu, in Mishra and Samal 1.1: 174–75. For spread of devotional cults, Umakanta Subuddhi, in Mishra & Samal 1.1:189-91; Agrawala 1970: 47-8; Shastri 1992: 171-76; Bakker 1997: 20,60-62.

97. Rudrasoma is Āmarda Tīrthanātha Kālabhairava from Āmardaka in Gujarat. 38 Mausula Rudra incarnations of Lakulīśa, descended in the spiritual lineage of Rudrasoma, are added to the 28 incarnations of Śiva, to complete 66 incarnations of the Lakula Paśūpata canon. Villages like Guḍāśarkara, jaggery and sugar, and land in village Lāṭa, named after Lāṭa or Gujarat, are reserved for teachers like Sadyāśivācārya and Sadāśivācārya from Āmardaka, the home of Sopariyā or Śaiva ascetics of Sopārā in Gujarat. See, with reference to Rājor inscription and Junvāni copperplates, Susmita Basu Mazumdar, in Kośala 2008: 87-98; Umakanta Subuddhi, in Mishra & Samal 1.1:190; L.K. Panda, in Mishra and Samal 1.2:503-5; and, B.C. Pradhan, *Ibid.*, 535-6, for discussions on dissemination of Lakula Paśupata cult and contribution of Āmardaka school in the spread of Tāntrik Śaivism in Dakṣiṇa Kośala and Kaliṅga.

98. Pandey 2002: 24. The abstract designs in rock paintings continue to figure in ceramic designs, auspicious drawings on wall or floor, piṣṭapañcāṅgula or palm prints in color paste, through medieval period, till this day, in temple and rural arts.

99. L.K. Mahapatra and Jagannath Dash, in Mishra and Samal 2.2: 819-20; Jagannath Dash, *Ibid.*, 847-48, 851- 53, 855-56; Jadumani Mahapatra, in Mishra & Samal 1.1:279; L.K. Mahapatra & Jagannath Dash, in Mishra & Samal 2.2:820; Pandey 2002: 13.

100. Śabaras discovered Śivaliṅgam on the crown of Madhuka tree and worshipped Madhukeśvara at Mukhaliṅgam. Śabara Daitāpatis have been included among the nine privileged servants of Lord Jagannātha at Purī, the Lord having been propitiated originally by Śabara chief Viśvavāśu. Śabaras mourn burial of the deity and celebrate transfer of his life substance, Brahmamaṇi, to navakalevara, the new body. As Śuddha Suār, they act as sevāyets, servitors to the deity, from anasāra day to the end of rathayātrā. They have been worshipping Lord Liṅgarāja of Bhuvaṇeśvar as bādus, or servitor priests, as Śabarīnārāyana at the confluence of Jonk and Mahānādi, and Śabarīnātha, in celebration of piṇḍabrahmāṇḍavāda, philosophy of soul over soul connection. See S.C. Panda, in Mishra and Samal 1.1: 87-88; L.K. Panda, in Mishra & Samal 1.2:499; L.K. Mohapatra, in Mishra and Samal 2.2: 708-9; Jaganath Dash, in Mishra and Samal 2.2: 856; K. Majumdar, in Mishra and Samal 2.2: 762. For bhoktā worship, see Jagannath Dash, in Mishra and Samal 2.2: 863.

101. Śabāras are said to have founded the Dhenkanāl state and selected the Pāl Lāhāra chief. Śabara headmen and Kondh Pātmāñjhis have been respectively crowning kings of Pal Lāhārā and Kālāhāṇḍi with jungle crowns. The Bhuiyān headman has been crowning the king of Keonjhar with suālatā jungle creeper and siāri leaf umbrella, and has acted as a horse to be mounted by him. L.K. Mahapatra and Jagannath Dash, in Mishra and Samal 2.2: 808, 819-20; L.K. Mahapatra, in Mishra and Samal 2.2: 201-209. Aśoka's designation of himself as upāsaka, devānām piyo, devaputra, votary, darling, son of Gods, in the 13th Kaliṅga rock edict, or Samudragupta's self designation as Lokadhāmadeva, God dwelling in this world, had shown the way to the local chiefs, for acting on behalf of their Gods. P.K. Mishra, in Mishra and Samal 1.1: 98-99, 100-102; Raicharan Das, in Mishra & Samal 2.2:989; L.K. Mahapatra 2005: 35, for chiefs as regents of God.

102. L.K. Mahapatra, Jagannath Dash, in Mishra and Samal 2.2: 825-36; Jagannath Dash, *Ibid.*, 851-52, 855-62; Sitakant Mahapatra, *Ibid.*, 880.

103. This is contrary to Frazer's suggestion about such beliefs being based on the weak foundation of false analogy, magic, superstition rather than on the rock of nature and scientific observation. He speaks of breaching, by the comparative method, 'venerable walls, mantled over by the ivy, moss and wild flowers of a thousand tender and sacred associations'. It is possible, in terms of his own statement, to hear, by attuning one's hearing, even in the stormiest weather, the distant chiming of the church bells of Rome, by the Lake of Nemi. See Frazer 1959: XXVI- VII, 739-40.

9

Origins and Influence of Tala Architecture

I have tried to reconstruct the plan, elevation, and other architectural constituents, as well as the mutual relationship of the two Tala temples. I have also looked at the sculpture which articulates the architecture, the way the architecture itself is sculpted and the way sculpture has acquired its distinctive personality or role from its place in the architecture. I have tried to understand the immediate origins of the style of Tala sculpture, and the meaning of Tala art and architecture. It is necessary now to set off the Tala style against earlier and later Indian art, identify its distinctive features, analyse the manner in which it reinterprets what it inherits, and influences the development of medieval Indian art and architecture. Having tried to understand Tala on its own terms, I shall now look at it in a comparative context, as a stage in the history of Indian art. I shall show that, contrary to recent hypotheses, complete isolation from the past or the future is not one of the features of Tala, however unique such features may be.

METHOD OF THE STUDY

Multilinear Evolution of Style

In discussing the influence of Tala on later Indian art, I have suggested that shallow and deep relief, the lean and the heavy body coexist in the style represented by Tala, and result in simultaneous stylistic movements in Dakṣiṇa Kośala at Malhār, Sirpur and Rajim through the 6th to the early 8th century AD.

The lean bodied Tala style of the older Malhār fragments appears to have travelled to the Lakṣmaṇa temple by early 7th century via Svastika vihāra or Gandheśvara temple in the 6th, come back to the Bhīma Deval temple early in the 7th and then moved through several phases at Rājīvalocana from mid to late 7th century.

In a second simultaneous movement, the heavy bodied idiom of Tala style is at work in the Rāmacandra temple maṇḍapa at Rajim in the 6th century, and then, after moving on to the Ānandaprabha vihāra in the early 7th century, this idiom appears to overcome the Rajim style in the prātolī door jamb and western gateway pillars by late 7th early 8th century.

A third movement appears to have also originated from the Lakṣmaṇa temple, laden with Tala memories, to simultaneously transform the brick temples of Chattisgarh, like Rāmacandra at Sirpur, Indal Deul at Khārod, Siddheśvara at Palāri, Kirwāi Dhobin near Dāmākheḍā, through approximately AD 625 to 700. The same movement, modified by the Rājīvalocana experience, informs the work at Śavarīnārāyaṇa at Khārod, and the stone temple at Aḍbhār in the 8th century. The movement continues into the 9th century and influences the Pujārīpāli brick temple of Raigarh district.

All the three movements pick up elements from the Tala style, multiply their use inside the temple, as well as on its external facade, and come together, to contribute to the making of the Odisha style. No unilinear evolution from a single source is suggested in these stylistic movements. And yet, the sculpture appears to grow harder and stiffer with time, substitute appearance of movement for movement itself, or ornament for modelled form, while the architecture experiments initially with general elaboration of constituent features, and then, with their multiplication, flattening, constriction and compression.

Having examined the implications of the Tala style for the evolution of temple architecture in Dakṣiṇa Kośala, I have discussed individual temples, to demonstrate how the Tala motifs and configurations are adapted and transformed at these, before being transmitted outside Dakṣiṇa Kośala. The vibrant internal space of the Tala access areas is externalized to quicken the outer facade of Central Indian and Odisha temples to life. The graduated, terraced, processional access of Tala, partially translates internal spatial planning of vihāras or caityas, into the arrangement of segments in freestanding temples, and thereby, influences the spatial composition and elevation of vihāras of eastern India. The coincidence of linear and plastic tendencies and a continuing sense for volume and simplicity, even after it is rejected in much of Central India, characterise Tala and other Dakṣiṇa Kośala sites including those of Bastar and Surguja, which are treated as peripherial even to provincial Dakṣiṇa Kośala. I have further shown that the efflorescence of a second classical style takes place in 9th century Surguja, when the rest of Dakṣiṇa Kośala is getting frozen into set, schematic moulds, and this is due, to no small extent, to the natal connection retained by Surguja with the extraordinary fervour of the early classical style at Sisdeori, Tala or Malhār.

Comparative Perspective

I am aware of the pitfalls in my venture. My attempt to dissociate the development of style from the uncertain and controversial evidence of inscriptions or dynastic sequence, could well culminate in the artificial construction of an autonomous, self-determined, unilinear and irrevocable sequence of styles. To avoid this pitfall, I have moved, what may appear to be far afield to other sites. I have discussed the problem in fixing the internal sequence and chronological situation of individual sites, while investigating their connections with, and graphing their distance from Tala. I have examined the simultaneous contribution of 'Gupta Vākāṭaka' sites to the unfolding of the morphological sequence in the art of Dakṣiṇa Kośala. I have not confined myself to a study of the exclusive bearing of Tala motifs or patterns on Dakṣiṇa Kośala, because that would have linked Dakṣiṇa Kośala with Tala in an impossibly harmonious, impermeable, architectonic construct, which does not really exist. Moreover, since most of the material on Dakṣiṇa Kośala is newly excavated and unpublished, such deliberate concentration on Tala would confuse the tracks and distort the perspective about the multilinear stylistic sequence. The proposed classification of this sequence, in spatial and temporal categories, is to be taken as a mere code or a key for unravelling the little examined language of this corpus. It is not sacrosanct and the different phases may well overlap. With new information, the chronological boundaries may become sharper and clearer, though, it is hoped, the broad design will survive.

INFLUENCE OF EARLY INDIAN ART

Motifs Not New

The vocabulary of Tala is not new. Though it is related to the Gupta-Vākāṭaka vocabulary, which is nearer its time, its elements have already appeared in the art of the three centuries before and after Christ. Colossal yakṣas and yakṣīs, carried by dwarf gaṇas, makaras, or installed on pedestals, have a long history extending from the second century BC examples at Bharhut. The gaṇas, siṁhas, gajas at the Jethani pillar base can be traced as early as Sanchi stūpa I in the 1st century BC. Prancing addorsed siṁhas, lotus rhizomes emerging from makara mouth or held by dwarfs, full or half lotus medallions, narrative panels on the inner lateral sides of Tala door jamb have already served as the principal decoration at both Sanchi 1 and 2. The perception of the human being as an integral part of the world of plants, animals and nature (Figs. 157, 203, 207), or of the heraldic role of the siṁha, the use of flowers and fruits to frame panels, the display of the elephant protome as a structural, basal element (e.g. Figs. 154-55 at Pitalkhorā vihāra and Kārle caitya) large male figures in triple flexion (Figs. 384, 386), makaras (Fig. 538), have been as characteristic of Tala as of early Indian sculpture and architecture.[1]

Yakṣas, nāgas, śālabhañjikās, which are so much in evidence at Tala, dominate the art of Sanchi, Bharhut or Amaravati, and continue to dominate the art of Mathura in the first three centuries AD.[2] Lions of Tala pillar bases appear at the throne bases below Kuṣāṇa kings or Buddhas. Makaras on architraves or bases, lotus medallions on pillar posts, figured panels or floral rhizomes on the inner side of door jambs, prancing lions in the capital, figures carved on at least two sides of corner pillars, have been part of the stūpa architecture of Mathura and Sanghol. Half embedded proto-Śiva or gaṇa busts appear above Devarani river goddesses, and several Jethani figures are carried by other figures. A similar convention of showing an animal directly below the feet and a human head or couple above a yakṣī on pillar posts has been in vogue at Mathura and Sanghol.[3]

INFLUENCE OF GUPTA VĀKĀṬAKA ART

It is, however, in the late 4th to early 6th century AD, in, what is conveniently classified as Gupta and Vākāṭaka art of northern India, Vidarbha and the Deccan, that most of the ornamental motifs of Tala or its broader themes, inherited from early Indian art, come into abundant use as an integral part of architecture. In its overall style, Tala relates to the later phase of this period. However, the Jethani temple retains a closer affinity with the earlier phase of the Gupta Vākāṭaka period than Devarani, which seems to more immediately anticipate the later trends in Indian art. This would appear to place Jethani in the late 5th and Devarani in the early 6th century. The truth of this can be illustrated by a comparison of Tala with Gupta or Vākāṭaka temples from the first half of the 5th century, the second half of the 5th century, and, finally, with the so-called post-Gupta style all over India, including the regional style of Dakṣiṇa Kośala.

INFLUENCE OF EARLY 5TH CENTURY 'GUPTA' SITES

Stylistic Change in Temple Plan

In the first half of the 5th century, Udayagiri cave temples 4, 6, 7, 19, Sanchi temple 17, Tigavā Kaṅkāli Devī temple, Eran Narasiṁha temple, temples at Dārrā, or Tumain, with their simple plan of a garbhagṛha and a maṇḍapa, and with an occasional antarāla, foresee, in essentials, the plan of Devarani temple. Similarly, seeds of the Jethani plan are found in surviving remains of early 5th century Eḍuka shrines, in brick or stone,[4] consisting of successive bhadrapīṭhas, or receding, pilastered terraces, culminating in a garbhagṛha on top, notably in examples at Pavāyā (Fig. 136), Lauriā Nandangarh, or Baigrām. These recall mulitiered Buddhist stūpa shrines and anticipate the gradual elevation, obtained through successive pillared, pilastered and stepped terraces, topped by a constricted garbhagṛha, at Jethani. A specific and important Tala feature like the aśoka leaf, dangling from a cluster of fruits, is also seen on the plinth of the Pavāyā temple and on the kalaśa base of a Mathura column.[5]

In Pillar Order

Specifically again, the entire pillar order of Tala is visualized at early Gupta sites. The square, heavy kumbhaka of Jethani pillars is seen at the base of early Gupta pillars, and the very tall kumbhaka of the Devarani maṇḍapa pillars harks back to Udayagiri cave 19 and Tigavā Kaṅkāli temple maṇḍapa. The further segmentation of the pillars into octagonal or sixteen sided portions is more architectonically rendered at Udayagiri, with straight edges, imperceptibly merging into one another. These segments are provided occasionally with rudimentary petal tips, which assume some prominence towards the end of this phase at the Tigavā temple, anticipating the successive bands of overlapping petals, that are often filled with designs in high relief at Tala. In the first half of the 5th century, the pillar or pilaster segments are not sharply differentiated, demarcated or independently emphasized like Tala (Figs. 276). The fluting on the shaft is vertical, and is very seldom varied by the diagonal bands of Tala. The profile on the surface is even, unhurried, smooth, and the flutes extend, in spite of the segmentation, from all directions, to the top. The need, so radically present at Tala, to vary this profile by projections, recessions, decorative bands, intrusive sculptures or varying widths or heights of such elements, is not yet felt. This remains true even in the detached 'Gupta' pillars or pilasters of Pipariyā[6] or the 'Vākāṭaka' pillars of Kevala Narasiṁha or Rudra Narasiṁha temple at Ramtek (Figs. 288-89). In these, apart from a grāsapaṭṭi, a śobhāpaṭṭikā or lotus medallions, the shaft is left plain, and the decoration, maintaining a certain uniformity of design, remains restful to the eyes. Twin-bodied, single-headed, addorsed lions do appear earlier at the abacus corners of the pillars, in the maṇḍapas of Sanchi temple 17 and the Tigavā Kaṅkāli temple, at the basement of a votive stūpa from Gokarṇeśvara in Allahabad Museum or on the Udayagiri hill top pillar (Fig. 275). Protruding human heads appear earlier at the four corners of the base of a Besnagar pilaster. These are, however, carved in relatively low relief and merge imperceptibly in the pillar surface. Later at Tala, similar lions or gaṇas are carved in high relief on the pillar base, and protrude from darpaṇas or corners of the pillar shaft, and break the visual or tectonic continuity of the pillar (Figs. 252-53, 257).[7] The decorative floral bands of Tala are anticipated by a Uparkot cave pilaster and a Mathura column, carved with diagonal, spiral floral bands. However, even in these, the decoration respects the uniformity of the pillar surface and does not warp its continuous ascent. However, at Tala, these spiral bands are not used all over, but only on part of the shaft and are carved in higher relief, which is visually accentuated, unlike before, by sharp projecting segments above and below (Figs. 241, 243-46, 252).[8]

In Door Jambs

In a similar way, despite motifs in Tala door jambs being anticipated by the elements in early 5th century Gupta temple door jambs, the cutting is deeper, harsher, more clearly articulated and stylized at Tala, more so at Devarani than at Jethani, suggesting a greater proximity of Jethani to the Gupta style. In the early 5th century temples (Figs. 201-06) of Sisdeori, Udayagiri, Tigavā, Tumain, Dārrā, Bilsadh, Eran or Sanchi, the door jambs have, among them, all the elements of the Tala door jambs, including the winding vallīśākhā, the spiral mālāśākhā, the pillared stambhaśākhā, the figured rūpaśākhā, the foliate puṣpa or patraśākhā. The chequerboard design of the Jethani eastern pillar appears on Eran Narasiṁha temple, Bilsadh, Pipariyā and Tumain doorframe, or Mirpurkhās Buddha panel, mostly for dividing panels of the rūpaśākhā or framing sculpted panels.[9] The spiral bands of the Devarani mālāśākhā appear already in the Udayagiri pillar top doorframe, in Udayagiri cave 6 door, at Uparkot, at Sākor Śiva temple, around the padmavitāna in the Kaṅkāli Devī temple at Tigavā, in a Mathura door jamb lintel, or in the stambhaśākhā of a Jankhāt door jamb fragment.[10] The rows of flowers, usually five petalled, strung together on the stambhaśākhā of the Devarani door jamb, are noticed at Udayagiri cave 4 doorframe as an independent projected band; on Udayagiri cave 19 maṇḍapa door, as an independent band, though not projected; on Eran Narasiṁha temple doorframe, as a band preceding mithunaśākhā, and going all over to frame the door lintel; in the Tigavā Kaṅkāli Devī temple doorway, as two independent bands, framing the padmavitāna or the phalakas; or on the pillar abacus of a Varanasi door jamb (Figs. 202-03).[11] Even the enormous pillar, lying at the Devarani doorstep, with a tall square base, and a pillar shaft embedded in its top recess, is, to some extent, an amplification, on a colossal scale, of the Udayagiri cave 6 stambhaśākhā, with its square base and a top niche showing a pillar in high relief (Fig. 255).[12] The kīrtimukha, Aśokalumbī on kalaśa, floral bands with central bosses, living creatures entwined with rhizome, makara or haṁsa with foliate tail, nara riding vyāla, gaṇa caryatids or attendants, overhanging canopy of leaves and fruits found at Tala, have surfaced already in early 5th century Mathura doorframes, Pipariyā and Sarnath columns, in door jamb or lintel fragments from Mukundarā at Koṭā, or in the lotus rhizome on the processional panel from Garhvā in Lucknow Museum (Fig. 157, 187, 272, 559).[13] The single, long stem, wrapped all the way up by the leaves of an winding creeper, which frames river goddesses on Devarani maṇḍapa side walls, or the Jethani antarāla door jamb (Fig. 167), and the location of the rūpaśākhā on the inner surrounds of the Devarani antarāla door jamb, figure earlier in the door jamb at Bilsadh, U.P.[14]

JETHANI CLOSER THAN DEVARANI TO EARLY 5TH CENTURY 'GUPTA SITES'

Door frames Compared

And, yet, while the Tala temples share motifs with early 5th century door jambs, they use and carve such motifs differently, with growing complexity and preciosity. The early 5th century door bands are arrayed side by side, inviting a direct, frontal inspection, and stressing horizontals and verticals. The Tala door bands are arrayed obliquely to one another, stressing spirals, diagonals and curves, even while respecting the vertical or horizontal accents in the stambhaśākhā, in an attempt to draw in the viewer's attention, narrowing and focusing it. The panels of the rūpaśākhā in the earlier door jambs are smaller, more uniform in size, divided by similar decorative bands. The Devarani rūpaśākhā panels are of different sizes, divided by different decorative bands. The figures in the earlier panels are fewer, standing at an incline, at an easy flexion, contained within the frame, set off against a blank background. The Devarani figures are many, arranged in a crowded composition, heaving to a side like a surging wave, projecting or spilling out of and across the frame, against a background, which is all but invisible under the multiple layering of figures and heads (Figs. 157, 202-03).

Similarly, the lotus rhizomes, the vertical or spiral floral bands in the earlier door frames at Udayagiri, Mukundarā, Gaḍhwā or Tumain are carved in lower relief, and modelled with a feathery, soft touch. The stems or tendrils of the rhizome sedately glide up in longer, statelier curves. Their edges are rounded off and assimilated to rounded contours of female bodies (e.g. at Garhvā) (Fig. 463). At Devarani, the winding stem forms quicker, shorter curves as it rushes up in explosive bursts of floral waves. All flowers, leaves and petals are executed in much higher relief, with sharper turns and twists, deeper undercutting, and more distinct volume. In particular, one can see how the spiral bands in the earlier door frames are in the nature of incised surface patterns, while at Devarani these bands are thick, twisted braids, with independent substance. Deeply gouged hollows form dark troughs of shadow, which are harshly outlined against the keen, sunlit profiles of the rhizome. One is reminded by this of the late 5th century door jambs of Bhūmarā, Nācnā, Deogarh or Ajanta, where the coiling, swirling floral eddies disgorge square or round beads of froth and foam, suggesting the churning motion of a whirlpool. One can further see how, in a single vertical row, flowers are set close to one another in the earlier doorbands, and how, at Devarani, this row is doubled, strung out across a lower layer of petals, connected by eye-shaped floral links, and let down from small kīrtimukhas, enhancing its visual impact (Figs. 162-66).[15]

Altogether, the earlier doorbands are more like decorative designs which are visually more restful, being architecturally integrated with the temples. As against this, the Devarani door jamb projects and recedes, galvanized by a greater play of light and shadow, assuming almost an autonomous, visually indeterminate aspect, independent of the temple itself. While this effect, as we have noticed before, may not have been consciously striven for, a need to use the stone as a malleable, tractable substance, adaptable to a more ornamental effect, appears to have been felt more keenly at Devarani than in early 5th century sites.

On the other hand, the flowers and stems on the Jethani door jamb stambhaśākhā, lying prone across the south steps, the spiral floral bands of its pillars, the floriate tail or face of its makaras or muktāgrāsas, are carved with a longer sweep, against a relatively empty background, in lower relief than Devarani, suggesting a greater proximity of Jethani to the early 5th century doorbands. The rhizome on the pillarets flanking the Varuṇa image at Jethani is carved volumetrically, leaving little neutral background, but without much undercutting, recalling, in this respect, the substantial volume of the rhizome, carved on early 5th century pillars at Mathura and Bilsadh. It is also evident that, on the Jethani door jamb, the craving for demonstration of virtuosity, or the preference for the sharp, oblique slant, and coloristic, bichromatic visual effect are much more subdued than in Devarani (Figs. 192, 197-200, 243-45).

However, once the modelling of the flora on Jethani south door jamb is compared with door jambs from early 5th century Sisdeori (Fig. 201), it appears to be harder and stringier, done with a more precise, sharply drawn, and dryly chiselled contour. Unlike early 5th century, when the floral and faunal elements exchange their life and shape freely without losing their natural, individual shape, the composite kīrtimukha on Jethani south pillar and the composite latā on the Jethani south door stambhaśākhā are rendered as highly stylized and decorative forms, in which natural shapes are translated into artificial combinations. Their lack of bombast or crowding should not blind us to their elongation, desiccation or hardening, characteristics shared with late 5th century sites, though the beading, squaring or looping which overtake the flora at late 5th century sites, have left the Jethani flora relatively untouched (Figs. 259-62).

Jethani also seems to be closer to early 5th century sites (Figs. 551-52), in retaining a greater feeling for natural animal form than Devarani. The loops and curves in the foliate makara tail are still few, and the foliate face or hair of a kīrtimukha or lion still retain some resemblance to hair or mane (Figs. 546-47). At Devarani the makara snout or tail, the head or whiskers or the kīrtimukhas are completely invaded by geometricized floral loops, twists and spirals (Figs. 171-72, 268-72). However, already at Jethani, the natural scales of the early 5th century makara tail have disappeared, and the disintegration of the organic faunal form into floral patterns has begun (Figs. 532, 535).

INFLUENCE OF EARLY 5TH CENTURY 'VĀKĀṬAKA' SITES

Early 5th Century Pillars

Closer to Dakṣiṇa Kośala, in early 5th century Vākāṭaka temples of Vidarbha (Pl. 3; Fig. 276), the elements of Tala architecture are foreseen in a similar way. Remains of two Vākāṭaka brick temples at Boṅgo Huḍki and Bholā Huḍki and a brick temple on the bank of Bāhārḍi tank at Mānḍhal show stirrings of the later architectural style in Vidarbha and Dakṣiṇa Kośala.[16] At Bhogārāma, Guptārāma, Kapotārāma, Trivikrama, Varāha, Rudra and Kevala Narasiṁha temples, at Ramtek, Sindūra Vāpī or Karpūra Vāpī step wells, we find full or half lotus medallions on pillars, with corners occasionally filled by petals, forming squares like the Jethani southeast pillar or the Jethani garbhagṛha ceiling slab. However, the medallions do not touch one another, nor cover the entire pillar in a crowded design like Jethani (Fig. 258). Except for a grāsapaṭṭi or śobhāpaṭṭikā, much of the pillar is left plain and unadorned. The pillar of Kevala Narasiṁha temple has bands of linked multipetalled flowers, foliate forms with central bosses, or vandanamālā designs, which also appear in Jethani east pillar or Devarani door jamb. The modelling, however, is shallow in comparison with Tala. A pillar in Trivikrama temple has a leaf with a cluster of small fruits on the kalaśa at base, a motif, which transfers itself on the Jethani east pillar to the kalaśa at top. The Trivikrama temple also has very tall square bases for its corner pillars like Devarani or Jethani east. However, the relative proportions of the base and shaft are more balanced, and made to a more human scale (Figs. 288-89).

Half or full lotus medallions on dwarf pillars, lion heads or architraves, mithunas in rectangular recesses, dancing dwarfs, creepers on rosette patterns, staṁbhajāla or lattice work on temple walls, pillars, square at base, octagonal, faceted or cylindrical in the shaft, and square in the capital, at Besnagar, Sisdeori, Ramtek, anticipate such features in rock cut caves of western India including late 5th century Mahāyāna caves of Ajanta and in temples of Tala and Dakṣiṇa Kośala (Pl. 9; Figs. 279, 286-91).

Vedibandha

Apart from sharing similarities in the pillar order with Tala, temples at Nāgrā, Mānsar, Ramtek also possess vedībandhas (Figs. 137-43, 543) with a rectilinear profile, like the Devarani jagatī and vedībandha, with their flat mouldings and a very tall kumbha (Figs. 77, 80). The Tala like mouldings are usually followed in Vidarbha by a plain, recessed kandhara, or a kandhara with a vedikā of recessed niches and projected galapādas. Later at Jethani, on the surviving portions of the jagatī and vedībandha on the west, similar kandharas with niches and pilasters are found carved in the brick cladding, suggesting the existence of kandharas on the original stone facade of the temple (Figs. 73, 75). Even in Devarani vedībandha, a narrow antarapaṭṭa with dwarf pilasters can be made out. The Nāgrā brick temple in the early Vidarbha school also displays a similar arrangement below the jaṅghā niches. Unlike Ramtek, the kandhara pilasters at Tala are not carved with floral relief or cavorting pramathas. Unlike the small, simple temples of Ramtek, where kandhara pilasters and niches serve as almost the only ornament, Jethani and Devarani use these as a frame at the base of the huge, sculpted wall slabs, as a narrow band in the vedībandha, as much taller recesses and projections on the jaṅghā, the lintel, and even on the pīṭha of the later platform. Thus, as sculpted ornament, integral to architecture, and enhancing it, these mouldings are put to a greater variety of uses at Tala (Figs. 54, 82-83, 90, 92, 179, 197-99, 547). The makarapraṇāla with a śuṇḍamakara and a water channel, the eight cisterns or altars below the platform of the Rudra Narasiṁha temple, are other features anticipating the makarapraṇāla on the northwest of Devarani and some of the altars found at the flanks of Devarani and Jethani.[17] At Mānsar, in the early half of the 5th century, the boxed, brick cell foundations, retaining walls, designs and motifs are anticipated.[18]

Pillared, Processional Access Cave and Vihāra Architecture

Several elements of Tala architecture have already made their appearance in the early cave architecture of Maharashtra, Bihar, or Odisha in the three centuries before or after Christ. The pillared halls of Koṇḍane, Pitalkhorā, Bedsā have addorsed animals and riders looking down from the pillars in aisles on either side of the nave, witnessing the visitor's approach to the stūpa at the end of the hall. Mithunas look in from the niches in the sidewalls of the verandah of the entrance hall at Kārle caitya. These arrangements anticipate the unusual processional access of the Tala entrances, specially Jethani south, with its large figures on pillars and wall slabs, watching the approaching worshipper on the route or from the flanks (Figs. 8-11). The Gajalakṣmī panel, so prominent on Devarani lintel, have its ancestors on Sanchi I toraṇa architrave or the door lintels of Udayagiri-Khaṇḍagiri caves in Odisha, vihāra 7 at Nādsur, or vihāra 4 at Pitalkhorā. The specific motif of chequerboard design or basketlike patterns on Jethani pillars, has already appeared on the lintel of Lomaś ṛṣi cave entrance in Bihar, or on the flanks of the arch above the cell doorways of vihāra 7 at Nādsur.

Temples and Vihāras

In the latter half of the 5th century, these forms are seen in greater abundance, in more complete shape, executed in more complex convolutions, and in bolder relief. The pillar and door jamb are more ornamentally conceived, and the figural sculpture, when it forms part of cave architecture, becomes larger and heavier, though, not necessarily more monumental than the smaller images of early 5th century, thereby setting the trend for the decorative and figural style at Tala. The penetration of the internal space by pillars, by sculpted side slabs, which face one another, charging the intervening space, has been noticed as a trait of early cave architecture (Figs. 290-91). This feature is further accentuated in Ajanta, Ghaṭotkaca, Kānheri or Bāgh caves and manifests itself in the processional access to the Tala temples. This enumeration of architectural features, illustrative rather than exhaustive, shows the futility of recent attempts to link Tala with the dynastic Gupta - Vākāṭaka or southern art on the ground of one architectural motif or another. The vocabulary of motifs, used at Tala, does not sprout suddenly into existence, under the influence of near contemporary imperial ateliers. It shares a common corpus of cognate themes, inherited impartially by all Indian art centres. Stylistically, there is little in common between the austere, but ornate, stylized and yet vigorous style of Tala, and the sensuous, naturalistic, though equally vigorous style of earlier centres like Mathura and Sanchi. Yet, the surviving feeling for flora or fauna in their natural form, quick with the beat of life, remains with Tala as an emphatic legacy from early Indian architecture and sculpture. An indirect echo of the Jethani plan can be detected in the plans of the rock cut vihāras. They have a vast, laterally spread space in front, narrowing down into a short, constricted garbhagṛha, and possess cells at the sides rather than at the back of the garbhagṛha, like Jethani.[19]

Pillar Features

The temples or architectural members of Nācnā, Bhūmarā, Marhiā, Deogarh, Sarnath, Mūrti from the late Gupta period, demonstrate a convergence of stylistic tendencies closely verging on those at Tala. Apart from sharing the broad features of plan or figural style with late 5th century sites, Tala shares ingredients of its pillar order with them. The pillars and pilasters, specially of the Ajanta cave, are miśraka like Tala, and are equipped with tall square bases and decorative bands on the shaft like padma and ardhapadma, darpaṇa and ardhadarpaṇa, maṇipaṭṭikā, muktādāma, grāsapaṭṭi, chequerboard patterns and ghaṭapallava. The darpaṇas of Ajanta, like those on Tala pillars, enclose patravallī, yakṣas, makaras, ihāmṛgas or haṁsas. The corners of the square sections, which contain full lotus medallions, are filled, like the Jethani south pillar, with foliate ornament, and very little space is left between the full and half lotus medallions. Vertical or spiral fluting of pillars becomes common at Ajanta like Tala,[20] and two lion bodies with one head, found on Jethani pillar bases, often adorn the corners or crowns of the square pillar base at Ajanta. Instead of gaṇas at bases or lion worshippers at the corners above such bases like Tala, Ajanta pillars display gaṇas around the āmalāsāraka, that uphold the śīrṣaka as well as figures with attendants on the capital and couples at corners above the square bases. Prancing lions flanking a grāsakiṅkiṇika appear at Ajanta on the impost block below the capital like the Jethani south entrance pillar. A succession of octagonal, sixteen or thirty-two sided bands on pillars have been rendered in a plain manner earlier in the 5th century, offering the vaguest notion of petalled edges. These edges assume, both at Tala and Ajanta, full-fledged and unmistakable forms of petals. Vṛkṣakās, framed by thickly clustered leaves and fruits, occupy the pillar capital at Ajanta and remind us of the river goddesses, or rock embedded proto-Śiva busts from Devarani door jambs, aureoled by leaves and fruits. Rosettes threaded together by eye or lozenge shaped flowers, which appear in Devarani door bands, emerge at Ajanta above pillars, to frame panels on three sides in cave 2. Leaves dangling from clusters of fruits, carved on pillar kalaśa, are found in similar situation in Ajanta cave 19. Tiger heads, looming large and menacing over crossed claws, are seen on Jethani south lintels and siṁhagavākṣas, and also appear in Bāgh cave 2, on lintels in candraśālās, or interspersed with candraśālas.[21]

Frames and Foundational Elements

If the elements of the Tala pillar border or doorbands are found at Ajanta, the elements of the Tala door jamb are found at other 'late Gupta' sites as well. Patra, ratna, khalva, mithuna, rūpa, stambha, mālā, vallīśākhās are found on the door jambs at these sites. Like Tala, the rosettes on these door jambs are mostly strung together vertically by eye or lozenge shaped flowers. The spiral bands are filled with flowers. Palm leaf scales and chequerboard squares, found in Jethani south sculptures and east pillar, invade the late Gupta doorband and window frames. The stambhaśākhā projects emphatically out. Only the doorbands are still arrayed side by side instead of projecting and receding like Tala. The tall, rectilinear pīṭha or vedībandha of Jethani and Devarani, already anticipated at Bhitargānv and Ramtek, becomes, more and more, a general feature at such sites, not only for temple bases, but also for pillar bases, specially inside cave temples.[22]

DEVARANI CLOSER THAN JETHANI TO LATE 5TH CENTURY SITES

Greater Movement

It would appear from the overall analysis, that Jethani retains a natal connection with early 5th century sites to a greater extent than Devarani, or than some other later 5th century sites. At the same time, it breaks away from early 5th century by preferring the syncopated rhythm of pillar segments, the decorative fusions and flourishes of floral designs, and the dynamic internal spatial organization of late 5th century. However, Jethani is left behind by Devarani in its decorative dexterity and versatility, which stamp Devarani as something of a culmination of late 5th century trends. With growing virtuosity and an attempt to surpass themselves, the Devarani craftsmen appear to have inducted the dynamic mobility, confined in late 5th century sites to the movement of the rhizome, and at Jethani, to the internal arrangement of architectural members, into the very structure of the door jamb, and galvanized it with the undulating motion of a wave. The wave swells from the bāhyaśākhā to the seething crest of the stambhaśākhā, to roll and subside on the heaving, unquiet surface of the laterally placed rūpaśākhā. And yet, this vibrant unrest is not allowed to go wild, but is disciplined by the firm, sure verticals of the grooved channels of the stambhaśākhā and the clear horizontals of the lintel and sur lintel, radiating up and down. Thus, while Jethani nudges close to the styles of sites in late 5th century, Devarani seems to follow, poised at the threshold of the 6th century and immediately thereafter.

Unique Elements in Tala Architecture

This tentative dating of the Tala temples can be now assessed in the light of the features of the architecture that follows. The question of the impact, if any, of the style represented at Tala, on later Indian architecture, will also enter such an assessment. In order to gauge this impact, we have to stop for a moment, look at the unique way the Tala temples reinterpret the earlier architectural forms, and determine, if such reinterpretations do or do not influence the later architectural repertoire.

Terraced Plan

Looking for unique and unprecedented elements of architecture at Tala, we find that Jethani is really the first temple known to have survived in Indian architecture, with a direct three door access to the garbhagṛha, the southern access being much larger than the eastern and western.

For the first time in temple architecture, these three accesses to the Jethani sanctum and the eastern access to the Devarani maṇḍapa are designed as staircases (Figs. 6-11, 42, 85), which serve also as proto-maṇḍapas, antarālas or ardhamaṇḍapas, with walls on either side, made of vertical slabs, carved with figures on the inner face. The installation of the rūpaśākhā on the inside face of the Devarani antarāla door jamb, and the placement of the river goddesses on the side walls of the Devarani maṇḍapa, are also variations and modifications of the same lateral emphasis, adapted in the carved side wall slabs of the Tala steps, an emphasis missing in earlier temples. The southern steps to Jethani are, in a fashion never tried before, varied in width, and punctuated by pillars and pilasters, to create a proto-catuṣki. The sarvatobhadrikā Jethani south pillars are also unprecedented, being faced on all sides, with carved blocks and slabs, to occupy several steps (Figs. 43-44, 46, 56). The huge Devarani pillar, carved with a recessed pillar shaft, towering like an independent structural member, above the wall slabs at the parapet entrance (Figs. 255-56), has also never been seen before.

Pillars

The swelling volume of the rhizome on the Varuṇa wall slab (Figs. 259-60), the delicate, shallow relief on the door jamb pilaster (Figs. 60, 258), the projecting lions, or climbing mouse in high relief (Fig. 252), and the low relief floral bands on the west side pillars and pilasters (Figs. 243, 246-47), the geometricized makaras on south pillars (Fig. 56, 58) and the human looking makara or gaṇa below the south door jamb at Jethani (Figs. 532-33), demonstrate a simultaneous variation of pace, bolder and more experimental than ever before. The coexistence of features like the highly ornamental door jamb and stark pillars at Devarani (Figs. 85-86, 248, 250-51, 255), the blank facade outside and the profusion of sculptures inside Jethani (Figs. 52, 67, 72-73), the austere, olympian figures on side walls or pillars of Jethani (Figs. 54-56, 351-52) and the frenetically active, volatile and expressive dwarfs carrying them (Fig. 52), the enormous monolithic pillars and figures, and the finest minutiae of ornamental patterns, chiselled out on the smallest fragments or figures (Figs. 44, 157, 268, 448, 470), speak of the same adventurous, experimental ardour.

Replication of Elements

An inventive use is made of forms like ghaṭapallava, worshipful siṁhas, kīrtimukhas, padmalatā, that keep on sliding or mutating into one another (Pl. 17; Figs. 161, 167, 170, 175, 178, 252-53, 257, 260, 262, 269, 311, 429). Repetitive, but extremely innovative use is also made of the same spiral floral bands on the door jamb, pillar shafts, garlands, lotus medallions (Figs. 243-48, 252). Many uses are also made of the motif of a square floral band with a central boss, in the pillar shaft, crown, armlet, waistband (Figs. 311, 350, 470); of the lotus, in a cap, a hand, and a head (Figs. 347, 353, 362, 397, 426, 428, 489, 490, 546); of the palm leaf scales, on a mace, a pendant and the trunk of a bull (Figs. 197, 473-74). This reveals a playful fertility of imagination, without an earlier parallel, an imagination, which uses standard elements to myriad surprise effects, enlivening the structure. The crouching elephants backing up the Jethani garbhagṛha and flanking a devakūlikā, the elephant and tiger protomes forming the bases of pilasters in the Devarani door jamb lintel (Figs. 179-81), the makaras occupying darpaṇas on the Devarani maṇḍapa pillar shaft (Figs. 268-72), rearing lions on Jethani pillars (Fig. 236-38) are unusual, not seen in similar situations or sequences before. The use of lotus petals to generate as many as sixty-four flutings on the pillars, which rise tall and sheer in the Jethani south or Devarani east maṇḍapa, the insertion of vertical rows of petals or flowers to frame panels, sculpted slabs or doorframes, the introduction of curving loops, spiral twists and diagonal turns in floral elements (Figs. 53, 86), reveal a similar stretching of convention to unconventional, surprising limits. The narrow garbhagṛha at Jethani, equal sized antarāla and garbhagṛha at Devarani, are also surprises. The use of the narrow āmalaka, compressed between ghaṭas, as a crown of the pillar capital (Fig. 256), and piled, one above the other, as the pillar itself (Fig. 254), is also a novel element, not in vogue before. The monumentality, scale, primeval vitality of cave architecture appear, for the first time, to transform and vivify temple architecture.

Experiments in Conservation

Even the later additions to the two Tala temples in brick or stone, offer examples of novel experiments in conservation. For one thing, nothing like the complete brick cladding of a stone temple, carved with vedikās or pilasters appears to have been tried before. The idea of having boxed cells, filled with brick and stone rubble, and paved with stones, to create a protective and ambulatory platform around Devarani, is recent.[23] When one remembers that this platform culminates on the north and southeastern ends of Devarani into two subshrines, backed up against the staircase, and is approached only from the northeast by an extension, equipped with two side staircases, and, probably also with a pillared roof (Figs. 7, 10, 80-81, 90-91, 94), the novelty introduced in the earlier arrangement becomes evident. In the mouldings of this platform, the jāḍyakumbha, carved with half candraśālās or mithunas, seated with legs dangling on the edge, or standing in a specially cut notch, the snake chasing a mouse, slithering in and out of the jāḍyakumbha and kalaśa; the candraśālā, flanked by pecking parrots; the nibbling haṁsas or cakravākas, carved across the recess of kapotāli; the aśoka or campakalumbīs, pending from clusters of fruits on the kalaśa, emerge as an original combination of elements in pīṭha mouldings (Figs. 92-93, 95-97). The notion of spanning and binding together the sloping and unstable ground around Jethani, with extended tentacles of low brick walls, is an adventure in structural conservation, shared with Vidarbha.

Advances Made

Many of these ostensibly unique elements, found in the architecture at Tala, surface in later architecture. These elements appear in new mutations, combinations or locations in eastern, western, central or south India. Direct impact of Tala forms seems to be felt in Dakṣiṇa Kośala itself. And yet, it would be quite inappropriate, even in Dakṣiṇa Kośala, to attribute developments in later architectural history, directly to the plan, designs, motifs or style of Tala temples or any other individual temple. Tala architecture is significant only in marking, fearlessly and emphatically, an intensification of the transition from classical Gupta Vākāṭaka to experimental forms of early medieval architecture. A significant attempt has been made at Tala, to transfer the monumental and colossal scale or processional access of cave architecture, to temple architecture; to stress the importance of sculpture as an integral, constituent element of the inner spatial disposition of architecture; to enhance the plastic value of floral ornament in both sculpture and architecture through many innovative uses; to point to the possibilities of the flexible, repetitive but effective use of similar decorative motifs in diverse compositions or locations; and, to help in the process of breaking out of the classical mould, without losing hold of the classical vocabulary.

INFLUENCE OF TALA STYLE ON DAKṢIṆA KOŚALA

EPIGRAPHIC EVIDENCE

The bridges between the Tala style and the styles of later Indian art are fairly clearly revealed in the art of Dakṣiṇa Kośala from the 6th to the 8th century AD. As we shall see in detail later, there are difficulties in charting the sequence of this art. The inscriptions, including Lakṣmaṇa temple inscription, or the Nala and Kalacurī inscriptions of Rājīvalocana temple, have been generally found detached from their original location, or inserted in course of successive additions. The Sirpur Lakṣmaṇa temple inscription has been dated differently over the range of more than a hundred years, without a thoroughgoing comparison of the styles either of scripts or of monuments. As a result, the art of Sirpur has been placed variously from the beginning of the 7th to the end of the 8th century AD. Because of the additions to temples like the Rājīvalocana or the Rāmacandra at Rajim, as well as extensive and often inaccurate restorations, contradictory conclusions about the sequence have been reached. Assumptions have often been made about the recutting of the sculptures, or resetting of door jambs, without carefully analysing the implications of such assumptions for the chronology of related monuments. Thus, the art in these monuments, it would seem to me, has been dated without considering its connections with works of the region, including the earlier work of Tala, in a consistent manner.[24]

STYLISTIC MOVEMENT

The way the elements, inherited from earlier art, are adapted and reused in Dakṣiṇa Kośala, and thence transmitted to other parts of India, also remains to be examined. Once we undertake this examination, we find that the accent at Tala on carving interior pillars and side walls, gradually gives way to an accent on the carving of the external facade. At the same time, the verticalism stressed at Tala in the sheer height of the plinth, pillars or wall slabs, is slowly replaced by short recesses and projections, which break up the wall plane in a crescendo of lines rushing upwards. The slow, gradual, stepped ascent of the structure, the broad segments, emphasized by heavy mouldings, koṣṭhas and makaratoraṇas at Tala, or by siṁhakarṇas and karṇāṇḍakas in early 6th and early 7th century brick temples, make way for a mass of narrow, compressed and flattened structural and figured segments, indistinguishable, in a distant view, from the surface of the elevation. The structurally differentiated, tactile form, inviting intimate, proximate physical touch, gradually turns into a visually undifferentiated mass, animated by chiaroscuro, inviting a single, synoptic, distant view. In the words of Riegl, the haptic becomes optic.[25] The rendering of plants, flowers or living beings, in their organic unity, so important to Tala, becomes more and more deemphasized, and these finally end up as subordinate patterns, giving life and mobility to the temple itself, Such trends towards stylization are already perceptible at Tala in the occasional intermeshing of diverse forms, in the preciosity of decorative motifs, and in the vivisection of internal space by an asymmetrical array of sculptures. These trends come to the surface in what follows, so that the three dimensional sculpture, used to compose and model the space inside, takes on the nature of two dimensional drawing, carved on the external surface of architecture, in fairly high relief (Figs. 145-53).

PHASE 1 (AD 525-75): THE RUINS AT MALHĀR AND OTHER EARLY SITES

AMBIVALENCE

The initial phase of the impact of Tala style is spread approximately between AD 525 to 575. The architectural style, that carries the imprint of the Tala style, is characterised by a simultaneous attempt to make both voluminous as well as slender images like Tala; to imitate the virtuosity of its style by executing undercut foliage, full of crests and depths, galvanized by light and shade; to at once execute shallow and high relief; to use the processional access, lined with figured slabs; and to emulate the massive scale of Tala, misunderstood in amorphous, laterally spread or over elongated modelling.

The closest affinities to the Tala style can be seen at Malhār, in a few side slabs, door jambs and pillar fragments, lying (Figs. 210-13, 313-14) in the compound of the Bhīma Devala temple on Motisāgar tank, in a pillar embedded in the wall of a villager's house (Fig. 277), in a Malhār pillar in the Raipur MGM Museum (Fig. 278), in some sculpted architectural fragments in the local ASI site museum, and in the foliate mouldings in Odishan temples (Figs. 149-53). Maliphula phadikā, or the motif of leaves, wound around a stem, common to Tala and Odisha, is most frequent at Malhār, where they frame the figured side slabs, and the door jamb fragments lying in the site of the Bhīma Devala temple (Figs. 152, 211-12, 312, 314). The heavily undercut padma or kalpalatā on Devarani door jamb, intertwined with small figures, becomes the gelaba in Odisha, with the figures being shown much more prominently and visibly (Figs. 162, 187, 232-34). At Malhār, however, this motif appears with or without figures, as a partly finished foliate band, on a fallen door jamb, and as a frame for the river goddess slabs, forming part of door jamb. It is as deeply undercut, and as full of dark voids as its Tala counterpart.

On the other hand, the swelling, tangible volume of the padmalatā, which wends its way gently upwards, to frame the door jamb with Gaṅgā, near a ruined temple beside the ASI Museum at Malhār, is conveyed, unlike the Devarani temple, without resorting to excessive undercutting or negating the tactile surface of the stone (Fig. 261). This volumetric rather than corrosive utilisation of the stone surface, for rendering the natural shape of padmalatā, reminds us of the natural shape of padmalatā on the pillars flanking the Varuṇa image at Jethani, while its slow meandering movement recalls the delicately spun latā on the stambhaśākhā of the Jethani south door jamb (Figs. 259-60, 262).[26] At Malhār itself, this plastic form may be earlier, and precedes the precious mannerism of the padmalatā on the Bhīma temple site door jamb. Like Tala, tall slender figures of Śiva, Pārvatī, Dūrgā, Ardhanāriśvara are carved on wall slabs, and stand on bhāravāhī gaṇa bases (Fig. 211). The band dividing the figures from the bases, shows rosettes in squares, like Tala. At the flanks of the bases, a lion with scrolled feet rears up, holding jewelled festoons in its mouth like both Tala and Odisha. Also common is the thickly clustered bunch of leaves above the river goddesses. The additive blocks of Tala pillars, carved with gaṇas or makaras, facing different directions, have been eliminated at Malhār, integrating the top and base in a frontal stance. As against Tala, a growing preference is evident for a certain symmetry of posture and proportion. The bevelling of the door jamb at Devarani gives it a strong inward curve, and is partially retained in the Malhār door jambs. However, its impact is diluted by carving the river goddesses on the front, or by fluting, flattening and bifurcating the stambhaśākhā.

In a similar ambivalent way, the Malhār pillar in the Raipur Museum (Fig. 278)[27] relates to Jethani (Figs. 252, 257), while two pillars at Malhār, at the Bhīma Deval site, and in the wall of a villager's house, relate to Devarani, and anticipate 8th and 9th century pillars and door jamb segments of Sirpur in Mahāsamund and Deepadih in Surguja (Figs. 228-31, 279, 415). In the pillar in Raipur Museum, the approach to design used in the Jethani east pillar is employed. It is similarly carved into segments by a growing number of petalled flutes, by bands of flowers with a central boss, rosettes, muktāgrāsas, and ghaṭa āmalaka, which substitutes seated gaṇas and bull protomes at its corners for the garland bearing lions on ghaṭa āmalakas of Tala. The square capital is carved with a scrolled haṁsa which, in its easy, gliding movement, shallow, soft, curvilinear contours, recalls the composite latā on the stambhaśākhā of Jethani south jamb. The slightly steeper shape and stiffer movement of the haṁsa, the multiplication of small projecting figures on the ghaṭa āmalaka and the flatter petal tips, indicate a later date than Tala. The shafts of these pillars show pilastered panels of mithunas, gaṇas, grāsamukhas, jātakas, scrolled haṁsas, gaṇas in octagonal sections, rosette bands and fluted semicircular sections. The spiral, decorative bands of Jethani pillars or Devarani door jamb are now reduced to vertical or horizontal bands and the projected figural elements of Tala are recessed. The multiple layers of figures, convulsed by an oblique, sideways movement on Devarani door jamb, are replaced by a few figures, arranged frontally on the foreplane of a relatively shallow background. Sharply incised lines, stylized into decorative patterns, encompass the shallow panels, and replace the organic and bulging sculptures on Devarani door jamb or Jethani pillars. In fact, the scrolled haṁsas or kapotas flanking the candraśālā on later Devarani mouldings, appear to possess greater volume, smoother and more fluid contours, a bolder and surer hand than the haṁsas or peacocks on the Malhār pillars (Figs. 277-78). Even the simple, unadorned, shorter, later Devarani pillar, sculpted with four small, well modelled gaṇas at the corners above the base, appears to precede the Malhār pillar in the Raipur museum. Thus, though derived from the Tala tradition, the Malhār pillars, like the carved slabs, seem to follow all of Tala.

SIRPUR VIHĀRAS AND TEMPLES

Translation of Elements from Tala Ground Plan

This phase at Malhār appears to be followed by a group of vihāras (Figs. 281, 283, 285) and ruined temples (Figs. 110-13) at Sirpur[28], preceding those constructed under the Pānduvamśi king, Mahāśivagupta Bālārjuna (595-650 AD). The tradition of constructing and restoring Buddhist vihāras appears to have already become an old one in Mahāśivagupta's reign. Hence, inspite of being a Śaiva, he allows the maintenance and construction of Buddhist vihāras. The recent excavations[29] at Sirpur have provided a wealth of detail, demonstrating emphatic links of the Sirpur style with the Tala style, in the use of sculpture to mould architecture. The links are evident in the heavy, moulded plinths, makaramukha gargoyles emerging out of the plinth, the perforated stone work of lotus rhizomes in door jambs, the decorative repertoire of the door jamb and all over figural sculpture of the pillars, the hair style, ornament, gestures and postures of couples, and, in the innovative and experimental imagery of snakes chasing mouse, pendant aśoka leaf, lotus medallion, animal fights, jātaka stories (Figs. 107-08, 216-20, 279-80) Only, the figures are more elongated and attenuated, the manneristic flexion more accentuated, the decorative foliage more pervasive and fussier than Tala.

The combined use of stone and brick in the structures in this phase presages the later Devarani structure at Tala. Large sculptures, carved from dolomite blocks, were installed in caitya arch niches in the walls as bhadra devatās as they were installed in the walls along the Tala temple stairs. The hand made tiles and wood used in Bālārjuna's house[30] gives rise to speculation concerning the material used for the Tala temple, specially the roofing over the later Devarani platform. The stellar plan in the Sirpur temples (Figs. 110-11), anticipated by the 5th century temples at Mānsar, anticipates, in turn, such plan in Dhobin, Palāri, Indal Deul, Kharod, Deepadih, Sāmat Sarṇā temples (Figs. 12-13, 29, 31, 35-37, 106, 121-23, 132). The graduated access, through pillared segments, to the sanctum at Jethani Tala, is replicated and elaborated in the pillared and segmented access of the Pañcayatana Baleshwar temple complex (S.R.P. 9),[31] Śiva temples (S.R.P 11, 15) or the Buddha vihāras (S.R.P 4.5, 10) (Pls. 12-13; Figs. 20-21, 23-24). The raising of the maṇḍapa of the Śiva temple S.R.P 15 on brick boxes of nine squares, and the use of iron dowels to join stone flocks have their parallels in Jethani and later reinforcements at Tala. Different from Tala is a polychromatic use of materials like vesicular, mottled, iron rich laterite, with dark brown or brick colour, purple sandstone, with green chlorite spots, pink or buff shale for architecture and sculpture; black, polished granite or white stone for Śiva liṅga, dolomite for pillar uprights, cuddapah stone blocks for toraṇa dwāras; fragile silt stone for minute sartorial or ornamental detail, and, corbelled brick with lime plaster for decoration[32]. A broad, processional access, tall plinth, array of figured pillars at the entrance and flanks, recessed mouldings with pillarets, aśoka leaf, snakes, slithering in and out of the vedibandha are characteristics shared by Sirpur temples and vihāras (Figs. 106, 108-09) with Tala temples (Figs. 83, 96-97).

The ground plan of the vihāras (Figs. 20-24, 111, 219, 281, 285) constructed during Mahāśivagupta's time,[33] consists of a hypaethral central courtyard, flanked by a pillared vīthikā, giving entry to residential cells on either side, with a shrine and side cells at the back. This plan is best in evidence in the Ānandaprabha vihāra. This plan reminds us of the south approach of Jethani with its pillared catuṣki, sculpted side slabs and niches, and the central cells, with side cells at the back to the north. The courtyard is approached by an antarāla and a maṇḍapa, the former being larger than the latter, like Devarani . Sculpted slabs on the lateral walls look in from either side like Jethani and Devarani steps. The colossal, nearly 4 m high pillars, with tall square bases and capitals, with chamfered octagonal shafts, flank the entrance to the maṇḍapa. Huge mudgara (mace) bearing dvārapālas are carved on pilasters on the left side of the door to the antarāla, rising more than 3ms high. Pedestals for similar figures survive on the right. The bases are carved with flower, citron, purse bearing yakṣas, carry remnants of the feet of images, and survive against the side walls of the maṇḍapa. Door jambs are recessed and carved with figured and foliate sculpture. All these features remind us of the array of figures lining the processional approach to the Tala temples and the inward propulsion of their door jambs . Iron nails, sockets, probably for holding timber roofing, remind us of the sockets on the inner side of Devarani door jamb and iron clamps found on Jethani steps.

The flanks and soffit of the inner surround of the door jamb (Figs. 216-18) of the Lakṣmaṇa temple and several vihāras are carved, like a Jethani south pillar and Devarani door soffit, with half-circular and circular lotus medallions. However, they are filled in the Ānandaprabha vihāra by mayūras and makaras, and linked by the motif of a leafy meander around a central stem, while the base is formed by peacocks carrying pearls in their beaks (Figs. 223-24). The lotus medallions have lost the natural shape (Fig. 258) found at Tala. However, the leafy meander, which surfaces later at Odisha as maliphula phadikā, retains its distinct shape from the Devarani maṇḍapa side walls or the Jethani south door jamb. The scrolled plumage of the mayūra or makara is fussier than Tala (Fig. 226). Compared with the haṁsa/peacock on later Devarani moulding, the peacocks at the Ānandaprabha vihāra are described by more linear incisions, while their plumage acquires repetitive, stylized, sharply demarcated, squarish edges, which exist only in embryo on the plumage of the later Devarani haṁsa/peacock. The band of round flowers, linked by cylindrical ones, or the rows of beads, framing the peacock in the vihāra, have become somewhat common, artificial and inorganic in comparison with their counterparts on the Devarani door jamb. Later in Odisha, the scroll framing haṁsas becomes the haṁsalatā scroll, issuing directly from the peacock on the inner surround. Here at Sirpur, the haṁsas or peacocks (Fig. 108) retain the experimental asymmetry of compositions at Tala, facing in the same, left direction, rather than each other.

The antarāla to which the vihāra door gives entrance, has a shrine of Jāmbhāla on the right wall. Its plinth has, like Tala, a tall kumbha, a vedikā of pilastered niches and projected galapādas, and a kapota with caityas enclosing stūpas. While this arrangement recalls the arrangement of mouldings on the brick embankment at Jethani or the later Devarani pīṭha, the Tala mouldings have greater weight and volume.

At the back of the courtyard, the gate to the main shrine was flanked by Gaṅgā and Yamunā images, of which the Gaṅgā image survives, carved on a slab measuring approx. 2x1.5 m. The verticalism, stressed in the side slabs of Tala, is accentuated by the more slender figure and narrower slab. Gaṅgā is shown walking to her left, with one foot bent and poised on toes, and recalls the sideways movement of Gaṅgā and her attendants on the inner surround of the Devarani door jamb. The multi-layered carving of Devarani door jamb is however eschewed, as is the additive layering of architectural blocks at Jethani. The trefoil caitya of later Devarani moulding is transferred to the lintel of this doorway and equipped with three bhāraputrakas.

The additive perception of Jethani architecture however, is not given up completely. Inside the main shrine, the body of Buddha (Fig. 376) is assembled out of seven horizontal segments, and his siṁhāsana has a separate front, carved with lions, and a back, bearing the main image, a pilastered architrave, with gajaśārdula motif, and a (missing) bodhi tree canopy. The rearing lions seen at Tala as well as the vihāra, become udyata, jāgrata or gajākrānta siṁhas in Odishan architecture later. The additive segmentation of architecture and sculpture at Tala or the vihāra becomes part of Odishan architecture, in its gaṇḍi, bāḍā, vajramastaka, gavākṣas, engaged nāgastambhas, drums of pillars, or in the organization of sculpted slabs (Pls. 14, 30).[34]

On either side of the Buddha stood Padma and Vajrapāṇi Avalokiteśvara, of whom the Padmapāṇi survives (approx. 2.18 x 0.5 m), recalling the size, dvibhaṅga posture, the heavy but relaxed modelling of the Tala dvārapālas. The overwhelming power and vehemence of the Tala figures are, however, very much dissipated in the somewhat diffuse, sluggish, spread out modelling of the vihāra figures.

The composer of the Bhikṣu Ānandaprabha's inscription, Sumaṅgala, is mentioned in an undated Gandheśvara temple inscription on the plinth surrounding the pillared maṇḍapa of Gandheśvara temple. This inscription and the two undated inscriptions on two identical pillars, which mention Ambullaka, refer to the rule of Bālārjuna. From this, it is reasonable to assume association of parts of the present Gandheśvara temple with Bālārjuna's reign. The ghaṭapallava pillars (Fig. 284) in the temple have very tall square shafts like Tala, but acquire an additional moulded base. Like Tala, the pillars use half lotus medallions and rosette bands to adorn the upper shaft, and have an octagonal constriction, a vase foliage capital, and a bracket base, suggesting comparison also with Viśvakarmā cave at Ellora. Another pillar in the maṇḍapa has a short, fluted, octagonal and sixteen sided constriction, compressed between a very tall, square shaft with capital and a taraṅga potikā, offering a variation of Tala and a simpler version of the ornate pillars in Aurangabad caves 6, 7 and Ellora cave 5. A third set of pillars in the maṇḍapa uses the kalaśa with overflowing foliage from Tala at the base but draws on Ajanta pillar designs for its fluted shaft, interrupted by decorative bands, lasūna, āmalaka, ṭāṭi and potikā. The decorative splendour of the Ajanta brackets, or the plastic fulness of the sculpted elements on Ajanta pillars are missing, as is missing the freedom and vivacity of experiment, special to Tala, which inventively uses the ghaṭapallava or āmalaka at the base, at the crown, or on the shaft. And yet, when one looks at the fulness of volume in the foliate canopy, overhanging the Buddha in bhūmisparśamudrā (Fig. 374) in the Gandheśvara temple; at the luxuriant, but not convoluted foliage, in the scrolled tail of the haṁsas flanking him; at the boldly described rosettes in his elliptical halo; at the smooth, flowing contours of his body, or at the siṁhas on his throne; one can see an architectural idiom, slightly earlier than the Ānandaprabha vihāra, closer to Tala, at work. Apart from the elongation surviving from Tala days in the halo, the parikara or the body of Buddha, a pent up tension, characteristic of the vertically conceived figured slabs of Tala or Malhār, still survives here, a tension which deserts the supine, additive modelling of the Buddha or Bodhisattva attendants in the Ānandaprabha vihāra (Figs. 376-77).[35]

RĀMACANDRA TEMPLE, RĀJIM AND SIRPUR FRAGMENTS

Growing Fusion of Architecture and Sculpture

The characteristics of this phase appear to be shared also by the door jamb and a few maṇḍapa pillars at Rāmacandra temple Rajim. This is obvious inspite of the considerable controversy about the different chronological phases of temple (Fig. 407), caused by the confusion created by later recutting. In spite of the recutting, it is evident that the older portion of the door jamb cannot be far from Tala.[36] The inner surrounds, fluted, and carved with square bosses, enclosing full and half lotus medallions with flower filled corners, adapt their idea and design from Devarani antarāla door jamb and the pillar outside Jethani south door jamb. However, the wavy undulations of the Devarani lotus petals, or the natural form of the Jethani petals, touching one another, are abjured for a more schematic pattern. Fluted pillars with medallions in square bosses have precursors at Ramtek or Nāsik cave 3. However, the fluttering life of petals, rocked by water, which is shared by these older sites with Tala, is suppressed. The mithuna on the rūpaśākhā has been seen as comparable to the Devarani door jamb mithuna by Stadtner, ostensibly on the ground of oversecting of forms. This ignores the fact that the Devarani mithunas in the smaller panels and even the Hara Gaurī in the larger panel, are probably drawn in curves, which are still in comparison with the free, sweeping curves enclosing the mithuna in the Rāmacandra panel. The same fluency and flow of curves characterises the gaṇa riding the makara at the base. These figures remind us of the gaṇa on makara, makara and haṁsa, foliate and mithuna forms in Ajanta caves 1, 23, 24 and Aurangabad cave 15, and relate to the fine drawing and draughtsmanship in the relatively shallow relief of the composite latā on Jethani south door jamb or the foliate tail of the makara on the Jethani west pillar.[37]

Four pillars and two pilasters in the maṇḍapa of the Rāmacandra temple[38] are carved with highly reworked figures of three vṛkṣakās, a mithuna, with monkeys and Gaṅgā. Stadtner relates these to the later 7th, early 8th century figures at Rājīvalocana or Palāri, using the pronounced tribhaṅga posture as a link. If posture alone is to decide us, the crossed legs should link the Gaṅgā directly with the Bhairavī image in a Jethani south lintel. However, in spite of visible reworking, these figures are modelled with an easier movement of contour, a softer and more relaxed modelling of flesh, and a more effortlessly balanced posture of body than the Palāri figure. Unlike the knock-kneed Palāri figures (Fig. 326), legs of the Rāmacandra pillar figures (Figs. 286-87, 316-17) stand free of one another and seemingly free of the pillar. There is, at the same time, no similarity between the squared off forms, comparatively stolid and stiff movements, hard, metallic modelling, relatively shallow and dry surfaces of the later work of Rājīvalocana temple in the western gate (Pl. 29) and these figures. The swing of the garland, the delicately incised mantle, the convincing volume of the overhanging canopy of foliage, the use of the freestanding pillars as a form, mobile and mutable, fusing sculpture with architecture, bring this series of pillars much closer to the Jethani pillars and Devarani door jambs than to Palāri. At Jethani, the fusion of sculpture and architecture has not yet proceeded this far, and piling of separately carved blocks or slabs with small intrusive sculptures, against a plain pillar, remains the convention. The negation of architectonic integrity is more conspicuous at Devarani. The negation of architecture becomes much more glaring in the Rāmacandra temple pillars, with the arbitrary growth of tilted images, irregularly assembled loads of foliage, large monkeys, climbing helter skelter, and everything spilling out of the frame (Fig. 287).

At the same time, Jethani figures are designed more archaistically, in a somewhat rigid frontal posture, and stiff dress, characterised by sedately marching curves (Figs. 95-96). The Devarani Pārvatī or river goddesses (Figs. 307, 309, 312) are designed with more dynamic curves at the transitions of waist or the hips, bringing these closer to the Rāmacandra pillar figures. However, the Devarani figures are yet to be invaded by the abrupt, broken rhythm of the Rāmacandra maṇḍapa figures. The lower garment or the uttarīya are more deeply incised at Rāmacandra temple, and plastered across the body. At Devarani, the garments are delicately modelled with the body, revealing and moulding it, and gliding across it. The sharply incised lines of ornament at Rāmacandra temple are duplicated in the ornamental foliage or garlands on the pillars. These look jumbled and haphazard in comparison with the deft, sure, meticulously cut foliate strands of Devarani pillars. The sculpture on Rāmacandra maṇḍapa pillars thus appears to nudge close to late 6th rather than end of 7th century, following the earlier work of Sirpur and Malhār. It continues to possess the tension, compression, sharp, brusque manneristic movement, slender but tight modelling of Devarani or Bhīma Deval site fragments, but modifies these features with the amplitude and spread of some of the Jethani and Ānandaprabha vihāra work.

The tradition of carving vṛkṣakās on pillars in Western Indian caves (Fig. 291), modified by the use of figures on the Tala pillars, is replicated in the vṛkṣakās on Rāmacandra maṇḍapa pillars.[39] The all over floral design on the inner surround of the varāha cell door jamb comes from Tala as do the beaded rows of (acanthus) buds or guṇḍikā, the half and full lotus medallions, or the medallion with the makara, framed by the spiral mālā. The nibbling haṁsa reminds us of its counterpart on the later Devarani moulding, and the makara recalls the turns and loops in the tail of the makara in the Devarani pillar. Their scrolled tails, meshed with scrolled designs, recall similar elements at Ajanta, with frilled edges and blurred details. The trefoil patralatā or scrolled kuṭila or ratikerā designs and the lotus petals in the door jamb soffit retain the fluid movement, careful detailing, undulation of burgeoning life, characteristic of the Malhār pillar in the Raipur Museum (Fig. 278), or the latā on the stambhaśākhā of the Jethani south door jamb (Fig. 262). In fact, the makara and scroll in Bādāmi cave 2 medallion, assigned to late 6th century, appear harder and flatter by comparison. In spite of retaining such clear memories of Tala work, the scroll or figural work of the maṇḍapa and Varāha door jamb are overtaken by more stylized flourishes and greater congestion of ornament than Tala, by a stiffer, harsher and a more halting movement of contours. This nullifies the impact of quicker flexions in its figures, more tortuous turns of its haṁsa or makara, the more sinuous twists of its foliage. The makaras in the Devarani pillar are rendered with a lighter touch and greater movement; and, foliage is rendered more economically, without losing its natural shape or volume. On these considerations, the Rāmacandra maṇḍapa pillars or the Varāha cell door jamb appear to follow after Devarani.

The discussion in our chapter on sculpture will show that if the high and shallow relief coexist at Tala, so do two conceptions of body (Figs. 296, 298, 302, 309). One figural type is tall, slender, though heavy hipped. The other type is broader, heavier, squarer. These two conceptions unite to suggest the tall, but weighty figures of Rāmacandra maṇḍapa. A similar phenomenon is illustrated at Sirpur, at about the same time, in wall slabs at the Sirpur Museum, carved with a tall, amply proportioned Ambikā posing as a vṛkṣakā, Yamunā or with a Nāgarāja figure (Figs. 324-25). These slabs appear to have fulfilled a function similar to the carved wall slabs of Jethani. The deeply carved padmavallī and padmalatā framing the inner surround of the door jamb, the deep cut scrolled makara tail at its base, its middle band, carved with full and half lotus medallions, linked by a scroll, filled with flowers, set in roundels and squares, emerge out of the Tala and Malhār tradition. The broad hips of Yamunā and Bhairava, the fluid, curvilinear contour of their body, the stress on their weight and shape rather than on extravagant ornament, the quiet benignance of Yamunā or the contained wrath of Bhairava, which spurn exaggerated or violent gesture, bring them close to Tala. On the other hand, the somewhat perfunctory finish of the elements in the middle band of the door jamb, the attenuation and streamlining of the head, shoulders or lower legs of these two figures, speak of a slightly later date. The surviving foundations and walls of two other ruined temples with tall, plain, vertical mouldings, decorative aśokalumbī, plain recess or a recess with galapādas, remind us of the Tala brick moulding, and may be assigned to the same period, in mid to late 6th century, presaging later developments at Sirpur.

A slab carved with Yamunā, in the reconstructed Kuleśvara temple at Rajim, is a further illustration of this style. The precise detailing of the layers of her mayūrātapatra, spiral mālā or mekhalā, the diaphanous uttarīya gliding across her left breast and right waist, the quiet, easy balance of her tribhaṅga posture, her slender attendants, looking out from behind, the fish and crab above, suggesting water, bring her close to the ornament, mantle, stance of Devarani river goddesses, and obtrusive sculptures above Sūrya or Varuṇa parikara or on Jethani pillars. The subtle triangularization of the frame of her head, the precipitous drop of the contour outlining her waist or thighs, the repetitive beading in her ornament, on the other hand, stamp the Kuleśvara Yamunā as being slightly later than Tala.[40]

PHASE 2 (AD 595-625): SIRPUR, LAKṢMAṆA TEMPLE AND RELATED SITES

EXTERIORIZATION, MINIATURIZATION, LINEARIZATION: MUTATIONS IN ODISHA

The next phase in the art of Dakṣiṇa Kośala appears to be characterised by a growing importance of the decorative embellishment of the exterior facade and mouldings; an attempt to miniaturize the cyclopean proportions of figures for accommodating them on the vedībandha mouldings or door jambs; a frequent use of the nāgabandha design on door jamb and pillars, stressing the human figures and scrolled tail of the nāgas; and, by a compression of the laterally spread or heavy modelling, to pose lean, middle sized, boyish figures, with sharp, jerky, stabbing movements of arms and legs, to create sudden turns in the contour from the waist to the hips. The tension, somewhat dissipated in the modelling of the intervening period after Tala, reanimates the tighter, more disciplined stance, gestures and postures. The foliage loses traits of the preceding phase like depth, fine, opulent curves, clear, emphatic description, and becomes harder, thicker and slower. It gives an impression of being appplied to rather than carved on the architecture. The later Devarani mouldings are now firmly integrated into the vedībandha, foreseeing the pābhāga of later Odisha temples. The design elements, found in embryo at Tala and earlier, are incorporated into the maṇḍovara and the śikhara, to anticipate the distinctive bāḍā and gaṇḍi of Odisha. This phase should stretch from AD 575 to 625.

SVASTIKA VIHĀRA

The so-called Svastika vihāra (Fig. 219) appears to stand at the head of this phase. The Buddha in this vihāra is made additively of assembled blocks, from the shoulder upwards. The wide petals in his halo, and his broad shoulders, betray memories of Jethani dvārapālas. The elliptical curve of the halo, the constricting, triangularizing, sheer outlines of his chest, the deep, conical dive of his kaṭisūtra, the cylindrical shape of his head, the raising of his height by a double lotus cushion, bring the Buddha closer to the tradition, represented by elongated Tala figures, Bhīma Deval, Malhār, or by Lakṣmaṇa temple, Sirpur. The Bodhisattva Padmapāṇi recalls the dvārapāla images of Nācnā Kuthārā Pārvatī temple as well as the Pratihāra and Śiva images on the Devarani door jamb lintel, in the simultaneous hardening and rarification of the body, its tension and relaxation.[41]

LAKṢMAṆA TEMPLE

In this develpment, the Sirpur Lakṣmaṇa temple (Figs. 104-05) is the next major landmark. The late dating of this temple by Shastri to the end of the 8th century cannot be supported on stylistic or epigraphic grounds.[42] The temple stands tall on a 7 feet high plinth like Devarani and has a garbhagṛha, kapilī and a maṇḍapa. The surviving kumbhakas outside the sanctum suggest four pairs of pillars, and probably, eight peripheral pilasters,[43] ostensibly carved with figures, some of which appear to have been shifted to the local ASI sculpture shed. This penetration of the interior with carved architectural elements clearly recalls Jethani. The later Devarani mouldings of khura and jāḍyakumbha are adapted, the kumbha becoming taller on the pratirathas than on the bhaḍras, recalling a similar staggering of height in Devarani vedībandha in the maṇḍapa portion. The kalaśa is also adapted, clasped by more numerous, closely arrayed aśokalumbīs (Fig. 106), but it eschews the experimental variety of design of Devarani, like the snake chasing the mouse. The antarapaṭṭa is similar to Devarani, carved with squat ghaṭapallava pilasters and caitya niches with large pendant mukulas. The kapota is similarly carved with candraśālās, with side leaves and a floral crest, but the ardhacandraśālās, mithunas, scrolled haṁsas of Devarani are no longer seen, the design showing uniformity and aversion for experiment. The ardhapadmas below or the vedikā above the Lakṣmaṇa kapota are missing at Devarani, though the vedikā is seen in the simple recessed brick moulding of Jethani.

All these later Tala elements travel via early brick temples like Lakṣmaṇa to find their place in the pābhāga of Odishan temples (Figs. 145, 147, 149-51, 153) as haṁsa on the khura, scroll on the muhānti, pūrṇaghaṭa with campaka ālambas on the noli, padmapṛṣṭha etchings on the upper slope of the ghaṭa, and in the khaṇḍi recess. These elements of Tala foundation mouldings are used repeatedly on the jaṅghā and superstructure of Lakṣmaṇa, in varying sizes, intervals, locations, and designs. The projections and recesses (short vedikās on vedībandha or tall koṣṭhas on jaṅghā) of Devarani or Jethani, are now found in the Lakṣmaṇa vedībandha twice, and on the jaṅghā thrice. Squat ghaṭapallava pilasters frame plain niches with mukulas. Short vedikās appear above the mañcikās on the jaṅghā and above the varaṇḍikā or the karṇāṇḍakas in the śikhara. Similarly, the kapota used in later Devarani moulding with trefoil and split candraśālikās appears in the vedībandha, the jaṅghā, in two rows below and one row above the vārāṇḍikā. Full candraśālikās replace the half on the bhadra, the trefoil motif being used on karṇas. The trefoil motif gives way to siṁkakarṇa in the udgamas, on the pratiratha in the jaṅghā and the śikhara. The door, simple yet suggestive of depth in the later Devarani candraśālā, becomes more elaborate in the siṁkakarṇas above the mañcikā on jaṅghā, or śūrasenakas of śikhara. The chequerboard design of Tala now assumes the shape of the perforated bāṅkājālī of Odisha and demarcates the vārāndā from the śikhara in a broad kaṇṭha. The entire facade becomes animated by the projections and recesses, used in the style represented by the Tala temples. The later Devarani kapota, equipped with the full and split candraśālas, is translated into the kalās in madhya and pratiratha, placing three candraśālas, one large and two small, side by side. The load bearing elements of the Tala pillar bases, or pīṭha like bhāraputrakas, lions or elephants, now come together in a horizontal row above the jaṅghā niches, cantoned by pilasters, between kapotas, and above the ghanadvāras, or on tulāsaṁgrahas. The padmapṛṣṭha of the Tala panel or pillar base frames, or of the Odisha pābhāga, also appears in the vedībandha once, and twice below the twin kapotas, separating the jaṅghā from the śikhara. The pervasive kīrtimukha of Tala appears now on the top of the siṁkakarṇas, on the pratirathas, foretelling the design of Odishan vajramastakas. This reveals the growing tendency towards the miniaturization of elements from the corpus of motifs in the Tala style, for application to the external facade, foreseeing the Odisha style (Pl. 14; Figs. 146, 151-52).[44]

Memories of the Tala door jambs (Figs. 157, 162, 175) survive in the inner surrounds of Lakṣmaṇa temple door jamb (Figs. 216-18), which are carved with full and half lotus medallions and foliage, and these retain some of the plasticity and movement from Tala. The vertical band of flowers, named jālapatra in Odishan art, which frames the surround, is an elongated and complex version of the motif on the right door jamb of Devarani. Like Devarani, a variant of the patraśākhā rises from a ghaṭapallava outside the inner surround to merge into an āmalaka on the top, and a second patravallī, intermeshed with jambhakas (like the Odishan gelaba), goes all over, to overhang the lalāṭabimba. A third patravallī framing the mithuna śākhā and the lalāṭabimba, and a fourth, partitioning the Daśāvatāra panels on the fifth band, are less heavily undercut than Devarani. However, they retain distinct weight and volume, and replicate the circular, overhanging form of their Tala counterpart many times over. An equivalent of the vertical band of rosettes, spouted by kīrtimukhas on the Devarani stambhaśākhā, divides the patraśākhā from the Daśāvatāra panel in the surlintel, and is known as raṅganī, later in Odisha. The padmapṛṣṭha, seen on Devarani Gajalakṣmī lintel or in Odishan vedībandha mouldings, frames the Keśivadha panel and the Daśāvatāra lintel. The arrangement of mithunas above one another, on a gaṇa pratihāra base, and the sweeping ratikerā design on the mithunaśākhā, demonstrate an adaptation of the Jethani pillars (Figs. 44, 54, 56), carved with tiers of figures, for the design of the door jamb. The ratnaśākhā shows a maṇibandha of diamond and bean shaped gems. It recalls the Rajim Rāmacandra temple door frame and the puṣpabandhas of Tala, and reappears later in places like Mukhaliṅgam in Odisha. The bevelling of the padmapṛṣṭha or the stambhaśākhā, which frame the ghanadvāras on the bhadras, and the use of large rosettes on their six mullioned compartments, show the transference of Tala motifs and concepts to the facade, and initiate the process, which culminates in the ornate niches on the bāḍā of Odishan temples like Mukteśvara (Pl. 15; Fig. 151).

With the Lakṣmaṇa temple door jamb, the Gupta tradition of displaying the rūpa or mithunaśākhā on the front (Figs. 207-08), is adapted in preference to the Tala practice of displaying it on the inner side (Figs. 167-68). Instead of being brought together in one śākhā like Devarani, the mithunas and divine figures are separated. Odisha temples act on the same preference. Visually, the impression of a scroll being folded up inwards in the Devarani door jamb, is given up at Lakṣmaṇa for that of a canvas spreading out. The alternate projection and recession of elements, thrusting one element out into light, withdrawing another into darkness, is replaced by a steady decrease in the size of horizontal and vertical bands, generating a gradual recession. The contrast and juxtaposition of diverse motifs and panel sizes at Devarani is replaced by an accent on the repetitive use of the patravallī, on similar sized partitions. The ground is made ready for the distinctly differentiated bands in the Odisha door frames, which also eschew the bewildering variation of pace at Devarani, to accept uniform, broad accents. The hard encrustations of ornament, though still heavy, are congealed in comparison with Tala. The striations on the lower garment become more regular. The uttarīya across the breast, waist or hips, appears to be incised across the body, instead of being laid delicately upon it like Tala. The tortuous convolutions of Devarani door jamb not being sought, the tall standing figures tend to harmonise with and emphasize the two principal directions given by a post and lintel door frame.[45] The adaption of the scrolled haṁsa of later Devarani mouldings on the door jamb base, already mediated by the Ānandaprabha vihāra, is acknowledged in the Odishan pābhāga door frame or paga designs as a haṁsalatā.[46]

Bhīma Deval, Malhār

The Lakṣmaṇa temple thus works as a catalytic agent, transmitting the heritage of Tala and earlier Gupta temples to Odisha. It inaugurates a phase of reordering the temple facade, in which the next significant landmark is the Bhīma Kīcak Deval temple at Malhār. This temple is built like the Tala temples, on a tall plinth (Figs. 102-03) and, in plan, the temple has a large garbhagṛha, a smaller maṇḍapa, connected by a very narrow antarāla, the garbhagṛha showing a stellate plan. The vedībandha of the temple shows, like the later Devarani vedībandha, a khura, a jāḍyakumbha, much taller and precipitous in outline than its more curvilinear and shorter counterpart at Devarani, a dhārāṇvita kalaśa,[47] somewhat lighter in comparison with the plain, heavy, later Devarani kalaśa. After the kalaśa,[48] an antarapaṭṭa intervenes like Devarani. The ghaṭapallava pilasters have a laśūna neck and a more ornate shaft, adorned with foliate scrolls, flying vidyādharas, standing river goddesses, etc., while the carvings in the niches replace the simple, later Devarani caityas, with entire parikaras carrying bhāraputrakas, Garuḍāsana Viṣṇu, Kāma-Rati, trefoil and complex multilayered caityas. This is followed by a kapota, which consistently uses the pūrṇa and ardha caitya motifs of later Devarani, and the nibbling haṁsa of Devarani, but, decorates its base occasionally and additionally, with a triangular foliate nīvrapaṭṭikā. This in turn, is followed by a further vedikā (missing at Tala, but present at Lakṣmaṇa) with ghaṭapallava pilasters and niches, carved with caityas enclosing heads, or with octagonal depressions enclosing a central block.[49] This, finally, is followed by a mañcikā, formed like a reversed kapota, which, unadorned at Lakṣmaṇa, is adorned at Malhār with a padmapaṭṭi and a nīvrapaṭṭika on the base.

Though the aśokalumbī of Tala is missing at Malhār, the Tala heritage, supplemented by the Malhār corpus, sows seeds for the highly ornate Odisha pābhāga mouldings. The caityas, ardhacaityas, haṁsas appear on the counterpart of the kapota, called the vasanta in Odisha. The projecting base or muhānti of vasanta is decorated with dhanugranthi on padmapṛṣṭha, and its stepped recesses or ḍamarubhāga acquires ratnapaṭṭa or diamand or diaper designs. The recessed vedikā with galapādas is replaced in Odisha by a talabandhana, carved with figural motifs. The caityas, enclosing heads, become nandīkāmukhas with kirīṭas, and take their place above the khuras, at the base of the vertical campakalumbī designs. The kalaśa becomes kaṭakāvṛta, and is vertically rather than horizontally indented. A pheni, carved with padmapṛṣṭha, like Malhār, or, with raṅganī, like Tala, also makes its appearance.[50]

The door to the maṇḍapa of Bhīma Kīcak Deval has broken bases of pillars with bhāraputrakas at the base, carrying Gaṅgā Yamunā figures, lost except for portions of the feet and the vāhanas. These are framed by deep cut scrolls, continuing the tradition of the earlier Bhīma Kīcak Deval site door jambs and Devarani door jambs. The stambhaśākhā relocates Tala to show standing female figures on the peḍyā on the front face, with lotus medallions and panels carved with padmapṛṣṭha, gajākrānta, on the adjacent faces (Figs. 210, 314, 320). The bands of rosettes and lotus scrolls, known as the raṅganī and ratikerā in later Odisha, frame the panels, become stringy, hard, and get infested with repetitive, fussy frills, to move away from the facility and fluency of the Devarani designs. Two affronted karimakaras are designed with the same repetitive frills, invading their shallow carved tail and body. The background of the standing padmahastā lady in the peḍyā, and her lower garment are choked with floral and geometric designs. These designs are somewhat hastily incised, compared with the garment of Devarani river goddesses, and the body of the lady shows sharp vertical and diagonal incisions, unlike Tala. The quick, sharp, abrupt bends, making for angular thrusts of arms and legs, characterise all figures, replacing the curvilinear contours of Tala. The caityas are developed far beyond later Devarani, as it is organized in three storeys, and acquires a central vertical row of three candraśālās, with mukulas, backed by two flanking candraśālās, on two storeys. At places, this caitya design, like later Odisha, is flanked by udyata siṁha, crowned by a leafy vajramuṇḍī, in an adaptation of Jethani south pillar carvings, and uses pīḍhās intervening between the central and the back rows of candraśālās. Occasionally, it is reduced to a more complex jāla, in which the three overlapping candraśālās in the centre are vertically compressed, and the flanking candraśālās are perforated. The elaboration of design beyond the later trefoil Devarani candraśālā, with its weighty parrots, or the simple trefoil Lakṣmaṇa temple candraśālās, enclosing a stūpa, is evident. The Malhār caitya design follows Tala and Lakṣmaṇa, and precedes the more ornate and stylized Pratihāra designs of Āmrol, Mahuā, Nareśvar or Indore as also of Odisha, with its repetitive guṇḍikā frames and figural carvings.[51]

One comes to the later door jambs, that lie in front of the Bhīma Deval temple, carved with nāgabandha designs (Figs. 212-13). Garland or sword bearing gaṇas are seen, at the base of these door jambs, heaving upwards, with the support of the coils of a nāgarāja worshipper. The coils are carved with floral and jewelled scrolls, emerging from the gaping jaws of nāgas at regular intervals. This nāgabandha is framed on one side by a vertical padmapaṭṭi, and on the other, by a vertical grāsapaṭṭi. Jewelled and floral festoons come out of the grāsamukhas, which are made of floral rhizome, except for the eyes or the nostrils. The nāgapāśas framing the ghaṭapallava base of Jethani south pillar or binding persons at the base of a pillar slab at Jethani north, the nāgaprabhāvalī surrounding the Paśupati image at Devarani, the grāsamukhas on Jethani and Devarani pillars, spitting jewelled and floral festoons, the padmapaṭṭis framing the Devarani jamb panels, and the foliate grāsamukhas, have converged to yield the Malhār nāgabandha design. It becomes pervasive in the early medieval art, and transforms the foliate rhizome, which was indistinguishably meshed with birds, animals or gaṇas in earlier art, into a winding latā, in which the figural elements become as emphatically visible as the floral or ophidian. It anticipates the gelabā and nāgabandha design of Odisha, and in Dakṣiṇa Kośala itself, the nāgabandha door jambs and pillars (Figs. 227-28, 235, 372).[52] The tall, elongated figures, elephants and geometric designes carved on the door jamb and plinth mouldings of Patāleśvara Mahādeva temple continue, with variations and ramifications the tradition of pillars with tall figures and the geometric designs articulated at early Malhār, Tala and outer areas of Maheshpur and deepadih (Figs. 211, 214-15, 231, 293, 299, 352, 365).

PHASE 3 (AD 625-700): RĀJĪVALOCANA TEMPLE, RĀJIM

Acceleration of Movement: Multiplication, Dispersion, Segmentation

Most of the work at the Rājīvalocana temple at Rajim (Figs. 126-27) seems to be made in the same broad style as Sirpur Lakṣmaṇa temple, and appears to follow it closely, extending from AD 625 to 675, while the prātolī may have been done around AD 700. Style has to be the essential criterion for determining its chronology in relation to other Dakṣiṇa Kośala temples, including Tala. The two inscriptions fixed to the inner maṇḍapa wall, hailing from the Nala and Kalacurī period, cannot be associated confidently with the temple, in view of the absence of any firmly dated Nala or Kalacurī work, to which the temple can be significantly related. The temple itself is made of brick, stone being used for pillars, pilasters, beams and door jambs. It is built like Tala on a high jagatī, and its present plan consists of a garbhagṛha, kapili and maṇḍapa, facing west. The maṇḍapa is approached through two ardhamaṇḍapas by a double flight of stairs from the west and the east, like Sirpur Lakṣmaṇa and later Devarani platforms, and door jambs are provided at the head of the stairs. The temple is developed as pañcāyatana, with shrines at four corners. As a modified sāndhāra prāsāda, the garbhagṛha is surrounded by an ambulatory, open to the sky like later Devarani platform, but enclosed by walls. The temple complex is contained within a prākāra, equipped with a prātolī with a colossal western gate.

Dikshit and Krishna Deva have phased the work at Rājīvalocana over a period of a century or more, while Stadtner has assigned it to less than two decades. While Dikshit or Krishna Deva do not work out the stylistic phases of this work, Stadtner declares it to be a new Nala style, quite different from the earlier Dakṣiṇa Kośala style, without making comparisons with the earlier work. Tala has been ignored by scholars as irrelevant to Rājīvalocana, because of an undue reliance on dynastic chronology, in which Tala finds no place.[53] Having isolated Rājīvalocana from the early phase of Dakṣiṇa Kośala art or Tala, Krishna Deva assigns its nucleus to AD 600 and compares its śikhara with Mahābodhi temple in Bihar, while Stadtner places it in late 7th, early 8th century, and derives it from unknown work in Andhra. They should have, instead, related Rājīvalocana to Tala, Lakṣmaṇa and some Surāṣtra temples.[54] If they had done so, the Rājīvalocana would have been found to have been executed within the same continuing idiom of Dakṣiṇa Kośala within 7th century AD, in spite of its obvious renovations, or the thick coat of lime and plaster found upon it. They would also have found, that, in the elements which the Rājīvalocana temple shares with Lakṣmaṇa temple, it also looks back to the later Devarani mouldings. These are the heavy kumbha, the kalaśa with aśokalumbī, the kapotas with candraśālās or ardhapadmas, the vedikā with ghaṭapallava pilasters and niches on the bhadras, the projections and recesses on the jaṅghā. Among other shared elements, the double siṁhakarṇa above the jaṅghā niches, the use of Tala vedībandha motifs in vārāndikā and śikhara, the incipient vajramuṇḍī on the siṁhakarṇas on the śikhara or phāmsanakūṭas, anticipate Odisha elements.

Krishna Deva's suggestion is that the Rājīvalocana maṇḍapa door jamb is coeval with the temple in AD 600, while the sanctum door jamb (Pls. 26-27; Figs. 221-22) is of AD 725, having hardened in modelling. However, when we compare the yakṣas climbing or swinging from the maṇḍapa door jamb nāgavallī, the nāgarājas on the main temple door, or the Lakṣmaṇa door jamb mithunas (Fig. 217) with Devarani, we find memories of the Devarani door jamb mithunas, Sagaraputras or gaṇas (Figs. 399-401), in the slim, smoothly youthful figures, oval, egg shaped heads, elongated by tiered headdresses, contoured by a straight, constricting line, at these later sites. Even the thick, pouting lips, open, expressive eyes, swelling ball of chin of these later figures, faintly recall Devarani. The gay abandon and insouciance of the Rājīvalocana maṇḍapa yakṣas has probably been deliberately avoided, in the relatively staid programme of the main door jambs of all the temples, including Devarani. The absence of fussy beads or frills at the edges of the vallī, at the later sites, indicates a feeling for rounded, organic form, continuing from Tala. The correspondence of the curves of the nāga tails and spiral movement of the creeper in these sites, speak of a similar continuity of the sense for rhythm.

There is thus no way of placing the Rājīvalocana maṇḍapa or sanctum door jamb either before or very long after the Lakṣmaṇa temple or Devarani door jamb, despite visible deviations at Rajim in the movement of style. The approach to a gradually recessed door jamb, with overhanging plant or figural bands, is broadly the same in all the three temples, but subtle changes have taken place at Rājīvalocana. The thick nāga coils, the mithunas stationed on half-circular padmapīṭhas, the twin padmapaṭṭis framing these bands in Rājīvalocana jambs, swell out in short waves and lend the doors an oblique, inward pull like Devarani. The padmavallī in Rājīvalocana retains the volume of Devarani or Lakṣmaṇa, but is laid in more horizontal layers.

Its nodes are not as clearly distinguished and its curves are not as lively as in Lakṣmaṇa or Devarani. The mithunas are more crowded and awkward, and the oversecting of planes makes their gestures look comparatively uncomfortable and their hands disproportionate in size. Their lower garment is incised, and lacks the distinct sense of weight, characteristic of Lakṣmaṇa or Devarani. Their legs are no longer given an easy and effortless bend at the knees like before. The legs are outlined with abrupt transitions in contour, bowed in an ungainly manner, and thinned down considerably below the knees. The ratikerā design at the base of the Rājīvalocana temple door jamb, with its stiff, conventionalized tendrils, is closer to the design on the inner surround of the Rājīvalocana prātolī door jamb, than to its more natural sway and more substantial stalk in the inner sides of Lakṣmaṇa temple door jamb or its incredible fluency at Devarani.[55]

It does not follow from this that the Lakṣmaṇa temple or Devarani are far earlier in time than the Rājīvalocana. It is only suggestive of the broad similarity of design and modelling which unite the main shrine, maṇḍapa or prātolī western gate (Pls. 28-29) door jambs, and place them later[56] than both Lakṣmaṇa and Devarani. At the same time, in the prātolī door jamb, there is an excessive enhancement of the stylistic tendencies of the maṇḍapa door jambs, and this excess, in a garbled way, looks back to the highly charged volumes of the Devarani door jamb. Thus, the first śākhā, rising from a maṅgala ghaṭa, in the Rājīvalocana garbhagṛha door, is a patravallī, while, in the prātolī door, it is a more elaborate latā, interlaced with a snake and jambhakas. The snake on the prātolī door is slender and slithers up and down, to wend its way in and out, in the manner of the later Devarani pīṭha moulding. The jambhakas on the prātolī door are slender too, in short drawers, like Devarani, and become much larger than Devarani. The figural elements accentuate the round, bulging patralatā, instead of merging in it like Devarani. The patralatā surges into thicker coils on the prātolī door, to subside in a semicircular saubhāgyapaṭṭa with Gajalakṣmī, and the patravallī is multiplied to culminate in a Śeśaśāyī Viṣṇu, accompanied by worshippers on the lintel, in the manner of Devarani. The second śākhā of the garbhagṛha, carved with mithunas and cāmaradhāriṇīs, merges into a Garuḍa on the lintel, and two yakṣas prising open the jaws of karimakaras, whose serpentine, intertwined tails spill out and roll down the flanks. This śākhā combines the mithunas, makaras and yakṣas of Tala, with serpentine tails dangling down the flanks.

On the prātolī jamb, the mithunas are multiplied on two śākhās, including a man fondling two women above river goddesses, and paraśu or daṇḍa-bearing Pratiharas at the base, recalling Devarani mithunas above river goddesses, Jethani panels showing Paraśurāma, Bhairava fondling Bhairavī, and Paśupati himself. Hooded heads or busts of many nāgarāja worshippers (Figs. 434-35) have been recovered from Tala (Pl. 38; Figs. 197, 353, 400-01). The transfer of such nāgarāja figures to the door jamb, to form links in a human chain, takes place at Rājīvalocana on the main shrine or prātolī doors, with the discovery of the possibility of using their composite form, as a substitute or complement for the winding latā. The inner surround of the prātolī door is carved with a ratikerā design, the idea being adapted from the Devarani door, and the specific form being taken from earlier Sirpur temples and vihāras. Altogether, the conception of modelling has become slightly heavier and ponderous within the same idiom, on the prātolī. The mithunas have become more explicit, and have lost the light, slender frame of their companions on the main sanctum door at Lakṣmaṇa or Devarani. The ornament is heavier, the design on the lower garment of the lady more intricate. The nāgas are fatter, and more stolid. The jambhakas are still slender, but more common. The edges of their limbs are sharper and the body harder, more metallic, lacking the blithe movement of Tala maṇḍapa door gaṇas. The ratikerā design is no longer so supple, getting to be flat, rigid and wiry. The strong inward curve of the door jamb is a prominent link with Devarani, continuing in the main garbhagṛha door. It is obstructed by the surfeit and juxtaposition of motifs and figures on the prātolī lintels, which lack the centralizing focus of the garbhagṛha lintel.

The twelve pillars and twelve sculpted pilasters of the Rājīvalocana maṇḍapa are a conglomerate assortment, and the pilaster sculptures of Gaṅgā and Yamunā, Dūrgā, Sūrya, Rāma, Varuṇa and Narasiṁha avatāras of Viṣṇu or guardian figures are heavily reworked, painted and whitewashed, making suggestion of a firm sequence risky. The incised lower garment, plastered on the body of Dūrgā, the incised uttarīya, lapping across the female breast or waist, the scrolled tail of the heavy, scaly makara and haṁsa below Gaṅgā, the thick cluster of leaves above the vṛkṣakā, the tiered curls of the dvārapāla, the slender bodies and the voluminous padmapīṭhas, suggest a period close to the garbhagṛha door jamb and continue to recollect Tala forms. The maṇḍapa pillars are all provided, like some pillars in Ajanta, Aurangabad or Tala, with tall, square shafts, octagonal and sixteen sided sections, foliate darpaṇas or with occasional figures, ghaṭapallava capital and taraṅga potikās. However, the moulded base, the shaft with half lotus medallions, dividing padmapaṭṭis, octagonal section, with double bodied garland bearing lions at corners, siṁhavarāhas or naravyālas, haṁsas, makaras or gaṇas, the ghaṭa with muktāgrāsas, show a rearrangement of similar elements from earlier cave or Tala architecture. On the other hand, the portion above the square shaft is more constricted than above sites. The legs of the siṁhas are still and congealed. The pillar is more slender. The carving of the foliage, the scrolled makara tail or siṁhavyāla is cursory and shallow. The foliage overhanging the kalaśa is no larger modelled softly. It does not slide over and nudge the kalaśa like Ajanta, Aurangabad or Tala. Instead, it is executed with harsh, knife like edges, and strung out, inert and life less, like Ellora.[57]

Within this broad idiom of Rājīvalocana, the two pillars in the western ardhamaṇḍapa of the prātolī (Pl. 28) appear to move out from the 7th into the 8th century. The ghaṭapallava bases and capitals, with stiff, overhanging foliage, the palm leaf decoration, adorning the bottom of the basal ghaṭa, the sixteen sided shaft, interrupted by parṇa or ratnapaṭṭis or plain bands, the padmapaṭṭi separating the bracket from the upper ghaṭa, recall similar ghaṭas at crown and base of Tala pillars or pilasters. The syncopated rhythm of these pillars is shared by them with Ajanta and Aurangabad. A Pratihāra stands in tribhaṅga against the shaft, on a projection from the lower ghaṭa, with one hand raised in capeṭamudrā, the other resting on the chest, in an adaptation of the figures sculpted on Jethani pillars and western cave architecture. The proto-lasūna segment, separated from the shaft by four interlaced serpents, with raised hoods and pendant tails, seems to derive some inspiration not only from the dangling serpent tails on the corners of Jethani south pillars, but also from the luxuriant serpentine coils, spread around some of the Ellora pillars. With these pillars, the Rājīvalocana temple foresees the conception of the nāga nāgi stambhas on the Odisha temple facades (Pl. 30; Fig. 235).[58]

The corner shrine images of Viṣṇu as Vāmana or Yoganārāyaṇa, Narasiṁha (Fig. 560) or Trivikrama, recall Tala, Lakṣmaṇa and Gandheśvara in precision and magnificence of ornament, eminently appropriate gestures or postures, expression of meditative bliss or overpowering dignity, the firm and sure hand for modelling. However, the excessive beading in their hair or ornament, the flattening of petals in their halo, the hardening of the crust of their uttarīya, the stiff spiked edges of the paryastaka, cloth or āyāla pasted on their body, the sharp conical elbow, the beginning of a harsh line dividing their legs, the glittering metallic sheen of their surface, betray a stylization, which takes the corner shrine images away from the continuing Tala traditions. They anticipate the palsy of life and movement, which invades the prātolī pillar sculptures, and chokes the style at Rajim. The serpent coils become flat and flabby in comparison with their muscular bulging webs on earlier door jambs. The foliate patterns are roughly incised, and lose their earlier fulness or decorative finesse. The Pratihāra loses touch with both the lean and volumetric styles heralded by Tala. He becomes squat and broad in proportions, acquires accentuated angular edges to his elbows and knees, and, is overcome by columnar stillness in his legs, which are marked with a harsh, spiky line in the middle. His eyes are stretched interminably out to the ears, and his dumpy head is plumped down on a short, thick neck.

This ossification of the 'classical' Dakṣiṇa Kośala style at Rājīvalocana[59] is paralleled at Sirpur in a Gandheśvara temple pillar and door lintel. The pillar is equipped with four anthropomorphic nāgarājas with interlaced coils and pendant tails on the corners of the upper ghaṭapallava segment. The door lintel is also an inserted fragment of intertwined nāgas. The flaccid coils and perfunctory movements of these nāgas, rendered with so much elan at Tala or early Rajim, put these segments at the end of this phase.

A thorough discussion of Rājīvalocana in relation with Tala has not been done while discussing its sequence of style, to exclude clutter. It is easy to see, however, that the maṇḍapa pillars and pilasters, with the tiered arrangement of sculptures, is derived from the arrangement represented by Jethani. The conception of the maṇḍapa or prātolī door jamb, with their round or spiral swelling forms, bevelled śākhās, powerful, inward pull, come out of the configuration, presented by Devarani door jamb. The replacement of the projecting figural sculpture of Devarani by a flat floral band on the inner surround of the door jamb, or the substitution of seemingly rotating figures on half-circular padmapīṭhas, snake coils, or obliquely inclined nāgas in place of the spiral or diagonal floral bands of Tala, are, however, special innovations of Rājīvalocana. The choice of a flat over a projected inner surround, appears to have been prompted by the consideration of giving unhindered passage, to a crowd of worshippers through the door, without breaking anything, projecting from the lateral sides.

A similar translation of floral Devarani elements into figural elements at Rājīvalocana is seen also in the flurry of the flying limbs of yakṣas on the maṇḍapa door jamb, which corresponds to the swift rhythm of its meandering creeper on dancing leaves. It is also seen in the slow, painful, cautious ascent and descent of the yakṣas in the west gate door jamb, which is answered by the sedate, subdued rhythm of the flowers, leaves or the snake, stretched out in a gradual prolonged movement. Compared, however, with the deep cut padmalatā, which absorbs the figures of birds or gaṇas in shadowy grooves at Devarani, the figures and plants on Rājīvalocana door jambs stay on the surface, clearly distinguishable from each other, and yet married by answering rhythms. The overhanging projection over Devarani door, made of floral elements, is similarly transformed into projecting figural sculpture over the Rājīvalocana garbhagṛha or prātolī door. The coexistence of slender and heavy figures at Tala is paralleled by coexistence of such figures on Rājīvalocana door jambs. Among specific motifs, the two bodied and garland bearing lions, gaṇas, makaras or haṁsas, often enclosed in darpaṇas, ghaṭapallava and āmalaka on capital and base, are transmitted by Tala to Rājīvalocana. The nāga coils are found earlier at Tala, before they go through the permutations and combinations at Malhār and Rājīvalocana. In fact, if Sirpur temples and vihāras purvey the Tala elements to Odisha through their facades, the Rājīvalocana, more than any other Rajim temple, follows the Tala programme faithfully inside the structure.

Rāmacandra Temple, Sirpur

In the same broad chronological phase (AD 625-700), a simultaneous movement begins with the Rāmacandra temple at Sirpur (Fig. 107), which executes the Tala elements with a heavier hand than Lakṣmaṇa, multiplies the angles of the karṇas and pratirathas by turning squares in plan, and adds narrow pratibhadras emphasized by tall pilasters, which stretch all the way up on the jaṅghā, like Devarani. Like Lakṣmaṇa and Devarani, it stands on a tall plinth. Like later Devarani, it has a khura, a jāḍyakumbha, which is curved more than Lakṣmaṇa, a heavy kalaśa adorned with aśokalumbī, which now undergoes faceting, specially on the karṇas. This is followed by a vedikā with simple recesses and galapādas (without the ghaṭapallava pilasters or mukulas in the recesses of Lakṣmaṇa), a kapota, heavier than Lakṣmaṇa, with large single kapotas on the segments, followed by a further vedikā. The jaṅghā shows empty devaprakoṣṭhas capped by kapota, vedikā, siṁhakarṇa with mukula, which stretch like Devarani all the way up the jaṅghā, and are substituted for the oblong, pilastered slits on the Lakṣmaṇa karṇas. Between the twin kapotas of the vārāndikā, a plain kaṇṭha is followed by a band of reversed kapiśīrṣakas, a feature seen also at Rājīvalocana. Two other ruined temples at Sirpur also show some of the Tala mouldings.[60]

Indal Deul, Khārod

With the Indal Deul temple (Figs. 12, 125) at Khārod there is a partial change in material,[61] and the angled pratiratha or karṇa projections of the Sirpur Rāma temple are blunted. The pratiratha, an element missing from the bland Tala facades, becomes narrower than both Lakṣmaṇa and Rāma, and retreats closer into the body of the temple. Siṁhakarṇas, missing from Tala maṇḍovara, earlier visible only on the pratirathas in Lakṣmaṇa, now occupy the karṇas and bhadras also, visually integrating the vārāndikā with the śikhara. Candraśālās on the kapotas, separated by regular intervals at later Devarani or Lakṣmaṇa, are banded together on the vedībandha and the śikhara. Unlike Tala or Lakṣmaṇa, candraśālās appear also on the bhadra and pratiratha pilasters. Figures[62] replace the caitya door motifs found in the siṁhakarṇas or candraśālās of later Devarani pīṭha, or on the karṇas of jaṅghā, bhadra of śikhara and vārāndikā at Lakṣmaṇa. Figures also occupy the oblong slits, niches and corners of the empty Tala or Lakṣmaṇa devakoṣṭhas on bhadras and pratirathas, anticipating the configurations on Odishan bāḍa and gaṇḍi more closely. Vertical visual integration is now achieved by repetition of sculpted elements on the exterior, whereas, at Tala, it was achieved with greater economy, by broadly stressing the two principal directions of architecture. The aśokalumbī on the kalaśa becomes flat and rectangular, losing the leafy outlines of Lakṣmaṇa and the substance of later Devarani. The effect of vertical integration is diluted only by quarter āmalakas, which replace the candraśālās on the pratiratha in the śikhara, varying the visually continuous line of candraśālās on Lakṣmaṇa pratiratha from vedībandha to the śikhara, and nudging the bhadra. The dopicchasiṁha of

Odisha, seen at Jethani pillar bases, appears at the corners of pratirathas at Indal deul. The siṁhavaktra, also foreseen on Jethani south flanks and Lakṣmaṇa pillars, crowns the siṁhakarṇas, anticipating the vajramuṇḍī of Odisha.[63]

The door jamb of Indal Deul at Khārod in Bilaspur district is of stone. The first innermost śākhā is patravallī, which emerges from a ghaṭapallava base, goes all over and overhangs the door like Devarani, but merges into the tails of two affronted makaras, whose gaping jaws hold, between them, an āmalaka like Lakṣmaṇa.[64] The second śākhā is a ratnabandha, which inserts a circular design after the diamond design of Lakṣmaṇa, replacing a jewelled festoon. The carving, compared with Devarani or Lakṣmaṇa, is shallow, and the design of the patravallī acquires the incipient sweep of the later Odishan ratikerā design. The third śākhā shows full length figures of Gaṅgā and Yamunā (Figs. 338-39), who carry mālā and ghaṭa, are canopied respectively by padma and mayūrātapatra, flanked by a dwarf female attendant, and crowned by fish and nāginīs, like Devarani river goddesses or Sūrya, Jethani Varuṇa or dwarf attendants. Indal Deul seems to prefer the heavy limbed form and languid posture of the Devarani river goddesses, to the heavy form but quicker flexions of the Rāmacandra maṇḍapa vṛkṣakās (Fig. 317). Compared with Devarani and even with Lakṣmaṇa, the figures develop sharper angles at the knees or elbows. The inner and outer contours of their body are broken up much more abruptly by ornament, which is laid in thick, opaque encrustations, in the appliquè manner of stucco work. It is a sharp change from the fluid, delicate and translucent modelling of the cloth at Tala. The several throat clasps, necklaces, rows of bangles, multi strand mekhalās (with a central makaramukha clasp for Gaṅgā), mālās, ūrujālakas (jewelled thigh band), keśabandhas (hairdress), thick, rope like kaṭisūtras (thread tied at waist), ridged, vertical floral bands in the lower garment, ridged eyebrows, eyelids or lips, give an impression of late medieval opulence and harshness, characteristic of Rājīvalocana prātolī door. This deviates completely from the accentless, pliant modelling of the transitions in the contour, or the equally supple, frugally chosen floral ornament, which enhance the lissom body at Tala. Yet, the ornament does not choke the fleshy fulness of the form completely, or obscure its links with images of Devarani or Rāmacandra, Rajim. Śiva Pārvatī are shown at the centre of the lintel, flanked by Brahmā, Viṣṇu, and adoring nāgīs and nāga nāgī mithunas. The thick, intermeshed snake coils, with parallel scales on the underside, the boyish, elongated face and body of these figures, their easy stance and relaxed contours, do not suggest a date long after the Rājīvalocana garbhagṛha door lintel figures. The inner surround of the door is carved, in the Tala manner, with one full and two half lotus medallions, linked by a continuous foliate band, and by two narrow flanking floriate bands. The carving of the band is slightly harder than the Sirpur ruined temple jamb and is close to the Gandheśvara temple door jamb.[65] The door frame appears to have possessed a pilaster (seen beside Gaṅgā), made of rows of ghaṭa āmalakas like some Tala pillars.

Siddheśvara Temple, Palāri

With the Siddheśvara temple on Bālasamudra tank in village Palāri in Raipur, further changes occur, bringing Dakṣiṇa Kośala further away from Tala and closer to Odisha. The simple broad lines of the Tala facade, without too many offsets, are given up completely. The angled projections increase, a pratikarṇa being added to the pratiratha, and the pratibhadra being differentiated from the bhadra, faceting the temples further, vertically, and driving its side profiles deeper inside than Indal Deul.[66] The vedībandha, equipped with the usual elements, shared by Lakṣmaṇa and Indal Deul with later Devarani, now adds a tulāpīṭha below the upper kapota in the gala, and begins to acquire the dhārāṇvita look, which will be the special property of Odishan pābhāgas. At the same time, the aśokalumbī of Tala, which becomes the campaka design in Odisha, decorates not only the kalaśa moulding, but invades the ghaṭapallava capitals of pillars or pilasters in the jaṅghā and the śikhara. The kapotas multiply, far beyond their use as a cap moulding on top of pīṭha, vedībandha or jaṅghā at Tala, and create a continuous madhyabandhana in the jaṅghā, anticipating such bipartite bands in Odishan temples. These bands replace the isolated kapotas on the pilasters of Indal Deul, and bind the entire temple body horizontally in tighter lines. Vertically, siṁhakarṇas become abundant, replacing the sparing use of makaratoraṇas alone on Devarani jaṅghā. These are inserted in the vārāndikā, like Indal Deul, including the section below the madhyalatā. A pratikarṇa is added to the quarter āmalakas of Indal Deul to reinforce the strong, upward visual compulsion. It is provided with a vertical row of pañjaras with siṁhakarṇas. Unlike the simple, rucaka pilasters of Devarani, the jaṅghā pilasters are severally segmented, above the madhyabandhana, to culminate in cruciform śīrṣakas, while, between the siṁhakarṇas and the kapotas on the śikhara, horizontal layers of pīḍhās, step up and out in offsets, anticipating the multiply tiered[67] look of deuls in Odisha, and, in isolated instances, in Bengal. The udyata, jāgrata or dopiccha siṁhas or vajramastaka lion designs of Odisha, anticipated at Tala, appear now in numerous locations, never assigned to them at Tala. They appear in rearing or seated postures. They trample two bodied elephants on the jaṅghā, vārāndikā and śikhara. They are addorsed at pilaster corners, below and above the quarter karṇāmālakas. They crown and flank the siṁhakarṇas. They bring Dakṣiṇa Kośala closer to Odisha. The siṁhakarṇas now occupy all the segments of elevation, accelerating the use of the curved element, used sparingly at Devarani in makaratoraṇas. The larger siṁkakarṇas contain images of divinities in bhadra and karṇa.[68] The smaller ones on the pratikarṇas contain human or grāsamukas, recalling Jethani south siṁhagavākṣas. The siṁkakarṇas or siṁhagavākṣas on the śikhara restore the caityas of Lakṣmaṇa and later Devarani pīṭha, modifying the profile of their architectonically conceived doors, with mukulas. The pilasters show the Tala aśokalumbī on the ghaṭapallava capital, which is adorned with incised lotus leaves and triangular ardhapadmas at the base, like Tala kalaśa capitals. The softly modelled sculptures in terracotta are characterised by a fine sense of design, the impression of which is enhanced by the thick overhanging jewelled festoons, used also on Tala pillar, later reformulated as jhārāvalī in Odisha.

A remarkable sense of volume, surviving from Tala through Indal Deul, characterises the door jamb of the Siddheśvara temple. It continues the trend of Sirpur and Rajim, in which figured sculpture pushes foliate designs, already reduced to a vestigial presence at Indal Deul, into the background.[69] In place of bulging foliate bands of Tala or snake coil bands of Rajim, an outer band with larger figural sculpture is combined with an inner band with smaller figural sculpture. Together with this, a diagonal accent in the river goddesses, dikpālas and other divine figures on the vertical flanks, is juxtaposed against a vertical accent in standing Pārvatī pariṇaya (Pārvatī's marriage) or seated Lakulīśa figures on the two lintels. A visual impact of recession, and inward propulsion like Tala is created by the swaying, triple flexed river goddesses (Fig. 326), with their hips jabbing inside, and by the dikpālas,[70] rushing down on their vehicles. This recession is reinforced by some accessory elements like the swimming fish above Gaṅgā's shoulder, the swinging garlands held by river goddesses, the flying vidyādharas and gandharvas above, or by the upraised snout and head of the makara and kūrma below, directing attention inside. The centripetal pull is strengthened on the Devarani or Rājīvalocana lintels by the simultaneous convergence of figures to the centre. At Palāri this is created by extreme flexed figures of Śiva killing the elephant and Andhaka demons on the upper lintel, and, by the flying figures of Brahmā on goose and Viṣṇu on Garuḍa on the lower lintel. The entire phalanx of heaving and rushing forms is stabilized, again in the manner of Devarani or Rājīvalocana, by Kalyāṇasundaramūrti of Śiva Pārvatī in the centre of the upper lintel, and by Lakulīśa and his disciples on the centre of the lower lintel. On the door frame, the stabilizing accent is provided by the extremely attenuated and stylized version of a pillar type, found at Tala Jethani, composed of successive rows of octagonal ghaṭapallavas, and flat, compressed āmalakas. The presence of ornament, dissecting if not choking the figure, has become prominent at both Indal Deul and Palāri. At Palāri, the river goddesses acquire an enhanced, manneristic curve, an arch to the shoulders, arms and the hips, an angular peaking to the headdress, elbows and knees, which take them further away than Indal Deul from their Devarani counterparts. In the dwarf female attendants, this tendency is further aggravated at Palāri by the bowing of their legs below the knees.

The inner lateral faces of the Palāri door jamb are carved, again after Tala and Dakṣiṇa Kośala examples, with a design like Khārod. These substitute, for the figural sculpture at Devarani, full and half lotus medallions, which are linked by a central and flanking floral bands, and divided from the scrolled makara base by a rosette band. The slight sharpening of the edges of the broader lotus petals of Indal Deul, the thinner and more jumbled strands of foliage indicate a change in style.[71]

Two pillars of the original maṇḍapa of the Palāri temple, now lost, stand at the entrance to its present courtyard. They betray similar designs like a ghaṭapallava base with vandanamālikās, an octagonal shaft, carved alternately with horizontal foliate bands and vandanamālikās, scrolled haṁsas and makaras on the impost block, a ghaṭapallava capital and a masūraka, carved with rosettes. The pillar on the right has two ghaṭapallava bases and capitals, with bhāraputrakas at the corners of the upper capital. The pillar on the left interrupts the shaft with a four-armed divinity. Most of these features have been seen earlier at Tala and other Dakṣiṇa Kośala temples. Several Tala segments like the siṁhagavākṣa pilasters of Jethani, and the stambhasākhā of the Devarani maṇḍapa door jamb, duplicate ghaṭapallava bases and capitals. The prātolī pillars of Rājīvalocana also duplicate ghaṭapallava at crown and base. The ghaṭapallava capital on the Jethani east pillar is adorned with a vandanamālikā, and its shaft is clasped by horizontal floral bands. These features are found also on Rāmacandra maṇḍapa pillars. A later Devarani pillar has a plain masūraka above the ghaṭapallava, both being hung with garlands rather than the Palāri rosettes and a shaft, with busts of gaṇas at the corners. The carving of a figure on the freestanding pillar is also derived from Jethani prototypes via Sirpur and Rajim. So are the scrolled haṁsas and makaras, which are also found in darpaṇas above the pillar base in Jethani, at the pillar base in Sirpur and Rajim, or in square blocks on the pillar shaft at Ajanta, Aurangabad, Ellora and Bādāmi. Bhāraputrakas appear on ghaṭapallava capitals at Ajanta, Ellora, and in the Rāmacandra maṇḍapa pillar at Rajim.[72] While the combination of these motifs suggests the experience of Dakṣiṇa Kośala and western Indian sites behind these pillars, the figures on the Palāri pillars or door jambs, despite a shared stiffness, are yet to be overtaken by the harsh angularity and metallic hardness of the Rajim prātolī pillar figures. The foliage on the pillars is also not as shallow as the foliage on the prātolī pillars, in spite of the superior decorative quality of design at Rajim. As such, the Palāri temple still stays within the seventh century AD.

PHASE 4: QUASI-STELLATE BRICK TEMPLES (AD 700-800), DHOBIN, DĀMĀKHERĀ

Sharpening, Flattening Hardening of Contours, Exaggeration of Ornament and Gestures, Suppression of Movement

With the onset of the eighth century, the brick temple tradition of Dakṣiṇa Kośala seems to lose its moorings in the early classical Tala style, or the freshness and vigour of the early work, inspired by Tala and Lakṣmaṇa. The architectural facade is gradually overtaken by an angularization, linearization and dematerialization, in suppression of explicit volumes. The temple of Kirwāi Dhobin (Figs. 122-23) near Dāmākheḍā on the Raipur-Bilaspur state highway appears to embody this trend, verging on early 8th century AD. Despite extensive damage to the śikhara or modern appendages, it is evident that the temple has a garbhagṛha, based on the plan of two concentric squares placed mutually at an angle of 45°, which is a sign of growing complexity since Tala.[73] The maṇḍovara of the temple, including the vedībandha, is made of stone, while the śikhara is made of brick, layered with stucco.

At first blush, the temple may convey a misleading impression of being earlier than the Palāri temple, because of its lateral expansion, or seemingly broader volumes. A closer look reveals that all profiles and lines of this temple have become straighter, sharper and harsher than the lines of Palāri. The continuing prominence given to curved shapes at Palāri, makes way here for sheer verticals and horizontals, which appear to only formally look back to Tala elevation. The replication of the later Devarani kapota moulding with candraśālās, all over the body of the temple, reaching its peak with the madhyabandhana on the jaṅghā of Palāri, is a tradition which is now discarded. Not only is there no madhyabandhana on the jaṅghā, but the kapotas or the śikhara are plain, and do not have candraśālās. The candraśālās are now again installed singly, like later Devarani mouldings, rather than in clusters of twos or threes, like Bhīma Kīcak Devala or later brick temples, on the rucaka pilasters of the pratirathas. The siṁhakarṇas on the karṇas or the jaṅghā modify their curved shapes, in vogue in brick temples since Lakṣmaṇa, for more linear and vertical shapes. Instead of a tall, pilastered caitya like Devarani or later, a short caitya is carried by two dwarfs, who are formed like pillars with rectilinear contours. Similarly, the vajramuṇḍī is made by a flat pilaster like lion, with its paw crudely carved on its chest, which replaces the livelier, more organic lions of Tala or Palāri. The dhyānamudrā figures appear in the siṁhakarṇas only on karṇas, with their hands curved and joined together like a garland, their chests outlined by a sheer, vertical contour. Complex, needless decoration grows, and the single mukulas in Devarani caityas, makaratoraṇas or Palāri siṁhakarṇa are replaced in the siṁhakarṇas at Dhobin by numerous mukulas. Unlike the clearly demarcated Devarani makaratoraṇas or Palāri, the siṁhakarṇas are flattened out against pilastered niches of vārāṇḍikā. Instead of being rendered substantially and displayed prominently as on Devarani pīṭha, the candraśālās are recessed and inconspicuously located on the śikhara pratirathas.

The visual continuity, uninterrupted on Devarani maṇḍovara, is broken here by dividing the śikhara (Fig. 121) into several horizontal bands, carved with kapotas and āmalakas on each bhūmi. The śikhara pilasters, unlike the Devarani jaṅghā pilasters, have cruciform śīrṣakas with stepped up phalakas, which continue these horizontal bands. Unlike Tala or earlier brick temples, aśokalumbī is used now on the serrated facets of the ghaṭapallava capital of the jaṅghā pilasters, a faceting which overcomes the pābhāga of Odisha temples later. The ghanadvāras, recalling the empty niches of Devarani, and the ghanadvāras of Lakṣmaṇa, reappear on the jaṅghā, replacing narrow, conical caitya niches with mukulas for the crowning kapota.[74] The bāñkājālī of later Odisha, Lakṣmaṇa vārāndikā, found in embryo at Tala as chequerboard squares, now invade sections of the dvāra. Mālādhārī vidyādharas, which appear on Tala wall slabs above figures, are carved on small projecting panels on the bhadra and pratiratha pilasters, anticipating such panels in the bāḍā of Odisha temples. The siṁhavaktra of Jethani Tala gavākṣas and lintel panels, fills some of the caityas on the kapota above the jaṅghā, anticipating Odisha practice. While the later Devarani mouldings and motifs continue, the candraśālās are crudely outlined, unlike Devarani, by double incised lines. The flattened aśokalumbī acquires a crudely human grāsamukha on its crown. A paṭṭikā of juxtaposed ardhapadma triangles is added above the vedikā, or in the śikhara. The mouldings become comparatively unsubstantial in volume and sharper in outline. Projection and recession are confined to the jaṅghā and maṇḍapa door jamb of Devarani. At Dhobin, the entire body of the temple projects and recedes more than any other temple before. Yet, because of the flattening, linearization, desiccation of its contours, it is not animated by the movement which characterises Tala temples, Lakṣmaṇa or Palāri. The heavy bhūmi āmalakas, which now occupy the bhadra and karṇa projections of the śikhara, freeze the movement further, instead of emphasizing it. The classical style of Tala and early Dakṣiṇa Kośala architecture appears, with this temple, to be frozen by the onset of medievalism.

Śavarīnārāyaṇa and Lakṣmaneśvara, Khārod

A similar premonition of the medieval mode can be sensed also in the brick temple of Śavarīnārāyaṇa (Figs. 14, 124) at Khārod in Bilaspur district. Situated on a tank like Palāri, it faces east rather than west unlike Palāri, and uses stone only in the foundation. In the Devarani vedībandha, the kumbha is replaced by a kaṇṭha and a kalaśa on the maṇḍapa. Acting on this precedent, the vedībandha at Śavarīnārāyaṇa, like Dhobin Śiva temple (Figs. 122-23), makes the kumbha taller on the pratirathas, shorter on the bhadras and karṇas, staggering the height.[75] However, unlike Devarani or Śavarīnārāyaṇa, this staggering device is used for greater visual impact of the elevation, by emphasizing the continuity of its vertical profile. Unlike the kapota with candraśālās on the later Devarani plinth (Figs. 91, 93, 95), the kapota is also staggered at Śavarīnārāyaṇa. It is used as a thin madhyabandhana, raised to a higher level on the pratirathas, salilāntaras and karṇas. Unlike the Palāri jaṅghā, or the continuous band across Dhobin jaṅghā, it is made more like the discontinuous band on the jaṅghā of Indal Deul. This device of staggered heights, though inspired by the Devarani precedent, is carried beyond its minimal use at Devarani, to quicken the facade to a more unstable life. The visual impact of projection and recession is enhanced by it to an extent, considered unnecessary for the external aspect of the temple at Devarani. Acute angled pilasters in salilāntaras, rows of stepped, pyramidal āmalakas, tiny āmalakas, are inserted below the lowest karṇāmalakas as 'grace notes'. Missing in the unadorned Tala exterior, these features further galvanize the temple body with the flashy frippery of ornament. At the same time, a natal connection with temples like Tala is retained by excluding siṁhakarṇas from the jaṅghā and vārāndikā. Despite visible restoration, the broad, heavy skandha and mastaka of Śavarīnārāyaṇa, and what may well be the original āmalaka, indirectly demonstrate its surviving links with the tremendous volumes of Tala temples. These help continue a tradition of wide shouldered temple bodies, which is consummated in the beki, āmlā or mastaka of Odishan temples. Taken as a whole however, the temple becomes more curvilinear than the earlier brick and stone prototypes, showing a further distancing from Tala. The earlier photographs of Śavarīnārāyaṇa with the ASI and the surviving portion of the projection wall, show the existence of the kapili and a maṇḍapa, the walls of which, like Devarani, and the garbhagṛha walls, were carved with oblong niches framed by pilasters.[76]

The Śavarīnārāyaṇa maṇḍapa is a modern restoration, in which are arranged six pillars and pilasters, carved with Śiva or female chowri bearers, atop a bhāravāhī gaṇa. This recalls the arrangement in Tala. The original door jamb of the shrine has been concealed by a lintel and a pair of jambs, one of them being carved with Gaṅgā or Yamunā, below clustered fruits and leaves, pratihāras and standing mithunas. Despite disfigurement by application of heavy coats of vermilion, it is possible to make out that the voluminous, wide hipped and broad shouldered bodies, the naturalistically rendered bunch of leaves and fruits, the slender mithunas or chowri bearers, still look back to the river goddesses and leafy crowns of Tala. The very location of the river goddesses on the top, with a pratihāra below, in an independent panel, reminds us of the arrangement of similar figures on the lateral walls of the Devarani maṇḍapa. They are, in fact, not distant from the Rājīvalocana maṇḍapa or western gate figures in the 7th century. Fluted into sixteen facets, interrupted by octagonal śobhāpaṭṭikās, carved with rathapaṭṭis and vandanamālikās, with full and half rosette borders, a ghaṭapallava āmalaka capital and śīrṣaka, the maṇḍapa pillars remind us not only of Jethani east pillars but also of the design of Rāmacandra maṇḍapa pillar at Rajim. The foliage is, however, carved much more superficially, like the figured pillar in front of the Palāri temple.

The original door jamb figures are later than these lintel figures. These have moved completely away from the curvilinear, fluent contours of Tala or the early brick temples, and have accepted the rectilinear forms of Dhobin. The original doorframe displays, like the Rājīvalocana garbhagṛha or prātolī doorway, a Garuḍa holding the tails of two nāgas on the lintel, the coils of which frame worshipful, or club and garland bearing, flying nāgas and nāginis on the outer śākhā. On the inner śākhā, a squatting nāgī holds serpentine creepers, coming out of the mouth of scrolled karimakaras on the sides. The nāgas are seated on a padmapīṭha, over river goddesses placed on the peḍyā, recalling the mithuna panels above the large river goddess panels on the inner surrounds of Devarani. The Garuḍa is, however, a stiff, squared off figure, coming closer to the dhyānī images in the siṁhakarṇas of Dhobin than to the fleshy Garuḍas or fluently contoured Viṣṇu of Rajim, or the peacock vehicle of Kārtikeya at Jethani. Equally stiff are the nāgas, who, while recalling the boyish forms of Rajim or Devarani door jamb mithunas, have lost their curved shapes, or animation, being reduced to rigid, squarish, column like shapes, falling rather than flying down, in a straight, vertical drop. The Garuḍa's wings are roughly incised, hard mantles, and do not look like the curved, feathered, fluttering Garuḍa or peacock wings of Rajim or Jethani. The snake coils are lifeless, bent to near squares on the top lintel flanks. They fail to evoke memory either of the fleshy, vibrant hoods of snakes at Tala or Rajim, or of the snake coils around the Indal Deul lintel figures.[77]

The door jamb of the sanctum of the completely reconstructed temple of Lakṣmaneśvara, and two pillars in front, would appear to belong to the same period as the Śavarīnārāyaṇa door jambs. The outer jambs have a similar arrangement of river goddesses posing as vṛkṣakās, with pratihāras below, while the inner jambs are adorned with full and half lotus medallions, linked by foliate bands, which look back to the Tala tradition. The pillars are carved on two sides in the Tala and Dakṣiṇa Kośala tradition, with curled serpents, and Rāvaṇānugraha, Ardhanāriśvara, or Viṣṇu incarnations. It is doubtful if the garbhagṛha, the door jamb or the pillars can be associated with the 6th century inscription in the maṇḍapa, and these should be dated to early 8th century.[78]

Śiva Temple, Aḍbhār

The Śiva temple of Aḍbhār (Fig. 13) in Bilaspur district, like the Dhobin temple, is based on a plan of two concentric squares, placed at an angle of 45°, indicative of the growing complexity, distancing it from Tala. While the plan itself does not make it contemporary to or later than Dhobin, the sculpture and the architecture of the temple show a frozen, linear quality, which heralds the medieval style in the 8th century AD. It comprises a garbhagṛha, antarāla, maṇḍapa with ardhamaṇḍapas, mukhamaṇḍapa, now missing, accessible by steps, and a detached nandīmaṇḍapa. The Tala motif of the kalaśa with aśokalumbī appears here at the base of the antarāla door jamb (Fig. 227), base of the inner surround of this door jamb, in the hands of river goddesses, on the outer face of the jambs, at the base also of the capital of the garbhagṛha and nandīmaṇḍapa door jamb, or of the pilasters in the fallen antarāla lintel. It becomes ubiquitous, also flatter, more incised and conical than Dhobin. The later Devarani kapota with candraśālās now occupies the base of the antarāla door jamb, the lintels of the garbhagṛha and nandīmaṇḍapa door jamb. It becomes sparse in its description on the caitya door in the nandīmaṇḍapa lintel. The siṁhavaktra of Jethani fills the central gavākṣa of nandīmaṇḍapa lintel. The rosettes or half rosettes, used at Tala, appear also in frames of the ghaṭa base of the inner surround, in the central candraśālā on the kapota lintel of the garbhagṛha, and on its pillar capital. The inner surround and soffit of the antarāla door jamb are decorated, in the Devarani, and Daksina Kośala tradition, by full and half lotus medallions, linked by a median foliate band, without the other flanking foliate bands. The bevelling of the Tala door jambs is partially captured by putting the nāgarāja worshippers at the corner base of the nāgabandha. The carving itself is dry, shallow and flat. The foliate splendour of Tala is gone. Gone also is the splendid mesh of snake coils with yakṣas, birds or animals at Rājīvalocana. The snake coils on the lintel move in a sluggish manner, and have lost the animation or volume of Tala, Rājīvalocana or even Indal Deul. The Garuḍa is drawn in a cursory manner in the centre of the nāgaśākhā. The architrave shows images in panels, partitioned by ghaṭapallava pilasters, like Jethani south lintels, and images on projected tulā bosses above the river goddesses, in an adaptation of the carved tulā bosses of Dhobini jaṅghā to the door jamb. In Odisha later, architraves largely adapt a similar method of display in pilastered panels, while a regular tulā saṁgraha with carvings is displayed above the vedībandha, a single projected tulā boss being accepted on the centre of the lintel as a station for the adhināyaka devatā.[79]

The biggest change since Tala is the palsy which has struck the body at Aḍbhār, specially the legs below knees, freezing life and movement. At Tala, standing images and even floral forms vibrate with movement. At Aḍbhār, movement is shown through an exaggeration of gestures or postures, though, the bodies remain frozen. The moment the images (Figs. 336-37) unlock a conventional sthānaka or āsana, they become awkward and ungainly in movement. The moving legs of the vṛkṣakās, accompanied by a śuka or haṁsa, or of the lady climbing a man in a mithuna on detached panels, are stunted. They hold one leg ramrod straight, the other leg being made disproportionately longer or shorter, with a stiff bend below the knees, which are placed far lower than normal. The same paralysis afflicts the flexed legs of the river goddesses. The modelling is blighted by the same awkwardness. The hands of the gandharvas or nāyikās playing vīṇā are bloated, and their fingers are curved out of shape. The faces of all images show a dismaying uniformity with a flat, broad nose, and sharp curves for eyebrows and mouth. Incisions and ridges affect all descriptions, and the swinging garment of vṛkṣakās or the foliate elements lack substance. The misleading simplicity in ornament does not hide the hardening of the limbs, or the sharp, rectilinear accents of architecture. An example is the āmalaka shaped capital and the miśraka pillar (Fig. 292) of the nandīmaṇḍapa. The pillar has become slender, with knife edge profiles. It is equipped with small gaṇas at corners above a high base, strapped with a pendant noose of slipknotted ropes for holding the kalaśa, or carved, elsewhere, with medallions on the impost block. It suggests a miniaturization and simplification of the pillar orders at Ajanta and Ellora (Figs. 290-91). As compared with the substantial capital, contained within the pillar at Tala or Ajanta, the capital has spilled out of the pillar like Elephantā and Ellora, and has flattened out beyond Bādāmi. The movement away from the distinct volume and visually mobile contours of the Tala pillars is evident. A comparison of the mayūrātapatra over Yamunā, at Tala and Aḍbhār, shows a similar reduction of a plastic, life like element to a conventionalized, decorative form at Aḍbhār.[80]

RUINED TEMPLES, PŪJĀRĪPĀLĪ 9TH CENTURY AD
REASSERTION OF LINE AND VOLUME

With the Rāma temple at Sirpur, the temples at Khārod (Figs. 124-25) and Palāri, Dakṣiṇa Kośala closely anticipates the stellate plans, formed by intersecting squares, at the Odisha brick temples of Buḍhikomnā, Kasuli and Baudh. At Pūjārīpālī (Fig. 144) in Raigarh district, the Dakṣiṇa Kośala brick temple tradition seems to come back to itself in the 9th century, filtered now through Odisha forms. This reincarnation of the tradition, to which Tala contributed in a large measure, is illustrated by the two ruined temples at Pūjārīpālī on Raigarh-Sārangarh-Sarāi road, near Mahānadī.[81] One of these (called Kewaṭin) has an intact garbhagṛha, kapili and antarāla, with a truncated śikhara, while the other (called Gopāla), has the garbhagṛha alone, with the top, back and one side of the śikhara and jaṅghā gone. The kapota of later Devarani, survives with the distinct shape and volume in the śikharas of earlier Dakṣiṇa Kośala brick temples. It is now reduced to a decorative architectural element, integrated in horizontal layers of a rectilinear khākharā muṇḍi. In the triaṅga plan of Kewaṭin, the pratiratha is more sharply differentiated by salilāntaras. Its distinct shape as an engaged pilaster, long on jaṅghā, short and stunted on the śikhara, is emphasized, and the kapotas, planted on each pilaster in the śikhara, come to look like so many mastaka khuras of khākharā Deul. Bifurcation of kapota, flattening of āmalakas, use of flat bands in continuous horizontal tiers around the temples,[82] show how Dakṣiṇa Kośala architecture now veers away from the sense of sculpted volume, to which Tala had committed its architecture for a long time.

In spite of this rarefication, the body of the Pūjārīpālī temples is more curvilinear and their profiles are much more moulded and rounded, compared with near contemporary Odishan temples like Buḍhikomnā, which links them with the Dakṣiṇa Kośala style. The square panels above the river goddesses at Aḍbhār (Fig. 227), appear here on the door of the 'Gopāla' temple, carved with lively figures of Keśi and Pūtanāvadha (slaughter of Keśi and Putanā) from Kṛṣṇalīlā (Kṛṣṇa's exploits). Such panels become smaller parts of Odisha temple lintels later (Fig. 235).[83] The unadorned simplicity of the garbhagṛha walls, relieved only by occasional tulā projections on karṇas, carved with figures like Dhobin, recalls the stark simplicity of the Devarani walls, or the later brick cladding of Jethani. Interestingly enough, the river goddesses on the stone door of the Gopāla temple and in the village, recapture the austere easy stance and weight of Tala figures. They also display the sīmantacuḍāmaṇi on the forehead, the fine mantle stretched across the left breast and the right waist, the swelling ball of the flexed knees, the distinct weight of the gathered frills over a low hung lower garment, the painstaking description of the hair, hair band or ornament, the slender, but wide hipped form, features which have been the hall mark of the Tala style earlier. Suppressed by a surfeit of ornament, excessive flexion, appliqué effect of a terracotta style, or by unnecessary aggravation or attenuation of volumes at Khārod or Palāri, the Tala features reassert themselves in these Pūjārīpāli images. Carved on pillars with sculpted bases and attendants, these figures show the continuing use of figured slabs in architecture, so much in vogue at Tala, while the carved rectangular panels above them, continue the use of such panels from Aḍbhār, carrying it into Odisha. In place of the figures above the Varuṇa image at Tala, or the fish above the river goddesses at Indal Deul, Khārod (Figs. 338-39), or Palāri, two haṁsas appear above the Yamunā at Gopāla temple, establishing a link with a variant of Tala motifs in Dakṣiṇa Kośala. The hardening, which has come in at Aḍbhār, remains however, and turns the lotus or peacock feather umbrellas into similar, honed, hard shapes. The squaring of the shoulders or head, the congested rows of bangles on the wrist, the repetitive beading in the ornament, also show the intensification of the movement away from the Tala style. A few other slabs or fragments with Bhairava, Kārtikeya, Lakṣmī, Gaṇeśa, haṁsa, makara or kinnara in the village show a gradual approach to the balance of form and ornament, volume and chastening line, which distinguish much of the 9th century sculpture, the acme of which can be seen in Dakṣiṇa Kośala in tribal Surguja.[84]

PARALLEL AND ARCHAISTIC DEVELOPMENTS IN SURGUJA (7TH TO 11TH CENTURY AD): COEXISTENCE OF CRUDITY WITH FLUENCY OF LINE AND AMPLITUDE OF VOLUME – CLOSER APPROXIMATION TO STYLES IN ODISHA

The convergence of currents from Tala and allied Dakṣiṇa Kośala sites towards the Odishan style and a second classical style in 9th century can be charted in the isolated, hilly, forested tract of tribal Surguja district, using style as the criterion, since inscriptions, firmly associated with monuments, are missing.

The lean and heavy bodied style of Tala, filtered through Dakṣiṇa Kośala, is generally misinterpreted in Surguja till late 8th century. Flattening, excessive elongation and rectilinearization restrict the fluency of modelling, which moves away from the energy of Tala and freshness of Sātmahallā around mid-7th century AD. It is only in the 9th century that the style recovers its feet, and both sculpture and architecture are executed with a renewed sense for modelled form, harking back to Tala, Malhār, Sirpur or Rajim. The earlier crudity does not return in the 10th and 11th century work, which accounts for its greater vitality, compared with much of the work in Ḍāhala in the later period.

Sātmahallā. 7th Century AD

The earliest site to reveal a link with the style of Tala is Sātamahallā in village Bhadvāhi, which is littered with brick and stone fragments of completely ruined temples (Figs. 25-29).[85] Two door jamb fragments still retain river goddesses (Fig. 318) in very high relief, who carry ghaṭa and a garland of spiral strands, reminding us of Tala, and stand in tribhaṅga, on a three tiered padmapīṭha. They are accompanied by a diminutive, female umbrella bearer, and canopied by a tiered umbrella, which, in turn, carries a small mālāvidyādhārī and a miniature ghaṭa. In the broad similarity of features like the interwoven hair braids, crowned by a dhammilla (tiered female headdress) bun, tribhaṅga posture, garland, a hāra lapping across the breasts, an intertwined two string armlet, these river goddesses appear close to those at Palāri, while the seated figure atop the umbrella reminds us of Indal Deul, Khārod or Tala river goddesses and Jethani Varuṇa. But the contour of the body, specially the shoulder, the umbrella, or the headdress, is more curvilinear and softer than Khārod or Palāri in the Sātamahallā images, bringing them closer to the Tala idiom. The relaxed volumes of the effortlessly flexed legs are spoilt neither by the heaviness or sloth of Indal Deul, nor by the thinning below knees or the awkward knocking of knees, which afflict the Palāri river goddesses. However, the stiffer depiction of the lower garment, the sharper bifurcation of the waist by the nīvibandha, the steeper contours of the waist or the legs, place these images before Indal Deul, but after the Sirpur Lakṣmaṇa or vihāra images in the 7th century AD.

Belsar. 8th century AD

The Śiva temple (Fig. 30) on the top of a mound at Harrātolā, Belsar, near confluence of river Kerākāchār and Mahān on Ambikāpur-Kusmi road forms a further link with Tala in the stylistic chain in Surguja district. Clearances, undertaken in 1991,[86] have revealed the plinths of this and several other small adjacent shrines, which possess striking similarities with the later Devarani plinth. They share mouldings like khura, jāḍyakumbha, kalaśa, antarapaṭṭa with ghaṭapallava pilasters, kapota. The broad shafts of antarapaṭṭa pilasters are adorned with the rosettes found in Tala panel frames and jambs. The kīrtimukhas and human heads in the caityas on the kapota are, however, much cruder in execution than the figures on the kapota at Devarani. They are in conformity with the generally crude figural style, characterised by short, stunted legs, bloated faces, misshapen and disproportionately large hands, and sheer, sharp contours. A Hari Hara, Garuḍa and a Kārtikeya are examples. The caitya itself is roughly and perfunctorily incised, not modelled as an autonomous element like Devarani. The style is an uncouth prototype of Dhobin and can well be contemporary.

The jaṅghā of the main Śiva temple shows simple pilasters and recesses like Devarani, and siṁhakarṇas like later brick temples of Dakṣiṇa Kośala. A fluted door jamb, carved with half and full lotus medallions, has been found, which resembles the jamb of the central cella to the north of Jethani. The pillars are of the miśraka type, with ghaṭapallava capitals like Tala. It is, however, the door jamb to the main temple, which offers several important features connecting the site with Tala, with brick temples of Dakṣiṇa Kośala, as well as with Odisha. The vine around a stem, later used as maliphula phadikā in Odisha, has been used at Tala to frame Devarani maṇḍapa side wall figures or a doorband at Jethani south, and then, in other sites of Dakṣiṇa Kośala. It is now used as the main outer band of the upper lintel. It also acts as the overhanging foliate element, frequent in earlier sites including Devarani, and culminates in a simple trefoil caitya, familiar from later Devarani or Sirpur, Khārod, or Palāri kapotas. This is edged by a thin stambhaśākhā, formed by vertically placed rows of ghaṭapallava and āmalakas, like Palāri door jamb, and some pillars of Jethani. The rūpaśākhā follows, forming the lower lintel, and is constituted by alternating bhāraputrakas, muktāgrāsas, vṛkṣakās, mālādhārī river goddesses, vidyādhara and nāga mithunas, Viṣṇu and Vareśvara Śiva (Śiva as bridegroom) on Nandin, flanked by Gaṇeśa and Kārtikeya on Kailāsa, in the dvāra-lalāṭa-bimba. Elements from the Tala pillars or door jambs are brought together in compositions, which anticipate the Odishan raṅganī doorbands[87], with their square panels, terminating in a single or several superimposed, projecting square niches in the centre of the lintel. The innermost band of rosettes in squares, seen in abundance on Tala door jamb and panel frames, is used extensively as raṅganī in Odisha door jambs.

The two large independent slabs, carved with Śiva and Pārvatī at the door of the temple, show the continuing use of such slabs from Tala days, probably no longer as architectural elements of the wall, but as freestanding panels with a semicircular top, framed with the raṅganī design. The severely squared off shoulders and heads, the flat body, the sharp, abrupt transitions at the waist, the cylindrical, ponderous legs and hands, the high relief, betray the 8th century idiom which overtakes the squarish figures of Dhobin or Aḍbhār. In spite of the folkish flavour or the angularity of the figures on the door frame, which unite them with the larger slab figures, they retain a sense of weight and volume, an austerity, a monumentality, a curvilinear rhythm in the contour of their face, a cheerful freedom from convention, which suggest surviving links with the Tala tradition, and place them in the early 8th century AD.

A sculpture of Kārtikeya (Pl. 44) has been found on this mound, which is a complete surprise, coming from this site. It is absolutely free from the crudity and lack of proportion, which characterise the other images. Almost directly inspired by the Tala design, it is a work of equally great beauty at the turn of the 8th and beginning of the 9th century, and is united with several images of the great 9th century art at adjacent Deepadih, by the union of sensuous modelling with contemplative bliss. That it is a later version of its Tala counterpart (Fig. 350), is evident from the changes in the modelling. The soaring, elongated body of Tala Kārtikeya becomes slightly stooped, and considerably compressed here both vertically and laterally. The large volumes of the cascading hair or the armlet are thinned down. The fullness of the face is diminished. The bifurcation of the waist by the lower garment becomes sharper and more horizontally outlined. The body and face become harder, animated less with the vibration of arrested breath. The correspondence of sweeping rhythms, established at Tala between the curved and outstretched wings of the peacock on the one head, and the body of Kārtikeya on the other, is diluted. The meditative expression of the Tala Kārtikeya head remains, but is reduced to more of a surface effect. In spite of these late features, the union of physical strength with spiritual emotion, which Tala receives as a strong legacy from the classical 5th century style, is asserted once again with great energy of purpose in this image, to leaven the Deepadih style in

9th century. It also recovers the capacity for soft and relaxed modelling, for a relatively easy movement of the contour, for establishing a harmony of compositional lines (evident in the curved shoulder, which responds to the curved peacock wings, albeit with a slower rhythm than Tala), which was suppressed at Dhobin, Aḍbhār or in the main temple of Belsar in early 8th century.

Deepādih 8th to 11th Century AD

Not very far from Belsar, at the 100% Orāon tribal village of Deepadih, on Rājpur-Shankargarh-Kusmi road, on a plateau, 2,900 feet above the sea level, and close to the confluence of rivers Kānher, Galphullā and Sūryā, the art of Dakṣiṇa Kośala enters a glorious period, going through several stylistic phases from the 8th to the 11th century AD. It is here, more than anywhere else, that the elements from the late classical Tala idiom, reinterpreted by early medieval experiments in the stone and brick temples of Dakṣiṇa Kośala, find their fruition in a second 'classical' style, lasting from the late 8th to early 10th century, reaching its acme in the mid-9th century. It is here again that the art of Dakṣiṇa Kośala attains a fullness of proportions, an authenticity of expression, an impeccable sense for appropriate decoration, an integration of sculpture with architecture, which are seen at the Tala temples earlier, and, in Odisha from the 8th century on.

The clearance of the Deepadih mounds[88] has revealed temples and fragments at Orāonṭolā, assignable to the 8th century; at Sāmatsarṇā, from the 9th and 10th century; on the grounds between Orāonṭolā and Sāmatsarṇā, attributable to the 10th and 11th century; and, on the Chailā Pāhār, from all these periods (Figs. 31-40).

Deepādih, Phase I Early 8th Century AD

The earliest temple is at Orāonṭolā (Fig. 129), equipped with a garbhagṛha, antarāla, maṇḍapa, raised on a plain jagatī, which provides a pradakṣinā patha around the temple. The vedībandha of the temple retains the plain khura of late Devarani, making it taller, and providing it, at the garbhagṛha, with a grooved stone channel like Devarani. The jāḍyakumbha, kalaśa, antarapaṭṭa and kapota follow, like later Devarani or Dakṣiṇa Kośala temples. The projected slope of the jāḍyakumbha uses the design at later Devarani and its variations on the muhānti of Odisha temple to show scrolled haṁsas, affronted across foliate patterns (which resemble addorsed, agape, flower spouting makaras), scorpions below half lotus medallions, a monkey, eating beside a banana tree, peacocks pouncing on snakes, snakes emerging from fissures, and the four legged, reptilian goherā (a kind of a lizard). It shows an experimental zest, found only at Tala earlier. The kalaśa, like Dakṣiṇa Kośala temples, including later Devarani or Jethani pillar elements, flaunts the aśokalumbī at regular intervals on certain segments, leaving other segments unadorned. The antarapaṭṭa is carved, like Devarani, with plain galapādas and recesses on karṇa rathas, and, with full lotus medallions, embedded between kapiśīrṣakas, on bhaḍrarathas. The muhānti of the kapota, like that of later Devarani, is carved with mithunas and scrolled, nibbling haṁsas. Additionally, it has ādityauttānapādāsanā (in a posture with both feet drawn up and spread out to reveal the vulva) Lajjā Gaurī and padmāsanā Lakṣmī. The jaṅghā follows, equipped, from the evidence, suggested by the minimal surviving remains in site, with mañcikās. These are carried by clustered pilasters with kapota capitals, and carved with large candraśālās with couples. It is an elaboration beyond the Devarani koṣṭhas, occasioned by intervening developments in the Dakṣiṇa Kośala brick temples. The vedībandha mouldings retain the heaviness, characteristic of 6th and 7th century Dakṣiṇa Kośala. In the pratirathas, the jāḍyakumbha is made taller, raising the kalaśa, creating the staggered effect, which is in embryo at early Devarani, but fully in play in the Śavarīnārāyaṇa temple at Khārod or at the Śiva temple of Dhobin. Unlike these, more like designs on the Vasanta paṭṭikā in the upper vedībandha of Odisha, the tall slope of the kumbha in pratiratha is decorated with flying mālādhārī vidyādharas and squatting bekibhairavas, figures which are confined to carved wall slabs or pillar bases of Tala. The offsets introduced at the corners of the bhadra and karṇarathas are now sharper, the vedībandha taller and more ornamental than 7th century Dakṣiṇa Kośala temples. The deliberate, inventive asymmetry in the distribution of the ornamental carvings of the mouldings survives as an inheritance from later Devarani, or the Malhār Bhīma Kīcak Deval vedībandha. The modelling of figures moves away from the curvilinear fluency of 7th century Sirpur or the heavy, balanced, if frozen volumes of Khārod and Aḍbhār. It demonstrates a continuing feeling for the flow of lines, with an occasional maldistribution of volume or angularization of the edges in the body (Figs. 228, 328-39).

Indeed, it is the door jamb near the Bhīma Kīcak Deval (Figs. 210-13) that provides an ancestor of the door jamb of the Orāonṭolā temple sanctum. The nāgavallī loses the elasticity of Malhār, and forms rectangular coiled frames for the flying sword bearing gaṇas. The bevelled stambhaśākhā, with the faceted ghaṭapallava pillar, offer faint memories of the stambhaśākhā in Jethani south door jamb, but abdicate the Jethani volume. The small river goddesses, carved on the main door jamb, or the tall, ghaṭa bearing cross legged river goddesses, with diminutive attendants below and mālāvidyādharas above, a lady with a child and garland bearing ladies carved on slabs, recovered from the maṇḍapa (Figs. 328-39), recall Tala or the Dakṣiṇa Kośala iconographic tradition. However, the square, pinched shoulders and arms, spindly, thin legs, flat breasts and thighs, the sharp, vertical contours and jutting angles of the body of the river goddesses, indicate a continuation and intensification of traits received from Dhobin, Aḍbhār, Pujārīpāli and, in Surguja itself, from Belsar. While these features distance it from Tala, at Tala such medievalisms are dormant.

Among the hundreds of detached architectural fragments, found in the debris of the Orāonṭolā temple, there are some antarapaṭṭa or kaṇṭha mouldings, carved with clustered, receding pilasters, flanking doors with pointed arches, the pilasters themselves being carved occasionally with grāsamukhas and half lotus medallions. These should have belonged to the vedībandha in the maṇḍapa, and show the elaboration in decoration since Devarani or later brick temples. Many kapotas have been found, carved with full and half candraśālās and mithunas, with flying, sword bearing, crouching, megalophallic, pensive gaṇas, vṛkṣakās, male and female riders, combatants, dopiccha, mālādhārī or gajākrānta siṁhas, and figures seated in meditative postures. Many of these figures present themselves in plinths, pillars or wall slabs of Tala. These kapotas could have adorned the pīṭha, vedībandha, jaṅghā as well as the śikhara, continuing the Tala and Dakṣiṇa Kośala brick temple tradition.[89] The trefoil candraśālās contain the caitya with mukula like Tala, but also acquire variations like liṅga in yonīpīṭha or human heads. Makaramukha praṇāla of Tala has been found here, and also siṁhamukha praṇāla. Two ghaṭapallava pillars of the maṇḍapa have square impost blocks, carved with lotus medallions on all four sides, like a later Devarani or Ramtek pillar. In spite of the crude carving of a few kapota figures, with misshapen heads and disproportionate limbs, the small figures remind us, if remotely, of the figures on the Malhār village pillars, while the spirit of gay, innovative abandon, animating them, evokes memory of later Devarani mouldings. In Odisha, this experimentalism is harnessed, often using similar motifs, to a stylized, disciplined programme of decoration of pābhāga, bāḍā or gaṇḍi.[90]

Deepādih, Phase 2. Late 8th century AD

Towards the end of the 8th century, a similar movement from flatness, elongation and angularity of Orāonṭolā temple figures, to a broadening and relaxation of form, appears to take place both at Deepadih and at Bhadvāhi near Sātamahallā.

Anticipated already in the Kārtikeya image from Belsar, this movement heralds a second, 'classical', style, often equivalent in quality, if not in exact patterns, to the 'classical' Dakṣiṇa Kośala style of Tala. In the clearances at Bhadvāhi,[91] two temples and a monastery of Śaivite inspiration, built on a stellate plan, have been found. Made of brick core, with a cladding of stone, the surviving plinths are tall and plain, evoking memory of Devarani. A freestanding slab has been found, carved with ghaṭa and mālā bearing river goddess, suggesting use of such slabs, like Tala, in the walls. At Sāmatsarṇā, Deepadih, a Mahiṣamardanī, garland bearing ladies, two river goddesses have been recovered from the ruins of a temple, which are modelled in an identical way. The shoulder and hips, breasts and ghaṭa become heavy once more, faintly recalling the heavy bodied Tala style. And yet, the waist of the ladies and the head or trunk of a Nṛvarāha. The sharp, rectilinear contours of Orāonṭolā are softened and relaxed into curves, which smoothly glide down the transitions in the body (Figs. 330-31, 333, 335, 573). The halo around head, is cursorily done by semicircular cut, in the slab,[92] reminding us of figures atop the umbrellas of Varuṇa at Jethani, or of river goddesses at Khārod and Palāri. The slightly more bloated face, smaller and flatter breasts, the stiffer posture or contours, are but signs of the problem these female figures or river goddesses face, in trying to break out of the 8th century moulds, to relearn the lessons of Tala, Sirpur or Rajim, and to recapture their volume[93]. At the same time, river goddesses and a Śiva Dakṣināmūrti, carved on the slabs of the coupled Śiva temple in Sāmatsarṇā, a male royal figure, a twenty-armed Viśvarūpa Viṣṇu, try to recover the slender body (Figs. 370-72), popularized simultaneously with the weighty fleshy body, at Tala and in Dakṣiṇa Kośala. To some extent, the attempt succeeds and the contour of the body becomes more curvilinear, and the flesh in the cheeks or in the belly awakens to a new life. The easy flexion and mutuality of relation established in the couples, the distinct delineation and soft contours of the fruiting banyan leaves, garland bearing vidyādharas and lions depicted on this pillar tell us about the rejuvenated feeling for the surging sap of life (Pl. 31). The fine sense of proportion at Tala breaks down however, and the headdress becomes higher, accentuating the interminably stretched out body on an enlarged head. The hands or the thighs are made thicker in proportion to the attenuated chest or waist. The eyebrows are ridged several times, and unlike Tala, the figures have difficulty in emerging from the back plane. A separate shelf is created in the slab to put up one of the arms of Śiva Dakṣiṇamūrti, in an artificial manner, to suggest rest.

Deepādih, Phase 3. 9th century AD

At the beginning of the 9th century, Deepadih recovers the experimental fervor[94] poise, power, grace, fulness of soft, accentless modelling, easy flow of the contour, which were characteristic of some of the best work at Tala. While the mouldings of the plinth remain similar to, but simpler than later Devarani, the use of figured slabs in walls continues. Some of these show Śiva or Paraśurāma in atibhaṅga, resting one of his feet on a paraśu,[95] a Bhairava in tribhaṅga, a seated Umā sahita Śiva and a load bearing gaṇa (Pl. 46; Figs. 379, 405). The soft, cascading locks of Śiva or Bhairava, the curling clouds above Siva or the fluent folds of the snake on their head or arms; the exhaustive description of the snake scales; the fluttering swatches or tab ends of cloth between their legs, or on the waist or seat of Umā; the slender, curled, reticulated fingers of their hands; the tactility of volume, evident even in the slightly swelling balls of knees of Śiva, or in the edge of Umā's lower garment; the furry, floriate character of the ornament; the easy swing of the powerfully rendered bodies; and the strong accent on correct expression, with lips of Śiva, parted in a beatific smile or a malefic snarl, or the face of Umā, lit up by love, remind us, after a long time, of Tala. We are reminded of the swaying bodies of vṛkṣakas, nāyikās, Śiva Pārvatī of Jethani (Figs. 295-96, 305-06, 354), river goddesses of Devarani, Hara Gaurī on Devarani door jamb (Figs. 176, 307, 309, 312, 401), the meandering latā of Jethani door jamb or on Varuṇa parikara, the lotus cups above or below the river goddesses on the Devarani maṇḍapa side walls, the streaming locks of Kārtikeya or Saumya Śiva at Tala, and their blissful expression. The decorative elegance and sophistication, characteristic of the high 9th century style, transforms even a kalaśa, in the manner of Tala, with delicately rendered āmralumbīs, which seem to flow with sap, and nestle cozily against the gentle slope of its body, above a curving necklace of triple pearl strands. In one sweeping movement, these images shake off the desiccation, linearization, flattening or stultification of movement, which overtake Dakṣiṇa Kośala art at sites like Dhobin, Aḍbhār, Belsar in the 8th century, and express themselves with an eloquence paralleling Tala.

However, the classic qualities of Tala modelling are modified by medieval traits, which can be detected in the jutting angles of elbows and knees, emphatic bifurcation of the body by waist bands, and the abrupt dip of the contour, constricting the waist. With the progress of the 9th century, these medieval features, which take Deepadih further away from Tala, are emphasized in a few door jamb fragments, carved with Dūrgā wrestling and killing Mahiṣāsura, Cāmuṇḍā and her minions seizing and devouring demons. The body now becomes relatively slender, the modelling drier, divested of the overwhelming physical vitality of the earlier images, which harked back to Tala. The contour outlining the body becomes steeper and more vertical. The ornament and garment turn harder, losing the vibrant life they had earlier in the century, and hugging the body closer, repeating similar trends of 6th and 7th century Dakṣiṇa Kośala, after Tala. And yet, the balance of form and ornament, weight and movement, power and grace is retained, maintaining a spiritual link with the classical tradition. In fact, the Kārtikeya from this period recovers the same boyish figure, tight, slim, lithe body, which reminds us of Bhīma Devala site pillars, Sirpur, Rajim, or Nācnā Pārvatī temple images (Figs. 327, 404, 526).

Deepādih, Phase 4. Late 9th, Early 10th Century ad

Towards the end of the 9th and beginning of the 10th century, the Deepadih style trembles on the verge of transition, and the architecture and sculpture of the main pañcaratha Śiva temple in Sāmatsarṇā shows transitional features. The brief moment of dalliance with the 'classical' Tala or Dakṣiṇa Kośala style is almost over. The age of schematization, stylization is at hand. The repertoire of Tala and Dakṣiṇa Kośala motifs is now brought fully into use. The modelling of such motifs shows a slackening of attention to the conceptual well-spring of such motifs. One misses the exalted sense of identification with this wellspring, which gives the motifs life and meaning, at Tala. Innovative ardour makes way for uniformity, repetition, and a search for ornamental effect. The kīrtimukha, mithuna, loadbearing gaṇas, lion rearing over an elephant and the winding foliate strand, Kārtikeya on a mayūra, as a base, carved with the fight of Bāli and Sugrīva, on a Sāmatsarṇā door jamb, demonstrate this (Figs. 229-30). The slender, rounded, well proportioned, plastic form coexists with ill proportioned, inelegant, angular, dried up forms. The vedībandha of the Sāmatsarṇā temple (Figs. 32-33, 130-32, 134) garbhagṛhas stands on a tall jagatī. It has a khura, shaped like the kapota moulding of later Devarani. Candraśālās stretch across an intervening recess, to link the upper and lower padmapṛṣṭha slopes in this vedibandha. The recess is carved with perforated chequerboard designs. Later known in Odisha as bāṅkājālī, these designs have been seen earlier in Dakṣiṇa Kośala, including Lakṣmaṇa, and, on Jethani pillars, without the perforations. The low, sloping jāḍyakumbha with softly rounded lotus leaves at corners, found at later Devarani, becomes tall and straight like a cliff, with sharp edged leaves. It projects to allow a second recessed kumbha with slightly moulded edges to go up on its top. The kalaśa comes above this, much larger than its Devarani counterpart. Both kalaśa and kumbha are made of two layers of horizontally laid slabs, in the additive manner of Sirpur vihāra images, Dhobin jaṅghā candraśālās, or figural configurations in Odisha. The kumbha and kalaśa are offsetted thrice in the karṇarathas, making the angles sharper than the bhadra or karṇarathas of Palāri. This parallels Odishan temple pābhāgas, where offsetting is done, more and more by faceting, and less and less by architectural differentiation, unlike Tala.[96] The paṭṭikā which follows, may well be the lower layer of a kapota, or a plain paṭṭa, notionally bolstered up with gradually stepped down mouldings. Similar kapotas are used to gird the vedībandha or śikhara of Śavarīnārāyaṇa, Khārod, Palāri, Dhobin or of Odishan temples, rather than at later Devarani.[97] Above the lowest, recessed two tier khura, all the mouldings are tied together by dviaṅga, pilastered, empty prakoṣṭhas, crowned by khurachādyas, adorned with ghaṭas, bells and udyata siṁhas and by dviaṅga udgamas of storeyed candraśālās. Though the prakoṣṭhas remind us of the pilasterd prakoṣṭhas on Tala jaṅghā, an elaborate formation like this is never used to bind the vedībandha at Tala or later Dakṣiṇa Kośala temples. Projections with oblong slits, carved on three sides of these rathikās, alternate with recesses of the offsets, and translate the Tala and Dakṣiṇa Kośala tradition of such alternation, from the jaṅghā to the vedībandha itself. The use of straight, steep or horizontal incised lines, to enclose triangular perforations, the precipitous ascent of the contour of the udgama, suggest a deliberate choice of abstraction in preference to the distinctly recognizable volume of the candraśālās of Tala or Dakṣiṇa Kośala udgamas. In Odisha, the idea of a continuous linking band is, to some extent, paralleled by the talagarbhikās on pābhāgas, or, by the continuous campaka leaf. The growing abstraction shows the distance traversed in time since Tala or Lakṣmaṇa, bringing this element of the storeyed, offsetted prakoṣṭha closer to the elongated vajra and khākharā muṇḍis of Odisha (Figs. 146, 151).[98]

The reassembled door jamb (Fig. 231) of the garbhagṛha of the Sāmatsarṇā temple shows the transitional features most clearly. The winding latā of classical art at Tala, the ratikerā scroll of Odisha, emerges from the ghaṭapallava, to merge in the tails of affronted makaras on the innermost śākhā of the door jamb and lintel at Lakṣmaṇa temple, and, in the makaras on lintel, at Śavarīnārāyaṇa and Rājīvalocana. It executes a similar movement on the outermost śākhā of the Sāmatsarṇā temple. On the second inner śākhā of the temple door, it encloses grāsamukhas on the lintel. The vertical row of flowers, which appears on the pillars recovered from Devarani, or on Odishan door jambs, as the jalapatra, adorns the innermost śākhā at Sāmatsarṇā.[99] The meticulous description of the floral designs on the garment of the river goddesses or attendants, the scales on the nāgarāja hoods, the scrolled makara tail or the tortoise shell, the distinct weight given to the cloth and ornament, lapping across the body, the dilated shoulders or hips of the river goddesses, speak of the Tala legacy. However, the bloated face and breasts, huge shoulders, and rather muscular arms of the river goddesses, the crudely portrayed features and sharply conical profiles of the attendants, point to the complete change in idiom from the shapely, softly modelled figures of Tala, and the proportionately rendered figures of Khārod, Palāri or Sātamahallā. Unlike earlier Dakṣiṇa Kośala temples, the figures now occupy the lower base of all the śākhās on the flanks. The gajākrānta siṁha and Gajalakṣmī images, which appear on the door sill and lalāṭabimba, respectively parallel Odishan features.[100] The seated padmahastā Lakṣmī, the flying mālāvidyādharas or vidyādharīs, the standing paraśu bearing or dancing Śaiva pratihāras on the lintel, are modelled with a sense of proportion, which reminds us of the early 9th century style at Deepadih, with its earlier Tala heritage.

A blend of the older motifs and style with a anticipation of 'medieval' features can be detected in the pillars recovered from the maṇḍapa of the Śiva temple. The pillar is divided into octagonal sections with a ghaṭapallava capital and square impost block. The sections are separated by the linked rosette bands, laid facing front, a motif in vogue in Tala and later Dakṣiṇa Kośala temples. The muktāgrāsa of Tala pillars appears on the ghaṭa, and is interspersed with mālādhārī gaṇas on the impost block, looking back to such ornament on the 6th century pillar in a Malhār village house. The lions at the Tala pillar bases, appear at the base of the ghaṭa. The mithunas, divided by decorative bands at Devarani, and by ghaṭapallava pilasters in the Malhār pillars, surface here in two sections, partitioned by ghaṭapallava pilasters, and become much more explicit than before. The aśokalumbī on the ghaṭa of Jethani pillars decorates the ghaṭa here. The rhythm of the number eight is kept up though all major elements, from top to bottom. In spite of the conical lion heads, the squared off gaṇa bellies, the sharply drawn triangles of the aśokalumbī or āyāla, the continuity of feeling for tangible flesh and modelled form, even in miniature, link these features with the older legacy of Tala and Malhār, revived in 9th century Deepadih. A few other pillars, recovered from the temple, have octagonal shafts, crowned by ghaṭapallava capital, with lions at the base, and share the same style.

Kalacurī Art of Dakṣiṇa Kośala: 11th Century AD

If the brick temples of the post-Tala period prepare the ground for this achievement at Deepadih and its neighborhood, the Kalacurī art of late 10th 11th century Dakṣiṇa Kośala moves away from the early tradition of Tala. It is invaded by a congestion of ornament, congealing of modelling, distortion of proportions, angularization of contours, and encrustation with ridges and bulges in its sculptures, and ornate, angular, repetitious, crowded compositions in its architectural facades.

Deepādih, Phase 5. 10th -11th century AD

With a pañcāyatana temple (Fig. 34), which has a Cāmuṇḍa slab in the garbhagṛha, and independent slabs, carved with seven mātṛkās, illustrated partially by the mutilated image of Indrāṇī recovered from Sāmatsarṇā, Deepadih arrives squarely in the 10th century AD. Uniform features like sharp incisive edges of the lower garment, the vivisection of contours by stiff, lifeless ornament, high arched, ridged eyebrows, a fixed smile, described by a 'v'curve of the lips, a visible hardening of the belly or the leaves in the halo, incisions in the navel below the breasts or in the throat, announce a break with the inventive, experimental iconography and soft, relaxed contours and volumes of Tala and subsequent Dakṣiṇa Kośala. A sense of proportion, power of precise description, and a superb skill in cutting the stone to minute effects, continue from the classical Dakṣiṇa Kośala style. The pulsing life of Tala is, however, choked by the diminished skill in exploiting the stone as a ductile material, by the tendency to remain content with sharp, easy cuts, or with ornamental surface effects. The body becomes lean and diamond hard, with a glittering but lifeless beauty.

The standing couple, flying garland bearing angels, lionhead and load bearing dwarf carved on a pillar fragment at Sāmatsarṇā, teetering at the edge of 10th - 11th century AD, are characterised by a fusion of linear and volumetric, angular and curvilinear elements (Pl. 32). Two door jambs recovered near the main temple, with vertical stambha, patra, rūpaśākhās with bhāraputrakas, male, female, vidyādhara couples, gajākrānta siṁhas, makaras and grāsamukhas, show an accentuation of these tendencies, using the old Tala and Dakṣiṇa Kośala motifs in a different combination. The Borjoṭilā Sūrya temple (Fig. 133) on the grounds between Sāmatsarṇā and Orāonṭolā, shows a sequence of mouldings in the vedībandha, which is exactly identical with such sequence in the main temple in Sāmatsarṇā (Fig. 132). However, the mouldings look squat and crude in comparison with those of the main temple. The bāṅkājālī is no longer confined to its incipient forms or limited locations at Tala, but appear in the antarapaṭṭa of khura, the vārāndikā, in rathikā udgamas, the salilāntaras or sandhisthalas, the kalaśa moulding of the rathas. The quarter āmalaka also appears in the karṇa of the udgama, showing its multiplier development beyond the Sāmatsarṇā temple udgama. The broken Sūrya, Hari Hara or Viṣṇu images, found from the temple debris, are also harder, flatter and cruder, intensifying the regression from the plasticity of Tala and early Dakṣiṇa Kośala modelling. The numerous devakūlikās and architectural fragments, recovered from the site, suggest existence of a śikhara with storeyed siṁhakarṇas, equipped with mukulas, śūrasenakas with heads on the lowest tier, several bhūmis of karṇāṇḍakas, daṇḍachādyas below vārāndikā, double āmalakas on mastaka, use of samvarṇā, phāmsanā and valabhī roofs, establishing connections with the Dakṣiṇa Kośala style at Maheshpur through 10th-11th century AD as well as with Odisha.

Maheshpur (8th to 11th Century AD)

The stylistic sequence established at Deepadih for Kalacurī art is paralleled, with a subregional accent, at Maheshpur[101] (Fig. 135) near Rāmgarh hills, Sargujā. Pillars with tall plain shafts or shafts decorated with floral stands, embedded ghaṭapallava base and capital, multistoreyed miniature śikharas on rathikās or jaṅgha, doorjambs, carved with playful mouse or monkey, volumetric rhizomes and stable, columnar figures in the stellar Śiva temples and Viṣṇu temple on mound I Nishān Pākhnā, remind us of the 8th century style at Orāonṭolā, Deepadih and Cherkā Deur temple at village Devtikrā, and also recall Sirpur. Ādinātha, Varāha, Nadīdevī,

Nṛsiṁha, Mahīṣamardinī and Mithunas from Ādinatha Ṭilā (Fig. 293) and the Buddha in dhyānamudrā (Fig. 378) demonstrate a curvilinear fluency and arrested energy, characteristic of 9th century Deepadih (Fig. 526). The enlarged, elongated, sloping heads, the chiaroscuro of crowded layers of oversected human or elephant figures in Kṛṣṇalīlā narratives (Figs. 156, 527); the elaboration of parikaras around samabhaṅga (equally flexed) figures, the backward or forward sway or out thrust legs of Hara Gaurī figures (Fig. 406), the ornate but incised decoration of nāga, padmavallī on ghaṭa in the Viṣṇu temple pillar at mound I (Fig. 293), Nishān Pākhnā; the multiplication and superimposition of candraśālās and miniaturization of rathikās on the jaṅghā in temple 2 and Cherkā Deur, Kuriā Jhurki Ṭilā (Figs. 156, 294, 406, 525, 574), tell us of the sharpening and angularization of Kalacūri features in 10th century AD in developments analogous to Sirpur. The disturbance of bodily proportions, thickening and pedestrianization of features in Hari Hara, Sūrya, caitya garvākṣa images recovered from Kuriā Jhurki Ṭilā demonstrate the growing desication of the style in 11th century AD. Stone has been quarried from the adjacent tānkināra hillock, putting us in mind about the Chailā pāhār quarry at Deepadih. The pillar order of the Nishān Pākhnā Viṣṇu temple door jamb bears a close comparison with 8th century Gurjara Pratihāra pillars of Varanasi district of Uttar Pradesh and the early 9th century pillars in Bāndhogarh fort in Shahdol district of Madhya Pradesh.

DEVELOPMENTS IN BASTAR (5TH TO 7TH CENTURY AD): GROWING APPROXIMATION TO SOUTHERN STYLES

We have discussed the gradual approximation of the Dakṣiṇa Kośala style to the style of Odisha. The question of southern influence on the art of Tala has been discussed in the sections on historiography and architecture. In the absence of any evidence of earlier southern movements which could have contributed the elements of Tala art, the question whether Tala could have contributed to the formation of the medieval southern art may now be examined. The obvious route for the transmission of such influence had to be through Bastar to eastern Andhra Pradesh and northern Karnataka. As always, the occurrence of Tala elements in the art of Bastar, or of elements from both in southern art may suggest simultaneous contacts with a common heritage, rather than a direct impact of one on the other. The work in Bastar begins earlier than Tala. Instead of drawing directly from Tala or the brick temple tradition of Dakṣiṇa Kośala, like Surguja, the Bastar work draws from styles, even earlier than Tala. It presents a style as classical and accomplished as, though different in approach, Tala. It marches in step with Surguja, with its brick temple facades, Tala like mouldings, and simple plans. However, it veers away from the prevalent Dakṣiṇa Kośala figural style to parallel southern Pallava forms. It does not retain and refine the Dakṣiṇa Kośala architectural heritage through the 11th century, like Surguja, and it does not survive in its original form beyond the 7th century.

BHOṄGĀPĀL, 5TH CENTURY AD

The connection with Tala and Dakṣiṇa Kośala art appears to be established for the first time in north Bastar through a 5th century Buddhist monastery (Figs. 18-19, 101), revealed in excavations at Bhoṅgāpāl.[102] The multiple entries to the pradakṣiṇā patha suggest a conceptual connection with Jethani. The tall kumbha of its pīṭha, an occasional simple pilaster and heavy kapota, which are shared also by the Śiva temple in the third mound, recollect the Devarani pīṭha and vedībandha. The apsidal or cāpākāra sanctum suggests a śālā or sabhākāra roof on pillared and pilastered wall slabs, which are used at Jethani.[103] The Śiva temple in the second mound also displays the sequence of khura, kumbha, kalaśa and a very thin kapota, interspersed with plain antarapaṭṭas in vedībandha, and plain recessed and projected mouldings in the jaṅghā, which remind us of the somewhat more elaborate mouldings on the brick cladding of Jethani or in the later Devarani pīṭha. Finally, the padmāsana Buddha (Pl. 7), recovered from the apsidal caitya, shows features, which root it in an early to mid 5th century idiom, placing it earlier than the Tala images. The Buddha has barrel shoulders, enhanced by powerful, outspread arms, and firmly locked legs, a broad chest, dilated with arrested breath, and points to an idiom closer to Udayagiri and Mathura than Tala. The rounded profiles of the head, the plain halo, the curves of shoulders and legs, establish an orchestrated play of rhythms, using simple means. At Tala, the contours of the large Śiva and dvārapāla images are somtimes interrupted by ornament and garment. At Bhoṅgāpāl, the transition from the waist to the hips has been shown by a subtly curved physical dent. The ekāṁśikā saṁghāti (an upper garment, slung across one shoulder) across Buddha's shoulder and chest is so delicately drawn as to appear nearly transparent, and anticipates the sensitivity of the Tala sculptor in carving the uttarīya on the Devarani door jamb figures.

Garh Dhanaurā

The post-Tala developments in north Bastar take place at Garh Dhanaurā, a village three kilometres off Keśkāl on the Raipur Jagdalpur road. These developments move in the grooves cut by the ground plan of Bhoṅgāpāl temples (Figs. 15-17). However, informed now by the Tala experience, they acquire significantly new dimensions, pointing to the medieval idiom in Bihar in the northeast and Andhra in the southeast. Clearance of sixteen mounds,[104] survey of the surrounding area and comparison with several significant images in Bihar and Andhra facilitated the discovery of these links. Twelve of these mounds have yielded temples with the essential pattern established at Bhoṅgāpāl, of a garbhagṛha with a constricted antarāla, demarcated by brick pilasters, the garbhagṛha being occasionally provided with bhadra projection, and sometimes with bhadra, prati and karṇa projections on the flanks. While the nucleus of this plan has been used at Devarani by replacing the constricted antarāla with a constricted maṇḍapa, the preference at all these temples seems to be for a sequence of tall, flat mouldings like Devarani vedībandha. Three of the mounds are large, built in terrace formation (Figs. 99-100), in a sequence of successive squares or rectangles, of diminishing size and rising height, processionally accessible, and equipped with tall, plain, flat mouldings, slightly recessed from one another. Similar terracing is implicit in the elevation of the Jethani temple, Suraṅg Ṭilā temple, Sirpur (Figs. 110-13), and the early medieval vihāras of Bihar or Bengal. The Jethani brick mouldings, however, retain a bulging volume, and shun the complete flatness of the Garh Dhanaurā mouldings.

Garh Dhanaurā, Phase 1. 5th-6th century AD

In sculpture, the closest to Tala, is a two-armed seated 6th cent. AD Kevala Narasiṁha from Garh Dhanaurā (Fig. 556) kept in the garbhagṛha of a Śiva temple at Kānker, Bastar. The smooth, gliding curve of the arms and head, massive, well proportioned limbs, the impression of overwhelming force, gently contained, take both of them closer to the magnificent Kevala Narasiṁha of Ramtek (Fig. 554), than the more amorphous modelling of the Kānker image,

Kevala Narasiṁha on a Jethani south lintel panel (Fig. 547), or the tight tension of the Narasiṁha from Dev Dhanaurā, Kānker (Fig. 557). The proportions go a bit awry in late 4th century AD in a sthānaka Viṣṇu slab (Pl. 43), recovered from one of the twelve mounds. It anticipates the huge shoulders of 5th century AD Gupta dvārapāla, Viṣṇu (Figs. 380, 388) Vākāṭaka (Pl. 47) and Tala (Fig. 350) figures, enhanced by a massive, cylindrical head, crowned by a broad and tall kirīṭa, to contain the cascading curls of hair. The width of its chest is emphasized by the hāra and vaijayantīmālā (long garland of flower shaped jewels). The cloth, bunched across its hips and thighs, retain volume, and, on the slab behind, the cloth foretells the fluency of curves from 5th century Gupta images. Its halo has the leafy substance of Ramtek and Tala. In the hardening and stiffening, visible in the linear accent below its knees or chest, the scythe sharp curve of its cloth, the dwarfing of its legs, this image seems to be close to the style of a Viṣṇu on a plaque and a slab (Fig. 364), recovered from Jethani. Its ecstatic expression, accented by slightly parted lips, and the thin, stringy floral strands in its mukuṭa and hāra, reinforce the impression of the Garh Dhanaura Viṣṇu being uninformed by the 5th century experience.

Garh Dhanaurā/Dev dhanaurā, Phase 2. 6th-7th century AD

The characteristics, implicit in this Viṣṇu image, are aggravated in what should be a late 6th-7th century images of Viṣṇu (Fig. 369) from Dev Dhanaurā, Bastar. The proportions of the image are 1.57 x 0.55 x 0.29 m. The body of Viṣṇu is lengthened. So is the kirīṭamukuṭa. The halo is made elliptical rather than circular, further elongating the head. The tapering legs of the earlier Viṣṇu, now become almost like round columns. The contour descends down the shoulder, waist or hips more abruptly and vertically. The chest is flattened. The uttarīya, so imperceptibly drawn at Tala or Bhoṅgāpāl, is laid across the chest like a solid crust, and allowed to hang down like a peaked pyramid rather than curve out like the earlier Viṣṇu or Tala figure slabs. With this image, certain tendencies towards a squared off shoulder, harsh, stylized curves, irrevocable frontality, elongation and flattening, burgeoning in the Kārtikeya stele or the huge standing gods or dvārapālas at Jethani, are brought to culmination, in the late 6th early seventh century. The change in idiom from 4th - 5th to the 6th 7th century becomes evident from a comparison of the fine uttarīya slung across the waist of a Jethani dvārapāla (Fig. 357), with the harder uttarīya stretched across the chest of this tall Dev Dhanaurā Viṣṇu. A similar comparison can be drawn of the fluent curve of peacock fans behind Kārtikeya in the Jethani stele (Fig. 350), with the rigid, frozen curve of uttarīya beside the legs of the late 9th cent. Viṣṇu (Pl. 43). The late 4th century Viṣṇu, together with the Tala plaque, looks forward to the features of some of the Viṣṇu images of Gaya. The 6th - 7th century Viṣṇu image, has intensified in itself the trends of the elongated figural style of Jethani or Malhār pillars (Figs. 211, 352, 365). It parallels and anticipates the seventh century Māmallapuram images of the Pallavas, and, Cālukya images of Paṭṭadakal, Āihole or Ālampur.[105]

If these Viṣṇu images acknowledge the tendency in some Tala sculptures towards elongation, late 5th - 6th century images (Figs. 366-68) from Garh Dhanaurā and Dev Dhanaurā show greater acquaintance with the style of heavy bodied Tala sculptures (Figs. 350, 354), with their accent on a broader, squarer, heavier form. These are two Kevala Narasiṁhas, seated on a pedestal with a partially broken left arm, recovered from the garbhagṛha of one of the smaller

Viṣṇu temple mounds in Garh Dhanaurā (Fig. 556) and a Narasiṁha from Dev Dhanaurā (Fig. 557); a slab with a standing four-armed Viṣṇu, with two hands resting on heads of āyudhapuruṣas, found at Badbār, Keśkāl near Garh Dhanaurā (Fig. 368); a two-armed standing ascetic, probably Śiva himself, on a slab, crowned with a round mass of jaṭā (Fig. 367), located in the forest of Garh Dhanaurā; a four-armed Viṣṇu, carved on a slab, with one of his hands resting on the mace head, found at Garh Dhanaurā (Fig. 368). They show a common tendency towards a slackening of the pent up tension in the Tala images or the earlier Garh Dhanaurā Viṣṇu, a transition from tightly muscled bodies to a more relaxed, if flabby form, and a squaring not only of the shoulder but of the entire body. Common medievalizing tendencies are a disproportionate enlargement of the hands, a thickening of the legs, waist and head. These are accompanied by the introduction of a distinct conical edge to the legs and a curbing of the height of kirīṭamukuṭa. With the unwinding of tautened body, there is an enhancement the drop and slope in the shoulders.

The three Viṣṇu images (Figs. 366-368) from Bastar appear to pertain to late 5th to early 6th century AD. Despite a difference in the tightness or looseness of the modelling, these images are united by the shared memory of the strength and breadth of 5th century Jethani but are distanced from them by the hardening and lateral spread that overtake them.

IMPLICATIONS OF TALA STYLE OUTSIDE DAKṢIṆA KOŚALA

Central India. 6th to 11th Century AD

Outside Dakṣiṇa Kośala, it is somewhat audacious and far-fetched to indicate any direct parallels or influence of the Tala style. Nor does the occurrence of isolated motifs suggest such analogies or influence. However, modified by the experiments in 7th-8th century Dakṣiṇa Kośala, the Tala style appears comparable with the coexistent lean and heavy figural styles of Central India (Figs. 383, 385, 387-88, 402-04, 409-11, 439-44, 451, 517-18, 568, 571). The ghaṭapallava āmalaka displayed at both crown and base of the stambhaśākhā in Devarani door jamb or in Jethani siṁhagavākṣa pilasters, becomes a frequent characteristic of pillars and pilasters on jaṅghā, door jambs, prāggrīvas and maṇḍapas.[106] The decoration of the Jethani south pillar base with recessed ghaṭapallava on all four sides is repeated on different sides of pillars in the Śitaleśvara Mahādeva temple, Candrabhāgā or on pilasters in Kurāyā Bir, Kuchdon. Muktāgrāsas, darpaṇas, ardha or pūrṇapadmas, śobhāpaṭṭikās, padmalatās, figural carvings or nāgapāśas, found on pillars, pilasters and slab bases at Ajanta, Tala, Sirpur or Rajim, are now absorbed in the decorative programme of pillars and pilasters.[107] The sequence of mouldings, established in the later Devarani jagatī or the vedībandhas of Sirpur, Khārod, Palāri, minus the recessed galapāda, is now adapted generally, even duplicated in pīṭha and vedībandha, the tall kumbha of Devarani pīṭha now becoming a frequent preference. The repetition of the kapota of later Devarani, with pūrṇa and ardhacandraśālās on vedībandha, jagatī, jaṅghā, vārāndikā or śikhara of the temples in Dakṣiṇa Kośala, is adapted as a general practice to visually bind the Pratihāra temples.[108] The chequerboard design on some Tala pillars, or on Lakṣmaṇa temple vārāndikā, the perforated ardhapadma designs at Deepadih, often become visible in the jagatī vārāndikās, the jaṅghā recesses or śūkanāsās in Central India.[109] The empty recesses and projections are used simply but effectively to vary the jaṅghā profiles of Tala temples. These are reinforced in Dakṣiṇa Kośala temple jaṅghās, by rathikās with siṁhakarṇas, and in the Deepadih vedībandhas, by offsetted prakoṣṭhas with storeyed udgamas binding all the mouldings. Such udgamas are now adapted on the temple jaṅghās, and, occasionally, on the pīṭhas or vedībandhas. The prakoṣṭhas are now generally filled with figures, unlike Dakṣiṇa Kośala, where figures appear occasionally in the siṁhakarṇas.[110] The scrolled, nibbling haṁsas of later Devarani kapota, scrolled makaras of Tala pillars, the vertical row of rosettes in Tala door jamb or panel frames, the udyatasiṁhas, flanking kīrtimukha on a Jethani south pillar, the Garuḍa holding nāga tails from Rajim, Khārod or Deepadih door jambs, now make frequent appearance, in different locations.[111] The projecting lalāṭabimba, found occasionally in Dakṣiṇa Kośala and usually in Odisha, is very much in vogue.[112] It is possible to see how the vibrant exterior of the Tala temples, enhanced in the Dakṣiṇa Kośala temples, is transformed and harnessed to temple architecture in Central India. The large candraśālās are now knit into jāla in the madhyalatā of the śikhara. The effect of continuous segmentation of rathas, vertically dividing the temple, is maintained, not by projecting quarter āmalakas or kapotas, but by diminishing tiers of relatively flat udgamas. The compression, which the Dakṣiṇa Kośala temples had already adapted, in preference to the lateral expansion of Tala temples, is now accentuated in Central Indian temples. This is achieved by flattening of āmalakas, growing ornamentalization of candraśālās, and sharpening of segmental contours, or, in sum, by abdication of the Tala volume. In sculpture, the transition in Dakṣiṇa Kośala, through the twin modelling traditions of Tala, from the slender, somewhat hesitant 8th century figures, to the fulness and grace of 9th century, is also paralleled in different areas of Central India.[113] The strong inward propulsion of Tala door jambs, inherited by many Dakṣiṇa Kośala temples door jambs, is, however, relinquished for a parallel and frontal presentation. The powerful oblique movement of figures is suppressed.[114]

The Tala preference for the cyclopean continues in the first half of the sixth century in the gigantic toraṇa uprights and pillar fragments from Nāgari near Chittor, Khilchipurā, Sondni and Māndāsor fort. The spiral mālāśākhā of Devarani jamb and tālapatra, palmleaf designs in the cornucopia in Jethani contribute to the decoration of the thin stambhaśākhā of the uprights. The rosette band or raṅganī design from Tala forms their outer band. The grāsamukha, lotus medallion, mithunas, scrolled haṁsa, or kīrtimukha, flanked by seated or udyatasiṁhas, found at Tala, appear in the panels of the uprights or abacus from Māndāsor. A Gaḍhvā pillar and a broken Sondni architectural fragment display Śiva at chausar, establishing a further iconographic link with Tala, as also with the mithuna in the Rāmacandra temple, Rajim sanctum door (Figs. 402, 407).[115] The Bhairava Bhairavī on the Māndāsor pillar is a livelier version of the more sedate Bhairava Bhairavī on a Jethani lintel. The punched out chests, accentuated curve of the shoulders, fussy lines of the head dress or lower garment at the crotch, the diagonally inclined legs of the Nāgari or Māndāsor figures, suggest a date slightly later than the effortlessly flexed Devarani figures with their suave modelling and easy contours.

At Tala, the preference for colossal images and pillars, full of massive power and vehemence, is relieved by the featherlight, playful touch of a fastidious designer which survives at Nāgari or Māndāsor. In Ḍāhala region under early Kalacurīs of Māhiṣmatī or Tripuri, the monumental is conveyed with overpowering effect without this softening touch. The Sagar University slab and the Choṭi Deori pillar, carved with a 7th century AD inscription of Śaṅkaragaṇa I (of Tripurī), a secular and divine couple, and mātṛkā images of Nāndchānd and Sagar University Museum, share heavy, ponderous figures with columnar legs, squared off head and shoulder and stiff posture. This indicates the palsy which overtakes the weighty but lightfooted figures of Tala, in subsequent developments between the end of the 7th to early 8th century AD, in Central India. A Nāndchānd guardian figure, with swollen, bow shaped, disproportionately large arms and hands, cylindrical, lifeless legs, a relentlessly rectilinear contour and flat chest, betray a desertion of the extraordinary volume and curvilinear fluency of an early 5th century Nāndchānd Viṣṇu or the pent up tension of a mid to late 5th century Māndasor Viṣṇu (Figs. 381, 388). It also shows the early 8th century AD dénouement, culminating in a misunderstanding of the style favored in Tala figured slabs or western Indian cave art.[116] The cyclopean 10th century images of Viṣṇu incarnations, carved against the Bāndhogarh fort, the broken Śiva image lying in Gurgī Mehsāun, the Hara Gaurī panel from Gurgī, in Yashwant park, Revā[117] indicate continuation of the same turgid style, by more accomplished hands. These build on the way western Indian cave art marries sculpture and architecture to the panoramic backdrop of the terrain, and on the way Tala temples translate this concept into freestanding structures. That the Tala and Dakṣiṇa Kośala traditions are transmitted to Ḍāhala through the Pratihāra style is evident from the śilā maṇḍapikā shrines on the top of the Bāndhogarh fort in Shāhdol. The repeated use of kapota all across the temple, or of candraśālās in a jāla, in the madhyalatā of the śikhara, of the heavy āmalakas as karṇāṇḍakas and crowning elements, of bāṅkājālī in vārāṇḍā, ratikerā design in door jamb, of pillars with ghaṭapallava base and capital in maṇḍapa, show the legacy of elements from the art of Tala and Dakṣiṇa Kośala in the late 8th and 9th century AD.[118]

In 10th century, Kalacurī temples like Marai (Satna), Chandrehe (Sidhi), Bināikā (Sāgar), Nohṭā (Dāmoh), adopt the Dakṣiṇa Kośala and Pratihāra features, which were in embryo at Tala. Analogously, they repeat the kapota, to bind the temple horizontally, the rathikā with udgamas, integrate the mouldings vertically, punctuate projections with recesses, and vary the jaṅghā profile. They add raṅganī, padmapṛṣṭha, puṣpapaṭṭi and padmopāna designs to the vedībandha. The jāla moves out of the madhyalatā in these as well as in Odisha temples., to cast a net across the śikhara, suppress the undulating outline, and compress the laterally spread mass, characteristic of the Jethani groundplan.[119]

Interactions in Western India. 6th to 8th Century AD

In western Indian cave architecture, which presages and overlaps many kindred features of Tala on Dakṣiṇa Kośala architecture, developments seem to reveal an awareness of earlier experiments, including those of Tala and Dakṣiṇa Kośala. In early to mid-6th century AD, the Yogeśvarī cave main hall acquires three entrances and the garbhagṛha four, while its mukhamaṇḍapa door frame displays a makaratoraṇa in the udgama, rosettes and spirals in the door bands, recalling the multiple access approach adapted at Jethani, as well as the jaṅghā toraṇas and door jambs of Devarani. The Dhumarlenā cave 2 at Ellora has three doors to the hall, the garbhagṛha being placed at the back. In the same period, in Elephantā cave I also, three colonnaded portals give entry to the main hall, and the pillars, like their Yogeśvarī or Devarani counterparts, show massive square bases, with gaṇas at their top corners, while the adhiṣṭhāna exhibits plain recesses like Jethani and later Devarani. The wall pilasters of the Aurangabad cave, from mid to late 6th century AD, show medallions acting as darpaṇas on all the four sides of the shaft, double bodied lions and gaṇa figures at four corners above the base, or around the āmalaka, recalling Tala. In late 6th to early 7th century AD, the tradition of carving gaṇas or darpaṇas on all sides, is continued at Ellora, where it is supplemented by depiction of recessed or projected ghaṭapallava on four sides of the main pillar shaft (Fig. 291), rather than at the base like Jethani south pillar. At Nāsik in the late 6th century, the pillar is carved with floral medallions and bands in all directions, on the base and on the shaft.[120]

At none of these places, however, the relief sculpture on the pillar shaft is given up, like Jethani, for surrounding it with independent, carved slabs. The flanking figures on sidewalls are also carved, against the cave walls rather than on independent slabs, unlike Jethani. In Gujarat, in late sixth, early seventh century Maitraka and Gārulaka temples of Surāṣṭra like Gop, Kadvār, Visāvāḍā, etc., the tall kandhara, pilasters and recesses in the pīṭha or vedībandha, capture the verticalism and simplicity of the Tala temple facades, for a more drastically austere rendering. The large candraśālas in the vimānas of the 7th century AD Maitraka Surāṣṭra temples like Khimeśvara, Bhāṇasārā reveal a close corespondence with the analogous forms in Rājivalocana temple Śikhara (Fig. 126), reinforcing evidence of mercantile, monastic, artistic contacts with Gujarat. Later, in the 8th and the 9th century, this verticalism and simplicity are stressed differently in the Mahāmaru and Mahā Gurjara styles, using, however, the same means of tall pīṭha, recessed and projected walls or mouldings.[121] In the late 7th and 8th century, temples are constructed under Cālukyas of Bādāmi, specially at Mahākūṭa, Āihole, Paṭṭaḍakala and Ālampur. Equipped with simple tall pīṭhas and blank walls, occasionally varied by projected galapādas or khaṭṭakas, these establish another version of the same idiom. The lion protomes, seen on the Devarani uttaraṅga pilasters, now come to occupy all the four sides of the base of the siṁhapāda pillar at Ālampur. The standing figures in relief, the kīrtimukha, the leaf pending from a bunch of fruits on kalaśa, the rosettes, lotus medallions or darpaṇas, usual at Tala, are also not missing from the pillar decoration. The elongated, single entry plan of Devarani finds echoes in some Āihole plans, while the four door plan at Ālampur, with accesses to the garbhagṛha and hall from all sides, suggests an amplification of the multi access Jethani or caitya plans.[122] However, the Jethani plan, with its disproportionately large southern entrance, or its steps penetrating the access up to the sanctum, is discarded in all these temples. From the 6th century onwards, preference is given to the more conventional and axial distribution of space in temples like Devarani, in translating the structural plan of cave architecture to independent shrines.

Eastern India, Amplification, Stylization of Patterns and Motifs

The Tala motifs invade Odishan temples via Dakṣiṇa Kośala by a process of externalization. These are brought out from inside, multiplied, stylized, miniaturized, variously relocated and integrated as a decorative frosting over the temple facade in Odisha (Pls. 4, 14-16, 30; Figs. 232-35, 542, 563-64), giving it an ornate, simmering surface, quite different from the regular profiles of the recesses and projections, marching unhurriedly on the Tala facade. Of all motifs from Tala, the lion is the most in vogue in Odisha. The seated lions or lions with two hind quarters, found at the base of Jethani pillars, reappear as dopiccha siṁhas above the kaṇikas in the beki of the gaṇḍi in the rekhā deul, at the corners below the ghaṇṭā of the jagamohana, as seated addorsed lions, at the corner base of the rāhā niches, above the capital of the kaṇika paga or on lower bārāndā. The seated or prancing siṁhas, holding mālās in their hands or mouth; muktāgrāsas or grāsakiṅkiṇikas, spitting pearl, jewel or floral festoons, carved on the Jethani or Devarani pillars, on the base or capital, appear as udyata siṁhas or the heraldic bho design, flanking or crowning the vajramuṇḍī, on the gaṇḍi, above the pilaster, on the bāḍā. The siṁhavaktra, glowering over crossed paws from gavākṣas, also looks out from the vajramastaka niche, or from above the udgama, crowning the jaṅghā niches.[123] The crouching gaṇa with bulging eyes and a scowl, with his hands between his feet, visible outside the Jethani south door jamb, establishes himself in Odisha, on the vasanta, in caityas, and assumes the aspect of bekibhairavas on the beki. The bhāravāhī gaṇas become bhārarakṣakas, and leave pillar bases inside, to occupy the flanks of vajramuṇḍīs, or niches in the bārāndās. Gaṇas, riding makaras in the Jethani south pillar darpaṇas, now ride virālas.[124] The makaras function in Odisha, as at Jethani, as abhiṣeka praṇālas. The kīrtimukha praṇālas of Odisha retain the blunted, geometricized look of the makara base of Jethani south pillars.[125] The figures, carved on pillar or wall slabs inside Jethani, are now carved not only outside on rāhā niches or ghaṭapallava pilasters, but also, exceptionally, on all sides of interior pillars, together with the recessed kalaśa motif of the Jethani south pillar.[126]

The decorative elements of the pillar or door jamb at Tala are now found everywhere (Pls. 14-16; Figs. 145-53) . The aśoka or campakalumbī, found on Jethani pillar kalaśas or the kalaśa moulding of the later Devarani platform, appears initially, in its more or less natural form, on the nolī and khaṇḍi. Later, in Odisha, it becomes stylized, inorganic and composite, stretching vertically across the pābhāga, binding all the mouldings. Similarly, the vasanta is carved, initially, like the later Devarani kapota, with caityas alternating with haṁsa. These alternating motifs are replaced later with complex scroll, figural or floral work. It completely covers the surface, and is integrated with the stylized campaka design below. The faceting and fluting are confined earlier to Tala pillars. Later, these are inducted into the pābhāga and the jaṅghā, to fragment them into rippling, surging lines. With time, the recesses and galapādas of the Tala style are reflected in the carved pilaster of ḍamaru recesses between the vasanta and nolī. The chequerboard design on Jethani pillar becomes the perforated bānkājālī, to occupy, at places like the Koṇārak Sūryā deul, all recesses on the jaṅghā. The band of rosettes, strung by eye shaped flowers on the base of petals, on Devarani door jamb, becomes the raṅganī; the winding padmalatā the ratikerā; the beads between floral bands on Jethani pillar or Devarani door jamb, the guṇḍikā; the padmavallī, entwined with fauna, the gelabā; the bāhyaśākhā with short, swift loops, the āgama or kuṭila scroll; the leaves around a stem, on the Devarani maṇḍapa side wall or Jethani door jamb, the mali phula phadikā; and, pendant floral ālambas become jhārāvalī, to cover the entire Odisha temple facade, in a complex, carefully orchestrated network of decorative designs. What is confined at Tala to door jambs or pillars, is now used to vivify the entire external aspect of the temple. Even the tiers of ghaṭas and āmalakas, used at Tala to compose a pillar, are adapted and incorporated in the udgamas or bhūmis of the bāḍā, in tala or ūrdhvagarbhikās, or gaṇḍi, to create a serrated, fluttering, vertical outline. The alasakanyās below clusters of leaves, the river goddesses below kamala or mayūrātapatras, common to Odishan temples, have also been already seen at Tala (Figs. 341-42). Moreover, the massive Rudra Śiva/Paśupati images, framed and crowned by rearing interwoven naga coils and hoods; the pillar base, recovered from Devarani steps, carved with nāgarāja; the pillar base, found north of Jethani, carved with nāgapāśa; the Jethani south pillar ghaṭa base, framed by nāgabandha; the all over design composed by nāgas, in thick, braided coils in Rajim, Aḍbhār, Sirpur, Deepādih temples (Pls. 26-29; Figs. 48, 220, 227-28) indirectly anticipate and parallel the nāga or nāgī stambhas on the Odisha temple facades (Pls. 16, 30; Fig. 235). The Gajalakṣmī motif on the lalāṭabimba, almost invariably seen on Odisha temple doors, is also given prominence on the Devarani doorlintel. The makara toraṇas of Devarani jaṅghā reappear in Odisha, with the makara head turned outwards, in the extrados of vajramastakas above doors.[127]

In the entire Odishan tradition, however, the excessive beading, the shallow, incised scrollwork, the fussy, invasive ornament, the myriad perforations of the inherited chequerboard design, the fluttering net of vertical and horizontal lines, chased in light and shade, create a surface, convulsed with a restless movement, completely different from the reticent Tala facades. The earliest developments in Odisha, beginning in the 7th century, may not be connected directly or in a unilinear fashion, with the developments at Tala, knowledge of which appears to have been transmitted via other 6th and 7th century temples of Dakṣiṇa Kośala. Yet, Tala is the earliest known temple in this region to have harnessed the vocabulary developed in western caves, Vidarbha or in 'Gupta' temples, to adorn its inner pillars or door frames, to surpassing splendour. With this inaugural development at Tala, it becomes possible for the Dakṣiṇa Kośala and Odishan temples Lakṣmaṇa and Paraśurāmeśvara to use the same motifs, with boldness like Tala, to transfigure the drab aspect of external elevation.[128] The specific Odishan means, used to enhance curvature or height, are also anticipated in Dakṣiṇa Kośala.[129]

Elsewhere in the east, in Bihar or Bengal, the impact of the contact with sites like Tala would have been modified by regional traditions already in vogue in the 5th and 6th century. And yet, the fact that sites in these regions also participate in a similar broad evolution, is evident from the galapādas, projections and recesses on the jaṅghā of the Muṇḍeśvarī temple, Aphsad Viṣṇu temple, the tall plinth of Nalanda stone temple no 2, or the Sālban vihāra brick temple of Maināmatī. It is evident also in dhvajastambhas or pillars, directly carved with figures (not on separate slabs like Tala), on all four sides, at Muṇḍeśvarī, or Deo Barunārk, in Shāhābād district, or at Mahāsthāngarh, in Bogrā district.[130] The sheer, tall heavy massive plinth, the gradual, processional approach to elevation, the lateral spread of space, the constricted space of garbhagṛha, generated on the very top, or the trenches converging from different sides to the central mound, are features of the Maniyār Maṭh at Rājgir, the great stūpa 3, or the mahāvihāras of Nalanda, Vikramśilā or Ānticak in Bihar, Ratnagiri, Odisha, Sompurā at Pahārpur, Koṭilāmurā, Iṭākholā, Ānanda Vihāra, Bihār Dhāp, Bogrā, Ruāylbāri, Netrakoṇā, at Maināmatī, in Bangladesh. These features create an impression of spatial planning and treatment of mass, substantially similar to that of the Jethani mound. Apart from the general plan, some of the motifs are also shared by these Buddhist sites with Tala.[131] While no one to one relationship exists between Tala and these vihāras, they demonstrate similar experimental efforts, that are involved in breaking out of the matrix of cave architecture, to set up an independent structure of a temple stūpa or monastery on the open ground.

South India

Even when we look at the temples of the Cālukyas of Bādāmi at Paṭṭadakala, Āihole or Ālampur in the 7th and 8th century AD or the 7th century Pallava temples of Mahābalipuram, we notice a simultaneous tendency towards repetition of the kapota, to build the śikhara. However, under Cālukyas, the adaptation of the lātina rather than the kūṭina form, brings the śikhara visually closer to the later Pratihāra and earlier Dakṣiṇa Kośala experiments.[132]

CONCLUSION

It does not, of course, follow from this investigation, that Tala or Dakṣiṇa Kośala directly generate the forms of medieval Indian art. It only points to an amalgam of motifs and styles to which Tala and Dakṣiṇa Kośala contribute in a significant way, and from which centres of medieval Indian art draw impartially. Nor is a suggestion made here that Tala borrows nothing from past, and gives everything to future. Its uniqueness consists not in individual motifs or patterns, which come to it as a legacy from earlier Indian art, but in the unusual and unexpected combinations it makes of such motifs and patterns. In what may be considered today the heart of Chattisgarh, in modern Bilaspur and Raipur divisions, the influence of Tala, modified by Gupta Vākāṭaka heritage, has been felt by Dakṣiṇa Kośala most decisively, from the 6th to the 8th century, and transmitted to central, eastern and western India. In Surguja, the influence of Tala and Dakṣiṇa Kośala continues till the 11th century, interacting with Odisha. In Bastar, the influence, modified by earlier traditions, continues till the 7th century and interacts with the Pallava south. In Chattisgarh itself, elements of Tala or early brick temples of Dakṣiṇa Kośala are seen, from the 8th to the 12th century, as part of a late medieval heritage, which travels back and forth, laden with elements from neighbouring cultural provinces of Dakṣiṇa Kośala, Kaliṅga and Vidarbha. In fact, in Odisha, Daśārṇa or Ḍāhala under Pratihāras or Kalacurīs, or in Pallava and Cālukya art, or in western Indian cave architecture, the impact of Tala is not direct. It does, however, form an important chain in the link, and not, as has been assumed, an insignificant one. The importance of this contribution is to be assessed, not by looking at the iconographic traits which it may have contributed to later Indian art, but, by appreciating the way it appears to transfer the monumentality, scale, terracing or processional approach of cave architecture and sculpture to temple art; and, by examining the mutual transference of traits it effects between sculpture and architecture, fusing them in several ways. Above all, the unique combinations of earlier motifs and patterns, established by the Tala temples inside the structure, are translated, with endless repetition, multiplication and mutation, to the external facade of later temples, changing it. In a subtle but certain way, Tala is responsible for the special expression of Dakṣiṇa Kośala art, and, as such, for the bequest of this art to the broader stream of medieval Indian art.[133]

NOTES

1. Zimmer 1955. 2: pls. 2a, 4, 7-35.
2. For Kauśāmbī, Nāgodh and Mathura pillars, P. Chandra, *Allahabad Museum* 1970: pls. 70, 71, 79a and b. Craven 1975: pl. 64. Czuma 1985: pls. 8, 10, 11, 15, 30, 42; S.P. Gupta 1985: pls. on pp. 92-96.
3. Craven 1975: pls. 66; Czuma 1985: pls. 28, 30; S.P. Gupta 1985: pls. on pp. 60-62, 89.
4. Dhaky & Meister 1983-88. *Encyclopaedia*, 2.1: 22. The 7th century AD text *Viṣṇudharmottara* mentions the Eḍuka temple.
5. Joanna Williams 1982: pl. 79.
6. Gokarṇeśvara, Allahabad Museum No. 3266. Photo P.C. 2324. *Encyclopaedia* 2.1: pls. 112-14, 121-22. Williams 1982: 116-17, pl. 176. She supports her suggestion for a late date by discussion of motifs rather than style. Some Pipariyā forms are softer, and more relaxed than those at Nācnā, and should not be dated beyond the mid-5th century.
7. *Encyclopaedia* 2.1: pls. 9, 41; Williams 1982: pls. 41, 47, p. 50, notes 94, 95.
8. Williams 1982: pls. 79, 139.

9. *Ibid.*, pls. 84, 122, 135, 174; *Encyclopaedia* 2.1: pl. 37.
10. William 1982: pls. 2, 7, 8, 36, 9, 139, 190-91; *Encyclopaedia* 2.1: pl. 39.
11. *Encyclopaedia* 2.1: pls. 13, 20, 35, 37, 39, 41, 43; For Varanasi door jamb N.M. No. 49. 123. AAB neg. No. A1. 14.
12. *Ibid.*, pl. 15.
13. Williams 1982: pls. 79, 100 for Mathura and Sarnath columns. Also *Encyclopaedia* 2.1: pls. 23, 41, 99, 122. Pls. 22-5, 29, 34-7, for early door frames. PC neg. Nos. 88-96, 88-48, 38-54 for Koṭā Museum fragments from Mukundarā, and the Lucknow Museum panel from Garhvā.
14. Williams 1982: pls. 81-83; PC neg. 45/6916.
15. For Mathura, Bilsadh, Williams 1982: pls. 23, 83. For the early 5th century rhizomes and flowers on Udayagiri door jambs, see *Encyclopaedia* 2.1: pls. 13-14, 22-26. For candraśālā and pillar fragment from Mukundarā at Koṭā Museum, pls. 29, 31. For other Koṭā Museum fragments from Mukundarā, PC negs. A5-70, 89.6, 89.7. For Gaḍhvā, PC neg. 71 and Williams 1982: pl. 241. For door jambs and foliate forms from the late 5th century, see *Encyclopaedia* 2.1: pls. 5, 6. For Nācnā Pārvatī temple door jamb, *ibid.*, pls. 82-83, 88, and Stern 1972: pl. 13 for Deogarh temple. For Bhūmarā see ASI No. 5502 of 1921. For Bhūmarā and Marhiā, Chandra, AA, 32, 1970: 125-45. Also Williams 1982: pl. 188. For a Sarnath door jamb, Williams 1982: pl. 234. For Ajanta door jambs in caves 1 and 6, Stern 1972: pls. 4-5: for makara in cave 27, *ibid.*, in pl. 7a. Spink 1967: pl. 9 on p. 41 for detail of cave 1 door jamb. For Bāgh, Marshall et al., 1927. Stern 1972: pl. 6a. For suggested late 5th century AD dates, see *Encyclopaedia* 2.1: 23, 73-74, 79-80, 93.
16. Shastri 1977: 142-74. The Bholā and Boṅgo Huḍki temples used bricks measuring 44 x 23 x 8 cm and 40 x 24 x 8 cm. Bakker 1997: 80-81.
17. *Encyclopaedia* 2.1: pls. 99-100, 103, 105-7, 110-13, 119-21, 125-26.
18. Mānsar, near Ramtek, in Nagpur, Maharashtra, has been excavated by Shri A.K. Sharma under ASI license since 1998, with the support of Bodhisattva Nāgārjun Smārak Samsthā Wa Anusandhān Kendra, Nagpur. Two brick stūpas, one above the other, and an oblong caitya, were built on the bedrock of the Hiḍimbā Tekḍi mound at Mānsar during late Maurya and early Śuṅga periods between the 3rd and 2nd century BC. Courses of bricks, measuring 46 x 22 x 7cm, were raised on rectangular boxes, filled with boulders, brick bats and earth, and staircases were built along the hill slope. Palaces, temples, fortifications, red-painted, moulded kesariyā type coins, tiles, red lipped spouted vessels, palaces, with 42 pillar maṇḍapa, made of well-baked bricks measuring 42 x 26 x 8 cm, using thin mortar, follow in the Sātavāhana period between 2nd to 3rd century AD. Stone foundations and remains of a brick superstructure of an early 4th century Vākāṭaka temple from the period of Pravarasena I (AD 275-335) have been found with remains of sacrificial ceremonies on the western side of Hiḍimbā Tekḍi, separated from Śatavāhana levels by laterite and red moorum filling. A three-storeyed palace, reinforced by massive retaining walls, was added by Vākāṭaka king Pravarasena II around AD 435. Sixteen rectangular Śiva shrines with lotus bud śikharas, made of triangular and inverted triangles, were installed on fluted, sharp angled, octagonal bases along the terraces of the palace. The retaining walls have used lime concrete and lime plaster, dressed and undressed sandstone blocks, bricks measuring 46 x 24 x 8 cm. The bricks are fine and well chiselled. A large number of Śaiva sculptures have been found from this level.
   A Buddhist stūpa and a mahāvihāra were raised during the 6th and 7th century AD on rectangular and square boxes of bricks, measuring 32 x 20 x 7 cms. and 28 x 27 x 7 cms. The boxes were filled with debris, walls of dressed sandstone blocks and bricks measuring 43 x 23 x 9 cm. Finds from this level are a Viṣṇukuṇḍin copper coin of Mahendravarman II (AD 470-580), showing a lion on obverse, a vase and lamps, in a rayed circle, on the reverse; two terracotta fragments, embossed with a circular design, enclosing a bodhi tree, with radiating branches; a circular copper begging bowl; a square limestone plaque, showing a stūpa dome, crowned by an umbrella, and flanked by a raised elephant trunk, holding a beaded rosary. Burnt wooden stumps, beams, charred bricks, ash reveal the damage brought to the Mānsar site by Nalas under kings Bhavadattavarman of Bastar in 5th century AD and under

Arthapati Bhaṭṭāraka in 6th-7th century AD. The Poḍāgarh inscription of Bastar provides background to the Nala attack and plunder. Joshi and Sharma 2000, 2005.

19. Walter Spink 1967: 14, 17. for plans of Ajanta caves. Also Stern 1972: plans E-J. Hariṣeṇa of Ajanta and Narendraṣeṇa in Vidarbha both performed śrāddha for Pravaraṣeṇa I and Vindhyaśakti and could be considered sapiṇḍa, as their architecture is related. Bakker 1997: 40.
20. For pillar decoration at Ajanta, see *Encyclopaedia* 2.1: pls. 49-50, 152-53, 161; PC. neg. 42-43. For vertical and spiral fluting, Stern 1972: figs. 39-40, 44, 51.
21. For the jointed lion body at pillar base in Ajanta cave 17 see Stern 1972: fig. 30; for such base in cave I, Gupte and Mahajan 1962: II, bottom pl; in cave 2. Stern 1972: fig. 51; in cave 17, Zimmer 1955: 2, pl. 176. At Nāgarī, a variation is introduced with a double bodied and single-headed bull, flanking a muktāgrāsa, on a pillar capital. PC neg. 4501. For gaṇas on capital in cave I, see Stern 1972:fig. 44; in cave 24, *Encyclopaedia* 2.1: pl. 153. For figures on capital and couples above base in caves 1 and 2, Stern 1972: figs. 41-42. See Stern 1972: fig. 27 for prancing lions in cave 4, and fig. 49 for cave 1. See *Encyclopaedia* 2.1: pl. 149 for petalled flutes at Ajanta. For vṛkṣakās on pillars, figs. 60, 62. For cave 23, see Stern 1972: fig. 58, for dangling leaves, and PC neg. 4385, Stern 1972: pl. 6a for tiger heads; for the Bhiṭā and Kauśāmbi pillar, pls. 122 and 200 a in Chandra 1980.
22. Odette Viennot 1964: pls. 5-6 (Ajanta), 13 (Deogarh), 15 (Nācnā Kuthārā, Pārvatī temple); Williams. 1982: pls. 157, 159, 160 (Nācnā, Mahādeva temple window, Kumrā Maṭh door way, Rupni-kā-Mandir), 174 (Pipariyā door jamb), 181 (Bhūmarā, Śiva temple), 188 (Marhiā, Vāmana temple), 205-06 (Deogarh bhadra panel), 215 (Nāgarī toraṇa post); *Encyclopaedia* 2.1: pl. 91 (Cārchomā, Mahādeva temple, garbhagṛha pillar) for comparisons with late 5th century pillars; *ibid.*, 2.1: pl. 45 (Bhitargānv), 101, 106 (Ramtek, Varāha and Trivikrama temple) for early 5th century vedibandha; *ibid.*, pls. 54 (Nācnā Pārvatī temple), 67 (Bhūmarā, Śiva temple), 79 (Devgarh), 90 (Cārchomā, Mahādeva temple), 99 (Nāgrā, brick temple). Spink 1967: pls on pp. 12, 15, 16 for late 5th century vedibandha mouldings.
23. The foundation cells under the terraced brick temple of Gokul near Mahāsthān in district Bogrā, Bānglādesh are, unlike Devarani, part of the original plan of the temple. See *Encyclopaedia* 2.1 (text): 26.
24. E.g. in the work of Stadtner or M.G. Dixit.
25. See Schapiro1953.
26. Photographs. *AIIS* 329.61 and 329.21.
27. 157 m tall, listed in B.C. Jain 1960:Catalogue No. 31, Museum No. 1408.
28. Spread 62 kms North to South, 42 kms East to West, Sirpur (Lat. 29° & 20° N, Long. 82° & 11° E) in district Mahāsamund in Chhattisgarh is sited along the seven kms long northeastward meander of river Mahānadī, before it turns east. The temples and palaces are oriented parallel to the river current along a mild slope to protect them from erosion by flood waters. The river protects it on three sides in a half circle, southwest to northeast. Hills protect it on east in another half circle. The two ends of the North-South passage in between provide entry and exit. Excavations have revealed temples dedicated to Śiva, white, black, red and yellow Śivaliṅgas, enshrined in Suraṅgaṭilā temple subshrines, Cāmuṇḍā, trinity, Hari-Hara, Buddhist and Jaina Vihāras; residence of princes, chiefs and priests; temples with 3 to 5 rathas, orthogonal, acute angled and stellar projections, 1 to 5 garbhagṛhas, grain rooms, lime stone stocks, water cisterns, courtyards, rows of cells and pillars, fusion of brick, wood, stone, lateral, horizontal and vertical segmentation and expansion. Sharma 2012.
29. About 184 mounds have been found at Sirpur. The excavations have been done by M.G. Dikshit between 1953 and 1955, and A.K. Sharma between 2000 and 2012, respectively under the auspices of Sagar University and the A.S.I. Most of the structures top their steps with stone, use sieved lime, fruit sap and vegetal paste as binding material and iron dowels for joining stone blocks. The priests' houses, located south of Śiva temples, have stone foundations and floors. The structures are generally double storeyed, the upper storey being accessed from inside by a southwestern flight of steps. In the earliest period, a fragmentary gold coin of king Prasannamātra was found. The second period, between 6th to 7th century

AD, witnessed a massive explosion in the construction of monasteries, forts and houses in a quadrilateral enclosure, measuring 250-220 yards, with walls, 16 ft. broad and 12 ft. high. The third period has revealed 43 residential rooms built of older materials, an industry of polychrome glass bangles and 166 copper coins of Ratnadeva of the Ratanpur Kalacurīs in 11th century AD.

30. The house identified as that a Bālārjuna had a laterite and shale stone foundation, laterite door uprights and sockets, brick pillars and superstructure, carved wooden pillars and ceiling made of seasoned teak wood, upper storey roof, covered by hand made, baked tiles, tied through holes.
31. The pañcāyatana (Quincunx) Suraṅgaṭilā Śiva temple comprised Cuḍḍapah stone block jagatī (plinth), cut stone block adhiṣṭhāna, laterite slabs in antarāla, garbhagṛha door, mahāmaṇḍapa floor pillar bases, white stone on base wall of shale stones.
32. The slate slabs used in the Sirpur temples, originally black, have leached into white. A.K. Sharma 2007: 5, 7, 12,14,16,19. For the temple and vihāra plans and details of recent excavation, *ibid.*, p 4-38, figs. 4, 6, 9, 11, 13, 15,16,18, 19.
33. A certain uniformity of material and techniques in the combined use of stone and brick appears to unite the large residential complex, attributed to Bālārjuna, with the Buddhist vihāras, Śiva temples and priestly houses constructed around his time. Mahāśivagupta is always called Paramamāheśvara, and his seals are inscribed with a seated bull Nandī, flanked by triśūla and bhadra-ghaṭa. Dikshit located four vihāras constructed by him. Only one of the vihāras has an inscription, recording the establishment of a charitable unit, for food distribution in the vihāra, by one Ānandaprabha during the reign of Bālārjunā. The Malhār grant mentions a donation to an extant vihāra. The hypaethral nature of the Ānandaprabha vihāra courtyard is suggested by the covered drain through the northeast, by the Belsonḍā slab paving, and by the large number of thrown away objects, found in courtyard. Iron nails, mortices for holding head rafters on the cornice behind the door jamb, indicate heavy timber roofing above side galleries. There is provision of ten figured slabs in the maṇḍapa, with three pratihāras on either side of the door, and two figures each on the side walls. Iron clamps 1/2" x 7/8" have been found, slid in the space between the pedestal surface and sculpture. Dikshit 1954-56.
34. See Thomas Donaldson 1985: fig. 69 (Paraśurāmeśvara, rāhā of gaṇḍi), fig. 858 (bāḍā of jagamohana); *Ibid.*, 2: fig. 1951 (Liṅgarāja temple, vajramastaka on pīḍhā roof of jagamohana), figs. 2460-68 (pillars at Kākudiā, Ganeśvarpur, nāga or nāgī stambhas at Rāṇipur Jhariāl, Gandharādi, Caurāśi, Rājarāṇī, Kālārahaṅgā) for additive segmentation of architectural fragments.
35. Gandheśvara is apparently the popular name of the ancient temple called Gandharveśa or Gandheśvara in inscriptions. The new temple is constructed with architectural fragments of the old temple. In the inscription on the plinth, a daily offering of flowers by Jorjjaraka to Gandheśvara is recorded. S.L. Katare 1957. An undated inscription on a ghaṭapallava pillar, close to the sanctum, records daily dedication by Ambullaka of garlands to Gandheśvara. B.C. Jain 1954-55.
    For the Gandheśvara maṇḍapa pillars, PC negs. 2217, 2218. For Ajanta pillars of similar description, see Stern 1972: figs. 27 (cave 4), 30 (cave 17), 32 (cave 23), 39 (cave 19), 41 (cave 2), 60 (cave 23), 65 (cave 26). Assigned to late 5th century by Spink, the pillars in these caves seem to inspire the design of the Gandheśvara pillars. The pillar with a tall base and upper constriction, not so usual in cave architecture before Tala, can be seen in the verandah of the Viśvakarmā cave 10 of Ellora. See Stern 1972: fig. 87 (Ellora, Viśvakarmā). Aurangabad, 6, 7 are assigned by Spink to the second half of 6th century and Ellora 5 and Viśvakarmā to first half of the 7th. Spink 1967: 7, Time chart.
36. Dikshit 1960: 31-32, suggests that despite several structural changes in the maṇḍapa, most of the pillars and pilasters of Rāmacandra temple at Rajim are original, at least those carved with śālabhañjikās, amorous couples, flower bearers and attendant deities. He attributes the temple, and hence the maṇḍapa pillars and pilasters, to the Pāṇḍava period, and seems to suggest it as the 'most mature phase', following Rājīvalocana, somewhere in the 7th century, after the Śarabhapurīyas, whom he places between AD 500 and 600 (p. 17). He distinguishes the octagonal pillars with ghaṭapallava capitals, darpaṇas (because of

their lack of maturity and grace, compared with Pāṇḍava pillars) as insertions of the Kalacurī king Jayasiṁha of Ratanpur, whose inscription is embedded in the maṇḍapa wall. He says nothing about the door jamb.

On the other hand, Stadtner 1977: 26-31, 119, 144-45 speaks of the maṇḍapa pillars and the door jambs near Varāha image as 7th century, the pilasters (except the outermost one bearing Gaṅgā) as largely modern, while the main door jamb itself is assigned by him, because of Ajanta and Gupta period motifs and figural style, Tala like precision and detail, to the same period as Tala, i.e. AD 535-50. In pp. 139-48, he attributes the thinning, reduction of ornament and detail, roughness in surface, crudeness in the carvings in the pillars, to their extensive reworking. He disagrees with Dikshit about the pillars closest to the sanctum, pointing them out as modern and crude copies of the Turturiyā pillar and a lost sixth century original (see pls. 439-43 in *Encyclopaedia* 2.1). He finds the maṇḍapa pillars with figures, as close to a free standing pillar of Palāri because of motifs or posture, though the ornament of Palāri, is heavier, more deeply cut (pp. 138-39). He then mentions the door jamb near the Varāha image as close to later work at Rājīvalocana temple (pp. 144-45), and dates it after Palāri (AD 675-685), to around AD 695-710 (period of later work of Rājīvalocana).

Both Stadtner (*ibid.*, 26-30) and Krishna Deva (*Encyclopaedia* 2.1: 226-27) notice the original door jamb, set into a largely modern (probably 17th century, says Krishna Deva) door jamb. Stadtner mentions recutting of the original jamb image (p. 27). Krishna Deva places the original door jamb in AD 525-50, even earlier than Tala (AD 550-75), and assigns the two pillars closest to the sanctum (pls. 439 and 443 in *ibid., Encyclopaedia*), found modern by Stadtner, to the same period because of Vākāṭaka influence. While he assigns the other maṇḍapa pillars to the latter half of 7th century AD, he also assigns the temples at Khārod, Palāri, Aḍbhār and finally Dhobin (pls. 480, 485, 494, 497 in *ibid., Encyclopaedia*) to the same period, irrespective of their varying styles. He finds these, unlike Stadtner, earlier than all of Rājīvalocana (pl. 504), or Rajim (AD 700-25), in which he draws no distinction between early and late work.

The dating of the door jamb to the period of Tala or earlier by Stadtner or Krishna Deva is not far from the truth. Their method for arriving at this conclusion is however indefensible, being based on a counting of motifs supposedly frequent at Vākāṭaka Ajanta, later Deccani and Gupta sites, or on their assessment of a similarity of skill in rendering the posture of a mithuna. Stylistic analysis suggests that the door jamb (minus the surrounds) may indeed closely follow or overlap the forms at Jethani and precede those of Devarani. If motifs alone were to decide us, use of rosettes dividing horizontal bands, of vertical (and in case of Tala, also diagonal and spiral) rows of 'acanthus buds' (in Stadtner's words), mithuna and standing female figure in peḍyā of rūpaśākhā (carved on the inner side at Devarani), perforated triangular ardhapadma (replaced by chequer board designs, alternately raised and recessed, or by triangular incised designs on Tala pillars), should suggest as much connection of the door jamb with Tala as with an assortment of monuments, identified by Stadtner from different dates like Udayagiri, Eran, Ajanta, or from later Deccani sites.

37. *Encyclopaedia* 2.1: pls. 441-42; Spink 1972, figs. 10-14, assigns most of the Western Indian caves to late 5th century AD. Also *Encyclopaedia* 2.1: pls. 121-22 for Rudra Narasiṁha temple, Ramtek 5th century AD; Stern 1972: figs 185-86, for pilasters in Nāsik cave 3, assigned by Spink to the last quarter of the 5th, first quarter of the 6th century AD.
38. For the Rāmacandra varāha cell and maṇḍapa pillars, also see PC negs. 2192 and 2198.
39. For vṛkṣakās on pillars in earlier caves, see *Encyclopaedia* 2.1: pls. 160 (Ajanta), 178 (Jogeśvari). River goddesses have been treated in Gupta and Vākāṭaka door frames as vṛkṣakās. *Ibid.* 2.1, figs. 22 (Udayagiri, cave 19 doorframe). fig. 42 (Tigavā, Kaṅkāli Devī door jamb). These are translated later from the door jamb to pillars, brackets, and the exterior facade.

    In Odisha, this process is illustrated by Donaldson 2, 1994, in figs. 2117 (Gaurī temple), 2118 (Mukteśvara temple) showing vṛkṣakās on paga, and in 2452 (Madhukeśvara temple) on khākharā corner pilasters. In western India and the Deccan, the vṛkṣakās are absorbed by mid-6th century in the bārāndā facade. Zimmer, 2, 1955: pls. 130 (Bādāmi cave 3), 227 (Ellora cave 21).

Designs of makara and haṁsa at Ajanta are seen in pls. 149-50 (cave 23) in *Encyclopaedia* 2.1 or of the scrolls on pillars and pilasters in pl. I on page 2 (cave 1), pl. 1 on page 56 (cave 23), and pl. 19 on page 60. The makara medallion at Bādāmi (cave 2) is illustrated by Stern, 1972: fig. 159.

40. Both Ambikā (AIIS neg no. 324-50) and Nāgarāja (AIIS neg no. 241-12) are in the Sirpur sculpture shed of the ASI. PC negs. 2223-2225 show door jamb fragment, with Yamunā and Bhairava. Stadtner 1977: 286-87, figs. 45 and 46 for Kuleśvara Yamunā.

41. Being arranged in the shape of a svastika, it has been so called since the excavation. Stadtner finds it earlier than Ānandaprabha, dating it to AD 590-600, on the basis of the wider use of basalt and the longer and narrower face, torso or waist of the Svastika vihāra Buddha vis-à-vis the Ānandaprabha Buddha. He does not use these as consistent criteria for analysis, or to build up a sequence. Dikshit, the excavator, points out that though the floor level of Svastika vihāra is lower than the floor level of Ānandaprabha, it is not, ipso facto, indicative of an earlier date, as with the Nalanda monasteries. See Dikshit, n.d.: 29. To compare the Ānandaprabha Buddha and Nācnā images, see Dikshit 1960: pl. 53. Viennot 1964: pls. 16a and b.

    Suggestion has been made that the Sirpur itself was designed as a Svastika Nagara, as per Mayamata norms, the Suraṅga Ṭilā complex with the elevated Pañcāyatana Śiva temple, occupying its centre, other important structures being situated at the cardinal points. The Svastika emblem occurs on many foundation stone slabs as mason marks. A.K. Sharma 2007: 4, 22.

42. For a summary of the controversy, see *Encyclopaedia* 2.1: 236. Ajayamitra Shastri's date for Bālārjuna, AD 725-85, is based on the controversial sequence of Maukharī Varma kings of Magadha, and their hypothetical connection with Vāsaṭā, Bālārjuna's mother. It is not substantiated by comparative discussion of styles in art. Vāsaṭā's brother Bhāskaravarman, is not mentioned in the Maukharī genealogy. The similarity of names of King Sūryavarmā of Magadha with Sūryavarmā of Lakṣmaṇa temple inscription, on which the argument largely hinges, can also be completely accidental.

43. *Encyclopaedia* 2.1: fig. 89. Donaldson 1985. 1: 464-66, pls. 468, 473 PC neg. 2212 for Lakṣmaṇa temple.

44. The route for the travel of influence from Dakṣiṇa Kośala to Odisha, either through Andhra Pradesh in the south and the Buddhist Puṣpagiri vihāra region in the north, near the homeland of the Bhaumakāras, remains to be charted. *Ibid.* 2: 797-98. For Paraśurāmeśvara, *ibid.*, pls. 510, 516-18, 520 (for Kapotas), 513-16, 519 (for padmapṛṣṭha), 468, 522-23 (for balconies, niches). Dikshit 1960: pl. 40.

45. For the various designs on Odishan door jambs, Donaldson I, 1985: pl. 384 (siṁhanātha, jagamohana); Donaldson 2: pls. 2003 (Mukteśvara), 2601 (Mukhaliṅgam, Someśvara temple lintel): 2546, 2878 (Bānkaḍā), 2549 (Kuālo, Kanakeśvara temple), 2877 (Paraśurāmeśvara). *Encyclopaedia* 2.1: pls. 408, 473. Williams 1982: pls. 117, 154, 203 for Gupta door jambs.

    The trefoil design reappears in Odisha as the somewhat impoverished patralatā design on the outer jambs of Kutaituṇḍi temple at Khiching. See Donaldson 2, 1986: figs. 2605, 2903. Kuṭila and ratikerā scrolls in Odisha are illustrated by Donaldson 2, figs. 200 (Ratnagiri), 215 (Puri). In the Devarani door jamb, the trefoil patralalā appears beside the inner right surround, the kuṭila and ratikerā on or beside the stambhaśākhā, the spiral mālā in the soffit or the mālāśākhā.

    The band of lotus medallions, common to Tala and Sirpur, partially anticipates a scroll design in Odisha with intervening squares. See Donaldson I, 1985: figs. 17-20 (Śatrughneśvara and Lakṣmaneśvara portals and rāhā niches). *Ibid.*, 2, fig. 2820; PC 2202.

46. The development of the haṁsalatā can be seen in Dikshit 1960: pls. 41-45, 51; Donaldson 1985. 2: figs. 2129 (Niāli, Śobhaneśvara temple, niche on paga), 2870 (Śatrughneśvara, on sanctum jamb), 2873 (Svarṇajāleśvara, sanctum jamb), 2903 (Khiching, Kiñcakeśvarī jamb); *Encyclopaedia* 2: pl. 549 (Bhuvaneśvara, Śatrughneśvara, vedībandha).

47. The dhārāṇvita kalaśa is known as the tripaṭṭa kumuda in the south.

48. The mouldings are often misplaced from above the kalaśa.
49. Representing simultaneously, one assumes, a temple plan, and a kaḍalikākaraṇa.
50. Donaldson 1985. 2: figs. 2174 (Lakṣmaneśvara), 2175 (Paraśurāmeśvara), 2178 (Kuālo), 2185 (Vaitāl Deul), 2204 (Pratāparudrapur, Akhaṇḍeśvara), 2210 (Garūḍipañcana, Buddhanātha Śiva), 2217 (Tīrtheśvara) for Odishan pābhāga mouldings.
51. See Odette Viennot 1976. 2: pls. 49 Āmrol, Rāmeśvar, 60 (Mahuā, Mahādeo I), 68 (Nareśvara, temple 2). Also *ibid.*, figs. 44 (Nareśvara, temple I), 47 (Indor), for illustrations of Pratihāra candraśālās.
52. In Odishan door jambs, gelabā and nāgabandha designs are separated, substituting the thick winding vine for the nāga tail of Malhār, and twisting the nāga tail itself into a braided band. Donaldson 1985. 2: pls. 2910 (Konārak, Sūryā Deul), 2911 (Garūḍipañcana, Buddhanātha Śiva), 213 (Beyālisbāṭi, Gaṅgeśvarī), 2915 (Puri). For nāgabandha designs in Dakṣiṇa Kośala, see *Encyclopaedia* 2: pls. 474 (Khārod, Śavarīnārāyaṇa temple, garbhagṛha door jamb), 496 (Aḍbhār Śiva temple, antarāla door jamb), 505 (Rajim, Rājīvalocana garbhagṛha door jamb), 506 (Rājīvalocana, prātolī door lintel), 507 (Rājīvalocana, prātolī pillars).
53. The assumption by Dikshit, 1960: 27-30, of a flat roofed structure, open on three sides, being the original nucleus of the temple, everything else being added later, is worked out neither on the basis of the sequence in sculptural style nor by analysis of the accretions in structure. Since Dikshit dates the different stages of the temple between the Śarabhapurīya (c. AD 500), through Pāṇḍava, till the Kalacurī period (12th century AD), such an analysis was called for. The dating by Krishna Deva in *Encyclopaedia* 2.1: 230-31, 249-50 of the assumed triple segment architectural nucleus to c. 600, of the sanctum, maṇḍapa or prātolī door jambs to c. 700-725, and of the maṇḍapa, and prātolī pillars to these two different periods, is also not worked out by stylistic comparisons. Stadtner 1977: 177-78 assigns all the work at Rajim to the Nala period in c. AD 695-710, but, on the basis of isolated motifs and inconsistently pursued stylistic criteria, he finds Rajim to be the herald of a new style, different from the preceding work at Sirpur, and emerging out of the Indal Deul temple at Palāri, which he declares to be earlier.

    The confusion is caused by undue reliance on inscriptions. The Nala stone inscription mentions construction of a Viṣṇu temple by Nala king Vilāsatuṅga. It is assigned to AD 700 by Mirashi in *CII*, 4: 1955: 115. It does not follow, in the absence of specific references, that Rājīvalocana temple is the temple in question. The second stone inscription mentions construction of a Rāma temple by Jagatpāla or Jayasiṁha during the regime of the Kalacurīs of Ratanpur in Kalacurī Saṁvat 896 (AD 1145). Mirashi, *ibid.*, 450-57. While some of the restoration of the maṇḍapa pillars on northeastern corner shrine, door jamb, or, of the crowning elements of the śikhara is indeed later, this does not, ipso facto, make the original nucleus of restored members later. However, the ten pilgrim records on the pillars in the maṇḍapa mention personal names in 7th-8th century Nala characters, and are suggestive of the early period of the temple. See Mirashi, n. 1, in *EI*, 26, 1941: 56; Also Cunningham, *ASIAR* 17, 1889: 19-20, pl. 10, figs. 1 to 10.
54. The candraśālās on the phāmsanā kūṭas below the karṇāṇḍakas, or the kapota below the vārāṇḍikā, or the vedībandha kapota, lack the architectonically conceived caitya doors of Lakṣmaṇa, while the mukulas in the siṁhakarṇas of śikhara are replaced by multiple curved frills. Though less elaborate than Lakṣmaṇa, these are more stylized. At the same time, these are still conceived as distinct and large architectural shapes, which have more in common with bulging siṁhakarṇas and karṇāṇḍakas in the śikharas of Khimeśvara, Bhānasāra or Akhodar in early 7th century Surāṣṭra, than with the flat pattern of siṁhakarṇa on the Mahābodhi temple.

    Being a proto-lātina structure with a central veṇukoṣa, Rājīvalocana cannot also be related to any Andhra form. *Encyclopaedia* 2.1: pls. 224 (Mahābodhi temple, Bodh Gaya), 346 (Khimeśvara, temple no. 1), 349 (Bhānasāra, temple no. 2), 411 (Akhodar, Sūrya temple).
55. For Krishna Deva's opinion, *Encyclopaedia* 2.1 (text): 232, 249 (plates) pls. 453 and 456 (Rājīvalocana), pl. 465 (Lakṣmaṇa) for mutual comparison. *Ibid.*, pls. 459-60, 504, 509 and Dikshit 1960: pls. 60, 64 for comparison of Rājīvalocana garbhagṛha, maṇḍapa or prātolī door jambs.

56. *Encyclopaedia* 2.1: pls. 468, 472-73, 504-06, 508-09; Dikshit 1960: pls. 61, 65-66, 68-70, for the change in the style of different motifs.
57. The extremely crude restoration, or later imitation of earlier work on some of the pillars need not confuse our chronology. Stadtner 1977: 166, 172 for examples. Stern 1972: fig. 15; *Encyclopaedia* 2.1: pls. 454-55 for the maṇḍapa pillars, 15, 27, 51, 58, 62 for Ajanta pillars, 73-75 for Aurangabad pillars.
58. Dikshit 1960: pls. 72 (Vāmana), 73 (Viṣṇu) for figures in Rājīvalocana temple corner shrines, pls. 47 (Nāga), 48 (Viṣṇu) for figures at Lakṣmaṇa and Gandheśvara temples respectively. *Ibid.*, 74-77 for prātolī pillars with serpent coils. PC negs. 2217, 2219 for Gandheśvara fragments. For serpentine foliate coils, Stern 1972: pls. 142. (cave 32, Indrasabhā), 146 (cave 33, Jagannātha sabhā). For the octagonal bands, pls. 41 (Ajanta cave 2), 74 (Aurangabad, cave 3). For nāgas forming clusters or pillars on pillar corners in Odisha, Donaldson 2: pls. 2464-77, specially 2470 (Ganeśvarpur, Pañcapāṇḍava), and 2477 (Konārak Sūrya temple). Zimmer 2, 1955: pls. 29, 97, 136.
59. The ossification is visible in the triangularization, stylization, hardened edges of the figures. Dikshit 1960: figs. 59-61, 68, 74-82.
60. These two temples are near the vihāras, and show a plain vertical paṭṭa, followed by a plain antarapaṭṭa with recessed brick patterns, recalling Tala Jethani. Stadtner 1977: pls. 45-46.
61. *Encyclopaedia* 2.1: fig. 90, p. 237, fig. 95, p. 242, illustrate plan of Indal Deul. At Indal Deul, stucco ornament, raised on projecting brick armatures, replaces brick, used at Lakṣmaṇa or Jethani as the ground, while local sandstone is substituted for Sirpur claystone foundation. Stadtner 1977: 102.
62. The iconographic programme shows a conventionalization of the Tala Śaiva pantheon with an additional element of eclecticism. Kevala Narasiṁha of Tala Jethani south lintel appears with two arms on the east karṇa or jaṅghā, and with four arms or the east karṇa of śikhara, in siṁhakarṇas. The Gajalakṣmī, featuring in Devarani lintel, appears in the siṁhakarṇa on the vārāṇḍikā. Śiva himself appears as Maheśa bust or head on the pratiratha of east wall, probably as Lakulīśa (or Brahmā?) on south bhadra, and with Pārvatī on the north karṇa of the śikhara. Kubera accompanies him on the south karṇa of the śikhara and east karṇa of jaṅghā. Dancing Gaṇeśa accompanies him in the siṁhakarṇa of karṇa on west jaṅghā. Dūrgā appears on the north bhadra. Garūḍāsana Viṣṇu, Indra and Sacī on Airāvata, and standing Sūrya appear respectively on the south and north karṇas, and on east bhadra. See Encyclopaedia 2.1: pls. 480-81.
63. *Ibid.*, 2.1: pls. 501, 511 (Paraśurāmeśvara), 570 (Paramagurū), for comparison with Odisha.
64. *Ibid.*, pl. 468.
65. PC neg. 2219 (Gandheśvara temple door jamb), 2221 (ruined temple door jamb). The door jamb is not as new as Stadtner thinks. Stadtner 1977: 110-11.
66. *Encyclopaedia* 2: pls. 485-486 (Palāri), 488-489, 2191 (Siṁhanātha), bāḍā, 2128 (Megheśvara paga).
67. The multiplication of tiers can be seen in the gavākṣamaṇḍana, khākharāmuṇḍis, vimānikā mouldings in tala and ūrdhvagarbhikās, in the decorative designs on the nāgas, bādās and gaṇḍis of deuls. Donaldson 2: pls. 1519, 1522 and 1524 (Sāri Deul), 1702 (Mahāvināyaka, bāḍā), 1838 (Barākar, Śiva temple in West Bengal), 1870, 2210 (Garūḍipañcana), 1995 (Buḍhikomnā; Pātāleśvara), 2128 (Megheśvara, pāga), 2300 (Mukteśvara, Khākharāmuṇḍi, jaṅghā), 2003, 2374 (Mukteśvara, bāḍā and gavākṣamaṇḍana), 2391 (Bīrapratāppur, Grāmeśvara, talagarbhikā).
68. Dancing Gaṇeśa, Sūrya on a five horse chariot, Gajalakṣmī appear on the bhadras, Skanda on peacock, a garland bearing gandharva, a divinity in yogapaṭṭa, Kubera and Varāha appear on karṇas.
69. It seems probable, from the disturbed packing of the structure here, that there was a second sculpted band on a sur lintel at Indal Deul, which is now lost.
70. For the Siddheśvara Temple, Palāri doorway, see *Encyclopaedia* 2.1: pl. 491. Above Gaṅgā, the outer door frame shows Sūrya on a chariot of rearing horses, Iśāna on a bull, Agni on a chariot of parrots. Above Yamunā, it shows Vāyu on a chariot of stags, Varuṇa on a scrolled karimakara, and Viṣṇu on Garuḍa. The inner doorframe displays Yama on a buffalo above Gaṅgā and Indra with Sacī on Airāvata above

Yamunā. Though the images are eroded, Stadtner's description of Sūrya as Vāyu, Nirriti as Iśāna, Vāyu as Agni, Varuṇa as Iśāna, Viṣṇu as Kubera appears to be based on a misidentification of the attributes and vehicles. It is also possibly based on the perception that Sūrya and Viṣṇu may not appear as dikpālas. Of the two garland bearers on the inner door frame, the one above Yama, which is a larger figure than Yama and a male, is wrongly identified by him as Yama's consort, on the expectation of a correspondence to Indra and Sacī figures on the opposite jamb. See Stadtner 1977: 121. Both Sūrya and Viṣṇu appear as dikpālas in earlier texts, including *Manusmṛti* or *Gobhila Gṛhyasūtra*. See Banerjea 1956: 520-21. According to a corrupt line in a verse in the *Rūpamaṇḍana*, Varuṇa on a scrolled karimakara can be alternatively seen as Kubera on an elephant. *Ibid.*, 528. However, Stadtner's attribution of a bull to Nirriti or foliate elephant to Iśāna is not understandable. See B.C. Bhattacharya 1921/1978: 27-30.

71. *Encyclopaedia* 2.1: pls. 490, 493.
72. Stern 1972: pls. 37 (Ajanta, cave 6), 159 (Bādāmi, cave 2); *Encyclopaedia* 2.1: pls. 149, 150, 153, 161 (Ajanta, caves 23, 24, 26), 162 (Aurangabad, cave 3), 193 (Aurangabad, cave 2), 196, 206 (Ellora, caves 5, 26); Dikshit, 1960: pls. 78, 81 (Rāmacandra). The crude carvings inside the vandanamālikā loops in pl. 81 may be later or heavily redrawn, without affecting the early style of the carving of the pillar itself, which makes it comparable with the Palāri pillar. See Stadtner's opinion about the late date of pillar as a modern imitation of a 6th century Turturiyā pillar, Stadtner 1977: 146-47, figs. 112, 114.
73. *Encyclopaedia* 2.1 (text); fig. 99.
74. In one section of the ghanadvāra, the woman in the half ajar door motif, frequent in later Odisha and Bengal, surfaces for the first time known, in Dakṣiṇa Kośala. *Ibid.* (2.1) pls. 497-503. Also Donaldson 1: pls. 154 (Vaitāl Deul) 280 (Bānkadā) for woman in door motif in Odisha. Donaldson 2, 1985: pp. 64-65, pls. 1952-53; Mirashi, *CII* 4; 1955: 2, 535.
75. Being differentiated by this device from the kumbha in the rest of the vedībandha, the kumbha on the pratiratha is integrated visually with the quarter āmalakas on the pratiratha of the śikhara. These quarter āmalakas now become larger than Indal Deul and Palāri for fulfilling the visual design, becoming almost as large as the karṇāmalakas.
76. In the kapili, these niches, unlike the garbhagṛha, are crowned by siṁhakarṇas, while the madhyabandhana continues across the walls of both kapili and maṇḍapa.
77. *Encyclopaedia* 2.1 (text): 23 (plates): pls. 474 (Śavarīnārāyaṇa), 483 (Indal Deul), 503-50 (Rājīvalocana).
78. In this inscription on a stone slab, inserted on the left wall of the restored Lakṣmaneśvara maṇḍapa, Somavaṁśī ruler Iśānadeva, son of Indrabala, records construction of a temple for religious performance by ascetic Śūlapāṇi, and grant of villages for Lakṣmaneśvara. A second inscription in the surrounding prākāra of AD 1181 speaks of extensive reconstruction of the Śaiva temple under Kalacurī Ratnadeva III. See *JOHRS* 5. 1-2.
79. For Aḍbhār temple, Cousens, *ASIPRWI* 1904: 32-33, neg. 2247-49. *Encyclopaedia* 2.1: pls. 494-96. The panels on the architrave show musical gandharva couples with vīṇā, Śiva-Pārvatī, mālādhārī vidyādharas on the lower lintel, and seated Śiva, flanked by Brahmā, Viṣṇu, and cāmaradhāriṇīs in the upper lintel, which has fallen and broken into fragments. The bosses show a flying vīṇā-bearing gandharva mithuna and Kārtikeya. For the Odishan adaptations, see *Encyclopaedia* 2.1: pls. 578 (Bhuvaneśvara, Taleśvara), 582 (Kuālo, Kanakeśvara); Donaldson 1985. 2: pls. 2591 (Mārkaṇḍeśvara), 2597 (Mukhaliṅgam, Madhukeśvara), 2601 (Mukhaliṅgam, Someśvara).
80. *Encyclopaedia* 2.1: 494 for Aḍbhār, Stern 1972: pls. II (Ajanta), 88 (Ellora), 90 (Elephantā), 187 (Bādāmi) for comparison of the pillar capitals.
81. Cunningham, *ASIAR* 8: 68; *ASIAR* 12: 144 and n. 1. Cunningham reports having deposited the 10th century inscription of 44 stanzas about a Śaivite temple at Pujārīpālī in the Sambalpur Museum. Hiralal, 1916/32: 169-70, discusses Pujārīpālī inscription of Gopālavīra praising Varāhadevī, and attributes it to the 11th century. These inscriptions cannot have a bearing on the surviving temple remains, reported at Pujārīpālī by Henry Cousens in *ASIPRWI*, 1904: 32, or by Burgess, *ASIPRWI*, 1903-

4: 48, pls. 288, 290, 298, 300, or by Longhurst in *ASIAR*, 1909-10: 11-17. Four surviving pillars of a temple at Pujārīpāli, with carvings of mithuna and pratihāras, called the Rāmjhulā (Rama's swing), belong to the Kalacurī period.

82. The kapota elements are bifurcated to replace the quarter āmalakas of Khārod or Palāri, to frame the madhyalatā of the śikhara. The karṇāmalakas no longer present the full, rounded, complete profile of such elements in earlier temples. Instead, they are quartered and flattened out to conform with the reduced size of the kapota elements. The madhyabandhana wends its way around the Śavarīnārāyaṇa temple as a discontinuous kapota. It goes around the Pūjārīpālī temples as a flat, continuous band, like the Dhobin temple, and cuts across the wall, intervening between the niches. The serrated, horizontal lines dissecting the śikhara, parallel and anticipate such lines in Odishan temple gaṇḍis. In the temple with the antarāla, the antarāla walls are strapped with continuous flat bands, closely anticipating such work at Odishan temples like the Buḍhikomnā, Pātāleśvara temple. Donaldson 1985. 2: pls. 1308 (Garūḍipañcana), 1848 (Rāṇipur Jhariāl, Indra lath), 1853 (Buḍhikomnā, Pātāleśvara).
83. *Ibid*. 1: pl. 2633 (Rāmeśvara).
84. For the traits of the 9th century style, restoring the 5th century balance of 'ethos' and 'pathos' in a new manner, after the experiments of the intervening period, see Chandra 1970: 26-29.
85. Sātmahallā is situated in Kalcā Bhadwāhi village in Udaypur Tehsil of Surguja near Renr river. Strewn with tanks named after patterns of use (Debborā, immersion of God, Dorgā, utensils), material (Pākhnā, stone), prefessions (Mānjhi, Mānjhāin, boatman and wife, Dhobghāṭ, washerman), trees (Tirhi, Jām, Karondā), the village has pañcāyatna Śaiva temples, monasteries and miniature temples in features and stone, at Dhanbo ṭilā, Sarāi Ghuṭri and Bhilvā Ghuṭri, ranging in age from c. 7th to 10th cent. AD. Pillars with tall shafts, aśokalumbi at base are characteristic features. See Varma 2010: 28-40.
86. These clearances were undertaken, at the instance of the author, on the basis of the plan and estimates, submitted by G.L. Raikwar R.O., Bilaspur and R.K. Singh, curator, Bilaspur Museum in March 1991. Only the main Śiva temple was visible above the mound from the door jamb upwards before the clearance. After this, the temple was revealed to its plinth. In the same mound, several other small temples were found in close vicinity. These are square in plan, survive only with their pīṭha, which is also the vedībandha, and a few pillars.
87. Donaldson 1985. 2: pls. 2536 (Śatrughneśvara), 2597 (Mukhaliṅgam, Madhukeśvara), 2617 (Koṇārak, Sūryā temple), 2868 (Bharateśvara), 2869 (Lakṣmaṇeśvara) for square niches in Odishan door jambs and lintels. 255 (Siṁhanātha), 2887 (Madhukeśvara) for examples of Raṅganī bands.
88. The clearance was undertaken by the Directorate of Archaeology and Museums, Madhya Pradesh, on the suggestion of, and on the basis of survey and estimates, submitted by the author. On the ground, the team was coordinated and supervised by the author from time to time. G.L. Raikwar, the then Registering Officer, Bilaspur and R.K. Singh, the then curator at Bilaspur, later Dy. Directors both, were directly associated with the work all through. The clearance has yielded temples and remains in three groups. One group is in the Orāonṭolā area of the village and consists of a Śiva temple with remains of a garbhagṛha and maṇḍapa, and remnants of pillars and foundations of a few other temples. The largest of these temples has yielded a damaged 17 line inscription (in two fragments) of the 9th century AD with words like 'Pavitrakavi Paramasukharāja' (Paramasukharāja, the holy poet).

    A second group consists of the remains in a grove of trees near the rivers, known as Sāmatsarṇā. A large pañcaratha Śiva temple, a pañcāyatana temple with Devī and Cāmuṇḍa images, a double Śiva temple with three garbhagṛhas, a double row of small Śiva temples, remains of temples in the semal and āmāṭilās (mounds with semal and mango trees), a stepwell at the western edge, and the foundations of a temple at the eastern end, are the remains in this group.

    The third group of remains is scattered on the vast grounds intervening between the Sāmatsarṇā and Orāonṭolā. These are a pañcāyatana Viṣṇu temple in Borjoṭilā near Sāmatsarṇā, four Śiva temples with foundations or sanctums near an ancient tank with stone embankments, known as the Rāṇipokhrā (the queen's tank) near Orāonṭolā, two monastic residences near Borjoṭilā and Rāṇipokhrā. The temples are mostly in stone, while brick is used in the flooring of the monastic residence. They are built mostly on a square or rectangular plan, while two temples are made on the stellate plan, popular in Dakṣiṇa Kośala. The clearance was begun in March 1988, and completed in two seasons, by March 1989. This was followed up by structural and chemical conservation, construction of storage sheds for housing isolated images, cattle trenching for security from mobile vehicular traffic, and plantation and land shaping for ecological restoration.

Very close to Deepadih, right on the banks of Ghograā nullāh (Hindi, rivulet), meeting river Kānhār, in village Gamhardih, three temples with a square plan have been found in ruins. At the outskirts of village Deepadih, on the road to Chāngroh, near Kānhār, there are hills called the Chailā Pahār, where our survey has revealed 9th century inscriptions with the words 'Aum Namaḥ Viśvakarmāyaḥ'(Glory be to the architect of the universe), in nail-headed characters, and working floors, littered with stone platforms and blocks, with hammer and chisel marks, or with perforated grooves used as striking points. The hills are carved with preliminary drawings, preparatory to removal of sculpted slabs, and are full of half finished images and architectural fragments, conforming to the style of Sāmatsarṇā, offering occasional replica images, like Kubera.

89. The kapotas with angled corners, provided with mālāvidyādharas or siṁhas, should have belonged to the pratirathas, maintaining the practice of similar decoration of the pratirathas at Palāri or Dhobin. Kapotas are added even to the base of the faceted sixteen sided pillars, dividing antarāla from maṇḍapa. Apart from this, several flat, sharply gadrooned āmalakas or quarter āmalakas, used obviously as karṇāṇḍakas or flanking elements to the bhadra in the śikhara, like Khārod or Palāri temples, are provided here, unlike earlier Dakṣiṇa Kośala sites, with male or female busts.
90. See, for comparisons with other Dakṣiṇa Kośala or Odisha sites, *Encyclopaedia* 2.1: pls. 477, 480-81, 485 (Dakṣiṇa Kośala sites): pls. 514, 517, 519, (Paraśurāmeśvara, gaṇḍi and bāḍā.), 549 (Śatrughneśvara); Donaldson 2: pls. 2174 (pābhāga of Lakṣmaneśvara), 2233 (sandhisthala of Mukteśvara).
91. These clearances were undertaken, at the instance of the author in 1990, by the Deputy Director, later Jt. Director, Archaeology and Museums, G.K. Chandrol and by the then Registering officer, later Dy. Director, Bilaspur G.L. Raikwar.
92. At Bhadvāhi, this portion is left unfinished, like Deepadih, and only incised above one figure.
93. A Bhairava image in tribhaṅga, a Śiva image in dvibhaṅga, also carved on slabs, have been found from the same site at Deepadih and belong to the same period.
94. Of the same experimental period are the two rows of small votive temples at Sāmatsarṇā, with a Śivaliṅga in garbhagṛha, and a Nandī maṇḍapa. These are made on a rectangular plan, and occasionally on a stellate plan, or with an apsidal end. These are equipped with the usual sequence of later Devarani mouldings, plain but for the full and half candraśālās on the kapota. The site is littered with fragments carved with candraśālās and pilastered recesses, framing human or kinnara mithunas, or secular scenes like a hunter extracting a thorn from the foot. These appear to have been detached from the śikharas, which possessed such features, bridging the Dakṣiṇa Kośala śikharas with Odishan gaṇḍis. At the easternmost edge of the Sāmatsarṇā, in the same period, another temple on a stellate plan shows the aśokalumbī from Tala and Dakṣiṇa Kośala, and a variety of patterns in the leaves, which occasionally emerge from grāsamukhas. An image of Brahmā, with a magnificent headdress, strung by two intertwined locks, and a Nṛvarāha (anthropomorphic boar-incarnation of Viṣṇu), with flying mukuṭa-bearing vidyādharas above, have been recovered from Sāmatsarṇā and belong to the same style and age. These are carved on slabs, used like Tala in walls, and the Varāha slab curves into a functional bracket above, confirming this.
95. The Paraśudhārī (axe bearing) figure at Tala, probably of Paraśurāma, appears on a Jethani south lintel, in dvibhaṅga, resting the paraśu on the ground.
96. Compare Donaldson 1985. 2: pl. 2204 (Pratāparudrapur, Akhaṇḍaleśvara, pābāga) with pl. 2203 (Rājārānī temple, pābhāga) and pl. 2210 (Garuḍapañcana, Buddhanātha, pābhāga).

97. *Ibid.*, pls. 2185 (Vaitāl Deul, pābhāga), 2186 (Śukleśvara, Māṇikeśvara temple, pābhāga) for such paṭṭas.
98. *Ibid.*, pls 2066-86 (talagarbhikās of rāhās), 2114 and 2195 (Ganeśvarpur, Pañca Pāṇḍava), 2117 (Gaurī), 2131 (Pārvatī) illustrate talagarbhikās, which become independent entities, ousting the mouldings. At Deepadih, however, the rathikās occupy portion of the mouldings, emphasizing their presence. *Ibid.*, pls. 2205 (liṅgarāja, pābhāga), 2206 (Khilor, Khileśvara pābhāga) show campaka leaf. *Ibid.*, pls. 2153-58 show elongated muṇḍis in Odisha.
99. *Ibid.*, 2536 (Śatrughneśvara) for grāsamukha on lintel, 2906 (Tīrtheśvara), 2915 (Puri) for examples of jalapatra.
100. *Ibid.*, pls. 2341 (Ratnagiri), 2565 (Mukteśvara, jagamohana, door frame), 2571 (Maṇināgeśvara, sanctum door frame).
101. Maheshpur has been excavated by Shri G.L. Raikwar of State Archaeology Department, Chhattisgarh in 2005–9. The broad chronological sequence can be illustrated by figs. 9-17, 20-18 (phase I); figs: 41-54 (phase 2); figs. 32, 36-37, 43-63, 67-71, 73-76, 96-106 (phase 3); figs. 116-125 (phase 4) in Varma 2012a. The yields of the few mounds, remaining to be excavated at Kuriā Jhurki and Bhītardurā, may reinforce this broad sequence. For comparable pillars from 8th-9th century AD, Encyclopaedia 2.2, pls. 137, 178-80.
102. These clearances were undertaken by G.K. Chandrol, Dy Director Achaeology, Raipur and other officers of the Directorate of Archeology M.P. at the instance, and under overall coordination of the author, in early 1991. Bhoṅgāpāl is a 100% tribal village, in the deep recess of the reserved forest in police station Farasgāon in Koṇḍāgāon Tehsil, at a distance of 153 km from Jagdalpur and 317 km from Raipur. The excavations have revealed remains in three mounds. The largest, 36 m long, 34 m broad, 5.50 m tall, has yielded a Buddhist brick caitya with apsidal sanctum, rectangular maṇḍapa and pradakṣiṇapatha with four doors, and a surrounding platform with remains of rectangular rooms on northwest, east, and southeast. This caitya faces a stream which joins river Lasurā nearby. Across this stream, the second mound (20 m x 16 m x 2.25 m) has revealed two square brick sanctums, with a Śivaliṅga and a saptamatṛkā panel. The third mound (24 m x 22 m x 2.50 m) has also revealed two brick temples with stone doors, on a square plan, one being with a Śivaliṅga, the other empty. *Report* of G.K. Chandrol, Dy. Director, Archaeology and Museums, Raipur, submitted on 22. 2.1991 to the Directorate at Bhopal.
103. See K.R. Srinivasan 1972: 20, 23-24, 27-28. Also Percy Brown 1956: pls. 20-21, 46. Earlier caityas in the south, eastern and western Ghāṭs, and later shrines like Ter in Deccan, Kapoteśvara at Chejarlā in Andhra, Dūrgā temple at Āihole show a tradition for apsidal structures from 200 BC to the 6th century and beyond.
104 . The clearance was undertaken in 1990-91 by Dy Director, Archaeology and Museums, Raipur on the instruction of the author, after a departmental survey by the author and V.P. Nagaich, Registering officer, Raipur. The survey has been conducted in Bastar and surrounding areas by administrators like B.D. Sharma, senior scholars like Sundarlal Tripathi, University and college faculty like Hiralal Shukla, V.D. Jha or S.P. Tiwari, and by departmental officers like V.P. Nagaich and Naresh Pathak through the last three decades and more. The author has also personally conducted a survey of this area, through both the Education and Archaeology Deptts of the States of Madhya Pradesh and Chhattisgarh, which he has headed for several years.
105. Bihar images are illustrated in F.M. Asher 1980: pls. 149 (Viṣṇu, in Dharmāraṇya, Gaya), 150 (Viṣṇu in Rāmacandra temple, Gaya), 155 (Viṣṇu in compound of Bodhgaya Mahānt), 157 (Viṣṇu in Viṣṇupada temple, Gaya). See Aschwin de Lippe 1978: pls. 144 (buffalo demon), 146 (varāha), 151 (King Mahendravarman), 163 (King Narasiṁhavarman) for Pallava images, *Ibid.*, pl. 133; *Encyclopaedia* 2.1: pl. 628 (Āihole, Huccāpāyyā, dvārapāla), pl. 687 (Ālampur, Svarga Brahmā, dvārapāla) for Cālukya images.
106. For ghaṭapallava on jaṅghā pilasters, see Viennot 2, 1976: pls. 56 (Śitaleśvara temple, Candrabhāgā), 64 (Nareśvar temple), 203 (small temple near Kālikā Mātā, Chittor), (Sūrya temple, Mānkherā). *Encyclopaedia* 2.1: pls. 277 (Mahuā, Śiva temple 2), 282 (Gyāraspur, shrine 2), 305 (Kuchdon, Kurāiyā Bīr temple). For

such features on door jamb, Viennot 2, 1976: pls. 73. (Nareśvar, temple 4), 84 (Bateśvar, temple 1). On pillars in prāggrīvas and maṇḍapas, *ibid.*, pls. 134 (Menāl, triple temple), 146 (Osiā, temple 5), 16 (Terahi, Śiva temple), 177 (Āmvan, temple 3), 195 (Bhavānīpuram, Nakti Mātā). Also *Encyclopaedia* 2.1: pls. 269 (Chāparā), 298 (Candrabhāgā, Śitaleśvara Mahādeva).

107. *Encyclopaedia* 2.1: pls. 299, 304, for ghaṭapallava decoration on all sides of pillar. For other decoration on pillars and pilasters, see Viennot 2, 1976: pls. 100 (Gwalior, Telikā mandir), 134 (Menāl, triple temple), 158 (Roḍā, temple 1); *Encyclopaedia* 2.1: pls. 273 (Rāmgarh, shrine), 282 (Gyāraspur, shrine 2), 305 (Kuchdon, Kurāiyā Bīr).

108. Foundation or plinth mouldings in Pratihāra temples are illustrated by Viennot 2, 1976: pls. 104, (Indor, Gargaj temple), 108 (Osiā, Harihara I), 122 (Buchkalā, Hari Hara 2), Lāmbā (Hari Hara), 195 (Bhavānīpuram, Naktimātā), 199 (Bhumdānā, Mahādev temple). For duplication of such mouldings on pīṭha and vedībandha, see pls. 176 (Āmvan, temple 1), 202 (Chittor, small temple near Kālikā Mātā, Chittor). *Encyclopaedia* 2.1: pl. 320 (Pāṭhāri, Sātmarhiā, temple 6). For repetition of kapotas, see Viennot 2, 1976: pls. 51 (Āmrol, Rāmeśvara temple), 122 (Buchkalā, Hari Hara 2), 143 (Osiā, temple 4), 156 (Roḍā, temple 5); *Encyclopaedia* 2.1: 276 (Mahuā, Śiva temple 2).

109. For general use of chequer board designs, see *ibid.*, pls. 124 (Buchkalā, Pārvatī 1), 133 (Menāl, triple temple), 180 (Āmvan, temple 3), 187 (Baḍoh, Gāḍarmal temple), 201 (Bhumdānā), 236 (Osiā, Piplādevī), 260 (Deogarh, temple 28), 274 (Kaḍvāhā, temples 3 a and b); *Encyclopaedia* 2.1: pls. 311 (Batesar), 318 (Baḍoh, shrine near Daśāvatāra group, west), 320 (Pāthāri, Sātmarhiā, temple 6).

110. *Ibid.*, pls. 51 (Āmrol, Rāmeśvara), 108 (Osiā, Hari Hara 1), 174 (Ābāneri, Harṣat Mātā), 187 (Baḍoh, Gāḍarmal), 227 (Gyāraspur, Mālādevī), 242 (Umri, Sūrya temple), 282 (Kadvāhā, Bhuteśvar). *Encyclopaedia* 2.1: pl. 320 (Pāṭhāri, Sātmarhiā, temple 6).

111. *Encyclopaedia* 2.1: pls. 273 (Rāmgarh shrine 1 jamb), 279 (scrolled makara and haṁsa on Mahuā temple 2 vedībandha), 224 (prancing siṁhas flanking kīrtimukha on Mākangañj temple 2 śikhara), 305 (scrolled nibbling haṁsas on vedībandha and vārāndikā at Kuchdon, Kurāiyā Bīr temple), Viennot 1976: pls. 93 (Garuḍa holding nāga tail on door lintel of Batesar, temple 3), 110 (Garuḍāsana Viṣṇu and nāgabandha on door lintel, Osiā, Hari-Hara 1), 152 (Garuḍa on doorlintel, Osiā, temple 7).

112. Viennot 1976: pls. 194 (Barvā Sāgar, Jarāi kā Mātā), 243 (Umri, Sūrya temple) for such lalāṭabimbas.

113. Compare pls. 49 (Abāneri, Jaipur, 8th century) and 60 (Ambikā mātā, Jagat, Udaipur, late 9th century), in Lippe 1978 for such transition.

114. Viennot 2, 1976: pls. 2 (Batesar door jamb), 236 (Roḍā, temple 3) 243 (Umri Sūrya temple); *Ibid.*, pl. 35 (Osiā temple I) for the door jambs.

115. The style rather than inscriptions is the criterion for chronology here. The five inscriptions at Nāgarī suggest activity from 3rd century BC to 5th century AD and do not strictly pin down the uprights in question. See D.R. Bhandarkar, *MASI* 4, 1920. In case of Māndāsor, a firm stylistic pointer is available from the AD 534 inscriptions of Yaśodharman, engraved on two pillars at Sondni. See Fleet 1888: 143-50; Joanna Williams 1972-73: 50-66. Dhaky, *Encyclopaedia* 2.1: pls. 286-90, 441.

116. *Encyclopaedia* 2.1: pl. 327 (Nāndchānd, Indrāṇi); R.D. Banerj *MASI* 23. 1931: pl. 28 A. for mātṛkā image; D.M. Stadtner 1980-81: 270-78, pls. 6, 7 and Williams 1982: pl. 173, for Nāndchānd figures. Mirashi assigns the Śaṅkaragaṇa panel and Chhoti Deorī pillar to mid-8th century AD. *CII* 4.1, 1955: pls. 35, 36.

117. R.N. Misra, 1987: pls. 12A (Viṣṇu as Kachchhapa at Bāndhogaḍh), 15A (Hara Gaurī from Gurgī). Four inscriptions of Gollaka, attributable to AD 915-945, are engraved on the fish temple, rocks and pillars at Bāndhogaḍh and, on a Gopālpur Śeṣaśāyī image near Bāndhogaḍh. These dedicate the Bāndhogaḍh rock sculptures of Viṣṇu incarnations during the reign of Yuvarājadeva I. Mirashi, *CII* 4, 1955: 1. Nos. 38-41.

118. R.N. Misra 1987: pls. 4A, 6A.

119. *Ibid.*, pls. 6B (Marāi), 7A (Chandrehe), 8A (Bināikā), 9A (Nohtā). Donaldson 1985. 2: pls. 2180 (Raṅganī and padmapṛṣṭha in talabandhana of Śiśireśvara). Spink, 18 for plan of Jogeśvari and Elephantā cave 1; *Encyclopaedia* 2.1: pls. 173, 179, 186, 190-91. Stern 1972: plan M of Dhumarlenā.

120. *Encyclopaedia* 2.1: pls. 194, 205 (Aurangabad and Nāsik); Stern 1972: figs. 73, 75 (Aurangabad): figs. 135, 142 (pillars in Ellora cave 16, Laṅkeśvara or cave 32, Indrasabhā). For the projected designs, see fig. 146 (cave 33, Jagannātha Sabhā). *Encyclopaedia* 2.1: pls. 328, 336, 370. Text, figs. 70, 71.

121. Chandra (ed.) 1975: pls. 63, 64, 71. *Encyclopaedia* 2.1: pls. 396, 399, 594, 598, 609, 612, 626, 631, 640-41, 644, 646.

122. *Ibid.*, text, 293, figs. 115, 295, 27, fig. 116, 301, fig. 117. Also figs. 119 (Āihole), 131, 133 (Ālampur).

123. For addorsed dopiccha siṁhas, Donaldson 1, 1985: figs. 132, 135 and 137 for Śiśireśvara temple facade 2, figs. 1502, 1541 for beki of Yameśvara or Citrakāriṅi temple gaṇḍi. For udyata siṁhas, *ibid.*, figs. 38 (Svarṇajāleśvara, vajramuṇḍī), 130 (Vajramastaka on rāhā, Śiśireśvara), 157 (above bāḍā, pilasters on Vaitāl Deul), 241 (in scroll-work), 267 (Bānkaḍā pillar base), 467 (Baidyanāth interior pillar base), 491 (Chardā interior pillar base), figs. 1951-57 (above vajramastakas). For bho motif, *ibid.* I: figs. 72, 118-20 (on vajramastaka), 156, 407, 474 (on pillar); *ibid.* 2: 2437 (on pillar). For siṁhavaktra. *ibid.* 1: figs. 76, 78, 81 (on jagamohana of Paraśurāmeśvara).

124. *Ibid.* 1: figs. 234 (Śukleśvara pābhāga), 249-50 (in caityas); *ibid.* 2: fig. 1967 (Bāripādā Museum) for bekibhairavas. Figs. 143, 154 (Vajramuṇḍīs of Śiśireśvara gaṇḍi, Vaitāl Deul rāhā above kumbha shaft); *ibid.* 2: figs. 2335-36 (on jagamohana bārāndās of Mukteśvara and Brahmeśvara) for bhārarakṣakas; *ibid.* I: fig. 773 (Mukteśvara anurāhā recess); *ibid.* 2: figs. 2449 (on Vaitāl Deul, engaged pillar), 2869 (Lakṣmaneśvara jamb) for gaṇas on virālas.

125. *Ibid.* 2: figs. 2516-19 for kīrtimukhapraṇālas.

126. *Ibid.*, figs. 153-54, 157 (Vaitāl Deul), for figures on the exterior. Figs. 265-67, (for figures around pillars in jagamohana of Bānkaḍā); *ibid.* 2, figs 2448-50, 2452, 2456, 2458-59 for figural, floral and pot foliage carving on different sides of pillars and pilasters beside gavākṣas of Baudh, Mukteśvara, Rājārāṇī, Pārvatī, or Anantavāsudeva.

127. Compare, for example, *ibid.*, figs. 103 (Ratnagiri), or 108 (Mārkaṇḍeśvara), with 744 (Gaurī, bāḍā), and 812 (Rājārāṇī, rāhā) for the binding campaka leaf; *ibid.* 2, fig. 2211 (Darāti temple) for vasanta; *Ibid.* I; fig. 810 (Rājārāṇī): *Ibid.* 2: fig. 1311 (Garūḍīpañcana, Buddhinātha Śiva temple) for faceting and fluting; *Ibid.* I: fig. 385 (Siṁhanātha) for recesses and galapādas; *ibid.* I: fig. 813 (Rājārāṇī), 2, fig. 1382 (Koṇāraka, Sūrya deul) for bānkājālī; *ibid.* I: figs. 236, (Śukleśvara, frame of north rāhā niche), 384 (Siṁhanātha, jagamohana), 396 (Somanātha, door frame); *ibid.* 2: figs. 1349, 1391 (Koṇārak, door frame and jaṅghā), 1442 (Bāṇpur jaṅghā), 1558 (Citrakāriṇi) for transfer of door frame motifs to facade; *ibid.* 2: figs. 1378 (Koṇāraka, nāṭamandira), 1885-87 (Baudh and Mukteśvara, gaṇḍi) for use of ghaṭa āmalaka designs; *ibid.* 1: fig. 138 (Śiśireśvara for vajramastaka); *ibid.* 2: fig. 1661 (Birañci Nārāyaṇa, toraṇa over door) for alasakanyā, nāgastambha, Gajalakṣmī, makara etc.

128. One example, comparing two temples of a species, similar in kind, different in degree, makes the process of this change clear. Thus, when we compare the Lakṣmaṇa temple with the Paraśurāmeśvara temple in Odisha, we discover a stylization, symmetrization and compression of the elements used at Tala and Lakṣmaṇa. The kapotas with candraśālās and ardhacandraśālās, at Devarani or Lakṣmaṇa, used sparingly to mark transitions from the vedībandha to the jaṅghā, or from the jaṅghā to the śikhara, are now used in multiplied tiers in the udgama of the niches of the rāhās, or on the gaṇḍi. The siṁhakarṇas and ardhasiṁhakarṇas used on the rāhā; gavākṣas and ardhagavākṣas used on the anarta; the bālapañjara, used on the kaṇikapagas and anurāhās (to adapt Odishan terminology) in early Dakṣiṇa Kośala brick temples in Odisha, are now made more equal in size, compressed, miniaturized, surrounded by guṇḍikā, filled with figures, crowned with vajramastaka. They are reduced from the large, visibly structural shapes of their ancestral prototypes at Devarani or Lakṣmaṇa, to latās made of perforated half-circular shapes, full of glancing light and shadow. The padmapṛṣṭha between the vārāndā and the

bāḍā becomes sharper and more conical than its precursors in panel frames of Tala and appears also in the śikhara. The chequerboard design of Tala, turned into the perforated design in the kaṇṭha of Lakṣmaṇa, is used as the rūpakaṇṭha, which is filled with figures. The nibbling scrolled haṁsa of later Devarani becomes more frequent, not only in the vasanta on the pābhāga, but also on the kapotas flanking the rūpakaṇṭha. The lions of Tala pillars, appear at the beki, or above the śūrasenaka in a similar pervasive manner. The tactile bulbous āmalakas of Tala, the karṇāṇḍakas of Lakṣmaṇa, are now flattened out into bhūmi bārāndis. The projections and recesses in the kaṭi become deeper balconies or niches on the bāḍā, or a flat, multilayered decorative design in the gaṇḍi.

129. Donaldson points out that in these Odishan temples, unlike Dakṣiṇa Kośala, the kaṇikas replace the rāhās as points of the stellate plan, and bhūmi āmlās form the crowning members of bhūmis rather than their basal elements. Donaldson's suggestion, that in Odisha, unlike Dakṣiṇa Kośala, the height can be increased without enlarging their base, should be read in the light of the fact that in Dakṣiṇa Kośala, the structural elements are in a formative and experimental stage. Enhancement of the curvature and visual impression of height are achieved at Palāri or Śavarīnārāyaṇa by compression of the elements, which are spread out at Dhobin. As Donaldson himself points out, the alignment of the pagas of bāḍā and gaṇḍi is achieved to create a vertical thrust from base to biṣama of deul at Lakṣmaṇa temple at Sirpur, long before Odishan temples like the Indralāth at Rānipur Jhāriāl. See Donaldson 1985. 1: 752-55.

130. *Archaeology, Bangladesh*, Shamshul Alam 1976: pls. 1a & b: (Comillā vihāra, Sālban). Ahmed 1979: figs. on pages 193-4. Bhāṣu Vihāra near Mahāsthāngarh; 1980: pls. 17, 46, 67, 72, 108, 109, 123-25, 246: *Encyclopaedia* 2.1: pl. 244 (Aphsad, Viṣṇu temple). Asher 1980: pls. 72, 110, 209, 215, 245, for the similarity in spatial organization or motifs. The padmalatā is flanked by vertical rows of rosettes on Sarnath, Dhamekh stūpa (AIIS negs. A27-64, A 27- 68). The caityas, scrolled haṁsas, or mithunas at Nalanda temple 2 (AIIS negs. 292-23, 292-76, 293-54), recall the later Devarani mouldings. This only suggests sharing of motifs, modelled differently, according to regional style or period.

131. Pradhan 2012: figs. on pages 17, 63 for Mahāstūpa at Ratnagiri: *Bāngladesh Archaeology*. Rahman 1992: figs. on pages 18, 26 for iṭākholā Vihāra, Maīnāmatī; Alam & Mian 1999: figs. on pages 32-34 for Ānanda Vihāra, Maināmatī; Alam, Mian & Khaleque 2000: figs. on pages 14 and 29 for Bihār Dhāp, Bogrā; Alam 2001: figs. 3-6 on pages 20-21 for Ruyālbāri.

132. *Encyclopaedia* 1: pls. 7 (Dhārmarāja ratha), 16 (Gaṇeśa ratha): 2,604 (Paṭṭadakal, Galganātha) 631 (Āihole, Hucāpāyyā), 667 (Ālampur, Garuḍa Brahmā); Lippe: pls. 123 (Hari Hara, Durgā temple, Āihole), 131 (Viṣṇu Aṣṭabhujaswāmi, Virūpākṣa, Paṭṭadakal).

133. The patterns of influence of the art of Tala and Dakṣiṇa Kośala on later developments may be seen as a mosaic of pieces in different stages and ages, rather than as a radial design conferring its meaning upon all the pieces. The shape of historical time, yielded by these patterns, should be read as different from biological time spans, as intermittent and variable rather than as uninterrupted and predictable. In describing such a shape of time, Kubler suggests that the electrodynamic model of energy transmission with impulses, generating centres, relay points, increments and losses in transits, resistances and transformations in the circuit is more applicable to the history of things, than the biological model of maturation of a plant from tentative appearance through a fuller growth to a culminating intricacy Kubler 1962: 8-9, 13, 27-28, 129.

10

Conclusion

AUTONOMY AND ORIGINALITY OF STYLE

In course of my investigations of the art of Tala and Dakṣiṇa Kośala, I have stepped back in time, and traversed the ancient cultural landscapes of which Dakṣiṇa Kośala formed a part. I have examined the likely or imagined connections of the art of Dakṣiṇa Kośala with provincial Śarabhapurīya, Nala or imperial Gupta-Vākāṭaka, Pallava-Cālukya dynastic developments. I have shown that the evolution of this art is not linked directly with the vicissitudes of dynastic fortunes; that this art is not a marginal, inferior, local aberration of the oecumenical styles of imperial capitals; and, that it is not an isolated incident in the development of Indian Art. I have traced the development of an original artistic style in Dakṣiṇa Kośala, which adapts the preceding styles emanating from various artistic ateliers, and gives the later art its strong individual identity through innovative zest. This style is not stricken by the growing enervation and angularisation in late fifth and sixth century Indian Art, which is often speculatively linked with the breakdown of imperial authority. Instead, it demonstrates a brio, an élan vital, a commitment to volume, an experimental spirit and a quality of humane observation which are missing in so called late or post Gupta North Indian Art centers, and culminates in an extraordinary efflorescence in the ninth and tenth centuries. The style is born in a ferment, fused in a cauldron of ideas, rural and urban, popular and royal, domestic and monastic, generated across India, specially in a stretch of land from Gujarat in the west to Odisha in the east. The style absorbs and develops these ideas in an original manner. It combines cyclopean scale with minutiae of description, unconscious simplicity with conscious complexity. It unites a perception of the grand spectacle staged by Gods and elements in the theatre of the universe with a tender, intimate, humorous understanding of the role played by earthly communities in this cosmic drama. It illustrates, with line and volume, the fervid yearning to express the in expressible, by breaking through canonical boundaries, textual prescriptions, iconographic symmetry or regularity.

PROBLEMS OF MISUNDERSTANDING

Amnesia

The art of Tala or Dakṣiṇa Kośala has been misunderstood as incidental, peripheral and derivative to what is considered to be mainstream Indian Art, emerging from dynastic centres. It has been misinterpreted as tribal, bizarre, naive, grossly physical, over crowded, nonlithic, xylographic, fetishistic, animistic and non naturalistic.[1] The combination, interpenetration and fusion of seemingly antithetical or unrelated features, organic and inorganic, human and non human, sacred and profane, artificial and natural forms in this art are inscrutable to an unempathetic contemporary interpreter. The signs and symbols, votive rituals, gestures, code of social exchange, contractual sacrifice, nexus of debts and rights, which were transparent and legible to the artists earlier, have been occulted by collective amnesia over time. The author of the graphein or granne, graphic mark or sign, that makes language, is no longer with us or has lost his/her authority. Hence, the understanding of interpreters, who are limited by their class, location and time, has been overcome by a nihilistic and arbitrary mise en abime, a void of signifiers. The interpretation of the Paśupati image of Tala as an ingenuous anatomical congregation, or of the roundel occupied by fifteen ascetics as a Brahmanical power emblem suggest an euhemeristic enterprise in interpreters to understand the artists better than they understood themselves. Symbols have tended to be confused with signs and signs with witty artifices.[2]

Alien Discourse

The interpreter's knowledge is doomed to arrive too late on the scene of experience at Tala or in Dakṣiṇa Kośala. Inevitably, an alien body of spiralling, self validating discourse has started growing around the art of Tala, and the surrounding landscapes. This has tended to suppress and supersede the original voice of the artists. The shifting kaleidoscope of the art of Tala and Dakṣiṇa Kośala is like a pristine, protean and dynamic conversation of mankind, which condensed apparently inconsistent and elusive ideas in a story, which acquired immediacy for the bhakta living in faith. The outlines of this conversation have become fixed with growing stylization over time, as we have started making increasing use of nature instead of holding it sacred, and, have lost the capability to see the simmering connection among the various elements of nature. In as much as Tala and associated sites are being treated as monuments, site museums, fair grounds, or, as tourist destinations in a consciousness industry, promoted by a society of spectacle, the actual image of Tala and other associated art sites is being replaced in a heterotopic inflation of discourse, by artificially generated antisigns.[3]

TOWARDS UNDERSTANDING

Unmasking of Reality

Since the art is being reduced to simulacra, eviscerated of their original meaning, the contemporary interpreter of Dakṣiṇa Kośala art has to play a double role. S(he) has to disengage his/her consciousness from the simulacra in the present day world, among which it is disrupted, scattered and forfeited. S(he) has to repossess his/her consciousness and selfhood, and penetrate the iconographic veneer masking the original reality, by recognizing what is repressed behind what is expressed. S(he) has to recall and celebrate the truth of this art, which is like a coin, that has lost its picture and is reduced to its metal.[4]

Unity of Form and Content

Tala and the art of Dakṣiṇa Kośala has been misinterpreted due to an exclusive obsession with its physical shape or inner idea. Those concerned with external forms have interpreted this art in terms of iconographic motifs, patterns or architectural features, without considering how the same patterns and motifs have been modelled differently in India in different sites and periods. As such, the same features at Tala have been variously explained by scholars as early or late, idiosyncratic or masterful, tribal or Brahmanical. On the other hand, a sculpture like Paśupati has been explained conceptually by concentrating attention on some of its external features to the exclusion of others. Preconceived ideas about the identity of the image have been matched with a random selection of texts and motifs. The various images have been explained iconographically in isolation from each other, their context in the temple or iconological history. The art has thus been incompletely explained, biologically or ideally.[5]

Such interpretation has ignored the original nature of this art, in which the outer form is not divorced from its inner content. An exclusive Hegelian emphasis on idea or Kantian emphasis on form hinders appreciation of this art, in which the tension between form and content is mastered by the artist and the audience, through a shared understanding about the unity of art and life. The Paśupati image is conceived and worshipped as many things at once. The simultaneity or ambiguity of themes, assembled in this image from the floral, faunal or human world, express the vernacular Indian concept of the unity of vision and its manifold articulation. The art is created as an expression of a cognitive philosophical and contemplative order, and not as a mere semantic or logical activity. There is an attempt, at sites like Tala, Sisdeori, Malhār, Sirpur, Rajim, to present the record of witnessing the miracle of pure Being, and not to illustrate a mere dogma. It is still possible to believe, that the ancients held converse with the Gods face to face. The art expresses this belief in its attempt to translate ideas of eternal forms, as also to achieve pleasurable and cathartic effects, to present a mimetic representation of ideal reality, as well as a creative process of its disclosure, without observing exact optical fidelity to anything in nature.[6]

Subject Object Fusion

In order to understand Tala or the art of its time, it is necessary to move away from the Western metaphysical, ideological and art historical enterprises, and to stop treating Indian Art, like Indian spirit, as an irrational bewilderment with regard to all phenomena and relations in nature. The image of Paśupati at Tala has been misread by some art historians as a biologically pregnant storehouse of forms, and the Tala art has been misinterpreted as cumbersome, grotesque, and hence, tribal. Such misunderstanding comes out of a tendency to see symbolic Indian art as illustrative of the somnolent Indian spirit, that is yet to awaken from dreaming into understanding, and that can be understood only by the wakeful modernizing spirit. In such formulation, the art of Tala and Dakṣiṇa Kośala is illustrative of instinctive life, responsive to nature, which finds itself in oscillation and fermentation, in meaningless repetition of barren and multiple shapes of petals, flowers, animals, geometric designs, carved on pillars, door jambs, sculptures, rather than in their meaningful reconciliation and identity. So misinterpreted, this art would appear to belong to the magical, mythic, fanciful, aboriginal world, and, represent a consumed residue, a sterile station, a superseded beginning, in the itinerary of the spirit from heteronomy to autonomy, to the Golgotha of absolute self knowledge. It would seem to have replaced respect for idea of the subject by respect for the object.[7]

It is necessary for the contemporary interpreter in Dakṣiṇa Kośala to place the homologic over such hegemonic art historical discourse. S(h)e may not act as subject, objectifying, fragmenting, reconstituting life and art, or as object, drifting helplessly in the tide of history, and mechanically reproducing past experience. S(h)e has to identify with the movement of history as both subject and object, to ensure its creative reproduction.[8]

THE PRECONCEPTUAL AND NON-REPRESENTATIONAL

As soon as the interpreter moves away from analyzing, fragmenting, appropriating, intellectual traditions of the West, which have tended to treat particular forms as superseded stages in a progress towards a higher generality, (s)he finds it possible to rethink the negative values, assigned to the mythology and belief systems, animating the art of Tala and Dakṣiṇa Kośala.[9] S(h)e can then cut through the abscissas of thought, and go back to the symbolic, non representational tradition, enunciated in ancient Indian texts and articulated in Dakṣiṇa Kośala art. S(h)e can then transcend the physical presence of this art to understand its emotional quality, suffused with feeling about an indelible solidarity of all life forms. S(h)e achieves this by fusing form with content and bringing their mutual tension to repose. One does not recover this repose, in its joy and youth, by reaching its physical expression with clumsy and avid hands, or by dismembering the bare body of its compositional elements. It is possible to taste the art in the manner of tasting the Being (Brahmāsvādasahodara). Conventional knowledge derived from physical senses, is an obstacle in the way of such tasting. The interpreter can not mistake his/her physiological and "native eyes" for the sole organ of sight vision. S(h)e has to move from the conceptual to the preconceptual level, at which the immediacy of the feeling of homini religiosi is conveyed overwhelmingly to him/her.[10]

Unity Transcending Plurality

For an interpreter who seeks the preconceptual in this art, it vibrates with a nagging sense of the numinous behind the teeming world of immediate sensation, a perception of the shared life of discrete phenomena, in their growth and attenuation, flowing and stowing, conflict and resolution. Becoming points back to Being in this art and the spectacle disappears, when the self moves away from it to return to itself. Matter manifests and multiplies itself, like ephemeral waves in the ocean, which break into shapes and disappear, without affecting the serenity of the spatial composition or depleting the whole.[11] A vision is offered, of polymorphous monotheism, a singular universal essence, which becomes multiform, to lapse back into an essential pristine unity. The vision transcends the pulsing variety of the external and partial manifestations of the Being, to reach its quintessential form. In a dialogue among elements, the boundaries of sthūla (embodied) and sukṣma (disembodied) are dissolved; and, the bhakta (devotee, literally, divided), shown in this art as a deformed dwarf or isolated, fragmented being, unites his/her mutilated self with the avibhakta (undivided) essence of the Lord. The simultaneous plurality and unity of the vision, acquired in pratibhā or a flash of illumination, by a being, in communion with the supreme Being, has been given an enduring presence in these temples of Tala and Dakṣiṇa Kośala.[12]

Interchangeability and Flux

In the search for harmony underlying the apparent differences in nature, the art of Tala and Dakṣiṇa Kośala acknowledges pariṇāmanityatā, the constant becoming of many into one, and rejects the erroneous adhyāropa or super imposition of plurality on a non dual identity. The eternity of the Being is virtually connected with the fluency of becoming in the physical canvas of this art. It is created by a ceaseless repetition, multiplication, disentangling, recombining, interpenetration and fusion of figural, geometrical, floral and faunal forms in numerous metamorphoses; the emergence and submergence, birth, growth, decay and disappearance, upward and downward flow, procession and recession of organic and inorganic elements; the kinetic interplay of light and shadow, opulent and stark surfaces, turbulent and placid narratives. The nāmarūpa, names and forms, appear and disappear like swallows in a barn, and represent a movement in opposite directions, anuloma and pratiloma, of the same wheel of time. The motion begins and subsides in the unmanifest, in perpetual cyclic flux. The cycle of movement, involves a constant inter changeability of features. It makes the present absent and the absent present, and entails a simultaneous acceptance and negation of the world. The incessant tendency of this art to overturn one order of nature into another, presents a scene of perpetual frustration, or, as an Indian may like to see it, of perpetual fulfillment. It transforms every form into every other, galvanises the intransigent flux, and the seemingly chaotic and capricious variety of forms, with a single breath, tension and feeling, and brings them into a characteristic whole. The breeze ruffles the garments. The flexing of limbs creases the muscles. The flow of sap creaties the swollen planes in the plants. The arrested breath in the body lends it movement. All these speak of a sharing of life and motion by different forms in this art, and the resultant assimilation of their shapes and curves.[13]

IDENTITY AND DIFFERENCE

It does not follow, from this postulate of constant mutability of forms, that the art is 'bizarre', a chaos of inchoate ideas and incompatible emotions. It emanates from an organized philosophy.[14] The ordered kosmos of this art is created by the organization of matter by formal principles, through the aspiration of all entities towards a condition of self originating, matter less form. The ceaseless movement between immanence and transcendence, the co existence of the noumenal and phenomenal remind us of western traditions of metaphysics[15] and physics,[16] which demonstrate various existential or experiential states as foster mothers of all becoming, despite being devoid of all forms. This web of relationships, created in the art of Tala and Dakṣiṇa Kośala, is a relation of anvaya and vyatireka, identity and difference, which are two sides of the same coin. Congregation of images in the body of Tala Paśupati or the Māndhal Śiva, or of various animal, vegetal and human elements, in the architecture and sculpture of Dakṣiṇa Kośala or Vidarbha, represent a circular movement, between forms manifest or sadṛśa pariṇāma and forms unmanifest, or visadṛśa pariṇāma. This movement binds Jīvātman with the Paramātman, the individual with the universe.[17]

Sacred and Profane

In this congeneric world of identity and difference, Śiva stands forth as a guardian of generative and destructive principles, as many and one, cruel and kind, passion and penance, knowledge and play, fullness and residuality, names, forms and lack of them. The fire and water, male and female, solar and lunar interact and are encompassed in the persons of Paśupati, Mārtaṇḍa Bhairava, Ardhanārīśvara, Varuṇa. Antinomies are combined to negotiate the apparent gap between the physical and the metaphysical, and faciliate the creative and pro creative operations in nature and their reenactments in arts. The wheel, conch, pitcher, lotus, and the pillar are presented as symbols that are indistinguishably sacred and profane. The names of places, dynasties, kings and priests on seals, coins and inscriptions, scattered through the landscape, hail the king as a rājarṣi and parivrājaka, a saint or mendicant. Traditions of yajña or sacrificial ceremonies and pūjā or devotional worship converge. Freedom and inexplicability of life are reconciled with the objective and defined laws of beauty. The multiplicity of apparently dissimilar elements appears to be a visual and intellectual clutter to the uninitiated. It resolves itself into a dialectical unity of opposites, a coexistence of contraries, to the initiated.[18]

Apparent Ambivalence in Style, Consonance and Dissonance

The interplay of apparently antithetical features of form and content, emanation and resolution is parallelled by an ambivalence between the plastic and linear, lateral and vertical, architectonic and sculptural, curvilinear and rectilinear accents in the style of Tala and Dakṣiṇa Kośala. The individual manifestations and their congregation in the body of Tala Paśupati suggest simultaneous presentations of via affirmativa, in which the aspects are distinguished, and, of via negativa, in which they become one. Mimetic elements like the frame, direction, movement, size and chiaroscuro contribute to the semantic value of this art, which tries to reflect the ineffable splendor of the life divine and conceives the world as a theophany.

At Tala itself, this ambivalence is present more at Jethani than at Devarani. The internal spatial organization and patterns of earlier cave temples appear to have been translated into the freestanding structural Jethani temple. This may account for the processional access, laterally spread mass, integration of sculpture and architecture in the organization of its internal space, the greater preference for round head, broad shoulders, weighty ornament, a simple, sparse narration, a lighter and easier stroke of the hammer or chisel at Jethani. Devarani accepts a more architectonic style by compressing its body, contracting its horizon, closing its doors and segmenting itself. It moves on to a more complex, crowded composition, a greater mannerism and expressionism in gestures and postures, to sharper and more angular contours, a more vibrant texture, carved with hollows and crests, a more agitated surface, chased in light and shade, and a more finicky use of floral ornament.

The internal features of Tala and other corollary temples, their motifs and themes are adapted and replicated in later temples of Dakṣiṇa Kośala and Odisha, to transform their external facades by myriad vertical and horizontal divisions, recesses and projections, solids and voids, lines and curves. This movement is a sign of the gradual loss of the concord of ideal and formal features, with the loosening of the earlier sensibility. The growing virtuosity and restlessness, miniaturization and multiplication of architectural elements, angularization, and linearisation of forms in the art of Dakṣiṇa Kośala or its neighbourhood do not speak of a radical change in style, or leave

Tala temples behind in splendid isolation. Instead, these changes show a deepening of the trends already visible at Tala, towards a gradual relaxation in the energy of perception and execution, in mantra or utsāhaśakti. The abhāsa or reflection of Śiva in jīva or vice versa fades in later art, which is overcome by an obsession with surface effects. The stylistic movement, in its evolution from an earlier fervor to later abstraction, reflects the history of an initial expansion and later contraction of consciousness. And yet, the slackening, in the later period, of the earlier concentration, spontaneity and will to form, incited by surging devotion, does not suppress the strong and continuing individual identity of the art, in its volumetric accent or experimental ardour.

This movement towards gradual attenuation and elongation of the temple body, accentuation of its upward and rotatory mobility, and the mesh of geometric and figural forms anticipates the transition from the so called classical to medieval stylistic trends. This movement becomes evident in the stylistic developments in sculpture and architecture, as one moves back and forth between the parts and whole, regional variations and the broad unity of ideas and styles. The religious and stylistic movement of this period is a unity. It refers simultaneously to disparate facets of experience. Once the art of this period is stript of the veneer of interpretations confined to its physical surface, its various parts are seen as essential links in the stylistic movement rather than as isolated incidents.[19]

SIGNALS AND ECHOES

To speak after George Kubler, the climatic entrance, in this stylistic movement, of prime objects like Paśupati, or the unique innovations of Tala, Malhār, Sirpur, Rajim, may appear vertiginous at first sight. However, the synthesis of passion and intelligence, ethos and pathos in the art of Māndhal, Ramtek, Mānsar or Sisdeori proves that these objects and sites were preceded by a series, the beginnings of which may not be immediately evident to us. Similarly, the parallel though remote echoes that follow in the cognate language of philosophy, folklore or art of Longman caves in China, Celtic or Japanese armour, classical or medieval Europe, primitivistic modern art, or art of tribal India, are separated from their own precursors or the art of Tala and Dakṣiṇa Kośala by the linguistic drift produced by cumulative changes in the articulation of audible sound. Outstanding objects like those of Tala are like mutant genes, as distinguished from standard examples, which influence later art without being perfectly understood. They are like primary signals, that are closest to the initial commotion. The work preceding this art is known by perturbations indirectly, as of dead stars whose light has ceased to reach us. The work succeeding this art is like successive signals that have distorted the original message in transmission. It may not be possible to trace archaeologically the exact genealogy of artistic solutions evolved in Dakṣiṇa Kośala for the ideological problems of showing the simultaneous merger and emergence of forms, or re-enacting and dramatising operations of nature. It is only when the work becomes repetitious and loses its innovative impulse, after 9th century, during the interchronic pause, 'when the light house is darkened between flashes, that the signals are clearer. We see and try to understand this art, in brief pauses between the sun and the rain, its traces vanishing when we go to the place where we thought we saw it first. Historical recall of this art can never, therefore, be complete'.[20]

NATURE AND CULTURE

Temple as an Adequate Symbol of the Universe

Understanding of this stylistic movement dawns on us only when we see it as closely linked with the Indian philosophy of life and arts. Once we do so, the art reveals itself as a passage from nature to culture, an imaginary to a symbolic order. Culture is visualized in this art as a cultivation rather than domination of nature. Its subject is nature, not isolated from, but modified by (wo)man, in an attempt to capture its essential manner of operation, rather than imitate it. The art goes beyond a trivial etiology, designed to entertain through stories and rituals. It brings nature into the domain of ritual pantomime. It draws on a heritage of mythic images stored in the deeply graven river bed of the Indian soul and allegorizes and expresses them with a thousand tongues. It radiates around the cosmic and mythical history of the universe, in which the stars, planets and elements are dramatis personae. It anthropomorphizes the temple as the house and body of God and the human body, on which the temple is modelled, as a double of the universe. It stages a symbolic rehearsal of the primordial drama of creation, enacted by Śiva, his family, attendants, woshippers, in the theatre of the universe. It introduces a sympathetic compulsion by narrating, reiterating and validating this drama. Thereby, it seeks to coerce all elements of nature towards a desirable consummation, for continuing bounty and well being of the world.[21]

It is possible, with the art of Tala and Dakṣiṇa Kośala, to reaffirm the affective world view, in which the universe is not indifferent but sympathetic to man; man, nature and God are ritualistically linked in harmony and oneness; one works with rather than against the elements in the phenomenal world; and, the idea of good, law or regularity regulates the idea of capriciousness or aleatory interest. Thus, at Tala, the paśus like gaṇas, siṁhas, gajas, kīrtimukhas, makaras are represented as incomplete, mutilated and deformed when they are separated from Paśupati, and as complete when they merge in him. The serpentine coils framing Paśupati represent the cyclic flux of time. As these images celebrate the constant appearance and disappearance of forms in the universe, so Sūrya and Aśvins represent the diurnal solar movement, and Kapila and Bhagīratha epitomize solar symbols. The purging of waters or retas through tapas or creative heat is represented in the form of Kapila, who burns Sagaraputras to ashes. The three fold movement of fiery breath is epitomized in the liquid form of Śiva as Gaṅgā Tripathagā, led by Bhagīratha, to regenerate the Sagaraputras, who, in turn, symbolize the inexorable passage of time. The union of Agni and Soma, fire and waters, reinforce and release the nutritive, therapeutic and generative forces of the universe. These forces are crystallized in the form of Varuṇa, Skanda, Ardhanārīśvara, and, of Paśupati himself. They are reflected in the divine and human couples, stationed at the threshold of the womb chamber or garbhagṛha, and, in the pollination, proliferation and persistence of floral and faunal growth. The form of Paśupati represents the primordial act of the sacrifice of Soma or waters in Agni or the flame of life breath. The guild of paśus represent life breaths serving the imperial breath in Paśupati. The ascent after the Sun in the body of Paśupati, the descent of Gaṅgā after Bhagīratha in the Devarani door jamb, are analogous to the interaction of Agni and Soma, fire and water, the movement of prāṇa in the human body. The anabolism and ketabolism, the systolic and diastolic expansion and contraction of the body, and the equinoctial and solstitial movements in the body of the solar universe, are equivalent.

The union of matter and energy in the body of the universe and the agnisomīya paśu are dramatized in this manner to present a story of sacrifice of eros to psyche, to open the door to bounty and plenitude, and, to offer an antidote to collective sorrow and anxiety. A mental rather than physical sacrifice of passions, conduces to the healing of the mutilated, fragmented consciousness of the votary, and to a shower of graces and good fortune, which is symbolized in the consecration of Laxmī in the saubhāgya paṭṭa, the head of the temple door. The language of literature, philosophy and culture is harnessed to the language of art. The bodies of nāga, makara, gaja, siṁha are presented partially in front or in profile, to form architectural parts, as synecdochic symbols. A lotus metonymically suggests the lotus pool of Sarasvatī, the magnum foramen, the solar circle, or the seat of Lakṣmī. A falling column of water elucidates the story of the rejuvenation of Sagaraputras. The haṁsa becomes a substitute for soham in a verbal, visual pun to suggest more than one meaning. Significant iconological allusions are distributed, like hypograms, rhythmically important letters, aligned along the length of the line, at different symbolic locations of the temples. Rearranged together, they yield a plot or word theme, or message, in terms of Saussure. The primal core of things is accompanied by the reminder of things, shaped, according to the degree of their participation in the core, into diverse aspects or hypostases.

Art Cathartic, not Fetishistic

The syncretic, hydraheaded, multiarmed images of Tala or Dakṣiṇa Kośala are not false images, or commodities, in Marxist terms. They do not represent the perverse exchange of commodity fetishism or the inversion of images, relations and consciousness through a historical process of exchange of human essence for the essence of fantasy or superstition. Subjective projections of ideology have not been stamped through these images on the products of human labour. Nor are the images mere things, intended to replace the human being, drain him/her of humanity, or assume this humanity, in a catachresis, to either produce material relations among human beings, or to enter into social relations with one another. The integration of floral and faunal elements in Paśupati, Varuṇa, Kīrtimukha, in architectural moldings, door slabs, door jambs, pillars in this art may appear to be forced and non human. It is, however, prompted by the human being's attempt to reach up to the universal, and to humanize rather than dehumanize the world. A vital empathy for life, a Dionysian will and fervour, throb in the flowers and plants, animate human gestures and expressions, ornament and clothes, and redeem this art from geometricity and abstraction. Here, the human beings are defining themselves, not according to what they are actually, but potentially. The human body has been used to give body to an idea of God and humanity, whose Being is a form of becoming what it already is. The images of Paśupati, his hosts and allies do not represent the Being. They are the Being. They are not allegorical, but tautogorical. To the impression of the factual world, which surrounds this art, the human spirit has opposed an act of expression, by no mere passive contemplation, but by emotive and willed participation, to confirm the human and non human persons as aspects of God and to endow them with holiness. The so called idols of Dakṣiṇa Kośala art are not external to the idolators, but embody their innermost goals of communion. They are real, as what is sought in them, in terms of creative and regenerative powers, is deemed to subsist in them. The objective of this art, therefore, is cathartic and oriented to defetishization. It is heroic in giving value to something that lacks it, transforming what it imitates, by infusing it with vibrations and intimations of the life and spirit of the universe. It is an attempt to ensure that the denatured individual, inserted rather than rooted in nature, reassumes his/her or its nature; as part of rather than apart from nature.[22]

The different creatures on the body of Paśupati are not pimples on the ocean of cosmic pus or will, or examples of passive acquiescence in joining a non existent, un differentiated ocean. Instead, they express joy in union with what they potentially are, as they are pierced by what Baudelaire calls 'the steely barb of the infinite.' The art, despite suggestions to the contrary, is not an example of inadequate symbolism. It does not represent an attempt, castigated by Hegel, to finitize the divine or divinize the finite; to force nature and humanity to assume forms appropriate to each other; to reconcile the irreconcilable, extreme abstraction and its gross manifestation; or, to present an inadequate, untranslatable symbolism, with a dissonance of form and meaning. A Hegelian misinterpretation of this art as grotesque, unnatural, absurd is to cannibalize and hegemonically translate, by an act of chresis, the genuine source text of Dakṣiṇa Kośala art into an artificial target text of the interpreter.[23]

FUSION OF PRECONSCIOUS, UNCONSCIOUS, CONSCIOUS, 'RAW AND COOKED'

It is inappropriate, on the fragile basis of such mistranslation, to explain this art as a mimetic expression of archetypes, derived by memory or association, from the collective, unconscious dream thinking of the race, in its infancy. The mind of the artist does not act in this art as a tabula rasa, or as a passive wax like receptacle, to receive signet impression of another mind, but actively uses objects to represent the world, and itself to itself. This art is not a body of involuntary interjections, signals or engrams, actuated by sensual animal apprehensions of interactions among organic and inorganic elements in nature, perceived in an artificially altered state of mind. It is not confined within a biological, functional circle of stimuli and response between the receptor and affector systems of the forces, impulses and artifacts of nature and their human correspondents. On the contrary, it is animated by a conscious concern to understand nature, not by material causes alone, but through a search for the final causes. The various ways in which shapes and meanings are transformed, consolidated or transmuted into composite forms at Tala and Dakṣiṇa Kośala are not born out of a psychically altered hypnotic, paranormal state, the unformed chaos of inchoate ideas, incompatible emotions, automatism, free association, or ideational mimetics. The art does not express ideas, generated by basic Id Instincts, that may have been repressed by conscious ego or social demands. The split second tachistoscopic exposure and multi dimensional attention to invisible subliminal images, the merger of a pot with lions, lions with crocodiles, crocodiles with elephants, Kubera, crocodiles or lion heads with lotus rhizomes do not illustrate Freudian principles like the condensation of incompatible images into a composite image, displacement of the psychological significance of one object and its assumption by substitute objects, translation and secondary revision of thoughts, to integrate incoherent dreams into a coherent whole. Far from being engendered by dream work subject to psychoanalytic exploration, this art is tied to an organized philosophy, fed by a continuous stream of oral and textual traditions. These traditions have been brought to a luminous focus by meditation, concentration and transubstantiation for artistic creation.[24]

Prepositional, logical, linguistic elements combine with appositional, seemingly non rational, visio spatial processes of the composite and mutually complementary imagery of this art. This convergence of seemingly contrary principles in the art of Dakṣiṇa Kośala is not to be explained in terms of a binary algebraic analysis of the neurophysiological mechanism of human brain, involved in its environment. The human mind does not express itself here in empirical cross differential categories, to reduce different aspects of experience, to an orderly operation, in which arrangements matter more that content or meaning. The Indian belief system, relevant to this art, is no mere bricolage, improvised into structures out of random materials.[25] The inventive, inspirational and pre conscious is artistically blended in this art with selective and critical consciousness. Open ended, multi evocative, polyphonic on a conscious and critical level, this art is a single serial structure with firm boundaries on an inspirational, inventive level. The apparent dissonances fuse there into remote consonances.[26]

UNITY AND VARIATION

It is through such fusion that the art of Tala and analogous sites seems to have generated a form and structure, to influence tradition, life and nature, in Dakṣiṇa Kośala, which, in turn, may have imitated this art, the art making rather than mirroring a world of growing consensus and convergence. Having brought the art world into existence, the artist may have also been influenced by this world, which may probably have been more orderly than the chaos of his/her personal life or the turbulence of his/her time. This development is reflected in the inscriptions and material culture of Dakṣiṇa Kośala in this period. The heterodox ways of Pāśupatism and Buddhism appear to have converged with older traditions, to discover a heuristic syntax of gestures and transcend sectarianism, for exploring the complex nature of reality. As this art retains its roots in collective racial traditions, the nonlinear, multilevel dispersion, adjacency, complementarity and seriality of its forms, displace, differ and exclude the presence of a single totalizing central logos, origin, or, an originating privileged human subject, a coherent cognito. It does not exclude the human, but the personal. A suggestion is made in this art of the ever renewed beginning, of life multiplied in history, through a number of nomadic distribution centers and structures, in which man is a measure but not the measure of things. In its mutations and variations, this art depicts the human being as neither a subject nor an object, but as a structure of relationships, 'a metaphor without breaks, that inhabits the interstices'. An attempt has been made in it to offer, not the biography of the artist, but the psychobiography of the tradition, as an on going process of interaction between the collective and universal language or langue, and specific temporal or spatial variations in utterances or parole.

The synchronic unity and totality of the tradition in terms of the themes of water cosmology, primordial sacrifice, cyclic emergence and merger of forms has been read in this art with diachronic historical developments of these themes at different times and places. The emic and phonemic linguistic units of organic and inorganic features have been read with the heterogeneous etic and phonetic speech sounds and expressions at various sites. It has been necessary to move back and forth from a complex, ever evolving, ever proliferating group of textual traditions, to an interior simplicity of the tradition at its beginnings. The to and fro movement between the nomothetic or general law of creativity, and the ideographic representation of a particular product of time has been undertaken to achieve a palingenesis or rebirth of the past, as a record of the human potentiality, which is constantly present with us, as a possibility to be fulfilled in the future.[27]

FROM THOUGHT TO UNTHOUGHT

The interdependence of the text and the art world being historically conditioned, the process of the unconcealment of the intentions of the text has been acknowledged in our discussion as historical, being shaped by history. History and the momentum of the past have been affirmed and negated at the same time in our interpretation, to touch the past from proximity, and, to reflect on it from a distance, to participate in it from within, and to define it analytically from without. The reenactment of the original act of the art has, therefore, been done by letting the object be, in its otherness, as also by imposing ourselves on the object, in an attempt to understand a statement about life, which is, after all, distinct from life itself. The sympathetic and critical approaches have been combined. The possibility has been acknowledged that the language used by the artist, his/her ideas and images, may be understood as analogous to ours. However, this being a distant kinship, the pristine context of ideas and images may be examined through models given by archaeology, botany, ethnography and art history.

The analyzing, fragmenting, appropriating intellectual traditions of art historical scholarship have treated Dakṣiṇa Kośala art as a strange and unfamiliar local aberration, and, as a superseded stage in the higher generality of mainstream artistic developments. As against this intellectual solipsism, an attempt has been made to participate in the incessant movement, between the part and the whole, in analyzing the language of this art; to go back to the original thinking, which has been obscured by later concepts; to liberate rather than annul, incorporate or surpass the unthought; and, to proceed from what has been thought, to what is yet to be thought.[28]

Critical and Sympathetic Reconstruction, to Elicit Meaning

Tala and other monuments of Dakṣiṇa Kośala have been treated as open works, which have existed in a series of past uses, and unfolded in a variety of future uses, in the history of textual exegeses and interpretations, as much as in their own history. The work of art, so historicized, may have been altered by our effort to understand it. The text of this art, or the self to which we have returned after experiencing the art, may no longer be the same text or the self with which we originally began. A multilinear transmission of impulses rather than unilinear biological growth or decay characterises this art[29]. The union of signifier and signified in the images of this art has been differed by the indeterminacy of the linguistic sign in this art, which is half not there and half not that, in a strange half life, and generates a multilayered meaning, deferred through the ages[30]. Since we have posed the divergent historicity of human existence against an assumption of unchanging substance of collective culture, thinking itself has been pitted against universalistic, psychologistic model of thought, as an artifact of history. The script of the Dakṣiṇa Kośala art has been treated as an incomplete translation of a translation of the signs of a non verbal world of ideas and expressions. The signs have been generated through a convergence of known and unknown cults. The text or the context of art has been translated, not as literal meta phrase, word by word, but as paraphrase, sense by sense. We have not read the art as a rigid system of inviolable boundaries and constraints, received intact from the past, in literal mimetic translations. Instead, we have subjected the temporally and spatially layered philosophical and iconological texts and regional contexts of the monuments to an interrogative reading. Such reading has involved reiteration, refutation and supplementation, change and reversal of directions, and acceptance of the risks of rupture and discontinuity in interpretation. The polysemy, the multiply divided meanings have, thereby, been recovered from the differentially plural body of linguistic kinship and affiliation, in the after life of such retranslation. The interpretative play with the texts of the monuments has acknowledged the inter texts of prior or subsequent art, including the phenotexts and genotexts of the verbal lore or psychological drives, operative behind the texts. Liberated from an affiliation with individual authors, the texts have been placed in the background of collective work of the art world, for discovery and production of meaning. We hope that instead of being depleted or exhausted by our retellings and readings, the meaning of this art, being differentiated and deferred, has been enlarged and completed.[30]

In our formulation, the various interpretations of the image of Paśupati as Agni, Rudra, Lakulīśa, Yakṣa, Yogī, do not express incommensurable vocabularies. Rather, these express the human being's attempt at self realization by posing the same question in different ways, in course of living through history. An exploration has been undertaken of the themes of interaction of matter and energy, retas and tapas, heat and waters, the therapeutic purging of waters in the body of Paśu, Paśupati or the universe. This may not be seen as a deterministic attempt to force the art to conform to a pre established meta narrative, through a random matching of texts and evidence, or to impose a structure where none exists. It should instead be seen as an attempt to pursue imprudence as a method, to excavate the text of the art, read it against the grain, and bring to the surface a multiplicity of little narratives, subjugated discourses and hidden contradictions. Unconditional iconological voyages have been undertaken into the vast sea of Indian philosophical speculation, in an attempt to understand the unforeseen estrangements from the habitual, and the extra ordinary transgression of the limits of standard artistic theory and practice. In this manner, the lost alphabet of the art has been deciphered by enlarging or miniaturizing its typography. An attempt has been made to derive the analogical, conventional or existential connections of icons, indexes and symbols, forms, functions and technologies, techmemes, formens and funcemes.

An investigation has been undertaken into the process of fusion of Gupta & Vākāṭaka alphabets of writing and making art; growing southeastern leanings in subsequent artistic developments, emerging from Dakṣiṇa Kośala. In this study we have tried to combine ratiocination and participation, poiesis and techne, onomatopoetic and interjectional approaches, psychologism and formalism. We have attempted, as people in history, a palingenesis, a resurrection of the past, by assembling its disjecta membra, and by inducing them to speak to us, in a coherent voice. We have studied, in the words of Rilke for Rodin's art, 'this differently great surface, variedly accentuated, accurately measured, out of which everything must arise'. We have used historical tools to recover understanding of a symbolic universe, as an organon of self knowledge. We have searched for aspects of an omniform God, immanent and transcendent, to gauge the eternal cyclic process of creation underlying biological parturition, and comprehend cardinal before ordinal numbers. In the process, like ST. Martin, we have heard 'bowers that sounded' and seen 'notes that shone'. In a world engulfed by technification, desacralisation, standardisation, aphasia and amnesia, loss of speech and memory, this may have helped us recover a sense of the mutuality of beings and Being, communion of human and non-human families, and sense the unity of God as instrumental and material cause, and embodiment of the predicates of a world, which is its body and remainder.[31]

NOTES

1. See Chapter 4, text; Notes in Chapter 6; opinions of scholars in Nigam 2000 about identification of Rudra Śiva image at Tala in Chapter 7.
2. Mitchell 1986:29. The consensus omnium or universality in judgement or taste, which united the ancient Dakṣiṇa Kośala artists with the craftsmen, has been reduced today to a consensus optimorum, the agreement of art historical experts, whose taste is determined by their social status and background. Dufrenne 1979: 255.
3. See Michael Foucault 1966/1970. Heterotopia is formation of tissue in a part of the body where it is not normally found. With the decline of representation, there has been a proliferation in discourse, and it is difficult to make the Being shine through a cumulative repetition of words. Jameson 1991 describes the growing divorce of the cognitive use of language from its marketable use, merger of the psychic with the economic, promotion of representations as products, and the expansion of capital into hitherto un commodified areas of art and culture. Derrida speaks of the de centering of the structure of the mythic book, which is no longer a natural site, in which an infinite number of sign substitution has come into play, and everything has becomes discoursed. One must be separated from oneself in order to be reunited with the blind origin of work in its darkness. Derrida 1967/1978: 8, 280.
4. Baudrillard explains about the procession of simulacra from their original reflection of the basic reality, through its masking and perversion, a further masking of its absence, to its final dissolution. Baudrillard and Strauss elucidate how the iconographic mask transforms the reality by representing or omitting, stating or excluding, revealing or concealing. Baudrillard 1975. Strauss 1988. Mehta 1985, "Philosophical Issues in Representation", in *India and the West*: 1-23.
5. Historiographical notes in chapters 5-8.
6. Of the three ages of God, Heroes and Man, described by Vico in discussing the origin of myth and poetry, the age of God is still very real for the artists of this period. All things are still full of Gods, every hill is the dwelling place of an oread, every tree the home of a dryad. Cassirer 1955: 153-54. The language of this art constitutes meaning, and does not merely reflect meaning in a conventional allegory, trope or metaphor, calcified by over use. It is a period, not yet overcome by the spirit of Socratism, when the sacred seeking for the principle of transformation and fulfilment of human nature is still considered a feasible venture. Attempt to explain this quest, in terms outside the Indian tradition, is fraught with the danger stressed by Sartre, that the black Orpheus must sing in French, if his voice is to carry across the frontier, and then, his voice is no longer entirely his own. Dufrenne 1979: 33-48.
7. Some art historians are obsessed by the idea of the interpreter as the Subject of History, armed with a teleological mission of understanding through reasoning, by objectifying, fragmenting and reconstituting existence and art. The Western concept of knowing does not allow non Western cultures to exist in their inappropriable mystery of otherness. The Christian eschatological concept of believing theologically poses an unbelieving, objectifiable other; the European enlightenment idea of human progress to a secular utopia; Hegel's identification of secular history of the West as a sacred history of the progressive self realisation of God, spirit or reason; the Marxist notion of material progress and historical materialism; the Freudian venture of enlarging self knowledge; the Cartesian or Leibnizian notion of the human subject as Ego Cogito or Monad, treat the Western or Westernizing interpreting human subjects as carriers of an absolute idea and telos, to live by reason. See Mehta 1985: 216-18. Also Spivak 1999.
8. The contemporary interpreter has to treat the beginnings of the Indian traditions, brought to fruition at Tala or Dakṣiṇa Kośala, not as primitive, clumsy or superseded, but as mighty and uncanny, in which the duality of knowing subjects and known objects lapses in the hermeneutic of the global We; in which, the human being exchanges his role of lord of beings for that of shepherd and sounding board of the Being; and, in which, art is at once man's way of experiencing and responding to the Being. The attempt to understand this art is an attempt to go beyond the subject object dichotomy, go back into the

neighbourhood of Being; recover the perception of the unhiddenness, disclosure or alatheia (Greek, unconcealedness) of Being; reach into the region of the pure and timeless or the hyperouranious typos; and, to begin the beginning once again, more radically, with all the strangeness, darkness and insecurity that attend a true beginning. After Heidegger, "Being and Time", in Mehta 1976: 208-9, 318-19.

9. Robert Redfield speaks of the transformation today of the retrospective mythology of recurrence into a prospective mythology of change and revolution, and the advent of an exclusively cognitive, positivistic world view, in which wo(man) confirms a universe, empty of personality, and considers him/herself competent to construct him/herself and society by deliberate design. Redfield 1953: XII, 94, 100, 104-5, 108,125-26; Langer 1979: 278-9. On the other hand, the sharp temporal dividing line seen by Comte, in his law of three phases, between the theoretical, historical and mythical consciousness, has been dissolved in nineteenth century West by the romantic rediscovery of the vanished world of myth, and by Schelling's attempt to give mythology a place in the history of philosophy, by uniting mythos and logos. The Indian perception of the unity of life and nature is paralleled in the West by the Stoic doctrine of an all pervasive breath, diffused through the universe in early Greek thought, which identifies the knowing subjects and reality. Aboriginal cults like Polynesian Mana, Iroquois Lorinda, Sioux Wakanda, in North America; and, in Algonquian Manitu, in Canada, perceive supernatural powers, as being dormant in men and things. Cassirer 1955: 95-96.

10. The interpreter has to recall the utterance of Paul Valery; "What I see blinds me. What I hear makes me deaf. What I know makes me unknowing. Knowledge is a cloud, obscuring the essence of being, the shining moon, like darkness or cataract on the eye. Take it away, so that I may see. Valery 1946: 60-61. Also Zimmer 1956: 548-51. Morgan, Aldrich, Nehlis in Langer, ed., *Reflections,* 1958. Mehta 1990:190. Once the interpreter combines monotheism of reason with polytheism of imagination, (s)he discovers that the iconoclastic is implicit in the iconism of Dakṣiṇa Kośala art; that the representational merges in it in the non representational; and that the knower, known and the act of knowledge converge in it as one, their perceived distinction being fictitiously created by nescience.

11. The art illustrates the principle of mirror, in which a face is reflected, the mirror being transparent and pure, while the mirror is not reflected in the face, because it is opaque and impure. The light of the principle reveals, but, being luminous, can not itself be revealed. Avalon 1914: 125, 145, 184; Sartre 1948: 282. Langer 1952: 259-61. *VuP* 5.1 speaks about the integral zero in algebra as equivalent to the plenum. Pūrṇasya pūrṇamādāya pūrṇamevāvaśiṣyate. The whole remains whole after taking out the whole from the whole.

12. Kaviraj 1984: 1-6, 10-13 describes such perception as Eureka, an act of sudden illumination, followed by abreaction and Katharsis, in his discussion of pratibhā. This is a period when the artists can open their constructive eye to the dynamic life of forms and say, with Wordsworth, 'I saw them feel or link them to some feeling: the great mass lay embedded in quickening soul, and all that I beheld respired with inward meaning'. Wordsworth, Prelude III: 127.

13. Arthur Schopenhauer points out, we are willing to change the state of affairs all the time, and as soon as we achieve what we are willing, we are propelled into willing something else.

14. The forms of art in Tala and Dakṣiṇa Kośala are not freakish features of nature, borrowed from the laboratory of Faust, the Cabinet of Caligary or from Arcimoldo heads. They are not designed to infect us with millenarian or chiliastic anxiety, with apocalyptic thoughts of insecurity, or, to astonish and stun. Though the biological boundaries are also transgressed in the heads of Arcimoldo in European art, and the elements there are always eager to become something else, the iconography of Arcimoldo does not, like Tala, point beyond itself to an ever throbbing rhythm of unity in nature. Barthes, "Matthew Klein", in Blonsky, ed., *Signs* 1978.

15. Among metaphysical theories, we are reminded of Plato's doctrine of the receptacle or Chora, a pre symbolic state of language, anterior to the world of syllables which works through and subverts syntactical synthesis, to enter into diverse representations; Epicurus's doctrine of the real void; Plotinus's

theory of beauty created by imposing limits, peras, upon the unlimited apeirol; the Alexandrian theory of primordial Being, who shares his nature with the world, is a component in the nature of all fugitive things, and contributes to the inevitable recurrence of the world towards order; and, of the Leibnitzian theory of pre established harmony.

16. In this context, one recalls the space time theory of mathematical physics. Max Planck points out, that the physicist has to measure all measurable things, and render all unmeasurable things measurable. Whitehead describes the external world as a web of relationships. He explains that the Newtonian theory of simple location and individuality of bits of matter, independent of external relations, has given way to the concept of what physical entities throughout the universe mean for those regions, and as modifications of conditions within space and time. The focal region of the thing itself obstinately refuses to be conceived as instantaneous fact, separated from the external stream. At every instantaneous point event, within or without the focal region, the modification to be ascribed to the thing itself is antecedent or successive to the corresponding modification introduced by that thing at another point event. It is in a state of constant agitation. In spite of certain differences in everything, the attempt is to express analogous elements, in the interweaving of various components in the composition of nature. Relations modify the nature of the relata as the relata modify the nature of the relation. See Whitehead 1960: 134-38, 153-54, 160-63.
17. Identity and difference are the obverse and reverse of the same coin in the art of Tala and Dakṣiṇa Kośala, as in medieval European philosophy. Giordono Bruno (1548-1600) was burnt because he had rediscovered and reiterated the lesson, enunciated at Tala, that God is both transcendant and immanent. The 12th century hermetic book of the 24 philosophers affirms the dictum that God is the sphere, whose center is everywhere and circumference nowhere. Campbell 1968: 28-31.

    The fructification of jīvas or beings in the manifest world and their dissolution into the Being or Paramātman, are explained as saṅkalpajanya, or creation of the divine will, and, a result of karmas or activities of such jīvas. Karma is undertaken in ignorance, and inexorably determines the relative and fragmentary manifestations of beings. It is pratyabhijñā or knowledge, acquired by effort, which destroys the perception of difference in these manifestations. Pre determination is combined thus with free will and volition. Kaviraj 1984: 63, 102-14.
18. Heraclitus says, "men do not understand how that, which is told in different directions, comes into accord with itself, harmony in contrariety, as in the case of the Bow and the Lyre. Heraclitus, in Blackwell 1907: 81. Cassirer 1944: 228.
19. In the theistic constitution of the living universe, in its cooperative form of activity, all life is single in its essence but various, ever varying and interactive in its manifestations. The stylistic ramifications in Tala art and the regional variations of later Indian art, in Dakṣiṇa Kośala and India, put us in mind of a fascinating mirror game in which these parts are reflected, refracted, constituted in and by each other, change each other and move asymptotically towards an undefined wholeness. One is reminded of Leibnitz's observation that each portion of matter is like a garden full of plants, a pond full of fishes, but each branch of plants, each member of animals, each drop of humors, is also such a garden or pond. Leibniz, in Wiener 1951: 547.
20. Kubler 1962: 17-18, 20, 22, 33, 40, 60, 93, 95, 129.
21. Arts Imitator Naturam Sua operatione. Arts imitate the operation of nature. Saint Thomas Aquinas. This art can well be seen as analogous to art in the ideal State of Plato, as an attempt to represent the reality to be what it should have been, rather than what it appears to be. The meaning of a reality, otherwise dumb, inchoate, restricted and resisted, is clarified and concentrated in this art by the creation of a new experience rather than by a servile, redundant and inferior imitation of the reality. Dewey 1934: 131-32; Sartwell 1995. In Taoism, Buddhism, as in Hinduism, the human body is treated as a double of the cosmic body of mountain and valleys, Yin and Yang, Puruṣa and Prakṛti. Immortality is perceived as analogous to re union with the rhythmic movement of the cosmos. The human body and the universe are perceived as

arenas for incessant interaction between fire and water, heat and cold, food and feeder, birth and death, malevolence and benevolence, sacrifice and dismemberment, regeneration and transformation, ascent and descent, masculine and feminine, nature and culture. To understand the artist, the art historian has to turn his mind, like a tuning fork, to this interactive rhythm, between the body and the non body. Thereby, he may relive, reenact and lend efficacy to the pristine dialogue between nature and culture, for engendering its effective future recurrence. See Sauvage 1961.

22. See Marx 1970: 175, 187-91; Eagleton 1978: 69, for the Marxist view of art. Mitchell 1986: 32, 162-163, 170, 187-198, for the iconological approach to recovery of meaning. Read 1965: 54; Cassirer 1944: 80-82, 263-64; Cassirer 1955: 387-400; Dufrenne 1979: 348-52 for a humanist rather than fetishistic view of icons.
23. An act of chresis is utilization by fragmentation, reconstitution, objectification, transplantation and appropriation of a tradition, outside its own context, by interpretation. The objective is to expose the sterility of the grains of the logos seed in the native soil of the text, rid it of dross, and plant it in the soil, where it can blossom and bear fruit. In the Indological interpretation of Paul Hacker, the scholar of Advaita Vedānta, the Indian logos seed can fructify only in the soil, fertilized by Judaeo- Christian thought. This is an approach also represented by Edmund Husserl, Maurice Marleau Ponty, and, in Indian art history, by scholars opposing classical to tribal subaltern art. The approach continues a tradition of interpretation, powerfully inaugurated by Hegel, who criticizes Indian art for divorcing form and meaning by forcing nature and humanity to assume forms appropriate to the other and inappropriate to itself. Hegel represents history as the march of the self thinking western spirit, swallowing, absorbing, superseding the Eastern spirit, evident in the Indian spirit of non- being, living in a state of dream. Martin Heidegger, Hans Georg Gadamar, Wilfred Cantwell Smith, Ernest Hocking, J.L. Mehta in philosophy, and, students of multiple regional roots of art traditions in Indian art oppose, to this approach of utilization, a hermeneutic, circular movement of going out to the other tradition, to come back to one's own. They demonstrate that self understanding is fulfilled by understanding the other, and that defects, if any, in one's own experience, can be discovered and cured through one's own exertions. Mehta 1985: 118-20, 121-37, 183-92.
24. Instead of reading this art as inchoate dream work after Freud 1900/1965, Karl Abraham 1913, C.G. Jung 1911, one may, with Cassirer 1955: 6-10, 16-18, 23-26, 29-37, read it in terms of its own religious and philosophical context.
25. The application of western structural analysis of myths to non-western societies has its limitations. Levi Strauss constructs structural dialectics in the backdrop of historical determinism and reduces culture to structural elements of opposition and correlation. Derrida shows how Strauss himself shows symbolic thought to be at once force and action, quality and state, noun and verb, omnipresent and localized. He also demonstrates how, with the de centering of the structure of mythic discourse, the opposition between the signifier and signified, sensible and intelligible, nature and culture, posed by Strauss, has become redundant. He adds that if there are structures, they can be understood only on the basis of a fundamental structure, which permits totality to open and overflow itself. It is not possible, after the structuralist, to delegate everything that is not comprehensible as an ideal type, to the status of an aberrational accident. Levi Strauss 1967; Derrida 1978: 26, 28, 280-81, 285-86, 290, 292-3.
26. The mutually complementary images of this art suggest a Janusian process of creativity, Janus being the Roman God of beginnings and communication, looking simultaneously in and out, towards departure and return. Rothenberg 1976: 311-27. Ehrenzweig 1976 discusses the way the conscious and inspirational blend in art.
27. Cassirer quotes Frederick Schlegel to designate the mission of the historian as that of a retrospective prophet. In his hermeneutic circular movement between past and present, the universal and local, continuity has been shown as consistent with dispersion and particularity. The artist, and the art historian after him, are trying to enrich and enlarge their self knowledge, not by effacing themselves, but, by drawing back further, through history, to leap higher.

28. Cassirer 1955: 179-91. Mehta 1976: 208-09, 318-19, 350-56, 442-43 discusses the process of moving from the thought to the unthought. Edward Said 1985: 283-88, 373-81 makes the suggestion of ever renewed beginnings in this movement. Julia Kristeva 1985: 210-11 suggests the need to recognize the coexistence of unity and particularity in such an exercise.
29. The electro dynamic rather than the biological model has been suggested as appropriate to the history of things, see chapter 9, note 133.
30. Said 1985: 9, 15, 38, 283-88, 306, 371-81 for interrogative reading of multiply divided meaning. The tradition has been reinaugurated and origins have been reawakened by recapitulation of Tala art, and, of the art after Tala. Jacques Derrida describes philosophy as the sun splashed morning, as the poetic inauguration. Being inaugural, it is anguishing. The freedom to augur is not the freedom to bring forth the already there, the interior design anterior to the work. The mythic book does not have a center, sheltered from play. The absence of play and difference is another name for death. The same line is no longer the same. The shadow of the book is the third party between the hands holding the books, the deferral within the now of writing, the difference between the book and the book, that other hand. What is to come is not a future present, and yesterday is not a past present. Derrida 1978: 26, 28, 292-93, 296, 300.
31. Negation of this sense of interconnectedness, assertion of instrumental, proximate, power centric values over ultimate, companionate values, has led to the manipulation of beings and things, and, to the darkening of the world, standardization of man, supremacy of the mediocre. See Mehta, quoting Nietzsche, 1976:356. Indian art illustrates the unified fourfold of the earth, heavens, mortals and Gods, to save and not master the earth or wear it out, to receive the sky as sky and not turn night into day, nor day into harassed unrest. Heidegger 1975: 150-51, 227-29. The Indian perception of the universe is illustrated in the diverse unity of the art of Dakṣiṇa Kośala. The same form unites saṁdeśyaḥ, videśyaḥ, daiva, mānuṣaḥ (*AV* 4. 16.8), the friend, stranger, divine, human. Rūpam rūpam pratirūpa vabhuva. *RV* 6.47.18. This one form becomes the form of all forms. Yatra viśvam bhavatyekanīḍam saḥ otaprataśca vibhuḥ prajāsu. *RV* 4.1.20. Humanity is united in this one nest. That One is the warp and weft of everyone. This perception conforms with the scientific perception, in which hidden worlds connect to the things that hide them, tide pools connect with unfathomable seas, which connect with our chromosomes. Rosenblatt 2000. The idea of maintaining the world as a self regulating, biological holon, in its fecundity and abundance, is to be read in the unfolding backdrop of non linear mathematics, fluid mechanics, high energy physics and isomorphism of verbal and genetic codes.

Glossary

After the first mention, South India or Odisha has been indicated respectively as S and O.

Abhayamudrā	Hand raised in gesture of assurance or protection
Abhiṣekapraṇāla	Channel for letting out lustral water from sanctum
Adhiṣṭhāna	Moulded base (South India)
Ādityauttnānapāda	Knees drawn up to reveal vulva
Āgama	Vertical scroll; Kuṭila (Odisha)
Akṣamālā	Rosary
Ālamba	Dangling festoons or garlands (O)
Alasakanyā	Beautiful girl used as decorative motif; Lit, languorous lady
Āmlā/Āmalaka	Grooved round disc-shaped, like myrobalan or Phyllanthus Emblica, crowning superstructure of Lātina-Nāgara temples (O)
Āmalasāraka	Cogged wheelstone, broader than āmalaka, crowning north Indian spire.
Āmrabhañjikā	Woman below mango tree, often shown holding or breaking a branch
Āmralumbī	Pendant cluster of mango fruits
Anarta	Vertical segments running from base to top of temple (O) between koṇaka and rāhā
Antarabhiṭṭi	Inner wall
Antarāla	Vestibule
Antarapaṭṭa	Recess between mouldings
Antarāla	Vestibule in front of sanctum
Anurāhā	Narrow vertical segment running from base to top of temple between anarta and koṇaka or rāhā (O)
Ardhacaitya	Half dormer window motif
Ardhadarpaṇa	Half mirror motif enclosing designs
Ardhagavākṣa	Half dormer (cow's eye) motif
Ardhamaṇḍapa	Half hall joined with main hall
Ardhapadma	Half lotus motif
Ardhasiṁhakarṇa	Split single dormer window pediment

Āsanapaṭṭa	Seatslab
Aśokalumbī	Design of pendant leaf (Jonesia Aśoka Roxb. with red flowers)
Atibhaṅga	Extreme flexion
Āyāla	Mane (leonine)
Bāḍā	Wall of temple (O)
Bāhyaśākhā	Outer door band
Bālapañjara	A vertical chain motif inserted in the recess between outer and inner latās of śikhara, made of miniaturized, apsidal temple fronts
Bānkājālī	Perforated chequer board design (O)
Bārāndā	Moulded parapet separating wall from spire
Beki	Neck of temple below mastaka (O)
Bekibhairava	Crouching human (O) figure on neck of temple (O)
Bhadra, Bhadraratha	Central offset of wall
Bhāraṇi	Pillar capital
Bhārapaṭṭa	Beam
Bhāraputraka, Bhārarakṣaka, Bhāravāhī gaṇa	Load-bearing dwarf
Bhāratulā	Lintel
Bhiṭṭa	Foundation course
Bhittistambha	Pilaster
Bho	Caitya with crowning kīrtimukha and flanking dwarfs (O)
Bhūmi	Horizontal segment of spire
Bhūmi-bārāndi	Mouldings in bhūmi (O)
Bhūmi-āmlā, Bhūmi-āmalaka	Āmlā demarcating one bhūmi from another
Bhūmi-sparśamudrā	Earth-touching gesture of Buddha, signifying victory over Māra, lord of passion
Biṣama	Uppermost Course or course of spire above the topmost bhūmi-āmlā, below the beki (O)
Caitya	Barrel vaulted window motif, resembling the window of early rock-cut sanctuary, the sanctuary, or the stūpa in it
Caityagavākṣa	Dormer-window
Camaradhāriṇī	Woman carrying fly-whisk
Campaka-ālamba	Leaf of Michelia Campaka dangling across campaka-lumbī foundation mouldings (O)
Campaka lumbi	
Candraśālā	Moon-chamber shown as dormer-window of barrel-vaulted hall
Capeṭamudrā	Hand raised in a gesture of giving a slap
Cāpākāra	Apsidal
Catuṣki	Bay of four pillars
Cauri	Fly-whisk
Chādya	Eave
Cinmudrā	Explicatory gestured of hand in discourse
Ḍamarū	Hourglass-shaped drum
Ḍamarūbhāga	Mouldings, stepped down from either side, resembling a ḍamarū (O)

Daṇḍa	Staff; pillarshaft
Daṇḍachādya	Straight as opposed to curved eave (khurachādya)
Daṇḍikā	Pillaret
Darpaṇa	Circular decorative mirror-motif, enclosing designs
Deul/Deval	Temple; Sanctuary (O)
Devakoṣṭha	Niche for divinity
Devakūlikā	Miniature or peripheral shrine
Dhanugranthi	Scroll, looped-like bowstring (O)
Dhārāṇvita, Dhārāvṛta	Faceted
Dhyānamudrā	Meditative seating posture
Dhvaja	Banner
Dhvajastamba	Banner on staff used as standard
Diggajas	Four legendary elephants of the quarters
Dikpālas	Eight guardians of the directions
Dīpadhārīṇī	Woman bearing lamp
Dopicha-Siṁha	Lion with two hind parts (O)
Dvāra-lalāṭabimba	Central figure on door lintel
Dvāra-pāla	Door-guardian
Dvāra-śākhā	Decorative band of door jamb
Dvi-aṅga	With two offset planes (and triratha or three projections)
Dvibhaṅga	Double flexed standing posture
Eḍuka	Temple-type resembling terraced stūpa
Ekamukhaliṅga	Śivaliṅga with one human face
Ekāvalī	Necklace of single pearl strand
Gajākrānta-Siṁha	Lion pouncing on elephant
Gajapāda	Pillar or pilaster with elephant- protome base
Gajapīṭha	Moulding of elephant figures
Gala	Recessed moulding
Galapāda	Vertical pilaster or partition in recessed moulding
Gaṇa	'Category'. Dwarf attendant of Śiva
Gaja-śārdula	Lion pouncing on elephant
Gandharva	Celestial minstrel
Gaṇḍi	Trunk; curvilinear spire or pyramidal roof (O)
Garbhagṛha	Womb-chamber; sanctum
Garuḍa	Mythical bird
Gavākṣa	Candraśālā. Mullioned window with vertical posts or latticework (O)
Gavākṣamaṇḍana	Sculpted panel above gavākṣa
Ghanadvāra	False door on central offset
Ghaṇṭā	Bell; Bell-shaped member in finial of pīḍhā-deul (O)
Ghaṭa	Vase; cushion-shaped crowning segment of pillar
Ghaṭapallava	Vase and foliage. Pillartype having such motif
Gelaba	Creeper intertwined with human figures (O)
Grāsa	Gorgon head
Grāsakiṅkiṇika	Jingling bells suspended from grāsamukhas
Grāsamukha	Gorgon face

Grāsapaṭṭi	Band of grāsamukhas
Gumphana	Interlacing
Guṇḍika	Row of beads
Haṁsa	Goose
Haṁsalatā	Frieze of geese (O)
Hāra	Garland. Miniature shrines forming balustrade (S)
Ihāmṛga	Mythical animal
Illikāvalana	Convoluted pediment, like a caterpillar
Jāḍyakumbha	Lowest pīṭha moulding resembling a kumbha
Jagamohana	Hall in front of sanctum, usually a pīḍhā-deul
Jagatī	Plinth. Basal moulding of adhiṣṭhāna (S)
Jāgrata Siṁha	Awake, rising lion (O)
Jalapatra	Waterplant framing doors and panels (O)
Jāla	Mesh design
Jālī	Fret or trellis-work
Jambhaka	Goblin
Jaṅghā	Wall between vedībandha and śikhara
Jaṭāmukuṭa	Crown of matted locks
Jhārāvali	Row of hanging drops (O)
Kadalikākaraṇa	Corbelling
Kakṣāsana	Seat back
Kalaśa	'Pitcher'; torus moulding
Kalā	Horizontal segments in elevation
Kalpalatā	Wishfulfilling
Kalpavallī	Vine
Kamalātapatra	Lotus umbrella
Kandhara	Broad recess
Kaṇikapāga	Projecting corner segment
Kaṅkanapatrapaṭṭi	Row of serrated leaves
Kaṇṭha	Neck; recess between mouldings
Kapili	Projecting wall connecting sanctum and vestibule
Kapiśīrṣaka	Parapet
Kapotāli, Kapotapāli, Kapotapālikā	Overhanging roll-cornice; cyma-eave cornice
Kapotabandha	Adhiṣṭhana with kapota as crowning member (S)
Karimakara	Fanciful crocodile with elephant trunk
Karṇa, Karṇalatā,	Corner wall division
Karṇaratha	Cornerband of spire
Karṇāmalaka	Āmalaka at corners of bhūmis in śikhara
Karṇāṇḍaka	Spirelet at corner of spire
Kaṭakāvṛta	Faceted
Kaṭi	Waist; wall or jaṅghā
Kaṭyāvalambita	Posture with hand resting on waist
Kautūka, Kautūhala	Fanciful figure
Khākhara	Semi-cylindrical member resembling khākharu (pumpkin) (O)

Khākhara-deul	Temple on rectangular plan with vaulted roof (O)
Khākhara-muṇḍi	Miniature representation of deuls with khākhara as the crowning member
Khalvaśākhā	Plain recessed doorband
Khāṇḍi	Grooved chase between two mouldings (O)
Kharaśilā	Capstone of foundation platform
Khaṭṭaka	Ornate niche
Khatvāṅga	Human skull placed on bone
Khura	Basal moulding of vedībandha
Khurachādya	Curved eave
Kinnara	Composite creature combining human with bird or equine forms
Kirīṭamukuṭa	Conical crown
Kirīṭa	Crown
Kīrtimukha	Face of glory. Lionlike head. Grāsamukha
Kumāra	Load-bearing gaṇa
Kumbha	Waterpot moulding above khura
Kumbhaka	Pillar base
Kumbhapañjara	Niche with kumbha (S)
Kumbhastambha	Pillar with kumbha at base and crown (O)
Kumbhikābandha	Waterjars aligned horizontally or vertically (O)
Kumuda	Torus moulding in adhiṣṭhāna (S)
Kuṇḍa	Tank; cistern
Kuṭila	Creeper with long, sweeping waves in its stalks (O)
Lalāṭabimba	Figure carved on middle lintel or architrave.
Lambana	Pendant motif
Lakula	Staff; club
Lasuna	Vase-shaped portion of pillar capital
Lātina	North Indian śikhara with curved vertical bands or latās
Liṅga	Phallic pillar. Aniconic representation of Śiva
Lokapālas	Guardian of the four quarters
Madhya-bandhana	Middle string course on wall
Madhyalatā	Central band of śikhara
Madhyaratha	Central projection
Mahāpaṭṭi	Broad band
Makara	Crocodile or dolphin
Makaramukha	Crocodile head. Ornament, shaped-like crocodile head
Makarapraṇāla	Makara-shaped gargoyle
Makaramukhapraṇāla	Gargoyle, shaped like makara head
Makara-toraṇa	Toraṇa arch emerging from makaras
Maliphula phadika	Floral scroll around a vertical stem (O)
Mālā	Garland
Mālādhārī	Garland-bearing
Mālā-Vidyādhara	Flying garland-bearing celestial
Mālāśākhā	Doorband in the form of a mālā
Mālāsthāna	Segment below capital, adorned with garlands
Mañcikā	Daislike projection supporting figures

Maṇḍapa	Hall
Maṇḍovara	Wall between jagatī and chādya
Maṇibandha	Row of diamonds and rosettes
Maṇipaṭṭikā	Band of jewels
Mastaka	Crown of temple (O)
Mastaka-khura	'Head' Crowning member above gaṇḍi (O)
Masūraka	Lentil, cushion-like segment of pillar
Mātṛkā	Mother goddess
Mattavāraṇa	Stage segment: equated with nāgadaṅtaka or Niryyuha
Matuluṅga	Citron
Mayūrātapatra	Umbrella of peacock feathers
Miśraka	'Mixed' pillar type with segments moving from squaṛe to circular
Mithuna	Auspicious couple
Mithunaśākhā	Doorband, bearing couples
Muhānti	Vedībandha moulding (O)
Mukhacatuṣki	Four-pillared entry porch
Muktādāma	Pearl festoon
Muktāgrāsa	Grāsamukha spouting pearls
Mukula	Floral bud
Nāga	Snake
Nāgabandha	Design of serpents intertwined with floral or faunal elements. Nāga represents circuit of the year, and governs position of temple with regard to directions
Nāgadantaka	Wall with projecting elephant protome
Nāgapāśa	Serpent noose. Intertwined serpent design
Nāgaprabhāvalī	Halo of snake hoods
Nāgapuruṣa or Nāgarāja	Anthropomorphic cobra-king
Nāgaśākhā	Doorband with nāga design
Nāga or Nāgīstambha	Pillar or pilaster encircled by serpents (O)
Nāgavallī	Interlaced serpents resembling wavy loops of creeper
Nandī-maṇḍapa	Pavilion for Śiva's bull
Nandikamukha/Nandikāmukha	Male or female head in centre of vajramastaka (O)
Naravyāla	Rampant lion pouncing on a man
Nāṭamandira	Dance hall (O)
Nidhikalaśa	Treasure-vase
Nidhiputra	Anthropomorphic treasure
Niryyuha	A projected pavilion.
Nivrapaṭṭikā	Band of leaf drops
Noli	Foundation moulding; kumbha
Pābhāga	Footsection comprising pañcakarma or five elements at base (O)
Padma	Lotus
Padmadala	Lotus petal
Padmahastā	Lotus-bearing
Padmalatā	Lotus vine; padmavallī
Padmaparikara	Lotus frame
Padmapaṭṭi, Padmapaṭṭikā	Lotus frieze

Padmapīṭha, Padmavedikā	Lotus pedestal
Padmātapatra	Lotus umbrella
Padmamukuṭa	Lotus crown
Padmanidhi	Lotus treasure
Padmopāna	Lotus-shaped subplinth moulding (upāna) (S)
Padmaprabhāmaṇḍala	Lotus halo
Padmapṛṣṭha	Moulding carved with lotus leaf in double curve profile (O)
Padmāsana	Lotus seat. Yogic posture
Padmavaravedīkā	Railing of pillars carved with lotus medallions
Padmavitāna	Lotus ceiling
Pāga	Vertical division of wall or spire. Ratha
Pakṣadvāra	Side entrance
Pañcaratha	With five offsets and three segments (trianga)
Pañcāyatana	Temple with four attendant shrines at corners
Pañjara	Fronton of vaulted apsidal shrine
Parṇapaṭṭi	Band of foliage
Parikara	Image-frame
Paryastaka	Cloth band dangling between legs
Patralatā	Foliate doorband
Patravallī	Leafy scroll. Patralatā
Paṭṭikā	Rectilinear fillet (S)
Peḍyā	Lower portion of door jambs
Phalaka	Abacus of pillar
Phālana	Minor offset demarcating planes
Phāmsana	Pyramidal roof type
Phāmsanakūṭas	Pyramidal tiered aedicule
Pheni	Moulding, usually carved with lotus petals, curving upwards in cyma profile (O)
Piḍhā	Projecting ledge in pyramidal roof; pediment
Piḍha-deul	Temple with gaṇḍi made of superimposed piḍhās (O)
Potikā	Bracket capital
Pradakṣiṇapatha	Circumambulatory
Prāggrīva	Projection connecting sanctum and vestibule
Prākāra	Walled enclosure
Prakoṣṭha	Niche
Pralambapādāsana	Seating posture with legs hanging down; bhadrāsana or paryaṅkāsana
Pramatha	Gaṇa
Praṇāla	Water chute
Prāsāda	Palace; temple
Prastara	Entablature above wall or pillar
Pratibandha	Adhiṣṭhāna with vṛtta (circular) kumuda (S)
Pratibhadra	Offset flanking bhadra
Pratihāra	Door-guardian
Pratikarṇa	Narrow vertical segment flanking *karṇa*
Pratimukha	Rectilinear moulding below ūparikampa or vājana (S)
Pratiratha	Offset flanking bhadra
Pratiśākhā	Narrow doorband carved with foliate relief

Prātoli	Gate-house
Pratyālīḍha	Standing with legs astride
Pṛṣṭhaśākhā	Outer doorband; bāhyaśākhā
Pūrṇa ghaṭa	Full jar, signifying plenitude
Puṣpaśākhā, Puṣpapaṭṭi	Floral doorband
Puṣpabandha	Floral frieze
Rāhā	Vertical central projecting division in wall or spire; ratha (O)
Rājalīlāsana	Royal seating posture with one leg drawn up
Raṅganī	Floral design in small squares
Ratha	Projecting division in wall and spire
Rathikā	Framed niche
Ratikerā	Floral design in vertical frame
Ratnapaṭṭi	Diamond band
Ratnaśākhā	Doorband carved with diamond pattern
Rekhā deul	Curvilinear spire (O)
Rucaka	Square pillartype
Rūpakaṇṭha	Recess carved with figures
Rūpaśākhā	Doorband with figural ornament
Sabhākāra	Rectangular vaulted roof without gables
Sahasrāra	Thousand petalled lotus; symbol of highest psychic centre in head
Śākhā	Doorband
Śākhāvibhakti	Division of door jamb into various bands
Śālā	Rectangular chamber
Śālāmaṇḍapikā	Temple with slab roof, sanctum, open parch
Salilāntara	Recess between walls to allow escape of water
Samabhaṅga	Equally flexed standing posture
Samatala	Flat
Samvarṇā	Roof with diagonally tiered members, crowned by bell-finial
Sāndhāra	With ambulatory
Sandhisthala	Junction. Wall segment connecting sanctum and hall (O)
Sarvatobhadrikā	Shrine with images on four faces
Saubhāgyapaṭṭa	Lintel frieze showing Lakṣmī
Śikhara	Spire in north; crowning dome (S)
Siṁhagavākṣa	Baywindow at upper story; Siṁhapañjara
Siṁhakarṇa	Single candraśālā pediment
Siṁhamukha	Lion head; Siṁhavaktra
Siṁhamukha-praṇāla	Praṇāla with lion mouth for its snout
Siṁhapāda	Pillar with lion base (S)
Siṁhāsana	Lion throne
Siṁhasaṁghāta	Group of lions
Siṁhavarāha	Lion pouncing on boar
Śīrṣaka	Pillar bracket
Skandha	Shoulder; flat crowning platform of śikhara
Śobhāpaṭṭikā	Ornamental frieze on pillar
Sopānamāla	Series of steps
Śrīvṛkṣaśākhā	Vertical foliate doorband

Stambha	Pillar
Stambhaśākhā	Doorband in the form of pilaster
Sthānaka	Standing posture
Śūkanāsā	Caitya-like antefix on front face of śikhara
Śuṇḍamakara	Makara with elephant trunk
Śūrasenaka	Caitya dormer pediment
Talabandhana	String course at base of jaṅgh above pābhāga
Tālacchanda	Rhythm of ground plan
Talagarbhikā	Decorative miniature temple on wall below central niche (O)
Tālapatra	Palm leaf
Taraṅgapotikā	Wavy pillar bracket; corbel bracket with roll-moulding
Tāṭi, tāṭikā	Minor dishmoulding over lasūna on pillar
Toraṇa	Gateway
Triaṅga	With three planes of offsets
Tribhaṅga	Triple flexed standing posture
Tripaṭṭa kumuda	Kumuda with three facets
Tulā	Joist end
Tulāpīṭha	Frieze of joist ends
Tulāsaṁgraha	Series of joist ends
Udadhikumāra	Minor divinity allied to Varuṇa
Udyata Siṁha	Lion rampant (O)
Udgama	Pediment of intermeshed caitya dormers
Ūparikampa	Upper fillet moulding ūrdhvakampa (S)
Ūrdhvacchanda	Rhythm of elevation
Ūrdhvagarbhikā	Miniature shrine used as decorative wall element above jaṅghā niche (O)
Utkuṭikāsana	Posture of sitting on haunches
Uttaraṅga	Architrave; lintel
Uttarīya	Scarf
Vāhana	Vehicle; mount
Vājana	Projecting upper band (S)
Vajramastaka	Dormer window with crowning kīrtimukha. Vajramuṇḍī enclosed head, flanking figures (O)
Valabhī	Temple with wagon-vault roof (śalāśikhara)
Vallīśākhā, Vallipaṭṭi	Doorband carved with a creeper
Vandanamālikā	Festoon of garlands
Vārāndikā	Moulded parapet separating jaṅghā from śikhara
Vartula	Circular plant ornament ((O)
Vasantapaṭṭikā	Broad band, carved with floral scroll (O)
Vāstumaṇḍala	Sacred diagram on which temple is planned
Vedī	Altar
Vedībandha	Basal wall mouldings
Vedīkā	Balustrade, railing. Moulding with projections and recesses
Veṇukoṣa	Outer sheath of curvilinear spire, recalling 'bamboo nodes'
Vidyādhara	Flying celestial

Vihāra	Monastery
Vimāna	Main temple or spire
Vimānikā	Mouldings with miniature vimānas (O)
Vitāna	Ceiling
Virāla	Lion (O)
Vīthīka	Gallery
Vṛkṣakā	Dryad; woman entwined with tree
Vṛttakumuda	Circular kalā moulding (S)
Vyākhyānamudra	Hand raised in gesture of teaching, exposition
Vyāla	Composite fanciful creature
Yakṣa	Demigods with benignant and malignant aspects
Yakṣāyatana	A Yakṣa shrine
Yaṣṭi	Staff
Yajñayūpa	Sacrificial post or stake

Bibliography

PRIMARY SANSKRIT TEXTUAL SOURCES

Vedas/Saṁhitās

Atharva Veda. Trans., W.D. Whitney, 2 vols. Harvard Oriental Series. Cambridge, Mass, 1905.
Ahirbudhnya Saṁhitā. Ed. T.M.D. Ramanujacarya. Adyar Library, Madras, 1966.
Bṛhat Saṁhitā, Ed., with Bhaṭṭotpala's Commentaries, by Sudhakar Dwivedi, 2 vols. Varanasi: 1895-7.
Kashyapa Saṁhitā, Trans. and Ed., P.V. Tewari.
Maitrāyaṇī Saṁhitā. Ed. Leopold Von Schroeder. 4 vols. Leipzig, 1881-86.
Ṛg Veda. Ed., F. Max Müller. 6 vols. London, 1849-74.
Suśruta Saṁhitā. Ed., Jadavji Trikamji Ācārya. Chaukhamba Orientalia, Varanasi, 1980.
Taittirīya Saṁhitā. Ed., A. Weber. Berlin, 1872-2, with Mādhava's commentary, Calcutta, 1854-99.
Yajurveda, Taittirīya Saṁhitā. Ed., E. Roerl, E.B. Cowell et al. 6 vols. Bibliotheca Indica, Calcutta, 1860-99. Trans., A.B. Keith, 2 vols. Harvard Oriental Series 18, 19. Cambridge, Mass, 1914.
Vājasaneyī Saṁhitā. Ed. with Mahidhara's commentary. By A. Weber. London, 1852.

Brāhmaṇas

Aitareya Brāhmaṇa. Ānandāśrama Sanskrit Series 37. Poona, 1898/1931.
Aitareya and Kauśitakī Brāhmaṇas of the Ṛgveda. Trans., A.B. Keith. Harvard Oriental Series 25. Cambridge, Mass, 1920.
Kauśitakī Brāhmaṇa. 3 vols. Ed., E.R. Sreekrishna Sarma. Franz Steiner Verlag, Wiesbaden, 1968.
Śatapatha Brāhmaṇa. Ed., A. Weber. London, 1855. Trans., Julius Eggeling. Sacred Books of the East, 12, 26, 41, 43, 44. Oxford, 1882-90.
Taittirīya Brāhmaṇa. Ed., Rajendralal Mitra. 3 vols. Bibliotheca Indica, Calcutta, 1859.

Āraṇyakas

Aitareya Āraṇyaka. Text. Ānandāśrama Sanskrit Series 37, 1898. Poona. Ed. and Trans., A.B. Keith. Oxford, 1909.
Taittirīya Āraṇyaka. Ed., Baba Shastri Phadke. 2 prts. Ānandāśrama Sanskrit Series 36. Poona, 1897-98.

Sūtras

The Nighaṇṭu and the Nirūkta (Yāska). Ed. and Trans., Lakshman Sarup, 1962. Ist ed. reprint, Delhi, 1967.

Āpastambha Gṛhyasūtra. Trans., H. Oldenburg. Sacred Books of the East. Vol. 30. 2.

Āpastambha Dharma Sūtra. Ed. G. Buhler. Bombay Sanskrit Series, 1892, 1894.

Āpastambha Śrauta Sūtra. Ed., A. Srinivasaraghavacharya Oriental Research Institute Publications, Sanskrit Series, 104, Vol. 3. Mysore, 1960.

Āpastambha Śūlbasūtra. Ed., Satyaprakash and R.S. Sharma. Ratha Kumari Publication Series 5. Maha Lakshmi Publishing House, Delhi, 1968.

Āśvalāyana Gṛhyasūtra. Ed., A.G. Stenzler, Leipzig, 1864.

Baudhāyana Dharmasūtra. Ed., E. Hultzsch. Leipzig, 1884.

Baudhāyana Gṛhyasūtra. Ed., R. Shamasastri, Mysore, 1920.

Baudhāyana Śrautasūtra. Ed., W. Caland, Calcutta, 1904-23.

Brahmasūtra with Śaṅkarabhāṣya. Nirṇayasagar Press, Bombay, 1948.

Brahmasūtra Śārīrikabhāṣya of Śaṅkara. Motilal Banarsidass, Delhi, 1964.

Gobhila Gṛhyasūtra. Trans., H. Oldenburg. Sacred Books of the East 30.2.

Gṛhya Sūtras. Trans., H. Oldenberg and F. Max Müller. 2 vols. Sacred Books of the East 29-30. Motilal Banarsidass, Delhi, 1981, 1982.

Mādhyamika Sūtra. Sacred Books of the East 49.2.

Śivasūtras. The Yoga of Supreme Identity. Ed. and Trans., Jaidev Singh. Motilal Banarsidass, Delhi, 1979.

Śivasūtravimarśinī of Kṣemarāja. Ed., J.C. Chatterjee. Kashmir Series of texts and Studies 1. Research Department of Jammu and Kashmir State, VII, Shrinagar.

Śūlba Sūtras of Baudhāyana, Āpastambha, Kātyāyana and Mānava. Ed. and Tr., by S.N. Sen and A.K. Bag. Indian National Science Academy, New Delhi, 1983.

Suvarṇaprabhāsottama (Lotus) Sūtra. Ed., Johannes Nobel. E.J. Brill, Leiden, 1944.

Yogasūtra of Patañjali, with the commentary of Vyāsa and gloss of Vācaspatimiśra jr., Ramaprasada. Panini Office, Allahabad, 1924.

Upaniṣads

Atharvaśiras Upaniṣad. In the Śaiva Upaniṣads. Ed., A. Mahadeva Shastri. Adyar Library Series 9. Repr., Adyar, 1950.

Bṛhadāraṇyaka Upaniṣad. Ed. and Trans., S.C. Vasu. Sacred books of the East 14. Ist ed., repr., New York, 1974.

Chāndogya Upaniṣad. Ed. and Trans., S.C. Verma. Sacred Books of the East 3. The Upaniṣads, part 2. 1st ed., repr., New York, 1974.

Maitrāyaṇīya Upaniṣad. Trans., Van Buitenen, Mouton, Gravenhage, 1962.

Muṇḍaka Upaniṣad. Ed., J. Hertel. Leipzig, 1924. Trans., R.E. Hume. In Thirteen Principal Upaniṣads. London, 1921.

The Principal Upaniṣads. Trans., F. Max Mueller. Sacred Books of the East, Vols. 1, 15. Oxford.

The Principal Upaniṣads. Ed. and Trans., S. Radhakrishnan. London and New York, 1953.

The Śaiva Upaniṣads. Ed., G. Srinivasamurti. Trans., T.R. Srinivasa Ayyanger. Adyar Library Series 85. Adyar, 1953.

Sūrya Upaniṣad. Unpublished Upaniṣads. Adyar Library, 1933.

Śvetāśvatara Upaniṣad. Ed. and Trans., Siddheshvar Varma Shastri. Sacred Books of the East 18. 1st ed., repr., New York, 1972.

Taittirīya Upaniṣad. Ed., with commentary of Śaṅkara. Ānandāśrama Sanskrit Series, 5th Ed. Poona, 1929.

Vāstusūtra Upaniṣad. Tr., Alice and Bettina Baumer and Sadasiva Rath Sharma. Motilal Banarsidass, Delhi, 1982.

Epics

Mahābhārata. Ed., V.S. Sukhtankar et al. 19 vols. Bhandarkar Oriental Research Institute. Poona, 1927-71.
Mahābhārata, Harivaṁśa Purāṇa. Ed., Parasuram Lakshman Vaidya. 2 vols. Poona, 1967-71.
Vālmikī-Rāmāyaṇa. Ed., G.H. Bhatt et al. 4 vols. Baroda, 1960-65.
Rāmāyaṇa of Vālmikī. Trans., R.T.H. Griffith. Varanasi, 1915. Repr., 1963.

Purāṇās

Agni Purāṇa. Ed., Acarya Baladeva Upadhyaya. Kashi Sanskrit Series 174. Varanasī, 1966. Trans., Manmatha Nath Dutt, Calcutta, 1903-4.
Bhāgavata Purāṇa. Ed., Madhava Sarma. Chowkhamba Sanskrit Series. Benares, 1911-15.
Bhaviṣya Purāṇa, Historical and Cultural data from Rajkumar Aurora, Sterling Publishers, Delhi, 1972.
Brahma Purāṇa. Ānandāśrama Sanskrit series, Poona, 1895.
Brahmāṇḍa Purāṇa. Ed., J.L. Shastri. Motilal Banarsidas, Delhi, 1973.
Brahmavaivarta Purāṇa. Ed., Jivananda Vidyasagara. 2 vols. Calcutta, 1888.
Kālikā Purāṇa. Ed., B. N. Shastri, 3 vols. Nag Publishers, Delhi, 1991-92.
Kūrma Purāṇa. Ed., Nilamani Mukhopadhyaya. Bibliotheca Indica, Calcutta, 1888-1904.
Liṅga Purāṇa. Ed., Acarya Sriram Sharma. Sanskrutic Sansthan, Bareli, 1969.
Mārkaṇḍeya Purāṇa. Trans., F. E. Pargiter. Calcutta, 1904.
Matsya Purāṇa. Ed., Hari Narayana Apte. Anandasrama Sanskrit Series 54. Poona, 1907.
Padma Purāṇa. Ed., Acarya Sriram Sharma. Sanskrutic Sansthan, Bareli, 1970.
——. Ed., V.N. Manalik. Anandasrama Sanskrit Series. 4 vols. Poona, 1973-74.
Śāmba Upapurāṇa. Shri Venkatesvar Press. Bombay.
Śāmba Purāṇa kā Saṁskrtik Adhyayan, Chardradev Pandey. Niraja Prakashan, Allahabad, 1986.
Śiva Purāṇa. Ed., Rama Teja Pandey. Chowkhamba Vidyabhavana, Varanasi, 1963.
——. Ed., Acarya Sriram Sharma. Sanskrutic Sansthan. Bareli, 1970.
——. Trans., Board of Scholars, Ed., J. L. Shastri: Motilal Banarsidass, Delhi.
Śrī Harivaṁśa Purāṇam, Ed. And Trans, K.P.A. Menon, Nag Publishers, Delhi, 2008.
Skanda Purāṇa. Ed., Vasudeva Shastri Pansikara. 3 parts. Anandasrama Sanskrit Series 25. Poona, 1893.
Saura Purāṇa. Ed., Kashinath Shastri Lele. Anandasrama Sanskrit Series 18. Poona, 1889.
Viṣṇudharmottara Purāṇa. Ed., Shri Venkatesvara. Bombay, 1912.
——. Ed., Priyabala Shah. A Study on a Sanskrit Text of Ancient Indian Arts, 2 vols. Gaekwad Oriental Series 137, 1958-61.
Vāmana Purāṇa. Ed., A.S. Gupta and Trans., S.H. Mukhopadhyaya et al. Varanasi, 1968.
——. Ed., Acharya Sriram Sharma. Sanskrutic Sansthan, Bareli, 1970.
Varāha Purāṇa, Ed., Anandaswarupa Gupta, Sarvabhāratīyakāśirājanyāsaḥ, Varanasi, 1981.
Vāyu Purāṇa. Ed., Anandasrama Sanskrit Series 49. Poona, 1905. Trans. and annotated by S. Venkita Subramonia Iyer, Motilal Banarsidass, Delhi, 1985.

Āgamic, Tāntrik and Sacred Texts

Aghoraśivācāryapaddhati (kriyākramodyotikā), with Prabhā commentary of Nirmalamani. Ed., K. Krishna Sastri and P. Rama Sastri, Tamilnadu, 1927.
Abhilāṣitārthacintāmaṇi. Someswara Deva. Ed., R. Shama Sastri. Govt. Branch Press, Mysore, 1926.
Akulavīratantra. Hindu online. Internet Archive.
Gaṇakārikā in Nakulīśa Pāśupata Darśana in Sarvadarśanasaṁgraha, 1HQ 2: 12-32. Ed., C.D. Dalal. Gaekwad Oriental Series 15.
Guhya Samāja Tantra. Ed., Benoytosh Bhattacharyya. Gaekwad Oriental Series. Bombay, 1931.
Iśanaśivagurudevapaddpati of Iśanaśaivagurudeva Miśra. Ed., T. Ganapati Shastri. 4 vols. Trivandrum Sanskrit Series 69, 72, 77, 83. Trivandrum, 1920-25.

Īśvarapratyabhijñākārikā of Utpaladeva. Vimarśinī by Abhinavagupta. 2 vols. Ed., M.S. Kaul. Kashmir Series of Texts and Studies. Shrinagar Research Department, Jammu and Kashmir State, 1918, 1921.
Jayākhya Saṁhitā of Pāñcarātra Āgama. Ed., Embar Krishnamacharya. Baroda Oriental Institute, Baroda, 1967.
Kāmadhenu Tantra, Prayāga, Kalyana Mandira Prakashana, 1978.
Kaula Vijñāna Nirṇaya. Ed., Prabodh Chandra Bagchi, Calcutta Sanskrit Series, 1934.
Kulārṇava Tantra. Ed., Taranatha Vidyaratna with introduction of Arthur Avalon. Calcutta, 1917. Reprint, Motilal Banarsidass, Delhi, 1984.
Lakṣmī Tantra, Pāñcarātra Āgama. Ed., V. Krishnamacharya. Adyar Library Series 87. Adyar Library and Research Centre, Madras, 1975.
Mahābhāṣya of Patañjali. Ed., F. Kielhorn. 3 vols. Rev., K.U. Abhyankar. Bhandarkar Oriental Research Institute, Poona, 1972-85.
Mahānirvāṇa Tantra. Arthur Avalon, Madras, 1927.
Mahāyānavimarśaka of Nāgārjuna. Ed. & Tr., Pundit Vidhushekhar Bhattacharya. Visvabharati Studies I. Visvabharati, Calcutta, 1931.
Mahimnastava. Trans. and Ed., W. Norman Brown. American Institute of Indian Studies. Publication 1. Poona, 1965.
Mātaṅgalīlā. Ed. T.G. Shastri: Trivandrum, Sanskrit Series 10.
Nāgārjuna's Mādhymikā Kārikā, Ed. Rev. J.W.D. Jong, Christian Lindtner, Chennai, Adyar Research Library.
Pāśupata Sūtras. Ed., R. Ananthakrishna Shāstri. Trivandrum Sanskrit Series 143. Trivandrum, 1940. Trans., Haripada Chakraborti. Calcutta, 1970.
Prapañcasāra Tantra of Śaṅkarācārya. Rev. A. Avalon. Ed., Atalananda Saraswati. Tantrik Text Series 19. Motilal Banarsidass, Delhi, 1989.
Śatarudrīya, Vibhūti of Śiva's Iconography. C. Sivaramamurti. Abhinav Publications. Delhi, 1976.
Somaśambhupaddhati. Ed. and Tr. into French by Helene Brunner Lachaux. Institut Français d'Indologie, Pondicherry, 1963.
Spandakārikā. The Divine Creative Pulsation, the Kārikās and the Spanda Nirṇaya of Kṣemarāja. Ed. and Tr. into English, by Jaidev Singh, Motilal Banarsidass, Delhi, 1986.
Svacchanda Tantra, with the commentary of Kṣemarāja. 7 vols. Ed., Madhusudan Kaul Śhāstri. Kashmir Series of Texts and Studies 31,38,44, 48, 51, 53, 56. Research Department, Jammu and Kashmir State, Shrinagar, 1921.
Tantrāloka of Abhinavagupta, with commentary by Rājanaka Jayaratha. Ed., M.R. Sastri and M.S. Kaul. Kashmir Series of Texts and Studies. 12 vols. Research Department, Jammu & Kashmir State, Shrinagar, 1921-38.
Tantrasamuccaya. Ed., T. Ganapati Sastri, Trivandrum, 1919.
Tantrasaṁgraha. Ed., M.M. Gopinath Kaviraj. Vārānaseya Sanskrit Viśvavidyālaya, Varanasi, 1970.
Tantrasāra of Abhinavagupta. Ed., M.S. Kaul. Kashmir Series of Texts and Studies 17. Research Department, Jammu and Kashmir State, Shrinagar, 1981.
Tattvasaṁgraha of Śāntarakṣita. 2 vols. Tr., Ganganath Jha. Baroda Oriental Institute, Baroda, 1937, 1939.
Tripiṭaka: Sūtrapiṭaka, Prajnāpāramitā, Vajracchedikā. The Diamond Sūtra, Trans. from Sanskrit and Chinese by Red Pine. Counterpoint, Washington D.C.
Vajracchedikā Yogasārasaṁgraha of Vijñānabhikṣu. Tr., Ganganath Jha. Akay Book Corporation, Delhi, 1986.

Encyclopaedias

Encyclopaedia of Indian Philosophies. 4 vols. Ed., Karl H. Potter. Motilal Banarsidass, Delhi, 1983-87.
Encyclopaedia of Plants and Flowers. Ed., Frances Perry. London: Macdonald & Co. 1974. Reprint 1984.
Encyclopaedia of Purāṇic beliefs and Practices. 3 vols. Ed., Sadashiv Ambadas Dange. Navarang, Delhi, 1986-7.

Encyclopaedia of Religion and Ethics. 13 vols. Ed., James Hastings. New York: Charles Scribner's Sons, 1908–26.
Encyclopaedia of Religion. 16 vols. Ed., Mircea Eliade. Macmillan, New York, 1987.
Encyclopaedia of the Upaniṣads, Ed., N.S. Subrahmanian. Sterling Publishers, Delhi, 1985.
Purāṇic Encyclopaedia. Ed., Vettum Mani. Harvard Oriental Series 10. Reprint. Motilal Banarsidass, Delhi, 1992.
Śabdakalpadrumaḥ. Śakābdāḥ 1808. Reprint 1988., Raja Radha Kanta Deb. 5 vols., Delhi. Nag Publishers.
Sacred Books of the Hindus. 1909-26. 31 vols. and supplements. Allahabad: Pāṇini office. Reprint in 46 vols., New York: AMS Press, 1974.
Sacred Books of the East, Vol. 49. 2, Buddhist Mahāyāna Texts, Ed. Friedrich Max Müller, Motilal Banarasidass, Delhi, 1965.
Saravadarśanasaṁgraha of Mādhava. Ed., Jivānanda Vidyāsagara. 2nd edn. Calcutta, 1899. Trans., E.B. Cowell and A.E. Gough, Calcutta Sanskrit Series 10, 3rd ed. London, 1908.
Sāttvata Saṁhitā, Ed, P.B. Ananthacharian, Conjeevaram, 1902.
Śāradā Tilaka. Ed., Arthur Avalon. Motilal Banarsidass, Banaras, 1934.

Śilpa Śāstras

Abhinaya Darpaṇa of Nandīkeśvara. Tr., A.K. Coomaraswamy and G.K. Duggirala. Harvard University Press, Cambridge, 1917.
Aparājitapṛcchā of Bhuvana Deva. Ed., Popatbhai Ambashankar Mankad. Baroda Oriental Institute, Baroda, 1950.
Bṛhat Saṁhitā by Varāhamihira. Ed., H. Kern. Bibliotheca Indica. Calcutta, 1865. Trans., H. Kern. Journal of the Royal Asiatic Society of Great Britain and Ireland 4: 430-70; 5: 45-90; 231-88; 6: 36-91, 279-338; 7: 81-134. 1870-75. Ed. and Tr., M. Ramakrishna Bhat. 2 vols. Motilal Banarsidass, Delhi, 1981-2. Ed. and Trans., Pandit Bhushan V. Subrahmanya Shastri. 2 vols. Bangalore, 1947.
Citralakṣaṇa. Ed. and Tr., Asok K. Bhattacharya. Sarasvat Library, Calcutta, 1974.
Dhvanyāloka of Ānandavardhana. Ed., Pattabhirama Shāstri. Chaukhambā Sanskrit Series, Varanasi, 1940.
——. Hindi Commentary by Vishvesvara Siddhantaśiromaṇi. Ed., Narendra, Varanasi: Jnānamaṇḍala Limited.
Mānasollāsa of Someśvara. 3 vols. Ed., G.K. Shirgondekar. Gaekwad Oriental Series. Baroda Oriental Institute, Baroda, 1939, 1961, 1967.
Mayamatam, Treatise of Housing, Architecture and Iconography. 2 vols. Ed., and Trans., Bruno Dagens. Indira Gandhi National Centre for the Arts and Motilal Banarsidass, Delhi, 1994.
Nāṭyaśastra of Bharata with Abhinavagupta's Commentary. Ed., M. Ramakrishna Kavi. Gaikwāḍ Oriental Series 36, Vol. 1 (1926), Vol. 2 (1934).
Pratimā Lakṣaṇa of Viṣṇudharmottara. Ed. and Tr., D.C. Bhattacharya, Harman Publishing House, Delhi, 1991.
Rūpamaṇḍana. Ed. & Tr. in Hindi by Balaram Srivastav. Motilal Banarsidass, Delhi, 1992.
Sāhitya Darpaṇa of Viśvanātha, with Kusumapratibhā Commentary. Ed., Haridas Bhattacharya, Hemachandra Bhattacharya, Calcutta, 1945.
Samarāṅgaṇa Sūtradhāra by Bhoja. Ed., V.S. Agrawala. Gaekwad Oriental Series 25. Baroda Oriental Institute, Baroda, 1966.
Śilpaprakāśa. Medieval Odishan Sanskrit Text on Temple Architecture by Rāmacandra Kaulācāra. Ed., Alice Boner and Sadasiva Rath Sarma. E.J. Brill, Leiden, 1966. Rev. Ed. by Bettina Baumer, Rajendra Prasad Das, Sadananda Das. 2nd edition, Indira Gandhi National Centre for the Arts and Motilal Banarsidass, Delhi, 2005.
Śṛṅgāraprakāśa of Bhoja. Ed., G.R. Josya. 4 vols. International Academy of Sanskrit Research, 10 Mysore, 1955-1977.

Viṣṇudharmottarapurāṇīyam Citrasūtram. Ed.and Trans., Parul Dave Mukherji. Indira Gandhi National Centre for the Arts and Motilal Banarsidass, Delhi, 2001.
Viśvakarmāvāstuśāstra. Bhandarkar. *ASIAR* 1906-7: 179-92.

Smṛti

Manu Smṛti, with the commentary of Medhātithi. Ed., Ganganath Jha. Asiatic Society, Bengal, Calcutta, 1934.
Yajñavalkya Smṛti with the Mitākṣarā commentary. Ed., N. Shastri. Choukhamba Sanskrit Series, Varanasi, 1908.

Semi-Historical and Literary Works

Buddhacaritam by Aśvaghoṣa. Ed., E.B. Cowell. Sacred Books of the East, 49. Oxford, 1893. Trans., E.H. Johnston. 2 vols. 2nd ed. Delhi, 1972.
Harṣacaritam by Bāṇa Bhaṭṭa. Trans., E.B. Cowell and F.W. Thomas. London, 1897. Ed., P.V. Kane. Bombay, 1918.
Caturvarga Cintāmaṇi of Hemadri. Ed. Pandit Bharatacandra Śiromaṇi. Bibliotheca Indica, Calcutta 1873, 1879.
Daśakumāracaritam by Daṇḍin. Ed., and Trans., M.R. Kale. 3rd ed. Bombay, 1928. Repr. 1966.
Kāvyamīmāṁsā of Rājasekhara. Ed., S.D. Dalal and R.A. Shastry. Gaekwad Oriental Series 1. Baroda, Oriental Institute, Baroda, 1934.
Kirātārjunīyam. Ed., Jīvānanda Vidyāsāgara. Calcutta, 1875.
Kumārasambhavam by Kālidāsa. Ed., and Trans., M.R. Kale. Motilal Banarsidass, Delhi, 1985.
Mālavikāgnimitram by Kālidāsa. Ed., Shankar Pandurang Pandit. 2nd ed. Bombay Sanskrit Series, 1889.
Naiṣadhacaritam by Srī Harṣa. Ed., E. Roer,N.N. Bedarkar, Calcutta, Baptist Mission Press, 1836-55.
Raghuvaṁśam by Kālidāsa. Ed. and Trans., Gopal Raghunath Nandargikar. Motilal Banarsidass, Delhi, 1971.
Sāhitya Darpaṇa. Ed., Ācārya Krishna Mohan Shstri. Kāshi Sanskrit Series, 145. Varanasi, 1967.

FOREIGN ACCOUNTS

FaHsian. 1965. *A Record of Buddhist Kingdom.* Trans. by James Legge. Reprint, New York: Dover.
Hsuan-tsang. 1000. *Si-yu-ki: Buddhist Records of the Western World.* Trans. by Samuel Beal. London: Kegan Paul.

ARCHAEOLOGICAL AND SECONDARY SOURCES

Abraham, Karl. (1909). 2006. *Dreams and Myths. A Study in Race Psychology.* New York: Kissinger Publishing.
Adorno, Theodor W. 1982. *Théorie Esthétique.* Traduit de'allemand par Marc Jimenez. Paris: Klincksieck.
Agrawala, P.K. 1965. *Pūrṇa Kalaśa.* Varanasi: Prithvi Prakashan.
——. 1967. *Skanda Kārtikeya,* Banaras Hindu University.
——. 1968. *Gupta Temple Architecture.* Varanasi: Prithvi Prakashan.
——. 1994. "Some Epigraphical Notes on the Early Art of Chhattisgarh", *Purātan* 9: 67-70.
Agrawala, R.C. 1969-70. "Carved Pillar of Gupta year 61". *JOIB* 19: 355-56.
——. 2000. "An Enigmatic Statue from Tala".In Nigam, ed., *Riddle of Indian Iconography*: 111-116.
Agrawala, V.S. Samvat 1990/AD 1933. "Śiva kā Svarūpa" (Identity of Śiva), Hindi, in Hanumanprasad Poddar, ed., *Śivāṅka*: 491-503.
——. 1943. "The Kalpavṛkṣa Motif in Art and Literature", *JISOA* 2: 1-8.
——. 1944. "Pūrṇakumbha or the Full Vase". *JUPHS* 18.1: 1-5.
——. 1947-48. "Terracotta Figurines of Ahichchhatra, District Bareilly, U.P." *Ancient India* 4: 104-79.
——. 1948. *Gupta Art.* Lucknow: *JUPHS.*

——. 1949. "Catalogue of the Mathura Museum". *JUPHS* 22: 102-210.
——. 1949. "Art Evidence in Kālidāsa". *JUPHS*, 22.
——. 1949. *Pṛthivī-putra*. Hindi. Son of Earth. Delhi: Sastā Sāhitya Maṇḍal Prakāshan.
——. 1960. "One Rudra and Many". *Purāṇa* 2. 1-2:211-24.
——. 1961. "A Survey of Gupta Art and Some Sculptures from Nācnā Kuthārā and Khoh." *Lalit Kalā* 9: 16-26.
——. 1962-63. *Sparks from the Vedic Fire*. Varanasi: School of Vedic Studies, Banaras Hindu University.
——. 1963. *The Thousand Syllabled Speech*. Varanasi: Prithvi Prakashan.
——. 1963. *Gaṇeśa*. Hindi Viśvakoṣa 3. Varanasi: Nāgari Prachāriṇi Sabhā: 388-89.
——. 1963. *India as Known to Pāṇini: A Study of the Cultural Material in the Aṣṭādhyāyi*. Varanasi: Prithvi Prakashan.
——. 1963. *Matsya Purāṇa-A Study*: Varanasi: All India Kāshirāja Trust.
——. 1963. *Solar Symbolism of the Boar*. Varanasi: Prithvi Prakashan.
——. 1964. "Palace Architecture in Daṇḍin's Avantīsundarīkathā". *JOIB* 13.4:832-40.
——. 1964. *Prācīn Bhāratīya Lokadharma*. Hindi. Ahmedabad: Ancient Indian Folk Religion. Jñānodaya Trust.
——. 1965. *Studies in Indian Art*. Varanasi: Vishwavidyalaya Prakashan.
——. 1965. *Indian Art: A History of Indian Art from the Earliest Times to the Third Century A.D.* Varanasi: Prithvi Prakashan.
——. 1966. *Śiva Mahādeva*. Varanasi: Veda Academy.
——. 1966. Ed., The Samarāṅgaṇasūtradhāra. *GOS*.
——. 1968. "Palace Architecture in Bāṇa's Harṣacarita". *Melanges d'indianisme, a la Memoire de Louis Renou*. Paris: 7-22.
——. 1969. *Deeds of Harṣa, Being a Cultural Study of Bāṇa's Harṣa Carita*. Varanasi: Prithvi Prakashan.
——. 1970. *Ancient Indian Folk Cults*. Varanasi: Prithvi Prakashan.
——. 1979. *Bhāratīya Dharma Mīmāṁsā, Indian Religion*: An Analysis, Varanasi: Prithvi Prakashan.
——. 1981. *Vedic Lectures*. Varanasi: Prithvi Prakashan.
——. 1983. *Vāmana Purāṇa: A Study*. Varanasi: Prithvi Prakashan.
——. 1984. *Pre Kuṣhāṇa Art of Mathurā*. Varanasi: Prithvi Prakashan.
Ahmed, Nisar. 1973. The date of Ārang Copperplate Inscription of Bhīmaṣena II: A Review." *JOIB* 23: 339-41.
——. 1994. "The Attribution of the Repoussé Gold Coins of Mahendrāditya and Kramāditya: A Review", *Purātan* 9: 50-55.
Adam, Leonhard. 1948. *Primitive Art*. Harmondsworth: Penguin Books.
Aiyangar, S.K. "Vākāṭakas and Their Place in the History of India". *ABORI* 15: 21-54.
Aldrich, V.C. 1958. "Beauty as Feeling". In Langer, ed., *Reflections on Art*: 3-9.
Allan, John. 1914. *Catalogue of the Coins of the Gupta Dynasties and of Saśāṅka, King of Gauḍa*. London: Trustees of the British Museum, reprint, 1967.
——. 1936. *Catalogue of the Coins of Ancient India in the British Museum*. London: Trustees of the British Museum. Reprint, 1967.
Altekar, Anant Sadashiv. 1957. *The Coinage of the Gupta Empire and Its Imitations*. Corpus of Indian Coins, Vol. 4. Banaras: Numismatic Society of India, Banaras Hindu University.
——. 1960. "The History of the Vākāṭakas". In Yazdani, ed, *History of the Deccan*, Oxford: 149–200.
Arnheim, Rudolf. 1974. *Art and Visual Perception. A Psychology of the Creative Eye*. Berkeley: University of California Press.
Apte, V.M. 1946. "Varuṇa in Ṛgveda" *NIA* 8: 136-56.
——. 1957. "From the Ṛgvedic Rudra to Purāṇic Śiva." *SAUJ* 6: 81-85.
Arbman, Ernst. 1922. *Rudra*. Uppsala: Untersuchungen Zum Altindischen Glauben und Kultus.
Archaeological Survey of India, 1903. *ASIPR, Western India*. Bombay.
——. 1904. *ASIPR Western India, for the year ending 30th June*, 1904, Bombay.
——. 1906. *ASIPR, Western India, for the months July, 1905 to March, 1906*. Bombay.
——. 1908. *ASIAR,, Eastern Circle*, 1907-08. Calcutta.

——. 1912. *ASIAR, Eastern Circle*, 1910-11. Calcutta.
——. 1954. *ASIAR 1926-27*. New Delhi.
——. 1955. *IAR 1954-55*. New Delhi.
——. 1959. *IAR 1958-59*. New Delhi.
——. 1961. *IAR 1960-61*. New Delhi.
——. 1994. "Observations on the History and Culture of Dakṣiṇa Kośala (5th to 7th centuries A.D.)" in Balbir and Bautze, ed., *Festschrift Klaus Bruhn.*: 1-66.
Archaeologist, Raipur. 1984. File on Protection (No. 5) of Devarani Jethani Temple. Directorate of Archaeology and Museums, Raipur.
Archaeology Department of People's Republic of Bānglādesh. 1976. *Maināmati*, Shamsher Alam, AKH; 1992. *Iṭākhola Vihar*, Lālmāi Maināmāti, Rahman, Habibur, in Bengali; 1999. *Excavations at Ānanda Vihāra*, Maināmāti, Comillā 1979-82, Alam, Md. Shaifiqul and Miah, Md. Abul Hashem; 1979. *Bānglādesh Archaeology*. Ed. Ahmed, Nazimuddin; 2000. *Excavations at Bihār Dhāp, Bogrā*, 1979-86, Alam, Md. Shafiul, Miah, Md. Abul Hashem Khaleque, Md. Abdul; 2000. *A Preliminary Report on Excavations at Halud Vihāra, Naogāon*. Miah, Md. Abul Hashem, Musa, Md. Abu; 2001. *Excavation at Ruyālbāri, A Preliminary Report*. Qadir, Md. Abdul, Rahman Habibur.
Asher, Frederick M. 1980. *The Art of Eastern India, 300-800*. Minneapolis: University of Minnesota.
Asher, F.M. and G.S. Ghai. 1985. Ed., *Indian Epigraphy: Its Bearing on the History of Art*. Oxford and I.B.H., with American Institute of Indian Studies.
Auboyer, J. et al. 1979. *Oriental Art. A Handbook of Styles and Forms*. London: Faber and Faber.
Auerbach, Erich. 1946. *Mimesis*. Trans. from German, by Willard Trask. New York: Doubleday. 1957.
Avalon, Arthur.1914. *Principles of Tantra*. Part I. Madras: Ganesh & Co.
Babb, Lawrence A. 1975. *The Divine Hierarchy: Popular Hinduism in Central India*. New York: Columbia University Press.
Bagchi, Prabodh Chandra. 1951. *India and China: A Thousand Years of Cultural Relations*. New York: Philosophical Library. 2nd ed., Westport, Conn.: Greenwood Press, 1971.
——. 1975. *Studies in the Tantras*. Calcutta: University of Calcutta.
Bajpai, K.D. 1946. "Mahākośala in Ancient Literature", *JKHRS* 1. 2: Bolaṅgir: 203-04.
——. 1965. *Cultural Heritage of Mahākośala*. New Delhi: Cultural Forum.
Bajpai, K.D. 1978. "Chattisgarh ke Prācīn Nagar," in Hindi (Ancient Cities of Chattisgarh). *PRP* 6.1: 145-48.
Bajpai, K.D. and S.K. Pandey. 1978. *Malhār*. Sāgar: University of Sāgar.
Bajpai, Santosh. 1977. "Revā se prāpta Śarabhapurī Rājā Narendra Kā Tāmrapatra," in Hindi (Copperplate of Śarabhapurī king Narendra, found in Rewā". *PRP* 5.1: 182-83.
Bajpai, Shivakant and Rajkumar Patel. 2008. "Dūrgarakṣitkā Senākapāṭ Abhilekh-Nāmābhidhān evam Sāmant Sāsakon ke Saṁdarbh Meṅ Punarvivecan". Hindi. In *Kośala* I: 49-53.
Bakker, Hans. 1989. "The Antiquities of Rāmṭek Hill". In *JSAS* 5: 79-102.
——. 1990 "Throne and Temple, Political Power and Religious Prestige in Vidarbha". *The Sacred Centre as a Focus of Political Interest: Proceedings of the Symposium on the 375th Anniversary of the University of Groningen*, Ed., Bakker, Groningen: 83-100.
——. 1990 "Rāmṭek, An Ancient Centre of Viṣṇu Devotion in Maharashtra". *The History of Sacred Places in India as Reflected in Traditional Literature*, ed., Bakker, Leiden: 62-85.
——. 1992. "Memorials, Temples, Gods and Kings, An Attempt to Unravel the Symbolic Texture of Vākāṭaka Kingship", in Hock, Kolpp, Oort. Ed., *Ritual*: 7-19.
Bakker, Hans and Harunaga Isaacson. 1993. "The Rāmṭek Inscriptions 2: The Vākāṭaka Inscriptions in Kevala–Narasiṁha" *BSOAS*, 56-1, 46-74.
——. 1995. The Twelve Faced Śiva Image from Mānḍhal". In *SAA* 2: 637-48.
——. 1997. *The Vākāṭakas*. Grotingen: Egbert Forsten.
——. 2000. "An Enigmatic Giant from Tala". In Nigam, ed., *Riddle*: 101-105.

Balasubramaniam, K.M. 1959. *Special Lectures on Śaiva Siddhānta.* Ānnāmālāi: Ānnāmalāi University.

Balbir, Nalini and J.K. Bautze. 1994. Ed., *Festschrift Klaus Bruhn*. Reinbek: Wezler.

Banerjea, Jitendra Nath. 1940. "Śiva and His Emblems on Early Indian Coins and Seals. *IHQ* 12: 131-34.

——. 1941. "Padminī Vidyā", *JISOA 9:* 141-66.

——. 1948. "Sūrya. Ādityas and the Navagrahas", *JISOA* 16: 47-100.

——. 1954. "Some Aspects of Śakti Worship in Ancient India". *PRB* 59.

——. 1956. *The Development of Hindu Iconography.* 2nd ed., Calcutta: University of Calcutta.

——. 1968. *Religion in Art and Archaeology (Vaishṇavism and Śaivism).* Lucknow: University of Lucknow.

Banerji, Rakhal Das. 1924. *The Temple of Śiva at Bhūmarā. MASI* 6. Calcutta: Superintendent, Government Printing.

——. 1930-31. *History of Orissa, from the Earliest times to the British Period.* 2 vols. Calcutta: R. Chatterji. Reprint, Delhi: Bhārātīya, 1980.

——. 1931. *The Haihayas of Tripuri and Their Monuments. MASI* 23. Calcutta: Government of India, Central Publications Branch.

——. 1933. *The Eastern Indian School of Medieval Sculpture.* MASI New Imperial Series 47. Delhi.

——. 1933. *The Age of the Imperial Guptas.* Varanasi: Banaras Hindu University.

Barthes, Ronald. 1953. *Le degré zéro de lé écriture.* Paris: Seuil. *Writing Degree Zero.* English translation by Annette Lavers & Colin Smith. London: Jonathan Cape, 1967.

——. 1957. *Mythologies*. Paris, Seuil. English translation by Annette Lavers, London: Jonathan Cape, 1972.

——. 1977. *Image, Music, Text*. Trans., Stephen Heath. New York: Hill and Wang.

——. 1978. "Rhetor and Magician in Arcimoldo". Trans. by John Shepley Parma, Franco Maria Ricci. In Blonsky, ed., *Signs;* 481-87.

——. 1985. *The Grain of the Voice*. New York: Hill and Wang.

——. 1986. *The Rustle of Language.* Trans., Richard Howard. New York: Hill and Wang.

Barua, B.M. 1933. "Ancient Indian Theories of Art". *JISOA.*

——. 1934. "Art as Defined in the Brāhmaṇas". *IC*: 1.2: 18-20.

Basa, Kishor K. and Pradeep Mohanty. 2000. Ed., *Archaeology of Orissa*, 2 vols. Delhi: Pratibha Prakashan.

Basu Majumdar, Sushmita. 2000. *Coins of Malhār*. Nasik: *IIRNS*.

——. 2008. "Temples, Monasteries and Patronage Issues at Sirpur. Looking through the Epigraphic Lens". In *Kośala* 1, Raipur: Directorate of Culture and Archaeology, Govt. of Chhattisgarh: 87-98.

Baudrillard. 1975. *Le Miroir de la Production. Mirror of Production.* Trans. by Mark Poster. New York: Telos Press.

Baumer, Bettina. 1982. Ed., *Rūpa Pratirūpa. Alice Boner Commemorative Volume.* New Delhi: Biblia Impex.

Bayer, Raymond. 1958. "The Essence of Rhythm". In Langer, ed., *Reflections:* 186-201.

Beal, Samuel. 1884. *Si-yu-ki. Buddhist Records of the Western World.* Trans. from the Chinese of Hiuen Tsang. 2 vols. London: Trubner and Co. Reprint, Delhi: Orient Books Reprint Corporation, 1969.

Becker, Howard S. 1984. *Art Worlds*. Berkeley: University of California Press.

Bedekar, V.M. 1967. "Legend of the Churning of the Ocean in the Epics and the Purāṇas: A Comparative Study." *PUJ* 4: 7-61.

Beglar, J.D. 1873-74. "Report of a Tour in the Central Provinces, 1873-74: Rāmṭek". In *ASI Reports (Old Series)* 7, by Alexander Cunningham and Others: 109-15.

——. 1874-76. *ASI Reports (Old Series) 13. Report of a Tour in South Eastern Provinces.*

Begley, Wayne Edison. 1966. *The Chronology of Mahāyāna Buddhist Architecture and Painting at Ajantā.* Ph.D. dissertation, University of Pennsylvania.

Behera, K.S. 2008. *The Liṅgarāja Temple of Bhuvaneśvara.* Delhi: IGNCA & Aryan Books International.

Benisti, Mirélle. 1952. *Le Medaillon Lotiforme dans la Plastique Indienne du 3 Siécle Avant J.C. Au 7 Siécle Apres J.C.* Paris: Musée Guimet.

Berkson, Carmel, George Michele and Wendy Doniger O' Flaherty. 1983.*Elephanta. The Cave of Shiva.* Princeton, N.J.: Princeton University Press.

Bhandarkar, D.R. 1904-07, "Ekaliṅgaji Stone Inscription and the Origin and History of the Lakulīśa Sect". *JBB: RAS* 22: 156-66.
——. 1906-07. "Lakulīśa" *ASIAR*: 179-92.
——. 1913. "Some Published Inscriptions Reconsidered" *IA* 32: 57-64.
——. 1920. "The Archaeological Remains and Excavations at Nāgarī". *MASI* 4: 120.
——. 1931-32. "Mathurā Pillar Inscription of Chandragupta II: G.E. 61". *EI* 21: 1-9.
——. 1927-36. Ed., *List of Inscriptions of Northern India*. Appendices to *EI* 19-23.
Bhandarkar, R.G. 1913. *Vaiṣṇavism, Śaivism and Minor Religious Systems.* Strassburg: Karl J. Trubner.
——. 1927. *Early History of the Deccan*: Collected Works 3. ed, W.B. Utgirkar, Bhandarkar Oriental Research Institute, Pune: 1-99.
Bhattacharya, B. 1975. *Śaivism and the Phallic World.* 2 vols. New Delhi: Oxford and IBH Publishing Co.
Bhattacharya, Brindavan Chandra. 1921. *Indian Images: The Brāhmaṇic Iconography.* Calcutta: Thacker, Spink and Co. Reprint, New Delhi, Cosmo Publications, 1978.
Bhattacharya, Dipak Chandra. 1980. *Iconology of Composite Images.* Delhi: Munshiram Manoharlal.
——. 1984. *Mythological and Ritual Symbolism. (A Study with Reference to the Vedic and Tāntric Agni).* Calcutta: Sanskrit Pustak Bhāṇḍār.
——. 1989. "Viśvarūpa of Śiva in the Pārel Sculpture" in *'Prācī Pratibhā: Essays in Honour of Prof B.N. Mukherjee.* Ed., D.C. Bhattacharya and Devendra Handa. New Delhi: Harman Publishing House.
——. 1986. "*Mūrti* and *Pratimā*", in *Rūpāñjali*: 43-48.
Bhattacharya, G. and M. Sivayya. 1961-62. "Malhār Plates of Jayarāja, Year 9." *EI* 34: 28-32.
Bhattacharya, G. 1961-62. "Malhār Plates of Pravara II, Year 3." *EI* 34: 53-54.
Bhattacharya, N.N. 1982. *History of the Tāntric Religion.* Delhi: Manohar Publications.
Bhattacharya, P.K. 1977. *Historical Geography of Madhya Pradesh from Early Records.* Delhi: Motilal Banarsidass.
Bhattacharya, Tarapada. 1963. *The Canons of Indian Art, or, a Study on Vāstuvidyā.* 2nd ed. Calcutta: Firma K.L. Mukhopadhyay.
Bhattacharji, Sukumari. 1960. "Rudra, from the Vedas to the Mahābhārata." *ABORI* 41: 85-128.
——. 1970. *The Indian Theogony. A Comparative Study of Indian Mythology, from the Vedas to the Purāṇas.* Cambridge: Cambridge University Press.
Biardeau, Madeleine. 1989. *Hinduism: The Anthropology of a Civilization.* Trans from French by Richard Nice. Delhi: Oxford University Press.
Biardeau, Madeleine and Charles Malamoud. 1976. *Le Sacrifice dans L'Inde Ancienne,* Paris.
Birdwood, George. 1880. *The Arts of India.* Jersey: The British Book Company.
Biswas, D.K. 1948. "Sūrya and Śiva." *IHQ 24*: 142-47.
Blackburn, S.H. 1977. "Tribal Creation Myth in Central India: A Problem of Cultural Diffusion". In *MII* 57.3.
Blackwell, Charles M. 1907. *Source book in Ancient Philosophy.* New York: Charles Scribner's.
Blair, C. 1961. *Heat in the Ṛgveda and Atharva Veda*: American Oriental Society Publication 45. Cambridge, Massachusetts.
Blonsky, Marshall. 1985. Ed., *On Signs.* Baltimore: Johns Hopkins University Press.
Bloomfield, Maurice. 1891. "On Jalāśaḥ, Jalāśabheṣajaḥ, Jalāśam, and Jalasam." *AJP* 12: 425-29.
Bolon, Carol Radcliffe. 1992. *Forms of the Goddess Lajjā Gaurī in Indian Art.* Pennsylvania.
Boas, Franz.1955. *Primitive Art.* New York: Dover Publications.
Boreve, Yuri. 1981. *Aesthetics.* Moscow: Progressive Publishers.
Bosch, David Kan Frederik. 1960. *The Golden Germ: An Introduction to Indian Symbolism.* The Hague: Mouten and Co.
Bose, D.N. 1950. Ed., *Tantras.* Calcutta: Oriental Publishing Co.
Bose, Nirmal Kumar. 1932. *Canons of Orissan Architecture.* Calcutta: R. Chatterjee.
Bose, Sushil K. 1937-38. "Indore Plates of Pravarasena 11". *EI* 24: 52-56.
Bouquet, A.C. 1956. *Comparative Religion.* Harmondsworth: Penguin Books.

Brown, W. Norman. 1931. "The Sources and Nature of Puruṣa in the Puruṣasūkta (Ṛgveda 10.91)." *JAOS* 51: 108-18.
——. 1965. "Theories of Creation in the Ṛgveda". *JAOS* 85: 23-24.
Brown, Percy. 1956. *Indian Architecture (Buddhist and Hindu Periods)*. Vol. I, 3rd ed., Bombay: D.B. Taraporevala Sons and Co.
Brown, R.L. 1991. Ed., *Gaṇeśa. Studies of an Asian God*. New York: State University of New York Press.
Brunner, Lachaus Helen. 1968. *Somaśambhupaddhati*, Deuxieme parti, Pondicherry.
Buitenen, J.A.B. Van. 1968. The *Pravargya, An Ancient Indian Iconic Ritual.* Poona: Deccan College Postgraduate and Research Institute.
Bulgakov, F.I. 1889. Iujustriovannaja Istorija Knigopecatanija i Tipografskago Iskusstra, 10. Republished in the *IDC Slavonic Microfiche Series*.
Bunce, Frederick W. 1998. *An Encyclopedia of Hindu Deities, Demi Gods, Godlings, Demons and Heroes*. Vol. 1-3., New Delhi: D.K. Print World.
Butterworth, E.A.S. 1970. *The Tree at the Navel of the Earth*: Berlin: de Gruyter.
Caland, Willem and Victor Henry. 1906-07, *L.'Agniṣṭoma: description complete de la forme normale du sacrifice de Soma dans le culte Vedique*. 2 vols. Paris: E. Leroux.
Campbell, Joseph. 1956. *The Hero with a Thousand Faces*. New York: Meridian Books.
——. 1962. *Oriental Mythology*. London: Seckar and Warberg.
——. 1968. *The Masks of God*. New York: Viking Press.
——. 1974. *The Mythic Image*. Princeton: Princeton University Press.
——. 1976. *Myths*. New York: Bollingen.
Capra, Fritjof. 1984. *The Tao of Physics*. New York: Bantam Books.
Cassirer, Ernst. 1944. *An Essay on Man*. New Haven: Yale University Press.
——. 1949. *Philosophy of Ernst Cassirer*, Ed., Paul Arthur Schlipp. La Salle,Illinois: Open Court Publishing Company.
——. 1955. *The Philosophy of Symbolic Form*. Two vols. New Haven: Yale University Press.
Cavendish, Richard. 1980. Ed., *Mythology*, New York: Rizzoli.
Certeau, Michel De. 1985. "What We Do When We Believe", in Blonsky, Ed., *On Signs*: 192-202.
Chhabra, Bahadurchand & Govind Swamirao Gai. 1981. Ed., *Inscriptions of the Early Gupta Kings*. Rev. by Devadatta Ramakrishna Bhandarkar. *CII* 3:
Chhabra, B.Ch. 1935-36. "Sonpur Plates of Mahābhavagupta(II) Janmejaya, the year 17". *EI* 23: 248-88.
——. 1947-48. "Bāmhoni Plates of Pāṇḍava King Bharatabala: Year 2". *EI* 27: 132-45.
Chakraborti, Haripada. 1970. *Pāśupata Sūtram*. Calcutta: Academic Publishers.
Chakravarti, N.P. 1931. "Khārod Inscription of Ratnadeva. Cedī Saṁvat 933". *EI* 21: 159-65.
Chakravarti, C. 1932. "The Soma or Sauma Sect of the Śaivas". *IHQ* 8:220-23.
Chakravarti, Chintaharan. 1943. "Pāśupata Sūtra". *IHQ* 19: 270-71.
Chakravarty, Kalyan Kumar. 1989. Ed., Śaiva Tradition in Indian Art, *Purātan*-6 Bhopal: Commissioner Archaeology & Museums, Madhya Pradesh.
——. *Purātan 9*. 1994. Special issue on *Art of Chhattisgarh*. Ed. I.M. Chahal, Guest Ed., K.K. Chakravarty, Commissioner, Archaeology& Museums, Govt. of M.P., Bhopal.
——. 1996. "Sculpture, 4th – 6th centuries A.D: High Phase in Central India", in *The Dictionary of Art 15*, New York: Macmillan Publishers Limited: 467-75.
Chakravarti, Mahadev. 1994. *The Concept of Rudra Śiva Through the Ages*. 2nd ed. Delhi: Motilal Banarsidass.
Chandra, Moti. 1944. "A History of Indian Costumes from the 3rd to the End of the 7th century A.D." *JISOA* 8:1-97
——. 1964-66. "Nidhiśṛṅga (Cornucopia)". *BPWM* 9: 1-33.
——. 1973. *Costumes, Textiles, Cosmetics and Coiffure in Ancient and Medieval India*. Delhi: Oriental Publishers.

——. 1977. *Trade and Trade Routes in Ancient India.* New Delhi: Abhinav.

Chandra, Pramod. 1970. "A Vāmana Temple at Marhiā and Some Reflections on Gupta Architecture". *AA* 32: 125-245.

——. 1970. *Stone Sculpture in the Allahabad Museum.* Poona: American Institute of Indian Studies.

——. 1971. "The Cult of Śrī Lakṣmī and Four Carved Discs in Bhārat Kalā Bhavan". In Anand Krishna, ed., *Chhavi. Golden Jubilee Volume.* Bhārat Kalā Bhavan, 1920-70. Banaras: Banaras Hindu University.

——. 1972. "Some Remarks on Bihar Sculpture from the Fourth to the Ninth Century". *Aspects of Indian Art*, ed., P. Pal. Leiden: Brill: 59-64.

——. 1975. *Studies in Indian Temple Architecture.* New Delhi: American Institute of Indian Studies.

——. 1983. *On the Study of Indian Art.* Cambridge, Massachusetts: Harvard University Press.

——. 1985. *The Sculpture of India (3000 B.C. to 1300 A.D.).* Washington: National Gallery of Art.

Chandrol, G.K. 1980. Note of 26th November, 1980 in *File No 20/58/80 A* Bhopal: Directorate of Archaeology and Museums, Madhya Pradesh.

Charpentier, Jarl. 1909." Über Rudra-Śiva". *WZKM* 23:151-79.

Chattopadhyaya, Sudhakar. 1970. *Evolution of Hindu Sects up to the time of Śaṅkarācārya.* New Delhi: Munshiram Manoharlal.

Chaturvedi, Jagadish Chandra. 1972. *Madhya Pradesh Ke Kalāmaṇḍapa,* (Art Pavilion of Madhya Pradesh). In Hindi. Gwalior: Kailāsh Pustak Sadan.

Chaudhuri, Nanimadhab. 1939. "Rudra-Śiva as an Agricultural Deity." *IHQ* 15: 183-96.

Chipp, Herschel B. 1968. *Theories of Modern Art.* Berkeley: University of California Press.

Chitgopekar, Nilima. 1998. *Encountering Śhaivaism.* New Delhi: Munshilal Manoharlal.

Chitrav, Siddhesvara Shastri. 1964. *Bhāratavarṣīya Prācīna Caritrakoṣa.* In Hindi. Poona: Bhāratīya Caritrakoṣamaṇḍala.

Chūggoku Sekkutsu: Ryūmon Sekkutsu (The Grotto Art of China, the Longman Grottoes). 7.1 (29,31). Tokyo: Heibonsha.

Clothey, F.W. 1983. "The Yāga, a Fire Ritual in South India". In F.W. Clothey, ed., *Experiencing Śiva: Encounters with a Hindu Deity.* Columbia: J. Bruclong: 129 ff.

Collingwood, R.G. 1958. *The Principles of Art.* New York: Oxford University Press.

Collins, Charles Dillard. 1988. *Iconography and Ritual of Śiva at Elephanta.* Albany: State University of New York.

Colum, Dadraic. 1930. *Orpheus: Myths of the World.* New York: Macmillan.

Coomaraswamy, A.K. 1908.*The Aims of Indian Art.* Broad Campden.

——. 1920. Art and Craftsmanship. In *Rūpam* 1:4-5.

——. 1927. *History of Indian and Indonesian Art.* London: E Goldston. Reprint, New York: Dover Publications, 1965.

——. 1928. "Indian Architectural terms". *JAOS* 48.

——. 1928-30. "Early Indian Iconography." *Eastern Art* 1. 1 (July 1928): 32-41; 1. 3 (January 1929): 174-89; Corrigenda and Addenda 2(1930): 240-42.

——. 1928-31. *Yakṣas.* 2 parts. Washington D.C.: The Smithsonian Institution. Reprint, New Delhi: Munshiram Manoharlal. 1971.

——. 1930-31. "Early Indian Architecture," *Eastern Art*, 1930: 208-35; 3 (1931): 180-217.

——. 1932. "Reactions to Indian Art". *JAOS* 52.

——. 1933. "The Mystery of Mahādeva", *Indian Arts and Letters* 6: 10-13.

——. 1934. *The Transformation of Nature in Art.* Cambridge,Massachusetts: Harvard University Press. Reprint, New York: Dover, 1956.

——. 1935. *The Ṛg Veda as Land–Nāma-Bok*, London: Luzac & Co.

——. 1935. *Elements of Buddhist Iconography.* Cambridge, Massachusetts: Harvard University Press. Facsimile Edition, Ann Arbor, Michigan: University Microfilms. 1970.

——. 1938. "The Yakṣa of the Vedas and Upaniṣads." *QJMS* 28.

——. 1942. *Spiritual Authority and Temporal Power in the Indian Theory of Government*. New Haven, Connecticut: *JAOS*.
——. 1943. *Why Exhibit Works of Art?* London: Luzac & Co.
——. 1956. *Christian and Oriental Philosophy of Art*. New York: Dover Publications.
——. 1983. *Coomaraswamy 1. Selected Papers: Traditional Art and Symbolism. Coomaraswamy 2. Selected Papers: Metaphysics*. Ed., Roger Lipsey. Princeton, N.J: 2, Princeton University Press.
Coleman, Francis J. 1968. *Contemporary Studies in Aesthetics*. New York: Mcgraw Hill.
Cooper, David E. and Robert Hopkins. 1995. Ed., *A Companion to Aesthetics. The Blackwell Companion to Philosophy*. Oxford: Blackwell.
Copleston, Frederick. 1946. *Schopenhauer: Philosopher of Pessimism*. Reprint, London: Search Press, 1975.
Cousens, Henry. 1897. *List of Antiquarian Remains in the Central Provinces and Berar. ASIAR, New Series* 19. Calcutta.
——. 1904. Aḍbhār. In *Progress Report of the Archaeological Survey of Western India*, 1904: 32-33.
——. 1905. Rāmṭek. In *Progress Report of the Archaeological Survey of Western India*, 1905: 41.
Croce, Benedetto. 1902. *Estetica. Aesthetic*. English translation by Douglas Ainslie. UNESCO Series of Representative Works, Italian Series. London: Peter Owen Vision Press, 1967.
Cunningham, Alexandar. 1871. *The Ancient Geography of India*. London: Trubner. Reprint, Varanasi: Indological Book House, 1963.
——. 1879. *CII* 6.
——. 1891. *Coins of Ancient India from the Earliest Times down to the Seventh Century A.D.* London: B. Quaritch. Reprint, Varanasi: Indological Book House, 1969.
——. with Beglar, J.D. 1878-89. *ASIAR* 7. Report of a Tour in Bundelkhanḍ and Mālva, 1871-72; and in the Central Province, 1873-74; *ASIAR* 8. Report of a Tour through the Bengal Provinces in 1972-73; *ASIAR* 9. Report of a Tour in the Central Provinces in 1873-74 and 1874-75; *ASIAR* 10. Report of a Tour in Bundelkhanḍ and Mālwa in 1874-75 and 1876-77. *ASIAR* 12. Report of a Tour in the Central Doāb and Gorakhpur in 1874-75 and 1875-76; *ASIAR* 13. Report of a Tour in the South-eastern Provinces in 1874-75 and 1875-76; *ASIAR* 17. Report of a Tour in the Central Provinces and Lower Gangetic Belt in 1881-82; *ASIAR* 21. Report of a Tour in Bundelkhand and Rewā in 1883-84 and of a Tour in Rewā, Bundelkhand, Mālva aand Gwalior, in 1884-85.
Czuma, Stanislaw J. 1985. *Kuśān Sculpture: Images from Early India*. Cleveland: The Cleveland Museum of Art.
Dalmia, Yashodhara. 1988. *Painted World of the Wārlis. Art and Ritual of the Wārli Tribes of Maharashtra*. Delhi: Lalit Kala Akademi.
Dandekar, R.N. 1953. "Rudra in the Veda." *PUJ*: 94-148.
——. 1961-62. "Aspects of Agni Mythology." *JOIB*": 347-70.
——. 1977. *Vaishṇavism and Shaivism*. Imphal: Atambapu Research Centre.
Danielou, Alain. 1964. *Hindu Polytheism*. Bollingen Series 75. New York: Pantheon Books.
Danto, Arthur C. 1986. *The Philosophical Disfranchisement of Art*. New York: Columbia University Press.
Darian, Steven G. 1978. *The Ganges in Myth and History*. Honolulu: The University Press of Hawaii.
Das, K.B. and V.K. Mahapatra. 1979. *Folklore of Orissa*. 2nd Edition. 1993. Delhi: National Book Trust.
Dasgupta, Kalyan Kumar. 2000. "An Enigmatic Image of Śiva", in Nigam, Ed., *Riddle* 73-81.
Dasgupta, S.N. 1922-55. *A History of Indian Philosophy*. 5 vols. Cambridge: Cambridge University Press. Reprint, 1969-73.
——. 1960. *Fundamentals of Indian Art*. Bombay. Bhāratīya Vidyā Bhavan.
Debrett, E.A. 1909. *Central Provinces Gazetteers, Chattisgarh Feudatory States*. Bombay: Times Press.
Deglurkar, G.B. 1972. "Pavnār Se Prāpta Kaṁsavadha Śilāpaṭṭa", "Kaṁsavadha Stone Inscription Found at Pavnār", (Hindi). *Smaraṇikā. Nāgpur Akhaṇḍa Saṁgaṭhan Samiti Rajatāṅka* (Silver Jubilee Number of the Nagpur City Integration Committee).

——. 1982-89. "Mānḍhal Yethil Mūrti", in Marathi (Images from Mānḍhal) in *VSMV*. "Aṣṭamūrti", Vol. 25, 1982: 188-71; "Tripurāntaka Śivamūrti", Vol. 26, 1983: 60-62; "Gajahāmūrti Śiva Andhakanātha", Vol. 27, 1984: 121-24; "Nagmeshhāchi Pahili Pratimā" Vol. 28: 183-85; "Balaramāchi Dhenukāsuravadha, Vol. 29, 1986: 140-43.

——. 1992. "Vilakṣaṇaśiva". In *Purātan* 8: 29-31.

——. 1994. "Enriching Iconography of Dakṣīṇa Kośala. *Purātan* 9: 28-30.

Deglurkar, G.B. and A.P. Jamkhedkar. 1972. *Pavnār Yethil Kaṁsavadha*, Nagpur: Yagavahi.

Dehejia, Vidya. 1979. *Early Stone Temples of Orissa*. New Delhi: Vikas Publishing House.

Demoulin-Bernard. 1949. *Lion dans L'Art de l'Inde Ancienne*.Musée de France 8.

Deo, P.K. (Forwarding Note), "Elliot's Report on Kālahānḍi state, the 28th July, 1856", *OHRJ*, 16.2.

——. "Forgotten Forts of Kālāhānḍi district, Jumlāgarh – Mārāguḍā complex (Part 12)", *OHRJ*, 16. 3.

——. "Forgotten Forts of Kālāhānḍi (Asuragarh Forest and a hoard of punchmarked coins", *OHRJ*, 16. 3&4.

Deo, S.B. 19 "A Unique sculpture from Mānsar (Maharashtra)". *Śrī Mālampalli Somaśekhara Śarmā Commemoration Volume*: 275-77.

Deo, S.B. and Dhavalikar. 1967. *Paunār Excavation*. Nagpur: Nagpur University.

Deo, S.B. and J.P. Joshi. 1972. Ed., *Pauni Excavations* (1969-70). Deptt. of Ancient Indian History and Archaeology, Nagpur.

——. N.D. Souvenir. *Vidarbha. History & Archaeology*. Nagpur University, Nagpur.

Derrida, Jacques. 1967. *De la Grammatologie*. Paris: Minelit. *Of Grammatology*. Trans. By Gayatri Chakravarty Spivak. Baltimore: Johns Hopkins University Press, 1976.

——. 1978. *L'écriture et la difference*. Paris: Seuil. *Writing and Difference*. Trans. by Alan Bass: University of Chicago Press.

Desai, P.B. 1947-48. "Bārdulā Plates of Mahāśivagupta:Year 9". *EI* 27:287-91.

Desai, Madhuri. 1958. *The Gupta Temple at Deogarh*. Bombay: Bhulabhai Memorial Institute.

Dev, Harit Krishna. 1925-26. "Stone-East Bank Copperplates of Indradeva and Udayarāja". *EI* 18: 222-30.

Deva, Krishna. 1960. "Lakṣmaṇa Temple at Sirpur." *JMPIP* 2: 34-44.

——. 1962. "Extensions of Gupta Art: Art and Archaeology of the Pratihāra Age". New Delhi: *Seminar on Indian Art History*.

——. 1969. *Temples of North India*. New Delhi: National Book Trust.

——. 1988. In *Encyclopaedia of Indian Temple Architecture*, Vol. II, Part 1: North India: Foundations of North Indian Style.

——. 1995. *Temples of India*. 2 vols. Delhi: Aryan Books International.

Deva, Krishna and A.K. Sharma. 2009. *Sculptural Art of Mānsar*. Delhi: Bharatiya Kala Prakashan.

Devasenapathi, V.A. 1960. *Śaiva Siddhānta*. Madras University Philosophical Series 7. Reprint, 1966.

Dewey, John. 1934. *Art As Experience*. 7th Impression. 1958. New York: Capricorn.

Dey, N.L. 1899. *Geographical Dictionary of Ancient and Medieval India*. Calcutta: W. Newman and Co. 3rd ed. New Delhi: Oriental Books Reprint Corporation. 1971.

Dhaky, M.A. 1965. *'The Vyāla Figures on the Medieval Temples of India*. Indian Civilization Series 2. Varanasi: Prithivi Prakashan.

——. 1975. "The Genesis and Development of Maru-Gurjara Temple Architecture". In *Studies in Indian Temple Architecture*. Ed., Pramod Chandra: 114-65. New Delhi: American Institute of Indian Studies.

——. 1982. "Praṇāla in Indian, South-Asian and Southeast Asian Sacred Architecture". *Rūpapratirūpa*. Ed., Bettina Baumer. 1982: 119-66, and pls. 1-46.

——. 1984. "Bhūtas and Bhūtanāyakas: Elementals and their Captains." *Discourses on Śiva*. Ed., M.W. Meister: 240-56.

Dhaky, M.A. and M.W. Meister, Ed. 1983 and 1988. *Encyclopaedia of Indian Temple Architecture*. Vol. 1, pts 1 and 2 (South India). New Delhi: American Institute of Indian Studies; Philadelphia: University of Pennsylvania Press. Vol. 2, pts 1 and 2. Delhi: Oxford University Press.

Dhavalikar, M.K. 1966. Pavnār yethil Andhakāsuravadhamūrti. In *VSMV*: 49-58.
Dhavamony, Maria Susa. 1971. *Love of God, According to Śaiva Siddhānta*. Oxford: Clarendon Press.
Dikshit, M.G. and D.C. Sircar. 1955-56. "Senākapāṭ Inscription of the time of Śivagupta Bālārjuna." *EI* 31: 31-36.
Dikshit, M.G. 1954-56. "Reports on Sirpur Excavation". In *IAR*.
——. 1954-55: 24-25; 1955-56: 12. Report on file in M.G.M. Museum, Raipur.
——. 1955. "Sirpur men Upalabdha Prācīn Avaśeṣ". "Ancient ruins found at Sirpur". Hindi. *Shukla Abhinandan Grantha*. 184-91.
——. 1955-56."Kurud Plates of Narendra, Year 24." *EI* 31: 263-68.
——. 1955-56. "The Buddhist Bronzes from Sirpur". *BPWM* 5: 1-11.
——. 1955-56. "Senākapāṭ Inscription of the Time of Śivagupta Bālārjuna *EI* 31: 31-36; "Sirpur Inscription of the time of Bālārjuna". *Ibid.*, 197-98.
——. 1956."Bauddha Saṁskriti Ki Jhalak". "Glimpse of Buddhist Culture". In Hindi. *Pragati*.
——. 1956. "A Chinese Coin from Sirpur" *JNSI* 18: 64-66.
——. 1955-57. "Some Buddhist Bronzes from Sirpur, Madhya Pradesh". *BPWM* 5: 1-17.
——. 1957. "A New Copperplate grant from Chhattisgarh". *IHQ* 33: 84-85.
——. 1960. *Sirpur and Rājim temples*. Heritage of Indian Art Series, Vol. 2. Bombay: Bhulābhāi Memorial Institute.
Donaldson, Thomas Eugene. 1985. *Hindu Temple Art of Orissa*. 2 vols. Leiden: E.J. Brill.
——. 2001. *Iconography of the Buddhist Culture of Orissa*. 2 vols. Indira Gandhi National Center for Arts, New Delhi.
——. 2002. *Tantra and Śākta Art of Orissa*. Delhi: D.K. Printworld.
Dowson, John. 1961. *A Classical Dictionary of Hindu Mythology and Religion, Geography, History and Literature*. 10th Ed., London: Routledge and Kegan Paul.
Dube, S.C. 1947. *Field Songs of Chhattisgarh*. Lucknow: The Universal Publishers.
Dubost, Paul Martin. 1997. *Ganeśa*. Mumbai: Project for Indian Cultural Studies.
Duffield, Holly Gene. 1968. Ed., *Problems in Criticism of the Arts*. San Francisco: Chandler Publishing Company.
Dufrenne, Mikel. 1979. *Main Trends in Aesthetics and the Sciences of Art*. New York: Holmes and Meier.
Dulaure, J.A. 1933. *The Gods of Generation*. New York: The Panurge Press.
Dumont, Louis. 1966/1980. *Homo Hierarchicus*. Trans., by Weiden Feld, Chicago: the University of Chicago Press.
Dumont, P.E. 1957. "A Note on Taittirīya Saṁhitā 5.2.8.5 and Śatapatha Brāhmaṇa 7.5.1.1", *S.K. Belvalkar Felicitation Volume*: 15-18.
Duvignaud, Jean. 1967/72. *The Sociology of Art*. Trans., by Timothy Wilson, New York: Harper and Row.
Dye, Joseph M. 1980. *Ways to Śiva: Life and Ritual in Hindu India*. Philadelphia Museum of Art.
Eagleton, Terry. 1978. *Criticism and Ideology. A Study in Marxist Literary Theory*. London: Verso.
Eco, Umberto. 1976. *A Theory of Semiotics*. London: Indiana University Press.
——. 1985. "Towards a New Middle Ages". In Blonsky, ed., *On Signs*: 488-504.
Ehrenzwrig, Anton. 1976. "Unconscious Scanning and Dedifferentiation in Artistic Perception". In Rothenberg and Hausman, ed., *The Creativity Question*: 149-53.
Eliade, Mircea. 1959. "Methodological Remarks on the Study of Religious Symbolism". In *Essays in Methodology*, ed., Mircea Eliade and J.M. Kitagawa. Chicago: 86-107.
——. 1959. *The Sacred and the Profane: The Nature of Religion*. New York: Harcourt, Brace & World.
Eliot, Sir Charles. 1921. *Hinduism and Buddhism*. 3 vols.
Eliot, T.S. "Hollow men", *Collected Poems*. 1909-35/1936, New York: Harcourt, Brace and Company.
Elwin, Verrier. 1940/1986. *The Baigā*. London: John Murray. Reprint. Delhi: Gian Publishing House.
——. 1946. *Folksongs of Chhattisgarh*. London: Oxford University Press.

——. 1947/1992. Reprint. *The Muriā and their Ghoṭul.* Bombay. Oxford University Press.
——. 1949/1991. *Myths of Middle India.* Oxford University Press. Reprint. Bhopal: Vanya Prakashan, 1991.
——. 1961. *When the World was Young: Folk Tales from India's Hills and Forests. Delhi:* Publication Division, Govt. of India, Reprint: Vanya Prakashan.
——. 1950. *Bonḍo Highlands.* London: Oxford University Press.
——. 1951. *Tribal Art of Middle India.* Delhi: Oxford University Press.
——. 1954. *Tribal Myths of Orissa.* London: Oxford University Press.
Evola, J. 1956. "Oriental and Mediterranean. Ancient Erotic Symbolism." *EAW* 7.2:156-61.
Farquhar, J.N. 1966. *An Outline of the Religious Literature of India.* Delhi: Motilal Banarsidass.
Fairservis, W.A., Jr. 1971. *The Roots of Ancient India, Archaeology and Early Indian Civilization.* New York: Macmillan. 2nd rev. ed. Chicago and London: University of Chicago Press, 1975.
Fergusson, James and James Burgess. 1880. *The Cave Temples of India.* London: W.H. Allen. Reprint, Delhi: Oriental Books Corporation, 1969.
Fischer, Ernst. 1963. *The Necessity of Art. A Marxist Approach.* Harmondsworth: Penguin Books.
Fiske, John. 1873. *Myths and Myth Makers.* Boston:James R. Osgood and Company.
Fleet, John Faithfull. 1888. *Inscriptions of the Early Gupta Kings and Their Successors. C11* 3. Calcutta: Superintendent, Government Printing. Reprint, Varanasi: Indological Book House, 1963.
——. 1894-95. "Records of the Soṁavaṁśi Kings of Kaṭak". *EI* 3: 323-59.
——. 1898-99. "Yenneri Rock Inscription of the time of Pulakeśin II." *EI* 5: 6-9.
Flueckiger, Toyee Burkhalter. 1996. *Gendre and Genree in the Folklore of Middle India.* Ithaca: Cornell University Press.
Foucault, Michael. 1966. *Les Mots et les choses*, Paris: Gallimard. Bibliotheque des Sciences Humaines. English translation, *The Order of Things. An Archaeology of the Human Sciences.* New York: Random House, 1973.
Fowler, Roger. 1973. Ed., *A Dictionary of Modern Critical Terms.* London: Routledge and Kegan Paul.
Fraser, Douglas. 1966. Ed., *The Many Faces of Primitive Art.* New Jersey: Prentice Hall.
Frazer, James George.1890. *The Golden Bough.* Abridged and Revised by T. H. Gaster as *the New Golden Bough.* New York: The New American Library, 1959.
Frazer, R.W. 1951. "Śaivism", in *Encyclopaedia* of *Religion and Ethics.* Ed., J. Hastings. New York: 91-96.
Freud, Sigmund. 1900. *Die Traumdeutung*, 7th edition, Vienna: F. Deuticke, 1945. *The Interpretation of Dreams.* Trans., James Strachey, New York: Avon Books, 1965.
Fromm, Erich. 1951. *The Forgotten Language.* New York: Grove Press.
Gadamer, Hans George. 1964. *Aesthetik and Hermeneutik.* Trans., P.E. Linge. *Philosophical Hermeneutics.* Berkeley, California: University of California Press.
Gairola, C.K. 1954. "Evolution du Pūrṇa Ghaṭa (Vase de L' Abondance) dans L'Inde et L'Inde Exterieure". *ARA*: 209-26.
Galton, Francis. 1976. "Genius as Inherited". In Rottenberg and Hausman, ed., *The Creativity Question.*: 42-48.
Ganguly, Dilip Kumar. 1975. *Historical Geography and Dynastic History of Orissa, Up to the Rise of the Imperial Gaṅgas.* Calcutta: Punthi Pustak.
Ganguly, M.M. 1912. *Orissa and Her Remains – Ancient and Medieval.* Calcutta: Thacker, Spink & Co.
Ganguly, O.C. 1920. "A Note on Kīrtīmukha; Being the Life History of an Indian Architectural Motif." *Rūpam* 1: 11-19.
——. 1925. "The Mithuna in Indian Art." *Rūpam* 25. 22/23: 54-61.
Gaston, Anne Marie. 1982. *Śiva in Dance, Myth and Iconography.* Delhi: Oxford University Press.
Gaur, R.C. 1983. *Excavation at Atrañjikherā. Early Civilization of the Upper Gaṅgā Basin.* Delhi: Motilal Banarsidass.
Getty, Alice. 1936. *Gaṇeśa: A Monograph on the Elephant Faced God.* Oxford: Oxford University Press.
Ghosh, Ajit. 1931-33. *NS* 44: 309.
Ghosh, A. 1955. "Sirpur", in *IAR*: 24-26.
——. 1956. "Sirpur", in *IAR*: 26-27.

Goetz, H. 1943/44. "A Dynamic Theory of Indian Art History". *BMPGB* I.
——. 1959. "Imperial Rome and the Genesis of Classical Indian Art." *EAW* 10: 153-82, 261-68.
——. 1963. "The Gupta School". *Encyclopaedia of World Art* 7. McGraw Hill: 248-68, pls. 133-42.
Goldwater, Robert. 1967. *Primitivism in Modern Art*. New York: Random House.
Gombrich, Ernst H. 1960. *Art and Illusion: A Study in the Psychology of Pictorial Representation*. New Jersey: Princeton University Press.
——. 1963. *Meditations on a Hobby Horse, and Other Essays on the Theory of Art*. London: Phaidon Press.
——. 1966. *Norms and Forms*. London: Phaidon Press.
——. 1986. *The Art and Architecture of the Indian Subcontinent*. Pelican History of Art. Harmondsworth: Penguin Books.
Gonda, Jan. 1939. "The Meaning of the Word Alaṁkāra." In *A Volume of Eastern and Western Studies, Presented to F.W. Thomas, NIA Extra Series I*, Ed. S.M. Katre and P.K. Gode. Bombay: Karnatak Publishing House.
——. 1965. *Change and Continuity in Indian Religion*: London.
——. 1970. *Viṣṇuism and Śaivaism. A Comparison*. London: University of London, Athlone Press.
——. 1974. *The Dual Deities in the Religion of the Veda*. Amsterdam: North Holland Publishing Company.
——. 1977. *Medieval Religious Literature in Sanskrit. A History of Indian Literature*, Vol. I. Wiesbaden.
Gorakshkar, Sadashiv. 1982. "The Pārel Mahādeva Reassessed and Two Newly Discovered Images from Pārel". *LK* 20: 15-24.
——. 1967. *A History of the Imperial Guptas*. Allahabad: Central Book Depot.
Goyal, Shriram. 1988. *Gupta aur Vākāṭaka Sāmrājyon kā Itihāsa*. History of Gupta and Vākāṭaka Dynasty. Hindi. Meerut/Jodhpur: Kusumanjali Prakashan.
Gras, Vernon W. 1973. *European Literary Theory and Practice*. New York: Delta Publishing Co.
Griffiths, John. 1896-97. *The Paintings in the Buddhist Cave Temples of Ajantā, Khāndesh, India*. 2 vols. London: W. Griggs.
Grigson, Wilfred Vernon. 1938/1949. *The Māriā Goṇḍs of Bastar*. London:Oxford University Press.
Grover, Satish. 1980. *The Architecture of India. Buddhist and Hindu*. Vol. 1. New Delhi: Vikas.
Gubernatis, A. de. 1872. *Zoological Mythology*. 2 vols. London: Trubner & Co.; in public domain in USA.
Guirand, Felix. 1959. Ed., *Larousse Encyclopaedia of Mythology*. Trans. from French by Auge et al. 5th Impression. 1972. Paris: The Libraire Larousse.
Gupta, Anand Swarup. 1975. "Eulogy of Paśupati Śiva." *Purāṇa* 17: 100-05.
Gupta, Chandrasekhar. 1971. "Vidarbha Ki Prācīn Śilpakalā" "The Ancient Art of Vidarbha". In *Purāṇa*. In Hindi. Nagpur: Viśva Hindi Sāhitya Sammelan.
——. 1974. "Mānḍhal Se Prāpta Mūrtiyān" "Images found at Mānḍhal". In *Purāṇa*. Hindi.
——. 1992. "Pavnār under the Vākāṭakas". In Shastri, ed., *the Age of the Vākāṭakas*: 119-53.
——. 2000. "Identity of the Unique Sculpture from Tala". In Nigam, ed., *Riddle* 117-20.
Gupta, Parmanand. 1973. *Geography of Ancient Indian Inscriptions (up to 650 A.D.)*. New Delhi: D.K. Publishing House.
Gupta, Parameshwari Lal. 1974-79. *The Imperial Guptas*. 2 vols. Varanasi: Vishwavidyalaya Prakashan.
Gupta, Pyarelal. 1923. *Bilāspur Vaibhav*. Hindi. Bilaspur District Gazetter. Bilaspur, Chhattisgarh Gaurav Pracārak Maṇḍalī.
——. 1973. *Prācīn Chhattisgarh*. In Hindi. Raipur: Ravishankar Vishwavidyalaya.
Gupta, Shakti H. 1971. *Plant Myths and Traditions in India*. Leiden: E.J. Brill.
Gupta, S.P. 1985. Ed., *Kuśāṇa Sculptures from Sānghol: A Recent Discovery*. Vol. 1. New Delhi: National Museum.
Gupta, Y.R. 1927-28. "Riḍḍhapur Plates of Bhavadattavarman." *EI* 19: 100-04.
Gupte, Ramesh Shankar and B.D. Mahajan. 1962. *Ajantā, Ellorā and Auraṅgābād Caves*. Bombay: D.B. Taraporevala Sons and Co.
Halbfass, Wilhelm. 1988. *India and Europe. An Essay in Understanding*. New York: University of New York Press.
Haldane, John. 1995. "Modernism & Post Modernism", in Cooper, ed., *Companion to Aesthetics*, 288-93.

——. 1995. "Plotinus". In Cooper, *ibid.*, 335-36.

Halemann, R.J. 1953. "The Art object in Indian Aesthetics". *JAAC* 12.

Handa, Devendra. 1989. Ed. *Ajaya-Śrī*. Delhi: Sundeep Prakashan.

Hara, Minoru. 1958. "Nakulīśa Pāśupata Darśanam", in *IIJ* 11: 8-32.

Harle, James C. 1974. "Late Kuśāṇa, Early Gupta: A Reverse Approach." In *SAA*. Ed., Norman Hammond. New Jersey: Noyer Press.

——. 1974. *Gupta Sculpture*. Oxford: Clarendon Press.

——. 1977. "The Post-Gupta Style in Indian Temple Architecture and Sculpture." *JRSEAMC*, 570-89.

Harper, Katherine Anne and Robert L. Brown. 2002. *The Roots of Tantra*. Albany: State University of New York Press.

Harris, Theodore L. and Richard E. Hodges Ed. 1981. *A Dictionary of Reading and Related Terms*. Newark: International Reading Association.

Heesterman, J.C. 1962. "Vrātya and Sacrifice". *IIJ* 6: 1-37.

——. 1964. "Brāhmin, Ritual and Renouncer: *WZKSO* 8: 1-31.

——. 1983. "Other Folk's Fire". Staal, ed., *Agni* 2: 76-94.

Hauser, Arnold. 1969. *The Philosophy of Art History*. Cleveland: The World Publishing Company.

Hazra, R.C. 1940. *Studies in the Purāṇic Records on Hindu Rites and Customs*. Dacca. 2nd ed. Delhi: 1975.

Heidegger, Martin. 1927. *Being and Time*. New York: Harper.

——. 1975. *Poetry, Language and Thought*. New York: Harper Colophon Books.

Heimann, Betty. 1964. *Facets of Indian Thought*. London: George Allen and Unwin Ltd.

Hegel, E.W.F. 1835-38. *Hegel's Aesthetics: Lectures on Fine Art*. 2 vols. Berlin. Trans. by T. M. Knox, Oxford: Oxford University Press, 1975.

Higgins, Kathleen Mary. 1995. "Psychoanalysis and Art". In Cooper, ed., *A Companion to Aesthetics*.

Hillebrandt, Alfred. 1927. *Vedische Mythologie. Vedic Mythology*. 2 vols. Breslan. Trans. from German by S.R. Sharma. Delhi: Motilal Banarsidass, 1980-81.

Heraclitus. N.D. *Fragment 51*, in Diels, Die Fragmene der Vrsokratikar, 5th edition, Trans, by Charles M. Bakewell, *Source book in Ancient Philosophy*, New York: Charles Scribner's Sons, 1907:81.

Hiralal, Rai Bahadur. 1907-08. "Inscriptions from the Bastar State. The Kākaṭīya Inscriptions" *EI* 9:160-66; "Kānpur Plates of Pampārājadeva". 166-70; "Sihāvā stone Inscription of Karṇarāja: the Śaka Year 1114": 182-87; "Sāraṅgarh Copperplates of Mahāsudeva." 281-85; Āraṅg Copperplates of Bhīmaṣena". Gupta Samvat 282": 342-45.

——. 1908. A Visit to Ramtek. In *IA* 37:202-08.

——. 1911-12. "Sirpur Stone Inscription of the Time of Mahāśivagupta". *EI* 11: 184-201.

——. 1916/1932. *Descriptive Lists of Inscriptions in the Central Provinces and Berār*. Nagpur: Government Press.

——. 1933. "The Extent and Capital of Dakṣiṇa Kośala". *IA* 62: 161-66.

——. 1938. *Madhya Pradeśa ka Itihāsa*. In Hindi. *History of Madhya Pradesh*.

Hoek, A.W. Van Den, D.H.A. Kolff and M.S. Oort. 1992. Ed., *Ritual, State and History in South Asia. Essays in Honour of J.C. Heesterman*, Leiden: E.J. Brill.

Hofstadter, Albert and Richard Kuhns. 1964. *Philosophies of Art and Beauty*. New York: The Modern Library.

Holly, Michael Ann. 1984. *Panofsky and the Foundations of Art History*. Ithaca and London: Cornell University Press.

Hopkins, Edward Washburn. 1915. *Epic Mythology*. Strassburg: K.J. Trubner. Reprint, Varanasi: Indological Book House, 1968.

Howard, A.F. 1986. *The Imagery of Cosmological Buddha*. Leiden: Brill Academic Publishers.

Hultzsch, E. 1901-02. "Balodā Plates of Tivaradeva." *EI* 7: 102-05.

——. 1907-08. "Tirumālāi Rock Inscription of Rājendra Cola I, Year 13". *EI* 9: 229-33.

——. 1925-26. "Kondaguru Grant of Indravarman". *EI* 18:2-5.

Huntington, Susan L. 1985. *The Art of Ancient India*. New York: Weather Hill.

Hyderabad Archaeological Series. 1915. Calcutta: Nizam Government.

IDC Medicine Slavonic Microfiche Series, Switzerland.

I-Ching. 1986. *Chinese Monks in India.* Trans. and ed. by Latika Lahiri. Delhi: Motilal Banarsidass.

Indira Kalā Sangeet Viśvavidyālaya, Khairāgarh & Directorate of Culture, Archaeology & Museums. *KV* 2006-07. Vol. 6.

Ingalls, Daniel H.H. 1962. "Cynics and Pāśupatas; The Seeking of Dishonour." *HTR* 55: 281-98.

——. 1976. "Kālidāsa and the Attitudes of the Golden Age". *Journal of the Americal Oriental Society (JAOS) 96: 15-26.*

Jain, B.C. 1954. "Some New Repoussé Gold Coins from Chāndā District". *JNSI* 16: 215-18.

——. 1954-55. "Sirpur Gandheśvara Temple Pillar Inscription of Ambullaka." *EI* 28: 219-22.

——. 1955-56. "Adhabhāra Plates of Mahānannarāja." *EI* 31:219-22.

——. 1957. *Inventory of the Hoards and Finds of Coins and Seals from Madhya Pradesh* (Non-Muhammedan), *Numismatic Note and Monograph Series, No. 6,* Numismatic Society of India.

——. 1960. *Pāṣāṇ Pratimāen,* Stone Sculptures. In Hindi. Raipur: M.G.M. Museum.

——. 1960. Catalogue of the Mahānt Ghāsīdās Museum, Raipur. 3 parts.

——. 1961. "Copperplate Inscription of Kākaṭīya Rājapāladeva". *OHRJ.* 10.2: 57-60.

——. 1961. 2005 *Utkīrṇa Lekh.* Inscribed Writings. In Hindi. Raipur: Mahānt Ghāsidas Smārak Saṅgrahālaya, Directorate of Archaeology and Museums, Chhattisgarh, Enlarged Edition, 2005.

——. 1962. "Malhār Plates of Pravararāja; Year 3". *IHQ* 37: 261-66.

——. 1963. "Sirpur Inscription of Ācārya Buddhaghoṣa, Year 3". *EI* 38/2: 59-62.

——. 1966. "Hitherto Unknown Repoussé coins of Kramāditya". *JNSI* 22: 184.

——. 1977. "Mahāsamund Plates of Sudevarāja, Year 3". *PRP* 5.1: 41-47; "An important Copperplate Inscription from Malhār, year 57."*Ibid.,* 54-56.

Jaiswal, K.P. 1933. "Vikramkhol Inscription". *IA* 1962: 58-60.

Jamkhedkar, A.P. 1981. "Maharashtra Temple Architecture. An Assessment of Some Problems". In 1980 *Proceedings of the Seminar on Temple Art and Architecture.* Ed., K.K.H. Venkatachari. Bombay: 81-86.

——. 1985. "Narrative Sculptures from Paunār: A Reappraisal". In *Indian Epigraphy-Its Bearing on the History of Art.* Ed., F. Asher and G. Ghai. Delhi: 83-86.

——. 1985. "Buddhist Bronzes from Rāmṭek." *LK* 22: 13-20.

——. 1987. "A Newly Discovered Temple at Rāmṭek, District Nagpur", in *Kusumāñjali. Śivarāmamūrti Commemoration Volume.* Ed., M.S. Nagaraja Rao. Vol. 2. Delhi: Agam Kala Prakashan,113-68.

——. 1988. "The Buddha in Bronze: Phophnār and Rāmṭek", in *The Great Tradition: Indian Bronze Masterpieces.* Ed., K. Khandalawala: 46-53.

——. 1988. "Beginnings of North Indian Temple Architecture, Early Vidarbha Style, c.AD 350-500: Vākāṭaka (Main Branch)". *Encyclopedia of Indian Temple Architecture.*

——. 1991."Vākāṭaka Sculpture", in *The Art of Ajantā.* Vol. 1. New Delhi: Books and Books, 194-212.

——. "Symbols, Images and Rituals of the Mother in Vākāṭaka Period". In *LK*: 23-40.

——. 1991. "The Vākāṭaka Area and Gupta Sculpture". In K. Khandalawala. Ed., *The Golden Age, Gupta Art-Empire, Province and Influence.* Bombay: 85-92.

——. 1992. "Discovery of Vākāṭaka Temples at Rāmṭek". In Shastri, ed. *Age of the Vākāṭakas.* 155-64.

——. 1993. "Iconography of Viṣṇu in Maharashtra". In *Colloquium on Viṣṇu in Art, Thought and Literature.* Hyderabad: Birla Archaeological and Cultural Research Institute, Hyderabad.

Jameson, Frederic. 1991. *Postmodernism, or The Cultural Logic of Late Capitalism.* Durham: Duke University Press.

Janssen, F.H.P.M. 1993. "On the Origin and Development of the so-called Lajjā Gaurī". In A.J. Bail and G.J.F. Mevisson. Ed., *SAA* 1991. Stuttgart: 457-72.

Jash, Pranavananda. 1964. *History of Śaivism.* Calcutta: Roy and Choudhary.

Jayakar, Pupul. 1990. *The Earth Mother.* San Francisco, Harper & Row.

Jefferson, Ann and David Robbey. 1982. Ed., *Modern Literary Theory. A Comparative Introduction.* New Jersey: Barnes and Noble.

Jenkins, Richard. 1825. "Account of Ancient Hindu Remains in Chattisgher (sic)". *ASR* 15: 501-19.

Jha, V.D. 1989. *Bastar Kā Mūrtiśilpa. The Sculpture of Bastar.* In Hindi. Bhopal: Abhyudaya Prakashan.

James, William. 1961. *The Varieties of Religious Experience.* New York: Collier Books.

Joshi, J.P. and A.K. Sharma. 2000. "Excavation at Mānsar". District Nagpur, Maharashtra, *Purātatva* 30: 127-30. New Delhi: Indian Archaeological Society.

——. 2005. "Mānsar Excavations. 1998-2004: The Discovery of Prabarapura". *Purāmanthana* 3: 1-26.

Joshi, N.P. 1969. "A Unique Figure of Śiva from Musānagar." In the *BMAUP* 3: 25 ff.

——. 1984. "Early Forms of Śiva". In M.W. Meister. Ed., *Discourses on Śiva.* Bombay: 47-61.

Jung. Carl G. 1911/1967. *Symbols of Transformation.* Trans. by R.F.C. Hall. 2nd ed. Princeton University Press.

——. 1976. "On the Relation of Analytic Psychology to Poetic Art". In Rothenberg and Hausman, ed., *The Creativity Question*: 120-26.

Kalyān. 1933. V.S. 1990 *Śrī Śivāṅka.* In Hindi. Mathura: Shrikṛṣṇa Janma Saṁsthān.

——. 1950. V.S. 2006. *Hindu Saṁskṛti.* Hindi. Gorakhpur: Gītā Press.

Kane, P.V. 1930-62. *History of Dharmaśāstra.* 5 vols. 2nd ed. 1968-75 Poona: Government Oriental Series.

Kantisagar, Muni. 1953. *Khāṇḍharon kā Vaibhav,* (Grandeur of Ruins). In Hindi. Kashi: Bhāratīya Gyānapeeth.

Karapatri, Swami. 1941-42. *Siddhānta* 2. Varanasi: Karapātriji's Āshram.

Katare, S.L. 1955-56. "Sirpur Plates of Mahāsudevaraja, Year 7". *EI* 31: 103-08.

——. 1957. "Sirpur Gandheśvara Temple Inscription". *IHQ* 33: 229-34.

——. 1959. "Excavation at Sirpur." *IHQ* 35: 8.

Kaviraj, Gopinath. 1963. *Tantra O Āgama Śāstrer Digdarshan. A Guide to Tantra and Āgama texts.* In Bengali. Calcutta: Sanskrit College.

——. 1975. *Bhāratīya Sādhanār Dhārā.* The Course of Indian Spiritual Exertion. In Bengali. Calcutta: Sanskrit College.

——. *1981 Svasaṁvedana.* Self Understanding. In Bengali. 2 vols. Calcutta: Pashyanti Prakashan.

——. 1983. *Tāntrik Sādhanā O Siddhānta.* Tāntrik Practice and Theory. In Bengali. 2 vols. Burdwan: University of Burdwan.

——. 1984. *Aspects of Indian Thought.* Burdwan: The University of Burdwan.

——. 1990. "Liṅga Rahasya". In Kalyāṇ. *Śrī Śivāṅka,* Ed., Hanumanprasad Poddar: 472-77.

Keeble, Brian. 2005. *On the Nature and Significance of the Crafts. W.R. Lethaby, Edward Johnston, Anand Coormaraswamy.* London. Temenos Academy.

Keith, Arthur Berrierdale. 1925. The Religion and Philosophy of the Vedas and Upaniṣads. 2 vols. *Harvard Oriental Series* 31-32. Cambridge, Massachusetts.

——. 1917. "Indian Mythology." In *The Mythology of All Races.* Ed., Louis Herbert Gray, Vol. 6. I. New York: Cooper Square Publishers. Rev. 1964.

——. 1928. *A History of Sanskrit Literature.* Oxford. The Clarendon Press.

Khamari, Subash. 2008. "Multiplicity and Linkages. "The Study of Temples at Rāṇipur Jharial Complex, Orissa". In *Kośala* 1: 127-36.

Khan, Abdul Waheed. "Vākāṭaka Inscription in Cave 16 at Ajantā". *HAS* 14. Hyderabad: Govt of Andhra Pradesh.

Kielhorn, F. 1889. "Sirpur Stone Inscription of Śivagupta". *IA* 18: 179-81.

——. 1900-01. "Āihole Inscription of Pulakeśin II: Śaka-Samvat 556". *EI* 6: 1-12; "Kanur Spurious Inscription of Amoghavarṣa 1, Śaka Samvat 782". *Ibid.,* 25-38; "Two Grants of Daṇḍimahādevī". *Ibid.,* 133-42.

——. 1905. "Buddhist Inscription of Bhavadeva Raṇakeśarin." *JRASGBI*: 617-33.

——. 1907-08. "Tamil Praśasti of Rājendra Cola" in *EI* 9: 22 Iff; "Bālāghaṭ Copperplates of Pṛthvīṣeṇa II", in *ibid.,* 267 ff.

——. "Ellora Daśavatāra inscription of Rāṣṭrakūṭa king Dantidūrga in *ASIPRWI* 6:92.

——. "Aḍbhār Copperplate of Pāṇḍuvaṁśi King Nannadeva", in *EI* 31: 219 ff.
Kirk, G.S. 1970. *Myth*. London: Cambridge University Press.
Klein, Matthew. 1985. "And Above All, Please Do Not Disturb". In Marshall Blonsky, ed., *On Signs*: 481-87.
Kleinbauer, W. Eugene. 1971. *Modern Perspectives in Western Art History*. New York: Holt, Rinehart and Winston.
Koestler, Arthur. 1976. "Biosociation in Creation". In Rothenberg and Hausman, ed., *The Creativity Question*: 108-13.
Konow, Sten. 1907-08. "Khariār Copperplates of Mahāsudeva." *EI*. 9: 170-74; "Bālāghāṭ Plates of Prithivīṣeṇa II". *Ibid*., 267-71; "Orissa Plates of Vidyādharbhañjadeva". *Ibid*., 271-77.
——. 1915-16. "Talegaon Copperplates of Krishnarāja. Śaka 690". *EI* 13: 275-82.
Kośala. 2008-2012. *Journal of the Directorate of Culture and Archaeology*, Govt. of Chhattisgarh, Vols. 1-5, Raipur.
Kosambi, Damodar Dharmanand. 1962/83. *Myth and Reality*. Reprint, Bombay: Popular Prakashan.
——. 1976. *The Culture and Civilisation of Ancient India, a Historical Outline*. New Delhi: Vikas.
Kramrisch, Stella. 1924. "The Viṣṇudharmottaram: A Treatise on Indian Painting." *CR*, 3rd series 10. 2: 331-86.
——. 1931. Die figurale Plastik der Guptazeit. Wiener Beitrāgi zur kunst-und Kulturgeschicpic Asiens V: 15-39.
——. 1932. "Classical and Medieval Indian Art." *Mālavīya Commemoration Volume*. Varanasi: Banaras Hindu University.
——. 1933. *Indian Sculpture*. The Heritage of India Series. Calcutta: YMCA Publishing House; London: Oxford University Press.
——. 1946. *The Hindu Temple*. 2 vols. Calcutta: University of Calcutta.
——. 1973. "Śiva the Archer". *Deutsche Indologentagung*. Wiesbaden: 140-50.
——. 1981. *Manifestations of Śiva*. Philadelphia: Philadelphia Museum of Art.
——. 1981. *The Presence of Śiva*. Princeton, N.J.: Princeton University Press.
——. 1983. "Figural Sculpture of the Gupta period." In *Exploring India's Sacred Art. Selected Writings of Stella Kramrisch*. Ed., Barbara Stoler Miller. Philadelphia: University of Pennsylvania Press.
Krishnamacharlu, C.R. 1931-32. "The Nala Inscription at Poḍāgaḍh; Year 12" *EI* 21: 153-57.
Kristeva, Julia. 1977. *Laura Marcus, Polylogue*. Paris, Editions du Seuil. Part Trans. Thomas Gora, A. Jardine and L. Roudiez, as *Desire in Language*. Oxford: Basil Blackwell, 1984.
——. 1985. "Speaking Subject". In Blonsky, Ed., *On Signs*: 210-20.
Kuanr, D.C. 1975. State Editor, *Gazetteer of India, Orissa, Sundergarh*. Chief Editor, N. Senapati, Cuttack.
——. 1980. State Editor, *Orissa District Gazetteers, Kālāhānḍi*, Chief Editor, N. Senapati, Cuttack.
Kubler, George.1962. *The Shape of Time*. London:Yale University Press.
Kuiper, F.B.J. 1978. *Varuṇa and Vidūṣaka*. North Holland Publishing Company.
——. 1983. *Ancient Indian Cosmogony*. New Delhi: Vikas Publishing House.
——. 1975. "The Basic Concept of Vedic Religion". *History of Religions*. 15. 2: 107-20.
Kung, Ta-chung. 1981. *Long-Men Shih-K'u-I-Shu (The Grotto Art of Longmen)*. Shanghai: Jen-Min-Ch'-upan-Shi.
Lacan, Jacques. 1985. "Sign, Symbol, Imaginings". In Blonsky, ed., *Signs*: 203-9.
Laechuli, Samuel. 1980. *Religion and Art in Conflict*. Philadelphia: Fortress Press.
Lahiri, A.N. 1955-56. "Kauvātāl Plates of Sudeva, Year 7". *EI* 31: 314-16.
Langer, Susanne K. 1952. *Feeling and Form*. New York: Charles Scribner's Sons.
——. 1958. Ed., *Reflections on Art. A Source Book of Writings by Artists, Critics and Philosophers*, Baltimore, The Johns Hopkins Press.
——. 1979. *Philosophy in a New Key*. Cambridge: Harvard University Press.
Lévi-Strauss, Claude. 1958. "The Structural Study of Myth". In T.A. Sebeok, ed., *Myth: A Symposium*. Bloomington: 81-106.
——. 1975. *The Raw and the Cooked. Introduction to a Science of Mythology*. New York: Harper & Row.
——. 1978. *Myth and Meaning*. Indian Reprint, 2003. University of Toronto Press.

Lévi, Sylvain. 1966. *La doctrine du sacrifice dans les Brāhmaṇas*. 2nd ed. Paris: Bibliotheque de L'Ecole des Hautes Études. Sciences Religieuses 73.

Liẹbert, Gosta. 1986. *Iconographic Dictionary of the Indian Religions*. Śrī Satguru Publications.

Lippe, Aschwin de. 1978. *Indian Medieval Sculpture*. Amsterdam: North Holland Publishing Company.

Long, J.G. 1970. *Visions of Terror and Bliss*. Ph.D. Dissertation, University of Chicago.

——. 1972. "Śiva as Promulgator of Traditional Learning and Patron Deity of the Fine Arts." *ABORI* 52: 67-80.

——. 1975."Life out of Death: A Structural Analysis of the Myth of the Churning of the Ocean of Milk." in Smith, ed., *Hinduism: New Essays*.

Longhurst, A.H. 1909-10. "Ancient Brick Temples in the Central Provinces" *ASIAR* 9: 11-17.

Lorenzen, David N. 1972. *The Kāpālikas and Kālāmukhas. Two Lost Śaivite Sects*. Delhi: Thomson Press.

Luders, Heinrich. 1957, 1959. *Varuṇa*. 2 vols. Gottingen: Vandenhoech and Ruprecht.

Macdonnell, Arthur Anthony. 1897. *Vedic Mythology*. Grundriss der Indo-Arischen Philologie und Altertumskund. Strasbourg. Repr, Varanasi: Indological Book House, 1963.

——. 1912. With Arthur Berrierdale Keith. *Vedic Index of Names and Subjects*. 2 vols. London: John Murray Reprint. Delhi. Motilal Banarsidass, 1982.

Machek, V. 1954. "Origin of the Gods, Rudra and Pūṣan". *Art* 22: 544-62.

Mahajan, Malati. 2000. *Chhattisgarh: A Study in the Culture and Historiography from Placenames in Inscriptions*. Delhi. Sharada Publishing House.

Mahanti, B. 1971. State Ed. *Gazetteers of India, Orissa, Sambalpur*: Chief Ed. N. Senapati. Cuttack.

Mahapatra, Kedarnath. 1971. "Po-lo-mo-lo-ki-li of Yuan Chwang's Accounts". In *New Aspects of the History of Orissa*. Ed., N.K. Sahu: 65-71.

Mahapatra, L.K. 2005. *People and Cultural Traditions of Orissa*. New Age Publications.

——. 1987. "Exprincely States of Orissa: Mayūrbhañj, Konjhar and Bonāi", in *Tribal Politics & State Systems in Pre-colonial Eastern & North-Eastern India*. 1-50. Kolkata: Centre for Studies in Social Science, with K.P. Bagchi & Co.

Maitra, Akshaya Kumar. 1921. "The River Goddess Gaṅgā", *Rūpam* 6:2-10.

Majumdar, R.C. 1951-68. Ed., Bhāratīya Vidyā Bhavan. Vols. on the *History and Culture of the Indian People*. Bombay: *The Vedic Age* (Vol.1), 1951; *The Classical Age* (Vol. 3), 1954; *The Age of Imperial Kanauj* (Vol. 4), 1964; *The Struggle for Empire* (Vol. 5), 1966; *The Age of Imperial Unity* (Vol. 6), 1968.

Majumdar, Ramesh Chandra and Anant Sadashiv Altekar. 1967. Ed., *The Vākāṭaka Gupta Age (circa 200-550 A.D.)*. Delhi: Motilal Banarsidass.

Mallaiya, N.V. 1942. "Modern Critics and Ancient Texts on the Aesthetic Value of Hindu Images". *JISOA* 10: 191-201.

——. 1949. *Studies in Sanskrit Texts on Temple Architecture*. Ānnāmālāinagar: Ānnāmālāi University.

Mallmann, Marie-Therese de. 1963. *Les Enseignements Iconographiques de L'Agni-Purāṇa. Annales de Musée Guimet AMG*, Vol. 67. Paris: Presses Universitaires de France.

——. 1975. *Introduction a L'iconographie de Tantrism Bouddique*. Paris: Bibliothique du Centre de Recherches sun L'Asia Centrale et Haute Asie.

Marg. 1969. Vol. 22.2. Has separate title *Bhitargāon*.

Margolis, Joseph. 965. *The Language of Art and Art Criticism. Analytic Questions in Aesthetics*. Detroit: Wayne State University Press.

Margolis, Joseph and Paul Ricoeur. 1981. *Hermeneutics and the Human Sciences*. Trans. and Ed., John B. Thompson. Cambridge: Cambridge University Press.

Marshall, John et al. 1927. *The Bāgh Caves in the Gwalior State*. India Society, London and the Department of Archaeology, Gwalior. Reprint, Delhi: Delhi Printers' Prakashan, 1978.

Marshall, John, Alfred Foucher and N.G. Majumdar. 3 vols. 1940. *The Monuments of Sanchi*. 3 vols. Calcutta: Manager of Publications.

Marx, Karl. 1970. *The German Ideology*. Ed., C.J. Arthur. New York: International Publisher.

Masson, J.L. and M.V. Patwardhan. 1969. *Śāntarasa and Abhinavagupta's Philosophy of Aesthetics.* Bhandarkar Oriental Series, 9. Poona: Bhandarkar Oriental Reserch Institute.

——. 1970. *Aesthetic Rapture. The Rasādhyāya of the Nāṭyaśāstra.* 2 vols. Poona: Deccan College.

Matejka, Ladislav and Irwin R. Titunik. 1984. Ed., *Semiotics of Art.* Cambridge: The MIT Press.

Mayrhofer, M. 1953, 1963,1976. *Concise Etymological Sanskrit Dictionary.* 3 vols. Heidelberg.

——. 1953. "Der Gottesname Rudra". *ZDMG* 103: 140-50.

Maxwell, Thomas S. 1973. "Transformational Aspects of Hindu Myth and Iconology: Viśvarūpa," *AARP* 4: 59-79.

——. 1975. "The Deogarh Viśvarūpa: A Structural Analysis," *Ibid.* 8: 10 ff.

——. 1982. "The Five Aspects of Śiva in Theory, Iconography and Architecture". In *AI* 25: 41-57.

——. 1983. "The Evidence for a Viśvarūpa Iconographic Tradition in Western India, 6th-9th centuries AD" *AA* 44: 213-34.

——. 1988. *Viśvarūpa.* Delhi: Oxford University South Asian Studies Series.

——. 1997. *The Gods of Asia.* Delhi: Oxford University Press.

Mcluhan, Marshall. 1962. *The Gutenberg Galaxy: The Making of Typographic Man.* Toronto: University of Toronto Press.

McCrindle, John Watson. 1901. *Ancient India as Described in Classical Literature.* Westminster: A. Constable.

Mehlis, George. 1958. "The Aesthetic Problem of Distance". In Langer, ed., *Reflections on Art:* 79-90.

Mehta, J.L. 1971. *The Philosophy of Martin Heidegger.* New York: Harper and Row.

——. 1976. *Martin Heidegger: The Way and the Vision.* Honolulu: University Press of Hawaii.

——. 1985. *India and the West. The Problem of Understanding.* Harvard University: Centre for the Study of World Religions.

——. 1990. *Philosophy and Religion. Essay in Interpretation.* New Delhi: Indian Council of Philosophical Research, in association with Munshiram Manoharlal.

Meister, Michael W. 1976. "Construction and Conception. Maṇḍapikā Shrines of Central India." *EAW* 26. 3.4: 409-18.

——. 1984. *Discourses on Śiva.* Ed., Bombay: Vakils, Feffer and Simons.

——. 1984. "Śiva's Forts in Central India: Temples of Dakṣiṇa Kośala", *ibid.*, 119-42.

Menon, Padmini. 1961. *Purāṇa Sandarbhakoṣa.* "Book of Purāṇic References". In Hindi. Kānpur: Grantham.

——. 2000. "Too Late to Tala", in Nigam, ed., *Riddle:* 82-88.

Merleau Ponty, Maurice. 1968. *The Visible and the Invisible.* Evanston: Northwestern University Press.

Meyerhoff, Hans. 1959. Ed., *The Philosophy of History in our Time.* New York: Doubleday.

Mirashi, V.V. 1933-34. "Ṭhākurdiyā Plates of Mahāpravararāja." *EI* 22: 15-23. "The Khāmked Plates of the Time of Pratāpaśīla". *Ibid.*, 93-96; "Tirodi Plates of Pravarasena II". *Ibid.*, 167-76; "An Unfinished Vākāṭaka Plate from Durg." *Ibid.*, 207-12.

——. 1934. "Malhār plates of Mahāśivagupta". *EI* 23: 113-22.

——. 1935. "Paṭṭan Plates of Pravarasena II." *EI* 23: 81-88.

——. 1935. With L.P. Pandey. "Malhār plates of Mahāśivagupta". *EI* 23:113-22.

——. 1937. "Pauni Stone Inscription of the Bhāra king Bhagadatta. *EI* 24: 11-14.

——. 1939. "Gold coins of Three Kings of the Nala Dynasty." *JNSI* 1: 29-35.

——. 1941. "Rājim Stone Inscription of the Nala King Vilāsatuṅga". *EI* 26: 49-58.

——. 1941. "The Coins of Kalacurīs". *JNSI* 3: 21-31.

——. 1941. Bāsim Plates of Vākāṭaka Vindhyaśakti". *EI* 26: 137-55.

——. 1941. "Vākāṭaka Inscription in Ajantā Cave 16". *HAS* 14: 1 ff.

——. 1942. "A Note on the Date of the Somavaṁśi Kings of Southern Kośala". *EI* 26: 227-30.

——. 1945. "Historical Data in Daṇḍin's Daśakumāracarita". *ABORI* 26:20 ff.

——. 1946-47. "Three Ancient Dynasties of Mahākośala." *BDCRI.* 7: 47-56.

——. 1947. "Vidarbha and Mahākośala". *JKHRS* 2: 1 ff.

——. 1947-48. With L.P. Pandey. "Lodhiā Plates of Mahāśivagupta." *EI* 27: 321-25.
——. 1949. "A Note on the Khairātāl Hoard of the Coins of Mahendrāditya". *JNSI* 11: 108 ff.
——. 1949. "A Note on the Tivarkhed Plates of Nannarāja." *IHQ* 25(2): 138-43.
——. 1954. "Pravarapura, an Ancient Capital of the Vākāṭakas". In *Sarūpa Bhāratī*. Dr. Lakshman Sarup Memorial Volume, Hosiārpur, 1-9. Reprinted in *Studies in Indology* 11:272-84.
——. 1955. "Madhya Pradesh kā Vākāṭaka Rājavaṁśa". "The History of the Vākāṭaka Dynasty in Madhya Pradesh". *Shukla Abhinandan Granth*: In Hindi 162-83.
——. 1955. *Inscriptions of the Kalacurī-Cedī Era. CII* 4.
——. 1955-56. Āraṅg. *EI* 33: 255-56.
——. 1957. "Vākāṭaka Pṛthvīṣeṇa, Suzerain of Vyāghra". *S.K. Belvalkar Felicitation Volume*: 286 ff.
——. 1957. *Vākāṭaka Nṛpati Ānityāmicā Kāla*. Vākāṭaka Kings and Their Times. Marathi. Nagpur University.
——. 1959-60. With D.C. Sircar. "Notes on Senākapāṭ Inscription." *EI* 33: 251.
——. 1960-62. *Studies in Indology*. 3 vols. Vidarbha Samshodhana Mandal.
——. 1963. *Inscriptions of the Vākāṭakas. CII* 5.
——. 1964. *Vākāṭaka Rājvaṁśakā Itihāsa tathā Abhilekha*. History and Inscriptions of the Vākāṭaka Dynasty. Trans. from Hindi into English by Ajay Mitra Shastri. Varanasi: Tārā Publications.
——. 1965. *Kalacurī Nareśa aur Unki Kalā. Kalacurī Kings and Their Art*. In Hindi: Bhopal: Madhya Pradesh Sāhitya Pariṣada.
——. 1965. "The Paṇḍava Dynasty of Mekala". *Indica*. Silver Jubilee volume of Indian Historical Research Institute. Bombay.
——. 1979. "The Date of Tivaradea", *JESI* 4: 1-5.
——. 1982. "The Date of Tivaradeva." *Indological Research Papers*, Nagpur: *VSMV* 1.
Mishra, B.N. 1984. "A Note on the So Called Buddhist Inscription on the Stone Slab from Malhār." Comments on S.K. Pandey's article. *PRP* 12: 115-18.
Mishra, Mahendra Kumar. 2002. *Visioning Folklore*. Bhubaneshwar: Lark Books.
Mishra, P.K. and J.K. Samal. 1997. *Comprehensive History and Culture of Orissa*. Vol. 1-4, New Delhi: Kaveri Books.
Mishra, R.N. 1981. "Sculptures in Dakṣiṇa Kośala. A Brief Survey of Stylistic Transformations, Chronology and Artisans". *Chhavi* 2 (Rai Krishnadas Felicitation Volume), Ed., Anand Krishna. Bhārat Kalā Bhavan: 139-43.
——. 1981. *Yakṣa Cult and Iconography*. New Delhi: Munshiram Manoharlal.
——. 1987. *Sculptures of Ḍāhala and Dakṣiṇa Kośala and Their Background*. Delhi: Agam Kala Prakashan.
——. 1991. "Aspects of Vākāṭaka Art at Ajantā and elsewhere". *The Art of Ajantā* 1: 186-93.
Mitchell, W.J.T. 1986. *Iconology*.Chicago: The University of Chicago Press.
Mitra, Debala. 1966. *Bhuvaneswar*. 3rd ed, New Delhi: Director General of Archaeology in India.
——. 1981. 'Lakulīśa and Early Temples in Orissa', in Meister, ed., *Discoveries:* 112.
Mitra, Haridas. 1958. "Gaṇapati". In *VBA* 8. Shāntiniketan: 1-120.
Mitra, K. 1925/26. "The Bird and Serpent Myth. *QJMS* 16: 79-92 and 182-200.
Mitter, Partha. 1977. *Much Maligned Monsters: A History of European Reactions to Indian Art*. Oxford: Clarendon Press.
——. *Art and Nationalism in Colonial India*, 1850-1922. Cambridge University Press.
Monier Williams, M. 1887. *Brahmanism and Hinduism; or, Religious Thought and Life in India, as Based on the Veda and Other Sacred Books of the Hindus*. London: Murray.
Morgan, Charles. 1958. "The Nature of Dramatic Illusion". In Langer, ed., *Reflections*: 91-102.
Mukherjee, B.N. 1980. "A Note on the Hisse-Borālā Inscription of the Time of Vākāṭaka Devaṣeṇa". *JESI* 7: 3-5.
——. 2007. *Numismatic Art of India* 1. Delhi: Indira Gandhi National Centre for the Arts.
Morrison, Madison. 1999. *Particular and Universal*. Crane Publishing Co.

Nagaych, B.P. 2008. "Deepādih ki Sthāpatyakalā". The Architectural Art of Deepādih, Hindi. In *Kośala* I: 35-40.
——. 2010. "Garhdhanaurā ki Viśiṣṭa Viṣṇu Pratimāyen'. The unique Viṣṇu Images of Garhdhanaurā. Hindi, in *Kośala* 3:31-42.
Nair, S. Bhaskaran. 1980. Ed., *Bhāratī-Bhānam* (Light of Indology) being K.V. Sharma Felicitation Volume. Hoshiarpur: Viśveśvarānanda Viśvabandhu Institute of Sanskrit and Indological Studies.
Nanavati, J.M. and M.A. Dhaky. 1969. *The Maitraka and the Saindhava Temples of Gujarāt.* (Supplementum 26). Ascona: *AA*.
Narain, A.K. et al. 1968. Ed., *Religious Study of the Symbols on the Local Coins of Northern India, c. 300 BC to 300 AD.* Varanasi: Banaras Hindu University.
——. 1991. "Ganeśa. A Proto History of the Idea and the Icon". In R.L. Brown. Ed., *Ganesha—Studies of an Asian God*. New York: 19-48.
Nath, Amarendra. 1991-92. "Ārambha: A Vākāṭaka site in Vidarbha." In *Purātattva* 22: 69-74.
Nelson, A.E. 1909. Ed. *Central Provinces District Gazetteers, Raipur District*, Volume A. Bombay: British India Press.
——. 1909-10. *Central Provinces District Gazetteers, Bilaspur District*, Volume A. Allahabad: Pioneer Press.
Nema, S.R. 1966. "Śarabhapurīya Kings and the Location of Śarabhapura". *JIH* 44: 455-73.
——. 1978. *Political History of the Somavaṁśi kings of South Kośala and Orissa*. Delhi.
Nigam, L.S. 1977. "Hitherto unknown Repoussé Gold Coins of Nandanarāja and Stambha". *PRP* 5. 1: 69-74.
——. 1984. *Dakṣiṇa Kośala Kṣetra kā Aitihāsik Bhūgol*. The Historical Geography of Dakṣiṇa Kośala. In Hindi. Unpublished Ph.D. Thesis. Raipur: Chattisgarh College.
——. 1987. "Numismatography of Repoussé Gold Coins". In *Vājapeya* (Prof. K.D. Bajpai Felicitation Volume). Delhi, 155-159.
Nigam, L.S. and Rahul Kumar Singh. 1988. "Rare Silver and Copper Repoussé Coins of Prasannamātra". In *JNSI L*: 30-32.
Nigam, L.S. 1990. "Some Seals, Sealings and Repoussé Gold Coins from Malhār". In *JNSI LII*: 126-130.
——. 1994. "The Image of Śiva from Tala: Issues in Identification and Interpretation of Symbols therein". In *Heritage of India: Past and Present* (Essays in Honour of Prof. R.K. Sharma). Ed., P.K. Mishra and S.K. Sullerey, Delhi: 229-34.
——. 1994. "Antiquity of Garh-Dhanorā (Bastar) and Debris Clearance of Viṣṇu Image Mound". In *Purātan* 9: 71-73.
——. 2000. Ed., *Riddle of Indian Iconography (Zetetic on Rare Icon from Tala)*. Delhi: Shāradā Publishing House.
Nirmalananda, Swami. 1981. *Devdevī O Tānder Vāhan*, Gods, Goddesses and Their Vehicles, in Bengali. Calcutta: Shrī Shrī Praṇab Maṭh.
Oberer, Hariof and Egon Verheyen. 1964. Ed., "Das Problem des stils in der bildenden kunst", in *Erwin Panofsky: Aufastze zu Grundfragen der Kunstwissenschaft*. Trans., Michael Ann Holly in *Panofsky and the Foundations of Art History*.
O'Flaherty, Wendy Doniger. 1969. "The Symbolism of the Third Eye of Śiva in the Purāṇas". *Purāṇa* 11: 273-84.
——. 1971. "The Submarine Mare in the Mythology of Śiva," *JRASI*: 9-27.
——. 1971. "The Symbolism of Ashes in the Mythology of Śiva". *Purāṇa* 13: 26-35.
——. 1973. *Asceticism and Eroticism in the Mythology of Śiva*. London: Oxford University Press.
——. 1974. *Hindu Myths*. Middlesex, England: Penguin Books.
——. 1976. *The Origins of Evil in Hindu Mythology*. Delhi: Motilal Banarsidas.
Orange, H.P.L. 1965. *Art Forms and Civic Life in the Late Roman Empire*. Princeton: Princeton University Press.
Otten, Charles M. 1971. Ed., *Anthropology and Art*. New York: The Natural History Press.
Panda, Lakshman Kumar. 1985. *Śaivism in Orissa*. Delhi: Sundeep Prakashan.
Panda, Sadhu Charan. 1978. "Antiquities of Mārāguḍā Valley Preserved in the University Museum", in *New Aspects of the History of Orissa* 2. Deptt of History, Sambalpur University: 48-52.

Panda, Shishir Kumar Panda. 2000. In Basa and Mohanty 1: 55-65.
Pandey, G.C. 1976. *Bouddhadharma Vikāśa ka Itihasa.* History of the Development of Buddhist Religion. In Hindi. Lucknow: Hindi Samiti, Information Deptt.
Pandey, K.C. 1950. *Comparative Aesthetics* 1: *Indian Aesthetics*: Varanasi: Chowkhambā Sanskrit Series.
——. 1986. *An Outline of the History of Śaiva Philosophy.* Delhi: Motilal Banarsidass.
Pandey, L.P. 1971. *Sun-Worship in Ancient India.* Delhi: Motilal Banarasidas.
——. 1994. "Fresh Light on the History of Chhattisgarh Based on Numismatic Evidence", *Purātan* 9: 56-64.
——. 1930. "A Silver Coin of King Prasannamātra; The Grandfather of King Sudevarāja of Śarabhapura". *PAIOC.* I. 5th Session, Lahore: University of Punjab: 456-64.
——. 1932. Ed., "Antiquity of Mahākośala."*MHSP* 1: 1-8; "Mahānadī-The Famous River of Mahākośala", *ibid.*, 41-43.
——. 1933-34. "The Mahākośala Historical Society's Plates of Mahābhavaguptarājadeva". *EI* 22: 135-38.
——. 1935. "Āraṅg plates of Mahāsudevarāya". *EI* 23: 18-22.
——. 1935. "Malhār Plates of Mahāśivagupta". *EI* 23: 113-22.
——. 1938-39. "Ṭhākurdiyā Copper Charter of Mahāpravararāja of Śarabhapura family". *QJAHRS* 9: 37-60.
——. 1939. "Ancient Śarabhapura". *IHQ* 15.1: 475-76.
——. 1943. "Haihaya Coins of Mahākośala". *IHQ* 19:281-83.
——. 1943-44. "A New Copper Charter of Mahāśivagupta Bālārjuna, dated 57th Year". *PAIOC*, 12th Session: 595-96.
——. 1945. "A New Charter of Mahāsudevarāja of Śarabhapura". *IHQ* 21: 274-75.
——. 1945-46. "Second Copper Inscription of Mahāśivagupta Bālārjuna of Mahākośala" *QJMS* 36: 1-4.
——. 1946. "The Longest and Earliest Brāhmī Inscription in Mahākośala, Chattisgarh, C.P." *JKHRS* 1.3: 217-18.
——. 1946. "Lodhiā Plates of Mahāśivagupta Bālārjuna". *JKHRS* 2: 121.
——. 1946. "The Name of Mahākośala and Its Use in Sanskrit Literature". *JKHRS* 1.2: 201-2.
——. 1954-55. "Lodhiā Plates of Mahāśivagupta; Year 57". *EI* 28: 319-25.
——. 1955-56. "Kurud Plates of Narendra". *EI* 31:
——. 1952. "A Note on the Lodhiā Plates of Mahāśivagupta Bālārjuna". *OHRJ* 1.1: 63-69.
——. 1988. *Kauśala Kaumudī.* Paṇḍit Lochan Prasad Pandey Sarma Birth Centenary Volume. Ed., by V.S. Thakur et al. Allahabad: Shanti Prakashan.
Pandey, S.K. 1977. "Archaeology of Chattisgarh". *PRP* 5.1: 97-104.
——. 1978. "Dress and Ornaments as Depicted in the Art of Chhattisgarh". *PRP* 6.2: 111-124.
——. 2002. *Dakṣiṇa Kośala.* Hindi. Madhya Pradesh, Hindi Granth Academy.
Pandey, S.K. and S.N. Manwani. 1989. "The Temple of Jethani in Bilaspur District". In *Dimensions in Indian Archaeology and History.* Ed., S.K. Pandey and K.S. Ramachandran, Delhi: 140-46.
Pandeya, Raghunandan Prasad. 2002. *Malhār Darshan.* 3rd edition. Hindi. Malhār: Malhār Purātattva Samiti.
Panigrahi, K.C. 1960. "Sculptural Presentations of Lakulīśa and Other Pāśupata Teachers". *JIH* 38:3: 635-43.
——. 1961. *Archaeological Remains at Bhubanesvar.* Bombay: Orient Longman.
Panofsky, Erwin. 1955. *Meaning in the Visual Arts.* New York: Double Day Anchor.
Pargiter, F.E. 1913. *Purāṇic Texts of the Dynasties of the Kali Age.* London: Oxford University Press. Reprint: Motilal Banarsidass, 1962.
——. 1922. *Ancient Indian Historical Tradition.* Oxford; Reprint, Delhi: Motilal Banarsidass, 1962.
Parimoo, Ratan et al. 1991. The *Art of Ajantā. New Perspectives.* 2 vols. New Delhi: Books and Books.
Parpola, Asko. "The Pre-Vedic Indian Background of the Śrauta Rituals". In Staal, ed., *Agni* 2:41–75.
Patel, C.B. 1990. *Dynastic History of the Nalas.* Calcutta: Punthi Pustak.
Pathak, K.B. and K.N. Dikshit. 1919-20. "Poona Plates of the Vākāṭaka queen Prabhāvatī Gupta, Year 13". *EI* 15: 39-44.

Pathak, V.S. 1960. *History of Śaiva Cults in North India (700 A.D. to 1200 A.D.)*. Varanasi: Banaras Hindu University.

Patil, Devendrakumar Dayaram. 1948. *Monuments of the Udayagiri Hill*. Gwalior: Archaeological Department.

Patil, D.R. 1963. *The Antiquarian Remains in Bihār*. Pāṭnā: Kashi Prasad Jayaswal Research Institute.

——. 1968. *Monuments of the Udayagiri Hill*. Gwalior: Archaeological Department.

Patnaik, Jeeban Kumar. 2008. "A Unique Star Shaped Siddheśvara Temple, Palāri". In *Kośala* I: 112-20.

Pattanayak, D.P., P.J. Claus and J. Handoo. 1980-81. Ed., *Indian Folklore* 1 & 2. Mysore: Central Institute of Indian Languages.

Paz, Octavio. 1982. *Conjunctions and Disjunctions*. New York: Seaver Books.

Peirce, C.S. 1931-58. *Collected Papers*. 8 vols. Ed., Charles Hardshorne and Paul Weiss. Cambridge: Harvard University Press.

Pelliot, P. 1920. *Les Grottes de Touen Houang*. Mission Pelliot En Asie Centrale. Tome Troisieme. Paris: Libraire Paul Geuthner.

Philipson, Morris and Paul J. Gudel. 1980. Ed., *Aesthetics Today*. New York: The New American Library.

Pisharoti, K.R. 1937. "Hindu Architecture According to Tantra Samuccaya". *JISOA* 5.

Poddar, Hanumanprasad. Saṁvat 1990/AD 1933. *Kalyāṇa, Śrīśivāṅka*, Issue on Lord Śiva. In Hindi. Gorakhpur: Gītā Press.

Podro, Michael. 1982. *The Critical Historians of Art*. New Haven: Yale University Press.

Postel, M. 1989. *Ear Ornament of Ancient India*. Project for Cultural Studies. Bombay: Franco Indian Pharmaceuticals.

Postel, Michael and Zarine Cooper. 1999. *Bastar Folk Art*. Mumbai: Franco Indian Research Pvt. Ltd.

Pradhan, Sadasiba. 2012. *Buddhist Heritage of Odiśā*. Bhubaneswar: Odisha Tourism with Times Group.

Pradhan, Atula Kumar and Shivakant Bajpai. 2015. *Excavations in Chhattisgarh*. New Delhi: Aayu Publications.

Prasad, Gokul. 1925. *Dūrg Darpaṇ*. Hindi. Durg District Gazetter. Amaravati.

——. 1925. *Raipur-Rashmi*. The Raipur lamp. Raipur District Gazetteer. In Hindi.

Preziosi, Donald. 1989. *Rethinking Art History, Meditations on a Coy Science*. New Haven and London: Yale University Press.

Proceedings of Workshop on Conservation and Preservation of Ancient Monuments and Art and Architecture of Chhattisgarh. Abstracts 2004. Raipur: Deptt. of Culture and Archaeology.

Proceedings of the Seminar on Art and Architecture of Chhattisgarh. 2007. *Abstracts of Indian Archaeological Society, Indian Society for Prehistoric and Quarternary Studies, Indian History and Culture Society*. Raipur: Directorate of Culture and Archaeology. Proceedings of the National Archaeological Seminar. 2007. *New Archaeological Findings of Last Five Years in India*. Raipur, Department of Culture and Archaeology.

Przyluski, Jean. 1931. "Varuṇa, God of the Sea and the Sky". *JRAS*: 613-22.

——. 1938. *Dragon Chinois et Nāga Indien. MS 3*.

Puri, B.N. 1968. *India in the Time of Patañjali*. Bombay: Bhāratīya Vidyā Bhavan.

Pusalkar, A.D. 1955. *Studies in the Epics and Purāṇas of India*. Bombay: Bhāratīya Vidyā Bhavan.

Raghuvirprasad. 1930. *Jhārkhaṇḍa Jhaṅkāra*. Hindi, A Gazetteer of Five Cutiā Nagpur States, Transferred to the Central Provinces. Jabalpur. Indian Press.

Radhakrishnan, S. 1927/2008. *Indian Philosophy*. 2 vols. Delhi: Oxford University Press.

Raikwar, G.L. 1985-86. *Report on Conservation File. Bilaspur; Survey Report* (File No 39). Bhopal: Directorate of Archaelogy and Museums (Ms).

——. 1987-88. *Tala Conservation Report* No 477/Arch/Regi/88. Bhopal: Directorate of Archaeology and Museums (Ms.).

——. 1989. "Bilāspur Jile ki Śaiva Pratimāen". Śaiva images of Bilaspur district. In Hindi. In *Purātan* 6:187.

Raikwar, G.L. and R.K. Singh. 1990. *Junvāni (Malhār) Copperplate of Mahāśivagupta, Year 57:* Tentative Reading. Bilaspur: Bilaspur Museum.

Raikwar, G.L. 2000. "A Classical Icon from Tala". In Nigam, ed., *Riddle:* 143-53.
——. 2013. Sisdeori Utkhanan (I Iindi). Directorate of Culture and Archaeology, Govt. of Chhattisgarh.
Ramakrishnan, V. 1978. *Perspectives in Śaivism*. Madras: Dr. S. Radhakrishnan Institute for Advanced Study in Philosophy. Madras University.
Ramesh, K.V. 1992. "On the Vākāṭakas and Their Inscriptions". In Shastri, ed., *Age of the Vākāṭakas.*
Ramanujan, A.K. 1973. *Speaking of Śiva*. Baltimore: Harmondsworth.
Ramanujan, A.K. and Stuart Blackburn. 1986. Ed., *Another Harmony, New Essays on the Folklore of India*, Delhi: Oxford University Press.
Rapson, E.J. 1922-53. Ed., *Ancient India*. Vol. 1 of *The Cambridge History of India.* Ed., H.H. Dodwell. London: Cambridge University Press.
Rao, V.N. Hari. 1970. "The Symbolism of Gajalakṣmī". *JIH* 48, part I, no. 142: 73-80.
Rao, L.S. 2000. "A Mysterious Sculpture from Tālā–A Rare Form of Varuna". In Nigam, ed., *Riddle:*121-26.
Rao, M. Raja. 1952. "The Astronomical Background of Vedic Rudra and Purānic Śiva." *BV* 13:
Rao, T.A. Gopinatha. 1914-16. *Elements of Hindu Iconography.* 2 vols. Madras: Law Printing House. Reprint, 2 vols. in 4, New York: Paragon Books Reprint Corp., 1968.
——. 1915-16. "Śarabharam Plates of the Lord of Chikura, Year 6." *EI* 13: 104-08.
Ray, H.C. 1931-36. *The Dynastic History of Northern India (*Early Medieval Period*).* 2 vols. Calcutta: University of Calcutta. 2nd ed. New Delhi: Munshilal Manoharlal, 1973.
Ray, P.K. 1975. Ed., *Archaeological Survey Report–Prācī Valley*, Bhubaneshwar.
Raychaudhuri, H.C. 1958. *Studies in Indian Antiquities.* Calcutta: University of Calcutta.
Read, Herbert. 1931/1959. *The Meaning of Art.* Harmondsworth: Penguin Books.
——. 1936/1970. *Art and Society*. London: Faber & Faber, Grove Press.
——. 1957. *The Tenth Muse.* New York: Grove Press.
——. 1965. *Icon and Idea*, New York: Schocken Books.
Redfield, Robert. 1953. *The Primitive World and Its Transformations*. New York: Cornell University Press.
——. 1971. "Art and Icon", in Otten, Ed., *Anthropology of Art*: 39-65.
Renou, Louis. 1954. *Vocabulaire du rituel Védique*. Paris: Klincksieck.
Ricoeur, Paul. 1981. *Hermeneutics and the Human Sciences*. Trans. and Ed., John B. Thompson. Cambridge. Cambridge University Press, 1981.
Riegel, Alois. 1953. *A Prolegomena to the Study of Roman Art*. 1927. Die Spatromische Kunstindustrie. Vienna: Osterreichische Staatsdruckerei. Late Roman Art Industry. Roma: Georgio Bretschschpeider. 1985.
Rilke, Rainer Maria. 1945. *Rodin*. Trans., J. Lamont and Hans Trausil. New York: Fine Editions Press: 11.
Risbud, Anand Kumar. 1984. "Tala Gāmv kā Śiva Mandir – Śiva temple of Tala Village". In Hindi: *Purātan* 1: 58-61.
Rivett-Carnac, J.C. 1879. "The Snake Symbol in India, Especially in Connection with the Worship of Śiva." *JRASB* 48.1: 17-31.
Robinson, Marguerite S. and L.E. Joiner. 1968. "An Experiment in the Structural Study of Myth". *Contributions to Indian Sociology* 2:1-37.
Rode, B.P. 1948. "The Khairātāl Hoard of the Coins of Mahendrāditya". *JNSI* 10: 137-42.
——. 1950. "Gold Coins of Prasannamātra". *JNSI* 12.1: 8-10.
Rosenfield, John M. 1963. "On the Dated Carvings of Sarnath". *AA* 26, no. 1: 10-26.
——. 1967. *The Dynastic Arts of the Kuśāṇas*. Berkeley and Los Angeles: University of California Press.
Rosselin, E. 1513. Der Schwangerenn Frawen und Hebammen Rosengarten. Hagenau. Republished in *IDC Medicine Microfiche Series*, Poststrasse 4 Zug, Switzerland.
Rothenberg, Albert and Carl R. Hausman. 1976. Ed., *The Creativity Question*. Durham, N.C.: Duke University Press.
Rothenberg, Albert. 1976. "The Process of Janusian Thinking in Creativity". In Rothenberg and Hausman, ed., *Creativity Question*: 311-27.

Rowland, Benjamin. 1954. *Art in East and West*. Boston: Beacon Press.

——. 1970. *Art and Architecture of India: Pelican History of Art*. 3rd edn. Harmondsworth: Penguin Books.

Russell, R.V. 1968. *Central Provinces, Imperial Gazetteers of India*. Calcutta: Oxford.

Sahay, Bhagawant. 1975. *Iconography of Minor Hindu and Buddhist Deities*. New Delhi: Abhinav Publications.

Sahu, J.K. "New light on Mahāśivagupta Bālārjuna," *OHRJ* 23, Nos. 1 to 4.

——. 1997. *Historical Geography of Orissa*. New Delhi: Decent Books.

Sahu, N.K. 1955. "Buddhist Art in Orissa". *Mārg 8*.

——. 1954. "History of Kośala and the Somavaṁśīs of Utkal". *OHRJ* 3.8:127-36.

——. 1958. *Buddhism in Orissa*. Cuttack: Utkal University.

——. 1962. "The Nalas," *OHRJ* 11. 2: 95-102.

——. 1964. Ed., *Utkal University History of Orissa, From the Earliest Time up to 500 A.D.* Vol. 1. Cuttack: Utkal University.

——. 1966. *Korāpuṭ*. With N. Senapati. *Orissa District Gazetteers*. Orissa Government Press.

——. 1971. Ed., *New Aspects of the History of Orissa*. Sambalpur: Sambalpur University.

Sahu, N.K. and S.C. Behera. 1971. "Survey of the History of South Kośala" in *New Aspects of the History of Orissa*, ed., N.K. Sahu. Sambalpur University.

——. 1973-74. "Two Obscure Dynasties of South Kośala," *SUJ* 6 and 7.

Said, Edward W. 1978. *Orientalism*. London and Henley: Routledge and Kegan Paul. Harmondsworth: Penguin.

——. 1985. *Beginnings: Intention and Method*. Columbia University Press. London. New edition.

Sanderson, Alexis. 1988. "Śaivism and the Tāntric Traditions". In Stuward Sutherland et al., Ed., *The World's Religions*, London: 660-704.

Sankaranarayanan, S. 1977. *The Viṣṇukuṇḍins and Their Times. An Epigraphical study*. Delhi: Agam Kala Prakashan.

Saran, Anjaninandan. N.D. Ed., *Kośala Khaṇḍa*. Hindi. Gorakhpur, U.P.: Gītā Press.

Sarma, I.K. 1992. "Some Unique Representations of Śiva of the Vākāṭaka Period". In *Age of the Vākāṭakas*: 219-24.

——. 2000. A Polycephalous Image from Tala. "Analysis and Identification". In Nigam, ed., *Riddle*: 97-100.

Sartre, Jean Paul. 1948. *Psychology of the Imagination*. New York: Philosophical library.

Sartwell, C. 1995. "*Representation*". In Cooper 1995: 354-68.

Sastri, T.V.G. 1967. "The Antiquity of Nagari and its Toraṇa". *JOIB* 16: 336-41.

Saussure, Ferdinand de. 1915 *Course de Linguistique Genéralé, Course in General Linguistics*. Ed., Charles Bally, Albert Sechehaye, Albert Rledlinger. Trans., Wade Baskin. New York: Philosophical Library, 1959.

Sauvage, Michelin. 1958. "Notes on the Superposition of Temporal Modes in Works of Art". In Langer, ed., *Reflections*: 161-73.

Schapiro, Meyer. 1953. "Style". In *Anthropology Today: An Encyclopaedic Inventory*, ed., A.L. Kroeber. Chicago: University of Chicago Press: 287-312.

Schwartzberg, Joseph E. 1978. Ed., *A Historical Atlas of South Asia*. Chicago: University of Chicago Press.

Schuster, Carl. 1951. *Joint Marks. A Possible Index of Cultural Contact between America, Oceania and the Far East*. Amsterdam. Koninklijk Institut voor de Tropen. Mededéling No. XCIV. Culturele en Physische Anthropologie 39.

Seidemberg, A. 1983. "The Geometry of the Vedic Rituals". In Fritz Staal, ed., *Agni 2: 95-126*.

Sen, Surendranath. 1952-53. *India through Chinese Eyes*. Sir William Meyer Endowment Lectures. Madras: University of Madras, 1956.

Senapati, N. Ed. *Gazetteers of India, Orissa*. Cuttack: Korāpuṭ (1966). Bolaṅgir (1968), Sambalpur (1971), Sundergarh (1975), Kālāhāṇḍi (1980).

Seiti, Midelho and Josio Nagahiro. 1941. *A Study of the Buddhist Cave Temples at LungMen, Ho-Nan*. Tokyo: Zauho Press.

Shah, D.P. 1960. "Sculptures from Sāmalāji and Roda". *BMPGB* 18: 1-136.

Shah, V.P. 1984. "Lakulīśa, Śaivite Saint". In M.W. Meister, ed., *Discourses:* 92-102.

Sharkey, John. 1975. *Celtic Mysteries. The Ancient Religion.* London: Thames and Hudson. Repr. 1979.

Sharma, A.K. 2000. "Excavations at Mānsar and Sirpur". In *Purātattva* 3, ed., C. Margabandhu, A.K. Sharma, R.S. Bisht. Delhi: Agam Kala Prakashan.

——. 2007. "Sirpur– The Grand Bāleśvar Temple". In *Purāmanthana,* No. 4, Ist Edition. Ed., A. K. Sharma, B.R. Mani and G.S. Khwaja: 68-85.

——. 2007. *Excavations at Sirpur, Chhattisgarh.* Special Report 1. New Delhi: Indian Archaeological Society.

——. 2012. *Ancient Temples of Sirpur.* Delhi: B.R. Publishing Corporation.

——. 2014. *Buddhist Monuments of Sirpur.* Delhi: Buddhist World Press.

——. 2015. *Jainism at Sirpur.* New Delhi: Aayu Publications.

Sharma, A.K. and Prabhat Kumar Singh. 2010. *Buddhist Bronzes from Sirpur.* New Delhi: Agam Kala Prakashan.

Sharma, A.K., Prabhat Kumar Singh and Praveen Tirkey. 2014. *Secular Monuments of Sirpur.* Delhi: B.R. Publishing Corporation.

Sharma, G.R. 1960. The Excavation at Kauśāmbī, 1957-59. *MASI* 74.

Sharma, I.K. 1982. *The Development of Early Śaiva Art and Architecture with Special Reference to Andhradeśa.* New Delhi: Sundeep Prakashan.

——. 1989. "Some Unique Representations of Śiva of the Vākāṭaka Period'. In *Ratna Chandrikā.* R.C. Agrawala Festschrift. Ed., Devendra Handa and Asvini Agrawal. New Delhi: Harman Publishing House.

Sharma, Madhuri and Deo Prakash. 1994. "Sirpur ki Kāṅsya Pratimāyon par Nālandā Pāla kalā Śailī kā Prabhāv". The Impact of Nālanda Pāla Art Style on Bronze Images of Sirpur. *Purātan* 9: 119-25.

Sharma, Meera. 1994. "Sirpur ki Prastar Buddha Pratimāyen". Hindi. The Stone Buddha Images of Sirpur. *Purātan* 9: 126-131.

Sharma, Raj Kumar. 1974. *Madhya Pradesh Kā Purātattva Kā Sandarbha Grantha.* Reference Volume on Madhya Pradesh Archaeology. In Hindi. Bhopāl. Madhya Pradesh Hindi Grantha Academy.

——. 1992. In Ajay Mitra Shastri, ed., *Vākāṭakas:* 221.

——. N.d. ed., *Shell Character Inscriptions from Vidarbha and the Deccan.* Delhi: Agam Kala Prakashan.

Shastri, Hirananda. 1917-18. "Harahā Inscription of the Reign of Iśānvarman, Vikrama Saṁvat 611". *EI* 14: 110-20.

——. 1987. "Chronology of the Pāṇḍuvaṁśins of South Kośala". In *Vājapeya (Prof. K.D. Bajpai Felicitation Volume),* Vol. 2: 313-27.

Shastri, S.S. 1955."The Philosophy of Śaivism", in *The Cultural Heritage of India* 3. Ed., H. Bhattacharya. 2nd ed. Calcutta: The Ramakrishna Mission Institute of Culture, 1953-78: 387-99.

Shastri, Ajaya Mitra. 1966. "Fresh light on the History of the Viṣṇukuṇḍins". *JIH* 44: 683-91.

——. 1968. "A Religious Sealing from Paunār". *JNSI* 30: 215-18.

——. 1968. "Religious Study of the Symbols on the Local Coins of Central India". *Seminar Papers on the Local Coins of Northern India.* Ed., A.K. Narain. Varanasi.

——. 1970. "Some Observations on the Hisse-Borālā Inscription of Vākāṭaka Devaṣeṇa". *Dr. Umesh Mishra Commemoration Volume.* Allahabad, Ganganath Jha Research Institute: 617-27.

——. 1975. "Some Observations on the Sirpur Plates of Mahasudevarāja, Year 7". *Studies in Indian Epigraphy, JESI* 2: 50-54.

——. 1975. "A Note on the Aḍabhāra Plates of Mahā-Nannarāja". *JOIB* 25: 67-69.

——. 1975. "Magha Itihās par Navin Prakāśa", New Light on Magha History. In Hindi. *VSMV*: 77-84.

——. 1975-76. "Māndhal Copperplate Charter of Pravarasena II, year V16" In *EI* 41 68-76.

——. 1976. "A Note on the Ipur and Palamuru Plates of Viṣṇkuṇḍin Mādhavavarman". M.S. Śarmā Commemoration Volume. *JAHRS* 35: 165-68.

——. 1977. "The Śarabhapurīyas", *PRP* 5.1: 1-40.

——. 1977. "Temple Administration in Chhattisgarh under the Śarabhapurīyas and the Pāṇḍuvaṁśins". *Ibid.* 5.2: 63-69.

——. 1977. "Vidarbha Kā Ek Sāṁskṛtik Kendra, Māṇḍhal". Māṇḍhal, a Cultural Centre of Vidarbha. In Hindi. *Purāṇa*: 128-33.

——. 1977. "Māṇḍhal Utkhanan". Māṇḍhal Excavation. In Hindi. In *VSMV* 20; Nagpur: 142-74.

——. 1979. "A Note on the Date of Tivaradeva". In F.M. Asher and C.S Ghai, ed., *JESI* 6: 5-11.

——. 1979. "Two Fragmentary Sirpur Inscriptions of the Time of Mahāśivagupta Bālārjuna", *VIJ* 17: 196-202.

——. 1979. "Pāṇḍuvaṁśins and Somavaṁśins". *PRP* 7: 11-26.

——. 1980. "The Date of Bāmhoni and Malhār Plates of Śūrabala Udīrṇavaira." *Bhāratī-Bhānam (Light of Indology), Dr. K.V. Śarmā Felicitation Volume.* Hoshiarpur: Viśveśvarānand Indological Research Institute: 439-44.

——. 1982, "Some Observations on the Senākapāṭ Inscription of the Time of Śivagupta Bālārjuna". *Studies in Indian Epigraphy*: 1-4.

——. "The Date of the Malhār Plates of Vyāghrarāja", *JESI* 7: 69-75.

——. 1984-86. "Fresh Epigraphic Evidence on the Vākāṭakas". In *NUJ* 35:130-64.

——. 1985. "Magha Coins from Malhār (In collaboration with Anand Kumar Risbud)". *ND* 9: 34-40.

——. 1985. "The Date of the Lakṣmaṇa Temple of Sirpur". In F.M. Asher and G.S. Ghai, ed., *Studies in Indian Epigraphy*: 105-09.

——. 1987. *Early History of the Deccan. Problems and Perspectives.* Delhi: Sundeep Prakashan.

——. 1987. "Chronology of the Pāṇḍuvaṁśins of South Kośala". In *Vājapeya (Prof. K.D. Bajpai Felicitation Volume).* Vol. 2: 313-27. Delhi: Agam Kala Prakashan.

——. 1988. "Pāṇḍavas of Mekala", in *History and Culture (B.P. Sinha Felicitation Volume).* Ed., 1988, A.M. Shastri, R.K. Sharma and Agam Prasad. Delhi: Agam Kala Prakashan, 472-91.

——. 1991. *Varāhamihira and His Times.* Jodhpur: Kusumanjali Prakashan.

——. 1992. *The Age of the Vākāṭakas.* Ed., New Delhi: Harman Publishing House.

——. 1994. "Capitals of the Vākāṭakas". *QJMS* 85.3:17-37.

——. 1995. *Inscriptions of the Śarabhapurīyas, Pāṇḍuvaṁśins and Somavaṁśins.* 2 vols. Delhi: Indian Council of Historical Research and Motilal Banarasidass.

——. 1995. "Nācnā ki Tālāi and Ganj inscriptions of the time of Vākāṭaka Pṛthvīṣeṇa – Some observations". In *JESI* 21: 1-13.

——. 1996. *Ancient Indian Heritage, Varāhamihira's India.* New Delhi: Aryan Books International.

——. 1997. *Vākāṭakas, Sources and History*, New Delhi: Aryan Books International.

Shastri, Ajay Mitra and Chandrashekhar Gupta. 1973. "Ā *Vākāṭaka Seal from Gorakhpur*". *JNSI* 35: 238-40.

——. 1977-78, "Yawatmal plates of Pravarasеṇa II, Year 26". In *EI* 42: 30-34.

——. 1985. "Dvitīya Rudraṣenācā Māndhala Tāmrapatra". "The Māṇḍhal copperplate of Rudraṣeṇa II". In Marathi. In B.L. Bhole, Ed., *Saṁśodhān cī Kṣitije. Dr. V.B. Kolte Amṛtamahotsava Gaurava Grantha*: Nagpur: 223-29.

Shastri, J.L. 1970 till date. Ed., *Ancient Indian Tradition and Mythology.* (Purāṇas in translation). 50 vols. Delhi: Motilal Banarsidass.

Shastri, S.S. Sūryanarayan. 1942-43. "Śaṅkara and the School of Vedānta." *PO* 7. 3. 1.

Shrotriya, Alok and Mohan Lal. 2008. "Malhār ki Mṛdbhāṇḍa paramparāyen". "Earthen Pot Traditions of Malhār". Hindi. In *Kośala* 1: 26: 31.

Shrivastava, A.L. 1989. *Bhāratīya Kalā Pratīka.* Indian Art Symbols. In Hindi. Allahabad: Anurag Prakashan.

Shukla, D.N. 1956. *Vāstu Śāstra.* 3 vols. Bhāratīya Vāstu-Śāstra Series. Lucknow: Vāstu-Vāṅmaya-Prakāśana-Śālā.

Shukla, Hiralal. 1978. *Prācīn Bastar. Arthāt Daṇḍakāraṇyakā Sānskritik Itihās.* Ancient Bastar, being a Cultural History of Daṇḍakāraṇya. In Hindi. Nagpur: Vishvabharati Prakashan.

Shukla Abhinandan Granth. 1955. *Shukla Felicitation Volume.* In Hindi. Presented to Pandit Ravi Shankar Shukla. Nagpur: Madhya Pradesh, Hindi Sāhitya Sammelan.

Shukla, N.K. 2012. Ed., *Proceedings of the National Seminar on River Valley Civilization of Chhattisgarh and New Researches in Indian Archaeology*. Raipur: Directorate of Culture and Archaeology, Govt. of Chhattisgarh.

Shusterman, Richard. 2004. Ed., *The Range of Pragmatism and the Limits of Philosophy*. Oxford: Blackwell.

Sickman, Lawrence and Alexander Coburn Soper. 1956. *The Art and Architecture of China*. Pelican History of Art. Middlesex, London: Penguin Books.

Siddhantashastree, R.K. 1975. *Śaivism Through the Ages*. New Delhi: Munshiram Manoharlal.

Siddiqi, W.H. 1978. "Two Newly Discovered Sculptures from Ṛṣikeś". *JISOA*. Dr. Motichandra Commemoration Volume: 76-80.

Singh, Rahul Kumar. 2000. Tala Icon: A Comprehensive Attempt of Its Identification". In Nigam, ed., *Riddle*: 135-42.

Singhal, A.P. 1977. "Three Centuries of Sirpur-Revelation by Excavation," *PRP* 5.1: 93-96.

Singhdeo, J.P. 1979. "The Traditional Account of the Origin of Dakṣiṇa Kośala". *JAIH* 11. University of Calcutta: 119-20.

——. 1982. "Archaeological Remains of Sunabedā Plateau". *OHRJ* 16.4:22.1.

——. 1987. *"Cultural Profile of South Kośala (From Early Period till the Rise of the Nāgas and the Chauhāns in 14th Century A.D)*. Delhi: Gian Publishing House.

——. 2000. "Composite Tāntric Yogic Figure of Mahākāla and Mahākāli". In Nigam, ed., *Riddle*: 127-34.

——. 2000. "Archaeology of Kālāhāṇḍi and Nuāpāḍā district, Orissa. In Basa and Mohanty 1: 418-30.

Sircar, Dinesh Chandra. 1930-31. "Pāṭṭā Plates of Mahāśivagupta Yayāti" in R.D. Banerji, *History of Orissa* 1:221; *EI* 7:141.

——. 1941. "The Vatsagulma Copperplate Grant of King Vindhyaśakti II. *IHQ* 17:110-16.

——. 1942/1965. *Select Inscriptions Bearing on Indian History and Civilization, from the 6th cent.* BC *to 6th cent.* AD. Calcutta: Calcutta University.

——. 1944. "A Note on the Genealogy of the Somavaṁśīs". *IHQ* 20: 76-82.

——. 1945. "Text of the Purāṇic List of Peoples". *IHQ* 21: 297-314.

——. 1946. "King Dūrgarāja of the Śarabhapurīya Dynasty". *IHQ* 22: 62-63.

——. 1949. "Keśaribādā Plates of Nala Arthapati-Bhaṭṭāraka". *EI* 28: 12-17.

——. 1953-54. "Terāsiṇghā Plates of Tuṣṭikāra". *EI* 30: 274-78.

——. 1954. "Deccan in the Gupta Age". *The Classical Age*, Vol. 3 of History and Culture of the Indian People. Ed., R.C. Majumdar. Bombay: Bhāratīya Vidyā Bhavan.

——. 1955-56. "Note on Kurud Plates of Narendra, Year 24." *EI* 31: 267-68.

——. 1957-58. "Erraguḍi Edicts of Aśoka". *EI* 32: 1-28.

——. 1959-60. "Malhār Plates of Jayarāja, Year 5." *EI* 33: 155-58.

——. 1959-60. "Notes of Senākapāṭ Inscription, No 2". *EI* 33: 255-56.

——. 1961-62. "Bonḍā plates of Mahāśiva Tivara", Year 5". *EI* 34: 111-16.

——. 1965. *Indian Epigraphy*. Delhi: Motilal Banarsidass.

——. 1968. "The Sātavāhanas and the Cedīs". In R.C. Majumdar, ed. Bhāratīya Vidya Bhavan, *The Age of Imperial Unity*, Vol. 6.

——. 1971. *Studies in the Geography of Ancient and Medieval India*. 2nd ed. Delhi: Motilal Banarsidass.

Sircar, Dinesh Chandra and L.P. Pandey. 1943. Pipardulā Copperplate Inscription of Narendra of Śarabhapura. *1HQ* 19: 139-46.

Sircar, D.C. and G. Bhattacharya. 1961-62. "Malhār Plates of Vyāghrarāja". *EI* 34: 45-52.

Sircar, D.C. and J.P. Singhdeo. 1976. "Aṅgura Plates of Jayarāja of Śarabhpur, Regnal Year 3". *IMB*: 57-9.

Sitaraman, B. and M.T. Sharma. 1977. "Malhār plates of Pāṇḍava King Śūrabala, Year 8". In *Studies in Indian Epigraphy*. 3. Mysore: 183-93.

Shivananda, Swami. 1962. *Lord Śiva and His Worship*. 2nd ed. Śivanandanagar: Divine Life Society.

Shivapadasundaram, S. 1934. *The Śaiva School of Hinduism*. London: George Allen and Unwin.

——. 1997. *VSMV* Annual 1997: 143-74.

Sivaramamurti, C. 1935. "Realism in Indian Art". *Journal of Oriental Research* (Madras) 9.
——. 1949. "Composite Figures in Indian Iconography". *BV* 10: 296-300.
——. 1955. "Parallels and Opposites in Indian Iconography", in *JAS*, letters, 21.2:
——. 1955. *Sanskrit literature and Art. Mirrors of Indian Culture. MASI* 73. Delhi: Manager of Publications, reprint, New Delhi: Lakshmi Book Store, 1970.
——. 1956. *Parallels and Opposites in Indian Iconography*. Calcutta: Asiatic Society.
——. 1974. *Birds and Animals in Indian Sculpture*. New Delhi: National Museum.
——. 1976. *Gaṅgā*. New Delhi: Orient Longman.
——. 1976. *Śatarudrīya: Vibhūti of Śiva's Iconography*. New Delhi: Abhinav Publications.
——. 1977. *The Art of India*. New York: Harry N. Abrams.
——. 1978. *Citrasūtra of the Viṣṇudharmottara*. New Delhi: Kanak Publications.
——. 1979. *Sources of History, Illumined By Literature*. New Delhi: Kanak Publications.
——. 1980. *Ethical Fragrance in Indian Art and Literature*. New Delhi: Kanak Publications.
——. 1981. *Rishis in Indian Art and Literature*. New Delhi: Kanak Publications.
——. 1982. *Śrī Lakṣmī in Indian Art and Thought*. New Delhi: Kanak Publications.
——. 1984. "Forms of Śiva in Sanskrit Sources". In M.W. Meister, ed., *Discourses on Śiva*, 182-190.
——. 1994. *Naṭarāja in Art, Thought and Literature*. Publications Division, Ministry of Information & Broadcasting, Govt. of India.
Smart, Vasudev. 1971. *Rūpasaṁhitā*. Varanasi: Banaras Hindu University.
Smith, Bardwell L. 1975. Ed., *Hinduism, New Essays in the History of Religion*. Leiden: E.J. Brill.
——. 1983. Ed., *Essays on Gupta Culture*. Columbia: South Asia Books.
Smith, Vincent A. 1914. "Indian Sculpture of the Gupta Period, AD 300–650". *OZ*: 1-27
Snellgrove, David L. 1978. Ed., *The Image of the Buddha*. Tokyo: Kodansha International.
Sontag, Susan. 1966. *Against Interpretation*. New York: Dell Publishing House.
Soper, Alexander Coburn. 1943. "Literary Evidence for Early Buddhist Art in China". *Artibus Asiae Supplementum*. Ascona, Switzerland.
——. 1956. *The Art and Architecture of China*. Pelican History of Art. Middlesex, London: Penguin Books.
Spink; Walter M. 1967. *Ajantā to Ellorā*. Bombay: Marg Publications.
——. 1968. "Ajantā's Chronology: The Problem of Cave Eleven". In *AO* 7: 155-68.
——. 1971. "A Temple with Four Uchchakalpa Doorways at Nācnā-Kuthārā." In *Chhavi*, ed., Ananda Krishna. Varanasi, Bhārat Kalā Bhavan: 163-72.
——. 1972. "Ajantā: A Brief History." In *Aspects of Indian Art*. Ed., P. Pal. Leiden, E.J. Brill: 49-58.
——. 1974. "The Splendours of Indra's Crown: A Study of Mahāyāna Developments at Ajantā". *JRSEAMC*: 43-67.
——. 1975. "Ajantā's Chronology: The Crucial Cave." *ARO* 10: 143-69.
——. 1976. "Bāgh: A Study." *ARAA* 30: 53-84.
——. 1981. "Ajantā's Chronology: Politics and Patronage". *Kalādarśana*, ed., Joanna G. Williams. New Delhi: Oxford and IBH Publishing, with the American Institute of Indian Studies: 109-26.
——. 1991. "Vākāṭakas, Flowering and Fall", in *The Art of Ajantā* I: 71-99.
——. 1991. "The Archaeology of Ajantā". In *ARO* 21: 67-94.
Spivak, Gayatri Chakravarty. 1999. *A Critique of Post Colonial Reason: Towards a History of the Vanishing Present*. Cambridge: Harvard University Press.
Sproul, Barbara C. 1979. *Primal Myths*. San Francisco: Harper & Row.
Srinivasan, Doris Meth. 1987. "Śaiva Temple Forms: Loci of God's Unfolding Body". In Yaldiz and Lobo, ed., *Investigating Indian Art*: 335-47
——. 1990. "From Transcendency to Materiality: Para Śiva, Sadāśiva, and Maheśa in Indian Art". In *AA* 50, 1-2:108-42.
——. 1997. *Many Heads, Arms and Eyes: Origin, Meaning and Form of Multiplicity in Indian Art*. Leiden: E.J. Brill.

——. 2000. "Rūpa Yakṣa Unique Icon/Unique Identification". In Nigam, ed., *Riddle* 89-96.

Srinivasan, K.R. 1972. *Temples of South India*. New Delhi: National Book Trust.

Srivastava, Balaram. 1985. *Nature of Indian Aesthetics, with Special Reference to Śilpa*. Varanasi: Chaukhambā Orientalia.

Staal, Frits. 1983. Ed., *Agni: The Vedic Ritual of the Fire Altar*. 2 vols. Berkeley: Asian Humanities Press.

Stadtner, Donald M. 1977. *From Sirpur to Rājim: The Art of Kośala during the Seventh century*. Ph D Dissertation, University of California, Berkeley, Ann Arbor, Mich.: University Microfilms, 1977, Microfilm No. DC J77-15867.

——. 1978. "The Siddheśwara Temple at Palāri and Art of Kośala during the Seventh and Eight Centuries". *ARO* 12: 49-56.

——. 1980. "A Sixth century Temple from Kośala." *ARSA* 33: 38-48.

——. 1981. "Ancient Kośala and the Stellate Plan." In J.G. Williams, ed., *Kalādarśana*: 137-45.

——. 1981-82. "Nāndchānd and a Central Indian Regional Style". *AA* 43: 129-36.

——. 1980-81. "Kalacurī Art at Singhpur". *AA* 42: 270-78.

Stein, Sir Aurel. 1931. On the Ephedra, the Hum Plant, and the Soma. *BSOAS*, VI, 2: 501-14.

Stein, O. 1985. *Arthaśastra and Śilpaśastra*. Stuttgart: Kleine Schriften.

Stern, Philippe. 1972. *Colonnes Indiennes d'Ajantā et d'Ellora, Evolution et Repercussions, Styles Gupta et Post-Gupta*. Publications du Musée Guimet, Recherches et Document d'Art et d'Archaeologie 11. Paris: Presses Universitaires de France.

Stietencron, H. von. 1962. "Bhairava". *ZDMG Supplementary*. Vonträge, Teil 3: 863-71.

Stone, Gorge Cameron. 1961. *A Glossary of the Construction, Decoration and Use of Arms and Armor in all Countries and All Times*. New York: Jack Brssel.

Strauss, Claude Levi. 1962. *La Pensée Sauvage. The Savage Mind*. Paris: Librairie Plon.

——. 1967. *Structural Anthropology*. New York: Anchor Books.

——. 1975. *The Raw and the Crooked*. New York: Harper Colophon Books.

——. 1978. *Myth and Meaning*. University of Toronto Press.

——. 1988. *La Boie de Masques*: The Way of the Masks. Trans. by Sylvia Modelshi. Seattle: University of Washington Press.

Stutley, Margaret and James. 1977. *Harper's Dictionary of Hinduism: Its Mythology, Folklore, Philosophy, Literature and History*, New York: Harper and Row.

Stutterheim, Willem Frederick. 1929. "The Meaning of Kāla-Makara Ornament". *IAL*. 3.1: 27-52.

Svoboda, R.E. 1993. *Aghora (At the Left Hand of God)*, Calcutta: Rupa & Co.

Sukhtankar, V.S. 1925-26. "Vākāṭaka Inscription from Gañj". *EI* 18: 12-14.

Swami Hariharanand Sarasvati. 1941: The Inner Significance of Liṅga Worship. *JISOA* 9: *52-80*.

Tagore, Abanindranath. 1914. "Some Notes on Indian Artistic Anatomy". Trans. Sukumar Ray. Calcutta: *JISOA* 1914.

Thapar, Romila. 1983. "The Archaeolgical Background to the Agnicayana Ritual", in Staal, ed., *Agni* 2:3-40.

Thakur, Vishnu Singh. 1965. *Ancient History and Culture of Dakṣiṇa Kośala*. Unpublished Ph.D. thesis. Jabalpur University.

Tanner, Michael. 1998. *Schopenhauer: Metaphysics and Art*. London: Phoenix.

Thakur, Upendra. 1978. *The Heritage of India, L.N. Mishra Commemoration Volume*. Bodhgayā: L.N. Mishra Publication Committee, Magadh University.

Thieme, P. 1952. "Brāhmaṇ". *ZDMG* 102: 91-129.

Tiwari, S.P. 1979. "A Note on Vākāṭaka Nala Scuffle". *Orissa History Congress Proceedings of the Annual Session*.

Tripathy, Balaram. 2000 "Archeology of Baudh", in Basa and Mohanty 1:392-417.

Trivedi, H.V. 1957. *Catalogue of the Coins of the Nāgas of Padmāvatī*. Gwalior: Department of Archeology and Museums.

Tripathi, G.C. 2004. *Communication with God*. Delhi: Indira Gandhi National Centre for the Arts & Aryan Books International.

Tripathi, Krishnakumar and O.P. Mishra. 1996. "Dakṣiṇa Kośala Kṣetra men Buddha Dharma". Hindi. Buddhist Religion in Dakṣiṇa Kośala. *Purātan* 9: 132-37.

Tripathi, S. 1977. "Aṅgura Plates of Mahājayarāja." Studies in Indian Epigraphy. *JESI* 4: 70-75.

Trivedi, R.D. 1981. *Iconography of Pārvatī*. Delhi: Agam Kala Prakashan.

——. 1990. *Temples of the Pratihāra Period in Central India*. Delhi: Archaeological Survey of India.

Tsuji, N. 1983. "Agnicayana Section of the Maitrāyaṇī Saṁhitā with Special Reference to the Mānava Śrauta Sūtra", in Frits Staal, ed., *Agni* 2: 135-60.

Tucci, Giuseppe. 1930. Ed. *Pre-Diṅnāga Buddhist Texts on Logic from Chinese Sources*. *GOS* 49.

Valery, Paul. 1946. *Monsieur Teste*. Paris: Nouvelle Edition.

——. 1957. *Oeuvres* 1. Ed., J. Hytrer. Paris: Pleiada.

Varma, T.P. 1996. "Note on Repoussé Coins", *Purātan*: 65-69.

Varma, Kamta Prasad. 2008. *Bastar ki Sthāpatyakalā*. Architecture of Bastar. In Hindi. Raipur: Shatakshi Prakashan.

——. 2010. *Chhattisgarh ki Sthāpatya kalā. Surgujā zile ke Visesh Sandarbh meṅ*. Hindi. The Architectural Art of Chhattisgarh. In the Special context of Surguja district. Raipur: Directorate of Arcaheology and Culture.

——. 2012. *Saṁskṛtisaritā Śivnāth*. Hindi. Shivnath, the Stream of Culture. Directorate of Culture and Archaeology, Govt. of Chhattisgarh, Raipur.

——. 2012. *Maheshpur ki Kalā*. Hindi. The Art of Maheshpur. Directorate of Culture and Archaeology, Govt. of Chhattisgar, Raipur.

Vats, Madho Sarup. 1952. *The Gupta Temple at Deogarh*. *MASI* 70. New Delhi: Manager of Publications.

Venkataramayya, M.A. 1962. "Caturmukhaliṅga from Sirpur, Raipur District, M.P." *JIH* 40: 159-78.

Venkataramanayya, N. 1930. An *Essay on the Origin of the South Indian Temples*. Madras: Methodist Publishing Housing.

——. 1942. *Rudra-Śiva*. Madras. University of Madras.

Viennot, Odette. 1954. "Le Culte de L'Arbe dans L'Inde Ancienne". *AMG*, *Bibliotheque d'Etudes* 59. Paris: Presses Universitaires de France.

——. 1954. "Typologie du Makara et Essai de Chronologie". *ARA* 1.

——. 1958. "Le Makara dans la décoration des monuments de L'Inde ancienne: positions et fonctions". In *ARA* 3:183-206 and 4: 272-92.

——. 1958. "Le Temple de Rāmacandra a Rājim." *ARA* 5: 138-43.

——. 1964. *Les Divinités Fluviales Gaṅgā et Yamunā aux portes des Sanctuaires de L'Inde: Essai d'evolution d'un theme decoratif*. Publication du Musée Guimet, Recherches et Documents d'Art et d' Archaeologie 10. Paris: Presses Universitaires de France.

——. 1968. "Le Probleme des Temples a toit plat dans L'Inde du Nord." *ARA* 18: 23-84.

——. 1976. *Temples de L'Inde Centrale et Occidentale. Etude Stylistique et Essai de Chronologie Relative du Vie au Milieu du Xe Siécle*. 2 vols. Publications de L'Ecole Francaise d'Extreme Orient, Memoires Archaeologiques. 11. Paris: Adrien Maisonneuve.

Vogel, Jean Philippe. 1912. "The Temple of Bhitargāon". *ASIAR*. 1908-09. Calcutta.

——. 1925. "Gaṅgā et Yamunā dans L'Iconographie Brāhmaṇique". *EA* 20: 385-402.

——. 1926/1972. *Indian Serpent Lore or the Nāgas in Hindu Literature and Art*. London: A Probsthain. Reprint, Varanasi: Prithvi Prakashan.

——. 1929. "The Woman and Tree or Śālabhañjikā in Indian Literature and Art". *AO* 7: 201-31.

——. 1929-30. "Le Makara dans la Sculpture d'Inde." *RAA* 6: 133-47.

——. 1948. "The Vyālaka in Indian Art". Leiden: *ON*.

——. 1953. "The Goose (Sanskrit, Hamsa) in Indian Literature and Art". *IAL* 28: 17-24.

Volwahsen, Andrea. 1969. *Living Architecture: Indian*. New York: Grosset and Dunlap.

Wagner, Richard. 1880. *Religion and Art*. Trans. William Ashton Ellis, 1897. The Wagner Library.

Walker, Benjamin. 1983. Ed., *An Encyclopaedic Survey of Hinduism*. 2 vols. Delhi: Munshiram Manoharlal.
Ward, W.E. 1952. "The Lotus Symbol: its Meaning in Buddhist Art and Philosophy." *JAAC* 11: 2.
Wasson, R.G. 1971. *Soma, Divine Mushroom of Inmortality*, New York: Harcourt Brace Jovanovich.
Watters, Thomas A. 1904. *On Yuan Chwang's Travels in India* (A.D. 629-645). Ed., T.W. Rhys Davids and S.W. Bushell. 2 vols. London: The Royal Asiatic Society; reprint, Delhi: Munshiram Manoharlal, 1961.
Wayman, Alex. 1957. "Contributions Regarding the Thirty Two Characteristics of the Great Person." *Liebenthal Festschrift, Sino-Indian Studies* 5. 3, 4: 234-60.
Weiner, S. 1962. "From Gupta to Pāla Sculpture". *AA* 25. 2,3: 167-92.
——. 1977. *Ajantā: Its Place in Buddhist Art*. Los Angeles: University of California Press.
Weitz, Morris. 1970. Ed., *Problems in Aesthetics*. London: Macmillan.
Whitehead, Alfred North. 1960. *Adventures of Ideas*. New York: Mentor.
Wiener, P.P. 1951. Ed. *Leibniz-Selections*. New York: Charles Scribner's Sons.
Wilkins, W.J. 1900. *Hindu Mythology, Vedic and Purāṇic*, Calcutta.
Williams, Joanna G. 1972-73. "The Sculpture of Māndāsor." *ARSA* 26: 50-66.
——. 1975. "Sarnath Gupta Steles of the Buddha's life." *ARO* 10: 179-92.
——. 1978. Review of Odette Viennot. Temples de L'Inde Centrale. In *AA*: 75-81.
——. 1981. Ed., *Kalādarśana. American Studies in the Art of India*. New Delhi: Oxford and IBH Publishing Co. with the American Institute of Indian Studies.
——. 1982. *The Art of Gupta India. Empire and Province*. Princeton, N.J.: Princeton University Press.
——. 1983. "Vākāṭaka Art and the Gupta Mainstream." In *Essays on Gupta Culture*. Ed., Bardwell Smith. Columbia, M.: South Asia Books: 215-33.
——. 1983. "Figural Sculpture of the Gupta Period". In B.S. Millar. ed., *Exploring India's Sacred Art*.
——. 2000. "Thoughts about a Remarkable Sculpture from Tala, in Nigam, ed., *Riddle*: 69-72.
Williams, M. Monier. 1885. *Religious Thought and Life in India, Vedism, Brāhmaṇism and Hinduism* (Vol. 1). London.
——. 1899. *Sanskrit-English Dictionary*. Clarendon Press, Oxford. New edition, Delhi: Motilal Banarsidass 1963.
Winternitz, Moriz. 1895. "Nejamesha, Nāigameshā, Nemeso". *JRAS*: 149-155.
——. 1927. *A History of Indian Literature*. 2 vols. Vol. I. Calcutta: University of Calcutta.
Wilson, Colin. 1956. *The Outsider*. Boston: Houghton Mifflin company.
Wölfflin, Heinrich. 1915. *Principles of Art History: The Problem of the Development of Style in Later Art*. 7th ed. Trans. M.D. Hottinger. 1932. Repr. N.Y. 1950.
Woodroffe, J.C. (Arthur Avalon). 1927. *The Great Liberation. Mahānirvāṇa Tantra*. Madras.
Woodroffe, John. 1956. *The Garland of Letters (Varṇamālā)*. 9th ed. Madras: Ganesh and Co.
Yaldiz. M. and W. Lobo. 1987. Ed., *Investigating Indian Art*. Berlin: Museum fur Indische Kunst.
Yazdani, Ghulam. 1960. *The Early History of the Deccan*. 2 vols. London: Oxford University Press.
Zaehner, Robert Charles. 1969. "Sexual Symbolism in Śvetāśvatara Upaniṣad." In *Myths and Symbols. Studies in Honor of Mircea Eliade*. Ed., J.M. Kitagawa and Charles Long. Chicago: 209-15.
Zaheer, Mohammed. 1981. *The Temple of Bhitargāon*. Delhi: Agam Kala Prakashan.
Zieseniss, Alexander. 1931. *Annual Bibliography of Indian Archaeology*.
Zimmer, Heinrich. 1926. *Artistic Form and Yoga in the Sacred Images of India*. Trans. from German by G. Chapple, J.B. Lawson and J.H. Mcknight. Princeton, N.J.: Princeton University Press, 1984.
——. 1946. *Myths and Symbols in Indian Art and Civilization*. Ed., Joseph Campbell. New York: Pantheon Books; reprint, New York: Harper and Brothers.
——. 1955. *The Art of Indian Asia: Its Mythology and Transformations*. 2 vols. Ed., Joseph Campbell. Bollingen Series. Vol. 39, New York: Pantheon Books.
——. 1956. *Philosophies of India*. New York: Meridian Books.

Index